DOIN' CALIFORNIA WITH YOUR POOCH!

Eileen's Directory of
Dog-Friendly Lodging
& Outdoor Adventure
in California

Pet-Friendly Publications
P.O. Box 8459, Scottsdale, Az 85252
Tel: (800) 638-3637

Doin' California With Your Pooch... A Rewarding Experience

You and Your Dog Can:

- Beachcomb hundreds of miles of coastline.
- Hike trails through redwood and sequoia forests.
- Explore remote, secluded canyons.
- Witness incredible wildflower displays and behold wildlife in natural surroundings.

Don't leave your canine buddy at home or kenneled in a cage when you vacation. Bring your best friend along. Increase your pleasure and your safety. If your dog is a great companion at home, he can be an even better one on the road.

DOIN' CALIFORNIA WITH YOUR POOCH!
by Eileen Barish

Pet-Friendly Publications
P.O. Box 8459, Scottsdale, AZ 85252
Tel: (800) 638-3637

ISBN #1884465-04-8
Library of Congress Catalog Number: 96-067233

Clubs, organizations, travel agencies, animal groups
and all interested parties: contact the publisher for information on quantity discounts. Every traveler who owns a dog
should have this directory. Printed and bound in the
United States of America.

CREDITS

Author & Managing Editor — Eileen Barish

Associate Editor — Harvey Barish

Lodging & Research Editor — Phyllis Holmes

Research/Writing Staff — Alison Dufner
Tiffany Geoghegan

Illustrator — Gregg Myers

Layout & Design — Tawni Hensley

Photographer — Ken Friedman

SPECIAL ACKNOWLEDGEMENTS

Doin' California with my smooch Harvey
has been the best.

Special thanks to a doggone great staff.

And for Sam, the "best friend"
who is always with us.

TABLE OF CONTENTS

CALIFORNIA DIRECTORY OF LODGING AND OUTDOOR ADVENTURE

LET'S GET READY TO TRAVEL

HOW TO USE THIS DIRECTORY

Pooch comes along

If you're planning to travel in California with your pooch or if you live in California and would like to enjoy more of the state with your canine buddy beside you, *Doin' California With Your Pooch!* is the only reference source you'll need. Included are more than 2,000 dog-friendly accommodations, thousands of outdoor adventures and chapters covering everything from travel training to travel etiquette.

Simplify vacation planning

The user-friendly format of *Doin' California With Your Pooch!* combines lodging and recreation under individual city headings. Pick a city, decide on lodging and then reference the outdoor activities listed under that city. Or perhaps you've always wanted to hike a certain trail or visit a particular park. Just reverse the process. Using the index, locate the activity of choice, find the closest lodging and go from there. It's that easy to plan a vacation you and Rover will adore.

No more sneaking Snoopy

Choose lodging from hotels, B&Bs (aka Bed & Biscuits), motels, resorts, inns and ranches that welcome you and your dog - through the front door. From big cities to tiny hamlets, *Doin' California With Your Pooch!* provides the names, addresses, phone numbers and room rates of thousands of dog-friendly accommodations. Arranged in an easy-to-use alphabetical format, this directory covers all of California, from Adelanto to Yucca Valley.

Just do it

Okay, now you've got your pooch packed and you're ready for the fun to begin. How will you make the most of your travel or vacation time? *Doin' California With Your Pooch!* details thousands of adventures you can share with your canine. If you're into hiking, you'll find descriptions for hundreds of trails. The descriptions will tell you what to expect - from the trail rating (beginner, intermediate, expert) to the trail's terrain, restrictions, best times to hike, etc. If laid-back pastimes are more to your liking, you'll find green grassy areas perfect for picnics or plain chilling out. For parks, monuments and other attractions, expect anything from a quickie overview to a lengthy description. Written in a conversational tone, it'll be easy for you to visualize each area. Directions are also included.

No matter what your budget or outdoor preference, with this directory you'll be able to put together the perfect day, weekend or monthlong odyssey.

Increase your options

Many of the recreational opportunities listed in *Doin' California With Your Pooch!* can be accessed from more than one city. See what activities are located in cities adjacent to your lodging choice and expand your options.

How to do it

Numerous chapters are devoted to making your travel times safer and more pleasurable. Training do's and don'ts, crate use and selection, carsickness, driving and packing tips, desert survival, doggie massage, pet etiquette, travel manners, what and how to pack for your pooch, first aid advice, hiking tips, emergency telephone numbers, a pet identification form and tons more are all discussed.

Not just for vacationers. A "must-have" reference for California dog owners

Owning a copy of *Doin' California With Your Pooch!* will mean you won't have to leave your trusted companion at home while you explore our beautiful state. So many places welcome Fido and Rover that there's rarely an occasion when your buddy can't come along. Exercise and outdoor stimulation are as good for his health as they are for yours. So include old brown eyes when you decide to take a walk, picnic in a forest glade, hike a mountain trail or rent a boat for the day. Armed with this guide, Californians who love their hounds can travel with their pooches and discover all that California has to offer. No matter where you make your home in the state, you'll find dozens of places in your own backyard just perfect for a day's outing. *Doin' California With Your Pooch!* answers your travel dilemma of what to do with the pooch when you travel - take him along. Expand your travel horizons and give your devoted companion a new leash on life.

Do hotel & motel policies differ regarding pets?

Yes, but all the accommodations in *Doin' California With Your Pooch!* allow dogs. Policies can vary on charges and sometimes on dog size. Some might require a damage deposit and some combine their deposit with a daily and/or one-time charge. Others may restrict pets to specific rooms, perhaps cabins or cottages. Residence-type inns which cater to long-term guests may charge a long-term fee. Some might require advance notice. But most accommodations do not charge fees or place restrictions in any manner.

Prior to publishing, all the accommodations in this book received a copy of their listing information for verification.

BE AWARE THAT HOTEL POLICIES MAY CHANGE. AT THE TIME YOUR RESERVATIONS ARE MADE, DETERMINE THE POLICY OF YOUR LODGING CHOICE.

Go Take A Hike

Hundreds of the best day hikes in California are detailed in ***Doin' California With Your Pooch!*** Each hike indicates degree of difficulty, approximate time to complete the hike and round-trip distances. Unless otherwise indicated, trailhead access is free and parking is available, although it is sometimes limited. To assist you in your travel plans, phone numbers are included for most recreation sites. In many areas, dogs may hike without being leashed.

When leashes are mandatory, notice is provided.

Please obey local ordinances so dogs continue to be welcome.

Hike ratings

The majority of the hikes are rated beginner or intermediate. As a rule of thumb, beginner hikes are generally easy, flat trails suited to every member of the family. Intermediate hikes require more exertion and a little more preparation, but can usually be accomplished by anyone accustomed to some physical exercise, such as fast-paced walking, biking, skiing, swimming, etc. Some expert trails have also been included. Many times, their inclusion signals some outstanding feature. Expert hikes should only be considered if you feel certain of your own and your dog's abilities. But whatever your ability, remember, if the hike you've undertaken is too difficult you can always turn around and retrace your steps. You're there to have a good time, not to prove anything.

Seasons change, so do conditions

Seasonal changes may effect ratings. If you're hiking during rainy season, you might encounter slippery going. Or if you've decided to hike during the winter and there's snow underfoot, that can up the difficulty rating. If it's springtime, small creeks can become rushing, perhaps impassable rivers. Whenever you're outdoors, particularly in wilderness areas, exercise caution. Know yourself and know your dog.

Hike time

Times are included for general reference. If you're short on time or energy, hike as long as you like. Never push yourself or your canine beyond either's endurance. Never begin a hike too late in the day, particularly in canyon areas where the sun can disappear quickly.

Directions

Directions are generally provided from the closest city with dog-friendly lodging. Odometer accuracy can vary so be alert to road signs. Unless specifically noted, roads and trailheads are accessible by all types of vehicles. In winter, access roads may be closed from November through May. Or you may experience heavy snow conditions where 4WD or snow chains are required. Remember too that national forest roads can be narrow and twisting and are often used by logging trucks. Exercise caution. Slow down around blind corners.

Parking your vehicle

Lock valuables in your trunk. Lock all doors and close windows completely. If you're hiking in bear country, don't leave food *anywhere* in your car. Bears can smell the food and might think your vehicle is a closed restaurant. They've been known to rip windows off cars searching for food.

Permits/Fees

Wilderness permits are needed for most hikes in USFS wilderness areas. In addition, most state parks and some national parks charge a nominal fee.

Common sense, don't hike without it

Consider potential hazards. Know your limitations. The overview descriptions included with hikes and other recreational activities are provided for general information. They are not meant to represent that a particular hike or excursion will be safe for you or your dog. Only you can make that determination.

Weather, terrain, wildlife and trail conditions should always be considered. It is up to you to assume responsibility for yourself and your canine. Apply common sense to your outings and they'll prove safe and enjoyable.

Leashes

Many hikes and other outdoor adventures do not require that dogs be leashed, but wildlife exists in all outdoor areas. Use caution and common sense. When a leash is mandatory, a notation will be made. When restrictions apply, they will also be noted. But in any case, keep a leash accessible. You never know when the need will suddenly arise.

BASIC DOG RULES:

THEY CAN'T BE AVOIDED AND THEY'RE REALLY QUITE EASY TO LIVE WITH. BE A RESPONSIBLE DOG OWNER AND OBEY THE RULES.

Note: When leashes are required they must be six feet or less in length. Leashes should be carried at all times. They are prudent safety measures particularly in wilderness areas.

THE CALIFORNIAS

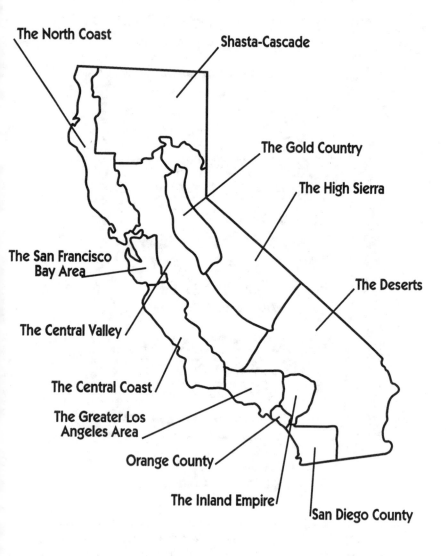

The North Coast

Shasta-Cascade

The Gold Country

The High Sierra

The San Francisco
Bay Area

The Deserts

The Central Valley

The Central Coast

The Greater Los
Angeles Area

Orange County

The Inland Empire

San Diego County

PREFACE

The Golden State Has It All

At nearly thirty million people, California boasts the largest population and the largest "pup"ulation of any state. From starlets to hippies, movie moguls to migrant workers, artists to political activists, purebreds to mutts, California is home to the nation's most eclectic collection of people and pooches. Blessed with an extraordinary landscape and an abundance of outdoor recreation, California offers something for everyone, especially anyone traveling with a pooch.

Experience California

The natural terrain of California is at once wildly primitive, and breathtakingly beautiful. More than any other state, California offers an incredible array of recreational opportunities you can share with your pooch. After glancing through *Doin' California With Your Pooch!*, outdoor enthusiasts and their canine companions will have a hard time deciding what to do first. There are more places to visit than any one lifetime will allow. Take your pick from hundreds of area descriptions. Explore mountainous regions. Dig your feet into the sand at pristine coastal beaches or dunes. Forget your cares in a forest preserve. Stand tall on a ridgetop with 360° panoramas. Fish for trout in an alpine lake. Cool your heels in a babbling brook. Observe wildlife in its natural habitat. Or just enjoy an early morning hike and an old-fashioned picnic lunch in the shade of a California sycamore.

The Other California

If your definition of doing California with your pooch means exploring sophisticated cities, this book will lead you there as well. In LA, stay with your pooch at the Four Seasons Hotel in Beverly Hills and receive VIP (Very Important Pooch) treatment. Window shop on glamorous Rodeo Drive and stroll trendy Melrose Avenue. Or head to San Francisco with room reservations at the Westin St. Francis and dinner reservations at one of the city's well-known eateries.

Perhaps the allure of Carmel, with its small boutiques, outdoor cafes, white sand beaches and rolling hillsides is more to your liking. With your pooch beside you, sip cocktails in the charming courtyard of the historic Cypress Inn or end your fun-filled day with a stroll on the manicured grounds of the Quail Lodge Resort.

Architecture Devotees

California's diverse terrain forms a stunning backdrop for the ethnic and period influences prevalent throughout the state. Spanish haciendas, California bungalows, arts and crafts cottages, victorian mansions, western ranches and architectural oddities from the funky fifties are all part of the scene.

Even history buffs and their history-sniffing canines will find that California is alive with its past. Ghost towns, mining towns, logging towns and old west towns are scattered throughout the state, symbolic of the colorful, turbulent times of the American West.

Coastal California

Nothing exemplifies California as much as its 1200-mile coastline. Wether you prefer your beaches sandy and secluded or rocky and rugged, you're sure to find your perfect beach in the Golden State. Although some areas are more dog-friendly than others, *Doin' California With Your Pooch!* will lead you and your water-loving dog to hundreds of miles of beaches where the "sea-dog" in both of you can be satisfied.

Along the coast, dividing the state in two, is dramatic Big Sur, a photographer's dream come true. This stretch of ruggedly spectacular shoreline looks today as it did thousands of years ago. Drive north from Big Sur and experience the idyllic, dog-friendly Monterey/ Pacific Grove/ Carmel area, where canines run leash-free on white sandy beaches. Further north another couple of hours is San Francisco, a foggy slice of dog heaven. But don't stop there. The next 400 miles, from San Francisco to the Oregon border, encompass the wilder, more isolated regions of California's North Coast. December through March, whalewatch from the coastal headlands or go tidepooling on windswept beaches.

Traveling south from Big Sur to Santa Barbara, you'll encounter breathtaking scenery and quaint towns. Have lunch or dinner at one of the fishing villages along the way and dine alfresco, with your canine beside you, as you feast on locally caught seafood. Further south, from sprawling Los Angeles and the "Hollywoodesque" Malibu colony, with its luxurious beachfront homes, to La Jolla and San Diego; the land, the climate and the charming beach towns epitomize the fabled California lifestyle.

CENTRAL COAST

Central Coast Cities: Arroyo Grande, Atascadero, Big Sur Area, Buellton, Cambria, Carmel, Carmel Valley, Carpinteria, Cayucos, Goleta, Grover Beach, King City, Lompoc, Monterey, Morro Bay, Ojai, Oxnard, Pacific Grove, Paso Robles, Pismo Beach, Port Hueneme, Salinas, San Juan Bautista, San Luis Obispo, San Simeon, Santa Barbara, Santa Maria, Seaside, Simi Valley, Solvang, Ventura

The coast with the most

Complete with medieval-like castles, Spanish missions, Danish styled windmills, lush vineyards, towering cliffs and expansive beaches, California's Central Coast is a fairy tale world come to life. Set out and hike for miles in Santa Barbara's backcountry or drop the top and take an unforgettable coastal cruise along one of the world's most spectacular drives - the scenic stretch of highway from Ventura County to Big Sur.

Catch a crashing wave

Defined by white sandy beaches and secluded coastal inlets, San Luis Obispo and the Monterey Peninsula offer seadogs a tail wagging chance to wet their paws. From December through March, pack your binoculars and stake out a private cove along Highway 1 and join in a favorite pastime - whalewatching. Or stroll amid the quaint harbor in Oxnard and ponder the primitive beauty and isolation of the Channel Islands. Don't forget a visit to off-the-beaten-path Ojai, where a charming art colony thrives in a valley of verdant beauty. The tree strewn mountains that surround this pretty town are laced with trails that will lead you and the pooch to remote swimming holes and top-of-the-world views.

CENTRAL VALLEY

Central Valley Cities: Bakersfield, Chico, Coalinga, Davis, Dinuba, Fairfield, Fresno, Hanford, Lemoore, Lindsay, Lodi, Los Banos, Madera, Marysville, Merced, Modesto, Oakdale, Orland, Oroville, Porterville, Reedley, Santa Nella, Selma, Stockton, Tehachapi, Tulare, Turlock, Vacaville, Visalia, West Sacramento, Willows, Woodland

Time to sniff the roses

The Central Valley is brimming with recreation for you and the pupster. Water woofers, head for Modesto. With two rivers and sixteen lakes and reservoirs, water sports are limitless. Flower Fidos will want to check out the tiny town of Wasco where over 20 million roses liven the landscape and scent the air. Laid-back Lassies will want to make tracks to Bidwell Park in Chico, a peaceful, shaded oasis.

The fishing's fine to drop a line

Any fisherman worth his salt will want to try his luck in the waterways of the Delta region where during autumn's migration, striped bass, steelhead and salmon are aplenty. Or float your boat and anchor away at any of the delightful waterfront towns, like Isleton, Locke, Brentwood, Brannan Island or Walnut Grove where you can mosey with Rosie on the wooden walkways of these unusual river cities. Consider renting a houseboat and spending a few days on the Delta, the perfect way to savor the quiet waterways of this beautiful region. Plan a trip to history-rich Madera and Merced, Gateway to Yosemite or explore the Sequoia/Kings Canyon National Parks area. Without question, when it comes to combining lush farmlands and water recreation, the Central Valley can't be beat.

DESERTS

Desert Cities: Barstow, Blythe, Brawley, Cathedral City, Coachella, Death Valley National Park, El Centro, Indian Wells, Indio, La Quinta, Mojave, Needles, Palm Desert, Palm Springs, Rancho Mirage, Ridgecrest, Rosamond, Twentynine Palms, Yucca Valley

The sun shines overtime

More than 300 cloudless, sun-filled days characterize this arid region, attracting sun-worshippers and their hot diggety dogs. So leave your rain ponchos at home and get ready for an action-packed desert experience. Day trip to the Imperial Sand Dunes for some rock and fossil collecting. Explore an authentic mining town in Calico. Plan a visit to Joshua Tree country where big horn sheep and darting reptiles abound. Or simply pamper yourself and your pooch at a five-star resort in Palm Springs or Rancho Mirage. Unless you're a desert rat who loves the heat, spring, fall and winter are the best times to visit California's arid regions.

Death Valley's vital signs

With elevations ranging from 282 feet below sea level (Badwater Basin) to 11,049 feet above sea level (Telescope Peak), Death Valley National Park is in a league of its own. Buckle up and cruise down "Artist Palette Drive" for a scenic car tour through mineral-clad hillsides and dreamy desert washes. Top off your water canteens and set your sights on a fascinating geologic exploration. Or leash up and check out the park on terra firma.

GOLD COUNTRY

Gold Country Cities: Angels Camp, Auburn, Columbia, Folsom, Grass Valley, Groveland, Jackson, Jamestown, Mariposa, Nevada City, Oakhurst, Penn Valley, Placerville, Pollock Pines, Rancho Cordova, Roseville, Sacramento, Sonora

Strike it rich

Journey back in time to the days when the '49ers were prospectors seeking their fortune in gold rather than football players seeking a Super Bowl victory. Aptly named, Highway 49 is the gateway to California's Gold Country, where town after historic town beckons you to explore the landscape that once pulsed with gold rush fever.

Capture the feeling of the old west and try your hand at gold panning in the quaint town of Columbia. Architecture aficionados and relic seekers won't want to miss appealing Sutter Creek where historic homes and antique troves await your perusal.

A capital idea

Plan a walk through 40-acre Capitol Park in Sacramento, California's restored capitol and admire the interesting flora, representative of countries from around the world. Or just stroll the cobblestone streets in Old Sacramento where small town niceties reminiscent of the fifties still linger along the cobblestone streets and wooden sidewalks. And when nothing but a hike or some splish splashing fun will do, make your way to the American and Sacramento Rivers and satisfy your craving for nature at its finest and wettest.

GREATER LOS ANGELES

Greater Los Angeles Cities: Beverly Hills, Catalina Island, Glendale, Hermosa Beach, Hollywood, Lancaster, Long Beach, Los Angeles, Malibu, Marina Del Rey, Palmdale, Pasadena, Redondo Beach, Rosemead, San Dimas, San Pedro, Santa Clarita, Santa Monica, Torrance, Venice, West Hollywood

See and be seen

Star gazers take heed. Famous faces and their companion pooches abound in this diverse cityscape. From the unexpected quiet of Larchmont to the estates of Hancock Park, to the charming small town ambience of Santa Monica, celebrity sightings are endless.

Not just for cityslickers

For a rugged slice of nature, head for the hills - the Santa Monica and San Gabriel Mountains to be exact. Just minutes east or west from the hustle, bustle of LA, you can trade pavement for pathway and experience canyons and rugged mountain trails. Or try a bark in the park. Plan an afternoon visit to secluded Laurel Canyon Park, where the famous and not so famous bring their dogs to run leash free or do some serious hiking in expansive Griffith Park. Wherever you are in the LA area, a green scene is never far away.

Venture to Venice and beyond

People watching pups will wag about Venice, an anything-goes beach town. Rollerbladers and jugglers vie for attention while funky shops vie for your money, selling everything from doggie visors to tie-dye shirts. No matter where you roam in this part of the state, one thing's certain, you'll be dazzled by the days and starstruck by the nights in Los Angeles County.

HIGH SIERRA

High Sierra Cities: Bass Lake, Bishop, Bridgeport, June Lake, Kernville, Lee Vining, Lone Pine, Mammoth Lakes, Markleeville, South Lake Tahoe, Springville, Truckee, Yosemite Area

Statiscally speaking

From the highest point in the continental U.S., 14,494' Mt. Whitney to the lowest, Badwater Basin at 282' below sea level, from Lake Tahoe, the largest alpine lake in North America to the Inyo National Forest, home to Bristlecone pines, the oldest living trees on earth, you'll experience the breathtaking beauty and vivid contrasts of California's High Sierra scenery. One visit and you'll quickly understand why this stunningly picturesque region captured the hearts and minds of John Muir and Ansel Adams.

Fall in love

For a profusion of autumnal colors, don't miss a visit to the California Alps, the area atop the crest and eastern slopes of the Sierra Nevada. Plan an afternoon sojourn through Hope Valley and along Monitor Pass and behold a wildly extravagant display of golden foliage.

Mile high heaven

Lake Tahoe is the largest and deepest alpine lake in North America. But alpine means cold. If you and Fido plan to make a splash, be prepared for chilly tootsies, 68° is as warm as it gets. Afterward warm up with a hike on the mountains and lakeside trails that lace the Lake Tahoe Basin. Your camera is one essential you won't want to forget. Point and shoot takes on new meaning in the majestic landscape of the Sierra Nevadas.

INLAND EMPIRE

Inland Empire Cities: Banning, Beaumont, Big Bear Lake, Claremont, Corona, Hemet, Idyllwild, Lake Arrowhead, Lake Elsinore, Moreno Valley, Ontario, Pomona, Redlands, Riverside, San Bernardino, San Jacinto, Temecula, Victorville

An empire of opportunity

Aquatic pups and fishing Fidos will have a paw stomping good time exploring this lake-laced region of California. Spend hours doggie paddling in Big Bear Lake, Lake Arrowhead, Lake Elsinore or any of the other beautiful lakes in the area. Pack a pole and catch some sup for you and the pup or strap on the life jackets and whip up whitecaps in a motor boat. Landlubbers, fear not. There's plenty of outdoor adventure awaiting you in the San Bernardino National Forest. Set your sights on 9,000 foot Mount Baldy or make tracks along one of the pretty nature trails. In summer, cool off with a day trip to Idyllwild Park in the San Jacinto Mountains, a mecca for avid hikers and their hounds. The high elevation of this charming retreat equates to cooler temperatures. And there are lots of trails leading from the park into the San Jacinto Wilderness and the summit of Tahquitz Peak.

Paint the towns orange and fragrant

Plan a visit to Redlands or Riverside in the spring when the air is filled with the intoxicating aroma of orange blossoms. In Redlands, plan your own self-guided tour of the restored victorian-era mansions. If Riverside figures into your itinerary, don't miss the city's landmark, the restored Mission Inn, a circa 1875 California mission-style adobe.

NORTH COAST

North Coast Cities: Arcata, Blue Lake, Bodega Bay, Calistoga, Clear Lake, Crescent City, Eureka, Ferndale, Fort Bragg, Fortuna, Garberville, Guerneville, Healdsburg, Klamath, Lakeport, Leggett, McKinleyville, Miranda, Napa, Orick, Petaluma, Rohnert Park, Santa Rosa, Sebastopol, Sonoma, St. Helena, Trinidad, Ukiah, Willits, Windsor

The toast of the coast

We're not just talking wineries. A region of rugged beaches, crashing waves, cool forests, icy streams, lush hillsides and gloriously verdant vineyards, the North Coast represents a dramatically varied and captivating landscape.

Savor the ethnicity of Sonoma with its Mexican-era adobes. Get a sense of tranquil small city living in Petaluma with a walking tour of the victorian homes. Visit the Russian River, rent a canoe and make your way among redwood forests to scenic Jenner-by-the-Sea. Stop and shop the enchanting villages of Duncan Mills, Guerneville, Monte Rio and Forestville along the way.

Find a touch of isolation

A drive up coast will lead you through quaint fishing villages that dot the shoreline on the way to Mendocino, the New England of the West and a thriving art community. The more sequestered regions of Mendocino County allow solitude-seeking canines a chance to curl up on a breezy bluff, inhale the tangy salt air and Orca-watch in the winter months. More active breeds might prefer tidepooling on remote, secluded beaches. Water woofers and birdwatchers, you'll want to plan a stop at Clear Lake in Lake County where over 100 miles of shoreline await your pleasure at the state's largest fresh water lake.

ORANGE COUNTY

Orange County Cities: Anaheim, Buena Park, Costa Mesa, Dana Point, Huntington Beach, Irvine, Laguna Hills, Newport Beach, San Clemente, Santa Ana

Something to bark about

Blessed with a temperate climate, there's hardly a time of year you and your canine can't enjoy the great outdoors in this pretty part of the state. Stretching from the Pacific to the Santa Ana Mountains, you can set out for an early morning stroll or plan a sunset walk and leave your footprints and pawprints in the smooth white sand along the coastal beaches. A visit to Tewinkle Park in Costa Mesa is the place to meet and greet other park hounds who come to play in the leashless Bark Park section.

Arts and crafts

Art walk through the quaint streets of Laguna Beach and be tempted by the vast array of artwork, sculptures and one-of-a-kind pieces. Then make tracks to Dana Point and have a first-hand glimpse at the thousands of crafts, from fishing boats to fabulous yachts, that colorfully fill the marinas.

Binocular and biscuit time

Animal lovers and birdwatchers alike will want to clean their lenses before setting out on their Orange County sight-seeing adventure. Stop by the San Juan Capistrano Mission for the annual return of the swallows or head to the coast for a whale-of-a-tail sighting. When chow time calls, take your Chow to Huntington Beach for a doggie treat extraordinaire at the Park Bench Cafe. This Fido-friendly eatery offers a special Canine Cuisine Menu for hungry hounds. Bone appetite.

SAN DIEGO COUNTY

San Diego County Cities: Carlsbad, Chula Vista, Coronado, Del Mar, El Cajon, Encinitas, Escondido, Fallbrook, Imperial Beach, Julian, La Jolla, Oceanside, Poway, Ramona, San Diego, San Marcos, Vista

Within city limits

The sixth largest city in the United States, San Diego offers an almost perfect climate and an endless "to do" list guaranteed to provide you and the dogster with a tail-wagging good time. From bustling marinas to secluded beaches, historic districts to modern meccas, rugged mountain trails to cool forest hikes, California's birthplace is a definite doggie delight. Boat on the bay or plan a day in the hills surrounding this culturally diverse city.

From crags to riches

Crowned as "the jewel", La Jolla is famous for its caves, coves and seaside cliffs. A visit to one of the coves might reward you with a seal sighting. These playful creatures often come to swim with the snorkelers who frequent the fish-filled waters. Take a sunny Sunday stroll along the people-filled, boutique-lined streets. Or inhale the tangy salt air as you hike atop majestic oceanside bluffs where you can admire the crashing Pacific on one side and beautiful beachfront homes on the other.

The bounty of the county

Sun, sand and surf will fill your days while starlit skies will fill your nights. But no bones about it, the beaches of Encinitas and Cardiff-by-the-Sea are top priority stops. While Fido spends hours frolicking with other lucky dogs, you can catch some rays.

SAN FRANCISCO BAY AREA

San Francisco Bay Area Cities: Berkeley, Burlingame, Fremont, Gilroy, Half Moon Bay, Hayward, Livermore, Los Gatos, Morgan Hill, Mountain View, Oakland, Pacifica, Pleasant Hill, Pleasanton, Point Reyes Station, San Anselmo, San Bruno, San Francisco, San Jose, San Rafael, Santa Clara, Santa Cruz, Saratoga, Sausalito, Sunnyvale, Tiburon, Vallejo, Walnut Creek

The heart stealer

This city by the bay rates four paws up as a genuine puppy paradise. Experience Golden Gate National Recreation Area, the world's largest urban park and immerse yourself in a world of remarkable contrasts - from redwood forests to beaches - guaranteed to satisfy every dream. Tote your binocs if your plans include Point Reyes National Seashore. Aside from hiking and beachcombing, this primitive area is a delight for naturalists.

Fido-friendly neighborhoods

Although San Francisco is world renowned for its incredibly beautiful and ornately colorful victorian architecture, to many the appeal of the city lies in the diversity of its neighborhoods, each a collage of boutiques, antiques and foodtiques. If your taste runs to retro, tailwag it to Haight Ashbury. Funky or fashionable, don't miss Polk or Fillmore. Or for more sedate saunterings, make your way to Sacramento.

If your interests are laid-back , point snouts north to Marin County. Sausalito and Tiburon are just two of the entrancing cities you'll find there. Whatever your pleasure in the Bay Area, don't forget your camera. From Alcatraz to Capitola, from the Golden Gate Bridge to sandstone headlands, this slice of foggy heaven eats Fuji.

SHASTA CASCADE

Shasta Cascade Cities: Alturas, Anderson, Chester, Corning, Dunsmuir, Fall River Mills, Greenville, Mount Shasta, Portola, Quincy, Red Bluff, Redding, Susanville, Weaverville, Weed, Westwood, Yreka

Wet, wild and wonderful

When you want to immerse yourself and your wagalong in the best of Mother Nature, Shasta Cascade is a must-see, must-do destination. Encompassing eight national forests, countless lakes, rugged canyons, cascading waterfalls, volcanoes and snow-capped mountains, the adventures are endless. Hike dense forests, toe-dip in alpine lakes, tackle ridgetop ascents, explore volcanic terrain or commune with nature in an isolated, wilderness area. Able anglers, pack your poles. Streams, lakes and rivers are everywhere. Or do something different - rent a houseboat, cruise pretty Shasta Lake and gape at the beauty of snow-capped Mt. Shasta. With over 370 miles of shoreline, you'll run out of time long before you run out of fun things to see and do.

The California sampler

History buffs might enjoy a taste of the Gold Rush era in Yreka where victorian mansions attest to the town's past. Cowboy canines will want to jingle their spurs in Dunsmuir, a town reminiscent of the Old West. Geology-minded mutts won't want to miss Lassen County where you never know what will be bubbling, boiling or spewing in this hot, hot region. Make tracks to Siskiyou County and ogle the glacier-polished granite crags that loom above the Sacramento River. Or surround yourself with a hundred alpine lakes in pristine Plumas County. Wherever you and Rover rove, unforgettably dramatic scenery will surround and astound.

INTRODUCTION

Doing California with your pooch can be easy. It doesn't take special training or expertise. Just a little planning and a little patience. The rewards are worth the effort. This directory is filled with information to make traveling with your dog more pleasurable. From training tips to what to take along, to the do's and don'ts of travel, almost all of your questions will be addressed.

Vacationing with dogs?

Not something I thought I'd ever do. But as the adage goes, necessity is the mother of invention. What began as my necessity turned into a new lifestyle. A lifestyle that has improved every aspect of my vacation and travel time.

Although my family had dogs on and off during my childhood, it wasn't until my early thirties that I decided it was time to bring another dog into my life. And the lives of my young children. I wanted them to grow up with a dog; to know what it was like to have a canine companion, a playmate, a friend who would always be there. To love you, no questions asked. A four-legged pal who would be the first to lick your teary face or your bloody knee. Enter Samson, our family's first Golden Retriever.

Samson

For nearly fifteen years, Sammy was everything a family could want from their dog. Loyal, forgiving, sweet, funny, neurotic, playful, sensitive, smart, too smart, puddle loving, fearless, strong and cuddly. He could melt your heart with a woebegone expression or make your hair stand on end with one of his pranks. Like the time he methodically opened the seam on a bean bag chair and then cheerfully spread the beans everywhere. Or when he followed a jogger and ended up in a shelter more than 20 miles from home.

As the years passed, Sam's face turned white and one by one our kids headed off to college. Preparing for the inevitable, my husband Harvey and I decided that when Sam died, no other dog would take his place. We wanted our freedom, not the responsibility of another dog.

Sammy left us one sunny June morning with so little fanfare that we couldn't believe he was actually gone. Little did we realize the void that would remain when our white-faced Golden Boy was no longer with us.

Life goes on...Rosie and Maxwell

After planning a two-week vacation through California, with an ultimate destination of Lake Tahoe, Harvey and I had our hearts stolen by two Golden Retriever puppies, Rosie and Maxwell. Two little balls of fur that would help to fill the emptiness Sam's death had created. The puppies were ready to come home only weeks before our scheduled departure date. What to do? Kennel them? Hire a caretaker? Neither felt right.

Sooo...we took them along

Oh, the fun we had. And the friends we made. Both the two-legged and four-legged variety. Having dogs on our trip made us more a part of the places we visited. We learned that dogs are natural conversation starters. Rosie and Maxwell were the prime movers in some lasting friendships we made during that first trip together. Now when we revisit Lake Tahoe, we have old friends to see as well as new ones to make. The locals we met made us feel at home, offering insider information on little known hikes, wonderful restaurants and quiet neighborhood parks. This knowledge enhanced our trip and made every day a grand adventure.

Since that first trip, our travels have taken us to many places. We've visited national forests, mountain resorts, seaside villages, island retreats, big cities and tiny hamlets. We've shared everything from luxury hotel rooms to rustic cabin getaways. I can't imagine going anywhere without our dogs.

Only one regret remained. Why hadn't it occurred to me to take Sammy along on our travels? He would have loved the adventures. That regret led to the writing of this book. I wanted others to know how easy it could be to vacation with their dogs.

When I watch Rosie and Maxwell frolic in a lake or when they accompany us on a hike, I think of Sammy and remember the legacy of love and friendship he left behind. So for those of you who regularly take your dog along and those who would if you knew how, come share my travel knowledge. And happy trails to you and yours.

Is my pooch vacation-friendly?

Most dogs can be excellent traveling companions. Naturally, the younger they are when you accustom them to traveling, the more quickly they will adapt. But that doesn't mean that an older dog won't love vacationing with you. And it doesn't mean that the transition has to be a difficult one.

Even if your dog hasn't traveled with you in the past, chances are he'll make a wonderful companion. You'll find yourself enjoying pensive moments watching him in new surroundings, laughing with others at his antics. But most of all, you'll find that spending quality time with your dog enhances every day of your travels. So get ready for a unique and rewarding adventure - filled with memories to last a lifetime.

A socialized pooch is a sophisticated traveler

Of course, every pooch is different. And you know yours better than anyone. To be sure that he will travel like a pro, accustom him to different environments. Take him for long walks around your neighborhood. Let him accompany you while you do errands. If your chores include stair climbing or taking an elevator, take him along. The more exposure to people, places and things, the better. Make your pet worldly. The sophistication will pay off in a better behaved, less frightened pet. It won't be long until he will happily share travel and vacation times with you.

Just ordinary dogs

Rosie and Maxwell, my traveling companions, are not exceptional dogs to anyone but me. Their training was neither intensive nor professionally rendered. They were trained with kindness, praise, consistency and love. And not all of their training came about when they were puppies. I too had a lot to learn. And as I learned what I wanted of them, their training continued. It was a sharing and growing experience. Old dogs (and humans too) can learn new tricks. Rosie and Maxwell never fail to surprise me. Their ability to adapt to new situations has never stopped. So don't think you have to start with a puppy. Every dog, young and old, can be taught to be travel-friendly.

Rosie and Maxwell know when I begin putting their things together that another holiday is about to begin. Their excitement mounts with every phase of preparation. They stick like glue - remaining at my side as I organize their belongings. By the time I've finished, they can barely contain their joy. Rosie runs to grab her leash and prances about the kitchen holding it in her mouth while Max sits on his haunches and begins to howl. If they could talk, they'd tell you how much they enjoy traveling. But since they can't, trust this directory to lead you to a different kind of experience. One that's filled with lots of love and an opportunity for shared adventure with your dogs. So with an open mind and an open heart, pack your bags and pack your pooch. Slip this handy book into your suitcase or the glove compartment of your car and let the adventure begin.

CALIFORNIA DIRECTORY OF DOG-FRIENDLY LODGING & OUTDOOR ACTIVITIES

Dogs May Be Unleashed Unless Otherwise Indicated

ADELANTO

LODGING

DAYS INN
11628 Bartlett Ave (92301)
Rates: $39-$45;
Tel: (619) 246-8777; (800) 329-7466

AGOURA HILLS

LODGING

RADISSON HOTEL
30100 Agoura Rd (91301)
Rates: $59;
Tel: (818) 707-1220; (800) 333-3333

AHWAHNEE

LODGING

SILVER SPUR BED & BREAKFAST
44625 Silver Spur Tr (93601)
Rates: $45-$60;
Tel: (209) 683-2896

ALAMEDA

LODGING

ISLANDER LODGE MOTEL
2428 Central Ave (94501)
Rates: $44-$59;
Tel: (510) 865-2121

RECREATION

COYOTE CANYON NATURE TRAIL HIKE- Leashes

Beginner/0.75 miles/0.5 hours

Info: Spend a pleasant afternoon with your buddy Trigger on this easy nature trail which trots to an overlook of Western Town,

Dogs May Be Unleashed Unless Otherwise Indicated

the locale of many famous westerns. The short hike allows time for a quick stroll through Western Town- you may recognize a building or two. For more information: (818) 597-9192.

Directions: From Agoura Hills, take Kanan Road and head south approximately .75 miles, turning left on Cornell Road. Follow Cornell Road about 2.5 miles to Paramount Ranch. The trailhead is located behind Western Town.

CROWN MEMORIAL STATE BEACH - Leashes

Info: Although dogs are not allowed on the beach, they can traverse the paved walking trails, partake of biscuits in the picnic areas, or just do what dogs do best, be A-1 companions. For more information: (510) 521-7090.

Directions: Access from the north is off Webster Street. Southern access is off High Street in Alameda.

Note: A parking fee and a $1 dog fee are charged.

PETER STRAUSS RANCH LOOP TRAIL HIKE- Leashes

Beginner/1.0 miles/0.5 hours

Info: Get your daily dose of Rexercise on this short, looping hike up a hillside and back down again. Pack a picnic lunch and let Snoopy snoop out a shady nook in the eucalyptus grove. Even couch potato pooches will give this trail two paws up. For more information: (818) 597-9192.

Directions: From Agoura Hills, take Kanan Road and head south approximately 2.75 miles, turning left on Troutdale Road to Mulholland Highway. Go left on Mulholland Highway, crossing over the Triunfo Creek Bridge to Peter Strauss Ranch. Park and walk back across the bridge to the trailhead behind the ranch house.

ROCKY OAKS TRAIL HIKE- Leashes

Beginner/1.0 miles/0.5 hours

Info: This little-bit-of-everything trail is a breeze. From the trailhead, follow the path to the pond and then ascend to the scenic overlook. On the way back, take the trail branch leading to an oak-clad picnic area. Find yourself a shady spot, break out the biscuit basket and chow down with your chow. For more information: (818) 597-9192.

Directions: From Agoura Hills, take Kanan Road and head south, turning right on Mulholland Drive. Follow Mulholland Drive to Rocky Oaks Site and make a right into the park. The trailhead is accessed from the parking lot.

ALTURAS

LODGING

BEST WESTERN TRAILSIDE INN
343 N Main St (96101)
Rates: $36-$46;
Tel: (800) 528-1234

DRIFTERS INN
395 Lake View Rd (96101)
Rates: $40+;
Tel: (916) 233-2428

ESSEX MOTEL
1216 N Main St (96101)
Rates: $36-$42;
Tel: (916) 233-2821

FRONTIER MOTEL
1033 N Main St (96101)
Rates: $28-$43;
Tel: (916) 233-3383

HACIENDA MOTEL
201 E 12th St (96101)
Rates: $26-$45;
Tel: (916) 233-3459

SUPER 8 MOTEL
511 N Main St (96101)
Rate: $46-$63;
Tel: (916) 233-3545; (800) 800-8000

RECREATION

BLUE LAKE NATIONAL RECREATION TRAIL HIKE - Leashes

Beginner/3.0 miles/1.5 hours

Info: When the dog days of summer make you yearn for the cool confines and serenity of pine forests and crystal clear blue water, satisfy your cravings with a day in this lake area. You and your hot diggety dog will delight in the beautiful deep-blue, 160-acre lake surrounded by dense forests and glorious meadows. Beginning at the Blue Lake Campground, you'll stroll around the west side of the lake to the boat ramp. On most of the trail, you and the pupster will be shaded by picturesque white fir and massive ponderosa pine. Deer tracks on the trail often outnumber hiker and hound tracks. Tree squirrels, ducks, geese, loons and hawks are frequently spotted. You'll want to come early and leave late. This is the next best thing to heaven. And if you're in the mood to throw a line, this natural lake sustains a fairly good population of rainbow and brown trout. Who could ask for anything more? For more information: (916) 279-6116.

Directions: From Alturas, head south on Highway 395 for 18.5 miles to Likely. Head east on Jess Valley Road for nine miles. Bear right when the road forks, and continue seven more miles on Blue Lake Road. Take a right at the Blue Lake sign and go to the campground.

HIGHGRADE NATIONAL RECREATION TRAIL HIKE

Beginner/1.1 miles/0.5 hours

Info: Most of this trail is designed for four-wheel driving with the first 1.1 miles for hikers. The trail is not heavily used and the views are spectacular. Once a hot spot for the precious metal, you'll come across remnants of old mining operations. If your canine has a snout for gold, you could strike it rich! For more information: (916) 279-6116.

Directions: From Alturas, go north on Highway 395 about 36 miles to Forest Service Road 9 and continue 4.5 miles. At the Buck Creek Ranger Station, take a left on Forest Service Road 47N72 and continue about six miles to the trailhead.

Note: A high clearance vehicle is not required to access the trailhead.

LILY LAKE TO CAVE LAKE TRAIL HIKE - Leashes

Beginner/0.25 miles/0.5 hours

Info: For a quickie outing, take this enchanting walk from Lily Lake's flower blooming lily pads to the barren shoreline at Cave Lake. Try your luck at fishing, rainbow trout at Lily Lake, brook trout at Cave Lake. And look for a pretty stream by the headwaters of Pine Creek. For more information: (916) 279-6116.

Directions: From Alturas, go north on Highway 395 for 40 miles to the town of New Pine Creek (California/Oregon border). Take a right (east) on Forest Service Road 2. Another 5.5 miles east will bring you to the lake.

Locate Other Dog-Friendly Activities...Check Nearby Cities

MILL CREEK FALLS LOOP TRAIL HIKE - Leashes

Beginner/0.5 miles/0.5 hours

Info: This relaxing jaunt from the Mill Creek Falls Trailhead to Clear Lake skirts the entire lake at a 6,000-foot elevation and is considered one of the most attractive areas in Modoc County. Add another .25 miles by taking the short walk to Mill Creek Falls. For more information: (916) 279-6116.

Directions: From Alturas, head south on Highway 395 for 18.5 miles to Likely. Go east on Jess Valley Road for nine miles. When the road forks, bear left and continue for 2.5 miles. Two miles ahead, take a right to the trailhead.

PINE CREEK TRAIL HIKE

Intermediate/4.0 miles/2.0 hours

Info: The Pine Creek Trail is an invigorating journey that begins along the South Fork of Pine Creek at 6,800 feet and climbs east into the lush South Warner Wilderness. This pretty trip encompasses many lakes and streams and is visually stimulating. For more information: (916) 279-6116.

Directions: From the south end of Alturas, head east on County Road 56 and go 13 miles to the Modoc National Forest boundary. Head south on West Warner Road and continue about 9 miles to the Pine Creek Trailhead sign. Go east and travel 1.75 miles to the parking area.

SOUP SPRING TRAIL HIKE

Intermediate/3.0 miles/1.5 hours

Info: The Soup Spring Trail escorts you up, over, and down a hill, eventually ending at pristine Mill Creek - a perfect picnic spot for you and your furry fellow. For more information: (916) 279-6116.

Directions: From the south end of Alturas, head east on County Road 56 and go 13 miles to the Modoc National Forest boundary. Head south on West Warner Road and travel about 10 miles until you reach the turn on Forest Road 40N24. Turn left (east) onto 40N24 and travel 3 miles to the Soup Springs Road. Turn left and drive to the turnaround where you can park.

Dogs May Be Unleashed Unless Otherwise Indicated

TIMBER MOUNTAIN TRAIL HIKE
Beginner/0.5 miles/0.5 hours

Info: In summer, this hike is nice with its pretty view of the Modoc plateau. But a visit in December has its rewards, wildlife style. Keep a close eye and perhaps a leash on your dog. Herds of mule deer migrate from Oregon and make their home in this area throughout the winter. Bring binoculars for some unbelievable wildlife sightings. For more information: (916) 279-6116.

Directions: From Alturas, take 299 west for 18 miles to Canby. Head north on Highway 139 and continue 20 miles; then go west on Forest Service Road 97 for about a mile. Go south on County Road 97A and travel 1.5 miles. Continue south on Forest Service Road 44N19 and go about three miles to the base of the mountain. The road takes you to the top and a Forest Service lookout.

ANAHEIM

LODGING

ANAHEIM ANGEL INN
1800 E Katella Ave (92805)
Rates: $31-$60;
Tel: (714) 634-9121

ANAHEIM HARBOR INN
2171 S Harbor Blvd (92802)
Rates: $44-$59;
Tel: (714) 750-3100

ANAHEIM INN AT THE PARK
1855 S Harbor Blvd (92802)
Rates: $31-$60;
Tel: (714) 750-1811; (800) 421-6662

ANAHEIM PLAZA HOTEL
1700 S Harbor Blvd (92802)
Rates: $79-$117;
Tel: (800) 228-1357

BEST WESTERN ANAHEIM STARDUST
1057 W Ball Rd (92802)
Rates: $40-$98;
Tel: (800) 528-1234

CAVALIER INN & SUITES
11811 S Harbor Blvd (92802)
Rates: $36-$65;
Tel: (714) 750-1000; (800) 821-2768

CROWN STERLING SUITES
3100 E Frontera St (92806)
Rates: $170-$180;
Tel: (714) 632-1221; (800) 433-4600
(800) 433-4600 (CA)

DESERT PALM INN & SUITES
631 W Katella Ave (92802)
Rates: $49-$64;
Tel: (714) 535-1133; (800) 635-5423

ECONO LODGE-EAST
871 S Harbor Blvd (92805)
Rates: $42-$62;
Tel: (714) 535-7878; (800) 424-4777

FRIENDSHIP INN-SUNRISE
705 S Beach Blvd (92804)
Rates: $32-$38;
Tel: (800) 424-4777

Locate Other Dog-Friendly Activities...Check Nearby Cities

GRAND HOTEL
7 Greedman Way (92802)
Rates: $85-$235;
Tel: (800) 421-6662

HAMPTON INN
300 E Katella Way (92802)
Rates: $55-$65;
Tel: (714) 772-8713; (800) 426-7866

HILTON AND TOWERS
777 Convention Way (92802)
Rates: $170-$255;
Tel: (800) 233-6904

HOLIDAY INN ANAHEIM AT THE PARK
1221 S Harbor Blvd (92805)
Rates: $75-$89;
Tel: (714) 758-0900; (800) 465-4329

MARRIOTT HOTEL
700 W Convention Way (92802)
Rates: $160-$189;
Tel: (714) 750-8000; (800) 228-9290

MOTEL 6-PREMIER
100 W Freedman Way (92801)
Rates: $36-$40;
Tel: (714) 520-9696; (800) 440-6000

MOTEL 6
2920 W Chapman Ave (92802)
Rates: $30-$36;
Tel: (714) 634-2441; (800) 440-6000

MOTEL 6
921 S Beach Blvd (92804)
Rates: $32;
Tel: (714) 220-2866; (800) 440-6000

THE PAN PACIFIC
1717 S West St (92802)
Rates: $135-$175;
Tel: (714) 999-0990; (800) 321-8976

QUALITY HOTEL-MAINGATE
616 Convention Way (92802)
Rates: $47-$95;
Tel: (714) 750-3131; (800) 231-6215

RAFFLES INN & SUITES
2040 S Harbor Blvd (92802)
Rates: $44-$74;
Tel: (800) 654-0196

RAMADA INN
1331 E Katella Ave (92805)
Rates: $47-$74;
Tel: (800) 228-0586

RED ROOF INN
1251 N Harbor Blvd (92801)
Rates: $31-$60;
Tel: (714) 635-6461; (800) 843-7663

RESIDENCE INN BY MARRIOTT
1700 S Clementine St (92802)
Rates: $79-$195;
Tel: (714) 533-3555; (800) 331-3131

RODEWAY INN
800 S Beach Blvd (92804)
Rates: $44-$68;
Tel: (800) 424-4777

STATION INN & SUITES
989 W Ball Rd (92802)
Rates: $35-$65;
Tel: (800) 874-6265

TRAVELODGE-ANAHEIM HILLS
5710 E La Palma (92807)
Rates: $55-$110;
Tel: (714) 779-0252; (800) 578-7878

TRAVELODGE AT THE PARK
1166 W Katella Ave (92802)
Rates: $35-$59;
Tel: (714) 774-7817; (800) 578-7878

RECREATION

YORBA REGIONAL PARK - Leashes

Info: Spend a leisurely afternoon at this popular and often crowded 166-acre park. Hike a trail or two, spectate at a baseball game or simply relax with Max and a picnic lunch. For more information: (714) 970-1640.

Dogs May Be Unleashed Unless Otherwise Indicated

Directions: From eastbound Highway 91, take the Weir Canyon Road/Yorba Linda Boulevard exit north to La Palma Avenue. Follow the signs to the park.

Note: $2 parking fee.

ANDERSON

LODGING

ANDERSON VALLEY INN
2661 McMurry Dr (96007)
Rates: $40-$60;
Tel: (916) 365-2566

BEST WESTERN KNIGHTS INN
2688 Gateway Dr (96007)
Rates: $42-$54;
Tel: (916) 365-2753; (800) 528-1234

ANGELS CAMP

LODGING

ANGELS INN MOTEL
600 N Main St (95221)
Rates: $50-$85;
Tel: (209) 736-4242; (800) 225-3764

GOLD COUNTRY INN
720 S Main St (95222)
Rates: $46-$76;
Tel: (209) 736-4611; (800) 225-3764

RECREATION

DUCK LAKE TRAIL HIKE - Leashes

Beginner/2.5 miles/1.5 hours

Info: A cinchy trail with a gradual ascent up a small hill, over a crest and back down to the lake. For more information: (209) 795-1381.

Directions: From Angels Camp, head northeast on Highway 4 for approximately 50 miles to Lake Alpine. Follow the east-shore road heading immediately away from the highway just east of the Chickaree Picnic Ground. Pass the spur road which branches east to the Pine Marten Campground to the Silver Creek Campground. For an area map and more information, stop by the Ranger Station.

Locate Other Dog-Friendly Activities...Check Nearby Cities

LIVING FOREST NATURE TRAIL HIKE - Leashes

Beginner/0.5 miles/0.5 hours

Info: Forest ecology is the theme of this no-sweat interpretive trail. So, leash your pup and take a quick, educational stroll. For more information: (209) 795-1381.

Directions: From Angels Camp, take Highway 4 north to Black Springs Road, approximately a half-mile north of the Calaveras Ranger Station in Hathaway Pines. The trailhead is located on Black Springs Road.

OSBORNE HILL TRAIL HIKE - Leashes

Beginner/2.6 miles/1.5 hours

Info: At an elevation of almost 8,000 feet, Osborne Hill provides magnificent views of the Lake Alpine area on this pleasurable jaunt. For more information: (209) 795-1381.

Directions: Travel northeast on Highway 4 for approximately 48 miles to Silvertip Campground. The small parking area (3-4 vehicles) and trailhead are 14 miles east of the campground. For an area map and more information, stop by the Ranger Station.

TRYON PARK - Leashes

Info: Relax with Rover along the banks of a refreshing, sun-dappled creek, or vege out on the soft grass under a mature oak tree in this lovely park.

Directions: Located at Highway 4 and Booster's Way.

UTICA PARK - Leashes

Info: Does the name Calaveras County sound familiar? Well once you visit this park and see the statue of Mark Twain, you'll know why. Keep Fido on a leash, there might be lost frogs jumping about.

Directions: Located at Highway 49 (Main Street) and Sam's Way.

ANTIOCH

LODGING

RAMADA INN
2436 Mahogany Way (94509)
Rates: $72-$92;
Tel: (510) 754-6600; (800) 272-6232

RECREATION

BLACK DIAMOND MINES REGIONAL PRESERVE - Leashes

Info: Over 40 miles of trails await you and the pooch in this pretty region. There's enough to keep you busy all day. Highlights include the Rose Hill Cemetery, the northernmost stand of Coulter pines and unusual plants like the Mt. Diablo manzanita and the desert olive. Keep a snout out for soaring eagles. Rock jocks might want to hound out the clearly defined, exposed beds of sandstone and coal. For more information: (510) 757-2620.

Directions: From Antioch, head south on Somersville Road for two miles to the park's entrance.

CONTRA LOMA REGIONAL PARK - Leashes

Info: Take the tailwagger for some romping fun and fishing pleasure in this 776-acre park. The 80-acre reservoir is chock-full of catfish, black bass, striped bass, bluegill, trout and red-eared sunfish. For more information: (510) 562-7275.

Directions: From Antioch, take Highway 4 east to Lone Tree Way. Follow Lone Tree Way to Golf Course Road and take a right. Continue to Frederickson Lane, turn right and follow to park entrance.

Note: Parking fee and $1 dog fee required.

APPLEGATE

LODGING

THE ORIGINAL FIREHOUSE MOTEL
17855 Lake Arthur Rd (95703)
Rates: $34-$43;
Tel: (916) 878-7770

APTOS

LODGING

APPLE LANE INN BED & BREAKFAST
6265 Soquel Dr (95003)
Rates: $70-$175;
Tel: (408) 475-6868; (800) 649-8988

MANGELS HOUSE BED & BREAKFAST
570 Aptos Creek Rd (95003)
Rates: $105-$135;
Tel: (408) 688-7982

RECREATION

RIO DEL MAR BEACH-Leashes

Info: This wide strip of clean sand offers plenty of paw-stomping space for your beach hound. For more information: (408) 688-3222.

Directions: Located on Rio Del Mar Boulevard.

ARCADIA

LODGING

EMBASSY SUITES HOTEL
211 E Huntington Dr (91006)
Rates: $107-$122;
Tel: (818) 445-8525; (800) 362-2779

HAMPTON INN
311 E Huntington Dr (91006)
Rates: $57-$75;
Tel: (818) 574-5600; (800) 426-7866

MOTEL 6
225 Colorado Pl (91006)
Rates: $36-$40;
Tel: (818) 446-2660; (800) 440-6000

RESIDENCE INN BY MARRIOTT
321 E Huntington Dr (91006)
Rates: $112-$142;
Tel: (818) 446-6500; (800) 331-3131

Dogs May Be Unleashed Unless Otherwise Indicated

<u>RECREATION</u>
CHANTRY FLAT TO STURTEVANT FALLS TRAIL HIKE
Intermediate/3.5 miles/2.0 hours

Info: Tails will be wagging in the breeze on this pristine hike through pretty Santa Anita Canyon along the Gabrielino Trail to the towering 55-foot falls. You and your soon to be dirty dog will enjoy a shade-filled hike into the canyon where you can pawse and admire the scenic surroundings. Pack plenty of Fuji, you'll want to capture the beauty of the cascading canyon waterfall. For more information: (818) 790-1151.

Directions: From the Foothill Freeway (210) in Arcadia, exit on Santa Anita Avenue and drive for six miles until the road ends at Chantry Flat. The trailhead is across the road from the parking area.

Note: DO NOT attempt to climb the waterfall, the rocks are extremely slippery.

CRYSTAL LAKE TRAIL to MT. ISLIP HIKE
Expert/8.5 miles/5.0 hours

Info: Crystal Lake is the only natural lake in the San Gabriel Mountains. Your trek on Windy Gap Trail traverses beautiful forestland. Listen for the sweet sounds of trickling brooks and melodic songbirds. Deer are plentiful too. If it's a blue sky day, you'll be treated to inspiring mountain and ocean views. For more information: (818) 574-1613.

Directions: From Arcadia, take the Foothill Freeway (210) east, past "The 605" to Azusa. Take Azusa Avenue (Highway 39) north for 24 miles to the turnoff for the Crystal Lake Recreation Area. Drive 2.5 miles to the parking area and the trailhead.

EAGLES ROOST to LITTLEROCK CREEK TRAIL HIKE

Intermediate/7.0 miles/3.5 hours

Info: Once you reach the trailhead, this scenic hike descends rather steeply and then levels out. You'll pass dense oak, fir, cedar and pine woodlands before coming to the upper section of Littlerock Creek. There's a small waterfall just upstream past a remarkable cluster of cedar trees. The views of the multi-colored rocky bluffs and outcroppings on your uphill return are incredible. For more information: (818) 574-1613.

Directions: From Arcadia, take the 210 Freeway northwest to Angeles Crest Highway (Highway 2) northeast. Follow to Eagles Roost Picnic Area, approximately 12 miles northeast of Chilao Recreation Area. To access the trailhead from the picnic area, take the old logging road descending west on the north side of the highway. After .75 of a mile, the trail is to the right.

SAN OLENE FIRE ROAD TRAIL HIKE - Leashes

Expert/7.0 miles/4.0 hours

Info: If you and Fido are in fine fettle, don't settle for a drive by. Although other paths in the area may be tempting, this trail offers unparalleled views. You'll be treated to awe inspiring panoramas reaching as far as the Channel Islands, Santa Catalina Island, Saddleback Peak and Palomar Mountain. Of course, the local backdrops like Mt. San Jacinto and Santa Monica Bay will also eat your Fuji rolls. Plan to spend the afternoon absorbing some classic California scenery. For more information: (818) 574-5300.

Directions: From Interstate 210 in Arcadia, exit on Santa Anita Avenue and head north. Drive six miles to road's end at Chantry Flat. Park in the large lot and look for the signed, paved fire road at the edge of the picnic area.

ARCATA

LODGING

BEST WESTERN ARCATA INN
4827 Valley West Blvd (95521)
Rates: $52-$78;
Tel: (707) 826-0313; (800) 528-1234

COMFORT INN
4701 Valley West Blvd (95521)
Rates: $35-$85;
Tel: (707) 826-2827; (800) 221-2222

HOTEL ARCATA
708 9th St (95521)
Rates: $45-$120;
Tel: (707) 826-0217; (800) 344-1221

MOTEL 6
4744 Valley West Blvd (95521)
Rates: $29-$40;
Tel: (707) 822-7061; (800) 440-6000

QUALITY INN-MAD RIVER
3535 Janes Rd (95521)
Rates: $45-$76;
Tel: (707) 822-0409; (800) 221-2222

SUPER 8
4887 Valley West Blvd (95521)
Rates: $32-$57;
Tel: (800) 800-8000

RECREATION

ARCATA COMMUNITY FOREST/REDWOOD PARK - Leashes

Info: A short drive from downtown Arcata, 575 acres of lush woodlands and scented air await you and your pooch. Visit in the morning and listen to the songbirds. Or get your daily dose of Rexercise on the 10 miles of trails which climb from 250 feet to 1,050 feet. For more information: (707) 822-7091.

Directions: From Highway 101, take Samoa Boulevard east. At Union Street, go north and make a right onto 14th Street. Continue into the forest to the parking area. Pick a trailhead and begin your day.

ARCATA MARSH AND WILDLIFE SANCTUARY - Leashes

Info: Birdwatching, walking and jogging are the popular activities in this 75-acre park that offers bay views and vistas of Arcata and the foothills. A series of marshes naturally treat wastewater before release into Humboldt Bay. The area is a nationally recognized habitat for several species of flora and fauna. For more information: (707) 826-7031.

Directions: The sanctuary is located at the foot of "I" Street in Arcata.

CLAM BEACH COUNTY PARK

Info: Your pooch can ride the waves or help you dig for clams at this expansive beach. Not only is this place dog-friendly, it's accessible too. For more information: (707) 445-7652.

Directions: From Highway 101 approximately 7 miles north of Arcata, take the Clam Beach Park exit west for about 2 miles.

HAMMOND TRAIL HIKE - Leashes

Beginner/4.0 miles/2.0 hours

Info: This beautiful coastal trail links Arcata with McKinleyville. Shake a leg and enjoy the seascape and delightful ocean breezes while getting your daily dose. For more information: (707) 445-7651.

Directions: Take the Guintoli Lane exit north of Arcata, or take the Murray Road exit in McKinleyville.

MAD RIVER COUNTY PARK

Info: This pretty drive from Arcata takes you through back country roads filled with old barns. If you like your beaches private, you've come to the right place. For more information: (707) 445-7651.

Directions: From Highway 101, exit on Guintoli Lane and go right almost immediately onto Heindon Road. Follow the signs to the park and a small parking lot at the end of the road.

ARNOLD

LODGING

EBBETT'S PASS LODGE
1173 Hwy 4, P. O. Box 2591 (95223)
Rates: $42-$59;
Tel: (209) 795-1563; (800) 225-3764

SIERRA VACATION RENTALS
P. O. Box 1080 (95223)
Rates: $130-$170;
Tel: (800) 995-2422; (800) 225-3764

WEHE'S MEADOWMONT LODGE
2011 Hwy 4 (95223)
Rates: $47-$58;
Tel: (209) 795-1394; (800) 225-3764

<u>RECREATION</u>

BULL RUN LAKE TRAIL HIKE - Leashes

Intermediate/7.0 miles/3.5 hours

Info: Don't be fooled by the relative easy-does-it beginning of this trail. After the first 1.5 miles, you and the dogster are in for a steep aerobic climb. Take some time to smell the flowers in the pretty meadowland before testing your leg muscles on the demanding ascent. For more information: (209) 795-1381.

Directions: From Arnold, take Highway 4 north to the Stanislaus Meadows turnoff (FR 8N13). The trailhead is on FR 8N13.

CALAVERAS BIG TREES STATE PARK - Leashes

Info: Embark on a journey along fire roads, over chaparral-studded hills, through conifer forests. The huge sugar pines you'll see are among the largest in the world. For more information: (209) 795-2334.

Directions: Travel northeast on Highway 4 for four miles. Follow the signs.

Note: Since dogs are not permitted on the trails, buy a map of the fire roads for $1. There's also a day-use fee of $5 per car & $1 per dog.

INSPIRATION POINT TRAIL HIKE - Leashes

Intermediate/3.0 miles/1.5 hours

Info: The exceptional Carson-Iceberg Wilderness is the locale of this hike. Make your way up to Inspiration Point for some outstanding panoramic views of the neighboring landscape. For more information: (209) 795-1381.

Directions: From Arnold, head northeast on Highway 4 for about 25 miles to Lake Alpine. Travel on the east shore road that heads immediately away from Highway 4 (just east of Chickaree Picnic Ground). Find the spur road branching east to the Pine Marten Campground, just prior to the Silver Creek Campground. Park at the Pine Marten Campground. For maps and more information, stop by the Ranger Station.

Locate Other Dog-Friendly Activities...Check Nearby Cities

WHITE PINES LAKE AND PARK - Leashes

Info: This park is as peaceful and beautiful as it sounds. You and the pupster can frolic through a forest of pines or listen to the waves lap along the shoreline as you enjoy the day and each other's company. For more information: (209) 795-1054.

Directions: Located in the vicinity of Highway 4 and Dunbar Road.

ARROYO GRANDE

LODGING

BEST WESTERN CASA GRANDE INN
850 Oak Park Rd (93420)
Rates: $58-$95;
Tel: (805) 481-7398; (800) 528-1234

ECONO LODGE
611 E Camino Real (93420)
Rates: $40-$110;
Tel: (805) 489-9300; (800) 424-4777

RECREATION

BIG FALLS TRAIL HIKE

Beginner/5.2 miles/2.5 hours

Info: Even telly bellies will love this trail through a forested canyon complete with two cascading waterfalls. Visit in springtime and brighten your world with rainbow colors. Visit in summer and tickle your toes in the cool waters. For more information: (805) 925-9538.

Directions: From Arroyo Grande, take Lopez Canyon Drive east approximately 10 miles to Hi Mountain Road. Turn right and continue one mile to Upper Lopez Canyon Road. Turn left for 11 miles to the trailhead.

LITTLE FALLS TRAIL HIKE

Intermediate/5.2 miles/2.5 hours

Info: This pretty hike lets you and the dogster experience a little bit of everything- water fun, scenery and cool forests. You'll ascend 1,350 feet from Lopez Creek through a forested canyon to a chaparral-covered ridge. The ridgetop views are extraordinary, reaching all the way to the Pacific. A mile from the canyon trailhead are the 50-foot high Little Falls, best viewed in early spring. For more information: (805) 925-9538.

Directions: From Arroyo Grande, take Lopez Canyon Drive east approximately 10 miles to Hi Mountain Road. Turn right and continue one mile to Upper Lopez Canyon Road. Go left for 9 miles to the trailhead.

LOPEZ CANYON TRAIL HIKE

Beginner/Intermediate/5.3 miles/2.5 hours

Info: When you and the dawgus yearn for a dose of Mother Nature with all the trimmings, plan a day in the wilderness along this enchanting trail. Lose yourself in lush vegetation and the delightful year-round stream of pretty Lopez Canyon. Don't forget to pack a biscuit basket, ancient oaks offer cooling shade all along the pathway. When day is done, say adieu and retrace your steps. For more information: (805) 925-9538.

Directions: From Arroyo Grande, take Lopez Canyon Drive east. After ten miles, Lopez Canyon Drive intersects with Hi Mountain Road. Turn right and continue one mile to Upper Lopez Canyon Road. Turn left. Upper Lopez Canyon is 13.5 miles past this junction.

Note: High clearance vehicles only.

ATASCADERO

LODGING

BEST WESTERN COLONY INN
3600 El Camino Real (93422)
Rates: $46-$83;
Tel: (805) 466-4449; (800) 528-1234

MOTEL 6
9400 El Camino Real (93422)
Rates: $26-$32;
Tel: (805) 466-6701; (800) 440-6000

RANCHO TEE MOTEL
6895 El Camino Real (93422)
Rates: $46-$95;
Tel: (805) 466-2231

SUPER 8 MOTEL
6505 Morro Rd (93422)
Rates: $39-$95;
Tel: (805) 466-0794; (800) 800-8000

RECREATION
CERRO ALTO LOOP TRAIL HIKE

Intermediate/3.0 miles/1.5 hours

Info: You and the pupster are in for a roller coaster-like hike on this looping trail that follows the East Fork of Morro Creek. The trail begins amidst bay, fern, oak and madrone trees, climbs through chaparral and then descends to the Cerro Alto Trail junction. Point your snout west for the switchbacking descent to the trailhead. If you're an experienced hiking duo and you're up to an additional 2-mile (roundtrip) challenge, tackle the steep ascent to Cerro Alto Peak for some incredible views. For more information: (805) 925-9538.

Directions: From Atascadero, head west on Highway 41 to the trailhead at the Cerro Alto Campground.

CERRO ALTO TRAIL HIKE

Expert/4.0 miles/2.0 hours

Info: This tough-as-nails hike is not for the fair-of-paw. Only experienced hikers and hounds will have the stamina for the steep 2-mile climb to Cerro Alto Peak. Your reward for the scramble, sweeping views of the Pacific coastline. For more information: (805) 925-9538.

Directions: From Atascadero, head west on Highway 41 to the Cerro Alto Campground. The trailhead is located just south of Host Cabin, along the main campground road.

AUBURN

LODGING

BEST WESTERN GOLDEN KEY MOTEL
13450 Lincoln Way (95603)
Rates: $46-$60;
Tel: (916) 885-8611; (800) 528-1234

COUNTRY SQUIRE INN
13480 Lincoln Way (95603)
Rates: $37-$52;
Tel: (916) 885-7025

HOLIDAY INN-AUBURN
120 Grass Valley Highway (95603)
Rates: $64-$78;
Tel: (800) 814-8787

Dogs May Be Unleashed Unless Otherwise Indicated

<u>RECREATION</u>
AUBURN STATE RECREATION AREA - Leashes

Info: For some great hikes and terrific views of the landscape, you can't go wrong at this 42,000-acre park. One popular hike begins behind the Auburn Fairgrounds at Pleasant Avenue. Walk a mile or all the way to Squaw Valley. For a quicker jaunt, exit off Interstate 80 at Foresthill Road and drive east. In about a mile, you'll pass over the Foresthill Bridge. Look for a small off-road parking area on your right. Walk back towards the bridge, and bear left at the little dirt road to the trailhead (you'll see a sign banning motorcycles). For more information: (916) 885-4527.

Directions: Behind Auburn Fairgrounds at Pleasant Avenue.

EUCHRE BAR TRAIL HIKE

Intermediate/6.0 miles/3.5 hours

Info: This trail begins with a steep, curving descent to the North Fork American River. Once you and the pupster reach the foot-bridge, the riverside trail heads upstream for an invigorating 2.4-mile trek. For more information: (916) 367-2224.

Directions: From Auburn head east on Interstate 80 to the Alta exit and turn right on Morton. Go left on Casa Loma to the Rawhide Mine sign and turn right. Continue .75 of a mile past the second railroad crossing to the parking lot. The trail begins .10 of a mile past the lot.

FOREST VIEW TRAIL HIKE - Leashes

Beginner/1.5 miles/0.75 hours

Info: The giant sequoia, the world's largest trees, dominate this forest. Pick up a brochure at the trailhead and make the most of this interpretive trail. At 5,200 feet you and your canine crony will enjoy endless views of the area's wild landscape, but you'll have to share them. This is a very popular trail. For more information: (916) 367-2224.

Directions: From Interstate 80 at Auburn, head east on Foresthill Road for 16 miles to the town of Foresthill. Then take Mosquito Ridge Road east 27 miles to the trailhead.

MCGUIRE TRAIL HIKE

Beginner/7.5 miles/4.0 hours

Info: This lakeside hike is perfect for anyone who simply loves a scenic walk in nature. The trail skedaddles up a gentle incline to Red Star Ridge at 5,600 feet, affording a great view of the French Meadows Reservoir. This 2,000-acre lake is chock-full of rainbow and brown trout. If you're a fishing hound, come prepared. For more information: (913) 367-2224.

Directions: From Interstate 80 at Auburn, head east on Foresthill Road for 16 miles to the town of Foresthill. Continue east on Mosquito Ridge Road for 36 miles across the Forest Meadows Reservoir Dam. Follow the road along the south side of the lake. Turn left at the southeast end of the lake and follow the signs to the trailhead at the boat ramp.

MICHIGAN BLUFF TRAIL HIKE

Intermediate/4.0 miles/2.0 hours

Info: Picturesque Eldorado Canyon is the backdrop for this rather simple hike. A series of switchbacks descend to your destination, a footbridge over the Eldorado Creek. Find a shady spot and partake in a game of fetch with Fletch. For more information: (916) 367-2224.

Directions: From Interstate 80 at Auburn, take Foresthill Road east for 20 miles. The trailhead is a quarter mile east of Michigan Bluff.

AVALON (Catalina Island)

LODGING

HOTEL MONTEREY
108 Sumner Ave, P. O. Box 1372 (90704)
Rates: $65-$165;
Tel: (310) 510-0264; (800) 858-0035

Dogs May Be Unleashed Unless Otherwise Indicated

AZUSA

<u>RECREATION</u>

LAKE TRAIL HIKE - Leashes

Intermediate/2.0 miles/1.0 hours

Info: For an optimum waterful adventure, plan this hike in springtime when snowmelt fills Crystal Lake, the only natural lake in the San Gabriel Mountains. Fishermen will also enjoy Crystal Lake in the spring, one of the times it's stocked with trout. No matter when you visit, you'll be delighted with the aromatic scents and the shady coolness along this trail. For more information: (818) 335-1251.

Directions: From Azusa, head north on Highway 39/Azusa Avenue approximately 25 miles to the Crystal Lake Recreation Area turnoff. Follow about 2 miles to the Crystal Lake Visitor Center parking area. The trailhead is southeast of the visitor center, which is only open on weekends.

PINYON RIDGE NATURE TRAIL HIKE - Leashes

Beginner/1.0 miles/0.5 hours

Info: From a verdant meadow and dense pine forest to a stand of yucca, this leg stretching jaunt is like a breath of fresh air. You and the pupster will stroll through big cone spruce, white fir and sugar pine as you loop along the Crystal Lake Basin. For more information: (818) 335-1251.

Directions: From Azusa, head north on Highway 39/Azusa Avenue approximately 25 miles to the Crystal Lake Recreation Area turnoff. Follow about 2 miles to the Crystal Lake Visitor Center parking area. The trailhead is southeast of the visitor center, which is only open on weekends.

TOTOTGNA NATURE TRAIL HIKE - Leashes

Beginner/0.75 miles/0.5 hours

Info: Learn as you take a turn around this nature trail. Pick up an interpretive guide for a quickie education on the area's earthquake fault and ecology. For more information: (818) 335-1251.

Locate Other Dog-Friendly Activities...Check Nearby Cities

Directions: From Azusa, head north on Highway 39/Azusa Avenue approximately 25 miles to the Crystal Lake Recreation Area turnoff. Follow about 2 miles to the Crystal Lake Visitor Center parking area. The trailhead is southeast of the visitor center, which is only open on weekends.

WINDY GAP TRAIL TO LILY SPRING HIKE - Leashes

Intermediate/Expert/9.0 miles/5.0 hours

Info: Fill up on kibble before you head out on this long hike- you'll need the energy. Whether you're up to a mile or going the distance, you'll walk in splendor along this pretty trail. You and your hiking hound will travel through a tranquil forest chock-full of songbirds and wildlife. Keep the leash taut if your pooch is of herding heritage, deer abound. Small springs lace the forest floor offering some paw dipping moments, while distant mountains and canyons echo the sounds of nature. When you junction with the Pacific Crest Trail on your right, follow it until Lily Spring where a biscuit break is sure to please. When you can pull yourself away from this captivating spot, turn the hound around, you're homeward bound. For more information: (818) 335-1251.

Directions: From Azusa, head north on Highway 39 for 25 miles to the Crystal Lake Recreation Area. Park in the dirt lot for hikers. The trailhead is on the left-side of the road.

BAKER

<u>LODGING</u>

ARNE'S ROYAL HAWAIIAN MOTEL
200 W Baker Blvd (92309)
Rates: $49;
Tel: (619) 733-4326

BUN BOY MOTEL
P. O. Box 130 (92309)
Rates: $29-$44;
Tel: (619) 733-4363

Dogs May Be Unleashed Unless Otherwise Indicated

BAKERSFIELD

LODGING

BEST WESTERN HERITAGE INN
253 Trask St (93312)
Rates: $44-$60;
Tel: (805) 764-6268; (800) 528-1234

BEST WESTERN HILL HOUSE
700 Truxtun Ave (93301)
Rates: $46-$50;
Tel: (800) 528-1234

BEST WESTERN INN
2620 Pierce Rd (93308)
Rates: $56-$77;
Tel: (800) 528-1234

BEST WESTERN OAK INN
889 Oak St (93304)
Rates: $56-$77;
Tel: (800) 528-1234

COMFORT INN-CENTRAL
830 Wible Rd (93304)
Rates: $36-$55;
Tel: (800) 221-2222

ECONO LODGE
200 Trask St (93312)
Rates: $33-$44;
Tel: (800) 424-4777

ECONOMY INNS OF AMERICA
6100 Knudsen Dr (93308)
Rates: $22-$37;
Tel: (800) 826-0778

ECONOMY INNS OF AMERICA
6501 Colony St (93307)
Rates: $24-$40;
Tel: (800) 826-0778

LA QUINTA MOTOR INN
3232 Riverside Dr (93308)
Rates: $47-$50;
Tel: (805) 325-7400; (800) 531-5900

LONE OAK INN
10614 Rosedale Hwy (93312)
Rates: $49;
Tel: (805) 589-6600

MOTEL 6
2727 White Lane (93304)
Rates: $26-$32;
Tel: (805) 834-2828; (800) 440-6000

MOTEL 6
5241 Olive Tree Ct (93308)
Rates: $24-$28;
Tel: (805) 392-9700; (800) 440-6000

MOTEL 6
1350 Easton Dr (93309)
Rates: $25-$31;
Tel: (805) 327-1686; (800) 440-6000

MOTEL 6-EAST
8223 E Brundage Ln (93307)
Rates: $26-$32;
Tel: (805) 366-7231; (800) 440-6000

QUALITY INN-AIRPORT
4500 Pierce Rd (93308)
Rates: $45-$65;
Tel: (800) 221-2222

QUALITY INN
1011 Oak St (93304)
Rates: $42-$62;
Tel: (800) 221-2222

RED LION HOTEL
3100 Camino Del Rio Ct (93308)
Rates: $105-$140;
Tel: (805) 323-7111; (800) 547-8010

RESIDENCE INN BY MARRIOTT
4241 Chester Ln (93309)
Rates: $65-$95;
Tel: (800) 331-3131

REGENCY INN
818 Real Rd (93309)
Rates: $40-$50;
Tel: (805) 324-6666

RIO BRAVO TENNIS & FITNESS RESORT
11200 Lake Ming Rd (93306)
Rates: $68-$78;
Tel: (805) 872-5000; (800) 282-5000

SHERATON INN BAKERSFIELD
5101 California Ave (93309)
Rates: $85-$110;
Tel: (805) 325-9700; (800) 500-5399

Locate Other Dog-Friendly Activities...Check Nearby Cities

<u>RECREATION</u>

KERN RIVER COUNTY PARK - Leashes

Info: The Hart Park section of this county park is an unusual blend of verdant, trail-laced meadows and a stark treeless mountain. Avoid the Lake Ming area, it's hot and not particularly dog-friendly. For more information: (805) 861-2345.

Directions: From North Bakersfield, travel east on Panorama Drive to Alfred Harrell Highway. Follow this curvy road to the gates of the park and signs to the different sections.

BALDWIN   PARK

<u>LODGING</u>

MOTEL 6
14510 Garvey Ave (91706)
Rates: $30-$34;
Tel: (818) 960-5011; (800) 440-6000

<u>RECREATION</u>

ISLIP SADDLE TRAIL to MT. WILLIAMSON HIKE

Intermediate/5.0 miles/2.5 hours

Info: Atop Mt. Williamson, you'll enjoy incredible views of two fascinating geological formations- Devil's Punchbowl and the San Andreas Fault. Reach the first summit on the faint trail along the ridge, about .5 miles from the main trail. From the rise, you'll see another rise about .25 miles to the northwest. This second rise offers the best views. For more information: (818) 574-1613.

Directions: From Baldwin Park, take Interstate 605 north to the 210 Freeway northwest. Follow to Angeles Crest Highway (Highway 2) heading northeast approximately 14 miles beyond Chilao. Islip Saddle is located at the junction of Highway 2 and Highway 39.

BANNING

LODGING

DAYS INN
2320 W Ramsey St (92220)
Rates: $38-$40;
Tel: (909) 849-0092; (800) 329-7566

SUPER 8 MOTEL
1690 W Ramsey St (92220)
Rates: $29-$37;
Tel: (800) 800-8000

TRAVELODGE
1700 W Ramsey St (92220)
Rates: $36-$45;
Tel: (909) 849-1000; (800) 578-7878

RECREATION

HURKEY CREEK PARK - Leashes

Info: Summer heat got you down? Head for the cool confines of this 59-acre, high-elevation park. The area encompasses Hurkey Creek along with several enjoyable hiking trails. Don't be tempted by the San Jacinto Wilderness, pooches are banned. For more information: (909) 659-2656.

Directions: From Banning, take Highway 243 south to Mountain Center. Continue south on Highway 74 four miles to the park.

Note: $2/Adult, $1/Child under 12 and $2/dog day - use fee

REPPLIER PARK - Leashes

Info: Your bowwow can rove over the ball field or sit quietly and contemplate nature with you in this pleasant park. For more information: (909) 922-1250.

Directions: Located on West George Street and San Gorgonio Avenue.

BARSTOW

LODGING

ASTRO BUDGET MOTEL
1271 E Main St (92311)
Rates: $22-$38;
Tel: (619) 256-2204

BARSTOW INN
1261 E Main St (92311)
Rates: $26-$34;
Tel: (619) 256-7581

BEST MOTEL
1281 E Main St (92311)
Rates: $24-$32;
Tel: (619) 256-6836

DESERT INN MOTEL
1100 E Main St (92311)
Rates: $28-$38;
Tel: (619) 256-2146

ECONO LODGE
1230 E Main St (92311)
Rates: $24-$52;
Tel: (619) 256-2133

ECONOMY INNS OF AMERICA
1590 Coolwater Ln (92311)
Rates: $24-$37;
Tel: (800) 826-0778

EL RANCHO MOTEL & RESTAURANT
112 E Main St (92311)
Rates: $19-$31;
Tel: (619) 256-2401

GATEWAY MOTEL
1630 E Main St (92311)
Rates: $22-$40;
Tel: (619) 256-8931

GOOD NITE INN
2551 Commerce Pkwy (92311)
Rates: $42;
Tel: (619) 253-2121

HILLCREST MOTEL
1111 E Main St (92311)
Rates: $24-$30;
Tel: (619) 256-1063

HOLIDAY INN
1511 E Main St (92311)
Rates: $68;
Tel: (619) 256-5673; (800) 465-4329

HOLIDAY INN EXPRESS
1861 W Main St (92311)
Rates: $40-$60;
Tel: (800) 465-4329

HOWARD JOHNSON'S
1431 E Main St (92311)
Rates: $49-$69;
Tel: (800) 446-4656

MOTEL 6
31951 E Main St (92311)
Rates: $24-$30;
Tel: (619) 256-0653; (800) 440-6000

MOTEL 6
150 N Yucca Ave (92311)
Rates: $25-$31;
Tel: (619) 246-1752; (800) 440-6000

QUALITY INN
1520 E Main St (92311)
Rates: $49-$68;
Tel: (619) 256-6891; (800) 221-2222

STARDUST INN
901 E Main St (92311)
Rates: $24-$45;
Tel: (619) 256-7116

SUNSET INN
1350 W Main St (92311)
Rates: $24-$35;
Tel: (619) 256-8921

SUPER 8 MOTEL
170 Coolwater Ln (92311)
Rates: $46;
Tel: (619) 256-8443; (800) 800-8000

VAGABOND INN
1243 E Main St (92311)
Rates: $36-$55;
Tel: (619) 234-9607; (800) 522-1555

Dogs May Be Unleashed Unless Otherwise Indicated

BASS LAKE

LODGING

FORK'S RESORT
39150 Rd 222 (93604)
Rates: $65-$105;
Tel: (209) 642-3737

THE LAKESHORE BED & BREAKFAST
39131 Lake Dr (93604)
Rates: $125-$195;
Tel: (209) 683-8220

BAYWOOD PARK

LODGING

BACK BAY INN
1391 Second St (93402)
Rates: $45-$110;
Tel: (805) 528-1233

BEAUMONT

LODGING

GOLDEN WEST MOTEL
625 E 5th St (92223)
Rates: $32-$40;
Tel: (909) 845-2185

WINDSOR MOTEL
1265 E 6th St (92223)
Rates: $26-$30;
Tel: (909) 845-1436

RECREATION

BOGART PARK - Leashes

Info: Hiking trails lace through shaded, song-filled forests in this lovely park. Able anglers can try their luck, while basket toters can just relax in the picnic area and nibble their kibble. For more information: (909) 845-3818.

Directions: Take Interstate 10 to the Beaumont offramp. Go north on Beaumont Avenue to Brookside Avenue, then east on Brookside Avenue to Cherry Avenue. Head north on Cherry Avenue to the park entrance.

Note: $1 dog fee.

NOBLE CREEK REGIONAL PARK - Leashes

Info: This sports-oriented park offers acres of grassy, open fields for you and the pooch to sniff out. For more information: (909) 845-9555.

Directions: Located at 38900 14th Street.

BELLFLOWER

LODGING
MOTEL 6
17220 Downey Ave (90706)
Rates: $35-$41;
Tel: (310) 531-3933; (800) 440-6000

BELMONT

LODGING
MOTEL 6
1101 Shoreway Rd (94002)
Rates: $42-$46;
Tel: (415) 591-1471; (800) 440-6000

BENECIA

LODGING
BEST WESTERN HERITAGE INN
1955 E 2nd St (94510)
Rates: $60-$95;
Tel: (800) 528-1234

THE PAINTED LADY BED & BREAKFAST
141 East F St (94510)
Rates: $70-$85;
Tel: (707) 746-1646

BENNETT VALLEY

LODGING
COOPERS GROVE RANCH BED & BREAKFAST
5763 Sonoma Mountain Rd (95404)
Rates: $100-$150;
Tel: (707) 571-1928

Dogs May Be Unleashed Unless Otherwise Indicated

BERKELEY

LODGING

BEAU SKY HOTEL
2520 Durant Ave (94704)
Rates: $60-$85;
Tel: (510) 540-7688

GOLDEN BEAR MOTEL
1620 San Pablo Ave (94702)
Rates: $45-$49;
Tel: (510) 525-6770; (800) 252-6770

MARRIOTT-BERKELEY MARINA
200 Marina Blvd (94710)
Rates: $100-$155;
Tel: (510) 548-7920; (800) 228-9290

RAMADA INN BERKELEY
920 University Ave (94710)
Rates: $45-$55;
Tel: (800) 272-6232

RECREATION

ANTIOCH PIER TRAIL HIKE

Beginner/0.5 miles/0.5 hours

Info: Delight in a short but sweet hike through marshlands to an exceptional fishing pier off the San Joaquin River. For more information: (510) 635-0135.

Directions: Take Interstate 580 towards Richmond, then head east on Interstate 80. Take the Highway 4 exit east to Antioch. Exit at Wilbur Street and go right. Make an immediate left on Bridgehead Road to the parking area at road's end.

AQUATIC PARK - Leashes

Info: Let Rover dip his paws in the lagoon water or birdwatch together from this park. For more information: (510) 644-6530.

Directions: From Interstate 80 in Berkeley, exit at Ashby and head north on Bay Street to the parking lot.

CLAREMONT CANYON REGIONAL PRESERVE

Info: Pick any one of the steep, hilly trails and make your way to the top. Views of the University and surrounding landscape are incredible and the spectacular vista of San Francisco Bay is one you won't soon forget. For more information: (510) 644-6530.

Directions: From Highway 13 (Ashby Avenue), head north on College Avenue. Make a right on Derby Street passing the

Locate Other Dog-Friendly Activities...Check Nearby Cities

Clark Kerr Campus. The trails are located at the southeast corner of the school grounds- near Stonewall Road.

Note: Dogs must be leashed in developed areas.

OHLONE DOG PARK

Info: Take a trip to where it all began- Ohlone. The first leash-free park in America. And the model for all subsequent dog-friendly parks. You'll find grassy areas, drinking water and lots of socialization...for humans and canines alike. For more information: (510) 644-6530.

Directions: Located at Martin Luther King Jr. Way and Hearst Street.

POINT ISABEL REGIONAL SHORELINE

Info: Playtime and social time blend together at this shoreline park. From a game of fetch on a grassy field to an afternoon of Fido-fraternizing, you couldn't ask for a more dog-friendly environment. For more information: (510) 644-6530.

Directions: Head north on Interstate 80 exiting at Central Avenue. Travel west to the park entrance.

POINT PINOLE REGIONAL SHORELINE

Info: This vastly beautiful shoreline park is puppy paradise. With over 2,100 acres of sandy beaches, wildflower-clad meadows, hiking trails and spectacular panoramas, you and your pup won't want the day to end. So before it does, explore the marshlands, wander through extraordinary eucalyptus groves and admire beautiful Mount Tamalpais as you stroll along the beach. A visit to this park will be long remembered. For more information: (510) 635-0135.

Directions: Head north on Interstate 80 exiting at Hilltop Drive. Go west and make a right on San Pablo Avenue and then a left on Atlas Road. Follow Atlas Road. which becomes Giant Highway to the entrance.

Note: $3/parking fee on weekends and holidays; $1/dog fee. Dogs must be leashed in developed areas.

Dogs May Be Unleashed Unless Otherwise Indicated

ROUND TOP LOOP TRAIL HIKE

Beginner/1.7 miles/1.0 hours

Info: Pick up a self-guided tour pamphlet at the trailhead and take the Round Top Loop Trail in a clockwise direction, following the numbered posts. Your explorations will lead you through the remains of an extinct volcano. For more information: (510) 635-0135.

Directions: Take Highway 24, just east of the Caldecott Tunnel, to the Fish Ranch Road exit west to Grizzly Peak Boulevard. Turn left on Skyline Blvd. Park entrance is .25 miles further.

SAN PABLO RIDGE LOOP TRAIL HIKE

Intermediate/6.2 miles/3.0 hours

Info: This trail's ridgetop rewards you with first-rate vistas of the San Francisco Bay and the surrounding landscape. Begin your panoramic journey heading up the Belgum Trail. Make a right on San Pablo Ridge Trail, and follow to the top. You'll climb 700 feet in 2.25 miles. To descend, go right on scenic Mezue Trail, then right on the Wildcat Creek Trail to the bottom. For more information: (510) 635-0135.

Directions: From Berkeley, take Interstate 80 north to the Amador/Solano exit and follow Amador for three blocks. Go right on McBryde Avenue, heading east. Once past Arlington Boulevard, continue straight on Park Avenue bearing left through a piped gate to the parking lot.

SHORELINE TRAIL HIKE

Beginner/1.0 miles/0.50 hours

Info: Within the 21-acre Point Isabel Regional Shoreline Park is the gentle Shoreline Trail, complete with terrific bayfront views of San Francisco and Golden Gate. Birdwatching is best in the fall. For more information: (510) 635-0135.

Directions: Take Interstate 580 to Richmond and pick up Interstate 80. Exit at Central Avenue heading west to Isabel Street and turn right. Follow to the parking area.

Locate Other Dog-Friendly Activities...Check Nearby Cities

TILDEN REGIONAL PARK - Leashes

Info: To experience all that this spectacular park has to offer, try your paw at one of the many hiking trails winding through its 2,077 acres. Hike along Nimitz Way for terrific vistas of the East Bay Hills or follow the Big Springs Trail through meadows and groves to its junction with the Skyline National Recreation Trail/Sea View Trail. If you're a diehard fisherman, don't forget your trusty rod, the waters of Lake Anza beckon. For more information: (510) 635-0135.

Directions: Take Grizzly Peak Boulevard to Canon Drive, Shasta Road or South Park Drive. The park is accessible from all three locations.

WILDCAT CANYON REGIONAL PARK

Info: Within 2,428 acres, this park encapsulates the natural glory of Northern California. The east side is alive with madrones, bay laurels and chaparral; while the western hillsides are rife with wildflowers and grass. The weather can be foggy or sunny and invariably windy. Take Wildcat Creek Trail or any of the side trails and wander your day away. For more information: (510) 635-0135.

Directions: Head north on Interstate 80 exiting at Amador/Solano. Go three blocks left (north) on Amador Street and make a right (east) on McBryde to the entrance.

Note: Dogs must be leashed in developed areas.

BERMUDA DUNES

LODGING

MOTEL 6
78100 Varner Rd (92203)
Rates: $32-$36;
Tel: (619) 345-0550; (800) 440-6000

BEVERLY HILLS

LODGING

THE BEVERLY HILTON HOTEL
9876 Wilshire Blvd (90210)
Rates: $215-$700;
Tel: (800) 922-5432

FOUR SEASONS-BEVERLY HILLS
300 S Doheny Dr (90048)
Rates: $325-$510;
Tel: (310) 273-2222; (800) 332-3442

HOTEL NIKKO AT BEVERLY HILLS
465 S LaCienega Blvd (90048)
Rates: $220-$350;
Tel: (310) 247-0400; (800) 645-5687

HOTEL SOFITEL MA MAISON
8555 Beverly Blvd (90048)
Rates: $190-$230;
Tel: (310) 278-5444; (800) 763-4835
(800) 521-7772 (CA)

LOWELL HOTEL
9291 Burton Way (90210)
Rates: $290-$630;
Tel: (800) 800-2113

THE PENINSULA
9882 Little Santa Monica Blvd (90212)
Rates: $300-$3000;
Tel: (310) 551-2888; (800) 462-7899

THE REGENT BEVERLY WILSHIRE
9500 Wilshire Blvd (90212)
Rates: $255-$600;
Tel: (310) 275-5200; (800) 421-4354

RECREATION

BEVERLY GARDENS PARK - Leashes

Info: You can follow a path for twenty blocks on this slender stretch of greenery. For more information: (310) 285-2541.

Directions: On the north side of Santa Monica Boulevard, from Wilshire Boulevard to Doheny Drive.

HASTAIN TRAIL HIKE - Leashes

Intermediate/2.5 miles/1.25 hours

Info: For aerial views of west LA and the San Fernando Valley, leash the Laddie and head for this looping canyon trail. You'll climb steadily along the east side of Franklin Canyon to a scenic overlook. The trail then turns left (north) and descends a fire road back to the trailhead. Birdlovers, don't forget your binoculars. Over 90 species have been sighted in the canyon. For more information: (818) 597-9192.

Directions: From the intersection of Beverly Drive and Coldwater Canyon Drive in Beverly Hills, head north on Beverly Drive approximately 1.2 miles to Franklin Canyon Drive. Go right for just under a mile to Lake Drive. Take a sharp right on Lake Drive for about .7 miles to the William O. Douglas Outdoor Classroom (WODOC) headquarters. Parking is available along Lake Drive.

LAUREL CANYON PARK

Info: This first-rate grassy park is such a celebrated doggie nirvana that even pooches of the rich and famous make regular appearances. You're sure to meet up with dozens of canines as you walk the grounds, watch from a picnic table or make yourself comfy under a large shade tree. This casual, anything-goes, dog-loving park is fully equipped with pooper scoopers and water. For more information: (818) 756-8190.

Directions: From Beverly Hills, follow Beverly Drive into the mountains where it turns into Coldwater Canyon. At the stop sign at the top of the hill, turn right on Mulholland Drive (if you come to a fire station, you've missed this turn). Continue on Mulholland for 3-4 miles to the park on your right-hand side. Park along the road or in the parking lot.

Note: Restricted off-leash hours: 6 a.m.- 10 a.m. and 3 p.m. to dusk.

WILL ROGERS MEMORIAL PARK - Leashes

Info: Window shop on Rodeo Drive and finish your day at this small but posh park in the heart of Beverly Hills. Don't be surprised to see a famous face or two. For more information: (310) 285-2541.

Directions: On the corner of Canon and Beverly Drives at Sunset Boulevard, directly opposite the Beverly Hills Hotel.

BIG BEAR LAKE

LODGING

BEAR CLAW CABINS
586 Main St (92315)
Rates: $55-$94;
Tel: (909) 866-2666

BIG BEAR CABINS
39774 Big Bear Blvd (92315)
Rates: $59-$149;
Tel: (909) 866-2723

BLACK FOREST LODGE
P. O. Box 156 (92315)
Rates: $38-$110;
Tel: (909) 866-2166; (800) 255-4378

BOULDER CREEK RESORT
Box 92 (92315)
Rates: $45-$300;
Tel: (909) 866-2665; (800) 244-2327

CAL-PINE CABINS
41545 Big Bear Blvd (92315)
Rates: $59-$175;
Tel: (909) 866-2574

COZY HOLLOW LODGE
40409 Big Bear Blvd, P. O. Box 1288
(92315); Rates: $79-$139;
Tel: (909) 866-9694; (800) 882-4480

CREEK RUNNER'S LODGE
374 Georgia St (92315)
Rates: $50-$200;
Tel: (909) 866-7473

EAGLE'S NEST BED & BREAKFAST
41675 Big Bear Blvd (92315)
Rates: $75-$165;
Tel: (909) 866-6465

EDGEWATER INN
40570 Simonds Dr (92315)
Rates: $75-$85;
Tel: (909) 866-4161

FRONTIER LODGE & MOTEL
40472 Big Bear Blvd (92315)
Rates: $50-$165;
Tel: (909) 866-5888; (800) 457-6401

GOLDEN BEAR COTTAGES
39367 Big Bear Blvd (92315)
Rates: $89;
Tel: (909) 866-2010

GREY SQUIRREL RESORT
39372 Big Bear Blvd (92315)
Rates: $75-$155;
Tel: (909) 866-4335

THE GRIZZLY INN
39756 Big Bear Blvd (92315)
Rates: $55+;
Tel: (800) 423-2742

HAPPY BEAR VILLAGE
40154 Big Bear Blvd (92315)
Rates: $59-$195;
Tel: (909) 866-2350

HONEY BEAR LODGE
40994 Pennsylvania (92315)
Rates: $29-$259;
Tel: (909) 866-7825; (800) 628-8714

MOTEL 6
42899 Big Bear Blvd (92315)
Rates: $34-$42;
Tel: (800) 440-6000

QUAIL COVE LODGE
39117 N Shore Dr (92315)
Rates: $69-$99;
Tel: (909) 866-5957

ROBINHOOD INN & LODGE
P. O. Box 3706 (92315)
Rates: $69-$109;
Tel: (909) 866-4643

SHORE ACRES LODGE
40090 Lakeview Dr (92315)
Rates: $60-$250;
Tel: (909) 866-8200; (800) 524-6600

SMOKETREE LODGE
40210 Big Bear Blvd (92315)
Rates: $49-$167;
Tel: (909) 866-2415; (800) 352-8581

SNUGGLE CREEK LODGE
40440 Big Bear Blvd (92315)
Rates: $79-$109;
Tel: (909) 866-2555

THREE PINES LODGE
39268-80 Big Bear Blvd (92315)
Rates: $78+;
Tel: (909) 866-4103

Locate Other Dog-Friendly Activities...Check Nearby Cities

TIMBER HAVEN LODGE
877 Tulip Ln (92315)
Rates: $79-$149;
Tel: (909) 866-7207

TIMBERLINE LODGE
P. O. Box 2801 (92315)
Rates: $49-$69;
Tel: (800) 352-8581

WISHING WELL MOTEL
540 Pine Knot (92315)
Rates: $49-$89;
Tel: (909) 866-3505; (800) 541-3505

RECREATION

CHAMPION LODGEPOLE TRAIL HIKE

Beginner/0.6 miles/0.5 hours

Info: One of California's tallest lodgepole pines sits at the end of this undemanding brookside trail. Visit May through November for a wildflower extravaganza. For more information: (909) 383-5588.

Directions: From the west end of Big Bear Lake, turn right off Highway 18 onto Tulip Lane. After .5 miles, go right on Forest Service Road 2N11 for five miles to the trailhead. Follow the signs for Champion Lodgepole.

COUGAR CREST TRAIL HIKE

Beginner/4.0 miles/2.0 hours

Info: Your pup will bounce with delight along this shaded 2-mile trail as it winds its way through stands of pinyon, juniper and Jeffrey pine. If you're in an exploring mood, take a side-trip on the Pacific Crest Trail to Bertha Peak, and admire the views from the summit. Go right on the PCT for a half-mile to an intersection with a dirt road. Head right on the dirt road for .5 miles to the peak. For more information: (909) 866-3437.

Directions: From Big Bear Lake Village, cross the lake at the Stanfield Cutoff and go left (west) on Highway 38. The trail is off to the right, a half mile past the Ranger Station.

PINEKNOT TRAIL to GRANDVIEW POINT TRAIL HIKE
Intermediate/6.0 miles/3.0 hours

Info: The trail sweeps over a flower-carpeted ridge with excellent Big Bear Lake vistas, into meadowlands bedecked with boulders and wildflowers, continuing through Deep Group Camp to Grand View Point. What's in a name? Plenty. You and your pooch will be left breathless from the stunning San Gorgonio views. Late spring to late autumn is best. But if you cross country ski, head for these hills. Snow only adds to the beauty. Anytime of year - dress warmly. There's always a cold wind. For more information: (909) 866-3437.

Directions: From Big Bear Lake, take Highway 18 east towards Big Bear Village, turning south on Mill Creek Road. Follow for .5 miles to the Aspen Glen Picnic Area. The trailhead is at the east end of the parking area.

SIBERIA CREEK to "THE GUNSIGHT" TRAIL HIKE
Beginner/3.0 miles/1.5 hours

Info: This easy nature excursion stretches along fern-banded Siberia Creek to "The Gunsight", an unusual rock configuration, a perfect outing for the fair of paw. For more information: (909) 866-3437.

Directions: From the west end of Big Bear Lake and Highway 18, take Tulip Lane south (left) about .5 miles. Turn right onto Forest Road 2N11 (west). For the next five miles follow the Champion Lodgepole signs, until you reach the trailhead.

SUGARLOAF NATIONAL RECREATION TRAIL HIKE
Expert/10.0 miles/6.0 hours

Info: A hike up 9,952-foot Sugarloaf Peak makes a great day trip for experienced hikers. The trail begins creekside and ascends a jeep road to the Sugarloaf Trail intersection. Go right and continue to the peak. Enjoy the view before heading back the way you came. For more information: (909) 866-3437.

Directions: From Big Bear Lake, take Highway 18 east towards Big Bear City to the Highway 38 junction. Head east on Highway 38 approximately 3 miles, turning right on Forest Service Road 2N84 - a rough dirt road. When FR 2N84 makes a sharp left, continue straight on FR 2N93. After the creek crossing, turn right onto an unsigned road and drive .25 miles to the parking area near the locked gate.

WOODLAND TRAIL HIKE

Beginner / 1.5 miles / 1.0 hours

Info: Visit in the summer and you won't want this 1.5-mile trail through the San Bernardino National Forest to end. Plan your walk in the cool mist of morning. For more information: (909) 337-2444.

Directions: From Big Bear Lake Village, cross the lake at the Stanfield Cutoff, go left on Highway 38. The trail is on the right.

BIG PINE

LODGING

BIG PINE MOTEL
370 S Main (93515)
Rates: $30-$42;
Tel: (619) 938-2282

RECREATION

ANCIENT BRISTLECONE PINE FOREST

Info: On a hot summer day, cool off at this 28,000-acre pine forest situated 10,000 feet above sea level. Walk silently on a soft carpet of pine. Marvel at the sight of the world's oldest trees. Take along a sweater- we're talking cool. For more information: (619) 873-2500.

Directions: From Highway 395 in Big Pine, take Highway 168 east approximately 15 miles to White Mountain Road and turn left. Continue about 10 miles to the south end of the forest. Roads in area closed in winter.

Dogs May Be Unleashed Unless Otherwise Indicated

EUREKA SAND DUNES NATIONAL LANDMARK

Info: If Fido is a sand-loving canine, this park is the answer to his wildest dog dreams and it includes California's tallest sand dune (over 700 feet tall). An artist with a stash of watercolors would have a field day trying to capture the contrast of colors and patterns. Avoid in hot months and always carry sufficient water. For more information: (619) 375-7125.

Directions: From Highway 395 in Big Pine, take Highway 168 east for 2.5 miles to the south fork- Death Valley Road. Follow about 40 miles and go right on Eureka Valley Road about 10 miles.

METHUSELAH TRAIL HIKE- Leashes

Beginner/3.0 miles/1.5 hours

Info: This Ancient Bristlecone Pine Forest is home to the world's oldest documented trees. Which one is the oldest? The rangers won't say. It should suffice to know you're walking among prehistoric pines that have survived centuries of wind, sand, fire, ice and people. This is a remarkable, unforgettable hike. For more information: (619) 873-2500.

Directions: From Highway 395 in Big Pine, take Highway 168 northeast towards Nevada. Go about 13 miles, and take a left on White Mountain Road. Head north for 10 miles past the entrance of Ancient Bristlecone Pine Forest to the Schulman Grove Picnic Area. Take a right and continue a short distance to the trailhead and parking.

NORTH FORK to SECOND FALLS TRAIL HIKE

Intermediate/6.0 miles/3.0 hours

Info: This alpine hike is a breath of fresh air for weary city dwellers and dogsters. The trail winds amidst groves of manzanita, Jeffrey pine and sage before reaching Second Falls. Chill out and dine alfresco with Fido before heading back.

If you and the pooch have the time and the energy, there's more to explore past Second Falls. Travel another 1.5 miles to First Lake, 1.8 miles to Second Lake or an additional 2.5 miles to glacier-fed Third Lake. The milky turquoise color of Third Lake is attributed to the glacial powder melt off of the Palisade Glacier. For more information: (619) 873-2500.

Directions: From Highway 395 in Big Pine, head west on Crocker Street up the canyon for about 10 miles to the day use parking area at road's end.

Note: A quota system is in effect from June through mid-September.

BIG SUR AREA

RECREATION

PFEIFFER BEACH - Leashes

Info: This white sand beach is breathtaking. Even safely on shore, you'll understand and respect the power of the Pacific. Watch mesmerized as waves crash and pound sea caves and splash through natural arches. The water here can be treacherous, resist the temptation to unleash your pooch. Take a sweater along. For more information: (408) 648-3130.

Directions: From Big Sur, take Sycamore Canyon Road west off Highway 1. Sycamore Canyon Road is unmarked; however it's the only paved, ungated road between the Big Sur Post Office and Pfeiffer Big Sur State Beach. Follow Sycamore Canyon for 2 miles to the parking area at road's end. Take the sandy shaded trail to the beach.

Note: Use caution on Sycamore Canyon Road- it's narrow and winding.

SAND DOLLAR PICNIC AREA AND BEACH - Leashes

Info: Picnic beneath spreading cypress trees, then work off the calories with a walk across the field and down to the crescent-shaped beach. For more information: (408) 648-3130.

Directions: Take Highway 1 approximately 11 miles south of Lucia. Parking and the beach are accessible from Plaskett Creek Campground across Highway 1.

Dogs May Be Unleashed Unless Otherwise Indicated

BISHOP

LODGING

BEST WESTERN CREEKSIDE INN
725 N Main St (93514)
Rates: $50-$139;
Tel: (619) 873-3543; (800) 528-1234

BEST WESTERN HOLIDAY SPA LODGE
1025 N Main St (93514)
Rates: $50-$85;
Tel: (619) 873-3543; (800) 528-1234

COMFORT INN-BISHOP
805 N Main St (93514)
Rates: $64-$75;
Tel: (619) 873-4284; (800) 576-4080

PARADISE LODGE
Lower Rock Creek Rd (93514)
Rates: $55-$75+;
Tel: (619) 387-2370

RODEWAY INN
150 E Elm St (93514)
Rates: $45-$65;
Tel: (800) 424-4777

SIERRA FOOTHILLS MOTEL
535 S Main St (93514)
Rates: $33-$48;
Tel: (619) 872-1386

SPORTSMAN'S LODGE
636 N Main St (93514)
Rates: $25-$70;
Tel: (619) 872-2423

SUNRISE MOTEL
262 W Grove St (93514)
Rates: $33+;
Tel: (619) 873-3656

THUNDERBIRD MOTEL
190 W Pine St (93514)
Rates: $34-$54;
Tel: (619) 873-4215

VAGABOND INN
1030 N Main St (93514)
Rates: $44-$66;
Tel: (619) 873-6351;
(800) 522-1555

VILLAGE MOTEL
286 W Elm St (93514)
Rates: $35+;
Tel: (619) 873-3545

RECREATION

BISHOP PASS TRAIL HIKE

Expert/11.0 miles/6.0 hours

Info: Climbing along the east side of South Lake, the trail forges through forests of aspen and lodgepole pine. You'll be surrounded by glaciated terrain and incredible scenery. Don't forget your camera - Hurd Peak, Mt. Goode and Mt. Thompson are all within snapping range. If dining on rainbow trout sounds appealing, tote your fishing rod as well. Be aware you're in high country - almost 12,000 feet - don't overexert yourself or your pooch. And drink lots of water. For more information: (619) 873-2500.

Directions: From Highway 395 in Bishop, take Line Street (Highway 168) west approximately 23 miles to the South Lake Road turnoff. Turn left and follow to the parking area at road's end.

Note: A quota system is in effect from June through mid-September.

BISHOP PASS TRAIL to CHOCOLATE LAKES HIKE

Expert/6.0 miles/3.5 hours

Info: Following the same route as the previous hike, before reaching Long Lake, take the cut-off to Chocolate Lakes Trail. You'll traverse the base of Inconsolable Range. As the trail loops, you'll hook up with Bishop Pass Trail near Ruwau Lake, at the northern section of Long Lake. High altitude sickness can occur at 12,000 feet. Rest often and drink fluids. For more information: (619) 873-2500.

Directions: From Highway 395 in Bishop, take Line Street (Highway 168) west approximately 23 miles to the South Lake Road turnoff. Turn left and follow to the parking area at road's end.

Note: A quota system is in effect from June through mid-September.

GREEN LAKE TRAIL HIKE

Expert/6.0 miles/3.5 hours

Info: Take the stock trail at the east end of the parking area and ascend through groves of conifers to the junction with the main trail. Just below Brown Lake, you'll find yourself in a luxuriant meadow. Continue your ascent to Green Lake and find yourself surrounded by ancient whitebark pines. Fishing fiends, rainbow trout is abundant. For more information: (619) 873-2500.

Directions: From Highway 395 in Bishop, take Line Street (Highway 168) west to the South Lake road turnoff. Turn left and follow to the parking area at road's end.

Note: A quota system is in effect from June through mid-September.

Dogs May Be Unleashed Unless Otherwise Indicated

HILTON LAKES to DAVIS LAKE TRAIL HIKE

Intermediate/10.5 miles/5.5 hours

Info: Treat your best buddy to an afternoon of fresh air and shimmering lake waters. The trail wanders through a lodgepole and whitebark pine woodland before entering the lake basin- Davis Lake is to the right. Go ahead, dip a paw or two before turning back. For more information: (619) 873-2500.

Directions: From Bishop, take Highway 395 north to the Tom's Place exit. Head west up Rock Creek Canyon to the trailhead parking area just below the Rock Creek Pack Station.

Note: A quota system is in effect from June through mid-September.

LAMARCK LAKES TRAIL HIKE

Intermediate/9.0 miles/5.5 hours

Info: Plan a day hike in the fall and treat yourself to the incredible quaking, shaking beauty of aspens. Groves of them. After the aspens, the trail becomes more difficult, the terrain is rocky and boulder strewn. Make it to the trail's peak and you won't be disappointed. The views of Mt. Emerson and Piute Crags are humbling. For more information: (619) 873-2500.

Directions: From Highway 395 in Bishop, take Line Street (Highway 168) west for 17 miles to the North Lake turnoff. Go right (southwest) to the parking area at the Pack Station. The trailhead is .5 miles further in the North Lake Campground.

Note: A quota system is in effect from June through mid-September.

LITTLE LAKES VALLEY to LOWER MORGAN LAKE TRAIL HIKE

Intermediate/9.0 miles/5.5 hours

Info: Amidst 13,000-foot peaks lies a lake-filled, glacier-carved valley. The Little Lakes Trail winds its way through this enchanting valley. Turn around at Lower Morgan Lake. Easy access to so many lakes has made this area very popular with hikers and anglers alike. Dogs give it two paws up as well. For more information: (619) 873-2500.

Locate Other Dog-Friendly Activities...Check Nearby Cities

Directions: From Bishop, take Highway 395 north to the Tom's Place exit. Head west up Rock Creek Canyon for 10 miles to the trailhead at the Mosquito Flat Parking Area.

Note: A quota system is in effect from June through mid- September.

MOSQUITO FLAT to MONO PASS TRAIL HIKE

Expert/7.0 miles/4.0 hours

Info: The first 2 miles of this hike are a breeze compared to the last mile and a half. Once past Ruby Lake, you and Rover are in for a steep, switchbacking climb to Mono Pass. Sit a spell, catch your breath and enjoy the views before heading back. For more information: (619) 873-2500.

Directions: From Bishop, take Highway 395 north to the Tom's Place exit. Head west up Rock Creek Canyon for 10 miles to the trailhead at the Mosquito Flat Parking Area.

Note: A quota system is in effect from June through mid-September.

MOSQUITO FLAT to RUBY LAKE HIKE

Intermediate/4.0 miles/2.0 hours

Info: A tailwagging good time awaits you and the dogster on this trail through a valley of glacier-formed lakes. The hike is not a walk in the park, but the view of Ruby Lake is worth the effort. Surrounded by sheer granite walls, this jewel-like lake is postcard material. Trout hounds, pack your fishing gear. Rainbow, brown and brook trout are yours for the catching. For more information: (619) 873-2500.

Directions: From Bishop, take Highway 395 north to the Tom's Place exit. Head west up Rock Creek Canyon for 10 miles to the trailhead at the Mosquito Flat Parking Area.

Note: A quota system is in effect from June through mid-September.

Dogs May Be Unleashed Unless Otherwise Indicated

PIUTE PASS TRAIL HIKE

Expert/12.0 miles/7.0 hours

Info: Perched atop 11,423-foot Piute Peak, the seemingly endless views are staggering. It's a long trek but a beautiful one. You'll climb through lodgepole pine and quaking aspen, and then walk creekside along Bishop Creek. This is high country and the glaciated canyon floor is covered with glistening granite and dotted with meadows. The sun bathers on the rocks are marmots. Hold onto your fanny or back pack - they're little thieves at heart. Come in springtime and fill your eyes with bursts of colorful wildflowers or make the trip in autumn and take home golden, aspen memories. For more information: (619) 873-2500.

Directions: From Highway 395 in Bishop, take Line Street (Highway 168) west for 17 miles to the North Lake turnoff. Go right (southwest) to the parking area at the Pack Station. The trailhead is .5 miles further in the North Lake Campground.

Note: A quota system is in effect from June through mid-September.

ROCK CREEK LAKE TRAIL to FIRST TAMARACK LAKE HIKE

Intermediate/9.5 miles/5.0 hours

Info: Calling all doggie paddling pooches. If you've got the time, this trail's got the lakes. From the get-go, you'll experience a lake hopping adventure you and Bowser will long remember. Beginning at Rock Creek Lake, the trail climbs steeply, levels out at Dorothy and Kenneth Lakes, then ascends once again topping out at First Tamarack Lake. Fishing aficionados, get set to reel 'em in - the lakes are chockfull of lahonton cutthroats, brook and golden trout. For more information: (619) 873-2500.

Directions: From Bishop, take Highway 395 north to the Tom's Place exit. Head west up Rock Creek Canyon to the trailhead parking area at Rock Creek Lake.

Note: A quota system is in effect from June through mid-September.

Locate Other Dog-Friendly Activities...Check Nearby Cities

SABRINA BASIN TRAIL to BLUE LAKE HIKE

Intermediate/6.0 miles/3.0 hours

Info: You can't pack enough Kodak to capture the postcardian beauty you'll encounter on this hike. As you and Rover rove along, you'll enter a spectacular world of shimmering alpine lakes backdropped by towering granite peaks. But the best Kodak moment can be found at trail's end where Thompson Ridge is reflected in the crystal clear waters of Blue Lake. We're talking Ansel Adams material. For more information: (619) 873-2500.

Directions: From Highway 395 in Bishop, turn west on Line Street (Highway 168) for approximately 18 miles to Lake Sabrina. Day use parking and trailhead are at road's end.

Note: A quota system is in effect from June through mid-September.

SABRINA BASIN TRAIL to DINGLEBERRY LAKE HIKE

Intermediate/10.0 miles/5.0 hours

Info: Initially, the trail to Dingleberry Lake is the same one that leads to Blue Lake. But on this journey, you'll have even more time to admire the beautiful landscape. Once at Blue Lake, continue hiking on the right fork of the branching trail. It's a two-mile trip among groves of lodgepole pine and glacial boulders to Dingleberry Lake. Save some film for your final destination - the skyscraping peaks of Sierra Crest create a stunning mountain/lake visual. For more information: (619) 873-2500.

Directions: See Sabrina Basin Trail to Blue Lake Hike.

Note: A quota system is in effect from June through mid-September.

SABRINA BASIN TRAIL to GEORGE LAKE HIKE

Expert/6.0 miles/3.5 hours

Info: The sign for this trail should read, "for diehard hikers and hounds only." The path parallels pretty Lake Sabrina before veering left (west) on a steep, switchbacking climb to George Lake. Once at the lake, energize with power snacks and biscuits, then do the descent thing. For more information: (619) 873-2500.

Directions: See Sabrina Basin Trail to Blue Lake Hike.

Note: A quota system is in effect from June through mid-September.

Dogs May Be Unleashed Unless Otherwise Indicated

TREASURE LAKES TRAIL HIKE

Intermediate/Expert/5.6 miles/3.0 hours

Info: They don't call 'em Treasure Lakes for nothing. Picture jewel-like lakes set in deep granite basins encircled by towering saw-toothed High Sierra peaks. What a beautiful sight. For more information: (619) 873-2500.

Directions: From Highway 395 in Bishop, take Line Street (Highway 168 west) to the South Lake Road turnoff. Turn left and follow to the parking area at road's end.

Note: A quota system is in effect from June through mid-September.

BLAIRSDEN

LODGING

FEATHER RIVER PARK RESORT
Hwy 89, Box 37 (96103)
Rates: $82-$182;
Tel: (916) 836-2328

GRAY EAGLE LODGE
Gold Lake Rd, Box 38 (96103)
Rates: $155+;
Tel: (916) 836-2511;
(800) 635-8778 (CA)

LAYMAN RESORT
Hwy 70, Box 8 (96103)
Rates: $48-$55;
Tel: (916) 836-2356

RIVER PINES RESORT
Box 117 (96103)
Rates: $50-$75;
Tel: (916) 836-2552;
(800) 696-2551 (CA)

BLUE LAKE

RECREATION

PERIGOT PARK

Info: You and the woofer can spend a playful day in this pleasant park. Fido can go unfettered if he's voice-control obedient. For more information: (707) 668-5655.

Directions: On Greenwood Avenue across from City Hall.

BLYTHE

LODGING

ASTRO MOTEL
801 E Hobsonway (92225)
Rates: $25-$42;
Tel: (619) 922-6101

BEST WESTERN SAHARA MOTEL
825 W Hobsonway (92225)
Rates: $49-$64;
Tel: (800) 528-1234

BEST WESTERN TROPICS MOTOR HOTEL
9274 E Hobsonway (92225)
Rates: $48-$64;
Tel: (800) 528-1234

COMFORT INN
903 W Hobsonway (92225)
Rates: $40-$95;
Tel: (619) 922-4146; (800) 221-2222

ECONO LODGE
1020 W Hobsonway (92225)
Rates: $35-$95;
Tel: (619) 922-3161; (800) 424-4777

HAMPTON INN
900 W Hobsonway (92225)
Rates: $50-$69;
Tel: (800) 426-7866

HOLIDAY INN EXPRESS
600 W Donlon St (92225)
Rates: $85-$139;
Tel: (619) 921-2300; (800) 465-4329

MOTEL 6
500 W Donlon St (92225)
Rates: $27-$32;
Tel: (619) 922-6666; (800) 440-6000

SUPER 8 MOTEL
550 W Donlon St (92225)
Rates: $41-$58;
Tel: (800) 800-8000

TRAVELODGE
850 W Hobsonway (92225)
Rates: $42-$60;
Tel: (800) 367-2250 (CA); (800) 578-7878

RECREATION

MAYFLOWER PARK - Leashes

Info: Hot and tired? Desert heat got you down? Take a break at this 24-acre park which backs up to the deliciously cold Colorado River. Go ahead, dunk a paw or two. Anglers, bring your rod and cast the day away. For more information: (619) 922-4665.

Directions: From westbound Interstate 10 in Blythe, take the Intake Boulevard (Highway 95) exit north for approximately 3 miles. Exit at 6th Avenue and turn right. Follow until it dead ends into the park which is north of 6th Avenue and Colorado River Road.

Note: $2/ adult, $1/ child under 12 and $2/ dog day use fee

PALO VERDE PARK - Leashes

Info: The crisp scent of cedar will fill your snout as you and the wagger while away the afternoon hours in this pleasant park. If you tote a boat, a ramp is provided. For more information: (619) 339-4384.

Directions: Located on Highway 78 south of Blythe on the Colorado River at Oxboe Lake.

BODEGA BAY

LODGING

HOLIDAY INN BODEGA BAY RESORT
521 Coast Highway 1 (94923)
Rates: $60-$180;
Tel: (707) 875-2217; (800) 465-4329

RECREATION

DORAN BEACH REGIONAL PARK - Leashes

Info: If you'd like your itinerary to include wildlife viewing, marshlands, hiking and a refreshing swim, this park is for you. For more information: (707) 875-3540.

Directions: Take Highway 1 south for one mile to Doran Park Road. Head west to the park.

Note: $3 per person day-use fee, $1 per dog.

BOLINAS

LODGING

ELFRIEDE'S BEACH HAUS BED & BREAKFAST
59 Brighton Ave (94924)
Rates: $75-$120;
Tel: (800) 982-2545

Locate Other Dog-Friendly Activities...Check Nearby Cities

BOULDER CREEK

LODGING

MERRYBROOK LODGE
13420 Big Basin Way (95006)
Rates: $64-$80;
Tel: (408) 338-6813

BRAWLEY

LODGING

TOWN HOUSE LODGE
135 Main St (92227)
Rates: $43-$47;
Tel: (619) 344-5120

RECREATION

IMPERIAL SAND DUNES - Leashes

Info: Lawrence of Arabia was filmed nearby. Got the picture? This incredible area extends more than 40 miles. Sculpted by the wind, the dunes are an everchanging sand canvas. Hike up and around the towering 300-foot Imperial Dunes or head to the less frequented area north of Highway 78. Summer's the worst, spring's the best time to visit. Pack plenty of water and if you don't trust your pooch to stay close by, keep him leashed. Dogs can disappear into mere specks in this vast area. For more information: (619) 344-3919.

Directions: Take Highway 78 east about 19 miles to Gecko Road. Turn right and continue one mile to the Ranger Station.

BREA

LODGING

HYLAND MOTEL
727 S Brea Blvd (92621)
Rates: $36-$40;
Tel: (714) 990-6867

WOODFIN SUITE HOTEL-BREA
3100 E Imperial Highway (92621)
Rates: $75-$109;
Tel: (714) 579-3200; (800) 237-8811

Dogs May Be Unleashed Unless Otherwise Indicated

<u>RECREATION</u>

CARBON CANYON REGIONAL PARK - Leashes

Info: This park is prettily ensconced in the undulating foothills of the Chino Hill Range. Head towards Carbon Canyon Dam and find yourself in a shady, cozy grove of coastal redwoods. For more information: (714) 996-5252.

Directions: From Highway 57, take the Lambert Road exit east for four miles (Lambert turns into Carbon Canyon Road). The entrance is one mile east of Valencia Avenue.

BRENTWOOD

<u>RECREATION</u>

SULLIVAN CANYON TRAIL HIKE - Leashes

Intermediate/6.0 miles/3.0 hours

Info: Escape the summer heat with your water woofer in tow and make tracks to a riparian oasis in Sullivan Canyon. Towering live oaks, walnuts and sycamores canopy the trail, while several stream crossings provide some cool splish splashing fun for you and the dawgus. After hiking about three miles, you'll reach a small grove of eucalyptus trees, your turn-the-hound-around point. For more information: (818) 597-9192.

Directions: From Brentwood take Sunset Boulevard west just over 2 miles to Mandeville Canyon Road. Turn right and continue a quarter-mile to Westridge Road. Make a left and travel a mile or so to Bayliss Road and turn left. Travel approximately .3 miles to Queensferry Road and turn left to the trailhead near road's end.

BRIDGEPORT

LODGING

BEST WESTERN RUBY INN
33 Main St (93517)
Rates: $55-$110;
Tel: (619) 932-7241; (800) 528-1234

SILVER MAPLE INN
310 Main St (93517)
Rates: $45-$80;
Tel: (619) 932-7383

WALKER RIVER LODGE
1 Main St, P. O. Box 695 (93517)
Rates: $75-$120;
Tel: (619) 932-7021

RECREATION

BODIE STATE HISTORIC PARK - Leashes

Info: Experience 500 acres of a once booming mining town that has been transformed into an historic park. Check out the authentic ghost town or frolic with your dog in the spacious areas of the park. For more information: (619) 647-6445.

Directions: Travel south on Highway 395 to Highway 270/Bodie Road. Head east for 13 miles. The last three miles are unpaved (may be closed in winter).

Note: $5 vehicle fee, $1 dog fee.

LUNDY LAKE TRAIL HIKE

Intermediate/8.0 miles/5.5 hours

Info: A wonderful, waterful, lake-hopping adventure in beautiful Hoover Wilderness can be yours on this high country hike. Begin 2 miles past Lundy Lake on the Lundy Lake Trailhead. Within 3 miles, you'll pass 2 mini waterfalls and arrive at Lake Helen. The last mile leads to Odell and Twin Lakes. If you've never visited Yosemite, this is a close second. Admire away and then retrace your steps. For more information: (619) 647-3000.

Directions: Take Highway 395 south to the junction of Highway 395 and Highway 167. At the junction, take Lundy Lake Road west approximately 7 miles to the trailhead at road's end.

Dogs May Be Unleashed Unless Otherwise Indicated

BROOKDALE

LODGING

BROOKDALE LODGE
11570 Hwy 9 (95007)
Rates: $44-$60;
Tel: (408) 338-6433

BUELLTON

LODGING

ECONO LODGE
630 Ave of Flags (93427)
Rates: $30-$80;
Tel: (800) 424-4777

MOTEL 6
333 McMurray Rd (93427)
Rates: $32-$40;
Tel: (805) 688-7797; (800) 440-6000

BUENA PARK

LODGING

BEST WESTERN BUENA PARK INN
8580 Stanton Ave (90620)
Rates: $36-$52;
Tel: (800) 528-1234

COVERED WAGON MOTEL
7830 Crescent Ave (90620)
Rates: $28-$32;
Tel: (714) 995-0033

**EMBASSY SUITES HOTEL-
BUENA PARK/DISNEYLAND**
7762 Beach Blvd (90620)
Rates: $99-$119;
Tel: (714) 739-5600; (800) 362-2779

HOLIDAY INN-BUENA PARK
7000 Beach Blvd (90620)
Rates: $89-$250;
Tel: (714) 522-7000; (800) 522-7006

MOTEL 6
7051 Valley View (90622)
Rates: $30-$34;
Tel: (714) 522-1200; (800) 440-6000

TRAVELODGE-BUENA PARK
7640 Beach Blvd (90620)
Rates: $35-$45;
Tel: (714) 522-8461; (800) 578-7878

RECREATION

RALPH B. CLARK REGIONAL PARK - Leashes

Info: A great choice for picnicking or fishing, this park bustles with fun-filled, sun-filled activities for you and the pupster. For more information: (714) 670-8045.

Directions: The park is located at 8800 Rosencrans Avenue in Buena Park, a half-mile east of Beach Boulevard.

Locate Other Dog-Friendly Activities...Check Nearby Cities

BURBANK

LODGING

**HILTON-BURBANK AIRPORT &
CONVENTION CENTER**
2500 Hollywood Way (91505)
Rates: $106-$176;
Tel: (800) 468-3576 (US);
(800) 643-6400 (CA)

HOLIDAY INN-BURBANK
150 E Angeleno (91510)
Rates: $96-$135;
Tel: (800) 465-4329

RAMADA INN-BURBANK AIRPORT
2900 N San Fernando Blvd (91504)
Rates: $75-$95;
Tel: (800) 272-6232

RECREATION

WOODLEY PARK - Leashes

Info: Take advantage of the exercise course in this spacious park. Or pack a sandwich and a couple of biscuits and do lunch. For more information: (818) 756-8190.

Directions: From Burbank, take the Ventura Freeway (134) until it becomes the Ventura Freeway (101). Stay on the 101 Freeway westbound to the San Diego Freeway (405). Take the 405 Freeway north to the Burbank Boulevard exit. Go west into the park. Make a right on Woodley Avenue, passing signs for the Japanese Garden. The park is on the right.

BURLINGAME

LODGING

**DOUBLETREE HOTEL-
SAN FRANCISCO AIRPORT**
835 Airport Blvd (94010)
Rates: $79-$139;
Tel: (415) 344-5500; (800) 222-8733

MARRIOTT-SAN FRANCISCO AIRPORT
1800 Old Bayshore Highway (94010)
Rates: $125-$138;
Tel: (415) 692-9100; (800) 228-9290

**RADISSON HOTEL-
SAN FRANCISCO AIRPORT**
1177 Airport Blvd (94010)
Rates: $125;
Tel: (415) 342-9200; (800) 333-3333

**RED ROOF INN-
SAN FRANCISCO AIRPORT**
777 Airport Blvd (94010)
Rates: $72-$82;
Tel: (415) 342-7772; (800) 843-7663

**VAGABOND INN-
SAN FRANCISCO AIRPORT**
1640 Old Bayshore Highway (94010)
Rates: $60-$100;
Tel: (415) 692-4040; (800) 522-1555

Dogs May Be Unleashed Unless Otherwise Indicated

RECREATION

ALPINE PARK - Leashes

Info: Enjoy an afternoon repast with Rover as you take in some soothing scenery and some fresh air in this community park.

Directions: Located at Carolan Avenue and Alpine.

BAYSIDE PARK - Leashes

Info: Baseball and soccer provide the excitement for avid sports fans, while a walk through this park will wag Fido's tail.

Directions: Located at 1125 Airport Boulevard.

BURLINGAME VILLAGE PARK - Leashes

Info: If you're in the neighborhood, pack your pooch's biscuit basket and head out for a paw pleasing afternoon in the sun.

Directions: Located on California Drive north of Broadway.

HERITAGE PARK - Leashes

Info: This quaint little park offers a lovely grassy area for picnickers and their pooches.

Directions: Located at 1575 Ralston at Occidental.

ROBERT E. WOLLEY STATE PARK - Leashes

Info: Happy tails to you when you take your wagalong to this beautiful park with stunning views of the bay. Four-footed friends will prance with delight as you lead them along one of the many walking paths. Two paws up for the greenbelt and scenic surroundings in this lush, sun-stroked area.

Directions: Located on Anza Boulevard off Airport Boulevard.

VICTORIA PARK - Leashes

Info: Take your tots and your Spots to this pretty little park equipped with a playground and basketball court.

Directions: Located at 30 Howard Avenue.

Locate Other Dog-Friendly Activities...Check Nearby Cities

WASHINGTON PARK - Leashes

Info: Lounge under one of the large grandfather-like trees at this mini-park or picnic at one of the redwood tables. Come autumn, the landscape explodes into brilliant reds and yellows.

Directions: At 850 Burlingame Avenue below Carolan Avenue.

Other parks in Burlington - Leashes
•CUERNA VACCA PARK, in Mills Estates at Alcazar and Hunt
•PERSHING PARK, at the corner of Newlands and Crescent
•RAY PARK, 1525 Balboa

BURNEY

<u>LODGING</u>

CHARM MOTEL
37363 Main St (96013)
Rates: $46-$74;
Tel: (916) 335-2254

GREEN GABLES MOTEL
37385 Main St (96013)
Rates: $45-$75;
Tel: (916) 335-2264

SHASTA PINES MOTEL
37386 Main St (96013)
Rates: $32-$58;
Tel: (916) 335-2201

SLEEPY HOLLOW LODGE
36898 Main St, P. O. Box 1105 (96013)
Rates: $30-$65;
Tel: (916) 335-2285

<u>RECREATION</u>

BUNCHGRASS TRAIL HIKE - Leashes

Intermediate/7.0 miles/3.5 hours

Info: This scenic trail to Durbin Lake makes for a great day hike with the hound. As you climb to the lake, take note of the lava flows spewed by Tumble Buttes and Hall Butte. Refreshing Durbin Lake is a great place to either cool your paws or cast your line. For more information: (916) 336-5521.

Directions: From Burney, take Highway 299 north to Highway 89. Head south on Highway 89 to Forest Road 16 (Ashpan Snowmobile Park). Turn northwest on FR 16 approximately 7 miles to FR 32N45. Turn right on FR 32N45 and proceed 2 miles to FR 32N42Y. Go left, following FR 32N42Y to the trailhead. The beginning of FR 32N42Y is very steep, so exercise caution.

Dogs May Be Unleashed Unless Otherwise Indicated

CYPRESS TRAIL HIKE - Leashes

Intermediate/4.6 miles/2.5 hours

Info: Involving a 1,000-foot elevation change, the first mile of this trail is not for the fair of paw. But if you're up for the initial challenge, it's smooth sailing the last 1.3 miles to Eiler Lake. Relax lakeside before heading back. For more information: (916) 336-5521.

Directions: From Burney, take Highway 299 north to Highway 89. Head south on Highway 89 to FR 34N19. Turn west on FR 34N19 approximately 8.5 miles to FR 34N22. Go left on FR 34N22 for 1.5 miles to the trailhead.

MAGEE PEAK TRAIL HIKE - Leashes

Expert/7.4 miles/4.0 hours

Info: Gear up for a butt-kicker of a hike that climbs over 2,500 feet from beginning to end. From your lofty perch on 8,550-foot Magee Peak, you and the dawgus will be treated to spectacular vistas. Once you've had your visual fill, continue on to Magee Lake. Chill out, catch your breath and do a little toe dipping at the lake before tackling the return trek. For more information: (916) 336-5521.

Directions: Take Highway 299 north to Highway 89. Head south on Highway 89 to Forest Road 16 (Ashpan Snowmobile Park). Turn northwest on FR 16 approximately 10 miles to FR 32N48. Turn right on FR 32N48 for 1.5 miles to the trailhead.

SPATTER CONE TRAIL HIKE - Leashes

Beginner/1.5 miles/0.75 hours

Info: For a quickie volcanic education, leash up the pup and head out on this self-guided tour of the Hat Creek Lava Flow. From spatter cones to vesicular basalt, collapsed lava tubes to cinder cones, you and your lucky dog will find it hard to believe your paws are still planted on Earth. Pick up a detailed trail brochure at the trailhead and make your hike more interesting. For more information: (919) 336-5521.

Locate Other Dog-Friendly Activities...Check Nearby Cities

Directions: From Burney, take Highway 299 north to Highway 89. Head south on Highway 89 to the Sanitary Dump Station across the highway from the Hat Creek Campground. The trailhead and parking area are located in the dump station.

SUBWAY CAVE TRAIL HIKE- Leashes

Beginner/0.7 miles/0.5 hours

Info: Break out your flashlight, you're gonna need it for this spelunking adventure. Subway Cave affords hikers and their hounds a unique experience- a self-guided tour through a lava carved cave. Be sure to check the batteries and dress appropriately before setting out. You don't want to be left in the dark or in the cold. For more information: (919) 336-5521.

Directions: From Burney, take Highway 299 north to Highway 89. Head south on Highway 89 to the cave. The cave is located off Highway 89 about a quarter-mile north of where Old Station junctions with Highway 44.

Note: The cave is closed during the winter months.

TAMARACK TRAIL HIKE- Leashes

Beginner/4.0 miles/2.0 hours

Info: Sofa surfers and social hounds will pawsitively love this popular, wilderness hike. The easy trail follows a relatively flat course to Eiler Lake where hot diggety dogs can cool off. Spend an hour or the day and then retrace your steps. For more information: (916) 336-5521.

Directions: From Burney, take Highway 299 north to Highway 89. Head south on Highway 89 to FR 33N25, approximately 3 miles past the Hat Creek Work Center. Turn west on FR 33N25 to FR 33N23Y. Go right, following FR 33N23Y to the trailhead.

Note: High clearance vehicles only.

Dogs May Be Unleashed Unless Otherwise Indicated

BUTTONWILLOW

LODGING

GOOD NITE INN
20645 Tracy Rd (93206)
Rates: $26-$32;
Tel: (805) 764-5121

MOTEL 6
3810 Tracy Ave (93206)
Rates: $23-$29;
Tel: (805) 764-5207; (800) 440-6000

MOTEL 6
20638 Tracy Ave (92306)
Rates: $23-$29;
Tel: (805) 764-5153; (800) 440-6000

SUPER 8 MOTEL
20681 Tracy Ave (93206)
Rates: $31-$49;
Tel: (805) 764-5117; (800) 800-8000

CALIMESA

LODGING

CALIMESA INN MOTEL
1205 Calimesa Blvd (92320)
Rates: $35-$47;
Tel: (909) 795-2536

CALIPATRIA

LODGING

CALIPATRIA INN
SR111, P. O. Box 30 (92233)
Rates: $46-$52;
Tel: (619) 348-7348

CALISTOGA

LODGING

MEADOWLARK COUNTRY HOUSE
601 Petrified Forest Rd (94515)
Rates: $125-$150;
Tel: (707) 942-5651

PINK MANSION
1415 Foothill Blvd (94515)
Rates: $85-$160;
Tel: (707) 942-0558

TRIPLE "S" RANCH
4600 Mountain Home
Ranch Rd (94515);
Rates: $42-$59;
Tel: (707) 942-6730

WASHINGTON STREET LODGING
1605 Washington St (94515)
Rates: $80-$90;
Tel: (707) 942-6968

Locate Other Dog-Friendly Activities...Check Nearby Cities

CALLAHAN

RECREATION

CHINA SPRING TRAIL to GRIZZLY CREEK HIKE - Leashes

Expert/6.0/3.5 hours

Info: Only hardy hikers and conditioned canines should attempt this butt-kicker of a hike. Beginning at 4,450 feet, the trail climbs to an elevation of 6,000 feet before dropping down to Grizzly Creek at 5,450 feet. Sit a spell and energize with some power snacks and water - the return trek isn't any easier. For more information: (916) 467-5757.

Directions: From Callahan, turn right on Callahan-Cecilville Road for 25 miles to East Fork Campground. Take the bridge over the river and continue 4 miles to Schoolhouse Flat. Go right on Forest Service Road 37N07 for 5 miles to the trailhead.

Note: Wilderness permit required.

DEACON LEE TRAIL to RUSSIAN LAKE TRAIL HIKE - Leashes

Intermediate/7.1 miles/3.5 hours

Info: If lakes float your boat, then set sail for this hike. You and the pupster will have a great time as you make tracks to your destination. Once at Waterdog Lake, head to the northeast side for the 500-foot plunge to Lower Russian Lake. This portion of the trail is very steep and not well-blazed. Dip a paw or two or try your line on the eastern brook trout that call this lake home. For more information: (916) 467-5757.

Directions: From Callahan, turn right on Callahan-Cecilville Road for 18 miles to Forest Service Road 39 (3 miles past Trail Creek Campground). Follow FR 39 approximately 3 miles to the trailhead (follow the Russian Lake Trailhead signs).

Note: Wilderness permit required.

SOUTH FORK FALLS TRAIL HIKE

Beginner/1.0 miles/0.5 hours

Info: Futon-loving Fidos, listen up. All of the fun of an outdoor excursion can be yours on this easy-does-it short hike. Play follow the leader on this riverside trail that heads downstream to South Fork Falls. For more information: (916) 467-5757.

Directions: From Callahan, take Highway 3 south to the Coffee Creek Guard Station. Turn right on Coffee Creek Road for 18 miles to the trailhead at Big Flat Campground.

VALLEY LOOP TRAIL HIKE

Beginner/2.5 miles/1.25 hours

Info: A quiet, delightful riverside jaunt awaits you and your deserving doggie. The trail loops around the river, providing a flat, easy hike. There are plenty of spots just right for breaking bread and biscuits. For more information: (916) 467-5757.

Directions: From Callahan, take Highway 3 south to the Coffee Creek Guard Station. Turn right on Coffee Creek Road for 18 miles to the trailhead at Big Flat Campground.

CALPINE

LODGING
SIERRA VALLEY LODGE
Box 115 (96124)
Rates: $38-$42;
Tel: (916) 994-3367; (800) 858-0322

CAMARILLO

LODGING
COMFORT INN
984 Ventura Blvd (93010)
Rates: $42-$59;
Tel: (800) 221-2222

MOTEL 6
1641 E Daily Dr (93010)
Rates: $30-$36;
Tel: (805) 388-3467; (800) 440-6000

Locate Other Dog-Friendly Activities...Check Nearby Cities

CAMBRIA

LODGING

BEST WESTERN MARINERS INN
6180 Moonstone Beach Dr (93428)
Rates: $32-$89;
Tel: (805) 927-4624; (800) 528-1234
(800) 344-0407 (CA)

CAMBRIA PINES LODGE
2905 Burton Dr (93428)
Rates: $65-$115;
Tel: (805) 927-4200; (800) 445-6868

CAMBRIA SHORES INN
6276 Moonstone Beach Dr (93428)
Rates: $45-$110;
Tel: (805) 927-8644; (800) 433-9179

FOGCATCHER INN
6400 Moonstone Beach Dr (93428)
Rates: $80-$145;
Tel: (800) 425-4121

CAMERON PARK

LODGING

BEST WESTERN CAMERON PARK INN
3361 Coach Ln (95682)
Rates: $51-$61;
Tel: (916) 677-2203; (800) 528-1234

CAMPBELL

LODGING

CAMPBELL INN
675 E Campbell Ave (95008)
Rates: $89-$175;
Tel: (408) 374-4300, (800) 852-4300;

EXECUTIVE INN SUITES
1300 Camden Ave (95008)
Rates: $68-$85;
Tel: (800) 888-3611

MOTEL 6
1240 Camden Ave (95008)
Rates: $37-$43;
Tel: (408) 371-8870; (800) 440-6000

**RESIDENCE INN BY MARRIOTT-
SAN JOSE/CAMPBELL**
2761 S Bascom Ave (95008)
Rates: $79-$154;
Tel: (800) 331-3131

RECREATION

LOS GATOS CREEK COUNTY PARK - Leashes

Info: Picnic by a pond, toss a frisbee or simply relax under a shade tree at this verdant park. For more information: (408) 356-2729.

Dogs May Be Unleashed Unless Otherwise Indicated

Directions: Take the Camden Avenue exit from Highway 17, then head west on San Tomas Expressway. Go south on Winchester Boulevard, turning left on Hacienda Avenue. Follow to the park.

Note: $3 parking fee. Hours are 8 a.m. to sunset.

CANOGA PARK

LODGING

BEST WESTERN CANOGA PARK MOTOR INN
20122 Vanowen St (91306)
Rates: $49-$64;
Tel: (818) 883-1200; (800) 528-1234

DAYS INN-SAN FERNANDO VALLEY
20128 Roscoe Blvd (91306)
Rates: $50-$95;
Tel: (818) 341-7200; (800) 329-7466

SUPER 8 MOTEL
7631 Topanga Canyon Blvd (91304)
Rates: $50-$60;
Tel: (818) 883-8888; (800) 800-8000

WARNER CENTER MOTOR INN
7132 DeSoto Ave (91303)
Rates: $40-$70;
Tel: (818) 346-5400

CAPISTRANO BEACH

LODGING

CLARION SUITES INN
23734 Pacific Coast Highway (92624)
Rates: $49-$149;
Tel: (800) 221-2222

CAPITOLA

LODGING

CAPITOLA INN
822 Bay Ave (95010)
Rates: $55-$135;
Tel: (408) 462-3004

EL SALTO BY THE SEA BED & BREAKFAST
620 El Salto Dr (95010)
Rates: $100-$185;
Tel: (408) 462-6365

SUMMER HOUSE BED & BREAKFAST
216 Monterey Ave (95010)
Rates: $75;
Tel: (408) 475-8474

Locate Other Dog-Friendly Activities...Check Nearby Cities

RECREATION
NEW BRIGHTON STATE BEACH - Leashes

Info: This area has a little something for everyone. Catch some rays or hike the pine and eucalyptus forest trail to the left of the main entrance. Some great views of Capitola await. Don't be tempted by the beach - no dogs allowed. For more information: (408) 475-4850, or (800) 444-7275.

Directions: From Highway 1, take the New Brighton Beach exit west.

Note: $6 car fee and $1 per dog fee.

CARDIFF - BY - THE - SEA

RECREATION
CARDIFF STATE BEACH

Info: You're sure to meet other prancing pups along this beach. Point your snouts to the north end and sniff out a doggie dreamland. Canines carouse leash-free and frolic together in puppy playgroups. You'll have a howl of a good time kicking back and watching the four-legged frenzy. For more information: (619) 729-8247.

Directions: The beach is located on Old Highway 101 west of the San Elijo Lagoon.

CARLSBAD

LODGING

ECONOMY INNS OF AMERICA
751 Raintree Dr (92009)
Rates: $30-$55;
Tel: (619) 931-1185; (800) 826-0778

MOTEL 6
1006 Carlsbad Village Dr (92008)
Rates: $29-$35;
Tel: (619) 434-7135; (800) 440-6000

MOTEL 6
750 Raintree Dr (92009)
Rates: $28-$34;
Tel: (619) 431-0745; (800) 440-6000

MOTEL 6
6117 Paseo del Norte (92009)
Rates: $28-$34;
Tel: (619) 438-1242; (800) 440-6000

RAMADA INN
751 Macadamia Dr (92009)
Rates: $79-$119;
Tel: (619) 438-2285; (800) 272-6232

TRAVELODGE-CARLSBAD/LA COSTA
760 Macadamia Dr (92009)
Rates: $35-$54;
Tel: (800) 367-2250 (CA); (800) 578-7878

Dogs May Be Unleashed Unless Otherwise Indicated

CARMEL

LODGING

BEST WESTERN CARMEL MISSION INN
3665 Rio Rd (93922)
Rates: $99-$149;
Tel: (408) 624-1841; (800) 528-1234

CARMEL RIVER INN
Hwy 1 & Carmel River Bridge (93921)
Rates: $60-$135;
Tel: (408) 624-1575

CARMEL TRADEWINDS INN
P. O. Box 3403, Mission
between 3rd & 4th (93921)
Rates: $69-$225;
Tel: (408) 624-2776; (800) 624-6665

COACHMAN'S INN
P. O. Box C-1, San Carlos &
7th Sts (93921)
Rates: $75-$150;
Tel: (408) 624-6421; (800) 336-6421

CYPRESS INN
P. O. Box Y, Lincoln &
7th Sts (93921)
Rates: $97-$250;
Tel: (408) 624-3671; (800) 443-7443

DOLORES LODGE
P. O. Box 3756 (93921)
Rates: $80-$125;
Tel: (408) 625-3263

FOREST LODGE BED & BREAKFAST
P. O. Box 1316 (93921)
Rates: $80-$240;
Tel: (408) 624-7023

HIGHLANDS INN
Highway 1 (93921)
Rates: $265-$695;
Tel: (408) 624-3801; (800) 682-4811

QUAIL LODGE RESORT & GOLF CLUB
8205 Valley Green Dr (93923)
Rates: $195-$860;
Tel: (408) 624-1581; (800) 538-9516

VAGABOND HOUSE INN
P. O. Box 2747, Dolores &
4th Sts (93921)
Rates: $79-$135;
Tel: (408) 624-7738; (800) 262-1262

WAYSIDE INN
P. O. Box 1900, Mission &
7th Sts (93921)
Rates: $95-$225;
Tel: (408) 624-5336; (800) 433-4732

RECREATION

CARMEL CITY BEACH

Info: This beach is puppy paradise. Watch your pooch's wagging tail as he gallops through the white sand. Take a tennis ball or frisbee for a game of catch. The swimming's great too. If you're not in a sandy mood, just stroll along the cypress-lined walking path. The city of Carmel provides clean up bags. For more information: (408) 624-3543.

Directions: From Highway 1, exit at Ocean Avenue. Follow to the end.

CARMEL VALLEY

LODGING

BLUE SKY LODGE
Flight Rd (93924)
Rates: $72-$93;
Tel: (408) 659-2935

CARMEL VALLEY INN
P. O. Box 115,
Carmel Valley Rd (93924)
Rates: $49-$119;
Tel: (800) 541-3113

VALLEY LODGE
8 Ford Rd (93924)
Rates: $99-$249;
Tel: (408) 659-2261; (800) 641-4646

RECREATION

GARLAND RANCH REGIONAL PARK

Info: This parkland is comprised of 4,500 acres of leashless abandonment through maple, oak and willow trees and nine miles of scenic trails that climb from sea level to 2,000 feet. What more could your pup ask for? Drop by the visitor center for a detailed park map and information on the fauna. For more information: (408) 659-4488.

Directions: From Highway 1, take Carmel Valley Road exit east for approximately 9 miles. The park is on your right.

CARNELIAN BAY

LODGING

LAKESIDE CHALETS
5240 N Lake Blvd (96140)
Rates: $95-$125;
Tel: (916) 546-5857; (800) 294-6378 (CA/NV)

RECREATION
See "Lake Tahoe Area" listings for recreation

CARPINTERIA

LODGING

BEST WESTERN CARPINTERIA INN
4558 Carpinteria Ave (93013)
Rates: $85-$129;
Tel: (800) 528-1234

MOTEL 6
4200 Via Real (93013)
Rates: $32-$38;
Tel: (805) 684-6921; (800) 440-6000

MOTEL 6
5550 Carpinteria Ave (93013)
Rates: $32-$38;
Tel: (805) 684-8602; (800) 440-6000

RECREATION

FRANKLIN PARK - Leashes

Info: Spread out your blanket and laze with your Lassie in this pleasant little park.

Directions: Located on Sterling Avenue at El Carro.

HEATH RANCH - Leashes

Info: You and Snoopy can snoop out the Old Heath Adobe as you saunter through a sweet-scented grove of eucalyptus.

Directions: Heath Ranch is located adjacent to Eucalyptus Street.

MEMORIAL PARK - Leashes

Info: This petite neighborhood park offers lawn for yawn-time, swings for offsprings and open space for pooch-face.

Directions: Located at Santa Ynez Avenue and Aragon Street.

MONTE VISTA PARK - Leashes

Info: Make tracks along the jogging course and do the exercise thing at the 20 fitness stations. Mellow fellows might prefer catching some rays while reclining in the large grassy area.

Directions: The park is located at the end of Bailard Avenue.

RINCON BEACH COUNTY PARK - Leashes

Info: After a picturesque blufftop picnic, take the stairway to the beach (a favorite with nudists). For more information: (805) 568-2460

Directions: Located at the south end of Carpinteria at Bates Road and Highway 101.

Other parks in Carpinteria - Leashes
•EL CARRO PARK, El Carro Lane and Namouna Street

CASTAIC

LODGING

CASTAIC INN
31411 Ridge Rt (91384)
Rates: $35-$69;
Tel: (805) 257-0229; (800) 628-5252

COMFORT INN
31558 Castaic Rd (91384)
Rates: $36-$85;
Tel: (805) 295-1100; (800) 221-2222

CASTRO VALLEY

LODGING

HOLIDAY INN EXPRESS
2532 Castro Valley Blvd (94546)
Rates: $48-$95;
Tel: (510) 538-9501; (800) 465-4329

RECREATION

CULL CANYON REGIONAL RECREATION AREA- Leashes

Info: Hike through grassy wooded hillsides, enjoy a picnic lunch or cast your line in the reservoir. You can't go wrong at this 360-acre park. For more information: (510) 635-0135.

Directions: From Interstate 580, take Cull Canyon Road north to the park entrance.

Dogs May Be Unleashed Unless Otherwise Indicated

CASTROVILLE

LODGING

CASTROVILLE MOTEL
11656 Merritt St (95012)
Rates: $36-$48;
Tel: (408) 633-2502

CATALINA ISLAND

LODGING

HOTEL MONTEREY
108 Sumner Ave, P. O. Box 1372 (90704)
Rates: $65-$165;
Tel: (310) 510-0264; (800) 858-0035

CATHEDRAL CITY

LODGING

DAYS INN SUITES
69-151 E Palm Canyon Dr (92234)
Rates: $52-$190;
Tel: (619) 324-5939;
(800) 329-7466

**DOUBLETREE RESORT
AT DESERT PRINCESS**
67-967 Vista Chino (92234)
Rates: $95-$245;
Tel: (619) 322-7000; (800) 637-0577

CAYUCOS

LODGING

CYPRESS TREE MOTEL
125 S Ocean Ave (93430)
Rates: $60;
Tel: (805) 995-3917

ESTERO BAY MOTEL
25 S Ocean Ave (93430)
Rates: $30-$85;
Tel: (805) 995-3614; (800) 736-1292

DOLPHIN INN
399 S Ocean Ave (93430)
Rates: $45-$110;
Tel: (805) 995-3810;
(800) 540-4276 (CA)

Locate Other Dog-Friendly Activities...Check Nearby Cities

CAZADERO

LODGING
CAZANOMA LODGE
100 Kid Creek Rd (95421)
Rates: $80-$115;
Tel: (707) 632-5255

CEDARVILLE

LODGING
SUNRISE MOTEL
Highway 299 (96104)
Rates: $35-$45;
Tel: (916) 279-2161

CERRITOS

LODGING
**SHERATON CERRITOS HOTEL
AT TOWNE CENTER**
12725 Center Court Dr (90703)
Rates: $59-$300;
Tel: (310) 809-1500; (800) 325-3535

CHATSWORTH

LODGING
SUMMERFIELD SUITES HOTEL
21902 Lassen St (91311)
Rates: $85-$158;
Tel: (818) 773-0707; (800) 833-4353.

RECREATION

BEE CANYON TRAIL HIKE - Leashes

Beginner/Intermediate/2.0 miles/1.0 hours

Info: Treat yourself and the pupster to a pleasant, creekside jaunt in this pretty parkland. The trail wanders through Bee Canyon for about a mile until it ends at the park boundary. Before heading home, sit a spell under a shady oak and do lunch alfresco style. For more information: (818) 785-5798.

Directions: From Chatsworth, take the San Fernando Valley Freeway east to the Balboa Boulevard exit. Go north on Balboa Boulevard to Orozco Street. Make a left and continue to the park's picnic area parking lot. The trailhead is at the north end of the picnic area.

CHATSWORTH OAKS PARK - Leashes

Info: Worthy of some playful puppy antics, this 51-acre park offers plenty of paw-friendly stomping ground for you and your furry friend to explore.

Directions: Located at 9301 Valley Circle Drive.

CHATSWORTH PARK NORTH - Leashes

Info: Give in to those pleading pooch eyes and take your faithful companion to this 24-acre park. Stroll along the hiking path, repast at a pleasant picnic spot, or have a kibble cook-out away from the bustle of the city.

Directions: Located at 22300 Chatsworth Street.

CHATSWORTH PARK SOUTH - Leashes

Info: Frolic in the meadows or hike the dirt trails of this 81-acre park. This is the local hangout where dogs meet to greet. Expect company.

Directions: From Highway 118, take the Topanga Canyon Boulevard exit south. After approximately 1.5 miles, turn right on Devonshire Street and follow to the park.

Locate Other Dog-Friendly Activities...Check Nearby Cities

DEVIL CANYON TRAIL HIKE - Leashes

Beginner/4.5 miles/2.25 hours

Info: Escape the dog days of summer on this serene canyon hike. Sycamore, oak and alder canopy the canyon floor, while a seasonal creek often affords some paw dipping fun. A gate marking private property is your cue to head back. Bring a picnic lunch and make a day of it. For more information: (818) 756-8188.

Directions: From Chatsworth, head east on the San Fernando Valley Freeway (118) to Topanga Canyon Boulevard. Park in the dirt lot just north of the Freeway.

MASON PARK - Leashes

Info: Fido can frolic through 20 acres of open space in this urban park equipped with baseball and football fields, a basketball court, and a picnic pad.

Directions: Located at 10500 Mason Avenue.

MISSION POINT TRAIL HIKE - Leashes

Intermediate/4.5 miles/2.25 hours

Info: For a bird's-eye view of LA's second largest park, head to 2,800-foot Mission Point. Do the distance on this somewhat demanding hike that ascends nearly 1,400 feet in just over 2 miles and you'll earn some vista points. This pastoral and wildlife-rich region is in sharp contrast to the city particularly in spring when wildflowers like California poppies, Indian paintbrush and yellow goldenbrush speckle and brighten the landscape. As you climb through the Santa Susana Mountains, you'll pass a tiny grove of Aleppo pine, trees native to the Mediterranean. Farther along, a stand of four lonesome oak trees signal the trail to Mission Point on the left. For more information: (818) 785-5798.

Directions: From Chatsworth, take the San Fernando Valley Freeway (118) east and exit on Balboa Boulevard. Turn north on Balboa to Orozco Street. Make a left to the park's picnic parking lot. The trailhead is at the north end of the picnic area.

O'MELVENY PARK - Leashes

Info: This 672-acre park contains trails that even couch potato pooches will adore. Try the woodsy canyon bottom trail along the creek or challenge yourself with one of the more demanding pathways. For more information: (818) 785-5798.

Directions: From Highway 5, take the Balboa Boulevard exit south to Orozco Street, go right. Follow to the picnic area parking lot.

CHESTER

LODGING

CEDAR LODGE MOTEL
Hwy 36, Box 677 (96020)
Rates: $29-$53;
Tel: (916) 258-2904

SENECA MOTEL
Box 504 (96020)
Rates; $35-$47;
Tel: (916) 258-2815

TIMBER HOUSE LODGE
First & Main Sts (96020)
Rates: $35-$60;
Tel: (916) 258-2729

RECREATION

DEER CREEK TRAIL HIKE

Beginner/3.5 miles/1.5 hours

Info: You and the pupster are in for a cinchy hike alongside Deer Creek. This shaded jaunt winds through a soothing setting and leads to a cascading waterfall. For more information: (916) 258-2141.

Directions: From Chester take Highway 36 west for twelve miles to Highway 32. Turn south (left) and drive about 12 miles to the Potato Patch Campground. The trailhead is on the right-side of the Red Bridge.

HAY MEADOW TRAIL to HIKING LAKES AREA HIKE

Intermediate/6.0 miles/3.0 hours

Info: Within the confines of the Caribou Wilderness, sandwiched between South Caribou Mountain and Black Cinder Rock, lies a trail looping to and through a world of tiny alpine lakes, dubbed the Hiking Lakes. If you like your water cold, you've got your pick of some great swimming holes. As far as fishing goes, Posey and Beauty Lakes offer the best trout. For more information: (916) 258-2141.

Directions: From Chester, take Highway 36 east for five miles to Forest Road 10. Turn north (left) and continue for 9.5 miles to FR 30N25. Take FR 30N25 to the trailhead.

HEART LAKE NATIONAL RECREATION TRAIL HIKE

Intermediate/7.0 miles/3.5 hours

Info: Hike creekside with your pooch on this scenic trail amid groves of dogwood and aspen, forests of fir and pine. Get an eyeful of Lassen Peak and Brokeoff Mountain and a snoutful of pine-scented air as you make tracks to trail's end at Lassen Volcanic National Park. For more information: (916) 258-2141.

Directions: From Chester, head west on Highway 36 for one mile to the Almanor Ranger District Station, located across from the airport. Once at the station, check with the forest rangers for specific directions to the trailhead. Since the roads are unsigned a forest service map is recommended.

LAKE ALMANOR - Leashes

Info: Brilliant blue waters at this picturesque lake can be yours if you know your way around or you're staying at one of the local resorts. This public/private area can be somewhat confusing. Stop at the Ranger Station or call for more information: (916) 258-2141.

Directions: The Ranger Station is located in Chester at 900 East Highway 36.

Dogs May Be Unleashed Unless Otherwise Indicated

CHICO

Lodging

DELUXE INN
2507 Esplanada (95926)
Rates: $38+;
Tel: (916) 342-8386

THE ESPLANADE BED & BREAKFAST
620 Esplanade (95926)
Rates: $45-$60;
Tel: (916) 345-8084

HOLIDAY INN OF CHICO
685 Manzanita Ct (95926)
Rates: $69-$85;
Tel: (916) 345-2491; (800) 465-4329

MATADOR MOTEL
1934 Esplanade (95926)
Rates: $30-$45;
Tel: (916) 342-7543

MOTEL ORLEANS
655 Manzanita Ct (95926)
Rates: $32-$39;
Tel: (916) 345-2533

MOTEL 6
665 Manzanita Ct (95926)
Rates: $30-$36;
Tel: (916) 345-5500; (800) 440-6000

O'FLAHERTY HOUSE BED & BREAKFAST
1462 Arcadian (95926)
Rates: $65+;
Tel: (916) 893-5494

OXFORD SUITES
2035 Business Ln (95928)
Rates: $59-$102;
Tel: (916) 899-9090; (800) 870-7848

SAFARI GARDEN MOTEL
2352 Esplanade (95926)
Rates: $32-$44;
Tel: (916) 343-3201

TOWN HOUSE MOTEL
2231 Esplanade (95926)
Rates: $28-$42;
Tel: (916) 343-1621

VAGABOND INN
630 Main St (95928)
Rates: $40-$65;
Tel: (916) 895-1323; (800) 522-1555

Recreation

BIDWELL PARK - Leashes

Info: Rover will run blissfully free on miles of trails through rugged terrain and cushy, grassy meadows. For more information: (916) 895-4972.

Directions: To Upper Park: from Highway 99 at Chico, take Highway 32 exit east to Bruce Road. Make a left onto Bruce Road and head north. The road curves sharply to the right and turns into Chico Canyon Drive. Bear left at Manzanita Avenue. Go left on Vallombrosa Avenue. Park on the road.

Note: No leashes in Upper Park area only.

Locate Other Dog-Friendly Activities...Check Nearby Cities

GENETIC RESOURCE CENTER NATURE TRAIL HIKE - Leashes

Beginner/1.5 miles/1.0 hours

Info: This 209-acre area is the site of many advances in agriculture and tree improvement. The Center is a key link in reforestation efforts, watershed and wildlife habitat improvement. Within the grounds, there's a self-guided nature trail which winds among mixed stands of mature trees and across small stream beds. The staff is often available to share the Center's history and scientific work with visitors. Mid-October through Mid-November marks the season for viewing fall leaf colors at the Center. The astounding variety rivals the foliage found in the northeastern United States. The autumnal colors represent California redbud, maple, dogwood, scrub oak and Brewer oak. The colors run the gamut from deep rusty red, golden yellow and brown, apple green to pale peach and deep raspberry. For more information: (916) 895-1176.

Directions: Located at 2741 Cramer Lane.

CHINO

LODGING

MOTEL 6
12266 Central Ave (91710)
Rates: $30-$34;
Tel: (714) 591-3877; (800) 440-6000

RECREATION

PRADO REGIONAL PARK - Leashes

Info: Sniff around the open space or just laze the day away with your Lassie in this pleasant region. For more information: (909) 597-4260.

Directions: Located at 16700 Euclid Avenue.

Dogs May Be Unleashed Unless Otherwise Indicated

CHOWCHILLA

LODGING

SAFARI MOTEL NATIONAL INN
220 E Robertson Blvd (93610)
Rates: $32-$40;
Tel: (209) 665-4821

CHULA VISTA

LODGING

GOOD NITE INN
225 Bay Blvd (91910)
Rates: $49-$79;
Tel: (619) 425-8200; (800) 648-3466

LA QUINTA INN
150 Bonita Rd (91910)
Rates: $49-$54;
Tel: (619) 691-1211; (800) 521-5900

MOTEL 6
745 E St (91910)
Rates: $33-$37;
Tel: (619) 422-4200; (800) 440-6000

RODEWAY INN
778 Broadway (91910)
Rates: $35-$56;
Tel: (800) 424-4777

TRAVELER MOTEL KITCHEN SUITES
235 Woodlawn Ave (91910)
Rates: $29-$59;
Tel: (619) 427-9170; (800) 748-6998

TRAVELODGE-CHULA VISTA
394 Broadway (91910)
Rates: $43-$69;
Tel: (619) 420-6600; (800) 578-7878

VAGABOND INN
230 Broadway (91910)
Rates: $36-$55;
Tel: (619) 422-8305; (800) 522-1555

CLAREMONT

LODGING

CLAREMONT INN
555 W Foothill Blvd (91711)
Rates: $49-$59;
Tel: (800) 854-5733

HOWARD JOHNSON LODGE
721 S Indian Hill Blvd (91711)
Rates: $49-$59;
Tel: (800) 446-4656

RAMADA INN & TENNIS CLUB
840 S Indian Hill Blvd (91711)
Rates: $54-$58;
Tel: (800) 228-2828

Locate Other Dog-Friendly Activities...Check Nearby Cities

RECREATION

ICEHOUSE CANYON TRAIL TO ICEHOUSE SADDLE HIKE

Expert/7.25 miles/4.25 hours

Info: For gung-ho hikers, this uphill canyon trek in the Cucamonga Wilderness is a great day trip and an excellent way to experience this high country region. Towering Timber Mountain, Telegraph Peak and Thunder Mountain loom overhead as you make your way to Icehouse Saddle. Your ascent from the canyon floor will be cool and shady, the background sounds of a creek will soothe your psyche. And the views from the upper reaches are stunning. Either retrace your steps or loop back on the Chapman Trail for a slight change of scenery. Experienced hikers, if the lure of the mountain peaks is too much to resist, just follow one of the side trails to the top. For more information: (818) 574-1613.

Directions: Take the San Bernardino Freeway (Interstate 10) east to Upland and exit at Mountain Avenue. Drive north on Mountain Avenue past where it meets Mount Baldy Road and continue to Mount Baldy Village. 1.5 miles past the Village is the Icehouse Canyon Resort, dirt parking and the trailhead.

MANKER FLATS TRAIL TO SAN ANTONIO FALLS HIKE - Leashes

Beginner/1.0 miles/0.5 hours

Info: Sunday strollers will love the ease of this short but fulfilling scenic hike. The trail ends at an impressive, three-tiered rumbling waterfall that is bound to thrill all breeds. You'll saunter through a shaded woodland before reaching the falls-the ideal kick-back spot to enjoy the beauty about you. For more information: (818) 577-0050.

Directions: From Claremont, take Mountain Avenue north until you join Mount Baldy Road in the San Antonio Canyon. Drive about 11 miles to Manker Campground. About .3 miles past the entrance to the campground, you'll see an unsigned paved road on your left. Park in the dirt lot, walk to the fire road and listen for the falls.

Note: Do not attempt to climb above the falls, it is extremely dangerous.

Dogs May Be Unleashed Unless Otherwise Indicated

CLEAR CREEK

LODGING

CLEAR CREEK MOTEL
667-150 Hwy 147 (96137)
Rates: $35-$45;
Tel: (916) 256-3166

CLEARLAKE

LODGING

SUNSET LODGE
13961 Lakeshore Dr (95422)
Rates: $40-$85;
Tel: (707) 994-6642

TRAVELODGE-CLEARLAKE
4775 Old Highway 53 (95422)
Rates: $34-$48;
Tel: (707) 994-1499; (800) 578-7878

CLEARLAKE OAKS

LODGING

LAKE HAVEN MOTEL
100 Short St (95423)
Rates: $36-$53;
Tel: (707) 998-3908

TWENTY OAKS COURT
10503 E Hwy 20 (95423)
Rates: $40;
Tel: (707) 998-3012

LAKE POINT LODGE
13440 E Hwy 20 (95423)
Rates: $45-$78;
Tel: (707) 998-4350

RECREATION

CACHE CREEK RECREATION AREA

Info: If your buddy's into sniffing wildflowers, this 50,000-acre area will be heaven-scent in spring. There's a challenging but rewarding 7-mile trail that winds through this vast, primitive area. You might encounter elk, blue herons, bald eagles and black bears. Keep a leash accessible. For more information: (707) 468-4000.

Directions: From Clearlake Oaks, travel eight miles east on Highway 20. The area is well signed.

Locate Other Dog-Friendly Activities...Check Nearby Cities

COALINGA

LODGING

BIG COUNTRY INN
25020 W Dorris Ave (93210)
Rates: $44-$60;
Tel: (209) 935-0866; (800) 836-6835

THE INN AT HARRIS RANCH
24505 W Dorris Ave (93210)
Rates: $86-$111;
Tel: (209) 935-0717; (800) 942-2333

MOTEL 6
25278 W Dorris Ave (93210)
Rates: $27-$33;
Tel: (209) 935-2063; (800) 440-6000

MOTEL 6
25008 W Dorris Ave (93210)
Rates: $27-$39;
Tel: (209) 935-1536; (800) 440-6000

COBB

RECREATION

BOGGS MOUNTAIN DEMONSTRATION STATE FOREST

Info: Well behaved Bowsers can accompany you leash-free in this interesting woodland. Explore several miles of hiking trails as you journey through ponderosa pine and mixed conifer forests. With 3,500 acres, you can plan an afternoon chock-full of woodsy fun. Picnicking is a popular activity as well, so pack a biscuit basket and plan a relaxing outdoor lunch. Wildlife species abound and birds are always busy singing. For more information: (707) 928-4378.

Directions: From Cobb, head north on Highway 175. The park covers a vast area east of Highway 175. Watch for signs to the entrance.

COFFEE CREEK

LODGING

BONANZA KING RESORT
Rt 2, Box 4790 (96091)
Rates: $65-$70;
Tel: (916) 266-3305

COFFEE CREEK RANCH
Coffee Creek Rd (96091)
Rates: $124-$278;
Tel: (916) 266-3343; (800) 624-4480

COLEVILLE

LODGING

ANDRUSS MOTEL
Walker Rte, Box 64 (96107)
Rates: $36-$42;
Tel: (916) 495-2216

MEADOWCLIFF MOTEL
Rte 1, Box 126 (96107)
Rates: $32-$45;
Tel: (916) 495-2255

COLTON

LODGING

PATRIOT INN & SUITES
2830 Iowa St (92324)
Rates: $32-$100;
Tel: (909) 788-9900

THRIFTLODGE
225 E Valley Blvd (92324)
Rates: $32-$42;
Tel: (909) 824-1520; (800) 578-7878

COLUMBIA

LODGING

COLUMBIA GEM MOTEL
22131 Parrotts Ferry Rd (95310)
Rates: $25-$70;
Tel: (209) 532-4508

COLUMBIA INN MOTEL
22646 Broadway St (95310)
Rates: $32-$76;
Tel: (209) 533-0446

RECREATION

COLUMBIA STATE HISTORIC PARK - Leashes

Info: Take a journey back in time as you and Rosie mosey along the dirt roads of this historic ghost town park. Don't miss the short nature trail through forest and meadow-lands. Spring and fall are the best times to visit. For more information: (209) 532-4301.

Directions: From Highway 49 south, drive north on Parrott's Ferry Road/County Road E18. After 1.5 miles, the entrance will be on your right.

Locate Other Dog-Friendly Activities...Check Nearby Cities

COMMERCE

LODGING

RADISSON CITY OF COMMERCE HOTEL
6300 Telegraph Rd (90040)
Rates: $60-$105;
Tel: (800) 333-3333

RAMADA INN
7272 Gage Ave (90040)
Rates: $51-$64;
Tel: (310) 806-4777; (800) 547-4777

WYNDHAM GARDEN HOTEL
5757 Telegraph Rd (90040)
Rates: $119-$129;
Tel: (213) 887-8100; (800) 996-3426

CONCORD

LODGING

BEST WESTERN HERITAGE INN
4600 Clayton Rd (94521)
Rates: $55-$60;
Tel: (510) 686-4466; (800) 528-1234

COMFORT INN
1370 Monument Blvd (94520)
Rates: $54-$80;
Tel: (510) 827-8996; (800) 221-2222

EL MONTE MOTOR INN
3555 Clayton Rd (94519)
Rates: $43-$55;
Tel: (510) 682-1601

HOLIDAY INN CONCORD
1050 Burnett Ave (94520)
Rates: $60-$95;
Tel: (510) 687-5500; (800) 465-4329

SHERATON CONCORD HOTEL
45 John Glen Dr (94520)
Rates: $60-$95;
Tel: (510) 825-7700; (800) 325-3535

RECREATION

CONTRA LOMA LOOP TRAIL HIKE

Beginner/1.6 miles/1.0 hours

Info: Pooches love this leg-stretching lake and hillside loop trail. From the parking area, head past the Cattail Cove Picnic Area. Continue on the trail to the right as it meanders lakeside to a short hilly ascent and descent. Then take a left turn for the return portion of the loop. For more information: (510) 635-0135.

Directions: Take Highway 4 east to Antioch, exiting at Lone Tree Way heading south. Make a right on Blue Rock Drive, following to Frederickson Lane and bear right to the gate.

Dogs May Be Unleashed Unless Otherwise Indicated

132   *Doin' California With Your Pooch!*

You'll be in Black Diamond Mines Regional Park once you pass the gate. Turn right, pass the kiosk and bear left. Follow to the parking area near the beach.

FRANKLIN RIDGE LOOP TRAIL HIKE

Beginner/3.1 miles/1.75 hours

Info: This agreeable trip ambles through sprawling grasslands and thickets of eucalyptus. It gets even better when you reach the 75-foot ridge with excellent views of Mt. Tamalpais, Mt. Diablo and the San Joaquin Delta. For more information: (510) 635-0135.

Directions: From Concord, take Interstate 680 north to Highway 4 west. Exit at Alhambra Avenue and drive north for two miles toward Carquinez Strait. Take a left on Escobar Street and proceed three blocks. Go right on Talbart Street (Carquinez Scenic Drive). Continue .50 miles to the parking area on the left. The hike heads south on the California Riding and Hiking Trail towards Franklin Ridge, climbing and then connecting to the Franklin Ridge Loop.

SHORELINE TRAIL HIKE

Beginner/2.2 miles/1.0 hours

Info: This easy hike shows off some of the best parts of Martinez Waterfront Park. Pack those binoculars, you'll see marshlands, bay frontage, and a variety of birds. For more information: (510) 635-0135.

Directions: From Concord, take Interstate 680 north to Highway 4 west. Drive north on Alhambra for two miles and turn right on Escobar Street. Continue for three blocks to Ferry Street and turn left. Cross the railroad tracks and bear right onto Joe DiMaggio Drive. Take a left on North Coast Street and enter the parking area next to the fishing pier.

CONEJO

RECREATION
GLENWOOD PARK - Leashes
Info: Break up a busy indoor day with an outdoor interlude and take Old Four Paws to this relaxing park.

Directions: Located at 1291 Windsor Drive.

LYNN OAKS PARK - Leashes
Info: If you're in the neighborhood, this 6.7-acre park is a great leg-stretcher.

Directions: Located at 359 Capitan Street.

NORTH RANCH PARK - Leashes
Info: Make those paws and your puppy's heart go pitter-patter with a stop at this friendly 12-acre neighborhood park.

Directions: Located at 1901 Upper Ranch Road.

OLD MEADOWS PARK - Leashes
Info: You and the dawgus can make your own fun strolling through 8 acres of scenic landscape.

Directions: Located at 1600 Marview Drive.

RUSSELL PARK - Leashes
Info: Have a tailwagging good time romping and playing on this park's 7.5 acres.

Directions: Located at 3199 North Medicine Bow Court.

SPRINGMEADOW PARK - Leashes
Info: Reward Rover with a trip to this lovely little park.

Directions: Located at 3283 Spring Meadow Avenue.

Dogs May Be Unleashed Unless Otherwise Indicated

STAGECOACH INN PARK - Leashes

Info: Get your daily dose in this pleasant 5-acre park.

Directions: Located at 51 Ventu Park Road.

THOUSAND OAKS COMMUNITY PARK - Leashes

Info: Hotdog! 35.8 acres are sure to please even finicky Fidos. Pack a snack, some sunscreen, a chew or two, and plan to spend an afternoon.

Directions: Located at 2525 North Moorpark Road.

TRIUNFO COMMUNITY PARK - Leashes

Info: 37.5 acres of open frolicking space await your pup's pawprints. Feast on a brown bagger as you feast your eyes on the landscape.

Directions: Located at 980 Aranmoor Drive.

WALNUT GROVE PARK - Leashes

Info: Happy tails will wag again as you and your four-legger frolic in the green scene of this 6.5-acre park.

Directions: Located at 400 Windtree Avenue.

Other parks in Conejo - Leashes
•BANYAN PARK, 3605 Erinlea Avenue
•BEYER PARK, 280 Conejo School Road
•CANADA PARK, 4351 Erbes Road
•CYPRESS PARK, 469 1/2 South Havenside
•EL PARK DE LA PAZ, 100 Oakview Drive
•ESTELLA PARK, 300 Erbes Road
•EVENSTAR PARK, 1021 Evenstar
•HICKORY PARK, 3977 South Camphor Avenue
•OAKBROOK PARK, 2787 Erbes Road
•SUBURBIA PARK, 2600 Tennyson Street
•SUNSET HILLS, 3350 Monte Carlo Drive
•WAVERLY PARK, 1300 Avenue de las Flores
•WENDY PARK, 815 American Oaks Avenue

Locate Other Dog-Friendly Activities...Check Nearby Cities

CORCORAN

LODGING

BUDGET INN
1224 Whitley Ave (93212)
Rates: $47-$60;
Tel: (209) 992-3171

CORNING

LODGING

CORNING OLIVE INN MOTEL
2165 Solano St (96021)
Rates: $28-$40;
Tel: (916) 824-2468; (800) 221-2230

DAYS INN
3475 Highway 99 W (96021)
Rates: $28-$60;
Tel: (916) 824-2000; (800) 329-7466

SHILO INN
3350 Sunrise Way (96021)
Rates: $54-$61;
Tel: (916) 824-2940; (800) 222-2244

CORONA

LODGING

MOTEL 6
200 N Lincoln (91719)
Rates: $26-$30;
Tel: (909) 735-6408; (800) 440-6000

TRAVELODGE
1701 W 6th St (91720)
Rates: $33-$41;
Tel: (909) 735-5500; (800) 578-7878

RECREATION

BRENTWOOD PARK - Leashes

Info: 13 acres of sports-filled fun and spacious lawns make this park a pleasant place for you and the pup to idle away some time.

Directions: Located at 1646 Dawnrigde.

Dogs May Be Unleashed Unless Otherwise Indicated

BUTTERFIELD PARK - Leashes

Info: 64 expansive acres are sure to bring a smile to your favorite pooch-face. Maybe there's even a fuzzy Penn in Fido's future.

Directions: Located at 1886 Butterfield Stage Drive.

CITY PARK - Leashes

Info: Bring a book, a blanket and a rawhide. Find yourself a secluded grassy knoll and do the lazy thing.

Directions: Located at 930 East 6th Street.

GRIFFIN PARK - Leashes

Info: The paved pathways in this 13-acre parkland are ideal for an afternoon stroll. Check out the panoramic views of the city and surrounding region from the 5-acre grassy hilltop, a great tail wagging spot.

Directions: Located at 2770 Griffin Way.

LINCOLN PARK - Leashes

Info: This small 5-acre park might be the perfect place for you and your furry-footed friend to spend an hour or two relaxing in the sun.

Directions: Located at Lincoln and Citron.

MOUNTAIN GATE PARK - Leashes

Info: Take a break from a dogday afternoon with a visit to this lovely 21-acre park.

Directions: Located at 3100 South Main Street.

ONTARIO PARK - Leashes

Info: Hightail it to this quaint 8-acre community park for your daily dose.

Directions: Located at Ontario and Via Pacifica.

Locate Other Dog-Friendly Activities...Check Nearby Cities

PARKVIEW PARK - Leashes

Info: Watch that tail wag as you and the mutt strut through this 6.3-acre park.

Directions: Located at 2094 Parkview Drive.

RIDGELINE PARK - Leashes

Info: Satisfy your pleading-eyed pooch by taking him for an outing in this 8-acre grassy park.

Directions: Located at 2850 Ridgeline.

RIVER ROAD PARK - Leashes

Info: This neighborhood park can fill the bill for a paw-pleasing afternoon.

Directions: Located at 1100 West River Road.

ROCK VISTA PARK - Leashes

Info: 8 undeveloped acres await you, furface, and a frisbee.

Directions: Located at 2481 Steven Drive.

Other parks in Corona - Leashes
- BORDER PARK, 2400 Border Avenue
- CONTERAS PARK, Buena Vista and Railroad
- HUSTED PARK, 1200 Merrill
- JOY PARK, Joy and Grand
- KELLOGG PARK, 1635 Kellogg
- MANGULAR PARK, 2200 Mangular Avenue
- MERRILL PARK, 10th and West Grand
- SERFAS CLUB PARK, 2575 Green River Road
- SHERIDAN PARK, 300 South Sheridan
- TEHACHAPI PARK, Tehachapi and St. Helena
- VICTORIA PARK, 312 9th Street

Dogs May Be Unleashed Unless Otherwise Indicated

CORONADO

LODGING

EL CORDOVA MOTEL
1351 Orange Ave (92118)
Rates: $70-$148;
Tel: (619) 435-4131; (800) 229-2032

LOEWS CORONADO BAY RESORT
4000 Coronado Bay Rd (92118)
Rates: $195-$245;
Tel: (619) 424-4000; (800) 815-6397

RECREATION

CENTENNIAL PARK - Leashes

Info: Grassy knolls, gazebo seating and an original ferryboat ticket booth are just some of the attractions of this park. The panoramic bay views are incredible, so tote a camera and your crony and head out to this scenic area.

Directions: On First Street at the foot of Orange Avenue.

CORONADO CENTRAL BEACH - Leashes

Info: Point your snouts north and sniff out the dog run. Fido's tail will be wagging as he finds furry friends for frolicking fun.

Directions: The beach runs along Ocean Boulevard. Free parking is available along the boulevard.

GLORIETTA BAY PARK - Leashes

Info: This park offers a small beach for your Sandy to enjoy. Pack a bone, a blanket and a book, and stake out a place on the grassy area.

Directions: Located south of Municipal Pool on Strand Way.

TIDELANDS PARK - Leashes

Info: Do the puppy stroll on the path beneath the bridge. Then do lunch at one of the picnic tables.

Directions: Located just below the Coronado Bridge.

Locate Other Dog-Friendly Activities...Check Nearby Cities

COSTA MESA

LODGING

ANA MESA SUITES
3597 Harbor Blvd (92626)
Rates: $59-$84;
Tel: (714) 662-3500; (800) 767-2519

BEST WESTERN NEWPORT MESA INN
2642 Newport Blvd (92627)
Rates: $52-$68;
Tel: (714) 650-3020; (800) 528-1234

COMFORT INN
2430 Newport Blvd (92627)
Rates: $42-$58;
Tel: (714) 631-7840; (800) 221-2222

LA QUINTA MOTOR INN
1515 S Coast Dr (92626)
Rates: $45-$55;
Tel: (714) 957-5841; (800) 531-5900

MARRIOTT SUITES
500 Anton Blvd (92626)
Rates: $59-$178;
Tel: (714) 957-1100; (800) 228-9290

MOTEL 6
1441 Gisler Ave (92626)
Rates: $31-$35;
Tel: (714) 957-3063; (800) 440-6000

NEWPORT BAY INN
2070 Newport Blvd (92627)
Rates: $33-$69;
Tel: (714) 631-6000; (800) 284-3229

RAMADA LIMITED
1680 Superior Ave (92627)
Rates: $44-$125;
Tel: (714) 645-2221; (800) 228-2828;
(800) 345-8025 (CA)

**RED LION HOTEL/
ORANGE COUNTY AIRPORT**
3050 Bristol St (92626)
Rates: $104-$400;
Tel: (714) 540-7000; (800) 547-8010

RESIDENCE INN BY MARRIOTT
881 W Baker St (92626)
Rates: $79-$156;
Tel: (714) 241-8800; (800) 331-3131

VAGABOND INN
3205 Harbor Blvd (92626)
Rates: $40-$60;
Tel: (714) 557-8360; (800) 522-1555

**THE WESTIN SOUTH COAST
PLAZA HOTEL**
686 Anton Blvd (92626)
Rates: $139-$164;
Tel: (714) 540-2500; (800) 228-3000

RECREATION

ESTANCIA PARK - Leashes

Info: Dog's tail dragging a bit lately? Give Fido something to wag about with a vista to this 10-acre community park.

Directions: Located at 1900 Adams.

LIONS PARK - Leashes

Info: Get the lead out with some power walking in this 10-acre park.

Directions: Located at 570 West 18th Street.

Dogs May Be Unleashed Unless Otherwise Indicated

SHIFFER PARK - Leashes

Info: This quaint 7-acre park beckons morning and early evening walkers for their constitutionals.

Directions: Located at 3134 Bear Street.

TANAGER PARK - Leashes

Info: Sniff your way through this 7.4-acre park. Or do the frisbee thing and make your dog's day.

Directions: Located at 1780 Hummingbird Drive.

TEWINKLE PARK - Leashes

Info: Run, doggie, run! That's right, within this expansive, 49-acre park there's an enclosed dog run where canines can run, play and socialize leash-free. Rover will have a howl of a good time, and you'll have a ball watching puppy playtime.

Directions: Located at 970 Arlington.

VISTA PARK - Leashes

Info: Plan an outing and a brown bag lunch in this 7-acre neighborhood park.

Directions: Located at 1200 Victoria Street.

WAKEHAM PARK - Leashes

Info: Drench yourself with sunshine as you dine with your canine in this 10-acre park.

Directions: Located at 3400 Smalley Street.

Other parks in Costa Mesa - Leashes
• BRENTWOOD PARK, 265 East Brentwood
• CANYON PARK, 970 Arbor Street
• DEL MESA PARK, 2080 Manistee Drive
• GISLER PARK, 1250 Gisler Street
• HARPER PARK, 425 East 18th Street
• HELLER PARK, 257 16th Street

Locate Other Dog-Friendly Activities...Check Nearby Cities

- LINDBERGH PARK, 220 East 23rd Street
- MARINA VIEW PARK, 1035 West 19th Street
- MESA VERDE PARK, 1795 Samar Avenue
- PAULARINO PARK, 1040 Paularino Avenue
- PINKLEY PARK, 360 East Ogle
- SMALLWOOD PARK, 1656 Corsica Place
- SUBURBIA I PARK, 3377 California Street
- SUBURBIA II PARK, 3302 Alabama
- WILLARD T. JORDAN PARK, 2141 Tustin Avenue
- WILSON PARK, 360 Wilson
- WIMBLEDON PARK, 3440 Wimbledon Way

COVELO

LODGING

WAGON WHEEL MOTEL
75860 Covelo Rd (95428)
Rates: $32-$39;
Tel: (707) 983-6717

RECREATION

GRINDSTONE CAMP TRAIL HIKE

Intermediate/1.0 miles/0.5 hours

Info: Running alongside Grindstone Creek, the trail traverses stands of mixed oak and conifer. There are plenty of places for water play as well as cozy little spots for some R&R. For more information: (707) 983-6118.

Directions: From Covelo, stay on 162 and proceed about one mile past town. The Ranger Station will be on the right side. Follow signs. At the station, check with the forest rangers on trail conditions, as well as specific directions to the trailhead. Or call the above number beforehand.

Note: Depending on snowfall, the hiking season is from June to September. Contact Ranger Station for trail conditions. High clearance vehicles only.

Dogs May Be Unleashed Unless Otherwise Indicated

HAMMERHORN LAKE TRAIL HIKE

Expert/1.0 miles/1.0 hours

Info: If you've been having fishy dreams, make your way to this trout-filled lake. If fishing's not your thing, you still can't go wrong strolling along the loop of this beautiful, pristine mountain lake. For more information: (707) 983-6118.

Directions: See GRINDSTONE CAMP TRAIL HIKE.

HELLHOLE CANYON TRAIL HIKE

Beginner/3.0 miles/1.0 hours

Info: Despite the name, this is an excellent hike for sunny days. Beginning at Indian Dick Road, you and Fido will find lots of lunch spots en route. Hellhole Canyon is your turnaround point. Use caution, cliffs exist trailside and the trail is popular with the mountain biking crowd. For more information: (707) 983-6118.

Directions: See GRINDSTONE CAMP TRAIL HIKE.

LANTZ RIDGE TRAIL HIKE

Intermediate/3.0 miles/1.5 hours

Info: Starting from an old logging deck, you and pooch-face will descend through an old growth Douglas fir forest to mature stands of oak and grasslands. Help Spot find a cool off spot at the refreshing creek, where some water fun is in order. The creek is surrounded with buckeye and if you're hiking in early summer your eyes won't believe the profusion of wild-flowers - like blue lupine, bright orange poppies and bush lilac. For more information: (707) 983-6118.

Directions: See GRINDSTONE CAMP TRAIL HIKE.

MIDDLE FORK EEL RIVER - Leashes

Info: A short jaunt from the campground will take you to a slice of hound heaven. A wet, wild and rugged experience awaits you and your wagalong when you reach the dense forests, meadows, rolling hills and steep-walled canyons of the Eel River. For more information: (707) 983-6118.

Locate Other Dog-Friendly Activities...Check Nearby Cities

Directions: Go north 1.5 miles along the Eel River until Highway 162. Head east on 162 for 12 miles to the campground.

PETERSON TRAIL HIKE

Beginner/3.0 miles/1.5 hours

Info: When nothing short of a water wonderland will do for you and your aquatic pup, nothing short of this hike will do. Beginning at Straight Arrow Camp, the trail wanders among ponderosa pine forests, pokes in and out of meadows and glades and passes the remains of an old cabin and orchard site before ending at Thomes Creek, a blissful water-filled oasis. Fantastic swimming holes and peaceful solitude are the highlights of this pretty trail. If you're looking for seclusion with a capital S, plan to visit on a weekday. Happy tails to you and old wet paws. For more information: (707) 983-6118.

Directions: See GRINDSTONE CAMP TRAIL HIKE.

POISON GLADE TRAIL HIKE

Expert/6.0 miles/4.0 hours

Info: Only rugged Rexes and Herculean hikers should attempt this difficult trek. The trail contours along the upper reaches of Grindstone Canyon as it travels through chaparral, large open glades and crosses canyons covered with live oaks. Many photo ops exist so tote that Brownie. For more information: (707) 983-6118.

Directions: See GRINDSTONE CAMP TRAIL HIKE.

SUNSET NATURE LOOP TRAIL HIKE

Beginner/0.5 miles/0.5 hours

Info: For a quickie leg stretcher, you can't go wrong on this self-guided trail which begins in the Lake Pillsbury area. The path is posted with interpretive signs as it leads you among several chaparral and mixed conifer species. This is an interesting walk for human and canine species alike. For more information: (707) 983-6118.

Directions: See GRINDSTONE CAMP TRAIL HIKE.

Dogs May Be Unleashed Unless Otherwise Indicated

THOMES GORGE NOMLAKI TRAIL HIKE

Beginner/4.2 miles/2.0 hours

Info: Named for the people indigenous to the area, this trail begins at the Mud Flat Trailhead on Forest Road 23N35. You'll voyage amidst chaparral combined with expansive views of the foothill country continuing through woodlands of gray pine. The trail wanders around seasonal vernal pools before dropping into the spectacular geologic formations of Thomes Gorge, ending near the deep, sparkling pools of Thomes Creek. The creek is a perfect place for a bit of paw dipping and a bit of lunch. Tote plenty of water, particularly in summer. And bring along your camera - Kodak moments are plentiful. For more information: (707) 983-6118.

Directions: See GRINDSTONE CAMP TRAIL HIKE.

TRAVELER'S HOME TRAIL HIKE

Beginner/Intermediate/7.6 miles/4.0 hours

Info: Do some California dreamin' as you saunter through stands of conifer and oak and traipse amid glades and meadows on this picturesque hike. There are some wet and wonderful times in store for you and your wagger on this trail which ends at the Wild and Scenic Area of the Middle Fork Eel River. No matter when you visit, pack plenty of Perrier, there are several long, steep grades. And expect company, mountain bikers like this trail too. For more information: (707) 983-6118.

Directions: See GRINDSTONE CAMP TRAIL HIKE.

COVINA

LODGING

EMBASSY SUITES HOTEL
1211 E Garvey (91724)
Rates: $79-$89;
Tel: (818) 915-3441; (800) 362-2779

CRESCENT CITY

LODGING

DAYS INN
220 M St (95531)
Rates: $39-$55;
Tel: (800) 339-7466

ECONO LODGE
119 L St (95531)
Rates: $32-$55;
Tel: (707) 464-2181; (800) 424-4777

EL PATIO BUDGET MOTEL
725 Hwy 101 N (95531)
Rates: $32-$55;
Tel: (707) 464-6106

PACIFIC MOTOR HOTEL
440 Highway 101 N (95531)
Rates: $42-$65;
Tel: (707) 464-4141; (800) 323-7917

ROYAL INN
102 L St (95531)
Rates: $33-$70;
Tel (707) 464-4113

SUPER 8 MOTEL
685 Hwy 101 S (95531)
Rates: $43-$70;
Tel: (707) 464-4111; (800) 800-8000

RECREATION

FRENCH HILL TRAIL HIKE

Intermediate/5.4 miles/3.25 hours

Info: First built as a route to lookout stations, this trail now serves as a high-tech highway rain gauge station. The trail meanders through Douglas fir, sugar pine, rhododendron and evergreen huckleberry which create a rainforest effect. If you and your canine enjoy romps through such scenic surroundings, you can't go wrong. For more information: (707) 457-3131.

Directions: From Crescent City, head north on Highway 101 for 4 miles to Highway 199. Turn right for 14 miles. Park at the Smith River National Recreation Area Information Center The trailhead is directly across from the visitor center.

McCLENDON FORD TRAIL HIKE

Beginner/2.0 miles/1.0 hours

Info: This ideal summer hike comes complete with a swimming hole. The trail wanders through a forest of Douglas fir and crosses the Horse Creek tributary, before reaching a secluded beach on the South Fork Smith River. Have a picnic lunch and an après-hike swim. Your pooch will love you forever. For more information: (707) 457-3131.

Dogs May Be Unleashed Unless Otherwise Indicated

Directions: From Crescent City, head north on Highway 101 for 4 miles to Highway 199. Turn east for 7 miles to South Fork Road (#427) and turn right approximately 14 miles to Forest Road 15. Go right for 2.5 miles to Forest Road 15N39. Turn left for 2 miles to signed South Kelsey Trailhead. Follow this trail for .25 miles to the McClendon Ford Trail on the left.

PELICAN BAY SAND DUNES TRAIL HIKE

Beginner/2.5 miles/1.25 hours

Info: Starting at the edge of Lake Earl and continuing south along the Pacific Ocean nearly to Crescent City, the dunes stretch for more than ten miles. If you and your buddy want some blissful solitude, this is the place. Even your dog will be humbled by the sheer enormity of the pristine sand dunes. The two of you can walk for miles and rarely encounter anyone else. For more information: (707) 464-7230.

Directions: Take North Crest (County Road D3) north through Crescent City to Morehead Road and turn west. Drive to Lower Lake Road, turn right and follow to Kellogg Road. Head west on Kellogg Road to parking at the end of the road. Walk south on the beachfront.

STONEY CREEK TRAIL HIKE

Intermediate/1.6 miles/1.0 hours

Info: If you and your pooch enjoy hiking amid woodlands and waterways, this simple trail is for you. The walk takes you to the mouth of Stoney Creek where it empties into the North Fork of the Smith River, a designated wild and scenic river. Chill out to the soothing sounds of running water and the rustling of tall trees. For more information: (707) 457-3131.

Directions: From Crescent City, head north on Highway 101 for 4 miles to Highway 199. Turn right for 14 miles to the Gasquet Post Office. Make a left on Middle Fork Road for one mile to North Fork Road. Turn left for 1.5 miles and go right on Stoney Creek Trail Road to the signed trailhead.

CRESTLINE

LODGING

CREST LODGE MOUNTAIN RESORT
23508 Lake Dr (92325)
Rates: $55-$150;
Tel: (909) 338-2418

CULVER CITY

LODGING

RAMADA HOTEL-LAX NORTH
6333 Bristol Pkwy (90230)
Rates: $89;
Tel: (310) 670-3200; (800) 272-6232

**RED LION HOTEL-
LOS ANGELES AIRPORT**
6161 Centinela Ave (90230)
Rates: $95-$135;
Tel: (310) 649-1776; (800) 547-8010

SUNBURST MOTEL
3900 Sepulveda Blvd (90230)
Rates: $55-$65;
Tel: (310) 398-7523

CUPERTINO

LODGING

CUPERTINO INN
10889 N De Anza Blvd (95014)
Rates: $79-$138;
Tel: (408) 996-7700

RECREATION

STEVENS CREEK COUNTY PARK - Leashes

Info: Able anglers can drop in on rainbow trout, black bass, large mouth bass, catfish and crappie. If you've got a non-motorized boat, drift away from city life atop the tranquil waters of Stevens Creek Reservoir. Or break some bread and biscuits with Fido at one of the lovely, shade-filled picnic areas scattered throughout the park. Birdwatchers will be dazzled by the diversity of the species that abound. Stevens Creek is

Dogs May Be Unleashed Unless Otherwise Indicated

one of the most popular birding parks in the bay area. Or burn off the kibble with a tailwagging stroll along the Old Canyon Trail. For more information: (408) 867-3654.

Directions: From Cupertino, take Interstate Highway 280 to Foothill Expressway west 3 miles to the northern park entrance.

Note: Vehicle fees are required for lake use and may be deposited at the self serve box at the boat launch ramp.

CYPRESS

LODGING

RAMADA HOTEL CYPRESS
5865 Katella Ave (90630)
Rates: $82-$96;
Tel: (714) 827-1010; (800) 228-2828

WOODFIN SUITE HOTEL
5905 Corporate Ave (90630)
Rates: $119-$179;
Tel: (714) 828-4000; (800) 237-8811

DANA POINT

LODGING

DANA POINT RESORT
25135 Park Lantem (92629)
Rates: $170-$280;
Tel: (714) 661-5000; (800) 533-9748

RECREATION

DANA POINT HARBOR - Leashes

Info: Mill around with your mutt and check out the interesting shops and scenery. The delightful ocean air is a perfect accompaniment to a biscuit break on the pier or in the park. Sorry, no pooches are allowed on Doheny State Beach. For more information: (714) 661-7013.

Directions: Take the San Diego Freeway to the Pacific Coast Highway exit and turn left. Follow until 2nd stoplight. Turn left on Dana Point Harbor Drive and follow to ocean.

DANVILLE

Lodging

DANVILLE INN
803 Camino Ramon (94526)
Rates: $65-$80;
Tel: (510) 838-8080; (800) 654-1050

DARDANELLE

Lodging

DARDANELLE RESORT
Highway 108 (95314)
Rates: $49-$65;
Tel: (209) 965-4355

DAVIS

Lodging

BEST WESTERN UNIVERSITY LODGE
123 B St (95616)
Rates: $50-$70;
Tel: (916) 756-7890; (800) 528-1234

DAVIS INN
4100 Chiles Rd (95616)
Rates: $37-$109;
Tel: (916) 757-7378; (800) 771-7378

ECONO LODGE
221 D St (95616)
Rates: $40-$50;
Tel: (800) 424-4777

MOTEL 6
4835 Chiles Rd (95616)
Rates: $28-$34;
Tel: (916) 753-3777; (800) 440-6000

DEATH VALLEY NATIONAL PARK

Lodging

FURNACE CREEK RANCH RESORT COMPLEX
P. O. Box 1 (92328) Rates: $70-$120;
Tel: (619) 786-2345; (800) 528-6367

STOVE PIPE WELLS VILLAGE
SR 190 (92328) Rates: $53-$76;
Tel: (619) 786-2387

Dogs May Be Unleashed Unless Otherwise Indicated

RECREATION

DEATH VALLEY NATIONAL PARK - Leashes

Info: Contrary to the park's name, 500 miles of natural wonders can be yours. Geologic formations and salt flats are just part of the unearthly landscape. Check out Badwater Basin at 282 feet below sea level, it's the lowest point in the United States. Stick to the roadways, pooches aren't permitted on the trails. The visitor center has brochures to make the most of your desert adventure. Pack plenty of water. For more information: (619) 786-2331.

Directions: From Highway 395, take either Highway 136 or 190 east. (Highway 136 merges with Highway 190). Follow the twists and turns of Highway 190 to the park which is approximately 100 miles from Highway 395.

Note: Avoid between April and September- it's too hot! $5 parking fee.

DEL MAR

LODGING

DEL MAR HILTON NORTH SAN DIEGO
15575 Jimmy Durante Blvd (92014)
Rates: $75-$140;
Tel: (619) 792-5200; (800) 445-8667

DOUBLETREE HOTEL DEL MAR
11915 El Camino Real (92130)
Rates: $119-$154;
Tel: (619) 481-5900; (800) 222-8733

RECREATION

DEL MAR CITY BEACH - Leashes

Info: The north section of the beach, particularly around the bluffs, gets two paws up from October to May when pups are allowed to explore the sand and surf leashless. The beach's mid-section bans dogs from June to September, but allows leashed pups during other months. Visit the south section all year long, just leash your pooch when you do. Pooper scoopers are mandatory at all three areas. For more information: (619) 755-1556.

Directions: Take Interstate 5 north to the Via de la Valle exit west to Camino del Mar, heading south. The north section stretches from 29th Street north to the Solano border. The middle section stretches from 17th Street to 29th Street. The south section goes from 6th to 17th Street.

Locate Other Dog-Friendly Activities...Check Nearby Cities

DELANO

LODGING

COMFORT INN
2211 Girard St (93215)
Rates: $51-$65;
Tel: (800) 221-2222

SHILO INN
2231 Girard St (93215)
Rates: $51-$65;
Tel: (805) 725-7551; (800) 222-2244

DESERT HOT SPRINGS

LODGING

ATLAS HI LODGE
18-336 Avenida Hermosa (92240)
Rates: $28-$39;
Tel: (619) 329-5446

BROADVIEW LODGE
12-672 Eliseo Rd (92240)
Rates: $25-$45;
Tel: (619) 329-8006

CARAVAN SPA
66-810 E 4th St (92240)
Rates: $38+;
Tel: (619) 329-7124

DESERT HOT SPRINGS SPA HOTEL
10-805 Palm Dr (92240)
Rates: $40-$120;
Tel: (619) 329-6495

EL REPOSO MOTEL
66-334 W 5th St (92240)
Rates: $35-$75;
Tel: (619) 329-6632

KISMET LODGE
13-340 Mountain View Rd (92240)
Rates: $45-$65;
Tel: (619) 329-6451

LAS PRIMAVERAS RESORT SPA
66-659 6th St (92240)
Rates: 45-$75;
Tel: (619) 251-1677; (800) 400-1677

MIRACLE MANOR
12-589 Reposo Way (92240)
Rates: $45-$50;
Tel: (619) 329-6641

MOTEL 6
63-950 20th Ave (92258)
Rates: $31-$37;
Tel: (619) 251-1425; (800) 440-6000

PONCE DE LEON MOTEL
11-000 Palm Dr (92240)
Rates: $39-$135;
Tel: (619) 329-6484;
(800) 922-6484 (CA)

ROYAL PALMS INN BED & BREAKFAST
12-885 Eliseo Rd (92240)
Rates: $45;
Tel: (619) 329-7975; (800) 755-9538

SAN MARCUS INN
66-540 San Marcus Rd (92240)
Rates: $32-$64;
Tel: (619) 329-5304

STARDUST SPA MOTEL
66-634 5th St (92240)
Rates: $37-$58;
Tel: (619) 329-5443

SWISS HEALTH RESORT & RETREAT
66-729 8th St (92240)
Rates: $49-$74;
Tel: (619) 329-6912; (800) 794-7743

TAMARIX MOTEL & SPA
66-185 Acoma (92240)
Rates: $30-$50;
Tel: (619) 329-6615

Dogs May Be Unleashed Unless Otherwise Indicated

DIAMOND BAR

LODGING

BEST WESTERN HOTEL DIAMOND BAR
259 Gentle Springs Ln (91765)
Rates: $59-$89;
Tel: (800) 528-1234

RADISSON INN DIAMOND BAR
21725 E Gateway Dr (91765)
Rates: $59-$79;
Tel: (800) 333-3333

DINUBA

LODGING

BEST WESTERN AMERICANA
Alta Ave & Kamm Rd (93618)
Rates: $45-$70;
Tel: (209) 595-8401; (800) 528-1234

DIXON

LODGING

BEST WESTERN INN
1345 Commercial Way (95620)
Rates: $45-$75;
Tel: (916) 678-1400; (800) 528-1234

RECREATION

HALL MEMORIAL PARK - Leashes

Info: Do the frisbee thing or the mutt meander in this 32-acre park.

Directions: Located at Hall Park Drive and East Mayes Street.

NORTH WEST PARK - Leashes

Info: Pups will find pure pleasure in this park's 23 acres. Pack a basket and a blanket and get set for an outdoor excursion.

Directions: Located at West H and North Lincoln Streets.

DOUGLAS CITY

LODGING

INDIAN CREEK LODGE
Hwy 299 E (96024)
Rates: $28-$75;
Tel: (916) 623-6294

DOWNEY

LODGING

EMBASSY SUITES HOTEL
8425 Firestone Blvd (90241)
Rates: $109-$160;
Tel: (310) 861-1900; (800) 362-2779

DOWNIEVILLE

LODGING

SAUNDRA DYER'S RESORT
P. O. Box 406 (95936)
Rates: $54-$125;
Tel: (800) 696-3308; (916) 289-3308

RECREATION

BRANDY CITY POND TRAIL HIKE - Leashes

Beginner/1.0 miles/0.5 hours

Info: You and your lucky dog will travel around a pretty pond as you check out an historic hydraulic mining pit. Take in some scenery and a little history as you take to this trail. For more information: (916) 288-3231.

Directions: From Downieville, take Highway 49 west to Cal Ida Road (County Road 490) on the left, just past the Indian Valley Outpost. (If you drive past Fiddle Creek Campground, you've gone too far.) After 4.5 miles you'll reach the old Cal Ida Mill Site. Take a left on dirt Road 491. Cross a bridge over Cherokee Creek and the road will intersect with Road 491-3.

Dogs May Be Unleashed Unless Otherwise Indicated

Stay left and proceed to Youngs Ravine. You'll see a gated Road 491-4 on the left. After you pass the gated Road 491-4, go 0.7 miles to Road 491-6 on your right. Follow this road for 0.1 miles and you'll be at Brandy City Pond.

CHIMNEY ROCK TRAIL HIKE

Beginner/2.0 miles/1.0 hours

Info: You and Rover just may have this trail to yourselves. The hike ends at Chimney Rock, an enormous volcanic cone 12 feet wide and 25 feet high. Enjoy the great views before heading back. For more information: (916) 288-3231.

Directions: Follow directions closely, this can be tricky. From Downieville, head west on Highway 49 for .2 miles to Saddleback Road. Go 8 miles north on Saddleback Road to the five-way intersection. Continue straight through the intersection onto Road 25-23-1 and proceed .3 miles to the "Y" intersection. Head straight through the intersection (do not veer right) for one mile to another "Y" intersection. Once again, head straight through the intersection for a mile, bearing right on Road 25-23-1-2 (by the "Dead End" sign). Follow about a half mile, heading straight through another intersection. After 100 yards, the road bears slightly left, but you want to keep right, continuing for approximately .6 miles past the turnout at the base of Bunker Hill to the trailhead.

Note: High clearance vehicles only.

EMPIRE CREEK TRAIL HIKE

Expert/5.0 miles/3.0 hours

Info: Towering timber and serenading songbirds offer soothing tranquility, while the trail offers a rigorous challenge. After a 2- mile strenuous ascent, the valley opens up and provides panoramic vistas of the surrounding area. Another half-mile will bring you and Bowser to the saddle and your turn-around point. Plan a break and a bit of landscape gazing before doing the descent thing. For more information: (916) 288-3231.

Directions: From Downieville, take Upper Main Street across the Downie River Bridge. Continue for 4.2 miles to a well-defined road fork. Go left (marked dead end) and pass under the tall gates marked "Empire Ranch." Continue 2 miles to a sharp 180 degree turn in the road. Follow the sign for "Empire Creek Trail" pointing to a narrow road on the right. Take the narrow road 1.6 miles to Red Oak Creek. It's another .7 miles to the trailhead.

Note: High clearance vehicles only.

FIDDLE CREEK RIDGE TRAIL HIKE

Intermediate/Expert/8.0 miles/4.0 hours

Info: Solitude-seeking canines will love this invigorating hike. As you hightail it to the ridgetop, you'll earn some spectacular views of the North Yuba River Canyon. Continue across the ridge for vistas of the Fiddle Creek Drainage. Stop anywhere along the way and do lunch scenic style. When you reach the junction with the Halls Ranch Trail, retrace your steps back to the Cal Ida Trailhead. For more information: (916) 288-3231.

Directions: From Downieville, follow Highway 49 west to County Road 490 (Cal Ida Road), near the Indian Valley Outpost. Travel about 1/4 mile to the trailhead. You can either park here or travel to the Cal Ida Campground and walk to the trailhead.

SECOND AND THIRD DIVIDE TRAILS HIKE

Intermediate/7.0 miles/3.5 hours

Info: Give yourself plenty of time to explore this delightful area. You'll climb through a beautiful shady oasis all the way to the ridgetop. After 0.2 miles of hilltop hiking, you'll meet up with the Second Divide Trail. Splish splash your way along this creekside pathway into the canyon. Keep those snouts out for the flora that brightens the landscape. If you're up to a side trip, take the short spur trail to the creek and break some biscuits with Beau before heading back. For more information: (916) 288-3231.

Dogs May Be Unleashed Unless Otherwise Indicated

Directions: From Upper Main Street in Downieville, go 1/2 mile east of the Post Office and cross the Downie River Bridge. Continue on the dirt road for 2.7 miles to the Second Divide Trailhead. Travel 1.5 miles to a well-defined road fork. Take the right branch, entering Empire Ranch private land and continue 0.2 miles to the trailhead sign on the right. Park your vehicle well off the road and leash up the pup when traversing private property.

DOYLE

LODGING

MIDWAY CAFE & MOTEL
Doyle Loop (96109)
Rates: $28+;
Tel: (916) 827-2208

7W CAFE & MOTEL
434-455 Doyle Loop (96109)
Rates: $22-$33;
Tel: (916) 827-3331

DUARTE

LODGING

TRAVELODGE
1200 E Huntington Dr (91010)
Rates: $35-$50;
Tel: (818) 357-0907; (800) 578-7878

DUBLIN

LODGING

BEST WESTERN DUBLIN PARK HOTEL
6680 Regional St (94568)
Rates: $89-$175;
Tel: (510) 828-7750; (800) 223-4656
(800) 422-4656 (CA)

DUNNIGAN

LODGING

BEST WESTERN COUNTRY
3930 Rd 89 (95937)
Rates: $56-$68;
Tel: (916) 724-3471; (800) 528-1234

VALUE LODGE-IMA
Rd 89 & Rd 6 (95937)
Rates: $39-$56;
Tel: (916) 724-3333; (800) 341-8000

DUNSMUIR

LODGING

**ABBOTTS RIVERWALK INN
BED & BREAKFAST**
4300 Dunsmuir Ave (96025)
Rates: $35-$55;
Tel: (916) 235-4300; (800) 954-4300

CABOOSE MOTEL
100 Railroad Park Rd (96025)
Rates: $45-$80;
Tel: (916) 235-4440;
(800) 974-7245 (CA)

CAVE SPRINGS RESORT
4727 Dunsmuir Ave (96025)
Rates: $37-$49;
Tel: (916) 235-2721

CEDAR LODGE
4201 Dunsmuir Ave (96025)
Rates: $28-$50;
Tel: (916) 235-4331

SHASTA ALPINE INN
4221 Siskiyou Ave (96025)
Rates: $30-$80;
Tel: (916) 235-0930; (800) 880-0930

TRAVELODGE
5400 Dunsmuir Ave (96025)
Rates: $40-$60;
Tel: (916) 235-4395; (800) 578-7878

RECREATION

BURNT LAVA FLOW GEOLOGIC AREA

Info: Unless you're accustomed to floating rocks and glass mountains, this eerie spot will make a lasting impression. Pick any direction and watch Dino survey the prehistoric-like geology. Avoid the potentially unstable ground you'll encounter in a few places and walk on the jet-black lava as you hop from one island of trees to another. If the pooch's paws are on the tender side, avoid the lava-hopping area. For more information: (916) 667-2246.

Directions: From Dunsmuir, go north on Interstate 5 about 8 miles. Exit on McCloud-Reno and go 29 miles east on Highway 89 to Bartle. Go northeast on Powder Hill Road

(Forest Service Road 49) and continue about 24 miles. Head east on Forest Service Road 42N25 and continue to the Burnt Lava Flow Geologic Area.

Note: Exercise caution — some areas can sink like quicksand in dry spells and become like wet concrete during rainy times.

DURHAM

RECREATION

DURHAM COMMUNITY PARK - Leashes

Info: This pretty park serves as a social gathering area for the people and pooches of the Durham community. Make some friends and then make some tracks in the open spaces of this 24-acre park.

Directions: Located at 1847 Durham Dayton Highway.

EL CAJON

LODGING

BEST WESTERN COURTESY INN
1355 E Main St (92021)
Rates: $40-$110;
Tel: (619) 440-7378; (800) 528-1234

BUDGET HOST HACIENDA
588 N Mollison Ave (92021)
Rates: $31-$36;
Tel: (800) 283-4678

DAYS INN-LA MESA
1250 El Cajon Blvd (92020)
Rates: $35-$49;
Tel: (800) 329-7466

MOTEL 6
550 Montrose Ct (92020)
Rates: $29-$35;
Tel: (619) 588-6100; (800) 440-6000

THRIFTLODGE
1220 W Main St (92020)
Rates: $35-$60;
Tel: (619) 442-2576; (800) 578-7878

VILLA EMBASADORA
1556 E Main St (92021)
Rates: $25-$42;
Tel: (619) 442-9617

RECREATION

LOUIS A. STELZER REGIONAL PARK - Leashes

Info: Hike through green fields and riparian forests at this 300+ acre park to some pretty views of the surrounding landscape. For more information: (619) 694-3049.

Directions: From Highway 67, take the Mapleview Street exit east for half a mile to Ashwood Street. Go left, following for a few miles to the park. (Ashwood Street turns into Wildcat Canyon Road).

NOBLE CANYON NATIONAL RECREATION TRAIL HIKE

Intermediate/10.0 miles/6.0 hours

Info: Spend hours exploring the canyon depths along this trail. The middle section is the prettiest and coolest. Take five any place along the creek and enjoy the scenery and the tranquility. Expect a lovely show of wildflowers in spring. For more information: (619) 445-6235.

Directions: From El Cajon, take Interstate 8 east to the Pine Valley exit, turning west on Old Highway. Follow past Pine Valley County Park and turn right onto Pine Creek Road to the parking area for the marked trailhead.

EL CENTRO

LODGING

BRUNNER'S MOTEL
215 N Imperial Ave (92243)
Rates: $46-$55;
Tel: (619) 352-6431

DEL CORONADO CROWN MOTEL
330 N Imperial Ave (92243)
Rates: $38-$58;
Tel: (619) 353-0030; (800) 653-3226

EXECUTIVE INN OF EL CENTRO
725 State St (92243)
Rates: $27-$40;
Tel: (619) 352-8500

LAGUNA INN
2030 Cottonwood Cir (92243)
Rates: $53;
Tel: (619) 353-7750

MOTEL 6
395 Smoketree Dr (92243)
Rates: $26-$32;
Tel: (619) 353-6766; (800) 440-6000

RAMADA INN
1455 Ocotillo Dr (92243)
Rates: $46-$75;
Tel: (619) 352-5152; (800) 272-6232

SANDS MOTEL
611 N Imperial Ave (92243)
Rates: $30-$44;
Tel: (619) 352-0715

TRAVELODGE
1464 Adams Ave (92243)
Rates: $36-$50;
Tel: (619) 352-7333; (800) 578-7878

VACATION INN
2000 Cottonwood Cir (92243)
Rates: $43-$48;
Tel: (619) 352-9523; (800) 328-6289

Dogs May Be Unleashed Unless Otherwise Indicated

<u>RECREATION</u>
RED HILL MARINA - Leashes

Info: Avid anglers are the most frequent visitors to the parks in this area. Local legend claims the region is "one of the best fishing areas in the world." For more information: (619) 348-2310.

Directions: From Highway 111, head west on Sinclair Road, then turn north on Garst and follow to the marina.

SUNBEAM LAKE COUNTY PARK - Leashes

Info: This eucalyptus-clad park totals 140 acres and is laced with walking trails. Sunbeam Lake is a bonus on hot summer days. For more information: (619) 339-4384.

Directions: Take Interstate 8 west for 8 miles to the Drew Road exit. Head north for about half a mile to the park.

Note: $2 day-use fee.

WIEST LAKE - Leashes

Info: Ready reelers, grab your gear, your good buddy and get set for some fishing from the dock, shore or private boat. In winter, this small lake is routinely stocked with trout. For more information: (619) 344-3712.

Directions: Located off Highway 111. Head east on Rutherford and south on Dietrich Road to reach the park.

EL CERRITO

<u>LODGING</u>
FREEWAY MOTEL
11645 San Pablo Ave (94530)
Rates: $38-$58;
Tel: (510) 234-5581

EL MONTE

LODGING

MOTEL 6
3429 Peck Rd (91731)
Rates: $30-$34;
Tel: (818) 448-6660; (800) 440-6000

RECREATION

CHILAO to MT. HILLYER via HORSE FLATS TRAIL HIKE

Intermediate/6.0 miles/3.0 hours

Info: For a short hike, take the mile-long chaparral and pine-covered trail to Horse Flats. For a longer trek, take the marked trail on the left to Mt. Hillyer and travel through an open forest of Jeffrey pine, manzanita and oak, interspersed with huge boulders. For memory-making views, walk a few hundred feet southwest to the top ridge. Springtime is prettiest- the trail comes alive with the exotic snow plant, yucca, mountain lilac and mountain mahogany. For more information: (818) 574-1613.

Directions: From El Monte, take Interstate 605 north to the 210 Freeway northwest (Foothill Freeway). Follow to Angeles Crest Highway (Highway 2) heading northeast to the upper Chilao Campground Road. Continue past the visitor center, and park in the paved parking spaces. The trailhead is to the right.

EL SEGUNDO

LODGING

CROWN STERLING SUITES-LAX
1440 E Imperial Ave (90245)
Rates: $124-$149;
Tel: (310) 640-3600; (800) 433-4600

SUMMERFIELD SUITES-LAX
810 S Douglas Ave (90245)
Rates: $179-$189;
Tel: (310) 725-0100, (800) 833-4353

TRAVELODGE AT LAX SOUTH
1804 E Sycamore St (90245)
Rates: $45-$62;
Tel: (310) 615-1073; (800) 578-7878

EL SOBRANTE

RECREATION

KENNEDY GROVE RECREATION AREA - Leashes

Info: Delight your senses as you and furface stroll amidst a pleasant grove of eucalyptus trees. Toss a frisbee on the expansive lawn or just chill out grass side. For more information: (510) 223-7840.

Directions: Below San Pablo Dam off San Pablo Dam Road.

ELK

LODGING

THE GREENWOOD PIER INN
Box 36, 5938 Highway 1 (95432)
Rates: $100-$225;
Tel: (707) 877-9997

ELK GROVE

RECREATION

ELK GROVE REGIONAL PARK - Leashes

Info: 125 acres offer a variety of pup-pleasing opportunities. Stroll through the open space or laze lakeside with Lassie. For more information: (916) 366-2066.

Directions: South of Sacramento in the town of Elk Grove.

EMERYVILLE

LODGING

HOLIDAY INN-SAN FRANCISCO BAY BRIDGE
1800 Powell St (94608)
Rates: $75-$130;
Tel: (800) 465-4329

<u>RECREATION</u>

FALSE GUN VISTA POINT TRAIL HIKE

Beginner/1.0 miles/0.5 hours

Info: Short, sweet and scenic, this trail is perfect for sofa surfers. On a clear day, the stunning views of the San Francisco Bay will knock your socks off. Head up Old Country Road from the parking area to the Marine View Trail. Go east to the Crest Trail and make a right on the False Gun Vista Point Trail. Kite enthusiasts, False Gun Point is known for its gusty winds. For more information: (510) 635-0135.

Directions: Go northbound on Interstate 80, bear left on Interstate 580 west - exit on Cutting Boulevard. Take a left on Cutting and proceed to Garrard Boulevard. Take a left and drive through the tunnel. The road becomes Dornan Drive. Continue on Dornan for a half mile to the parking area at Miller/Knox Park.

MILLER-KNOX REGIONAL SHORELINE

Info: Head straight for the trails on the rolling hills east of Dornan Drive and throw Rover's leash to the wind. For a scenic stroll, keep his leash on and make your way west of Dornan to shaded, grassy fields that come complete with a lagoon. The trails on this side offer spectacular vistas of Mount Tamalpais, Brooks Island and the San Francisco skyline. For more information: (510) 635-0135.

Directions: From Emeryville, go west on Interstate 80 through the town of Richmond. Exit on San Pablo Dam Road. Go east and drive through El Sobrante for 3.5 miles to the park entrance on the left. The pavement will take you to parking.

Note: Dogs must be leashed in developed areas.

EMIGRANT GAP

<u>LODGING</u>

RANCHO SIERRAS RESORT
43440 Laing Rd (95715)
Rates: $45-$85;
Tel: (916) 389-8572

ENCINITAS

LODGING

BUDGET MOTELS OF AMERICA
133 Encinitas Blvd (92024)
Rates: $31-$57;
Tel: (619) 944-0260; (800) 795-6044

FRIENDSHIP INN ENCINITAS
410 N Hwy 101 (92024)
Rates: $35-$55;
Tel: (619) 436-4999; (800) 424-4777

RECREATION

ENCINITAS VIEWPOINT PARK - Leashes

Info: You and Fletch can catch some rays and panoramic views of the quaint town. For a more social and free-spirited experience, check out the posted signs for leash-free hours. Plan a return visit and linger with the locals.

Directions: Located at Cornish Drive and D Street.

ORPHEUS PARK - Leashes

Info: This beautiful park is a great place to take your favorite barker. Visit during early morning hours or evenings and your pooch can run free. Hours are posted.

Directions: Located at 482 Orpheus.

Other parks in Encinitas - Leashes
• GLEN PARK, 2149 Orinda Drive
• H STREET VIEWPOINT, 498 H Street
• I STREET VIEWPOINT, 498 I Street
• LEUCADIA ROADSIDE PARK, 860 Old Highway 101
• OAKCREST PARK, 1140 Oakcrest Park Road

ESCONDIDO

LODGING

BEST WESTERN ESCONDIDO
1700 Seven Oaks Rd (92026)
Rates: $59-$116;
Tel: (619) 740-1700; (800) 528-1234

CASTLE CREEK INN RESORT & SPA
29850 Circle "R" Way (92026)
Rates: $80;
Tel: (619) 751-8800; (800) 253-5341

ECONO LODGE
1250 W Valley Pkwy (92029)
Rates: $44-$49;
Tel: (800) 424-4777

LAWRENCE WELK RESORT
8860 Lawrence Welk Dr (92026)
Rates: $90-$220;
Tel: (619) 749-3000; (800) 932-9355

MOTEL MEDITERAN
2336 S Escondido Blvd (92025)
Rates: $34-$75;
Tel: (619) 743-1061

MOTEL 6
509 W Washington Ave (92025)
Rates: $25-$29;
Tel: (619) 743-6669; (800) 440-6000

MOTEL 6
900 N Quince St (92025)
Rates: $28-$32;
Tel: (619) 745-9252; (800) 440-6000

PINE TREE LODGE
425 W Mission (92025)
Rates: $44;
Tel: (619) 740-7613

THE SHERIDAN INN
1341 N Escondido Blvd (92026)
Rates: $51-$57;
Tel: (619) 743-8338; (800) 258-8527

SUNSHINE MOTEL
1107 S Escondido Blvd (92025)
Rates: $29-$95;
Tel: (619) 743-3111

SUPER 7 MOTEL
515 W Washington Ave (92025)
Rates: $21-$72;
Tel: (619) 743-7979

SUPER 8 MOTEL-ESCONDIDO
528 W Washington Ave (92025)
Rates: $35-$55;
Tel: (619) 747-3711; (800) 800-8000

ETNA

<u>RECREATION</u>

ETNA SUMMIT TRAIL to PAYNES LAKE HIKE - Leashes

Intermediate/10.0 miles/5.0 hours

Info: Strap on the odometer and tick off some miles on your journey. Refreshing Paynes Lake is your reward for tackling this lengthy ridgeline hike. Pack some Perrier, puppy and people treats and chill out lakeside before pointing your snout home. For more information: (916) 467-5757.

Directions: From Etna, turn right (uphill) on Main Street (Etna-Somes Bar Road) for 10 miles to the trailhead at Etna Summit.

Note: Wilderness permit is required.

ETNA SUMMIT TRAIL to SMITH LAKE HIKE - Leashes

Intermediate/6.0 miles/3.0 hours

Info: Spend some quality time with Old Brown Eyes and get a workout to boot on this trail which covers a 1,000-foot elevation change from start to finish. Once at Smith Lake, chow down on high energy snacks and dip your tootsies before heading back. For more information: (916) 467-5757.

Directions: From Etna, turn right (uphill) on Main Street (Etna-Somes Bar Road) for 10 miles to the trailhead at Etna Summit.

Note: Wilderness permit is required.

LOWER LITTLE NORTH FORK TRAIL HIKE - Leashes

Intermediate/6.0 miles/3.0 hours

Info: Cascading Sur Creek Falls is reason enough to lace up your hiking boots and head out on this hike. Fishing Fidos, pack your gear, pick your spot and cast the afternoon away. If you're a lucky dog, you might go home with dinner. For more information: (916) 467-5757.

Directions: From Etna, turn right (uphill) on Main Street (Etna-Somes Bar Road) for 29 miles to Little North Fork Campground. The trailhead is located one mile up Little North Fork Road (40N51).

Note: Wilderness permit is required.

SOUTH RUSSIAN CREEK TRAIL HIKE - Leashes

Beginner/4.0 miles/2.0 hours

Info: Lose yourself in nature along this charming woodsy trail through verdant meadows and groves of old-growth trees. Visit in spring for a wildflower crayola experience. For more information: (916) 467-5757.

Directions: From Etna, turn right (uphill) on Main Street (Etna-Somes Bar Road) for approximately 20 miles to Forest Service Road 40N54, located just before the bridge over the North Fork of Salmon River. Turn left for 4 miles to FR 40N54A. Follow FR 40N54A for about 1 mile to the trailhead.

Note: Wilderness permit is required.

STATUE LAKE TRAIL HIKE - Leashes

Beginner/5.0 miles/2.5 hours

Info: Statue Lake is in a league of its own and definitely worth a look-see. Bring your camera - the unique granite pillars sprouting from the water are worth a Fuji click. From the trailhead, make tracks up to the Pacific Crest Trail junction and travel south for 2 miles to the lake. For more information: (916) 467-5757.

Directions: From Etna, turn right (uphill) on Main Street (Etna-Somes Bar Road) for approximately 20 miles to Forest Service Road 40N54, located just before the bridge over the North Fork of Salmon River. Turn left for 8 miles to the trailhead.

Note: Wilderness permit is required.

TAYLOR LAKE TRAIL to HOGAN LAKE HIKE - Leashes

Intermediate/6.0 miles/3.0 hours

Info: Lake-loving Lassies won't want to miss this hike, but there's a catch. You first have to find Hogan Lake. From the upper end of Taylor Lake, follow the trail to the ridge then take the right fork down to Hogan Creek. This is where it gets a little tricky. From the creek, the trail follows the drainage up to the lake. But it's not well-blazed, especially in the meadow areas. Make it to the lake, have some splish-splashing fun and then retrace your steps. For more information: (916) 467-5757.

Directions: From Etna, turn right (uphill) on Main Street (Etna-Somes Bar Road) for approximately a quarter mile past Etna Summit. Turn left on Taylor Lake Road (41N18) for about 2 miles to the trailhead.

Note: Wilderness permit is required.

EUREKA

LODGING

A WEAVER'S INN BED & BREAKFAST
1440 B St (95501)
Rates: $65-$100;
Tel: (707) 443-8119

BAYVIEW MOTEL
Hwy 101 (95501)
Rates: $42-$60;
Tel: (707) 442-1673

CARSON HOUSE INN
1209 4th St (95501)
Rates: $60-$110;
Tel: (707) 443-1601; (800) 772-1622

EUREKA INN
518 7th St (95501)
Rates: $70-$140;
Tel: (707) 442-6441; (800) 862-4906

FIRESIDE INN
5th & R Sts (95501)
Rates: $30-$55;
Tel: (707) 443-6312

MATADOR MOTEL
129 4th St (95501)
Rates: $29-$39;
Tel: (707) 443-9751

MOTEL 6
1934 Broadway (95501)
Rates: $29-$43;
Tel: (707) 445-9631; (800) 440-6000

NENDELS VALU INN
2223 4th St (95501)
Rates: $40-$65;
Tel: (707) 442-3261

RED LION MOTOR INN
1929 4th St (95501)
Rates: $78-$138;
Tel: (707) 445-0844; (800) 547-8010

SAFARI BUDGET 6 MOTEL
801 Broadway (95501)
Rates: $30-$58;
Tel: (707) 443-4891

SANDPIPER MOTEL
4055 Broadway (95501)
Rates: $34-$45;
Tel: (707) 443-7394

TOWN HOUSE MOTEL
933 4th St (95501)
Rates: $32-$75;
Tel: (707) 443-4536; (800) 445-6888

TRAVELODGE
4 Fourth St (95501)
Rates: $60-$70;
Tel: (707) 443-6345; (800) 578-7878;

VAGABOND INN
1630 4th St (95501)
Rates: $32-$70;
Tel: (707) 443-8041; (800) 522-1555
(800) 424-4777 (CA)

SAMOA DUNES RECREATION AREA

Info: Water-loving sea dogs, this place can't be beat. Take an ocean dip and explore 300 acres of coastal dunes. Walk the beach, hike on the nature trail or watch the gulls do their thing. For more information: (707) 825-2300.

Directions: From Eureka, turn west on Highway 255 and cross the Samoa Bridge. Once you're on the Samoa Peninsula, take a left on New Navy Base Road. The park is on the right-side of the street about five miles south of the bridge. Park in the main lot.

Note: No leashes but voice control obedience is mandatory.

FAIRFIELD

LODGING

BEST WESTERN CORDELIA INN
4374 Central Pl (94585)
Rates: $48-$66;
Tel: (707) 864-2029; (800) 528-1234

HOLIDAY INN OF FAIRFIELD
1350 Holiday Ln (94533)
Rates: $59-$86;
Tel: (707) 422-4111; (800) 465-4329

MOTEL 6-NORTH
1473 Holiday Ln (94533)
Rates: $32-$38;
Tel: (707) 425-4565; (800) 440-6000

MOTEL 6-SOUTH
2353 Magellan Rd (94533)
Rates: $27-$33;
Tel: (707) 427-0800; (800) 440-6000

Locate Other Dog-Friendly Activities...Check Nearby Cities

RECREATION

ALLAN WITT PARK - Leashes

Info: Equipped with plenty of open space and picnic areas, this 48-acre park sits smack dab in the heart of Fairfield. Active breeds will enjoy the jogging trails.

Directions: Located on West Texas and 5th Streets.

HILLS PARK - Leashes

Info: Spend the day hiking with your hound through oak-clad hills in the picturesque landscape of this 503-acre park. Explore the day away, chances are you'll find scores of scenic spots and plenty of serenity. For more information: (707) 428-7432.

Directions: From Fairfield, take Rockville Road until you see a sign for the parking lot. The park is about 1 1/2 miles from the intersection of Rockville Road and Suisun Valley Road.

LAUREL CREEK PARK - Leashes

Info: Journey down memory lane to this old-fashioned 44-acre neighborhood park. Head towards the west side to an open unshaded area where your pooch can enjoy a nice long walk.

Directions: The park is located on Cement Hill Road at Peppertree Drive.

LEE BELL PARK - Leashes

Info: You'll find 7 acres of romping room to explore with fur-face at this park.

Directions: Located at Union Avenue and Travis Boulevard.

LINEAR PARK - Leashes

Info: True to its name, Linear Park bisects the middle of Fairfield, offering visitors an interesting perspective on the city.

Directions: Main access to this park is at West Texas Street and Oliver Road.

Dogs May Be Unleashed Unless Otherwise Indicated

ROCKVILLE HILLS PARK - Leashes

Info: Hikers, able anglers and picnic-loving pooches will wagabout this park. The area encompasses 600 acres and offers miles of trails for eager paws to peruse. For more information: (707) 428-7428.

Directions: Located on Rockville Road between Green Valley and Suisan Valley Roads, five miles west of Fairfield.

FALL RIVER MILLS

LODGING

HI-MONT MOTEL
43021 Hwy 299 (96028)
Rates: $43-$65;
Tel: (916) 336-5541

FALLBROOK

LODGING

BEST WESTERN FRANCISCAN INN
1635 S Mission Rd (92028)
Rates: $45-$65;
Tel: (619) 728-6174; (800) 528-1234

LA ESTANCIA INN
3135 S Old Hwy 395 (92028)
Rates: $48-$78;
Tel: (619) 723-2888

FERNDALE

LODGING

FERNDALE LAUNDROMAT & MOTEL
632 Main St (95536) Rates: $48-$53;
Tel: (707) 786-9471

FIREBAUGH

LODGING

APRICOT INN/SHILO INN
46290 W Panoche Rd (93622)
Rates: $42-$58;
Tel: (209) 659-1444; (800) 222-2244

Locate Other Dog-Friendly Activities...Check Nearby Cities

FISH CAMP

LODGING

MARRIOTT'S TENAYA LODGE
1122 Hwy 41 (93623)
Rates: $199-$259;
Tel: (209) 683-6555; (800) 228-9290

FOLSOM

LODGING

RADISSON INN AT LAKE NATOMA
720 Gold Lake Dr (95630)
Rates: $79-$135;
Tel: (916) 351-1500; (800) 333-3333

RECREATION

AMERICAN RIVER PARKWAY TRAIL HIKE

Beginner/1.0 to 23.0 miles/0.5 to 11.0 hours

Info: This 23-mile riverside trail along the American River stretches from Discovery Park in Sacramento to Folsom. A multi-use trail, it attracts walkers, cyclists, joggers and equestrians. The bike and horse trails are separate. It's prettiest in spring and fall. Can be very hot in summer. For more information: (916) 366-2061.

Directions: Head west on Highway 50 to the Bradshaw north exit. Take Bradshaw to Folsom Boulevard and turn right. Travel to Rod Braudy Drive and go left. This road takes you into the park and the start of the trail.

FONTANA

LODGING

MOTEL 6
10195 Sierra Ave (92335)
Rates: $32-$38;
Tel: (714) 823-8686; (800) 440-6000

Dogs May Be Unleashed Unless Otherwise Indicated

FORT BIDWELL

Lodging

FORT BIDWELL HOTEL
Main St, P. O. Box 100 (96112)
Rates: $35-$45;
Tel: (916) 279-2050

FORT BRAGG

Lodging

BEACHCOMBER MOTEL
1111 N Main St (95437)
Rates: $30-$150;
Tel: (707) 964-2402

**CLEONE LODGE INN &
BEACH HOUSE B&B**
24600 N Hwy 1 (95437)
Rates: $75-$104;
Tel: (707) 964-2788

COAST MOTEL
18661 Hwy 1 (95437)
Rates: $32-$55;
Tel: (707) 964-2852

EBB TIDE LODGE
250 S Main St (95437)
Rates: $45-$60;
Tel: (707) 964-5321; (800) 974-6730

WISHING WELL COTTAGES
Hwy 20 (95437)
Rates: $60-$70;
Tel: (800) 362-9305

Recreation

CHAMBERLAIN CREEK WATERFALL TRAIL HIKE - Leashes

Beginner/0.5 miles/0.5 hours

Info: Buried deep in Jackson State Forest and surrounded by towering redwoods you'll find a plunging 50-foot waterfall. The trail is short and somewhat steep as it descends into the canyon, but the trip is worth every little huff and puff. For more information: (707) 964-5674.

Directions: From Fort Bragg, head south on Highway 1 to the Highway 20 turnoff. Go east on Highway 20 for 17 miles. A little past the Chamberlain Creek Bridge, take a left on Road 200 and go 1.2 miles. Bear left as the road forks and continue for nearly three miles. There is parking on the side of the road. Follow the hand railing to the trailhead.

MACKERRICHER STATE PARK - Leashes

Info: For a day of fun in the sun with your water-loving pooch, leave the crowds behind and head north to eight miles of secluded beach. Explore the tidal pools but keep your distance from the easily spooked harbor seals. For more information: (707) 937-5804.

Directions: For the best dog access, take Highway 1 approximately 3.5 miles north of Fort Bragg to the Ward Avenue entrance (one half mile north of the main entrance).

FORTUNA

LODGING

BEST WESTERN COUNTRY INN
1528 Kenmar Rd (95540)
Rates: $42-$76;
Tel: (707) 725-6822; (800) 528-1234

ECONO LODGE
275 12th St (95540)
Rates: $39-$59;
Tel: (707) 725-6993; (800) 424-4777

HOLIDAY INN EXPRESS
1859 Alamar Way (95540)
Rates: $35-$70;
Tel: (707) 725-5500; (800) 465-4329

NATIONAL 9 MOTEL
819 Main St (95540)
Rates: $30-$52;
Tel: (707) 725-5136

SUPER 8 MOTEL
1805 Alamar Way (95540)
Rates: $40-$60;
Tel: (707) 725-2888; (800) 800-8000

FOSTER CITY

LODGING

HOLIDAY INN-FOSTER CITY
1221 Chess Dr (94404)
Rates: $65-$145;
Tel: (415) 570-5700; (800) 465-4329

RECREATION

FOSTER CITY DOG EXERCISE AREA

Info: Here, the price paid for leashless abandon is dust. But the area is fenced and there are usually other canines about. For more information: (415) 345-5731.

Directions: 600 Foster City Boulevard. Park behind City Hall.

Dogs May Be Unleashed Unless Otherwise Indicated

FOUNTAIN VALLEY

LODGING

FOUNTAIN VALLEY INN
9125 Recreational Circle Dr (92708)
Rates: $40-$65;
Tel: (714) 847-3388;
(800) 826-1964 (CA)

RESIDENCE INN BY MARRIOTT
9930 Slater Ave (92708)
Rates: $136-$149;
Tel: (714) 965-8000; (800) 331-3131

RECREATION

MILE SQUARE REGIONAL PARK - Leashes

Info: Amidst greenery and woodlands, this 200-acre park is filled with idyllic trails. For more information: (714) 962-5549.

Directions: Located at Edinger Avenue and Euclid Street.

Note: $2 parking fee.

FREESTONE

LODGING

GREEN APPLE INN
520 Bohemian Hwy (95472)
Rates: $85-$92;
Tel: (707) 874-2526

FREMONT

LODGING

BEST WESTERN THUNDERBIRD INN
5400 Mowry Ave (94538)
Rates: $65-$75;
Tel: (510) 792-4300; (800) 528-1234

GOOD NITE INN
4135 Cushing Pkwy (94538)
Rates: $42-$49;
Tel: (510) 656-9307

ISLANDER MOTEL
4101 Mowry Ave (94538)
Rates: $35-$53;
Tel: (510) 796-8200

LORD BRADLEY'S INN BED & BREAKFAST
43344 Mission Blvd (94539)
Rates: $65-$75;
Tel: (510) 490-0520

MISSION PEAK LODGE
43643 Mission Blvd (94539)
Rates: $29-$50;
Tel: (510) 656-2366

MOTEL 6-NORTH
34047 Fremont Blvd (94536)
Rates: $29-$35;
Tel: (510) 793-4848; (800) 440-6000

MOTEL 6-SOUTH
46101 Research Ave (94539)
Rates: $29-$35;
Tel: (510) 490-4528; (800) 440-6000

RESIDENCE INN BY MARRIOTT
5400 Farwell Pl (94536)
Rates: $69-$158;
Tel: (510) 794-5900; (800) 331-3131

RECREATION

ARDENWOOD HISTORIC FARM - Leashes

Info: Take Fido on a journey along the garden-filled grounds of George Washington Patterson's Victorian Mansion. As a working farm, Ardenwood offers you a chance to learn about a farmer's life first-hand while you reap the benefits of your visit by purchasing just-picked vegetables. Visit in summer or fall and you might get to experience a harvest festival. For more information: (510) 562-7275.

Directions: The entrance is located on Ardenwood/Newark Boulevard just north of Highway 84 in Fremont.

Note: Entrance fee and $1 dog fee required.

BAY VIEW TRAIL HIKE

Beginner/3.0 miles/1.5 hours

Info: This historic walk loops around Coyote Hills Regional Park and features ancient Indian ruins. The park is also a wildlife sanctuary with marshes and grassy hills. Take the Shoreline Trail for superb views of the South Bay. For more information: (510) 635-0135.

Directions: From Fremont, take Highway 238 (Mission Boulevard) north through Union City to Garin Avenue. Go right on Garin Avenue and travel one mile to the park entrance.

COYOTE HILLS REGIONAL PARK

Info: Head for the hills and leash-free bliss. This 976-acre wildlife refuge is home to red-tailed hawks and white-tailed kites. The picturesque Bay View Trail offers the best panoramas in the park. Tread lightly in this delicate region. For more information: (510) 635-0135.

Dogs May Be Unleashed Unless Otherwise Indicated

Directions: Head west on Highway 84, exiting at Thornton Avenue/Paseo Padre Parkway. Go north about one mile. Turn left on Patterson Ranch Road/Commerce Drive to the park entrance.

Note: $3 parking fee and $1 dog fee. Dogs must be leashed in developed areas.

FREMONT CENTRAL PARK - Leashes

Info: If yours is a lake-loving lapdog then leash him up and lead the way to this expansive park. Tote your own boat and do a floating lunch with Fido or keep your paws grounded and take a scenery-filled stroll.

Directions: There are many access points to the park from Paseo Padre Parkway and from Stevenson Boulevard.

HIGH RIDGE LOOP TRAIL HIKE

Intermediate/3.3 miles/1.5 hours

Info: Within this 3,000-acre park, you and your pooch will encounter endless stretches of oak-clad meadows and rolling hills as well as spectacular bay views. Begin your panoramic journey by accessing Arroyo Flats from the parking area and turning left on the High Ridge Trail. After .25 miles, you'll connect with the High Ridge Loop. Continue in a clockwise direction. The next mile will take you from 380 feet to the 934-foot Vista Peak and then to the 948-foot Garin Peak. For more information: (510) 635-0135.

Directions: Head north on Highway 238 (Mission Boulevard) through Union City to Garin Avenue and turn right. Follow a mile to the Garin Park entrance.

MISSION PEAK REGIONAL PRESERVE

Info: Aerobic workout guaranteed! Take any of the uphill trails to Mission Peak in this 3,000-acre preserve and you'll be treated to some extraordinary vistas, from Mount Tamalpais to Mount Hamilton. Or do nothing but loll in the spacious grasslands. Bring plenty of water. For more information: (510) 635-0135.

Directions: Go east on Mission Boulevard to Stanford Avenue, turn right (east) and travel less than a mile to the entrance.

Note: Dogs must be leashed in developed areas.

PEAK TRAIL HIKE

Expert/7.0 miles/4.0 hours

Info: A strenuous workout awaits you along a steep trail that climbs over 2,100 feet in just 3.5 miles. The hike begins along the Spring Valley Trail before intersecting with the Peak Trail and continuing to Mission Peak. The summit provides breathtaking panoramas of the Santa Cruz Mountains, San Francisco and sometimes the Sierra Crest. Come spring, the hillsides are painted green and dotted with wildflowers. For more information: (510) 635-0135.

Directions: From Fremont, take Mission Boulevard (Highway 238) to Ohlone College Campus. Park in either lot D or H. At the back of the campus, go through the gate to reach the trail.

SUNOL LOOP TRAIL HIKE

Intermediate/4.75 miles/2.5 hours

Info: The 6,500-acre Sunol Preserve is a "get away from the world" kind of place. It's filled with enchanting special spots, like Little Yosemite - a miniature of its namesake, and Cave Rocks, a series of unusual geologic formations. Hike north on Indian Joe Creek, the babbling brook alongside the trail and ascend one mile to Cave Rocks. A right on Rocks Road will take you over the summit. For more information: (510) 635-0135.

Directions: From Fremont, go north on Interstate 680 and exit on Calaveras Road in Sunol. Go right on Calaveras Road and take it to Geary Road. Take a left on Geary Road to the park.

Note: A parking fee and $1 dog fee are charged.

SUNOL REGIONAL WILDERNESS

Info: Treat Fido to a hike on Camp Ohlone Trail (accessible from the main entrance off Geary Road) to beautiful Little Yosemite. Spend hours exploring the geologic wonders contained in this canyon or venture off on one of the other scenic trails. Check out the waterfalls and whirlpools of Alameda Creek. For more information: (510) 635-0135.

Directions: From Fremont, go north on Interstate 680 and exit on Calaveras Road in Sunol. Go right on Calaveras Road and take it to Geary Road. Take a left on Geary Road to the park.

Note: Leashes required on the Backpack Loop. A parking fee and $1 dog fee are charged.

FRESNO

LODGING

BEST WESTERN TRADEWINDS MOTOR INN
2141 N Parkway Dr (93705)
Rates: $48-$62;
Tel: (209) 237-1881; (800) 528-1234

BLACKSTONE PLAZA INN
4061 N Blackstone Ave (93726)
Rates: $36-$48;
Tel: (209) 222-5641

BROOKS RANCH INN
4278 W Ashian Ave (93722)
Rates: $31-$44;
Tel: (209) 275-2727

DAYS INN
1101 N Parkway Dr (93728)
Rates: $38-$48;
Tel: (209) 268-6211; (800) 329-7466

ECONOMY INNS OF AMERICA
2570 S East St (93706)
Rates: $26-$33;
Tel: (800) 826-0778

ECONOMY INNS OF AMERICA
5021 N Barcus Ave (93722)
Rates: $27-$41;
Tel: (800) 826-0778

EXECUTIVE SUITES OF FRESNO
P. O. Box 42 (93707)
Rates: $650-$1495 Monthly;
Tel: (209) 237-7444

HILTON HOTEL-FRESNO
1055 Van Ness Ave (93721)
Rates: $74-$119;
Tel: (209) 485-9000; (800) 445-8667

HOLIDAY INN-CENTRE PLAZA
2233 Ventura St (93709)
Rates: $72-$86;
Tel: (209) 268-1000; (800) 465-4329

HOLIDAY INN-FRESNO AIRPORT
5090 E Clinton Ave (93727)
Rates: $74-$110;
Tel: (209) 252-3611; (800) 465-4329

HOWARD JOHNSON HOTEL
4071 N Blackstone Ave (93726)
Rates: $36-$48;
Tel: (800) 654-2000

LA QUINTA INN
2926 Tulare St (93721)
Rates: $50-$65;
Tel: (209) 442-1110; (800) 531-5900

MOTEL 6
445 N Pkwy Dr (93706)
Rates: $26-$32;
Tel: (209) 485-5011; (800) 440-6000

MOTEL 6
4245 N Blackstone Ave (93726)
Rates: $29-$35;
Tel: (209) 221-0800; (800) 440-6000

MOTEL 6
4080 N Blackstone Ave (93726)
Rates: $28-$34;
Tel: (209) 222-2431; (800) 440-6000

MOTEL 6
933 N Pkwy Dr (93728)
Rates: $24-$30;
Tel: (209) 233-3913; (800) 440-6000

MOTEL 6
1240 Crystal Ave (93728)
Rates: $26-$32;
Tel: (209) 237-0855; (800) 440-6000

SUPER 8 MOTEL
1087 N Parkway Dr (93728)
Rates: $42;
Tel: (209) 268-0741; (800) 800-8000

TRAVELODGE
2345 N Parkway Dr (93705)
Rates: $25-$33;
Tel: (209) 268-0711; (800) 578-7878

<u>RECREATION</u>

BEAR WALLOW INTERPRETIVE TRAIL HIKE - Leashes

Beginner/4.0 miles/2.0 hours

Info: Hop on this trail and immerse yourself in cool forested beauty, splish splashing riverside fun, vistas to die for, flowers in springtime, shaded walking in summer. Beginning on the north side of the Kings River, signs will provide an education on the cultural heritage, wildflowers and grasses, California Mule Deer migration path, Blue Oak Woodland and a description of the scenic overlook. Wow, this trail is a must-see, must-do for anyone interested in flora and fauna. You'll experience a gradual ascent from the river along the foothill slopes where you can try to capture a Kodak moment - the John Muir Wilderness, Monarch Wilderness, Kings Canyon National Park and the snakelike Kings River are spread out in splendor before your eyes. When you can drag yourself away from the very special overlook, retrace your steps. The most pleasant times to visit are spring and fall. Summers can be very hot. For more information: (209) 855-8321.

Directions: From Fresno, take Belmont Avenue east (it turns into Trimmer Springs Road). Travel up and around Pine Flat Reservoir. After passing Kirch Flat Campground, go over the bridge and continue on the road along the Kings River. Turn left and cross a metal bridge. At the end of the bridge, turn right on Garnet Dike Road. Watch for the Bear Wallow Trailhead sign on your left.

BOULE TREE TRAIL HIKE - Leashes

Beginner/2.0 miles/1.0 hours

Info: You and the sniffer can sniff out this incredible tree if you make your way to the southern boundary of the Special Management Area. The giant sequoia stands 269 feet tall with a 29-foot diameter. For more information: (209) 784-1500.

Directions: From Fresno, take State Highway 180 east to Converse Basin Road (about five miles past the Giant Grove). Turn left onto Converse Basin Road (13S55) and follow the signs about two miles to the trailhead.

Note: High clearance vehicles only.

KEARNEY PARK - Leashes

Info: This 225-acre private estate turned county park is a very popular attraction, especially on weekends. Ogle the grandiose mansion or simply enjoy the company of 100-year-old trees.

Directions: Located on Kearney Boulevard, seven miles west of Fresno.

Note: $3 day-use fee.

KINGS RIVER SPECIAL MANAGEMENT AREA - Leashes

Info: This very special region contains a wild trout fishery in the Kings River, Garlic Falls and the Boule Tree, the largest sequoia found in any national forest area in the United States. Comprised of 49,000 acres within the Sierra and Sequoia National Forests, the area offers exceptional recreational opportunities. For more information: (209) 855-8321.

Directions: From Fresno, take Belmont Avenue east (it turns into Trimmer Springs Road). Travel up and around Pine Flat Reservoir. After passing Kirch Flat Campground, go over the bridge and continue on the road along the Kings River a short distance to the Special Management Area.

KINGS RIVER TRAIL HIKE - Leashes

Beginner/6.0 miles/3.0 hours

Info: This National Recreation Trail is the most popular hike in the region. When you and the pupster want a tootsie-wetting, tree-filled adventure, don't miss this enchanting trail. Beginning on the north side of the Kings River at the end of Garnet Dike Road, the trail skirts the river to Spring Creek. All along the path are photo ops and picnic spots. For more information: (209) 855-8321.

Directions: From Fresno, take Belmont Avenue east (it turns into Trimmer Springs Road). Travel up and around Pine Flat Reservoir. After passing Kirch Flat Campground, go over the bridge and continue on the road along the Kings River. Turn left and cross a metal bridge. At the end of the bridge, turn right on Garnet Dike Road to the trailhead at road's end.

PINE FLAT LAKE - Leashes

Info: Hotdog! This area is absolutely gorgeous. You can picnic in a grassy, songbird-filled setting and enjoy the cool shade of massive oak trees. Or you and your companion can make tracks along the streamside pathways and marvel at the views. Tote a camera, you won't want to miss the shutter-clicking opportunities. Bring a boat and float along the surface of the crystal blue lake, or pack a pole and try your fly at fishing. For more information: (209) 787-2589.

Directions: From Fresno, take Belmont Avenue east (it turns into Trimmer Springs Road). Follow Trimmer Springs Road 35 miles to the end and Pine Flat Lake.

WOODWARD PARK - Leashes

Info: A regional park and bird refuge, this 300-acre area has become a heavily visited tourist attraction. Lush green fields, woodlands, refreshing streams, lakes and numerous pathways are just too inviting to pass up. Crowded in summer and on weekends. For more information: (209) 498-1551.

Dogs May Be Unleashed Unless Otherwise Indicated

Directions: From northbound Highway 41, exit at Friant Road and head northeast. Turn left on East Audubon Drive and follow to the main entrance.

Note: $2 parking fee February-October.

FULLERTON

LODGING

FULLERTON INN
2601 W Orangethorpe Ave (92633)
Rates: $35-$45;
Tel: (714) 773-4900

**HOLIDAY INN-
FULLERTON/DISNEYLAND**
222 W Houston Ave (92632)
Rates: $61-$90;
Tel: (714) 992-1700; (800) 465-4329;
(800) 553-3441 (CA)

MARRIOTT HOTEL/CAL STATE UNIV
2701 E Nutwood Ave (92631)
Rates: $79-$89;
Tel: (714) 738-7800; (800) 228-9290

MOTEL 6-EAST
1440 N State College (92631)
Rates: $28-$36;
Tel: (714) 956-9690; (800) 440-6000

MOTEL 6-WEST
1415 S Euclid St (92632)
Rates: $30-$34;
Tel: (714) 992-0660 ; (800) 440-6000

RECREATION

TED CRAIG REGIONAL PARK - Leashes

Info: Spend some quality time with your pooch at this verdant park. Picnic under a shade tree, frolic on the grassy knolls or simply partake in an afternoon of people watching. The 2.2-mile nature trail is perfect for those seeking a bit of exercise. Pick up a brochure at the Ranger Station and it will expand your knowledge of the region's flora and fauna. For more information: (714) 990-0271.

Directions: Located at 3300 North State College Boulevard, south of Imperial Highway.

Note: $2 parking fee.

FULTON / EL CAMINO

<u>RECREATION</u>
BOHEMIAN PARK - Leashes

Info: Bring a blanket and relax with Max as you listen to the babble of the pleasant little creek that runs through this park.

Directions: Located at Wright and Yellowstone.

COTTAGE PARK - Leashes

Info: Picnic tables dot this lovely park equipped with a fitness course, ball fields and an open play area. Aquapups will love a paw-dip in the cool waters of the creek.

Directions: Located at 3097 Cottage Way.

CREEKSIDE PARK - Leashes

Info: Wag away the day playing with the pup creekside. Get some Rexercise in the grassy area or find some serenity in the nature area.

Directions: Located at 2641 Kent Avenue.

HOWE PARK - Leashes

Info: Hop on the one-mile loop trail and make your way amid several acres of greenery. Anglers will love dropping in on the fish in the pond.

Directions: Located at 2201 Cottage Way.

SANTA ANITA PARK - Leashes

Info: Picnic streamside with your water-loving pooch or frolic through the grounds and admire the scenery.

Directions: Located at 2000 Bell Street.

Dogs May Be Unleashed Unless Otherwise Indicated

SEELY PARK - Leashes

Info: This park has several sports amenities, but chances are that your furry Murray will sniff out the open play area. Pack some snacks and simply enjoy some California dreamin'.

Directions: Located at 3000 Pope Avenue.

GARBERVILLE

LODGING

BENBOW INN
445 Lake Benbow Dr (95542)
Rates: $110-$295;
Tel: (707) 923-2124; (800) 355-3301

BEST WESTERN HUMBOLDT HOUSE INN
701 Redwood Dr (95542)
Rates: $52-$79;
Tel: (707) 923-2771; (800) 528-1234

GARBERVILLE MOTEL
948 Redwood Dr (95542)
Rates: $38-$56;
Tel: (707) 923-2422

HEART OF THE REDWOODS RESORT
900 Hwy 101 (95542)
Rates: $55-$110;
Tel: (707) 247-3305

SHERWOOD FOREST MOTEL
814 Redwood Dr (95542)
Rates: $50-$88;
Tel: (707) 923-2721

RECREATION

CHEMISE MOUNTAIN TRAIL HIKE

Intermediate/3.0 miles/1.5 hours

Info: A pleasant 1.5-mile journey from the Wailaki Recreation Site to Chemise Mountain, begins at a 2,000-foot elevation and ends at the 2,598-foot summit. With majestic views of the Pacific Ocean to the west and many remote coastal ridges to the south, you and the tailwagger will feel like you're on top of the world. For more information: (707) 822-7648.

Directions: Take Briceland Road/Shelter Cove Road west about 20 miles. Go left on Chemise Mountain Road and travel one mile to the Wailaki Campground and trailhead.

KING CREST TRAIL HIKE

Intermediate/10.0 miles/5.5 hours

Info: Get psyched for a tough climb - 2,200 feet in in just 5 miles. King's Peak is the highest point on the northern coast, and on a clear day you can see forever. Be sure to tote plenty of water for you and the dawgus. For more information: (707) 822-7648.

Directions: Take Highway 101 north to the South Fork-Honeydew exit. Take Bull Creek Road west for 21.5 miles. Head south for 2 miles on Wilder Ridge Road and turn west onto Smith-Etter Road to the trailhead.

Note: Smith-Etter Road is closed Nov. to March. High clearance vehicles only.

KING RANGE NATIONAL CONSERVATION AREA

Info: This glorious coastal region fulfills every outdoor wish list. Within a three-mile area, King Range ascends from sandy beaches to over 4,000 feet. This is wilderness country - remote, rugged, pristine and absolutely unforgettable. Walk for miles along the often foggy Lost Coast Trail. Roam lush green meadows and groves of Douglas fir. Take a dip in one of the rushing creeks. Don't forget your camera, the scenery is outstanding. Although this is a leashless area, consider your dog's obedience factor. Wildlife abounds. Watch for marine mammals too, and don't let your pooch disturb the rookery. For more information: (707) 822-7648.

Directions: Head west on Briceland/Shelter Cove Road about 12 miles to Shelter Cove. Call the above number for specific directions to your destination.

Note: Voice control obedience is mandatory.

GARDEN GROVE

<u>LODGING</u>

HIDDEN VILLAGE BED & BREAKFAST
9582 Halekulani Dr (92641)
Rates: $55;
Tel: (714) 636-8312

Dogs May Be Unleashed Unless Otherwise Indicated

GARDENA

LODGING

CARSON PLAZA HOTEL
111 W Albertoni St (90248)
Rates: $32-$50;
Tel: (310) 329-0651

GASQUET

RECREATION

ISLAND LAKE TRAIL TO SOUTH FORK OF THE SMITH RIVER HIKE

Intermediate/2.0 miles/1.0 hours

Info: From the trailhead, you and the dawgus will begin your workout with a rapid descent for approximately one mile to the cool confines of the South Fork of the Smith River. This is a perfect place to wet those tootsies and take a biscuit break. If fishing's your passion, think trout. For more information: (707) 457-3131.

Directions: From Gasquet, proceed northeast on U.S. 199 to Little Jones Creek Road (FS 17NO5). Continue on FS 17NO5 approximately 10 miles to FS16NO2 and turn right. Travel approximately 2 miles to FS16N28 and turn left. Proceed to the end of the road and the trailhead.

GEORGETOWN

LODGING

AMERICAN RIVER INN BED & BREAKFAST
P. O. Box 43, Main & Orleans Sts (95643)
Rates: $89-$105;
Tel: (916) 333-4499; (800) 245-6566

RECREATION

BALD MOUNTAIN CANYON TRAIL HIKE - Leashes

Expert/3.2 miles/2.0 hours

Info: Limber up before heading out on this rigorous trail. After a steep drop to Rock Creek, relax creekside - you've earned the break. Coax Fido from the cool waters when you're ready for the uphill trek to trail's end at Sugarloaf Mountain. For more information: (916) 333-4312.

Directions: From Georgetown, take Wentworth Springs Road east for 3.5 miles to Balderston Road. Turn south on Balderston to Darling Ridge Road. Head south on Darling Ridge for approximately 2 miles to FR 12N89. Take FR 12N89 east about one mile to the trailhead at road's end.

BEAR FLAT OAK TRAIL HIKE - Leashes

Beginner/0.25 miles/0.25 hours

Info: For a quickie leg stretcher, you and the dawgus will want to check out this hike. A scenic overlook of Bear Flat Oak is just a hop, skip and a jump away. For more information: (916) 333-4312.

Directions: From Highway 193 in Georgetown, make a right on Church Street. Follow Church Street to the "Y" and go left on Mameluke. Take Mameluke to West Canyon Creek Road, turn right and cross the bridge. Continue on West Canyon Creek approximately 2.1 miles to Bottle Hill Road. Turn right and travel about 2.3 miles to a gravel path at the trailhead.

HUNTER TRAIL HIKE - Leashes

Intermediate/1.0-10.0 miles/0.5-5.0 hours

Info: This riverside trail is very pupular among hikers and their furry sidekicks. Pack your fishing poles and try to reel in dinner. Or pack your swim wear and spend the day doggie paddling in one of the refreshing watering holes. Either way, you can't go wrong. For more information: (916) 333-4312.

Directions: From Georgetown, take Wentworth Springs Road east for 15 miles to Eleven Pines Road. Turn north for approximately 5 miles to the Rubicon River. The trail parallels the river for 10 miles.

Dogs May Be Unleashed Unless Otherwise Indicated

KELLIHER TRAIL HIKE - Leashes

Expert/4.0 miles/2.5 hours

Info: You and Digger can expect a genuine workout on this old miner's trail. With a final destination of Volcanoville, you'll hike down to Otter Creek, then up to Paymaster Mine Road. Pack plenty of water for this difficult hike, you'll need it. For more information: (916) 333-4312.

Directions: From Georgetown, take Wentworth Springs Road east for 3 miles to Breedlove Road. Turn north for 2 miles to Bottle Hill Road and turn left. Follow for approximately 1.5 miles to the trailhead on the right.

LAWYER TRAIL HIKE - Leashes

Expert/1.6 miles/1.0 hours

Info: This hike definitely separates the dogs from the pups. But there are rewards. The trail descends into a beautiful gorge of the Rubicon River, complete with a fishing and swimming hole. For more information: (916) 333-4312.

Directions: Take Wentworth Springs Road east for 15 miles to Eleven Pines Road. Turn north for about 2 miles to the trailhead on the left side of Eleven Pines Road.

MAR DET TRAIL HIKE - Leashes

Intermediate/8.4 miles/4.0 hours

Info: Spend some quality time with your four-pawed pal in the great outdoors. The pine-scented air is a bonus on this lengthy, but relatively flat trail. For more information: (916) 333-4312.

Directions: Take Highway 193 south for 2 miles to Meadowbrook Road and turn east. Travel one mile to the trailhead at road's end.

MARTIN TRAIL HIKE - Leashes

Intermediate/2.2 miles/1.0 hours

Info: This yoyo-like hike starts with a steep descent to Rock Creek followed by a steep ascent to Rock Creek Road. The return trip reverses the process. For more information: (916) 333-4312.

Locate Other Dog-Friendly Activities...Check Nearby Cities

Directions: Take Wentworth Springs Road east for 3.5 miles to Balderston Road. Turn south on Balderston to Mace Mill Road. Follow Mace Mill approximately 2 miles to FR 12N31. Take FR 12N31 to the trailhead at road's end.

NEVADA POINT TRAIL HIKE - Leashes

Expert/9.2 miles/6.0 hours

Info: This strenuous hike is for physically fit hikers and hounds only. Pack some high energy trail mix, lace up your boots and get ready to tackle a 2,200-foot elevation change. Initially, you'll descend to and cross over a couple of foot-bridges before you climb to Nevada Point Ridge Road. For more information: (916) 333-4312.

Directions: From Georgetown, take Wentworth Springs Road east for 11 miles to Volcanoville Road. Turn north for approximately 1.5 miles to Rubicon Road. Make a right, following for about 2 miles to an uphill spur road to the right. The trailhead is located at the end of this short road.

ONE EYE CREEK TRAIL HIKE - Leashes

Expert/5.2 miles/3.0 hours

Info: Get ready for a challenging trek on this trail. The 1,000-foot descent into the Rock Creek drainage is tough and the ascent is even tougher. On the way down reward yourself with some fine views of Castle Rocks. For more information: (916) 333-4312.

Directions: From Georgetown, take Highway 193 south for 2 miles to Spanish Flat Road. Head east for eight miles, turning right on a spur road approximately a half-mile past the Bear Creek Picnic Area. Follow the spur road for a half-mile to a 4-way intersection. Continue straight through the intersection, making your first right. Follow this road to the trailhead.

SUGARLOAF TRAIL HIKE - Leashes

Expert/2.0 miles/1.5 hours

Info: This hike spells HARD from the get-go. It's like an outdoor stairmaster. You'll begin with a steep descent to Rock Creek and then an uphill climb to Sugarloaf Mountain where you can take a biscuit break before heading back. Water-loving Lassies can dip a paw or two along the way. For more information: (916) 333-4312.

Directions: From Georgetown, take Wentworth Springs Road east for 3.5 miles to Balderston Road. Turn south on Balderston to Mace Mill Road. Follow Mace Mill to the trailhead at road's end.

GILROY

LODGING

BEST WESTERN INN
360 Leavesley Rd (95020)
Rates: $48-$71;
Tel: (408) 848-1467; (800) 528-1234

LEAVESLEY INN
8430 Murray Ave (95020)
Rates: $38-$50;
Tel: (408) 847-5500; (800) 624-8225

MOTEL 6
6110 Monterey Hwy (95020)
Rates: $30-$36;
Tel: (408) 842-6061; (800) 440-6000

SUNREST INN
8292 Murray Ave (95020)
Rates: $42-$50;
Tel: (408) 848-3500; (800) 526-4489

SUPER 8 MOTEL
8435 San Ysidro (95020)
Rates: $35-$48;
Tel: (408) 848-4108; (800) 800-8000

RECREATION

CHRISTMAS HILL PARK - Leashes

Info: This expansive 36-acre park is chock-full of trails for you and your buddy to tread. Songbirds will give you an earful if you choose to check out the wilderness area. Picnic tables dot the park.

Directions: Located southwest of Gilroy on Miller Avenue.

COYOTE LAKE - Leashes

Info: This 635-acre lake is a water wonderland. Fish for trout, bluegill, crappie, and bass or pack a brown bag lunch and a handful of biscuits and make a day of it. From mixed grassland and chaparral to a central coast riparian forest and a dense growth of deciduous trees, this park is an eye-pleasing scene for all breeds. For more information: (408) 842-7800.

Directions: Take Leavesley Road east for 1.75 miles to New Avenue and turn left. Drive 0.6 miles to Roop Road and turn right. Continue 3 miles to the park entrance. Turn left onto Coyote Reservoir Road to the Visitor Center/Ranger Station after one mile.

Note: Fees posted at park entrance. Dogs are allowed in designated areas only and leash laws are strictly enforced.

GAVILAN SPORTS PARK - Leashes

Info: Gallivant on the Gavilan campus and then partake of some playtime in this 8-acre park.

Directions: Located at Gavilan College. The entrance to the park is off Santa Teresa Boulevard.

LAS ANIMAS PARK - Leashes

Info: 36 acres of turf, trees and trails await you in this pleasant park. Lounge with your hound in the shade or hike, bike or jog along one of the many paw-friendly pathways.

Directions: Located northwest of Gilroy on Park Drive.

MILLER PARK - Leashes

Info: Get your daily dose of Rexercise along the walking trail of this 5-acre green scene.

Directions: Located in West Gilroy, between Carmel and Princevalle Streets.

Dogs May Be Unleashed Unless Otherwise Indicated

MOUNT MADONNA COUNTY PARK - Leashes

Info: Sniff out the Sequoia Semepervirens that characterize the landscape of this park. They are among the tallest and oldest trees in the world and they tower with such magnificence that you'll be left breathless. The smaller madrone trees are also interesting. They often become knotted and twisted in their quest for sunlight from under the canopy of the massive redwoods. Several species of oak thrive in the parkland and in autumn they create an astounding array of color, while spring wildflowers bedeck the landscape. Whatever your aesthetic pleasure, you and the dogster will enjoy the scene in this spacious 3,219-acre park. For more information: (408) 842-2341.

Directions: Head west on Highway 152 for 10 miles. The park entrance is located at Highway 152 and Pole Line Road.

Note: Fees posted at park entrance. Dogs are allowed in designated areas only and leash laws are strictly enforced.

SAN YSIDRO PARK - Leashes

Info: Jog with your dog along the pathway that leads through this pretty 9-acre park, or vege out in the open grassy section.

Directions: On the east side of Gilroy at Murray and Lewis.

Other parks in Gilroy - Leashes
•ATKINSON PARK, North Monterey Street
   adjacent to Southern Pacific Railroad
•BUTCHER PARK, located at the east end of Old Gilroy Street
•EL ROBLE PARK, adjacent to El Roble Elementary School
•FOREST STREET PARK, located on Forest Street
•RENZ PARK, located on Hanna Street, north of First Street

GLEN AVON

<u>LODGING</u>

CIRCLE INN MOTEL
9220 Granite Hill Dr (92509)
Rates: n/a;
Tel: (714) 360-1132

GLEN ELLEN

LODGING

BIG DOG INN BED & BREAKFAST
15244 Arnold Dr (95442)
Rates: $100-$135;
Tel: (707) 996-4319

GLENDALE

LODGING

DAYS INN
600 N Pacific Ave (91203)
Rates: $47-$57;
Tel: (800) 329-7466

VAGABOND INN
120 W Colorado St (91204)
Rates: $48-$65;
Tel: (818) 240-1700; (800) 522-1555

RED LION HOTEL
100 W Glenoaks Blvd (91203)
Rates: $128-$155;
Tel: (818) 956-5468; (800) 547-8010

RECREATION

RATTLESNAKE TRAIL to WEST FORK CAMPGROUND HIKE

Intermediate/9.0 miles/4.5 hours

Info: You get highs and lows on this woodsy trail. From superior views of the Mt. Wilson Observatory and the peaks of the San Gabriels to the spreading metropolis below. Retrace those paw prints when day is done. For more information: (818) 574-1613.

Directions: Take the Glendale Freeway north to the 210 Freeway and go east to Angeles Crest Highway (Highway 2) north. Follow Angeles Crest Highway to Red Box Divide. Take Red Box Road east for five miles to the trailhead.

THREE POINTS to TWIN PEAKS TRAIL HIKE

Expert/1.0 to 16.0 miles/0.5 to 9.0 hours

Info: Peacefulness and a sense of accomplishment accompany you on this intense climb to Twin Peaks at 7,761 feet. The serenity is soothing, the views are stunning and the terrain is memo-

Dogs May Be Unleashed Unless Otherwise Indicated

rable. You might even catch sight of an elusive bighorn sheep. Follow your tracks back. For more information: (818) 574-1613.

Directions: Take the Glendale Freeway north to the 210 Freeway and go east to Angeles Crest Highway (Highway 2) north. Follow Angeles Crest Highway approximately 2.5 miles past the Chilao Visitor Center to Three Points. The trailhead is across the highway from the Horse Flats Road.

GLENHAVEN

LODGING

INDIAN BEACH RESORT
9945 E Hwy 20, Box 648 (95443)
Rates: $35-$100;
Tel: (707) 998-3760

GOLETA

LODGING

MOTEL 6
5897 Calle Real (93117)
Rates: $37-$43;
Tel: (805) 964-3596; (800) 440-6000

GOLETA VALLEY

RECREATION

GOLETA BEACH - Leashes

Info: Digger can dig his paws into the sand as you lead him through this beautiful beachfront park. Or wet those paws with a bit of wading fun. For more information: (805) 568-2461.

Directions: From Santa Barbara, head north on 101 to Highway 217. Get on Highway 217 and stay in the right lane, exiting at Sandspit Road. Turn left and you'll see the entrance. Turn right and head across the bridge to park. The park is located next to the airport.

GRANADA HILLS

RECREATION

BEE CANYON PARK - Leashes

Info: This lovely landscaped park offers 21 acres of undeveloped frolicking space for you and Fido to enjoy.

Directions: Located at 17015 Burbank Boulevard.

ZELZAH PARK - Leashes

Info: If you're dog-tired of driving or being indoors, take a break and shake a leg in this lovely landscaped 9.7-acre park.

Directions: Located at 11690 Zelzah Avenue.

GRASS VALLEY

LODGING

ALTA SIERRA RESORT MOTEL
135 Tammy Way (95949)
Rates: $40-$90;
Tel: (916) 273-9102

BEST WESTERN GOLD COUNTRY INN
11972 Sutton Way (95945)
Rates: $69-$76;
Tel: (916) 273-1393; (800) 528-1234

GOLDEN CHAIN RESORT MOTEL
13363 SR 49 (95949)
Rates: $34-$70;
Tel: (916) 273-7279

HOLIDAY LODGE
1221 E Main St (95945)
Rates: $38-$75;
Tel: (916) 273-4406; (800) 742-7125

SWAN-LEVINE HOUSE
328 S Church St (95945)
Rates: $65-$95;
Tel: (916) 272-1873

RECREATION

CROOKED LAKES TRAIL to UPPER ROCK LAKE HIKE

Intermediate/4.5 miles/2.25 hours

Info: This trail to beautiful Upper Rock Lake is accessible from a turnoff on the Lindsey Lakes Trail. A lot less used than Lindsey Lakes, this hike will lead you and Fido to picture-pretty Upper Rock Lake, nestled in an unsullied High Sierra setting. For more information: (916) 265-4531.

Dogs May Be Unleashed Unless Otherwise Indicated

Directions: From Grass Valley, take Highway 20 east for approximately 22 miles to Bowman Lake Road. Travel north to the "Lindsey Lakes, Feely Lake, Carr Lake" sign, turn east. Follow the signs to Lindsey Lakes. The Crooked Lakes trail is accessed from the Lindsey Lakes Trail.

EMPIRE MINE STATE HISTORIC PARK - Leashes

Info: Investigate an old gold mine or leisurely explore 800 acres of verdant gardens and meadows. For more information: (916) 273-8522.

Directions: From Highway 49, exit and head east on Highway 20/Empire Street about 1.5 miles to the park.

Note: $2 fee per adult, $1 fee per dog and child.

LINDSEY LAKES TRAIL HIKE

Intermediate/7.0 miles/3.5 hours

Info: A 250-foot climb in elevation routes you past Lindsey Lakes where refreshing swimming holes are waiting to cool you and the dogster. The trail is rather steep so expect to burn off some calories. For more information: (916) 265-4531.

Directions: From Grass Valley, take Highway 20 east approximately 22 miles to Bowman Lake Road. Travel north to the "Lindsey Lakes, Feely Lake, Carr Lake" sign, turn east. Follow the signs to the lake and trailhead.

GREEN VALLEY LAKE

<u>**LODGING**</u>

LODGE AT GREEN VALLEY BED & BREAKFAST
33655 Green Valley Lake Rd (92341)
Rates: $65-$95;Tel: (909) 867-4281

Locate Other Dog-Friendly Activities...Check Nearby Cities

GREENVILLE

LODGING

HIDEAWAY RESORT MOTEL
101 Hideaway Rd (95947)
Rates: $42-$45;
Tel: (916) 284-7915

OAK GROVE MOTOR LODGE
700 Hwy 89, Box 827 (95947)
Rates: $40-$47;
Tel: (916) 284-6671

SIERRA LODGE
303 Main St, Box 578 (95947)
Rates: $24-$40;
Tel: (916) 284-6565

SPRING MEADOW RESORT MOTEL
18964 Hwy 89 (95947)
Rates: $53+;
Tel: (916) 284-6768

GROVELAND

LODGING

**GROVELAND HOTEL/
YOSEMITE NATIONAL PARK**
18767 Main St (95321)
Rates: $75-$155;
Tel: (209) 962-4000; (800) 273-3314

MOUNTAIN RIVER MOTEL
12655 Jacksonville Rd (95321)
Rates: $30;
Tel: (209) 984-5071

SUGAR PINE RANCH
P. O. Box 784 (95321)
Rates: $69-$95;
Tel: (209) 962-7823

YOSEMITE INN
31191 Hardin Flat Rd (95321)
Rates: $28-$55;
Tel: (209) 962-0103

YOSEMITE WESTGATE MOTEL
7366 Hwy 120 at Buck Meadows
(95321)
Rates: $49-$150;
Tel: (209) 962-5281; (800) 253-9673

RECREATION

INDIAN CREEK TRAIL HIKE - Leashes

Expert/6.0 miles/3.0 hours

Info: This hike to the Tuolumne River is a bonafido butt-kicker. Covering a 1,600-foot elevation change, the trail is bound to get the juices flowing. At the river, do lunch and chill out waterside. When your energy is restored, turn the hound around and head for home. For more information: (209) 962-7825.

Directions: From Groveland, go east on Highway 120 for 8 miles to Ferretti Road. Turn left for 5.25 miles to Clements Road and make a right. Continue past the Pine Mountain Lake Stables, following the signs to trailhead and parking.

Dogs May Be Unleashed Unless Otherwise Indicated

PRESTON FLAT TRAIL HIKE - Leashes

Intermediate/9.0 miles/4.5 hours

Info: For a waterful adventure the wet wagger won't soon forget, try this riverside jaunt. With only a 400-foot elevation change, it's pretty much smooth sailing along the north side of the Tuolumne River. For more information: (209) 962-7825.

Directions: Head east on Highway 120 for 11 miles to Cherry Lake Road. Turn left, follow to Early Intake. Turn right immediately after the bridge to the trailhead just past the powerhouse.

TUOLUMNE RIVER CANYON TRAIL HIKE - Leashes

Intermediate/12.0 miles/6.0 hours

Info: Strap on the odometer and clock some miles on this journey. Get an early start and complete the entire hike from the Tuolumne River to the confluence of the Clavey River or hike in as far as you want. Pack a brown bagger and a couple of water toys and make a day of it. For more information: (209) 962-7825.

Directions: Head east on Highway 120 for 8 miles to Ferretti Road. Turn left for 2 miles to Lumsden Road and make a right. Follow Lumsden Road about 4.5 miles to the trailhead on the left side of the road.

Note: High clearance vehicles only.

GROVER BEACH

LODGING

OAK PARK INN
775 N Oak Park Blvd (93433) Rates: $50-$100;
Tel: (805) 481-4448; (800) 549-4448

GUALALA

LODGING

GUALALA COUNTRY INN
Hwy 1 (95445)
Rates: $71-$145;
Tel: (707) 884-4343; (800) 564-4466

SURF MOTEL AT GUALALA
39170 Hwy 1 (95445)
Rates: $79-$145;
Tel: (707) 884-3571

Locate Other Dog-Friendly Activities...Check Nearby Cities

GUERNEVILLE

LODGING

AVALON INN
16484 4th St (95446)
Rates: $50-$125;
Tel: (707) 869-9566

CREEKSIDE INN & RESORT
16180 Neeley Rd (95446)
Rates: $60-$150;
Tel: (707) 869-3623; (800) 776-6586

THE HIGHLANDS
14000 Woodland Dr (95446)
Rates: $55-$105;
Tel: (707) 869-0333

HACIENDA HEIGHTS

LODGING

MOTEL 6
1154 S 7th Ave (91745)
Rates: $30-$34;
Tel: (818) 968-9462; (800) 440-6000

RECREATION

SCHABARUM TRAIL HIKE - Leashes

Intermediate/5.0 miles/2.5 hours

Info: From the get-go, you and your hiking buddy are in for a "get your juices flowing" climbing adventure on this steep, looping trail. After about a mile, the trail forks- head right. In another mile you'll meet up with the Skyline Trail - go left and begin your downhill descent. Be sure to keep Fido leashed on this popular equestrian trail. For more information: (818) 854-5560.

Directions: From Hacienda Heights, exit the Pomona Freeway at Azusa Avenue and drive south to Colima. Turn right into Schabarum Park. The signed trailhead is located behind the restrooms near the park entrance. Stop by the office for a trail map.

Dogs May Be Unleashed Unless Otherwise Indicated

HALF MOON BAY

LODGING

HOLIDAY INN EXPRESS
230 Cabrillo Hwy (94019)
Rates: $69-$85;
Tel: (415) 726-3400; (800) 465-4329

RAMADA LIMITED
3020 Hwy 1 N (94019)
Rates: $75-$150;
Tel: (415) 726-9700; (800) 272-6232
(800) 350-9888 (CA)

ZABALLA HOUSE BED & BREAKFAST
324 Main St (94019)
Rates: $65-$170;
Tel: (415) 726-9123

RECREATION

BEAN HOLLOW STATE BEACH - Leashes

Info: Unless you're the acrobatic, athletic type who's looking for a challenging climb, stick to the level ground along the coastal promontory. Check out the seal rookery on the rocks below. Listen for the bark of the sea lions and the cries of the gulls as you stroll along the eroded sandstone rocks. For more information: (415) 879-0832.

Directions: Go south on Highway 1, approximately 18 miles to parking at Bean Hollow State Beach.

DAVENPORT BEACH TRAIL HIKE

Beginner/1.0 miles/0.5 hours

Info: A perfect way to transform your cityslicker canine into a beach bum bowser. Unspoiled sand dunes, expansive ocean frontage and nary a soul in sight, if you don't count the hang gliders off to the south. Toss a frisbee or contemplate the Pacific. In the winter, make your way up to the bluffs - you might spot passing gray whales blowing their spouts on their migration to warmer waters. For more information: (408) 462-8333.

Directions: From Half Moon Bay, turn south onto Highway 1. Go past Ano Nuevo State Park nine miles to Davenport. Parking is on the right-side of the highway.

MCNEE RANCH STATE PARK - Leashes

Info: For a rigorous get-away-from-it-all hike, climb the trails of Montara Mountain. Travel from sea level to almost 2,000 feet and reward yourself with some spectacular vistas. Pack your own water. For more information: (916) 653-6995.

Directions: From Half Moon Bay, head north on Highway 1 to Montara and park in the far north section of the Montara State Beach lot. Walk across Highway 1 and continue north to the gate and state property sign on a dirt road. Follow the narrow trails uphill to the left.

OCEAN BLUFFS TRAIL HIKE - Leashes

Beginner/6.0 miles/3.0 hours

Info: For a lovely day that combines Rexercise with serenery, you won't regret a moment spent along this blufftop trail. Benches dot the walkway and provide the seating while song-birds provide the music. Excite your senses with forever views of the ferocious Pacific and then soothe your cares admiring the beauty of wildflowers. Orange poppies, yellow primroses and pale yellow lupines line your path and add a splash of color to the already beautiful landscape. For more information: (415) 726-5202.

Directions: Access to the trail is off Kelly Avenue at Francis Beach or park off Highway 1 at Miramar and walk to the trail.

PILLAR POINT TRAIL HIKE

Beginner/2.5 miles/1.25 hours

Info: Check out the inshore kelp beds and the playful sea lions. At low tide, simply go around the corner to Pillar Point and total privacy. Wildlife includes cormorants, pelicans, grebes and of course your tailwagger. Birdwatchers, don't forget your binoculars... the sightings are unrivaled. The coastline is especially pretty at night when the harbor lights twinkle in the distance. For more information: (415) 728-3584.

Dogs May Be Unleashed Unless Otherwise Indicated

Directions: Take Highway 1 north to the Capistrano Road exit. Follow Capistrano Road west past the Pillar Point Harbor entrance to Prospect Way, turn left. Make a right on Broadway, then a quick left on Harvard. Follow Harvard to West Point Avenue and turn right for half a mile to the parking area.

Note: Consult tide tables. Pillar Point is underwater much of the time.

PURISMA CREEK TRAIL HIKE - Leashes

Beginner/2.5 miles/1.25 hours

Info: Escape the hustle and bustle of city life by rustling some leaves along this peaceful pathway leading through the Open Space Preserve. You'll have it made in the shade beneath towering redwoods and bigleaf maples. Visit in fall for an amazing array of autumnal colors. And take note of the rainbow wildflowers that bedeck the trailside. For more information: (415) 619-1200.

Directions: Take Highway 1 south for one mile. Turn east (left) on Higgins Purisma Road and follow for 4.4 miles to the small, unmarked parking lot at the sharp bend in the road.

HANFORD

LODGING

DOWNTOWN MOTEL
101 N Redington St (92320)
Rates: $30-$42;
Tel: (209) 582-9036

IRWIN STREET INN
522 N Irwin (93230)
Rates: $69-$110;
Tel: (209) 583-8791

RECREATION

CIVIC CENTER PARK - Leashes

Info: From the authentic 1911 fire engine to the quaint carousel, you'll love this charming old-fashioned park. As you stroll under the canopy of large shade trees and flower-filled gardens, the only thing missing will be a twirling parasol and perhaps a glass of fresh lemonade. For more information: (209) 582-0483.

Locate Other Dog-Friendly Activities...Check Nearby Cities

Directions: From Highway 198, exit at 11th Avenue and go north. Turn right on Seventh Street. The park is at Irwin and Seventh Streets.

HIDDEN VALLEY PARK - Leashes

Info: Perfectly groomed lawns, weeping willows and a pond combine for a delightful afternoon scene at this enchanting park.

Directions: From Highway 198, exit at 11th Avenue, and go north for 2 miles. The park is on your left. For parking, turn left at West Cortner Street.

HAPPY CAMP

LODGING

FOREST LODGE MOTEL
63712 Hwy 96 (96039)
Rates: $40-$55;
Tel: (916) 493-5424

RECREATION

CLEAR CREEK NATIONAL RECREATIONAL TRAIL HIKE

Intermediate/2.0-29.0 miles/1.0-15.0 hours

Info: Suffering from the summer doldrums? Pack your hiking gear and head for the cool confines of Clear Creek and this do-your-own-thing kind of hike. A popular short hike brings you to the steel footbridge that crosses Clear Creek - about a mile from the trailhead. Once across the bridge, the trail ascends into the Siskiyou Wilderness and continues 14.5 miles to Devil's Punchbowl. The farther you hike, the more seclusion you'll find. For hot diggety dogs, there are endless paw dipping opportunities in the creek's deep pools. For more information: (916) 493-2243.

Directions: Take Highway 96 southwest about 7 miles to FR 15N32. Turn right for 6 miles, crossing Clear Creek. Make a right on the road that leads up Clear Creek. Follow for about .5 miles to the trailhead. Be prepared to clear some rocks from the roadway.

Dogs May Be Unleashed Unless Otherwise Indicated

COOK & GREEN PASS to ELK LAKE TRAIL HIKE

Intermediate/7.0 miles/3.5 hours

Info: Blissful solitude is just one aspect of this picturesque hike. The relatively undemanding trail follows an old road affording panoramic views of both Oregon and California. Once at Elk Lake, admire the scenery, brown bag it and then point your snout homeward. For more information: (916) 493-2243.

Directions: From Happy Valley, take Highway 96 west to the Seiad Valley exit. Turn up Seiad Creek Road approximately 4.5 miles to FR 48N20. Turn left for about 8 miles to the pass. Park and walk up the gated road on your left around the hill. The trail to Elk Lake is on the right, just below Red Butte.

Note: High clearance vehicles only.

ELK CREEK to NORCROSS TRAIL HIKE

Beginner/2.8 miles/1.5 hours

Info: Sunday strollers will enjoy this easy, pleasant creekside jaunt. At the Norcross Trail spur, retrace your steps or if you're up to more, continue another 2.8 miles to trail's end at Hummingbird Camp. For more information: (916) 493-2243.

Directions: From Happy Camp, go south on Elk Creek Road 14 miles to the trailhead at the Sulphur Springs Campground.

GRIDER CREEK TRAIL HIKE

Intermediate/6.0 miles/3.0 hours

Info: Escape the summer heat on this wet and wild excursion. The trail takes you on a gentle up and down journey, complete with two creek crossings - one with a bridge and one without. Rover will relish the chance to cool his paws in the refreshing water at the second, bridgeless creek crossing where you may end up wetting more than your toes. The large log which serves as the bridge will test your balance. Happy wet trails and tails to you. For more information: (916) 493-2243.

Directions: From Happy Valley, take Highway 96 west to the Walker Creek Road turnoff (located 1.5 miles southeast of Seiad Valley). After exiting, make an immediate right on Grider Creek Road and follow the signs to the Pacific Crest Trail approximately 5.5 miles. Once you cross Grider Creek, take the next left to Grider Creek Campground. The trailhead is in the campground near the low water crossing.

POKER FLAT TRAIL to KELLY LAKE HIKE

Intermediate/4.0 miles/2.0 hours

Info: Treat yourself and the dogster to a pretty wilderness hike that bottoms out at shimmering, sun-dappled Kelly Lake. The trail descends through the Siskiyou Wilderness to the lake. But remember, those who go down must come back up. For more information: (916) 493-2243.

Directions: From Happy Valley, head up Indian Creek Road approximately 7.5 miles and turn left on the South Fork Indian Creek. Make your first right on FR 18N30, keeping to the right as you turn. Follow FR 18N30 to FR 18N33 and go left. Continue on FR 18N33 7 miles to the trailhead at Poker Flat.

RAINY VALLEY CREEK to ELK CREEK TRAIL HIKE

Intermediate/11.5 miles/6.0 hours

Info: Cover the distance on this one and you and your hiking hound will feel invigorated and accomplished - it's long, but pretty and fun-filled. The trail begins by following the Norcross Trail for 3 miles to Hummingbird Camp. From the camp, hook up with the Rainy Valley Creek Trail for the last 2.75 miles. Within .4 miles, you'll paw splash across Hummingbird Creek before reaching Elk Creek. The creek marks the end of your hike and the beginning of water sports for you and your pup. For more information: (916) 493-2243.

Directions: Head south on Elk Creek Road for 15 miles to the Norcross Trailhead, one mile south of Sulphur Springs Campground. It's a 3-mile hike from the Norcross Trailhead to the Rainy Valley Creek Trailhead at Hummingbird Camp.

Dogs May Be Unleashed Unless Otherwise Indicated

HARBOR CITY

LODGING

MOTEL 6
820 W Sepulveda Blvd (90710)
Rates: $35-$39;
Tel: (310) 549-9560; (800) 440-6000

TRAVELODGE
1665 W Pacific Coast Hwy (90710)
Rates: $38-$46;
Tel: (310) 326-9026; (800) 578-7878

HAYFORK

LODGING

BIG CREEK LODGE
Big Creek Rd (96041)
Rates: $25-$65;
Tel: (916) 628-5521

HAYWARD

LODGING

BEST WESTERN INN OF HAYWARD
360 West A St (94541)
Rates: $55-$63;
Tel: (510) 785-8700; (800) 528-1234

EXECUTIVE INN
20777 Hesperian Blvd (94541)
Rates: $72-$88;
Tel: (510) 732-6300; (800) 553-5083

HAYWARD ISLANDER MOTEL
29083 Mission Blvd (94544)
Rates: $34-$49;
Tel: (510) 538-8700

MOTEL 6
30155 Industrial Pkwy SW (94544)
Rates: $29-$35;
Tel: (510) 489-8333; (800) 440-6000

PHOENIX LODGE
2286 Industrial Pkwy W (94545)
Rates: $36-$42;
Tel: (510) 786-2844

PHOENIX LODGE
500 West A St (94541)
Rates: $36-$44;
Tel: (510) 786-0417

VAGABOND INN
20455 Hesperian Blvd (94541)
Rates: $49-$64;
Tel: (510) 785-5480; (800) 522-1555

RECREATION

DON CASTRO REGIONAL RECREATION AREA - Leashes

Info: You can relax with Max on the 3.5-acre lawn, or traipse lakeside and check out the interesting semi-aquatic scene. Turtles and frogs sun themselves on heated rocks while ducks nest in the

Locate Other Dog-Friendly Activities...Check Nearby Cities

reeds. Visit at sunset and you might catch a deer drinking from the peaceful water. For more information: (510) 636-1684.

Directions: Located in Hayward on Woodroe Avenue just south of Interstate 580.

GARIN & DRY CREEK REGIONAL PARKS

Info: At 3,000 acres, these two unique parks join forces affording you and your pooch an afternoon of outdoor fun. Beautiful farmland, fish-filled waters and leash-free romping are just a few of the alluring features you'll find. Take a tranquil stroll through grassy mounds on twenty miles of looping trails, cool your heels in Jordan Pond or Dry Creek or enjoy a game of fetch with Fletch. For more information: (510) 635-0135.

Directions: Take Highway 238 (Mission Boulevard) to Garin Avenue and turn left. Follow uphill .9 miles to the park.

Notes: $3 parking fee on weekends and holidays and $1 dog fee. Dogs must be leashed in developed areas.

HAYWARD REGIONAL SHORELINE - Leashes

Info: Hiking hounds, birdwatchers, ready reelers and alfresco diners can do their own thing in this park. Marsh vegetation, which is gradually returning to the site, has created a habitat populated with many species of flora and fauna. For more information: (510) 562-7275.

Directions: Access in Hayward is off West Winton Avenue.

HEALDSBURG

<u>LODGING</u>

BEST WESTERN DRY CREEK INN
198 Dry Creek Rd (95448)
Rates: $55-$79;
Tel: (707) 433-0300; (800) 528-1234

FAIRVIEW MOTEL
74 Healdsburg Ave (95448)
Rates: $38-$60;
Tel: (707) 433-5548

**MADRONA MANOR-
A WINE COUNTRY INN**
1001 Westside Rd (95448)
Rates: $130-$240;
Tel: (707) 433-4231; (800) 258-4003

Dogs May Be Unleashed Unless Otherwise Indicated

HEMET

LODGING

BEST WESTERN HEMET MOTOR INN
2625 W Florida Ave (92545)
Rates: $44-$100;
Tel: (909) 925-6605; (800) 528-1234

COACHLIGHT MOTEL
1640 W Florida Ave (92543)
Rates: $28-$40;
Tel: (909) 658-3237; (800) 678-0124

QUALITY INN
800 W Florida Ave (92543)
Rates: $45-$61;
Tel: (909) 929-6366; (800) 221-2222

RAMADA INN
3885 W Florida Ave (92545)
Rates: $45-$50;
Tel: (800) 858-8594

SUPER 8 MOTEL
3510 W Florida Ave (92545)
Rates: $39-$65;
Tel: (909) 658-2281; (800) 800-8000

TRAVELODGE
1201 W Florida Ave (92543)
Rates: $38-$42;
Tel: (909) 766-1902; (800) 578-7878

RECREATION

RAMONA TRAIL HIKE

Intermediate/6.0 miles/3.0 hours

Info: Hot summer months aside, this trail provides a pleasurable outing for you and your four-pawed sidekick. A 1,500-foot ascent along a dirt road affords terrific views of Garner Valley, while the aromatic Jeffrey pines delight the senses. For more information: (909) 659-2117.

Directions: Take Highway 74 south to the marked trailhead approximately 3.5 miles past Lake Hemet.

SPITLER PEAK TRAIL HIKE

Expert/10.0 miles/6.0 hours

Info: This calorie burning hike takes you to a panoramic divide northwest of Spitler Peak. Before heading back, either sit a spell at the divide and enjoy the scenery or continue along the Pacific Crest Trail. This hike should be called "Almost Spitler Peak" because you never quite make it to the summit. But it's still is worth the effort. For more information: (909) 659-2117.

Locate Other Dog-Friendly Activities...Check Nearby Cities

Directions: Take Highway 74 east towards Mountain Center to the intersection of Highway 74 and Highway 243. Head south on Highway 74 for 3 miles, turning left at the marked junction for Hurkey Creek County Park. Drive past the park, up Apple Canyon Road to the signed trailhead. Parking is just south of the trailhead.

HERMOSA BEACH

<u>RECREATION</u>

HERMOSA VALLEY GREENBELT

Info: A leashless jaunt along this somewhat shaded dirt path will take you from one end of town to the other - 30 blocks in all. Since dogs are a no-no on the beaches, this slender slice of greenery can fulfill your exercise quota for the day. For more information: (310) 329-4115.

Directions: Access points located along Ardmore Avenue and Valley Street.

HESPERIA

<u>LODGING</u>

DAYS INN SUITES
14865 Bear Valley Rd (92345)
Rates: $39-$69;
Tel: (800) 329-7746

<u>RECREATION</u>

BLUE RIDGE to MT. BALDY TRAIL HIKE

Expert/10.0 miles/6.0 hours

Info: Experience the best of the San Gabriels on this high country trek to Pine Mountain, Dawson Peak and the big daddy of them all - Mt. Baldy at 10,064 feet. Take the Pacific Crest Trail east from the trailhead for 2.5 miles, heading south on the Pine Mountain Trail. Continue south along the spine to Dawson Peak Trail over Dawson Peak to Mt. Baldy. Make it to the top and your views will be nothing short of amazing. This trail is not for the fair-of-paw. Only experienced high country hikers should give it a go. Look around at the weathered trees, the alpine terrain and put your everyday cares in perspective. Retrace your steps on your return trip. For more information: (619) 249-3504.

Directions: From Hesperia, take Interstate 15 south to Highway 138. Go north on Highway 138 to the Angeles Crest Highway (Highway 2). Turn west for eight miles (passing Wrightwood) to Big Pines. 1.5 miles past Big Pines is Blue Ridge Road (across from Inspiration Point). Turn left and drive six miles to Gruffy Camp and the Pacific Crest Trailhead.

HESPERIA LAKE PARK - Leashes

Info: Plan an afternoon beside a small waterfall or take a shaded stroll in this 200-acre park. For more information: (619) 244-5951.

Directions: From Hesperia, follow Main to Arrowhead Lake Road. Turn right (south) and continue to the park entrance.

LIGHTNING RIDGE NATURE TRAIL HIKE

Beginner/1.5 miles/0.75 hours

Info: Zigzag through a slope encrusted with Jeffrey pine and white fir to the Pacific Crest Trail. The refreshing alpine air only adds to the long-range views. For more information: (619) 249-3504.

Directions: From Hesperia, take Interstate 15 south to Highway 138. Go north on Highway 138 to the Angeles Crest Highway (Highway 2). Turn west for eight miles (passing Wrightwood) to Big Pines. 1.5 miles past Big Pines is Blue Ridge Road (across from Inspiration Point). The trailhead is two miles west of the visitor center, opposite Inspiration Point.

LIME STREET PARK - Leashes

Info: 20 acres of open space and private picnic areas await you and your favorite furface.

Directions: On Hesperia Road just north of Lime Street.

LIVE OAK PARK - Leashes

Info: A shaded oasis offers 9 acres of frolicking room for you and the dawgus.

Directions: On Main Street east (north side) of Hesperia Road.

MOJAVE RIVER FORKS - Leashes

Info: A thousand + acres of riverside scenery await you and your hound. Although the area is mostly geared for camping, there are plenty of trails for you and Fido to follow. For more information: (619) 389-2322.

Directions: Located on the north side of the Bear Valley cut-off, east of Ridge Crest Road.

PRAIRIE FORK to UPPER FISH FORK TRAIL HIKE

Intermediate/8.0 miles/4.0 hours

Info: If you want to share the same solitude as the elusive bighorn sheep, you've picked the right trail. This dense woodland is one of the most remote sections of the Angeles National Forest. Sparkling streams tease anglers with the possibility of trout for dinner. Throw in a line - you might get lucky. For more information: (818) 574-1613.

Directions: From Hesperia, take Interstate 15 south to Highway 138. Go north on Highway 138 to the Angeles Crest Highway (Highway 2). Turn west for eight miles (passing Wrightwood) to Big Pines. 1.5 miles past Big Pines is Blue Ridge Road (across from Inspiration Point). Turn left and drive 20 miles to the Lupine Campgrounds. The trailhead is just before the campground.

Note: High clearance vehicles only.

Dogs May Be Unleashed Unless Otherwise Indicated

TABLE MOUNTAIN NATURE TRAIL HIKE

Beginner/1.0 mile/0.5 hours

Info: Hike amid tall Jeffrey pine and oak woodlands on this Sierra Nevada-like terrain. For more information: (619) 249-3504.

Directions: From Hesperia, take Interstate 15 south to Highway 138. Go north on Highway 138 to the Angeles Crest Highway (Highway 2) and turn west. The trailhead is on Highway N4, approximately one mile north of the visitor center.

TIMBERLANE PARK - Leashes

Info: Pack the pooch's pouch and treat him to a picnic at this pleasant 7-acre park.

Directions: Located on Timberlane Road north of Main Street.

HIGHLAND

LODGING

SUPER 8 MOTEL
26667 E Highland Ave (92346)
Rates: $32-$36;
Tel: (909) 864-0100; (800) 800-8000

HOLLISTER

LODGING

BEST WESTERN SAN BENITO INN
660 San Felipe Rd (95023)
Rates: $45-$70;
Tel: (408) 637-9248; (800) 528-1234

CINDERELLA MOTEL-IMA
110 San Felipe Rd (95023)
Rates: $52-$66;
Tel: (408) 637-5761; (800) 341-8000

RIDGEMARK GUEST COTTAGES
3800 Airline Hwy (95023)
Rates: $70-$105;
Tel: (408) 637-8151; (800) 637-8151

Locate Other Dog-Friendly Activities...Check Nearby Cities

RECREATION

DUNNE PARK - Leashes

Info: Located in the downtown section, this small park is shaded by sycamore and olive trees.

Directions: Located off Highway 156 at 6th and West Streets.

VISTA PARK HILL - Leashes

Info: Spacious greenery and eucalyptus-bordered paths are everywhere in this hilltop park.

Directions: From Highway 156, head west on Hill Street to the entrance.

HOLLYWOOD

LODGING

BEST WESTERN HOLLYWOOD MOTEL
6141 Franklin Ave (90028)
Rates: $55-$85;
Tel: (213) 464-5181; (800) 528-1234

HOLIDAY INN
1755 N Highland Ave (90028)
Rates: $89-$169;
Tel: (213) 462-7181; (800) 465-4329

OBAN HOTEL
6364 Yucca St (90028)
Rates: $25-$45;
Tel: (213) 466-0524

RECREATION

LAKE HOLLYWOOD TRAIL HIKE - Leashes

Beginner/4.0 miles/2.0 hours

Info: Leash up the Laddie and get your daily dose along this tranquil path where escapism reigns supreme. Green and serene, you'll play peek-a-boo with the lake until you make your way to the other side of the reservoir. From the top of Mulholland Dam, you'll see the Hollywood sign and sprawling LA before you. Since the service road doesn't form a complete circle, you'll have to hike part of Lake Hollywood Drive to get back to where you began. For more information: (213) 665-5188.

Dogs May Be Unleashed Unless Otherwise Indicated

Directions: From Hollywood, take the Barham Boulevard exit off the Hollywood Freeway (101), heading north to Lake Hollywood Drive. Turn east, following the snaking road through a residential area. Lake Hollywood Drive eventually winds south toward the Hollywood Reservoir. Parking is available along Lake Hollywood Drive.

Note: Trail hours- Monday-Friday, 6:30 a.m. to 10:00 a.m. and 2:00 p.m. to 7:30 p.m.; Saturday and Sunday, 6:30 a.m. to 7:30 p.m.

MT. LEE TRAIL to the HOLLYWOOD SIGN HIKE - Leashes

Intermediate/3.0 miles/1.5 hours

Info: Just do it! And then tell everyone about your up close encounter with Hollywood's most famous sign. Boogie with Bowser up the slopes of Mt. Lee to a "Y" intersection and head left (west) on the fire road to the intersection with Mt. Lee Drive. From the top, panoramas of LA and the San Fernando Valley are yours for the gazing. A locked gate prevents you from touching the sign, but the perspective from this vantage point more than makes up for the paws-off policy. For more information: (213) 665-5188.

Directions: From Hollywood, head north on Beachwood Drive into the Hollywood Hills. At the intersection of Beachwood Drive and Hollyridge Drive, park along the road. The trailhead is located about 50 yards up Hollyridge Drive on the left-hand side.

RUNYON CANYON TRAIL HIKE - Leashes

Intermediate/3.0 miles/1.5 hours

Info: Runyon Canyon offers you and the dawgus abundant opportunity for exploration. Rich in history, views and wildlife, Runyon Canyon is an enchanting outdoor adventure. The plenitude of ruined structures of the old McCormick estate provide Snoopy snoopers unlimited sources of discovery. The pristine upper canyon retains a sense of the wild and is home to deer, coyote, snakes, lizards, owls and hawks. Within the park's boundaries you'll experience a rare example of wild chaparral- all so close, yet so far from the hubbub of

Hollywood. Once in the park, the trail branches left on paved Runyon Canyon Road and climbs the west canyon wall. Near the top, take in the views from the scenic overlook before heading right on the dirt road that steeply descends the east canyon wall to the trailhead. For more information: (213) 485-5572.

Directions: From Hollywood take Highland Avenue south past the Hollywood Bowl to Franklin Avenue and head west to Fuller. Make a right on Fuller to the park entrance at road's end. The trailhead is located just within "The Pines" gate entrance. There is no parking in the park. Car pooling and public transportation are encouraged.

HOLTVILLE

LODGING

BARBARA WORTH COUNTRY CLUB & HOTEL
2050 Country Club Dr (92250)
Rates: $48-$75;
Tel: (619) 356-2806; (800) 356-3806

RECREATION

HEBER DUNES COUNTY PARK - Leashes

Info: The trails of this 300-acre park wind their way through sand dunes and diverse vegetation. The Salt-Cedar trees provide lots of shade, a bonus in summer. For more information: (619) 339-4384.

Directions: From Highway 111, take the Heber Road exit east approximately 6.5 miles to the park.

WALKER PARK - Leashes

Info: A walk in Walker Park provides a leg-stretching opportunity for weary travelers.

Directions: In Holtville on old Highway 80.

HOMEWOOD

LODGING

HOMESIDE MOTEL
5205 W Lake Blvd (96141)
Rates: $222 (Three nights lodging);
Tel: (800) 824-6348

HOPE VALLEY

LODGING

SORENSEN'S RESORT
14255 Hwy 88 (96120)
Rates: $55-$120;
Tel: (916) 694-2203; (800) 423-9949

HUNTINGTON BEACH

LODGING

BEACH COMFORT MOTEL
118 11th St (92647)
Rates: $50-$75;
Tel: (714) 536-4170

BEST WESTERN REGENCY INN
19360 Beach Blvd (92648)
Rates: $63-$120;
Tel: (800) 528-1234

MOTEL EUROPA
7561 Center Ave 46 (92647)
Rates: $36-$50;
Tel: (714) 892-7336

RECREATION

HUNTINGTON BEACH DOG BEACH - Leashes

Info: Sand-loving dogs pawsitively love this beach. But like many of California's beaches, it can disappear at high tide. Check tide tables before visiting. For more information: 1-800-SAY-OCEAN.

Directions: West of Goldenwest Street on Pacific Crest Highway.

HUNTINGTON CENTRAL PARK - Leashes

Info: This vast city park is a cornucopia of nature, from woodlands to lakes, lush meadows to hillocks. Pick a path and explore them all. Goldenwest Road divides the park into two equally lovely areas. If you feel a tug at the leash, Fido has probably sniffed out the "bark park" section where pooches prance and play leash-free in the fenced area. To access this section, enter at Inlet Drive off Edwards Avenue. For more information: (714) 848-0690.

Directions: The eastern entrance can be accessed by the entry road across from Rio Vista Drive. The western entrance is accessed by heading west on Ellis Avenue.

THE PARK BENCH CAFE - Leashes

Info: Talk about a truly unique dining experience. Canines can saddle up to the cafe and choose from a menu especially designed for four-footed visitors. Puppies can fill up their paunches with tasty menu items such as: the Wrangler Roundup, a lean ground turkey patty for low-cal canines; Chilly Paws, a scoop of vanilla for pampered pooches; and just plain doggie kibble for discriminating tastes. Prices are reasonable and only well-behaved Bowsers are served. Don't worry, an extensive menu is available for hungry humans too. You can dance with Prancer during the summer when live, pet-friendly entertainment is provided on Wednesday-Saturday until 8:30 p.m. "Bone Appetit!" For more information: (714) 842-0775.

Directions: Located within Huntington Central Park at 17732 Goldenwest Street, just south of Slater Avenue.

HYAMPOM

<u>LODGING</u>
ZIEGLER'S TRAILS' END
#1 Main St (96046) Rates: $50-$80;
Tel: (916) 628-4929; (800) 566-5266

Dogs May Be Unleashed Unless Otherwise Indicated

IDYLLWILD

LODGING

FIRESIDE INN
54540 N Circle Dr (92549)
Rates: $55-$80;
Tel: (909) 659-2966

IDYLLWILD INN
P. O. Box 515 (92549)
Rates: $47-$124;
Tel: (909) 659-2552

KNOTTY PINE CABINS
54340 Pine Crest Dr (92549)
Rates: $42-$120;
Tel: (909) 659-2933

MILE HIGH LODGE
54635 N Circle Dr (92549)
Rates: $70-$110;
Tel: (909) 659-2931

RECREATION

BLACK MOUNTAIN TRAIL HIKE

Intermediate/Expert/7.2 miles/4.0 hours

Info: Climbing nearly 2,300 feet in elevation, this hike is no walk in the park. But if you're up to the workout, you'll get the rewards. Chaparral soon gives way to lush forests as you ascend from 4,480 feet to 7,772 feet. From your lofty perch on Black Mountain, take in the spectacular vistas of Mt. San Gorgonio and the Banning Pass. En route, you'll traverse a Research Natural Area where ecosystems are being studied. If the pupster isn't voice controlled, you'll want to use his leash. For more information: (909) 659-2117.

Directions: From Idyllwild, head north on Highway 243 to the Idyllwild Ranger Station at the corner of Highway 243 and Pinecrest Road. Once at the station, check with the forest rangers on trail conditions, as well as specific directions to the trailhead. Or call the above number beforehand.

CAHUILLA MOUNTAIN TRAIL HIKE

Intermediate/5.0 miles/2.5 hours

Info: Make tracks with furface to the top of 5,604-foot Cahuilla Mountain and you won't be disappointed - the views are worth the effort. From Cahuilla Saddle, the trail climbs through groves of live oak, Jeffrey pine and chaparral before topping out at the summit. You'll pass through a Research Natural Area that contains ecosystems for study purposes. Leashes are recommended. For more information: (909) 659-2117.

Locate Other Dog-Friendly Activities...Check Nearby Cities

Directions: From Idyllwild, head north on Highway 243 to the Idyllwild Ranger Station at the corner of Highway 243 and Pinecrest Road. Once at the station, check with the forest rangers on trail conditions, as well as specific directions to the trailhead. Or call the above number beforehand.

ERNIE MAXWELL SCENIC TRAIL HIKE
Beginner/5.2 miles/2.5 hours

Info: When loading your backpack, don't forget water sandals. This cinchy trail crosses Strawberry Creek as it descends through a densely forested area. The creekside is chockful of picnic spots for you and Spot. For more information: (909) 659-2117.

Directions: From Idyllwild, head north on Highway 243 to the Idyllwild Ranger Station at the corner of Highway 243 and Pinecrest Road. Once at the station, check with the forest rangers on trail conditions, as well as specific directions to the trailhead. Or call the above number beforehand.

FOBES TRAIL HIKE
Intermediate/3.0 miles/1.5 hours

Info: Hike with Spike on this scenic trail to the pine-clad Desert Divide. You'll ascend through woodlands of chaparral and oak and experience an 800-foot elevation change. When you junction with the Pacific Crest Trail, turn around and head back the way you came. For more information: (909) 659-2117.

Directions: Head north on Highway 243 to the Idyllwild Ranger Station at the corner of Highway 243 and Pinecrest Road. Once at the station, check with the forest rangers on trail conditions, as well as specific directions to the trailhead.

IDYLLWILD COUNTY PARK - Leashes
Info: Hop on one of the self-guided nature trails at this spacious 202-acre park and learn a little about the area.

Directions: Located at the north end of County Park Road, one mile north of Idyllwild.

Note: $2/ adult, $1/ child under 12 and $2/ dog day use fee.

Dogs May Be Unleashed Unless Otherwise Indicated

SOUTH FORK TRAIL HIKE

Intermediate/Expert/9.0 miles/5.0 hours

Info: If you've got the time and the hiking experience, high-tail it on this trail and get your juices flowing. Initially, the trail drops you and the dogster down to the South Fork of the San Jacinto River. From the river, it's a steep climb to trail's end at an elevation of 4,600 feet. Rouse Ridge Road marks your turnaround point. For more information: (909) 659-2117.

Directions: From Idyllwild, head north on Highway 243 to the Idyllwild Ranger Station at the corner of Highway 243 and Pinecrest Road. Once at the station, check with the forest rangers on trail conditions, as well as specific directions to the trailhead. Or call the above number beforehand.

WEBSTER TRAIL HIKE

Expert/5.0 miles/3.0 hours

Info: Only fit Fidos and Herculean hikers should undertake this strenuous hike to the North Fork of the San Jacinto River. But if you're made of tough stuff, you'll experience a variety of vegetation including from Jeffrey pine, chaparral and willow trees. En route, get an eyeful of the terrific vistas of the San Jacinto and Hemet Valleys. For more information: (909) 659-2117.

Directions: From Idyllwild, head north on Highway 243 to the Idyllwild Ranger Station at the corner of Highway 243 and Pinecrest Road. Once at the station, check with the forest rangers on trail conditions, as well as specific directions to the trailhead. Or call the above number beforehand.

IMPERIAL

<u>LODGING</u>

BEST WESTERN IMPERIAL VALLEY INN
1093 Airport Blvd (92251)
Rates: $42-$60;
Tel: (619) 355-4500; (800) 528-1234

Locate Other Dog-Friendly Activities...Check Nearby Cities

IMPERIAL BEACH

LODGING

HAWAIIAN GARDENS SUITE-HOTEL
1031 Imperial Beach Blvd (91932)
Rates: $60-$125;
Tel: (619) 429-5303; (800) 334-3071

INDIAN WELLS

LODGING

ERAWAN GARDEN HOTEL
76-477 Hwy 111 (92210)
Rates: $45-$140;
Tel: (800) 237-2926

INDIO

LODGING

BEST WESTERN DATE TREE HOTEL
81-909 Indio Blvd (92201)
Rates: $49-$98;
Tel: (619) 347-3421; (800) 528-1234
(800) 292-5599 (CA)

COMFORT INN
43-505 Monroe St (92201)
Rates: $44-$79;
Tel: (619) 347-4044; (800) 221-2222

INDIO HOLIDAY MOTEL
44-301 Sungold St (92201)
Rates: $45-$65;
Tel: (619) 347-6105

MOTEL 6
82-195 E Valley Pkwy (92201)
Rates: $26-$32;
Tel: (619) 342-6311; (800) 440-6000

PALM SHADOW INN
80-761 Hwy 111 (92201)
Rates: $49-$75;
Tel: (619) 347-3476

PENTA INN
84-115 Indio Blvd (92201)
Rates: $29-$42;
Tel: (619) 342-4747; (800) 897-9555

RODEWAY INN AT BIG AMERICA
84-096 Indio Springs Dr (92201)
Rates: $39-$76;
Tel: (800) 424-4777

ROYAL PLAZA INN
82-347 Hwy 111 (92201)
Rates: $44-$60;
Tel: (619) 347-0911; (800) 228-9559

SUPER 8 MOTEL
81-753 Hwy 111 (92201)
Rates: $36-$60;
Tel: (619) 342-0264; (800) 800-8000

Dogs May Be Unleashed Unless Otherwise Indicated

RECREATION

LAKE CAHUILLA - Leashes

Info: The views of the Santa Rosa Mountains that surround this lovely lake are absolutely breathtaking. Take your pooch for a day of fishing and fun in the sun. Several miles of scenic hiking trails escort you and your canine companion through this stunning region. For more information: (619) 564-4712

Directions: Take Monroe Street south until you reach Avenue 58 and turn right. The park is located at the end of Avenue 58.

Note: $2/day dog fee.

INDUSTRY

LODGING

**INDUSTRY HILLS SHERATON
RESORT & CONFERENCE CENTER**
1 Industry Hills Pkwy (91744)
Rates: $115-$150;
Tel: (818) 965-0861; (800) 325-3535

INGLEWOOD

LODGING

BEST WESTERN AIRPORT PLAZA INN
1730 Centinela Ave (90302)
Rates: $56-$95;
Tel: (310) 568-0071; (800) 528-1234;
(800) 233-8061 (CA)

ECONO LODGE-AIRPORT
439 W Manchester Blvd (90301)
Rates: $45-$60;
Tel: (800) 424-4777

ECONO LODGE LAX
4123 W Century Blvd (90304)
Rates: $35-$50;
Tel: (310) 672-7285; (800) 424-4777

HAMPTON INN-LAX
10300 La Cienega Blvd (90304)
Rates: $65-$85;
Tel: (310) 337-1000; (800) 426-7866

Locate Other Dog-Friendly Activities...Check Nearby Cities

INVERNESS

LODGING

MANKA'S INVERNESS LODGE
P. O. Box 1110 (94937)
Rates: $65-$160;
Tel: (415) 669-1034

MOTEL INVERNESS
12718 Sir Francis Drake Blvd (94937)
Rates: $59-$79;
Tel: (415) 669-1081

**ROSEMARY COTTAGE
BED & BREAKFAST**
75 Balboa Ave (94937)
Rates: $112-$175;
Tel: (415) 663-9338;
(800) 878-9338

RECREATION

POINT REYES NATIONAL SEASHORE - Leashes

Info: Drift away from city life and be awestruck by the dramatic coastal scenery. Products of folding, faulting and plate tectonics, rocky cliffs rise from the sea and create incredible viewing vistas. Not to mention the fabulous Fido-friendly beaches you can explore. Enter at the Bear Valley entrance and stop by the Visitor Center for details. For more information: (415) 663-1092.

Directions: From Inverness, head east on Highway 1 to Bear Valley Road. The Visitor Center is well signed.

Note: Check tide tables. High tide can be dangerous.

1) KEHOE BEACH - Leashes

Info: Park roadside, hike a half-mile through wildflowers and thistle to enter paradise. Limestone cliffs form the backdrop to tidal pools, white-capped waves and a beach that goes forever. Keep your pooch leashed, this shoreline region is home to harbor seals and endangered snowy plovers. For more information: (415) 663-1092.

Directions: Take Sir Francis Drake Highway west to the fork and bear right on Pierce Point Road. Go about four miles and park on the road.

2) LIMANTOUR BEACH - Leashes

Info: Birdwatching, beachcombing and sun-basking are the favorite pastimes on this beautiful stretch of beach. Dogs are allowed between the main Limantour parking lot and the rocky promontories south of Coast Camp. For more information: (415) 633-1092.

Directions: Located off Bear Valley Road near the Visitor Center.

3) POINT REYES BEACH NORTH - Leashes

Info: For a beach outing, plain and simple, this is the place for you and your sand-loving pup. For more information: (415) 633-1092.

Directions: Take Sir Francis Drake Highway west for approximately 10 miles. The beach turnoff is clearly marked.

4) POINT REYES BEACH SOUTH - Leashes

Info: Paw-friendly and perfect for picnicking pooches, this beach is a great place for you and Fido to frolic. A word of warning - do not go near the water. The hammering surf and rip currents are dangerous. For more information: (415) 633-1092.

Directions: Located off Sir Francis Drake Highway. The exit for the beach is clearly marked.

INYOKERN

LODGING

THREE FLAGS INN
1233 Brown Rd (93527)
Rates: $30-$120;
Tel: (619) 377-3300

Locate Other Dog-Friendly Activities...Check Nearby Cities

IRVINE

LODGING

ATRIUM MARQUIS HOTEL
18700 MacArthur Blvd (92715)
Rates: $75-$190;
Tel: (714) 833-2770; (800) 854-3012

**HOLIDAY INN SELECT-
IRVINE/ORANGE COUNTY AIRPORT**
17941 Von Karman Ave (92714)
Rates: $89-$149;
Tel: (714) 863-1999; (800) 465-4329

HYATT REGENCY IRVINE
17900 Jamboree Blvd (92714)
Rates: $89-$169;
Tel: (714) 975-1234; (800) 233-1234

LA QUINTA MOTOR INN
14972 Sand Canyon Ave (92718)
Rates: $58-$76;
Tel: (714) 551-0909; (800) 531-5900

MARRIOTT HOTEL
18000 Von Karman Ave (92715)
Rates: $79-$160;
Tel: (714) 553-0100; (800) 228-9290

MOTEL 6-JOHN WAYNE AIRPORT
1717 E Dyer Rd (92705)
Rates: $36-$40;
Tel: (714) 261-1515; (800) 440-6000

**RESIDENCE INN BY MARRIOTT-
IRVINE SPECTRUM**
10 Morgan (92718)
Rates: $74-$159;
Tel: (714) 380-3000; (800) 331-3131

RECREATION

WILLIAM R. MASON REGIONAL PARK - Leashes

Info: Chill out with the dogster lakeside or laze the day away under a shade tree. If you're the athletic type, plan a hike on one of the wilderness trails along the eastern side of this county park. For more information: (714) 854-2490.

Directions: At 18712 University Drive, just west of Culver Drive.

Note: $2 parking fee.

JACKSON

LODGING

AMADOR MOTEL
12408 Kennedy Flat Rd (95642)
Rates: $27-$57; Tel: (209) 223-0970

BEST WESTERN AMADOR INN
200 S Hwy 49 (95642) Rates: $46-$74;
Tel: (209) 223-0211; (800) 528-1234

EL CAMPO CASA RESORT MOTEL
12548 Kennedy Flat Rd (95642)
Rates: $33-$70; Tel: (209) 223-0100

JACKSON HOLIDAY LODGE
850 N Hwy 49 (95642)
Rates: $46-$70;
Tel: (209) 223-0486

LINDA VISTA MOTEL
10708 N Hwy 49 (95642)
Rates: $28-$47;
Tel: (209) 223-1096

Dogs May Be Unleashed Unless Otherwise Indicated

RECREATION

DETERT PARK - Leashes

Info: If historic Jackson is your destination, take an afternoon break at this grassy, shady oasis.

Directions: The park is located just east of Highway 49/88, north of Hoffman Street.

MINNIE PROVIS PARK - Leashes

Info: Visit the historic section of downtown Sutter Creek and then stroll about this small grassy park.

Directions: From Jackson, travel northwest on Highway 49 exiting at Church Street. Go east a half block and the park is on the street.

NEW HOGAN LAKE - Leashes

Info: With fifty miles of shoreline, you and your sidekick will find plenty to do. The landscape is a combination of gentle hills and open land. Summer can be hot and crowded. For more information: (209) 772-1462.

Directions: Head southeast on Highway 49 to Highway 26 west towards Valley Springs, following the signs to the lake.

Note: $3 day-use fee.

JAMESTOWN

LODGING

HISTORIC NATIONAL HOTEL
BED & BREAKFAST
77 Main St, P. O. Box 502 (95327)
Rates: $65-$80;
Tel: (209) 984-3446; (800) 446-1333
(800) 894-3446 (CA)

SONORA COUNTRY INN
18755 Charbroullian Ln (95327)
Rates: $49-$69;
Tel: (800) 847-2211

Locate Other Dog-Friendly Activities...Check Nearby Cities

JENNER

LODGING

STILLWATER COVE RANCH
22555 Coast Hwy 1 (95450)
Rates: $50-$80;
Tel: (707) 847-3227

TIMBER COVE INN
21780 Coast Hwy 1 (95450)
Rates: $68-$110;
Tel: (707) 847-3231

JOSHUA TREE

LODGING

JOSHUA TREE INN BED & BREAKFAST
61259 29 Palms Hwy (92252)
Rates: $95-$150;
Tel: (619) 366-1188

RECREATION

JOSHUA TREE NATIONAL MONUMENT - Leashes

Info: Put this 870-square-mile park at the top of your day's itinerary and you won't soon forget the dazzling display of nature. Access the park from the visitor's center for amazing vistas of granite rock formations, desert flora and fauna. The west end is home to the elegant Joshua tree. Come spring-time, the desert terrain comes alive with brilliant wildflowers. Your pup can partake of the nature excursion as long as he remains leashed and on the roads, not the hiking trails. For more information: (619) 367-7511.

Directions: Take Highway 60 east to Interstate 10 southeast. Continue on Interstate 10 to Highway 62 northeast. Follow approximately 39 miles to the town of Twentynine Palms. The visitor's center is on the Utah Trail, south of Highway 62, one mile east of town.

Note: $5 entrance fee.

JULIAN

LODGING

**EDEN CREEK ORCHARD
BED & BREAKFAST**
1052 Julian Orchards Dr (92036)
Rates: $90-$100;
Tel: (619) 765-2102

PINE HILLS LODGE
2960 La Posada, Box 2260 (92036)
Rates: $60-$125;
Tel: (619) 765-1100

RECREATION

INAJA NATIONAL RECREATION TRAIL HIKE

Beginner/0.5 miles/0.5 hours

Info: This path takes you to a lookout point with a good view of the San Diego River Canyon. Along the way, you'll notice a picnic spot that was dedicated to honor 11 firefighters who perished in a devastating 1956 forest fire. Sometimes in early winter, fog rolls into the canyon, covering nearly everything. Peaks and ridges poke through the thick blanket for a postcard pretty picture. For more information: (619) 788-0250.

Directions: Head west on Hwy 79/Hwy 78 to the Inaja Picnic Area.

JUNCTION CITY

LODGING

BIGFOOT CAMPGROUND
Hwy 299 (96048)
Rates: $69;
Tel: (916) 623-6088

STEELHEAD COTTAGES
Hwy 299 (96048)
Rates: $43-$76;
Tel: (916) 623-6325

JUNE LAKE

LODGING

GULL LAKE LODGE
P. O. Box 25 (93529)
Rates: $59-$75; Tel: (619) 648-7516

JUNE LAKE MOTEL & CABINS
P. O. Box 98 (93529) Rates: $50-$80;
Tel: (619) 648-7547; (800) 648-6835

REVERSE CREEK LODGE
4479 Hwy 158 (93529)
Rates: $45-$100;
Tel: (619) 648-7535; (800) 762-6440

Locate Other Dog-Friendly Activities...Check Nearby Cities

RECREATION

GULL LAKE - Leashes

Info: Retreat to 64 acres of lakeside tranquility and savor an hour or two of sheer relaxation. For more information: (619) 647-3000.

Directions: From the Highway 395 junction in June Lake, head southwest about three miles to the lake.

SILVER LAKE - Leashes

Info: Leave the crowds behind while you and your canine buddy hike leash-free trails. Breathtaking views of the unsullied Ansel Adams Wilderness and pretty Gem and Agnew Lakes are part of the scenery. Carry enough water for you and your pooch and some munchies for energy. For more information: (619) 647-3000.

Directions: The lake is in the middle of the June Lake Loop. Exit Highway 395 at the north or south end of the loop (Highway 158) depending on the direction you're traveling. Find the trailhead near the camping area.

KELSEYVILLE

LODGING

CREEKSIDE LODGE
79901 Hwy 29 (95451)
Rates: $34-$50;
Tel: (707) 279-9258; (800) 279-1380

JIM'S SODA BAY RESORT
6380 Soda Bay Rd (95451)
Rates: $49-$59;
Tel: (707) 279-4837

KENWOOD

LODGING

THE LITTLE HOUSE BED & BREAKFAST
255 Adobe Canyon Rd (95452)
Rates: $130;
Tel: (707) 833-2536

KERNVILLE

Lodging

HI-HO RESORT LODGE
11901 Sierra Way (93238)
Rates: $60-$80;
Tel: (619) 376-2671

KERN LODGE MOTEL
67 Valley View (93238)
Rates: $50-$95;
Tel: (619) 376-2223

LAZY RIVER LODGE
15729 Sierra Way (93238)
Rates: $36-$65;
Tel: (619) 376-2242

RIVER VIEW LODGE
2 Sirretta St (93238)
Rates: $65-$85;
Tel: (619) 476-6019

Recreation

BULL RUN TRAIL HIKE - Leashes

Intermediate/7.0 miles/3.5 hours

Info: For a bonafido water adventure that will set your pooch's tail a-wagging, hop aboard this trail that descends Cow Creek to a slice of puppy paradise. From the pine and oak-clad waterway, the trail climbs upstream to Bull Run Basin and continues up a ridge before topping out at FR 24S35. Good luck coaxing Bowser to leave, you may just have to promise a return visit. For more information: (805) 871-2223.

Directions: From Kernville, take Road 495 west 6 miles to Wofford Heights. Turn right on Highway 155 (Evans Road) for 8 miles to Greenhorn Summit. Make a left at the summit onto Forest Highway 90 (Road #24S15 - also called Portugese Pass Road). Follow Forest Highway 90 north about 1.25 miles to an intersection. Take the left fork onto Cow Creek Road and follow to the trailhead at road's end. The trailhead is approximately 15.25 miles from Kernville.

Note: High clearance vehicles only.

CANNELL TRAIL to CANNELL MEADOW HIKE

Intermediate/4.5 miles/2.25 hours

Info: Once rated as a National Scenic Trail, this delightful day hike's final destination offers views of Cannell Meadow in emerald splendor. Climb Cannell Trail (FS 33E32) to a saddle, then travel down to FS 24S56 to the historic Cannell Meadow Guard Station. You and your hiking hound should avoid this unshaded trail in the summer— it's hot! For more information: (619) 376-3781.

Directions: From Kernville, take State Mountain 99 north for 2 miles to the trailhead at the horse corrals.

FLYNN CANYON TRAIL HIKE

Intermediate/Expert/7.8 miles/4.0 hours

Info: Up, up and away. This trail takes you and the pupster on a steady climbing adventure that begins once you cross the bridge. You'll ascend a small hill and continue up the Flynn Creek drainage. The last half mile ascent to Speas Ridge is a steep butt-kicker. If you're hiking this trail in the summer, bring lots of water. Vege out at Speas Ridge and when you're ready, do the descent thing. For more information: (619) 376-3781.

Directions: From Kernville, take State Mountain Highway 99 north for 16 miles to the trailhead at the Fairview Footbridge.

HOBO FISHING TRAIL HIKE - Leashes

Beginner/1.0 miles/0.5 hours

Info: This short, riverside jaunt is definitely a piece of cake. Fishing hounds, don't forget your gear. The trail parallels the Kern River affording plenty of fishing and dipping opportunities. Sandy Flat Campground marks the end of the trail. For more information: (805) 871-2223.

Directions: From Kernville, take Road 495 west 6 miles to Wofford Heights. Continue southwest on Highway 155 to Lake Isabella. Turn right (west) on Highway 178 approximately 4.5 miles to Borel Road and go left. At the stop sign, turn right on Old Kern Canyon Road for about 1.5 miles to the trailhead at Hobo Campground. The trailhead is located approximately 17.5 miles from Kernville.

Dogs May Be Unleashed Unless Otherwise Indicated

KERN RIVER TRAIL HIKE - Leashes

Intermediate/10.6 miles/5.50 hours

Info: Set out early with Curly on this river odyssey. The trail skirts the Kern River through verdant hillsides where lunch alfresco beckons. At China Garden, do a 180° and point your snout towards home. Come springtime, wildflowers splash the landscape in kaleidoscopic colors. For more information: (805) 871-2223.

Directions: From Kernville, take Road 495 west 6 miles to Wofford Heights. Continue southwest on Highway 155 to Lake Isabella. Turn right (west) on Highway 178 approximately 12 miles. The trailhead is located at Highway 178 and Delonegha Road, approximately 23 miles from Kernville.

MILL CREEK TRAIL HIKE - Leashes

Beginner/4.0 miles/2.0 hours

Info: Paw dip with Skip on this wet and wild excursion. You'll wander along and across Mill Creek as the trail gently climbs through riparian woodlands. The beautiful wildflower show makes this a great spring hike, while the creek crossings offer a cool respite in summer. When the trail starts climbing from the creek, that's your signal to turn around. Gung-ho hikers and hounds can opt to extend their trip. The trail continues on another 4.6 miles to Squirrel Meadow, but expect steep going in sections. For more information: (805) 871-2223.

Directions: Take Road 495 west 6 miles to Wofford Heights. Continue southwest on Highway 155 to Lake Isabella. Turn right (west) on Highway 178 approximately 13 miles to Old Kern Canyon Road and make a left. The trailhead is about a half-mile past the Democrat Fire Station, 24.5 miles from Kernville.

PACKSADDLE CAVE TRAIL HIKE

Intermediate/4.6 miles/2.5 hours

Info: You and your pooch will definitely burn some calories on this occasionally steep trail through live oak, sagebrush, manzanita and digger pine. If you're a spelunker at heart, bring a flashlight and check out the cave at trail's end. Avoid in summer, too hot. For more information: (619) 376-3781.

Directions: From Kernville, take State Mountain 99 north for 16 miles to the trailhead.

PATCH CORNER TRAIL HIKE - Leashes

Beginner/4.0 miles/2.0 hours

Info: Stroll along the Kern River with your puppy pal or cast the day away while your buddy chows down on a chew. Visit in the spring during the annual heaven-scent wildflower extravaganza. China Garden marks the end of the hike. For more information: (805) 871-2223.

Directions: Take Road 495 west 6 miles to Wofford Heights. Continue southwest on Highway 155 to Lake Isabella. Turn right (west) on Highway 178 about 12.75 miles. The trailhead is located a quarter-mile before Old Kern Canyon Road on Highway 178, approximately 18.75 miles from Kernville.

PORTUGUESE TRAIL HIKE - Leashes

Beginner/4.2 miles/2.0 hours

Info: Even couch slouches will have a fun time on this easy-does-it trail. Stroll amidst lush meadows as you ascend to ridgetop and then retrace your steps. For more information: (805) 871-2223.

Directions: From Kernville, take Road 495 west 6 miles to Wofford Heights. Turn right on Highway 155 (Evans Road) for 8 miles to Greenhorn Summit. Go right on Forest Highway 90 approximately 4 miles. The trail begins just south of Girl Scout Camp. The trailhead is located approximately 18 miles from Kernville.

Dogs May Be Unleashed Unless Otherwise Indicated

RIVER TRAIL HIKE

Intermediate/10.4 miles/5.5 hours

Info: Gear up for an all dayer with furface. From the bridge, head due north and begin your riverside adventure. Level at first, the trail ascends moderately over bluffs then drops back down to rocky river outcroppings. Groves of incense cedar, live oak and digger pine are responsible for the delicious aromas. Avoid this trail during the height of spring run-off, parts of the trail may be submerged. For more information: (619) 376-3781.

Directions: From Kernville, take State Mountain Highway 99 north for 19 miles to the Johnsondale Bridge. The trailhead is on the east side of the bridge.

SUNDAY PEAK TRAIL HIKE - Leashes

Beginner/3.4 miles/1.5 hours

Info: This hike involves the 3 basics - short, simple and scenic. The trail gently climbs through mixed conifer woodlands to the top of 8,300-foot Sunday Peak. Cram your RAM with expansive views of the Sierras and Kern Valley before heading back. For more information: (805) 871-2223.

Directions: From Kernville, take Road 495 west 6 miles to Wofford Heights. Turn right on Highway 155 (Evans Road) for 8 miles to Greenhorn Summit. Go right on Forest Highway 90 approximately 4 miles. The trail begins just south of the Girl Scout Camp parking lot. The trailhead is located approximately 18 miles from Kernville.

TOBIAS TRAIL HIKE

Intermediate/Expert/9.2 miles/5.0 hours

Info: Aquatic pups will love the beginning of this trail, while only physically fit Fidos should attempt the last leg of the trek. Once on the Tobias Trail, you'll hike downhill to Tobias Creek, a refreshing 2 paws up watering hole. The trail then parallels the creek for 1.5 miles before the workout begins. The last 2.5 miles involve a steep, strenuous climb to Speas Ridge. Go the distance to the ridgetop and feel satisfied with your accomplishment. Fishing fans, remember your gear. Opportunities are plentiful at Tobias Creek. If hiking the trail in the summer, carry lots of H2O. You'll need it. This area can be hot, hot, hot. For more information: (619) 376-3781.

Directions: From Kernville, take State Mountain Highway 99 north for 16 miles to the trailhead at the Fairview footbridge. Hike along the Flynn Trail for .5 miles to where the Tobias Trail forks off.

TRAIL OF A HUNDRED GIANTS HIKE

Beginner/1.0 miles/0.5 hours

Info: Short and easy describes the trail, while towering and awesome describes the sequoias. The trail rambles amidst the Long Meadow Giant Sequoia Grove where sequoias with diameters of up to 10 feet exist. In fact, the largest sequoia measures 20 feet in diameter and rises to a staggering 220 feet. You and the dogster will be humbled by the majesty of this grove. Take some time to read the interpretive signs and learn as you sojourn. For more information: (805) 548-6503.

Directions: Located 45 miles northwest of Kernville on the Hot Springs Ranger District. From Kernville, take State Mountain Highway 99 north to Johnsondale. Head west on State Mountain Highway 50 to the Western Divide Highway turnoff. Follow for 2 miles to the Redwood Meadow Campground. The trailhead is across the road from the campground.

UNAL TRAIL HIKE - Leashes

Beginner/3.0 miles/1.5 hours

Info: This looping trail circles Greenhorn Summit where you and furface will collect pretty views of the surrounding area. For more information: (805) 871-2223.

Directions: From Kernville, take Road 495 west 6 miles to Wofford Heights. Turn right on Highway 155 (Evans Road) for 8 miles to Greenhorn Summit. The trail begins at the ranger station, approximately 14 miles from Kernville.

KETTLEMAN CITY

LODGING

BEST WESTERN OLIVE TREE INN
33415 Powers Dr (93239)
Rates: $56-$62;
Tel: (209) 386-9530; (800) 528-1234

KING CITY

LODGING

BEST WESTERN KING CITY INN
1190 Broadway (93930)
Rates: $42-$55;
Tel: (408) 385-6733; (800) 528-1234

COURTESY INN
4 Broadway Cir (93930)
Rates: $42-$94;
Tel: (408) 385-4646; (800) 350-5616

MOTEL 6
3 Broadway Cir (93930)
Rates: $24-$30;
Tel: (408) 385-5000; (800) 440-6000

PALM MOTEL
640 Broadway (93930)
Rates: $27-$49;
Tel: (408) 385-3248

SAGE MOTEL
633 Broadway (93930)
Rates: $29+;
Tel: (408) 385-3274

RECREATION

CITY PARK - Leashes

Info: Expansive and shade-filled, this 20-acre urban park has the makings for an afternoon delight. The dawgus will find splendor in the grass as he happily prances along.

Directions: Located on the 400 block of Division Street.

SAN LORENZO REGIONAL PARK - Leashes

Info: Smack dab between San Francisco and Los Angeles, this riverside park is an ideal stop for a bit of leg stretching. For additional information: (408) 755-4899.

Directions: Exit Highway 101 at Broadway and follow the signs.

KINGS BEACH

LODGING

FALCON MOTOR LODGE
8258 N Lake Blvd (96143)
Rates: $61-$99;
Tel: (916) 546-2583

STEVENSON'S HOLIDAY INN
8742 N Lake Blvd (96143)
Rates: $45-$95;
Tel: (916) 546-2269; (800) 634-9141

RECREATION

See "Lake Tahoe Area" listings for recreation

KINGSBURG

LODGING

SWEDISH INN
401 Conejo St (93631)
Rates: $42-$52;
Tel: (209) 897-1022; (800) 834-1022

KLAMATH

LODGING

CAMP MARIGOLD MOTEL
16101 Hwy 101 (95548)
Rates: $32-$55;
Tel: (707) 482-3585

KNIGHTS FERRY

LODGING

KNIGHTS FERRY RESORT COTTAGE
17525 Sonora Rd (95361)
Rates: $95;
Tel: (209) 881-3349

Dogs May Be Unleashed Unless Otherwise Indicated

LA HABRA

LODGING
LA HABRA INN
700 N Beach Blvd (90631)
Rates: $42-$50;
Tel: (310) 694-1991

MOTEL 6
870 N Beach Blvd (90631)
Rates: $30-$34;
Tel: (310) 694-2158; (800) 440-6000

LA JOLLA

LODGING
COLONIAL INN
910 Prospect St (92037)
Rates: $120-$220; Tel: (619) 454-2181

THE INN AT LA JOLLA
5440 La Jolla Blvd (92037)
Rates: $53-$83; Tel: (800) 525-6552

LA JOLLA PALMS INN
6705 La Jolla Blvd (92037)
Rates: $69-$149; Tel: (619) 454-7101

LA JOLLA SHORES INN
5390 La Jolla Blvd (92037)
Rates: $50-$100;
Tel: (619) 454-0715; (800) 525-6552

MARRIOTT HOTEL-LA JOLLA
4240 La Jolla Village Dr (92037)
Rates: $115-$135;
Tel: (619) 587-1414; (800) 228-9290

RESIDENCE INN BY MARRIOTT
8901 Gilman Dr (92037)
Rates: $95-$139;
Tel: (619) 587-1770; (800) 331-3131

SANDS OF LA JOLLA
5417 La Jolla Blvd (92037)
Rates: $49-$89;
Tel: (800) 643-0530

SCRIPPS INN
555 Coast Blvd S (92037)
Rates: $90-$165;
Tel: (619) 454-3391

U.S. SUITES OF SAN DIEGO
3262 Holiday Ct #205 (92037)
Rates: $84-$107;
Tel: (800) 877-8483

RECREATION
LA JOLLA SHORES BEACH - Leashes

Info: Get out early in the summer months and you can walk for miles on this pretty beach. Admire the beautiful beachfront homes or watch the surfer dudes catch a wave. You might even glimpse a seal or a playful group of dolphins. If you climb over the breakers just north of the pier, you can walk for miles. Dog hours are restricted to before 9 a.m. or after 6 p.m. Check the tide tables too. For more information: (619) 221-8901.

Directions: Located in La Jolla Shores, west of Camino del Oro.

Locate Other Dog-Friendly Activities...Check Nearby Cities

POINT LA JOLLA CLIFFS and BEACHES - Leashes

Info: The beauty of the cliffs and the surrounding landscape can best be captured in the early morning. Take the stairway down the cliffs to the beach or just watch the crashing waves from the grassy knoll atop the bluffs. Pooches permitted before 9 a.m. or after 6 p.m. For more information: (619) 221-8901.

Directions: Located on Coast Boulevard, near Girard Avenue.

LA MESA

LODGING

COMFORT INN-LA MESA
8000 Parkway Dr (91942)
Rates: $39-$99;
Tel: (619) 698-7747; (800) 221-2222

E-Z 8 MOTEL
7851 Fletcher Pkwy (92041)
Rates: $35-$50;
Tel: (619) 698-9444; (800) 326-6835

LA MESA SPRINGS HOTEL
4210 Spring St (91941)
Rates: $29-$39;
Tel: (619) 589-7288

MOTEL 6
7621 Alvarado Rd (91941)
Rates: $28-$38;
Tel: (619) 464-7151; (800) 440-6000

TRAVELODGE-GROSSMONT
9550 Murray Dr (91942)
Rates: $30-$50;
Tel: (619) 466-0200; (800) 578-7878

LA MIRADA

LODGING

RESIDENCE INN BY MARRIOTT
14419 Firestone Blvd (90638)
Rates: $69-$119;
Tel: (714) 523-2800; (800) 331-3131

LA PALMA

LODGING

LA QUINTA INN
3 Centerpointe Dr (90623)
Rates: $50-$60;
Tel: (714) 670-1400; (800) 531-5900

Dogs May Be Unleashed Unless Otherwise Indicated

LA QUINTA

LODGING

LA QUINTA HOTEL GOLF & TENNIS RESORT
49-499 Eisenhower Dr (92253)
Rates: $110-$2,200;
Tel: (619) 564-4111; (800) 854-1271

LAGUNA BEACH

LODGING

CARRIAGE HOUSE BED & BREAKFAST
1322 Catalina St (92651)
Rates: $95-$150;
Tel: (714) 494-8945

CASA LAGUNA INN BED & BREAKFAST
2510 S Coast Hwy (92651)
Rates: $69-$225;
Tel: (714) 494-2996;
(800) 233-0449 (CA)

COMFORT INN
23061 Ave de la Carlota (92653)
Rates: $49-$69;
Tel: (714) 850-0166; (800) 221-2222

QUALITY INN
1404 N Coast Hwy (92651)
Rates: $49-$119;
Tel: (714) 494-6464; (800) 221-2222

TRADE WINDS MOTOR LODGE
2020 S Coast Hwy (92651)
Rates: $35-$120; Tel: (714) 494-5450

VACATION VILLAGE
647 S Coast Hwy (92651)
Rates: $80-$285;
Tel: (714) 494-8566; (800) 843-6895

RECREATION

ALTA LAGUNA PARK - Leashes

Info: This lovely hilltop park provides views and walking trails for you and Old Brown Eyes.

Directions: At the north end of Alta Laguna Boulevard.

DOG PARK

Info: Yippee Skippy! Social breeds will be wagging about this park. Canines run leash-free from dawn to dusk every day except Wednesday, so make your pup's day by taking him on a bark park lark. For more information: (714) 497-0706.

Directions: On Laguna Canyon Drive next to the GTE Building.

HEISLER PARK - Leashes

Info: This pretty blufftop park is filled with palm trees and ocean views.

Directions: On Cliff Drive between Aster Street and Diver's Cove.

LAGUNA BEACH BEACHES - Leashes

Info: Sandy adventures are yours at the craggy coastal inlet beaches of Laguna Beach. Summer months are restrictive. No dogs June to mid-September between 8 a.m. and 6 p.m.

Directions: Via footpaths off Cliff Drive.

LANG PARK - Leashes

Info: Take advantage of the grassy sports field in this community park.

Directions: On Wesley Drive off Pacific Coast Highway.

MAIN BEACH PARK - Leashes

Info: Furry friends can join you for a stroll along the beach any time during the off-season. In summer, dogs are only permitted before 8 a.m. and after 6 p.m.

Directions: At the end of Broadway on Pacific Coast Highway.

MOULTON MEADOWS PARK - Leashes

Info: Plan a kibble cook-out and then vege out on the grassy hilltop in this paw-friendly park.

Directions: Located at Del Mar and Balboa Avenues.

Other parks in Laguna Beach - Leashes
- BLUEBIRD PARK, Cress Street between Temple Terrace and Bluebird Canyon Drive
- CRESCENT BAY, Off Pacific Coast Hwy on Crescent Bay Drive
- FERNANDO STREET PARK, From Pacific Coast Highway, take Nyes Place to Balboa Avenue. From Balboa, turn left on Del Mar Avenue, then right on La Mirada. Park is on

Dogs May Be Unleashed Unless Otherwise Indicated

Fernando Street off La Mirada
- •NITA CARMEN PARK, At the corner of Legion and Wilson Streets
- •OAK STREET PARK, Off Pacific Coast Highway on Oak Street
- •PACIFIC AVENUE PARK, At the end of Pacific Way
- •RUBY STREET PARK, Off Pacific Coast Hwy on Ruby Street
- •TEMPLE HILLS PARK, On Temple Hills Drive about halfway between Cress Street and Alta Laguna Boulevard
- •THALIA STREET PARK, Off Pacific Coast Highway on Thalia Street
- •TOP OF THE WORLD PARK, Off Alta Laguna Boulevard on Tree Top Lane

LAGUNA HILLS

LODGING

HOLIDAY INN LAGUNA HILLS
25205 La Paz Rd (92653)
Rates: 69-$99;
Tel: (714) 586-5000; (800) 465-4329

LAGUNA HILLS LODGE
23932 Paseo De Valencia (92653)
Rates: $50-$70;
Tel: (714) 830-2550; (800) 782-1188
(800) 468-4470 (CA)

LAGUNA NIGUEL

RECREATION

LAGUNA NIGUEL REGIONAL PARK - Leashes

Info: From remote control airplane flying to fine fishing, this expansive suburban park offers a day's worth of fun for you and Frisky. Hop on one of the hiking trails, get your daily dose on the exercise course, or learn a little something about the region from the interpretive programs. Sofa loafers can kick back and enjoy the beauty of the pretty landscaped grounds. For more information: (714) 831-2791.

Directions: Located at 28241 La Paz Road, 1500 feet south of Aliso Creek Road on La Paz Road.

Locate Other Dog-Friendly Activities...Check Nearby Cities

LAKE ALMANOR

LODGING

ALMANOR LAKESIDE LODGE
3747 Eastshore Dr (96137)
Rates: $70;
Tel: (916) 284-7376; (800) 238-3924

LAKE ALMANOR RESORT
2706 Big Springs Rd (96137)
Rates: $47-$90;
Tel: (916) 596-3337

LASSEN VIEW RESORT
7457 Eastshore Dr (96137) Rates:
$42-$92;
Tel: (916) 596-3437

LITTLE NORWAY RESORT
432 Peninsula Dr (96137)
Rates: $50-$100;
Tel: (916) 596-3225

LAKE ARROWHEAD

LODGING

ARROWHEAD TREE TOP LODGE
P. O. Box 186 (92352)
Rates: $59-$125;
Tel: (909) 337-2311; (800) 358-8733

LAKE ARROWHEAD RESORT
27984 Hwy 189 (92352)
Rates: $99-$329;
Tel: (909) 336-1511; (800) 800-6792

**PROPHETS' PARADISE
BED & BREAKFAST**
26845 Modoc Ln (92352)
Rates: $90-$160;
Tel: (909) 336-1969; (800) 987-2231

STORYBOOK INN BED & BREAKFAST
28717 Hwy 19 (92385)
Rates: $60-$145;
Tel: (909) 336-1483

RECREATION

FISHERMAN'S CAMP TRAIL HIKE - Leashes

Intermediate/5.0 miles/2.5 hours

Info: Creek crossing is the name of the game on this hike, so pack your water sandals. The trail traverses both Crab Creek and Deep Creek affording plenty of splish splashing opportunities. After Deep Creek, the trail ends at Fisherman's Camp. Able anglers, bring your gear and catch sup for you and the pup. If hiking during times of high water, call it quits at Deep Creek. Crossing the creek can be a dangerous undertaking. For more information: (909) 337-2444.

Directions: Head east on Highway 18 to Lake Road. Turn left, following to FS 3N16. Make a left on FS 3N16 to FS 3N34. The trailhead is on FS 3N34, approximately 1.3 miles west of Crab Flats Campground.

Dogs May Be Unleashed Unless Otherwise Indicated

HEAPS PEAK ARBORETUM TRAIL HIKE - Leashes

Beginner/1.4 miles/0.75 hours

Info: For a quickie education on the area's native flora and fauna, pick up a trail guide and take a stroll with the dawgus on this easy trail. Feel free to take home the brochure, but please leave a donation. For more information: (909) 337-2444.

Directions: From Lake Arrowhead, head west on Highway 18 to the trailhead. If you reach Skyforest, you've gone 1.4 miles too far west.

LITTLE GREEN VALLEY TRAIL HIKE - Leashes

Expert/3.0 miles/1.5 hours

Info: Only hardy hikers and conditioned canines should set out on this strenuous hike. From the get-go, the trail begins its steep ascent to a verdant meadow at FS 2N19. As you climb, take a water break every now and then and admire the views of Snow Valley and Slide Peak. For more information: (909) 337-2444.

Directions: From Lake Arrowhead, go east on Highway 18 to the trailhead between the two entrances to Snow Valley Ski Area.

SEELEY CREEK TRAIL HIKE - Leashes

Beginner/2.0 miles/1.0 hours

Info: Couch pooch alert. This hike is short, flat and easy, it even includes a bit of paw dousing in Seeley Creek. Cross the creek and then amble creekside to Heart Rock, a scenic overlook. Once you've had your visual fill, follow the paw prints back to the trailhead. For more information: (909) 337-2444.

Directions: From Lake Arrowhead, head west on Highway 18 to Highway 138. Take Highway 138 north to FS 2N03, a quarter-mile south of Camp Seeley. The trailhead is on FS 2N03.

Locate Other Dog-Friendly Activities...Check Nearby Cities

LAKE ELSINORE

LODGING

LAKEVIEW INN
31808 Casino Dr (92530)
Rates: $38-$48;
Tel: (909) 674-6749

LAKE FOREST

RECREATION

HERITAGE HILL HISTORICAL PARK - Leashes

Info: Old cold nose can't enter the buildings, but you can stroll together and admire the architecture of the four historical buildings that represent distinct eras in the early development of Saddleback Valley and El Toro. Pack a biscuit basket for an alfresco lunch apres' tour. For more information: (714) 855-2028.

Directions: At the corner of Lake Forest Drive and Serrano Road.

LAKE TAHOE AREA

LODGING

ALDER INN & COTTAGES
1072 Ski Run Blvd
(S Lake Tahoe 96150)
Rates: $38-$95; Tel: (916) 544-4485

BEESLEY'S COTTAGES
6674 N Lake Blvd
(Tahoe Vista 96148)
Rates: $70-$140; Tel: (916) 546-2448

BLUE JAY LODGE
4133 Cedar Ave
(S Lake Tahoe 96150)
Rates: $39-$99; Tel: (800) 258-3529

CAPTAIN'S ALPENHAUS
6941 W Lake Blvd
(Tahoma 96142)
Rates: $100-$150; Tel: (916) 525-5000

**DAYS INN-
STATELINE/SOUTH LAKE TAHOE**
968 Park Ave
(S Lake Tahoe 96157)
Rates: $60-$92; Tel: (800) 325-2525

EMBASSY SUITES RESORT
4130 Lake Tahoe Blvd
(S Lake Tahoe 96150)
Rates: $139-$500; Tel: (800) 362-2779

HIGH COUNTRY LODGE
1227 Emerald Bay Rd
(S Lake Tahoe 96150)
Rates: $30-$70; Tel: (916) 541-0508

HOLIDAY HOUSE-LAKESIDE CHALETS
7276 N Lake Blvd
(Tahoe Vista 96148)
Rates: $75-$115; Tel: (916) 546-2369

LA BAER INN
4133 Lake Tahoe Blvd
(S Lake Tahoe 96150)
Rates: $40-$53; Tel: (916) 544-2139

LAKEPARK LODGE
4081 Cedar Ave
(S Lake Tahoe 96150)
Rates: $40-$65; Tel: (916) 541-5004

LAKESIDE CHALETS
5240 N Lake Blvd
(Carnelian Bay 96140)
Rates: $85-$115;
Tel: (916) 546-2369;
(800) 294-6378 (CA/NV)

MATTERHORN MOTEL
2187 Lake Tahoe Blvd
(S Lake Tahoe 96157)
Rates: $38-$58; Tel: (916) 541-0367

THE MONTGOMERY INN
966 Modesto Ave
(S Lake Tahoe 96151)
Rates: $28-$40; Tel: (916) 544-3871

MOTEL 6
2375 Lake Tahoe Blvd
(S Lake Tahoe 96150)
Rates: $30-$44; Tel: (916) 542-1400;
(800) 440-6000

RAVEN WOOD HOTEL
4075 Manzanita Ave
(S Lake Tahoe 96150)
Rates: $79-$99; Tel: (800) 659-4185

SCOTTISH INNS
930 Park Ave
(S Lake Tahoe 96150)
Rates: $33-$58; Tel: (800) 251-1962

TAHOE MARINA INN
930 Bal Bijou Rd
(S Lake Tahoe 96150)
Rates: $56-$140; Tel: (916) 541-2180

SUPER 8 MOTEL
3600 Highway 50
(S Lake Tahoe 96151)
Rates: $53-$78; Tel: (800) 800-8000

TAHOE VALLEY MOTEL
2241 Lake Tahoe Blvd
(S Lake Tahoe 96150)
Rates: $85-$150; Tel: (916) 541-0353

TATAMI COTTAGE RESORT
7449 N Lake Blvd
(Tahoe Vista 96148)
Rates: $69-$129; Tel: (916) 546-3523

TORCHLITE INN
965 Park Ave
(S Lake Tahoe 96150)
Rates: $38-$78; Tel: (916) 541-2363

TRADE WINDS MOTEL
944 Friday Ave
(S Lake Tahoe 96150)
Rates: $34-$57; Tel: (916) 544-6459

WOODVISTA LODGE
7699 N Lake Blvd
(Tahoe Vista 96148)
Rates: $35-$75; Tel: (916) 546-3839

RECREATION

ANGORA LAKES TRAIL HIKE

Beginner/1.0 miles/0.5 hours

Info: Short and sweet, the trail leads to picturesque, cliff-framed Angora Lakes - perfect for those lazy, hazy days of summer. Be prepared for crowds, everybody likes it here. For more information: (916) 573-2600.

Locate Other Dog-Friendly Activities...Check Nearby Cities

Directions: From South Lake Tahoe, take Highway 89 north 3 miles to Fallen Leaf Lake Road, turn left. Make another left at the first paved road, following to Forest Service Road 12N14. Go right, past Angora Lookout, to the parking lot at the end of the road.

BAYVIEW TRAIL to GRANITE LAKE HIKE

Expert/2.0 miles/1.0 hours

Info: This scenic, albeit steep trail snakes up Maggie's Peak into Desolation Wilderness to Granite Lake. For a longer hike, continue a few miles further to the Eagle Falls Trail for outstanding vistas of Emerald Bay and Lake Tahoe. For more information: (916) 573-2600.

Directions: Go north on Highway 89 for 8 miles to the Bayview Campground The parking lot is at the far end of the campground.
Note: A wilderness permit is required.

BRYAN MEADOWS TRAIL HIKE- Leashes

Intermediate/6.0 miles/3.0 hours

Info: Spend a pleasant afternoon with your pooch on this scenic trail. Glimpses of pretty Bryan Meadows are yours for the taking as you hike through groves of lodgepole pine and mountain hemlock. The trail ends after meeting up with the Pacific Crest Trail. For more information: (916) 644-6048.

Directions: From South Lake Tahoe, take Highway 89 south to Highway 50 west. Exit Highway 50 at Sierra Ski Ranch Road for 2 miles to Bryan Road. Turn right, following for 2.5 miles to the trailhead and parking area. Hike up the Sayles Canyon Trail for one mile to the Bryan Meadows Trail.

CASCADE CREEK FALL TRAIL HIKE

Beginner/2.0 miles/1.0 hours

Info: In springtime, this easy hike offers magnificent views of a plunging 200-foot waterfall and sparkling Cascade Lake. For more information: (916) 573-2600.

Directions: From South Lake Tahoe, go north on Highway 89 approximately 8 miles to the Bayview Campground The parking lot is at the far end of the campground.

EAGLE FALLS to EAGLE LAKE TRAIL HIKE

Intermediate/2.0 miles/1.0 hours

Info: The trail to Eagle Lake is popular and quite beautiful. Expert hikers and hounds can continue several miles further to Eagle Falls for incredible views of the Sierra High Country. For more information: (916) 573-2600.

Directions: From South Lake Tahoe, head north on Highway 89 for approximately 8 miles to the trailhead at Eagle Falls Picnic Area, which is on the left.

Note: A wilderness permit required.

ECHO LAKES TRAIL HIKE

Intermediate/5.0 to 12.0 miles/2.5 to 6.0 hours

Info: Many alpine lakes can be reached via this very popular summertime trail. Hike an hour or a day - the choice is yours and Fido's. For more information: (916) 573-2600.

Directions: From South Lake Tahoe, take Highway 50 southwest to Echo Summit, turning off at Johnson Pass Road. Stay left at the fork to the Lower Echo Lake parking area.

Note: A wilderness permit is required.

ELLIS PEAK TRAIL HIKE

Intermediate/5.0 miles/2.5 hours

Info: You and Fido will burn a few calories on this aerobic hike which begins with a steep switchbacking ascent to the ridgetop. The next mile and a half follows the ridge guiding you among forests and verdant meadows with memorable vistas of Lake Tahoe everywhere you look. When the trail junctions with a dirt road you have two choices. Go left for .2 miles to Ellis Lake and cool off those hot paws or head right for the final stretch to 8,640-foot Ellis Peak. The peak affords

Kodak-worthy vistas of Lake Tahoe and the surrounding area. For more information: (916) 587-3558.

Directions: From Tahoe City, take Highway 89 south for 4.2 miles to Caspian Picnic Area. Head west on Blackwood Canyon Road approximately 7 miles to Barker Pass. Ellis Peak Trailhead is located on the south side of the road where the pavement ends on the summit.

FOURTH OF JULY LAKE TRAIL HIKE- Leashes

Expert/9.0 miles/5.0 hours

Info: The motto of this hike could be "no pain, no gain" because gain you will as you partake of three pretty lakes. Chill out for a bit at each and enjoy the surrounding beauty or hike straight through to trail's end at Fourth of July Lake. Once past Round Top Lake, it's a steep 1.5 mile descent to the end. This trail is glorious in the spring when wildflowers bloom at every turn. For more information: (209) 295-4251.

Directions: From South Lake Tahoe, take Highway 50 south to where Highway 89 forks. Take Highway 89 south for 11 miles to the intersection of Highway 89 and Highway 88. Head south on Highway 88 to Carson Pass Visitor Center. The trail-head begins in the south parking lot of the visitors center.

GLEN ALPINE TRAIL to GRASS LAKE HIKE

Intermediate/4.0 miles/2.0 hours

Info: Get your Rexercise on this invigorating hike to postcard-pretty Grass Lake. For more information: (916) 573-2600.

Directions: From South Lake Tahoe, take Highway 89 north 3 miles to Fallen Leaf Lake Road. Follow to the trailhead sign and turn left. The parking area is across from Lily Lake.

Note: A wilderness permit is required.

GRANITE CHIEF TRAIL HIKE

Expert/7.0 miles/4.0 hours

Info: You should have lots of hiking points under your collar before attempting this strenuous trek. Your excursion begins with a canyon ascent, continues creekside for a short distance before veering into a thick forest of Jeffrey pine and white fir. Fill your snout with the crisp, clean, aromatic air and take a moment to admire the views of Squaw Valley. Keep climbing and the shimmering surface of majestic Lake Tahoe will slowly creep into view. When you junction with the Pacific Crest Trail, retrace your tracks and head home. For more information: (916) 587-3558.

Directions: From Tahoe City, take Highway 89 north for five miles to Squaw Valley Road and turn left (west). Drive 2.2 miles to the fire station and park in the large parking area in front of the ski lift buildings. The trailhead is located on the right-side of the fire station and is clearly marked.

KIVA BEACH - Leashes

Info: History buffs will enjoy the shaded Tallac Historic Trail which begins near the east end of the beach. Or stroll to a large stretch of shoreline along the crystal waters of Lake Tahoe via the dirt path. For more information: (916) 542-6055.

Directions: From the junction of Highway 50 and Highway 89 in South Lake Tahoe, take Highway 89 north about 2.5 miles. The entrance is on your right.

MORAINE TRAIL HIKE

Beginner/2.0 miles/1.0 hours

Info: This cinchy, flat 2-mile trail meanders through a forest and alongside pretty Fallen Leaf Lake. Even couch potato pooches will enjoy this trail. For more information: (916) 573-2600.

Directions: From South Lake Tahoe, take Highway 89 north 3 miles to Fallen Leaf Lake Road. Follow for .7 miles to Fallen Leaf Campground. Trail parking is located just before camp-site #75 on the right. The trailhead is marked.

NORTH TAHOE REGIONAL PARK - Leashes

Info: Four miles of trails are part of this 108-acre park. Hike long enough and you'll find yourself in the Tahoe National Forest where your pup can throw his leash to the wind. For more information: (916) 546-7248.

Directions: The park is located at the corner of Donner Road and National Avenue in Tahoe Vista. From Highway 28, head north on National Avenue. Follow the road to the top, then turn left on Donner Road.

PAGE MEADOW - Leashes

Info: In springtime, this spacious meadow is transformed into a kaleidoscope of wildflowers. Bring a camera and take home some vivid memories. For more information: (916) 573-2600.

Directions: From Tahoe City, take Highway 89 south two miles to Pineland Drive and head west. Go right on Forest Service Road 15N60 or 16N48 to the meadow area.

PREY MEADOWS / SKUNK HARBOR TRAIL HIKE

Beginner/3.0 miles/1.5 hours

Info: This easy path through a mixed conifer forest offers you and the dawgus two pleasurable options. The left fork takes you to wildflower-strewn Prey Meadows. The right fork leads to the swimming cove of Skunk Harbor- perfect for a hot summer day. For more information: (916) 573-2600.

Directions: From South Lake Tahoe, go north on Highway 50. From the intersection of Highway 28 and Highway 50, continue north on Highway 28 approximately 2 miles. Look for the iron pipe gate on the west side. Park in any of the highway's turnouts.

ROUND TOP LAKE TRAIL HIKE- Leashes

Expert/6.0 miles/3.0 hours

Info: Definitely not for the fair of paw, this strenuous voyage is sure to get the juices flowing. Winnemucca Lake is just the spot for a picnic before the last mile to Round Top Lake. Plan

Dogs May Be Unleashed Unless Otherwise Indicated

a visit in spring when wildflowers speckle the landscape. For more information: (209) 295-4251.

Directions: From South Lake Tahoe, take Highway 50 south to where Highway 89 forks. Take Highway 89 south for 11 miles to the intersection of Highway 89 and Highway 88. Head south on Highway 88 to Carson Pass Visitor Center. The trailhead begins in the south parking lot of the visitors center.

SAYLES CANYON TRAIL HIKE - Leashes

Intermediate/9.0 miles/4.5 hours

Info: Meet your exercise quota for the day on this attractive trail through Sayles Canyon. You might want to tote water sandals. The trail crisscrosses Sayles Creek before reaching Round Meadow, a gorgeous mountain lea. Your ascent will take you ridgetop to a junction with the Pacific Crest Trail. When you're ready to head down, turn left and travel to Bryan Meadow. You'll be routed through an enchanting lodgepole pine and hemlock forest. For more information: (916) 644-6048.

Directions: From South Lake Tahoe, take Highway 89 south to Highway 50 west. Exit Highway 50 at Sierra Ski Ranch Road for 2 miles to Bryan Road. Turn right, following for 2.5 miles to the trailhead and parking area.

STATELINE LOOKOUT TRAIL HIKE

Beginner/1.0 miles/0.5 hours

Info: Incredible telescopic views of the lake are provided at the lookout, while a self-guided nature trail gives insight into the history of the north shore of Lake Tahoe. For more information: (916) 573-2600.

Directions: From Highway 28 on the north shore of Lake Tahoe, head north on Reservoir Drive, just east of the old Tahoe Biltmore Casino. Make a right on Lakeshore Avenue, then left on Forest Service Road 1601 - marked by an iron pipe gate. The parking lot is just below the lookout.

TALLAC HISTORIC SITE TRAIL HIKE

Beginner/1.5 miles/1.0 hours

Info: The lives and personalities of turn-of-the-century Tahoe landowners are explored on this historic, educational hike. Pick up a trail brochure before heading out. For more information: (916) 573-2600.

Directions: Take Highway 89 north to the Kiva Beach Picnic Area. There is one parking lot at Kiva and another at the Forest Service Center.

WINNEMUCCA LAKE TRAIL HIKE- Leashes

Expert/4.0 miles/2.25 hours

Info: The beginning of this hike is decidedly steep. The payoff - Winnemucca Lake. Cool off and unwind lakeside before tackling the return portion. Come springtime, wildflowers offer spectacular splashes of color. For more information: (209) 295-4251.

Directions: From South Lake Tahoe, take Highway 50 south to where Highway 89 forks. Take Highway 89 south for 11 miles to the intersection of Highway 89 and Highway 88. Head south on Highway 88 to Carson Pass Visitor Center. The trailhead begins in the south parking lot of the visitors center.

LAKEHEAD

LODGING

ANTLERS RESORT & MARINA
P. O. Box 140 (96051)
Rates: $90-$170;
Tel: (800) 238-3924

**O'BANION'S SUGARLOAF
COTTAGES RESORT**
19667 Lakeshore Dr (96051)
Rates: $59-$122;
Tel: (916) 238-2448

TSASDI RESORT
19990 Lakeshore Dr (96051)
Rates: $47-$175;
Tel: (916) 238-2575; (800) 995-0291

Dogs May Be Unleashed Unless Otherwise Indicated

RECREATION

SHASTA LAKE - Leashes

Info: It's hard to know where to begin at Shasta Lake, California's largest artificial lake. Hike the forest trails? Scramble up craggy mountains? Wade through hidden streams? Houseboat? With more than 29,000 acres, your choices are limitless. Stop at the visitor's center and pick up a map. You won't want to miss a thing in this beautiful area. For more information: (916) 225-4100 or (800) 874-7562.

Directions: Take Interstate 5 south to the Mountain Gate Wonderland Boulevard exit. Follow the signs to the visitors center.

LAKEPORT

LODGING

CHALET MOTEL
2802 Lakeshore Blvd (95453)
Rates: $35-$45;
Tel: (707) 263-5040

COVE RESORT
2812 Lakeshore Blvd (95453)
Rates: $50-$85;
Tel: (707) 263-6833

RAINBOW LODGE MOTEL
2569 Lakeshore Blvd (95453) Rates:
$30-$36;
Tel: (707) 263-4309

LAKESHORE

LODGING

LAKEVIEW COTTAGES
58374 Huntington Lodge Rd (93634)
Rates: $45-$80;
Tel: (310) 697-6556 or (209) 893-2330

LAKEWOOD

LODGING
CRAZY 8 MOTEL
11535 E Carson St (90715)
Rates: $34-$42;
Tel: (310) 860-0546

LANCASTER

LODGING
BEST WESTERN ANTELOPE VALLEY INN
44055 N Sierra Highway (93534)
Rates: $57-$69;
Tel: (805) 948-4651; (800) 528-1234

MOTEL 6
43540 17th St W (93534)
Rates: $27-$31;
Tel: (805) 948-0435; (800) 440-6000

LASSEN VOLCANIC NATIONAL PARK

LODGING
DRAKESBAD GUEST RANCH RESORT COMPLEX
CR Chester-Warner Valley (96020)
Rates: $110-$190;
Tel: (916) 529-1512

LAYTONVILLE

LODGING
GENTLE VALLEY RANCH COTTAGES
P. O. Box 1535 (95454)
Rates: $65-$150;
Tel: (707) 984-8456

THE RANCH MOTEL
P. O. Box 1535 (95454)
Rates: $26-$45;
Tel: (707) 984-8456

Dogs May Be Unleashed Unless Otherwise Indicated

RECREATION

WRIGHTS VALLEY TRAIL HIKE

Intermediate/8.0 miles/4.0 hours

Info: Tote a swimsuit in summer - this trail takes you to one of the prettiest streams in the region. Be prepared for a couple of stream crossings and some terrific trout fishing. For more information: (207) 983-6118.

Directions: From Laytonville, take the secondary road east towards Covelo. Turn left onto 162. 13 miles past Covelo is the Eel River Bridge. At the bridge, turn left (north) onto Forest Road M1. Drive about 24 miles to FR 36N15C, turn left and continue to the Rock Canyon Trailhead.

L E B E C

LODGING

FLYING J INN
42810 Frazier Mtn Park Rd (93243)
Rates: $50-$65;
Tel: (805) 248-2700; (800) 766-9009

LEE VINING

LODGING

MURPHEY'S MOTEL
P. O. Box 57 (93541)
Rates: $38-$73;
Tel: (619) 647-6316; (800) 334-6316

RECREATION

BENNETTVILLE TRAIL HIKE - Leashes

Intermediate/2.0 miles/1.0 hours

Info: Let Rover be the first dog on the block to explore a deserted gold-mining town. You'll enjoy checking out this gold rush town too. For more information: (619) 647-3000.

Directions: From Lee Vining, take Highway 120 (Tioga Road) west past Ellery Lake to Saddlebag Lake Road. Turn right to the trailhead at the Tioga Junction Campground, located just before camp site #1.

Note: Highway 120 may be closed from November through May. A quota system is in effect from June through mid-September.

GARDISKY LAKE TRAIL HIKE

Expert/2.0 miles/1.5 hours

Info: This short, but challenging climb is definitely four-paw terrain. The steep ascent ends at Gardinsky Lake, located at the base of Tioga Peak. For more information: (619) 647-3000.

Directions: From Lee Vining, take Highway 120 (Tioga Road) west past Ellery Lake to Saddlebag Lake Road. Go right for 1.2 miles to the trailhead on the right-side of the road.

Note: Highway 120 may be closed November through May. A quota system is in effect from June through mid-September.

GIBBS LAKE TRAIL HIKE

Expert/7.8 miles/4.25 hours

Info: If you and your pooch are in tip-top shape, have a go at this steady climb to Gibbs Lake at 9,530 feet. Beginning at 8,000 foot Upper Horse Meadow, you'll experience half a mile of switchbacks, then a steady 1,500-foot rise in elevation alongside Gibbs Creek. You might have this pretty granite and conifer region all to yourself. For more information: (619) 647-3000.

Directions: Take Highway 395 south from Lee Vining for one mile to Forest Road 1N16 west (a sign indicates Upper Horse Meadow). Follow for three miles to the trailhead at road's end.

Note: High clearance vehicles only. A quota system is in effect from June through mid-September.

Dogs May Be Unleashed Unless Otherwise Indicated

LAKES CANYON TRAIL HIKE

Intermediate/6.5 miles/3.0 hours

Info: Get Fido fit as a fiddle on this hike. You'll start your workout on Lakes Canyon Trail, east of Lundy Lake Dam. The trail heads through the Hoover Canyon Wilderness as it ascends to Crystal Lake. If you're still feeling energetic, stunning views at Tioga Crest await those with staying power. For more information: (619) 647-3000.

Directions: From Lee Vining, take Highway 395 north past Mono Lake to Lundy Canyon Road. Turn left (west), following to Lundy Lake. The trailhead and parking area are located at the east end of the lake.

Note: A quota system is in effect from June through mid-September.

LUNDY CANYON TRAIL HIKE - Leashes

Intermediate/Expert/6.0 - 10.8 miles/3.5 - 6.0 hours.

Info: From towering granite walls to sparkling jewel-like lakes, this high country wilderness hike is filled with staggering beauty, but your leg muscles pay the price. Once the first 3 miles through Lundy Canyon are behind you, it's time for a steep, switchbacking adventure to the 20 Lakes Basin. The last 2.4 miles of this hike are definitely not recommended for the fair of paw. For more information: (619) 647-3000.

Directions: Take Highway 395 north to the junction of Highway 167 at Mono Lake. Head west on Lundy Lake Road approximately 5 miles to Lundy Lake. The trailhead and parking are 2 miles west of the lake.

Note: A quota system is in effect from June through mid-September.

MONO LAKE - Leashes

Info: Volcanic formations, tufa spires and a 700,000-year-old lake - all natural wonders from prehistoric time await you on this eerily beautiful trail. Experience them first-hand by trekking through the region with Rex. Be sure to pick up brochures from the visitor's center - they'll make your journey much more exciting and edifying. For more information: (619) 647-3044.

Directions: Take Highway 395 to the Mono Lake Visitor's Center and follow the signs to the lake area of choice.

Note: The state reserve fee is $2 per person or $5 per vehicle per day. The national forest is free.

MOUNT DANA TRAIL HIKE

Expert/6.0 miles/3.25 hours

Info: Go the distance on this challenging mountainside journey and you and Champ will enjoy a sense of accomplishment at the summit. Break some bread and biscuits before heading back. For more information: (619) 647-3000.

Directions: From Lee Vining, take Highway 120 (Tioga Road) west. The trailhead is located on the south side of Highway 120 at the Tioga Pass entrance station to Yosemite National Park.

Note: Highway 120 may be closed November through May. A quota system is in effect from June through mid-September.

PARKER LAKE TRAIL HIKE

Beginner/3.6 miles/2.0 hours

Info: All gain, no pain! An easy trail with a mere 300-foot elevation gain from the get-go. This undiscovered High Sierra gem sits amid granite walls. If you and your pooch like your swimming holes cold, this place is A-one. For more information: (619) 647-3000.

Directions: From Lee Vining, head south on Highway 395 for nearly four miles to Highway 158 (June Lake Loop). Go south another 1.5 miles, then take a right on Parker Lake Road and travel two miles. Make a left on Forest Service Road 1S26 for one mile until it dead ends at the Parker Creek Trailhead.

Note: A quota system is in effect from June through mid-September.

SADDLEBAG LAKE TRAIL HIKE

Beginner/6.0 miles/3.0 hours

Info: Lake hop the day away on this "no sweat" looping trail. Take the path on either side of Saddlebag Lake and treat your water-loving pooch to an afternoon he won't soon forget. For more information: (619) 647-3000.

Directions: From Lee Vining, take Highway 120 (Tioga Road) west past Ellery Lake to Saddlebag Lake Road. Go right to the trailhead parking area across from the Saddlebag Dam.

Note: Highway 120 may be closed November through May. A quota system is in effect from June through mid-September.

TIOGA TARNS NATURE TRAIL HIKE

Beginner/0.5 miles/0.25 hours

Info: Take a pleasant stroll with furface along this looping nature trail. For a quickie education, stop and read the interpretive signs explaining the area's geology and natural history. For more information: (619) 647-3000.

Directions: From Lee Vining, take Highway 120 (Tioga Road) west. The trailhead is on Highway 120 just east of Tioga Lake.

Note: Highway 120 may be closed November through May. A quota system is in effect from June through mid-September.

WALKER LAKE to WALKER CREEK TRAIL HIKE

Expert/4.0 miles/2.5 hours

Info: The special Ansel Adams Wilderness provides a dramatic backdrop for this hike. Walker Lake is the trail's half-way point, a perfect catch-your-breath spot. Chill out lakeside or continue another mile to Bloody Canyon. For more information: (619) 647-3000

Directions: From Lee Vining, take Highway 395 south 4 miles to Walker Lake Road. Turn west (right) and drive to the trailhead on the east side of the lake.

Note: A quota system is in effect from June through mid-September. Dogs not allowed past park boundary.

Locate Other Dog-Friendly Activities...Check Nearby Cities

LEGGETT

LODGING

REDWOODS RIVER RETREAT
75000 Hwy 101 (95585)
Rates: $20-$55;
Tel: (707) 925-6249

LEMON GROVE

LODGING

E-Z 8 MOTEL
7458 Broadway (92045)
Rates: $35-$50;
Tel: (619) 462-7022; (800) 326-6835

LEMOORE

LODGING

BEST WESTERN VINEYARD INN
877 East D St (93245)
Rates: $44-$46;
Tel: (209) 924-1950; (800) 528-1234

LEWISTON

LODGING

LAKEVIEW TERRACE RESORT
Star Rt, Box 250 (96052)
Rates: $36-$82;
Tel: (916) 778-3803

LEWISTON VALLEY MOTEL
Trinity Dam Blvd (96052)
Rates: $35-$43;
Tel: (916) 778-3942

LINDSAY

LODGING

OLIVE TREE INN
390 N Highway 65 (93247)
Rates: $45-$56;
Tel: (209) 562-5188; (800) 366-4469

Dogs May Be Unleashed Unless Otherwise Indicated

LITTLERIVER

LODGING

S S SEAFOAM LODGE
6751 N Highway 1 (95456)
Rates: $85-$175;
Tel: (707) 937-1827

VICTORIAN FARMHOUSE INN
7001 N Hwy 1 (95456)
Rates: $85-$130;
Tel: (707) 937-0697; (800) 264-4723

LIVERMORE

LODGING

HOLIDAY INN
720 Las Flores Rd (94550)
Rates: $53-$65;
Tel: (510) 443-4950; (800) 465-4329

RESIDENCE INN BY MARRIOTT
1000 Airway Blvd (94550)
Rates: $69-$130;
Tel: (510) 373-1800; (800) 331-3131

MOTEL 6
4673 Lassen Rd (94550)
Rates: $30-$36;
Tel: (510) 443-5300; (800) 440-6000

SPRINGTOWN MOTEL
933 Bluebell Dr (94550)
Rates: $37+;
Tel: (510) 449-2211

RECREATION

ALMOND PARK - Leashes

Info: Get your daily dose of exercise as you lead your Lassie along the walking path in this 6-acre neighborhood park.

Directions: Located on Almond Avenue just south of East Avenue between Jefferson and Charlotte.

DEL VALLE REGIONAL PARK

Info: Rent a boat and set sail for a day of fun on the 5-mile long lake. Or enjoy one of the leash-free hiking trails at this pristine park. For more information: (510) 635-0135.

Directions: From Interstate 580 in Livermore, take the North Livermore Avenue exit. Turn south and follow to Mines Road (North Livermore Avenue turns into Telsa Road). Make a right on Mines Road for 3 miles to Del Valle Road. Turn right to the park entrance.

Note: $4 parking fee, $1 dog fee. Dogs must be leashed in developed areas.

HAGEMANN PARK - Leashes

Info: Lazy bones can take a leisurely stroll or merely soak up some afternoon sun in this 7.2-acre park.

Directions: Located on Olivina Avenue between Murrieta and Hagemann.

HOLMWELL PARK - Leashes

Info: Put a little park in your busy day with a visit to this relaxing, 6-acre green scene.

Directions: Located off Isabel at Crystal and Peridot.

MAX BAER PARK

Info: Socially conscious pups travel for miles to wag away the day and make new friends in this dog-friendly park. A special leash-free enclosure allows all breeds a chance to see and be seen. For more information: (510) 373-5700.

Directions: Located at 1310 Murdell Lane.

MORGAN TERRITORY REGIONAL PRESERVE

Info: This splendid 3,986-acre preserve is crisscrossed with miles of hiking trails which afford access to panoramas of the San Joaquin River, the Sierra Nevadas and the Delta. As you climb through groves of bay and oak keep watch overhead for soaring eagles and hawks. For more information: (510) 635-0135.

Directions: From Interstate 580, take the North Livermore Avenue exit and head north. Make a left on Manning Road and a right onto Morgan Territory Road to the entrance.

Note: Dogs must be leashed in developed areas.

MURIETTA FALLS TRAIL HIKE

Expert/11.0 miles/7.0 hours

Info: Hidden within the depths of the Ohlone Wilderness and backdropped by the verdant East Bay foothills is Murietta Falls, a breathtaking 100-foot cascade. But the price for a slice of heaven

Dogs May Be Unleashed Unless Otherwise Indicated

is a strenuous 5.5-mile hike. You'll climb to Rocky Ridge before plunging into Williams Gulch. Catch your breath and flex your muscles for an intense uphill trek to Wauhab Ridge at 3,300 feet. If you make it that far, only a mile and a couple turns separate you from your goal. Go right on the Springboard Trail (#35) for 0.25 miles then left on the Greenside Trail. Enjoy the memorable view, you've earned it.   A word to the wise - springtime is the only time to visit. By summer, the falls are a mere trickle and the area is unbearably hot. For more information: (510) 635-0135.

Directions: From Interstate 580 in Livermore, take the North Livermore Avenue exit. Turn south and follow to Mines Road (North Livermore Avenue turns into Telsa Road). Make a right on Mines Road for 3 miles to Del Valle Road. Turn right to Del Valle Regional Park. Both the trailhead and parking area are at the south end of the reservoir.

TASSAJARA CREEK REGIONAL PARK - Leashes

Info: Tassajara is an underdeveloped park, which equates to an unspoiled landscape for you and the pupster to explore. Plans for a future regional trail link are under consideration for the 25-acre area. For more information: (510) 635-0135.

Directions: The park entrance is on Tassajara Road just north of Interstate 580 in Livermore.

VISTA MEADOWS - Leashes

Info: 5.7 acres await your pup's paw-stomping pleasure.

Directions: Located at Westminster and Lambeth.

VOLVON LOOP TRAIL HIKE

Intermediate/5.5 miles/3.25 hours

Info: Uphill and demanding best describe the first leg of this hike. But you and Fido will collect incredible vistas as you climb the sandstone hills to 1,977 feet. From this point, the trail loops around the peak and begins its descent along Coyote Trail. In springtime, the hills are alive with color and offer one of the best wildflower displays in the bay area. For more information: (510) 635-0135.

Locate Other Dog-Friendly Activities...Check Nearby Cities

Directions: From Interstate 580 in Livermore, take the North Livermore Avenue exit. Drive north to Highland Road and turn left. Continue to Morgan Territory Road and turn right. Drive to the parking area just past the summit.

Other parks in Livermore - Leashes

- ALCAFFODIO PARK, Shawnee Road
- BIG TREES PARK, Kathy Way
- BILL CLARK PARK, Hillflower/Bellflower
- CARNEGIE PARK, 2155 Third Street
- EL PADRO PARK, 31 El Padro Drive
- INDEPENDENCE PARK, Holmes/Vallecitos
- JACK WILLIAMS PARK, Neptune Road
- JANE ADDAMS HOUSE, 1310 Murdell Lane
- KARL WENTE PARK, Darwin/Kingsport
- LESTER J. KNOTT, 655 North Mines Road
- LITTLE HOUSE PARK, 85 Trevarno Road
- LIVERMORE DOWNS, Paseo Laguna Seco
- MAITLAND R. HENRY PARK, Alameda/Mendecino
- MOCHO PARK, Holmes/Mocho
- M.W. "TEX" SPRUIELL PARK, Geraldine/Felicia
- NORTH LIVERMORE NEIGHBORHOOD PARK, Bluebell/Galloway
- PLEASURE ISLAND PARK, Pearl/Flint
- RALPH T. WATTENBURGER PARK, Honeysuckle/Poppy
- ROBERT LIVERMORE PARK, East Avenue
- ROBERTSON PARK, Robertson Park Road
- SUNSET PARK, Geneva Park, Geneva Street

LODI

LODGING

BEST WESTERN ROYAL HOST INN
710 S Cherokee Ln (95240)
Rates: $44-$65;
Tel: (209) 369-8484; (800) 528-1234

COMFORT INN
118 N Cherokee Ln (95240)
Rates: $69-$89;
Tel: (209) 367-4848; (800) 221-2222

LODI MOTOR INN
1140 S Cherokee Ln (95240)
Rates: $65-$72;
Tel: (209) 334-6322

Dogs May Be Unleashed Unless Otherwise Indicated

LOMITA

<u>LODGING</u>

ELDORADO COAST HOTEL
2037 Pacific Coast Highway (90717)
Rates: $44-$58;
Tel: (310) 534-0700; (800) 536-7236

LOMPOC

<u>LODGING</u>

BEST WESTERN VANDENBERG INN
940 E Ocean Ave (93436)
Rates: $30-$50;
Tel: (805) 735-7731; (800) 528-1234

INN OF LOMPOC
1122 North H St (93436)
Rates: $51-$57;
Tel: (800) 548-8231

MOTEL 6
1521 North H St (93436)
Rates: $25-$29;
Tel: (805) 735-7631; (800) 440-6000

QUALITY INN & EXECUTIVE SUITES
1621 North H St (93436)
Rates: $44-$79;
Tel: (800) 221-2222

REDWOOD INN
1200 North H St (93436)
Rates: $40-$45;
Tel: (805) 735-3737

TALLY HO MOTOR INN
1020 E Ocean Ave (93436)
Rates: $29-$40;
Tel: (805) 735-6444; (800) 332-6444

<u>RECREATION</u>

GAVIOTA PEAK TRAIL HIKE

Intermediate/Expert/10.0 miles/5.5 hours

Info: Get away from it all on this trail. Your first stop will be Gaviota Hot Springs before you voyage to the peak with its splendid panoramas of the Pacific. You might want to pack a jacket. It can get chilly and windy at the top, but the views are well worth the effort and the wind-chill factor. For more information: (805) 683-6711.

Directions: From Lompoc, head south on Highway 1 to its intersection with Highway 101. Turn left. The parking lot is on Frontage Road immediately east of the highway.

Note: $2 parking fee.

Locate Other Dog-Friendly Activities...Check Nearby Cities

JALAMA BEACH PARK - Leashes

Info: Any time of the year you'll find something interesting to do at this 28-acre park. Whalewatch in the fall. Birdwatch in the spring. Beachcomb and rockhound all year long. Or try your hand at fishing. For more information: (805) 736-3504.

Directions: Take Highway 1 south to the Jalama Road exit. Turn left continuing 15 miles to the park.

LA PURISIMA MISSION STATE HISTORIC PARK - Leashes

Info: What an unexpected treat! In addition to traversing miles of trails throughout this 966-acre park, Fido can accompany you inside the historic La Purisima Mission. For more information: (805) 733-3713.

Directions: From Highway 1, head east on Purisima Road for a couple of miles to the park entrance.

Note: $5 entrance fee.

LOS ALAMOS PARK - Leashes

Info: 51 acres of open space beckon you and the frolicker. Plan a kibble cookout or toss a tennie. For more information: (805) 934-6211.

Directions: Located in Drum Canyon on Route 135.

LONE PINE

LODGING

ALABAMA HILLS INN
1920 S Main St (93545)
Rates: $38-$60;
Tel: (619) 876-8700; (800) 800-5026

BEST WESTERN FRONTIER MOTEL
1008 S Main St (93545)
Rates: $39-$80;
Tel: (619) 876-5571; (800) 528-1234

DOW VILLA MOTEL
310 S Main St, P. O. Box 205 (93545)
Rates: $56-$70;
Tel: (619) 876-5521; (800) 824-9317

NATIONAL 9 TRAILS MOTEL
633 S Main St (93545)
Rates: $34-$54;
Tel: (619) 876-5555

Dogs May Be Unleashed Unless Otherwise Indicated

<u>RECREATION</u>

ALABAMA HILLS PARK

Info: Hollywood buffs will have a great time exploring the terrain where many famous Westerns were filmed. Recall favorite movie scenes as you wander among canyons and interesting rock configurations. For more information: (619) 872-4881.

Directions: From Highway 395, take the Whitney Portal Road west about 2.5 miles to Movie Road.

MEYSAN LAKE TRAIL HIKE

Expert/9.4 miles/5.0 hours

Info: Only experienced hikers and their hounds should undertake this bonafido vigorous hike. But if you've got the stuff, you'll get an eyeful - the panoramas are gorgeous. Mostly unmaintained and hard to follow, this trail climbs 3,500 steep feet. Situated at 11,460 feet, Meysan Lake is a picturesque alpine lake where you can indulge in a cool retreat from the scorching summer temperatures. Use caution on the final stretch of the trail from Camp Lake to Meysan Lake- it's rocky and not well-blazed. Be prepared, thunderstorms are a common occurrence in summer. For more information: (619) 876-6200.

Directions: From Lone Pine, take Whitney Portal Road west for 12 miles to the Whitney Portal Campground parking area. Directions to the trailhead are posted on the campground's bulletin board or follow the signs in the campground.

Note: A quota system is in effect from June through mid-September.

WHITNEY PORTAL NATIONAL RECREATION TRAIL HIKE

Intermediate/Expert/8.0 miles/4.5 hours

Info: An incredible hiking excursion can be yours on this scenic albeit somewhat difficult trail. Beginning from the upper trailhead, you'll gradually descend along trout-filled Lone Pine Creek before passing through a grotto. Check out the fascinating rock configurations, then travel over the wooden bridge to Whitney Portal Campground. Once through the campground, cross the road and stay straight. This is where the going gets tough. The trail switchbacks on a steep descent into the canyon, crosses a log bridge, ascends to the mouth of the canyon and ends with a downhill trek to Lone Pine Campground. The last section of the trail is unshaded, which equates to hot in the summer. Take a breather - you'll need the energy for the 2,700-foot climb back to the trailhead. You might feel like jello legs at the end of this outing. For more information: (619) 876-6200.

Directions: Take Whitney Portal Road west to the lower trailhead at the Lone Pine Campground. Continue west on Whitney Portal Road to the upper trailhead at the Whitney Portal Pond. Cross the bridge by the restroom to the signed trailhead.

Note: A quota system is in effect from June through mid-September.

LONG BEACH

LODGING

BEST WESTERN LONG BEACH
1725 Long Beach Blvd (90813)
Rates: $58-$78;
Tel: (310) 599-5555; (800) 528-1234

CLARION HOTEL EDGEWATER
6400 E Pacific Coast Highway
(90803) Rates: $63;
Tel: (310) 434-8451

COMFORT INN
3201 E Pacific Coast Highway
(90804) Rates: $50-$54;
Tel: (800) 221-2222

DAYS INN-LONG BEACH
1500 E Pacific Coast Highway (90806)
Rates: $45-$85;
Tel: (310) 591-0088; (800) 329-7466

**HILTON-LONG BEACH AT
WORLD TRADE CENTER**
Two World Trade Center (90831)
Rates: $110-$170;
Tel: (310) 983-3400; (800) 445-8667

**HOLIDAY INN-CONVENTION &
WORLD TRADE CENTER**
500 E First St (90802)
Rates: $79-$104;
Tel: (800) 465-4329

HOLIDAY INN-LONG BEACH AIRPORT
2640 Lakewood Blvd (90815)
Rates: $59-$125;
Tel: (310) 597-4400; (800) 465-4329

HOWARD JOHNSON HOTEL
1133 Atlantic Ave (90813)
Rates: $71-$87;
Tel: (800) 654-2000

MARRIOTT-LONG BEACH
4700 Airport Plaza Dr (90815)
Rates: $69-$119;
Tel: (510) 425-5210; (800) 228-9290
(800) 321-5642 (CA)

MOTEL 6
5665 E 7th St (90804)
Rates: $35-$39;
Tel: (310) 597-1311; (800) 440-6000

RAMADA INN
5325 E Pacific Coast Highway (90804)
Rates: $79-$139;
Tel: (310) 597-1341; (800) 272-6232
(800) 990-9991 (CA)

RESIDENCE INN BY MARRIOTT
4111 E Willow St (90815)
Rates: $79-$149;
Tel: (800) 331-3131

Dogs May Be Unleashed Unless Otherwise Indicated

**SHERATON LONG BEACH-
SHORELINE SQUARE**
333 E Ocean Blvd (90802)
Rates: $139-$165;
Tel: (510) 436-3000; (800) 325-3535

**TRAVELODGE HOTEL
RESORT & MARINA**
700 Queensway Dr (90802)
Rates: $59-$150;
Tel: (510) 435-7676; (800) 578-7878

**TRAVELODGE LONG BEACH
CONVENTION CENTER**
80 Atlantic Ave (90802)
Rates: $50-$65;
Tel: (310) 435-2471; (800) 578-7878

VAGABOND INN
185 Atlantic Ave (90802)
Rates: $45-$55;
Tel: (510) 435-7621; (800) 522-1555

<u>RECREATION</u>

RECREATION PARK

Info: Your pooch will have a tailwagging, leash-free time at the dog run area. Once at the 63-acre park, make tracks to puppy paradise near the casting pond and say "goodbye leash, hello doggie freedom." For more information: (310) 570-1670.

Directions: Located on East Seventh Street, just west of Bellflower Boulevard.

LOS ALAMOS

<u>LODGING</u>

SKYVIEW MOTEL
9150 Highway 101 (93440)
Rates: $75-$125;
Tel: (805) 344-3770

LOS ANGELES

<u>LODGING</u>

BEST WESTERN DRAGON GATE INN
818 N Hill St (90012)
Rates: $52-$70;
Tel: (213) 617-3077; (800) 528-1234

BEST WESTERN THE MAYFAIR
1256 W 7th St (90017)
Rates: $75-$130;
Tel: (310) 484-9789; (800) 821-8682

BEVERLY HILLS PLAZA HOTEL
10300 Wilshire Blvd (90024)
Rates: $105-$310;
Tel: (310) 275-5575

BEVERLY LAUREL MOTOR HOTEL
8018 Beverly Blvd (90048)
Rates: $51-$57;
Tel: (213) 651-2441; (800) 962-3824

Locate Other Dog-Friendly Activities...Check Nearby Cities

BRENTWOOD MOTOR HOTEL
12200 Sunset Blvd (90049)
Rates: $55-$85;
Tel: (310) 476-9981

BRENTWOOD SUITES HOTEL
199 N Church Ln (90049)
Rates: $85-$105;
Tel: (310) 476-6255

CENTURY PLAZA HOTEL & TOWER
2025 Avenue of the Stars (90067)
Rates: $119-$240;
Tel: (310) 277-2000; (800) 228-3000

CENTURY WILSHIRE HOTEL
10776 Wilshire Blvd (90029)
Rates: $65-$85;
Tel: (800) 421-7223

CHATEAU MARMONT HOTEL
8221 Sunset Blvd (90046)
Rates: $160-$550;
Tel: (213) 656-1010; (800) 242-8328

**CONTINENTAL PLAZA-
LOS ANGELES AIRPORT**
9750 Airport Blvd (90045)
Rates: $85-$130;
Tel: (310) 645-4600; (800) 529-4683

DOUBLETREE-LOS ANGELES AIRPORT
5400 W Century Blvd (90045)
Rates: $89-$114;
Tel: (800) 528-0444

EMBASSY SUITES HOTEL-LAX/CENTURY
9801 Airport Blvd (90045)
Rates: $99;
Tel: (800) 362-2779

HALLMARK HOTEL
7023 Sunset Blvd (90028)
Rates: $56-$75;
Tel: (213) 464-8344

HOLIDAY INN-BRENTWOOD/BEL AIR
170 N Church Ln (90049)
Rates: $98-$210;
Tel: (310) 476-6411; (800) 465-4329

HOLIDAY INN CITY CENTER
1020 S Figueroa St (90015)
Rates: $89-$129;
Tel: (213) 748-1291; (800) 465-4329

**HOLIDAY INN CROWNE PLAZA-LOS
ANGELES INTERNATIONAL AIRPORT**
5985 W Century Blvd (90045)
Rates: $124-$154;
Tel: (800) 465-4329

HOLIDAY INN-DOWNTOWN
750 Garland Ave (90017)
Rates: $69-$79;
Tel: (800) 465-4329

**HOLIDAY INN-INTERNATIONAL
AIRPORT**
9901 S La Cienega Blvd (90045)
Rates: $89-$109;
Tel: (310) 649-5151; (800) 465-4329

HOLIDAY SELECT INN .
1150 S Beverly Dr (90035)
Rates: $85+;
Tel: (310) 553-6561

HOLLYWOOD CELEBRITY HOTEL
1775 Orchid Ave (90028)
Rates: $65-$83;
Tel: (800) 222-7090

HOTEL BEL-AIR
701 Stone Canyon Rd (90077)
Rates: $285-$435;
Tel: (800) 648-4097

**HOTEL INTER-CONTINENTAL
LOS ANGELES AT CALIFORNIA PLAZA**
251 S Olive St (90012)
Rates: $175-$265;
Tel: (213) 617-3300; (800) 442-5251

KAWADA HOTEL
200 S Hill St (90012)
Rates: $75-$109;
Tel: (800) 752-9232

MARRIOTT-LOS ANGELES AIRPORT
5855 W Century Blvd (90045)
Rates: $105-$154;
Tel: (800) 228-9290

OMNI HOTEL & CENTRE-LOS ANGELES
930 Wilshire Blvd (90017)
Rates: $129-$169;
Tel: (800) 445-8667

Dogs May Be Unleashed Unless Otherwise Indicated

QUALITY HOTEL-AIRPORT
5249 W Century Blvd (90045)
Rates: $55-$125;
Tel: (800) 266-2200

RADISSON WILSHIRE PLAZA HOTEL
3515 Wilshire Blvd (90010)
Rates: $129-$139;
Tel: (213) 381-7411; (800) 333-3333

SKYWAYS KNIGHTS INN AIRPORT HOTEL
9250 Airport Blvd (90045)
Rates: $40-$55;
Tel: (800) 336-0025

TRAVELODGE HOTEL AT LAX
5547 W Century Blvd (90045)
Rates: $54-$65;
Tel: (800) 367-2250

VAGABOND INN FIGUEROA
3101 S Figueroa St (90007)
Rates: $59-$76;
Tel: (213) 746-1531; (800) 522-1555

VAGABOND INN
1904 W Olympic Blvd (90006)
Rates: $45-$55;
Tel: (213) 380-9393; (800) 522-1555

THE WESTIN BONAVENTURE HOTEL & SUITES
404 S Figueroa St (90071)
Rates: $89-$150;
Tel: (800) 228-3000

WILSHIRE MOTEL
12023 Wilshire Blvd (90025)
Rates: $50-$60;
Tel: (310) 478-3545

WYNDHAM CHECKERS HOTEL-LOS ANGELES
535 S Grand Ave (90071)
Rates: $95-$205;
Tel: (213) 624-0000; (800) 822-4200
(800) 631-4200 (CAN)

RECREATION

ARROYO SECO PARK - Leashes

Info: 279 acres of open frolicking space spell fun for you and Fido, while the landscape spells pretty for your eyes.

Directions: Located at 5566 Via Marisol Street.

BARNSDALL PARK - Leashes

Info: Plan a picnic or a quickie stroll with the pup in this 13-acre urban park.

Directions: Located at 4800 Hollywood Boulevard.

CITY HALL PARK - Leashes

Info: Political pooches will love sniffing around the landscaped grounds of City Hall.

Directions: Located at 200 North Main Street.

Locate Other Dog-Friendly Activities...Check Nearby Cities

CRESTWOOD HILLS PARK - Leashes

Info: Musically inclined mutts can try to catch a concert. This 15-acre park offers an outdoor stage for guitar-pickers. Various sports fields provide plenty of sniffing space for restless Rovers.

Directions: Located at 1000 Hanley Avenue.

ELYSIAN PARK - Leashes

Info: This 550+ acre park is a delightful treat for both dogs and their baseball-loving owners. Enjoy cool breezes and skyline views of LA from one of the hilltop perches. For more information: (213) 226-1402.

Directions: Located between Interstate 5, Highway 101 and Highway 110. To access Angel's Point, exit Interstate 5 at Stadium Way and follow the signs. Once in the park, make your first left on Elysian Park Drive.

ERNEST E. DEBS REGIONAL COUNTY PARK - Leashes

Info: Spend an hour or two at this spacious grassy park. Hike fire roads or tote a picnic lunch and spend the afternoon. For more information: (213) 847-3989.

Directions: From Los Angeles, take the Pasadena Freeway (110) north towards Highland Park to the Marisol Avenue exit, head west (right). Follow Marisol Avenue to Monterey Road and go right. Continue approximately one mile to the park.

GRIFFITH PARK - Leashes

Info: Once inside this 4,000+ acre park, you'll quickly forget the LA crowds and noise. Walk among 100 species of trees including oaks, pines and redwoods. Hike on over 50 miles of trails, but stick to the more developed areas. End your day with a dog-friendly, open-air train ride. Adult fares are $1.75, dogs go free. For more information: (213) 665-5188.

Directions: The park is surrounded by Highway 101, Interstate 5 and Highway 134. One access point is off Interstate 5 at Los Feliz Boulevard.

Note: For a free map of the trails and info on the train ride, call ranger headquarters at the above number.

Dogs May Be Unleashed Unless Otherwise Indicated

HAROLD A. HENRY PARK - Leashes

Info: 67 landscaped acres provide you and Fido with plenty of stomping ground and perhaps a chance to spectate at a basketball game.

Directions: Located at 890 South Lucerne Avenue.

HOLLENBECK RECREATION CENTER - Leashes

Info: Your pooch can work off some calories in this spacious, 20-acre park. Try the ball field for a leg-stretching romp. Able anglers will enjoy dropping in on the fish in the small lake located within the boundaries of this park.

Directions: Located at 415 South St. Louis Street.

HOLMBY PARK - Leashes

Info: Plan an afternoon stroll or a kibble cook-out in this pleasant 8.5-acre park.

Directions: Located at 601 Club View Drive.

JIM GILLIAM RECREATION CENTER - Leashes

Info: Tie those tennies and hightail it with your tailwagger along the trail in this 17-acre park.

Directions: Located at 4000 South La Brea Avenue.

KENNETH HAHN STATE RECREATION AREA - Leashes

Info: History buffs, this park was home to the 1932 Olympics. Hike the trails to the top or head downhill to the lake and stream. For more information: (213) 291-0199.

Directions: From Los Angeles, exit the Santa Monica Freeway (10) at La Cienega Boulevard. Head south to the park entrance.

Note: $3 vehicle fee on weekends and holidays.

Locate Other Dog-Friendly Activities...Check Nearby Cities

LEIMERT PLAZA - Leashes

Info: 10 acres of spacious grounds spell a paw-stomping good time for you and the pupster. This nicely landscaped park provides a chance for escapism.

Directions: Located at 4395 Leimert Boulevard.

LINCOLN PARK RECREATION CENTER - Leashes

Info: 46 acres of land for you to rove with Rover. Fishing gurus will enjoy the lake while canine cronies will love stretching their furry bods in the grass along the shoreline. Plan to nibble on some kibble in one of the picnic areas.

Directions: Located at 3501 Valley Boulevard.

NORMAN O. HOUSTON PARK - Leashes

Info: Take in a local game of basketball as you relax with Max in this pleasant 10-acre park.

Directions: Located at 4800 South La Brea Avenue.

PERSHING SQUARE PARK - Leashes

Info: 5 acres of landscaped grounds can satisfy a quickie constitutional in this pretty little park.

Directions: Located at 532 South Olive Street.

PORTOLA TRAIL HIKE

Beginner/5.0 miles/2.5 hours

Info: Nestled within the confines of urban Los Angeles, this delightful trail affords city slickers a chance to commune with nature in their backyards. Leave your city blues behind and be serenaded by songbirds as you mosey with Rosie through groves of eucalyptus, oak, palm, pine and walnut. Stake out a grassy knoll or set up a private picnic spot under a shade tree and delight in lunch alfresco. Woof. For more information: (213) 485-5054.

Dogs May Be Unleashed Unless Otherwise Indicated

Directions: From downtown Los Angeles, take North Broadway north to Elysian Park Drive which becomes Park Row Drive. Make a left and follow to the trailhead at Elysian Park. The trail is marked by an historical landmark honoring explorer Don Gaspar de Portola. Parking is available on Park Row Drive.

SILVERLAKE PARK - Leashes

Info: This puppy playground is a great place for your pal to make new friends and run with the pack.

Directions: Located at 1850 West Silverlake.

SOUTH PARK - Leashes

Info: Calling all sporting breeds. Furry friends can bury their snouts in the grassy playing fields while you root at the local ball game of choice. 18 acres assure a fun-filled visit.

Directions: Located at 345 East 51st Street.

SYCAMORE GROVE PARK - Leashes

Info: You and furface can get your daily dose on 15 acres of landscaped grounds.

Directions: Located at 4702 North Figueroa Street.

TEMESCAL CANYON PARK - Leashes

Info: 49 acres of unspoiled scenery are sure to please serenity seekers. You and Fido can feast your eyes on a calming sun-stroked landscape as you slowly stroll along the grounds. Pick a spot to rest your paws and be soothed by the cool California breeze as the hassles of city life drifts away.

Directions: Located at 15900 Pacific Coast Highway.

Locate Other Dog-Friendly Activities...Check Nearby Cities

WESTWOOD RECREATION CENTER - Leashes

Info: Convenient and canine-friendly this expansive 26-acre action packed area has just about everything a park loving pooch could want. Green, contoured lawns and open fields provide plenty of frisbee chasing space. Joggers will be delighted to see a gravel pathway circling the park, while mellow fellows can laze beneath a shade tree. Pack some snacks and plan on an afternoon delight. Once your wagalong sniffs out the fun, he won't want to leave.

Directions: Located at 1350 Sepulveda Boulevard.

Other parks in LA - Leashes
• NORTHRIDGE PARK/DEVONSHIRE HOUSE, 10058 Reseda Boulevard.
• PROSPECT PARK, Enchandia and Judson Streets.

LOS ANGELES COUNTY

RECREATION

SANTA MONICA MOUNTAINS NATIONAL RECREATION AREA - Leashes

Info: This 65,000-acre smorgasbord of nature is situated in the glorious Santa Monica Mountains. A pristine region of towering crags, sun-dappled waterfalls, boulder-strewn canyons, verdant meadows, creeks, forests and isolated beaches, you and Fido can't go wrong with a visit to this beautiful area. Amazingly, this enormous playground is just a short drive from Los Angeles. It is governed by a number of agencies including the National Park Service, California State Parks, Conejo Open Space, Santa Monica Conservancy, City of Malibu Parks and Los Angeles City Parks.

This mountainous, coastal region offers year-round recreation opportunities. According to the Ranger Office, there are 33 dog-friendly sections within the Santa Monica Mountains. Trails and other activities are listed below. For more information: (800) 533-PARK or (818) 597-9192.

Dogs May Be Unleashed Unless Otherwise Indicated

FIDO-FRIENDLY AREAS WITHIN THE SANTA MONICA MOUNTAINS - Leashes

NATIONAL PARK SERVICE
Arroyo Sequit
Castro Crest
Cheesboro Canyon/Palo
   Comado
Circle X Ranch
Deer Creek Park
Franklin Canyon
   Ranch/Reservoir
Fryman Canyon
Malibu Springs
Paramount Ranch
Peter Strauss Ranch
Rancho Sierra Vista/Satwiwa
Rocky Oaks
Wilacre Park
Zuma/Trancas Canyon Area

CALIFORNIA STATE PARKS
Tapia Park
Will Rogers State Historic
   Park

CONEJO OPEN SPACE
Wildwood Regional Park

S.M.MOUNTAINS CONSERVANCY
Calabasas Peak
Corral Canyon Park
Dixie Canyon
Escondido Canyon
Mulholland Gateway Park
Red Rock Canyon
San Vicente Mt. Park
Solstice Canyon
Stunt Ranch
Temescal Gateway Park

CITY OF MALIBU PARKS
Charmlee Natural Area

L.A. CITY PARKS
Coldwater Canyon Park
Laurel Canyon Park
Runyon Canyon Park
Serrania Park
Temescal Canyon Park

Note: Keep your pooch leashed and exercise common sense with regard to wildlife.

LOS BANOS

LODGING

BEST WESTERN JOHN JAY INN
301 W Pacheco Blvd (93635)
Rates: $45-$55;
Tel: (209) 827-0954; (800) 528-1234

REGENCY INN
349 W Pacheco Blvd (93635)
Rates: $30-$42;
Tel: (209) 826-3871

Locate Other Dog-Friendly Activities...Check Nearby Cities

RECREATION

LOS BANOS WILDLIFE AREA

Info: Nearly 6,000 acres of seasonal and permanent wetlands comprise the oldest State Wildlife Area in California. Bring your binoculars, over 200 species of birds can be observed at various times of the year. For more information: (209) 826-0463.

Directions: From Highway 152, take Mercey Springs Road/Highway 165 north 3 miles and turn right on Henry Miller Road. Follow for one mile to the wildlife area on the left-hand side. Access into the area is on gravel roads.

Note: $2.50 day-use fee/person 16 years & older. Open mid-January through mid-September. Dogs must be leashed from April 1 – June 30.

LOS GATOS

LODGING

LOS GATOS MOTOR INN
55 Saratoga Ave (95032)
Rates: $58-$70;
Tel: (408) 356-9191

TOLL HOUSE MOTOR HOTEL
140 S Santa Cruz Ave (95030)
Rates: $79-$158;
Tel: (408) 395-7070; (800) 238-6111

RECREATION

BELGATOS PARK - Leashes

Info: Songbirds will be singing sweet melodies as you roam amid 17 acres of natural woodlands. Cityslickers might prefer the 7 acres of developed lawn.

Directions: Located off Blossom Hill Road at the end of Belgatos Road.

BLOSSOM HILL PARK - Leashes

Info: Sup with your pup at one of the picnic tables or spread out your blanket on the lush green grass and cloudgaze with your best buddy in this 9.2-acre neighborhood park.

Directions: Located on Blossom Hill Road.

Dogs May Be Unleashed Unless Otherwise Indicated

LA RINCONADA PARK - Leashes

Info: You and the tailwagger can head out for a quick leg-stretching stroll on this park's quarter mile walking trail complete with a par course. If you'd rather just kick back, bring a snack and relax with Max creekside.

Directions: Located at Wedgewood Drive and Granada Way.

NOVITIATE PARK - Leashes

Info: Every dog must have his day, so treat your pooch to an outing at this beautiful 8-acre park. You'll meander through lovely, open meadows and gaze upon Los Gatos Creek. For a bit of Rexercise, sniff out the trail to Jacob's Open Space Preserve.

Directions: Located at the end of Jones Road off College Avenue. There is no on-site parking.

ST. JOSEPH'S HILL OPEN SPACE PRESERVE - Leashes

Info: You and your pup are destined for a serene day of hiking the dirt trails or traipsing through the meadows of this compact preserve. Bring your own water. For more information: (415) 691-1200.

Directions: From Highway 17, exit at Alma Bridge Road. Follow the signs.

STEVENS CREEK - Leashes

Info: Noted as the county's first park, this pleasant region offers a gamut of paw-friendly activities. Do a floating lunch with Fido or try you luck at catching dinner. No dogs allowed on trails. For more information: (408) 358-3741.

Directions: Located at Blossom Hill Road and University.

VASONA LAKE COUNTY PARK - Leashes

Info: Birdwatchers beware, you may never want to point those binoculars away from the sky. Ducks, geese, great blue heron, egrets and a variety of other feathered species inhabit this park. Thick woodland areas provide shade and serenity for peace seekers. Don't forget to pack a snack, this park is so beautiful, you'll want to stay for the day. Hiking trails provide the Rexercise while the park provides free, disposable pooper scoopers. Pet-friendly and packed with scenery, this park rates two paws up. For more information: (408) 365-2729.

Directions: From Highway 17 in Los Gatos, head west on Highway 9 to University Avenue. Turn right to Blossom Hill Road. Make a right to the park. The walk-in entrance is at Garden Hill Drive.

Note: Dogs are prohibited on the playground. Vehicle fee may be required.

WORCESTER PARK - Leashes

Info: Abundant with natural vegetation and shade-giving trees, this 112-acre park is a perfect getaway spot for city-dwelling dogs. Hop on the half-mile, self-guided nature trail and broaden your horizons.

Directions: Located a short distance from Los Gatos Boulevard on Worcester Loop.

Other parks in Los Gatos - Leashes
- BACHMAN PARK, Bachman Avenue and Belmont Street
- FAIRVIEW PLAZA PARK, the end of Fairview Plaza
- HOWES PLAYLOT, Union Avenue between Howes Avenue and Thomas Drive
- LIVE OAK MANOR PARK, Carlton Avenue and Gateway Drive
- OAK HILL PLAYLOT, Garden Lane and Oak Park Drive off Los Gatos Boulevard
- OAK MEADOW PARK, University Avenue and Blossom Hill Road

Dogs May Be Unleashed Unless Otherwise Indicated

LOS OLIVOS

RECREATION

ZACA PEAK TRAIL to FIGUEROA MOUNTAIN HIKE

Beginner/1.5 miles/0.75 hours

Info: For an easy walk with some extraordinary scenery, plan a pup-size excursion on the first section of this trail. You and Bowser will browser across the flanks of Figueroa Mountain amidst a dense woodland. If you're seeking a bit of solitude in beautiful surroundings, this place has your name on it. For more information: (805) 683-6711.

Directions: From Los Olivos, turn north on Figueroa Mountain Road at Mattei's Tavern. The trailhead is 0.6 miles above the fire station opposite Tunnell Road.

LOS OSOS

LODGING

BACK BAY INN
1391 Second St (93402)
Rates: $29-$110;
Tel: (805) 528-1233

LOST HILLS

LODGING

ECONOMY INNS OF AMERICA
14684 Aloma St (93249)
Rates: $23-$36;
Tel: (800) 826-0778

MOTEL 6
14685 Warren St (93249)
Rates: $23-$29;
Tel: (805) 797-2346; (800) 440-6000

LOTUS

LODGING

GOLDEN LOTUS BED & BREAKFAST INN
1006 Lotus Rd (95651)
Rates: $80-$95; Tel: (916) 621-4562

Locate Other Dog-Friendly Activities...Check Nearby Cities

LUCERNE

LODGING

BEACHCOMBER RESORT
6345 E Hwy 20, Box 358 (95458)
Rates: $40-$85;
Tel: (707) 274-6639

LAKE SANDS RESORT
6335 E Hwy 20, Box 48 (95458)
Rates: $50; Tel: (707) 274-7732

STARLITE MOTEL
5960 E Hwy 20, Box 467 (95458)
Rates: $40-$85;
Tel: (707) 274-5515

MADERA

LODGING

BEST WESTERN MADERA VALLEY INN
317 North G St (93637)
Rates: $52-$66;
Tel: (209) 673-5164; (800) 528-1234

ECONOMY INNS OF AMERICA
1855 W Cleveland Ave (93637)
Rates: $26-$42; Tel: (800) 826-0778

GATEWAY INN
25327 Avenue 16 (93637)
Rates: $35-$49;
Tel: (209) 674-8817

MALIBU

LODGING

MALIBU COUNTRY INN
6506 Westward Beach Road (90265)
Rates: $95-$155;
Tel: (310) 457-9622; (800) 386-6787

MALIBU RIVIERA MOTEL
28920 Pacific Coast Highway (90265)
Rates: $50-$70;
Tel: (310) 457-9503

RECREATION

ROBERT H. MEYER MEMORIAL STATE BEACHES - Leashes

Info: Beach-loving pups will have a marvelous time gallivanting along miles of surf and sand. This area consists of three separate state beaches: El Matador, El Pescador and La Piedra State Beach. El Matador is the largest and most picturesque with its rocky bluffs and hidden inlets. La Piedra and El Pescador closely resemble one another. Both offer picnic areas and trails from bluff to ocean. For more information: (310) 457-1324.

Dogs May Be Unleashed Unless Otherwise Indicated

Directions: Along the Pacific Coast Highway at the west end of the county, just south of Decker Canyon Road.

Note: $2 parking fee.

MAMMOTH LAKES

LODGING

AUSTRIA HOF LODGE
924 Canyon Blvd, P. O. Box 607
(93546) Rates: $50-$115;
Tel: (619) 934-2764; (800) 922-2966

CONVICT LAKE RESORT
Rt 1, Box 204 (93546)
Rates: $65-$350;
Tel: (619) 934-3800; (800) 992-2260

CRYSTAL CRAG LODGE
307 Crystal Crag Dr (93546)
Rates: $49-$175;
Tel: (619) 934-2436

ECONO LODGE-WILDWOOD INN
3626 Main St (93546)
Rates: $49-$99;
Tel: (800) 424-4777

ENGLEHOF LODGE
6156 Minaret Rd (93546)
Rates: $35-$80;
Tel: (619) 934-2416

THE INTERNATIONAL INN
3554 Main St (93546)
Rates: $45-$65;
Tel: (800) 457-1997

MOTEL 6
3372 Main St (93546)
Rates: $36-$44;
Tel: (619) 934-6660; (800) 440-6000

NORTH VILLAGE INN
103 Lake Mary Rd (93546)
Rates: $70-$100;
Tel: (619) 934-2925

ROYAL PINES RESORT
3814 Viewpoint Rd, P. O. Box 348
(93546) Rates: $49-$59;
Tel: (619) 934-2306

SHILO INN
2963 Main St (93546)
Rates: $79-$150;
Tel: (619) 934-4500; (800) 222-2244

THRIFTLODGE
6209 Minaret Rd (93546)
Rates: $39-$75;
Tel: (619) 934-8576; (800) 525-9055;
(800) 578-7878

ZWART HOUSE-THE FAMILY LODGE
76 Lupin St, P. O. Box 174 (93546)
Rates: $50-$80;
Tel: (619) 934-2217

RECREATION

DEVIL'S POSTPILE NATIONAL MONUMENT - Leashes

Info: Venture into 800 acres of natural wonders. Geology enthusiasts will be enthralled by the 60-foot wall of columnar basalt posts. Others will be captivated by magnificent Rainbow Falls. For more information: (619) 934-2289.

Directions: Head west on Highway 203/ Main Street through Mammoth Lakes. Make a right on Minaret Summit/Minaret Road. Drive about seven miles to the park.

Note: A nominal day-use fee is charged. During the summer, ride a shuttle from town for $6 round-trip per person-dogs go free Road closed in winter.

HORSESHOE LAKE- Leashes

Info: Puppy paradise found! This tranquil, enchanting lake, makes for a great all day outing. At the north end of the lake you'll find a trailhead through alpine forests. Breathe deeply. The air is so clean and sweet smelling, you'll want take some home. Walk long enough and you'll reach the Pacific Crest Trail. For more information: (619) 934-2505.

Directions: Head west on Highway 203/Main Street through Mammoth Lakes. The road curves to the left and becomes Lake Mary Road. Follow for seven miles to the lake at road's end.

HOT CREEK GEOLOGIC SITE- Leashes

Info: For an out-of-this-world experience, make tracks for the volcanic wonderland of Hot Creek. From boiling hot springs to gushing geysers, hidden vent holes to effervescent fumaroles, you and Astro might forget that your paws are still earthbound. The waters of Hot Creek are home to the native Owens Sucker and Tui Chub, while the terra firma is a wildlife sanctuary. Bring your binoculars and keep watch for great horned owls, bald eagles, dippers, spotted sandpipers and cliff swallows. For safety reasons, do not wander off the walkways and boardwalks. Swimming is not advised; the dangers of scalding and high concentrations of chemicals exist in the water. For more information: (619) 924-5500.

Directions: From Mammoth Lakes, take Highway 395 south to the Airport/Fish Hatchery exit. Head east, following the road to Hot Creek. Once on the gravel portion of the road, it's about one mile to the creek.

Dogs May Be Unleashed Unless Otherwise Indicated

STEELHEAD LAKE TRAIL HIKE

Expert/10.0 miles/6.0 hours

Info: You and the pupster better have a slew of hiking miles under your belts/leashes for this one. Covering a 2,300-foot elevation change, this wilderness hike is hard on both the legs and the lungs. Beginning along an old jeep road, you'll enter the John Muir Wilderness and continue along McGee Creek. It'll be doggie splashdown as the trail crisscrosses the creek. Exercise caution during times of high water.

Once the trail turns west into a lodgepole forest, the workout begins. The trail steepens as it climbs to a signed junction, leaving the jeep trail and continuing on to another junction with the Steelhead Lake lateral. The fork to the left (east) leads to First Grass Lake and then Steelhead Lake, a steep, switchbacking trek. Chill out lakeside, take a biscuit break, then retrace your steps. For more information: (619) 873-2500.

Directions: From Mammoth Lakes, take Highway 395 south for 8 miles to the McGee Creek exit. Head west for 4 miles, passing the McGee Pack Station, to the trailhead and parking area at road's end.

Note: A quota system is in effect from June through mid-September.

MANHATTAN BEACH

LODGING

RADISSON PLAZA HOTEL-LAX SOUTH
1400 Parkview Ave (90266)
Rates: $129-$159;
Tel: (800) 333-3333

RESIDENCE INN BY MARRIOTT
1700 N Sepulveda Blvd (90266)
Rates: $89-$189;
Tel: (310) 546-7627; (800) 331-3131

RECREATION

MANHATTAN BEACH PARKWAY PARK - Leashes

Info: Take your pooch for his morning constitutional on this narrow one-mile slice of greenery.

Directions: Stretches the length of Ardmore Valley Avenue.

MANTECA

LODGING

BEST WESTERN INN OF MANTECA
1415 E Yosemite Ave (95336)
Rates: $59-$68;
Tel: (209) 825-1415; (800) 528-1234

MARINA

LODGING

MOTEL 6
100 Reservation Rd (93933)
Rates: $32-$38;
Tel: (408) 384-1000; (800) 440-6000

RECREATION

MARINA STATE BEACH - Leashes

Info: Beachcomb on one of the central coast's largest state beaches while Rover romps and wets his paws. For more information: (408) 384-7695.

Directions: Located at the foot of Reservation Road, just off Highway 1. Walk down the boardwalk to the beach.

MARINA DEL REY

LODGING

FOGHORN HARBOR INN
4140 Via Marina (90292)
Rates: $60-$109;
Tel: (310) 823-4626

MARINA DEL REY HOTEL
13534 Bali Way (90292)
Rates: $79-$325;
Tel: (310) 301-1000; (800) 882-4000
(800) 862-7462 (CA)

MARRIOTT-MARINA DEL REY
13480 Maxella Ave (90291)
Rates: $139-$159;
Tel: (800) 228-9290

MARIPOSA

LODGING

THE CLUBB'S BED & BREAKFAST
5060 Charles St (95338)
Rates: $45-$75;
Tel: (209) 966-5085

THE GUEST HOUSE INN
4962 Triangle Rd (95338)
Rates: $98;
Tel: (209) 742-6869

MARIPOSA LODGE-IMA
5052 Hwy 140, Box 733 (95338)
Rates: $35-$75;
Tel: (209) 966-3607; (800) 341-8000

MINERS INN
P. O. Box 1989 (95338)
Rates: $70;
Tel: (209) 742-7777

MOTHERLODE LODGE
5051 Hwy 140, P. O. Box 986 (95338)
Rates: $32-$68;
Tel: (800) 398-9770

MOUNTAIN OAKS GUEST HOUSE
5070 Allred Rd (95338)
Rates: $45-$95;
Tel: (209) 966-6033

THE PELENNOR BED & BREAKFAST
3871 Hwy 49 S (95338)
Rates: $35-$45;
Tel: (209) 966-2832

RECREATION

CATHEYS VALLEY COUNTY PARK - Leashes

Info: An ideal picnic site for travelers on Highway 140. Satiate your hunger under a shaded grove of trees and then treat Rover to a trot around the ball field. For more information: (209) 966-2498.

Directions: From Mariposa, travel southwest on Highway 140 to the exit for Catheys Valley. The park is located on the south side of the Highway at 2820 Highway 140.

LAKE McCLURE - Leashes

Info: Delight in a lovely lakeside sojourn or venture over to the Bagby Recreation Area for a riverside stroll. Maybe you'd prefer an escape to shady seclusion at the Horseshoe Bend Recreation Area, at the northeast section of the lake. The choice is yours. For more information: (800) 468-8889.

Directions: Head northwest on Highway 49 to Highway 132 (just south of Coulterville). Go west about 3 miles to the lake entrance.

Note: $4 day-use fee, $2 dog fee.

Locate Other Dog-Friendly Activities...Check Nearby Cities

LOWER YOSEMITE FALLS TRAIL HIKE - Leashes

Beginner/0.6 miles/0.5 hours

Info: Ahhh, the world-famous, majestic Yosemite Falls. Don't let the possible crowds dissuade you. May and June are the best months - the turbulent falls are in full force. This is the only area in Yosemite where dogs are permitted but they must be leashed. For more information: (209) 372-0200.

Directions: From Mariposa, head east on Highway 140 to Yosemite National Park. Follow the signs to Yosemite Valley and the Yosemite Falls parking area. There's also parking in the Valley Visitor Center, where you can walk on the bike path to get to the Yosemite Falls parking area.

MARIPOSA PARK - Leashes

Info: Roam through this multi-level park until you happen upon the activity of choice. Picnic on the green lawns or at a table overlooking the town. Venture down the dirt road to a walking trail or cool your paws in a tree-shaded oasis. For more information: (209) 966-2948.

Directions: Travel south on Highway 49/140 and turn right on 6th Street. Continue to Stroming Road and make a right, then take a quick left onto County Park Road.

MARKLEEVILLE

LODGING

J. MARKLEE TOLL STATION HOTEL
14856 Highway 89, P. O. Box 395 (96120)
Rates: $40;
Tel: (916) 694-2507

RECREATION

ALPINE COUNTY HISTORICAL COMPLEX - Leashes

Info: You'll be afforded outstanding views of historic Markleeville and the surrounding area if you lead your Laddie through the grounds of this hilltop complex. Dogs are not allowed in the buildings, but they can accompany you on a picnic or a jaunt through the fascinating grounds. For more information: (916) 694-2317.

Directions: The complex is atop the hill at #1 School Street.

Note: Open Memorial Day-October 12 noon-5 p.m. Closed on Tuesdays.

COLE CREEK LAKES TRAIL HIKE - Leashes

Beginner/6.0 miles/3.0 hours

Info: What a beautiful way to spend a day. This gentle trail will escort you and the pupster to a blue bouquet of gem-like lakes nestled high in the wooded mountains. A fishing pole might save you the cost of dinner. For more information: (209) 295-4251.

Directions: From Markleeville, head north on Highway 89 to Highway 88. Take Highway 88 southwest past Silver Lake. At the Tragedy Springs Campgrounds there is a 4-wheel drive road across from the campgrounds. Take this road southeast past the Lookout. The trailhead is near the site of the old Plasse Trading Post.

Note: High clearance vehicles only. Before heading out, check with the El Dorado Information Center regarding weather and road conditions.

EMIGRANT LAKE TRAIL HIKE- Leashes

Intermediate/9.0 miles/4.5 hours

Info: Beat the dog days of summer with a little paw dipping refreshment in Emigrant Lake. If you've got the time and the pupster's got the stamina, this hike has the water. The first 2.5 miles parallel Caples Lake before ascending to a junction. Go left, cross the stream and continue to the lake. For more information: (209) 295-4251.

Directions: From Markleeville, head north on Highway 89 to Highway 88. Take Highway 88 southwest to Caples Lake. The trail begins at the west end spillway of Caples Lake.

GRANITE LAKE TRAIL HIKE- Leashes

Intermediate/2.0 miles/1.0 hours

Info: Short and relatively flat, this trail is a bonafido leg-stretcher. Once the trail crosses Squaw Creek via the wooden bridge, it branches off. Take the left fork to access Granite Lake. Dip a paw or two before retracing your steps. For more information: (209) 295-4251.

Directions: Head north on Highway 89 to Highway 88. Take Highway 88 southwest for 20 miles to Silver Lake. On the north side of the lake (by the spillway) is a sign for Kit Carson Lodge. Take the road east to the north entrance of Camp Minkalo. Trailhead and parking are on the east side of the lake.

HIDDEN LAKE TRAIL HIKE - Leashes

Intermediate/6.0 miles/3.0 hours

Info: Enjoy a one-mile leg stretching jaunt to Hidden Lake or spend your afternoon exploring the pretty terrain on the longer looping trail. For the long route, continue past Hidden Lake to the Off-Highway Vehicle Trail. Go right to Stockton Muni Camp and make another right. This section of trail breezes by Silver Lake and returns to the trailhead. For more information: (209) 644-6048.

Directions: Head north on Highway 89 to Highway 88. Take Highway 88 southwest for 20 miles to Silver Lake. On the north side of the lake (by the Spillway) is a sign for Kit Carson Lodge. Take the road east to the north entrance of Camp Minkalo. The trailhead is at the southeast end of the lake.

LAKE MARGARET TRAIL HIKE - Leashes

Beginner/5.0 miles/2.5 hours

Info: This gentle trail wanders among beautiful fields of wild-flowers. Between the allure of Lake Margaret and the colorful flowers, this is a favorite weekend destination for many hikers and their hounds. For more information: (209) 644-6048.

Directions: From Markleeville, head north on Highway 89 to Highway 88. Take Highway 88 southwest past Caples Lake to the trailhead on the north side of the highway between Caples Lake and the Kirkwood Inn.

LITTLE ROUND TOP TRAIL HIKE - Leashes

Intermediate/5.0 miles/2.5 hours

Info: Your scenic ascent through lodgepole and whitebark pines ends at the junction with the Pacific Crest Trail. For a lofty sneak peak of the Sierras and Caples Lake, continue traversing cross-country to the summit of Little Round Top. For more information: (916) 644-6048.

Directions: From Markleeville, head north on Highway 89 to Highway 88. Take Highway 88 southwest to the CalTrans maintenance station near Caples Lake. Turn north for two miles to Schneiders Cow Camp and parking. The trailhead begins a half-mile down the road.

Note: High clearance vehicles only.

SCOUT CARSON LAKE TRAIL HIKE- Leashes

Intermediate/12.0 miles/6.0 hours

Info: Gear up for an all day outing on this trail. Pack plenty of perrier, power munchies and some Scooby snacks. Take the Horse Canyon Trail for 5.5 miles until the junction near Covered Wagon Peak. The trail to the right will take you to Scout Carson Lake. For more information: (209) 295-4251.

Directions: Head north on Highway 89 to Highway 88. Take Highway 88 southwest for 20 miles to Silver Lake. The trailhead is near Oyster Creek, approximately .75 miles north of Silver Lake.

SHEALOR LAKE TRAIL HIKE - Leashes

Expert/3.0 miles/2.0 hours

Info: Looking for a challenge? This steep hike ascends .75 miles through granite chunks and woodland, then suddenly descends to Shealor Lake. The beauty of your surroundings makes the effort worthwhile. For more information: (209) 644-6048.

Locate Other Dog-Friendly Activities...Check Nearby Cities

Directions: Head north on Highway 89 to Highway 88. Take Highway 88 southwest to just past Silver Lake. The trailhead is between Kay's Resort and the Plasse turnoff.

MARTINEZ

<u>RECREATION</u>

CARQUINEZ STRAIT REGIONAL SHORELINE - Leashes

Info: This 1,304-acre park is laced with hiking trails and loaded with outstanding views of Port Costa, Martinez, Benecia and Carquinez Strait. For more information: (510) 562-7275.

Directions: There are two major access points to the park, both off Carquinez Scenic Drive; the Bull Valley Staging Area, just west of Port Costa and the Nejedly Staging Area just west of Martinez.

HIDDEN LAKES PARK - Leashes

Info: When you visit this beautiful 26-acre area, jog with your dog along the track or hop on one of the trails leading to Hidden Valley Park.

Directions: On Morello Avenue at Chilpancingo Parkway.

MARTINEZ REGIONAL SHORELINE - Leashes

Info: Acres of green and gold will surround you on your leisurely stroll through a marsh preserve, seasonal home to many species of plants and animals. Scenic vistas, picnic areas and a lovely pond contribute to the diverse environment. For more information: (510) 562-7275.

Directions: Access is off Ferry Street.

NANCY BOYD PARK - Leashes

Info: Get the kinks out with a jaunt around this 8.5-acre expanse of land. This park is a great place to go to catch some late afternoon rays.

Directions: At Pleasant Hill Road East and Church Street.

Dogs May Be Unleashed Unless Otherwise Indicated

RANKIN PARK - Leashes

Info: Either prance around the picnic area or have a ball on the ball field as you lead your Lassie through this 41-acre park.

Directions: Located at the west end of Buckley Street.

Other parks in Martinez - Leashes
- CAPPY RICKS PARK, Brown Street, Arreba Street, near Pacheco Boulevard
- GOLDEN HILLS PARK, Bernice Lane off Blue Ridge Drive
- HIDDEN VALLEY PARK, Highland Avenue at Merrithew Drive
- HOLIDAY HIGHLANDS PARK, Fig Tree Lane and East Woodbury Lane
- JOHN MUIR PARK, Vista Way and Pine Street, adjacent to John Muir School
- MORELLO SCHOOL PARK, Morello Avenue and Joey Garcia Drive
- MOUNTAIN VIEW PARK, adjacent to Parkway Drive off Howe Road
- PLAZA IGNACIO PARK, Alhambra Avenue and Henrietta Street
- SUSANA PARK, Susana Street and Estudillo Street

MARYSVILLE

LODGING

HOLIDAY LODGE
530 10th St (95901)
Rates: $29-$38;
Tel: (916) 742-7147

MARYSVILLE MOTOR LODGE
904 E St (95901)
Rates: $32-$40;
Tel: (916) 743-1531

McCLOUD

LODGING

STONEY BROOK INN BED & BREAKFAST
309 W Colombero Dr (96057)
Rates: $20-$70;
Tel: (916) 964-2300; (800) 369-6118

Locate Other Dog-Friendly Activities...Check Nearby Cities

RECREATION

PACIFIC CREST TRAIL to SQUAW VALLEY CREEK HIKE

Beginner/1.0 miles/0.5 hours

Info: When you want a Fido flexer that ends with a bit of creekside cavorting, tickle your toes on this delightful trail which leads to Squaw Valley Creek. The trail escorts you through a grand forest of cedar, Douglas and white fir. For more information: (916) 964-2184.

Directions: From McCloud, take the McCloud Reservoir Road six miles to the junction of the road on the right at the end of Squaw Valley. Drive this road about four miles. The trail crosses the road at the top of the hill.

PACIFIC CREST TRAIL to TROUGH CREEK HIKE

Intermediate/8.0 miles/4.0 hours

Info: This trail will take you through Squaw Valley Creek and continue on to Trough Creek. Wet your paws or just admire the old and majestic forests of cedar, Douglas and white fir, before turning the hound around and heading back the way you came. For more information: (916) 964-2184.

Directions: From McCloud, take the McCloud Reservoir Road six miles to the junction of the road on the right at the end of Squaw Valley. Drive this road about four miles. The trail crosses the road at the top of the hill.

McKINLEYVILLE

LODGING

SEA VIEW MOTEL
1186 Central Ave (95521)
Rates: $45-$95;
Tel: (707) 839-1321

Dogs May Be Unleashed Unless Otherwise Indicated

MENDOCINO

LODGING

BLACKBERRY INN
44951 Larkin Road (95460)
Rates: $90-$160;
Tel: (707) 937-5281

BLAIR HOUSE BED & BREAKFAST
45110 Little Lake St (95460)
Rates: $75-$130;
Tel: (707) 937-1800

**L.L. MENDOCINO COTTAGES-
VACATION HOMES & B&B**
10940 Lansing St (95460)
Rates: $131-$191;
Tel: (800) 944-3278

MENDOCINO VILLAGE COTTAGES
45320 Little Lake St (95460)
Rates: $50-$100;
Tel: (707) 937-0866

1021 MAIN STREET INN
44781 Main St (95460)
Rates: $130-$175;
Tel: (707) 937-5150

SEARS HOUSE INN
44840 Main St (95460)
Rates: $55-$110;
Tel: (707) 937-4076

**STANFORD INN BY THE SEA-
BIG RIVER LODGE**
P. O. Box 487, Comptche-Ukiah Rd
& Highway 1 (95460)
Rates: $195-$275; Tel: (707) 937-5026;
(800) 331-8884

RECREATION

CASPAR STATE BEACH - Leashes

Info: This pint-sized beach is ideal for a romp with your pooch, especially if you're traveling from Mendocino to Fort Bragg, or vice-versa. For more information: (707) 937-5804.

Directions: From Mendocino, take Old Highway 1/ Point Cabrillo Road north. Take the Doyle Creek exit to the beach.

GUALALA POINT REGIONAL PARK - Leashes

Info: Walk through a marsh or beside a coastal bluff. Wander among queues of pine and cypress. Or sit back and watch Fido delight in the piles of driftwood and seaweed strewn on the beach. For more information: (707) 785-2377.

Directions: From Mendocino, head south on Highway 1 to just south of Gualala. Turn at the sign for the park and the Sea Ranch Golf Links.

Locate Other Dog-Friendly Activities...Check Nearby Cities

JACKSON DEMONSTRATION STATE FOREST

Info: From educational nature trails to miles of logging roads, relish in 50,000 acres of outdoor adventures. Or further your knowledge of trees by wandering along the popular Tree Identification Trail (located off Highway 20, about 11 miles east of Highway 1). You'll see signs. For more information: (707) 964-5674.

Directions: The forest is located along Highway 20 just east of Mendocino and Fort Bragg to about nine miles west of Willits.

MENDOCINO HEADLANDS STATE PARK/
BIG RIVER BEACH - Leashes

Info: Extraordinary headlands and arched rocks offer dramatic seascapes at this Mendocino Beach. Roam the serpentine trails or romp along clifftop fields. Visit year round and enjoy cool weather and the delightful tang of salt air. For more information: (707) 937-5804.

Directions: For park access, take Highway 1 south from Mendocino, exit at Lansing Street and head west. For beach access, take Highway 1 south and exit at the sign for Mendocino Headlands State Park/Big River Beach.

MERCED

LODGING

BEST WESTERN PINE CONE INN
1213 V St (95340)
Rates: $49-$69;
Tel: (209) 723-3711; (800) 528-1234

DAYS INN-MERCED
1199 Motel Dr (95340)
Rates: $38-$60;
Tel: (209) 722-2726; (800) 329-7466

MOTEL 6-CENTRAL
1215 R St (95340)
Rates: $26-$32;
Tel: (209) 722-2737; (800) 440-6000

MOTEL 6-NORTH
1410 V St (95340)
Rates: $27-$38;
Tel: (209) 384-2181; (800) 440-6000

MOTEL 6-SOUTH
1983 E Childs Ave (95340)
Rates: $26-$32;
Tel: (209) 384-3702; (800) 440-6000

SANDPIPER LODGE
1001 Motel Dr (95340)
Rates: $36-$58;
Tel: (209) 723-1034

Dogs May Be Unleashed Unless Otherwise Indicated

RECREATION

APPLEGATE PARK - Leashes

Info: This 23-acre park is home to more than 60 species of trees. For your daily dose of Rexercise, take the 12-mile bike path.

Directions: Between M & R Streets on the south side of Bear Creek.

BEAR CREEK BIKEWAY - Leashes

Info: 6 acres of open space make for great frisbee retrieving or a bit of leg-stretching.

Directions: Located along Bear Creek from R Street to McKee Road.

BLACK RASCAL CREEK BIKEWAY - Leashes

Info: Make tracks along the pathway in this 20-acre region.

Directions: The park runs along Black Rascal Creek between Bismark Drive and Parsons Avenue.

COURTHOUSE PARK - Leashes

Info: Take furface for a stroll through this charming 6.5-acre parkland, home to the Merced County Courthouse. The Courthouse was built in 1875 and is located smack dab in the center of the park. Its Italianate architectural style was designed by Albert A. Bennet and is a delight to behold.

Directions: Located at 21st and M Streets.

FAHRENS PARK - Leashes

Info: Altogether, this park encompasses 75 acres of tree-filled landscape. 11 acres are developed for those who appreciate the amenities, while 64 acres remain in a natural state.

Directions: Located at Buena Vista Drive and Fahrens Creek.

Locate Other Dog-Friendly Activities...Check Nearby Cities

JOE HERB PARK - Leashes

Info: With a total of 26 acres, there's definitely room for a game of fetch with Fletch. Pick up lunch and picnic with your precious pup.

Directions: Located at Yosemite Parkway and Parsons Avenue.

MCNAMARA PARK - Leashes

Info: Kick back in this lovely 7-acre park and cloudgaze the afternoon away with your canine crony.

Directions: Located at 11th and Canal Streets.

RAHILLY PARK - Leashes

Info: You'll have it made in the shade at this tree-lined park. After one visit you'll understand why Merced has received national recognition as a Tree City USA.

Directions: Located at Parsons Avenue and Flying Circle.

SANTE FE STRIP PARK - Leashes

Info: Let your mutt strut his stuff along the strip in this 14-acre park equipped with a walking path.

Directions: Located at Buena Vista Drive and M Street.

Other parks in Merced - Leashes
- ADA GIVENS PARK, Hawthorn Avenue and Ada Givens School
- BURBANK PARK, Olive Avenue adjacent to Burbank School
- CIRCLE DRIVE PARK, East 23rd Street and Circle Drive
- FLANAGAN PARK, East Cone Avenue
- GILBERT MACIAS PARK, Child Avenue and G Street
- MCREADY PARK, Grogan Avenue and McReady Drive
- STEPHEN LEONARD PARK, 7th and T Streets

Dogs May Be Unleashed Unless Otherwise Indicated

MI-WUK VILLAGE

LODGING

MI-WUK MOTOR LODGE
24680 Highway 108 (95346)
Rates: $45-$95;
Tel: (209) 586-3031; (800) 341-8000

RECREATION

TRAIL OF THE ANCIENT DWARFS HIKE - Leashes

Beginner/2.5 miles/1.25 hours

Info: Age-old dwarf trees are the main attraction of this effortless hike. You'll want to tote your camera for this one- the natural bonsai garden is pawsitively photo worthy. During the summer months, a brochure is available at the trailhead. The same brochure is available year round at the Summit Ranger Station. For more information: (209) 965-3434.

Directions: From Mi-Wuk Village, head east on Highway 108 approximately 15 miles past Pinecrest to Eagle Meadow Road. Turn right, following the signs to the trailhead.

TRAIL OF THE GARGOYLES HIKE - Leashes

Beginner/3.0 miles/1.5 hours

Info: For a quick geology lesson, stroll this easy trail with your gem of a pooch. During the summer months, a brochure is available at the trailhead. The same brochure is available year round at the Summit Ranger Station. For more information: (209) 965-3434.

Directions: From Mi-Wuk Village, head east on Highway 108 approximately 4 miles past Pinecrest to Herring Creek Road. Turn right and proceed to the trailhead.

MIDPINES

LODGING

HOMESTEAD GUEST RANCH
P. O. Box 113 (95345)
Rates: $95-$130;
Tel: (209) 966-2820

LION'S DEN RETREAT BED & BREAKFAST
5125 Chamberlain Rd (95345)
Rates: $75-$110;
Tel: (209) 966-5254

MUIR LODGE HOTEL
6833 Highway 140 (95345)
Rates: $35-$69;
Tel: (209) 966-2468

MILL VALLEY

LODGING

HOLIDAY INN EXPRESS
160 Shoreline Hwy (94941)
Rates: $77-$95;
Tel: (415) 332-5700; (800) 465-4329

RECREATION

BAYFRONT PARK

Info: After an afternoon at this 4-acre dog run area, Rover is sure to have a new #1 for his top ten list. Just follow the signs to hours of leashless fun.

Directions: Take Blithedale Avenue east to Camino Alto and turn left. Follow to Sycamore Avenue and make another left. Park at the end of the cul-de-sac.

Note: Keep your dog leashed from the car to the dog run area.

BLITHEDALE SUMMIT OPEN SPACE PRESERVE - Leashes

Info: Escape from the heat on a redwood shaded trail that leads to Larkspur Creek. For more information: (415) 499-6387.

Directions: Take Blithedale Avenue west until you see a gate and a wooden bridge, just past Lee Street. Park and walk to the preserve.

Note: No leashes needed on fire roads. Public parking not provided.

Dogs May Be Unleashed Unless Otherwise Indicated

CAMINO ALTO OPEN SPACE PRESERVE - Leashes

Info: Take the wide, crest-top fire trail which connects with Mount Tamalpais. Bay laurels, chaparral and madrones line the path overlooking the bay, headlands and surrounding hillsides. For more information: (415) 499-6387.

Directions: Located at the end of Escalon Drive, west of Camino Alto. There are a number of entrances on Camino Alto.

Note: No leashes needed on fire roads. Public parking not provided.

CASCADE CANYON OPEN SPACE PRESERVE - Leashes

Info: Spend a cool afternoon in this redwood forest along the foothills of Mount Tamalpais. Make your way to refreshing Cascade Creek for a little paw dipping. For more information: (415) 499-6387.

Directions: Located at the western end of Cascade Drive.

Note: No leashes needed on fire roads. Public parking not provided.

LOMA ALTA OPEN SPACE PRESERVE - Leashes

Info: Naked hills surround a tree-sprinkled canyon in this pretty preserve. Make your day special with a hike in the shade of oak, bay, laurel and buckeye which grow alongside seasonal White Hill Creek. For more information: (415) 499-6387.

Directions: From Mill Valley, take Highway 101 north to Sir Francis Drake Boulevard, heading west approximately 8 or 9 miles. Turn north on Glen Avenue, following to the preserve at road's end.

Note: No leashes needed on fire roads. Public parking not provided.

OLD MILL PARK - Leashes

Info: Cross the wooden bridge for a leisurely saunter along redwood-lined paths bordering Old Mill Creek. A great escape on hot summer days.

Directions: Located near the public library on Throckmorton Avenue and Olive Street.

Locate Other Dog-Friendly Activities...Check Nearby Cities

RED HILLS SCHOOL SITE

Info: Rover can get his daily dose of exercise at this off-leash dog exercise area. You're sure to meet some locals.

Directions: From Mill Valley, take Highway 101 north to Sir Francis Drake Boulevard, heading west. Turn right on Shaw Drive and follow to the school.

SORICH RANCH PARK

Info: This primitive park combines expansive, low-lying meadows with spectacular hilltop views of the San Francisco skyline, Mount Tamalpais and San Rafael. Summers are hot. Bring your own water. For more information: (415) 258-4645.

Directions: From Mill Valley, take Highway 101 north to Sir Francis Drake Boulevard, heading west. Turn right on San Francisco Boulevard and continue to the park.

STINSON COUNTY BEACH - Leashes

Info: Listen for the cries of gulls as you leash up and head to Dog Beach, a local favorite. For more information: (415) 868-0942.

Directions: From Mill Valley, take Highway 1 south to the Stinson Beach exit. Follow signs to the beach, parking at the far north end of the lot. The Fido-friendly county beach begins at the houses.

MILLBRAE

<u>LODGING</u>

**BEST WESTERN
EL RANCHO INN & SUITES**
1100 El Camino Real (94030)
Rates: $79-$135;
Tel: (415) 588-8500; (800) 826-5500

**CLARION HOTEL-
SAN FRANCISCO AIRPORT**
401 E Millbrae Ave (94030)
Rates: $99-$119;
Tel: (415) 692-6363; (800) 223-7111

COMFORT INN-AIRPORT WEST
1390 El Camino Real (94030)
Rates: $99-$109;
Tel: (415) 952-3200; (800) 221-2222

**THE WESTIN-
SAN FRANCISCO AIRPORT**
1 Old Bayshore Hwy (94030)
Rates: $119-$500;
Tel: (415) 692-3500; (800) 228-3000

Dogs May Be Unleashed Unless Otherwise Indicated

RECREATION

SAWYER CAMP TRAIL HIKE - Leashes

Beginner/4.0 miles/2.0 hours

Info: Take a lakeside ramble on the 2-mile trail in one of the only dog-friendly areas in the vicinity. Be prepared to share your space, this trail is very popular. For more information: (415) 348-7600.

Directions: From Highway 280, exit at Highway 35 (Skyline Boulevard) or Millbrae Avenue. Park on the road.

MILPITAS

LODGING

BEST WESTERN BROOKSIDE INN
400 Valley Way (95035)
Rates: $39-$44;
Tel: (408) 263-5566; (800) 528-1234

BEVERLY HERITAGE HOTEL
1820 Barber Ln (95033)
Rates: $98;
Tel: (408) 943-9080

ECONOMY INNS OF AMERICA
270 S Abbott Ave (95035)
Rates: $39-$49;
Tel: (408) 946-8889; (800) 826-0778

HOLIDAY INN-SAN JOSE NORTH
777 Bellew Dr (95035)
Rates: $95-$145;
Tel: (408) 321-9500; (800) 465-4329

RECREATION

ED R. LEVIN COUNTY PARK - Leashes

Info: It's a bird, it's a plane, it's a hang glider! That's right skygazers, this stunningly beautiful park is home to the Wings of Rogallo hang gliding, an attraction that makes for a unique experience. The sight of a graceful hang glider soaring with the birds is aweinspiring. Of course, the scene on the ground is also something to bark about. Springs flow freely in the southern end of the park and the natural surroundings are irresistible to camera snappers and their canine companions. For more information: (408) 262-6980.

Directions: Take Calaveras Road east to the southern portion of the park.

Note: Entrance fees are posted at the kiosk. Dogs are restricted in some areas. Please heed the signs.

MIRANDA

LODGING

MIRANDA GARDENS RESORT
6766 Avenue of the Giants (95553)
Rates: $45-$175;
Tel: (707) 943-3011

WHISPERING PINES
Avenue of the Giants (95553)
Rates: $40-$65;
Tel: (707) 943-3182

MISSION HILLS

LODGING

BEST WESTERN MISSION HILLS INN
10621 Sepulveda Blvd (91345)
Rates: $59-$72;
Tel: (818) 891-1771; (800) 528-1234

RECREATION

BRAND PARK - Leashes

Info: Take the pooch for a stroll through the memory garden in this lovely 19-acre park.

Directions: At 15174 San Fernando Mission Boulevard.

MISSION VIEJO

LODGING

FAIRFIELD INN BY MARRIOTT
26328 Oso Pkwy (92691)
Rates: $57-$64;
Tel: (714) 582-7100; (800) 228-2800

RECREATION

HOLY JIM HISTORIC TRAIL to HOLY JIM FALLS HIKE

Beginner/2.5 miles/1.5 hours

Info: Set Rover's tail wagging with a delightful creekside sojourn to a glistening waterfall. En route, you'll pass several interesting sights, including the remnants of "Holy" Jim Smith's

Dogs May Be Unleashed Unless Otherwise Indicated

house and an incredible view of Talking Mountain. Check out the fire damaged forest area and Picnic Rock, a cement check dam that creates deep pools for fish. As the name implies, this is a pupular lunch spot for hikers and their hungry hounds. Just beyond Picnic Rock, the trail forks. Take the right fork to the falls. For more information: (909) 736-1811.

Directions: From Interstate 5 in Mission Viejo, head east on El Toro Road. Go south on Live Oak Canyon Road. After passing O'Neill Regional Park, travel about one mile to Trabuco Wash, go left into the wash and up rugged Trabuco Canyon Road. After about five miles, you'll pass a fire station and arrive at the marked Holy Jim turnoff to the left. Park in the dirt area. The trail begins just past the gate.

O'NEILL REGIONAL PARK - Leashes

Info: Hike on 6.5 miles of trails through oak and sycamore forests, lush meadows and rolling hillsides in this verdant 1,700-acre park. For more information: (714) 858-9365.

Directions: Take El Toro Road northeast. The road eventually becomes Live Oak Canyon Road and veers south. From the name change, it's about 3 miles to the main entrance, just south of the Rama Krishna Monastery.

Note: $2 parking fee.

MODESTO

LODGING

BEST WESTERN MALLARDS INN
1720 Sisk Rd (95350)
Rates: $65-$95;
Tel: (209) 577-3825; (800) 528-1234

BEST WESTERN TOWN HOUSE LODGE
909 16th St (95354)
Rates: $44-$58;
Tel: (209) 524-7621; (800) 528-1234

CHALET MOTEL
115 Downey Ave (95354)
Rates: $36-$48;
Tel: (209) 529-4370

HOLIDAY INN HOLIDOME
1612 Sisk Rd (95350)
Rates: $65-$150;
Tel: (800) 334-2030

MOTEL 6-NORTH
1920 W Orangeburg Ave (95350)
Rates: $27-$31;
Tel: (209) 522-7271; (800) 440-6000

MOTEL 6-SOUTH
722 Kansas Ave (95351)
Rates: $26-$30;
Tel: (209) 524-3000; (800) 440-6000

RED LION HOTEL
1150 9th St (95354)
Rates: $98-$141;
Tel: (209) 526-6000; (800) 547-8010

TROPICS MOTOR HOTEL
936 McHenry Ave (95350)
Rates: $32-$48;
Tel: (209) 523-7701

VAGABOND INN
1525 McHenry Ave (95350)
Rates: $38-$57;
Tel: (209) 521-6340; (800) 522-1555

RECREATION

LA GRANGE REGIONAL PARK - Leashes

Info: Explore the primitive reaches of this 750-acre park. Pack your binoculars and witness the noisy rituals of woodpeckers, and the swooping dives of eagles. Take a refreshing riverside hike along the Tuolumne River. Or visit the Old West in historic La Grange. For more information: (209) 525-4107.

Directions: From Highway 132, take the Lake Road exit and follow the signs. Park in the lot. The wilderness area is across the street.

TUOLUMNE RIVER REGIONAL PARK - Leashes

Info: Delight in six miles of undeveloped land. Romp through spacious meadows and oak groves or dangle your feet in the cool Tuolumne River. The area east of Tioga Drive contains the best of the park. For more information: (209) 577-5344.

Directions: Located at the south end of Tioga Drive, off Legion Park Drive.

MOJAVE

LODGING

MOTEL 6
16958 SR 58 (93501)
Rates: $25-$29;
Tel: (805) 824-4571; (800) 440-6000

SCOTTISH INNS
16352 Sierra Highway (93501)
Rates: $35-$55;
Tel: (805) 824-9317; (800) 251-1962

VAGABOND INN
2145 Highway 58 (93501)
Rates: $29-$48;
Tel: (805) 824-2463; (800) 522-1555

WESTERN INN
16200 Sierra Highway (93501)
Rates: $33-$45;
Tel: (805) 824-3601

RECREATION

RED ROCK CANYON STATE RECREATION AREA

Info: This region has more colors than a box of crayons. Unique rock formations and canyons are painted with powerful reds, whites, chocolate browns and muted tans. Spring heralds even more vibrant colors when the wildflowers are in full bloom. Load your Canon with color film. Visit at sunrise or sunset for the best lighting. Stick to the small roads, dogs aren't allowed on the trails. For more information: (805) 942-0662.

Directions: Head northeast on Highway 14 for 25 miles to park.

MONROVIA

LODGING

COMFORT INN
1125 E Huntington Dr (91016)
Rates: $30-$40;
Tel: (800) 221-2222

HOLIDAY INN
924 W Huntington Dr (91016)
Rates: $60-$125;
Tel: (818) 357-1900; (800) 465-4329

OAK TREE INN
788 W Huntington Dr (91016)
Rates: $54-$105;
Tel: (818) 358-8981

WYNDHAM GARDEN HOTEL
700 W Huntington Dr (91016)
Rates: $59-$128;
Tel: (818) 357-5211; (800) 996-3426

MONTARA

LODGING

FARALLONE INN BED & BREAKFAST
1410 Main St (94037)
Rates: $75-$150;
Tel: (415) 728-8200; (800) 350-9777

MONTE RIO

LODGING

ANGELO'S RESORT
20285 River Blvd (95462)
Rates: $50-$150;
Tel: (707) 865-9080

HIGHLAND DELL INN BED & BREAKFAST
21050 River Blvd, P.O. Box 370 (95462)
Rates: $85-$250;
Tel: (707) 865-1759; (800) 767-1759

Locate Other Dog-Friendly Activities...Check Nearby Cities

MONTECITO

LODGING

SAN YSIDRO RANCH
900 San Ysidro Ln (93108)
Rates: $195-$995;
Tel: (805) 969-5046

RECREATION

EAST FORK COLD SPRINGS CANYON TRAIL HIKE

Intermediate/3.5 miles/2.0 hours

Info: Hike in just a short distance and you'll quickly forget your cares. Steep canyon walls and lush vegetation surround you. Do lunch picnic-style while you listen to the creek, the songbirds and the wind whistling through the alders. This is one canyon hike you and the pupster won't soon forget. Gorgeous watering holes and huge flat boulders await a doggie paddler or a sun bather. Go early and make the most of a memorable hike. For more information: (805) 683-6711.

Directions: From Montecito, drive 3 miles north on Hot Springs Road to Mountain Drive. Turn left and continue 1.25 miles to trailhead.

MANNING COUNTY PARK - Leashes

Info: Take a brown bag lunch, a doggie chew and relax your day away at this cool, green oasis. When you want to spend the green, start with some window shopping along Coast Village Road. For more information: (805) 568-2461.

Directions: Go north on San Ysidro Road for about a mile. The park is on the left past the school.

WEST FORK COLD SPRINGS CANYON TRAIL HIKE

Intermediate/3.5 miles/2.0 hours

Info: After the first half-mile, you'll find it hard to believe that you've just left the city behind. This picturesque trail embodies escapism. In minutes you'll find yourself in a canyon of

Dogs May Be Unleashed Unless Otherwise Indicated

incredible riparian vegetation amid pools of refreshing water. Pick a sun-streaked boulder and vege out for the afternoon with a good book for you and a good chew for your puppy pal. If you're feeling energetic, the trail continues to a 200-foot waterfall in the Middle Fork of Cold Springs Canyon. Be prepared for lots of boulder-hopping and wet paws. For more information: (805) 683-6711.

Directions: From Montecito, drive 3 miles north on Hot Springs Road to Mountain Drive. Turn left and continue 1.25 miles to the trailhead.

MONTEREY / MONTEREY PENINSULA

LODGING

ARBOR INN
1058 Munras Ave (94930)
Rates: $79-$119;
Tel: (408) 372-3381

BAY PARK HOTEL
1425 Munras Ave (93940)
Rates: $69-$129;
Tel: (408) 649-1020; (800) 338-3564

BAYSIDE INN
2055 Fremont St (93940)
Rates: $35+;
Tel: (408) 372-8071

**BEST WESTERN-
MONTEREY BEACH HOTEL**
2600 Sand Dunes Dr (93940)
Rates: $59-$199;
Tel: (408) 394-3321; (800) 528-1234

BEST WESTERN-MONTEREY INN
825 Abrego St (93940)
Rates: $63-$113;
Tel: (408) 373-5345; (800) 528-1234

BEST WESTERN-VICTORIAN INN
487 Foam St (93940) Rates: $99-$209;
Tel: (408) 373-8000; (800) 528-1234
(800) 232-4141 (CA)

CANNERY ROW INN
200 Foam St (93940)
Rates: $65-$150;
Tel: (408) 649-8580

COLTON INN
707 Pacific St (93940)
Rates: $69-$110;
Tel: (408) 649-6500; (800) 848-7007

CYPRESS GARDENS INN
1150 Munras Ave (93940)
Rates: $63-$225;
Tel: (408) 373-2761; (800) 433-4732

CYPRESS TREE INN
2227 N Fremont St (93940)
Rates: $52-$185;
Tel: (408) 372-7586

DRIFTWOOD MOTEL
2362 N Fremont St (93940)
Rates: $60-$129;
Tel: (408) 372-5059

EL ADOBE INN
936 Munras Ave (93940)
Rates: $59-$99;
Tel: (408) 372-5409; (800) 433-4732

HOLIDAY INN RESORT
1000 Aquajito Rd (93940)
Rates: $89-$220;
Tel: (408) 373-6141; (800) 234-5697

MONTEREY BAY LODGE
55 Camino Aquajito (93940)
Rates: $49-$139;
Tel: (408) 372-8057; (800) 558-1900

MONTEREY FIRESIDE LODGE
1131 10th St (93940)
Rates: $55-$99;
Tel: (408) 373-4172

MUNRAS LODGE
1010 Munras Ave (93940)
Rates: $79-$149;
Tel: (408) 646-9696

MONTEREY MARRIOTT
350 Calle Principal (93940)
Rates: $150-$170;
Tel: (408) 649-4232; (800) 228-9290

SCOTTISH FAIRWAY MOTEL
2075 N Fremont St (93940)
Rates: $35-$84;
Tel: (408) 373-5551; (800) 373-5571

MOTEL 6
2124 N Fremont St (93940)
Rates: $38-$46;
Tel: (408) 646-8585; (800) 440-6000

WESTERNER MOTEL
2041 Fremont St (93940)
Rates: $35+;
Tel: (408) 373-2911

RECREATION

JACK'S PEAK REGIONAL PARK - Leashes

Info: Set your sights on the 1,000+ foot peak, the highest point on the Monterey Peninsula, and relish in the fabulous views of Carmel Valley, Monterey Bay and the Santa Lucia Mountain Range. Balmy ocean breezes will cool you as you wander along 8.5 miles of diverse paths, including an interpretive trail and the softly cushioned pine trail which begins at Jack Peak's parking lot. For more information: (408) 755-4899.

Directions: From Monterey, head east on Highway 68 for a few miles and turn right on Olmstead Road. Go left on Jack's Peak Road and follow signs to the park.

Note: $2 fee Monday-Thursday; $3 fee Friday-Sunday.

MONTEREY PARK

LODGING

DAYS INN & SUITES HOTEL
434 Potrero Grande Dr (91755)
Rates: $65;
Tel: (213) 728-8444; (800) 329-7466

Dogs May Be Unleashed Unless Otherwise Indicated

MORENO VALLEY

LODGING

MOTEL 6-NORTH
24630 Sunnymead Blvd (92553)
Rates: $30-$34;
Tel: (909) 243-0075; (800) 440-6000

MOTEL 6-SOUTH
23581 Alessandro Blvd (92553)
Rates: $26-$30;
Tel: (909) 656-4451; (800) 440-6000

MORGAN HILL

LODGING

BEST WESTERN COUNTRY INN
16525 Condit Rd (95037)
Rates: $54-$76;
Tel: (408) 779-0447; (800) 528-1234

BUDGET INN
19240 Monterey Hwy (95037)
Rates: $30-$55;
Tel: (408) 778-3341

EXECUTIVE INN
16505 Condit Rd (95037)
Rates: $70;
Tel: (408) 778-0404

INN AT MORGAN HILL
16115 Condit Rd (95037)
Rates: $83-$108;
Tel: (408) 779-7666

MORGAN HILL INN
16250 Monterey Rd (95037)
Rates: $36-$65;
Tel: (408) 779-1900

RECREATION

CHESBRO RESERVOIR - Leashes

Info: Calling all anglers. This narrow reservoir is ideal for dropping a line. Your aquadog is welcome to keep you company on the shore or in your boat. If fishing isn't your forte, you can just float your boat and relax with Max. For more information: (408) 779-9232.

Directions: From Morgan Hill, head west on Edmundson. After crossing the Creek Bridge, make a right on Oak Glen Avenue. Oak Glen snakes around to a stop sign. Take a left at the stop sign, staying on Oak Glen to the reservoir.

UVAS CANYON COUNTY PARK - Leashes

Info: Romp with your best lad along seven miles of oak-shaded trails in this parkland. Sniff out the interpretive one-mile loop trail that skirts Swanson Creek and deposits you and aquapup at a stunning waterfall. Satisfy your exercise-induced appetite with a quiet brown bag lunch at one of the picnic sites that dot the park. For more information: (408) 779-9232.

Directions: From Highway 101, exit at Cochrane Road. Head south on Business 101 to Watsonville Road and turn right (west). Go right on McKean-Uvas Road (past Uvas Reservoir) to Croy Road and turn left. Follow Croy to the park. The last four miles are rough going.

MORRO BAY

LODGING

ADVENTURE INN ON THE SEA
1148 Front St (93442)
Rates: $40-$125;
Tel: (805) 772-5607

BEST VALUE INN
220 Beach St (93442)
Rates: $28-$98;
Tel: (805) 772-3333;
(800) 549-2022 (CA)

BEST WESTERN-EL RANCHO
2460 Main St (93442)
Rates: $39-$99;
Tel: (805) 772-2212; (800) 528-1234

BEST WESTERN-TRADEWINDS MOTEL
225 Beach St (93442)
Rates: $35-$85;
Tel: (805) 772-7376; (800) 528-1234

BREAKERS MOTEL
780 Market St (93442)
Rates: $60-$120;
Tel: (805) 772-7317; (800) 932-8899

COFFEE BREAK BED & BREAKFAST
213 Dunes St (93442)
Rates: $75-$125;
Tel: (805) 772-4378

ECONO LODGE
1100 Main St (93442)
Rates: $38-$105; Tel: (800) 424-4777

GOLD COAST
670 Main St (93442)
Rates: $30-$85; Tel: (805) 772-7740

GOLDEN PELICAN INN
3270 N Main St (93442)
Rates: $40-$125;Tel: (805) 772-7135

MORRO HILLTOP HOUSE
1200 Morro Ave (93442)
Rates: $40-$75;Tel: (805) 772-1890

MOTEL 6
298 Atascadero Rd (93442)
Rates: $28-$42;
Tel: (805) 772-5641; (800) 440-6000

SUNDOWN MOTEL
640 Main St (93442) Rates: $30-$75;
Tel: (805) 772-7381; (800) 696-6928

SUNSET TRAVELODGE
1080 Market Ave (93442)
Rates: $39-$125;
Tel: (805) 772-1259; (800) 578-7878

RECREATION

CAYUCOS STATE BEACH - Leashes

Info: For an afternoon of isolated fun with your pooch, head for the south end of this wide, seaweed strewn beach. For more information: (805) 549-5200.

Directions: Head north on Highway 1/Highway 101 to Cayucos. Go southwest on Cayucos Drive. Turn left at Ocean Drive. Enter anywhere between Cayucos Road and E Street.

MORRO STRAND STATE BEACH - Leashes

Info: Delight in a sandy dune-dotted stroll along this 3-mile state beach.

Directions: Located between Atascadero Road and Yerba Buena Avenue, west of Highway 1.

MOUNT SHASTA

LODGING

ALPINE LODGE MOTEL
908 S Mount Shasta Blvd (96067)
Rates: $31-$89;
Tel: (916) 926-3145; (800) 500-3145

BEST WESTERN TREE HOUSE MOTOR INN
P. O. Box 236, I-5 & Lake St (96067)
Rates: $66-$149;
Tel: (916) 926-3101; (800) 545-7164;
(800) 528-1234

CEDAR POND CHALET
1701 N Old Stage Rd (96067)
Rates: $95+; Tel: (916) 926-3200

EVERGREEN LODGE
1312 S Mount Shasta Blvd (96067)
Rates: $28-$60; Tel: (916) 926-2143

MOUNTAIN AIR LODGE
1121 S Mount Shasta Blvd (96067)
Rates: $36-$125; Tel: (916) 926-3411

PINE NEEDLES MOTEL
1340 S Mount Shasta Blvd (96067)
Rates: $34-$58; Tel: (916) 926-4811

SHASTA LODGE MOTEL
724 N Mount Shasta Blvd (96067)
Rates: $29-$55;
Tel: (916) 926-2815; (800) 742-7821

SWISS HOLIDAY LODGE
2400 S Mount Shasta Blvd (96067)
Rates: $33-$90;
Tel: (916) 926-3446

TRAVEL INN
504 S Mount Shasta Blvd (96067)
Rates: $24-$60;
Tel: (916) 926-4617

VILLAS VACATION RENTAL CABINS
P. O. Box 344 (96067)
Rates: $30-$125;
Tel: (916) 926-3313

WAGON CREEK INN
BED & BREAKFAST
1239 Woodland Park Dr (96067)
Rates: $55-$65;
Tel: (916) 926-0838; (800) 995-9260

Locate Other Dog-Friendly Activities...Check Nearby Cities

RECREATION

BROWN'S NATURE REFUGE - Leashes

Info: Birdwatchers, bring the binocs. This marshland environment is home to many species of feathered friends. Take Fido on one of the two loop trails that lead through the area and see what songbirds you can identify. For more information: (916) 926-4865.

Directions: Located 1.5 miles from Mount Shasta just off W.A. Barr Road on the North Shore Environmental Education Area.

ELLEN TUPPER MINI PARK - Leashes

Info: Dazzle the dawgus with this park's award-winning design. A picnic table and a pure spring water fountain also highlight this lovely little site.

Directions: Located on Lake Street at the train tracks at Mount Shasta Visitors Bureau.

ELSA RUPP NATURE STUDY AREA - Leashes

Info: This uncrowded, peaceful park is situated amidst a pine forest. Enjoy the crisp, clean air as you take pooch-face along an enlightening excursion on the half-mile loop trail where you can check out the native plants and an icy cold stream. For more information: (916) 926-4865.

Directions: Just north of Fish Hatchery on Old Stage Road.

GLASS MOUNTAIN AREA

Info: Get out your geology book and pay attention. Without blending, glassy dacite and rhyolitic obsidian poured from the same volcanic vent and caused a rare geological phenomenon, a glass flow that spans 4,210 acres. You and the dawgus should avoid the slippery, razor sharp obsidian. Yes, it's really a glass mountain. For more information: (916) 964-2184.

Directions: From Mt. Shasta, take Interstate 5 south to Highway 89. Continue for 28 miles to Bartle. Go northeast on Powder Hill Road (Forest Service Road 49) and travel about 29 miles. Take a right on Forest Service Road 97 for about six miles, then go north on Forest Service Road 43N99 to the southern edge of Glass Mountain.

MEDICINE LAKE GLASS FLOW

Info: There are no designated trails, so just make your own way and enjoy the unique geology of this area. Spanning 570 acres, this region is covered with smoothed, prehistoric, stony-gray dacite ranging from 50 to 150 feet deep. The lunar-like surface will make your pooch feel like part of the NASA team. Bring a camera and lots of film. For more information: (916) 964-2184.

Directions: From Mt. Shasta, take Interstate 5 south to Highway 89. Head east for 28 miles to Bartle. Go northeast on Powder Hill Road (Forest Service Road 49) and travel about 33.5 miles (2.5 miles past Medicine Lake turnoff). The glass flow area is just off the road to the left.

MEDICINE LAKE LOOP TRAIL HIKE

Beginner/4.5 miles/2.5 hours

Info: Once the center of a volcano, this ancient crater is now filled with clean, crisp water, surrounded by conifers. A hike around the lake is a great way to spend the day. The route is clear even though there isn't a specific trail. And if you're into shorefishing, each year the lake is stocked with 30,000 brook trout. Nearby, you'll find ice caves that you and your pooch can explore as well as some small lakes. For more information: (916) 964-2184.

Directions: From Mt. Shasta, take Interstate 5 south to Highway 89. Head east for 28 miles to Bartle. Go northeast on Powder Hill Road (Forest Service Road 49) and continue 31 miles to Medicine Lake Road. Follow to the lake.

MOUNT SHASTA CITY PARK - Leashes

Info: This wooded park has the makings for a great picnic. Spread your blanket in the meadow or relax in the gazebo. After lunch, a walk on the trail behind the stream will work off those calories. No dogs allowed in the stream. For more information: (916) 926-3464.

Directions: From Interstate 5, take the Mount Shasta Boulevard exit and head southeast. Turn right at Nixon Road and bear right into the park.

SHASTICE PARK - Leashes

Info: For more active, social parkgoers, this 38-acre expanse offers multi-purpose fields and plenty of picnic tables. Rover can rove over endless acres of open space as he sniffs this way and that way through the park.

Directions: East on Rockefeller Drive and Adams Drive.

MOUNTAIN RANCH

RECREATION

MOUNTAIN RANCH PARK - Leashes

Info: You'll find splendor in the grass lolling with the pupster in this peaceful community park that's dotted with shade-giving mature oak trees. In autumn, the changing leaves add to the park's appeal.

Directions: Located on Mountain Ranch Road.

MOUNTAIN VIEW

LODGING

BEST WESTERN TROPICANA LODGE
1720 El Camino Real W (94040)
Rates: $55-$80;
Tel: (415) 961-0220; (800) 528-1234

RESIDENCE INN BY MARRIOTT
1854 El Camino Real (94040)
Rates: $89-$139;
Tel: (415) 940-1300; (800) 331-3131

RECREATION

COOPER PARK - Leashes

Info: Geared mainly for outdoor sports enthusiasts, this park offers plenty of open space for pooch-walkers to enjoy.

Directions: Located at 500 Chesley Avenue.

CUESTA PARK - Leashes

Info: Dine à la blanket with Bowser at this 32-acre park. Après lunch, burn some calories with an athletic amble.

Directions: Located at 685 Cuesta Avenue.

PIONEER MEMORIAL PARK - Leashes

Info: This 5-acre park is located directly behind the library, so check out a book and relax with the hound under the shade of an old oak tree.

Directions: Located at Castro and Church Streets.

RENGSTORFF PARK - Leashes

Info: Your pooch's passport to fun at this attractive, clean park is a free permit. A copy of Fido's vaccination certificate and license are all you need to obtain a permit from the park's community center. For more information: (415) 903-6331.

Directions: Located on Rengstorff Avenue between Central Expressway and California Avenue.

Note: Hours are 6 a.m. to sunset.

SYLVAN PARK - Leashes

Info: Checkerboard tables and horseshoe pits are just a couple of the amenities you'll find in this pleasant 9-acre park where furry friends can enjoy the great outdoors.

Directions: Located at Sylvan and Devoto Roads.

Other parks in Mountain View - Leashes
- FAIRMONT PARK, Fairmont and Bush Streets
- GEMELLO PARK, Marich Way and Solana Court
- JACKSON PARK, Shoreline Boulevard and Jackson Street
- KLEIN PARK, Ortega and California Streets
- REX MANOR PARK, Farley and Bonny Streets
- SAN VERON PARK, San Veron and Middlefield Roads
- THADDEUS PARK, Middlefield and Independence
- VARSITY PARK, Duke and Jefferson Streets

MT. BALDY VILLAGE

RECREATION

SUNSET PEAK TRAIL HIKE - Leashes

Intermediate/Expert/5.0 miles/3.0 hours

Info: Peak seekers, get geared up for a treat. Some of the best views of Mt. Baldy await you and the dawgus at the top of this trail. In the winter months, this massive peak glistens with seasonal snow, and reflects sunlight in such a way that it always looks blanketed in white. On a clear day, the views of the valley below are spectacular. For more information: (818) 335-1251.

Directions: From the south end of Mt. Baldy Village, turn west and head up Glendora Mountain Road for one mile to Cow Canyon Saddle. Park in the dirt parking lot on your right. Cross the road and walk past the locked gate up the fire road. After two miles, make a sharp left to remain on the road. The fire road will take you to the summit trail.

MURPHYS

RECREATION

MURPHYS PARK AND CREEK - Leashes

Info: Give your wagalong something to bark about with a jaunt to the babbling brook. Visit on a Wednesday in the summer and you might catch an outdoor concert.

Directions: Located on Main and Church Streets.

Dogs May Be Unleashed Unless Otherwise Indicated

NAPA

LODGING

BEST WESTERN INN
100 Soscol Ave (94558)
Rates: $65-$150;
Tel: (707) 257-1930; (800) 528-1234

BUDGET INN
3380 Solano Ave (94558)
Rates: $40-$96;
Tel: (707) 257-6111

ELM HOUSE BED & BREAKFAST
800 California Blvd (94559)
Rates: $60-$130;
Tel: (800) 788-4356

SHERATON INN NAPA VALLEY
3425 Solano Ave (94558)
Rates: $65-$120;
Tel: (800) 325-3535

RECREATION

ALSTON PARK - Leashes

Info: Bring along a fuzzy tennie or a chewed-up frisbee when you visit this area. Fidos can run free in the lower section of this paw-friendly park.

Directions: Located on the south side of Dry Creek Road. The leash-free area is in the lower area of the park off Dry Creek Road.

JOHN F. KENNEDY MEMORIAL PARK

Info: Frolic with your furball in the undeveloped acres of this park or hike the dirt trail beside the river. In summer, bring lots of drinking water.

Directions: Take Highway 221 to Streblow Drive and follow the signs past the Napa Municipal Golf Course and Napa Valley College to the boat marina/launch area. Park in the lot and look for the riverside trail.

SHURTLEFF PARK

Info: Delight in a day of unleashed fun at this canine-friendly park. On hot summer days, loll in the shade of the fir and eucalyptus trees.

Directions: Located on Shelter Street at Shurtleff, adjacent to Phillips Elementary School.

NATIONAL CITY

LODGING

E-Z 8 MOTEL
607 Roosevelt St (92050)
Rates: $35-$50;
Tel: (619) 575-8808; (800) 326-6835

E-Z 8 MOTEL
1700 E Plaza (92050)
Rates: $35-$50;
Tel: (619) 474-6491; (800) 326-6835

HOLIDAY INN-SOUTH BAY
700 National City Blvd (91950)
Rates: $55;
Tel: (619) 474-2800; (800) 465-4329

RADISSON SUITES NATIONAL CITY
810 National City Blvd (91950)
Rates: $55-$69;
Tel: (619) 336-1100; (800) 333-3333

NEEDLES

LODGING

BEST MOTEL
1900 W Broadway (92363)
Rates: $21-$30;
Tel: (619) 326-3824

**BEST WESTERN-
COLORADO RIVER INN**
2271 W Broadway (92363)
Rates: $40-$60;
Tel: (619) 326-4552; (800) 528-1234

DAYS INN
1111 Pashard St (92363)
Rates: $40-$65;
Tel: (619) 326-5660; (800) 329-7446

IMPERIAL 400 MOTOR INN
644 Broadway (92363)
Rates: $28-$38;
Tel: (619) 326-2145

MOTEL 6-NORTH
1420 J St (92363)
Rates: $25-$29;
Tel: (619) 326-3399; (800) 440-6000

MOTEL 6-SOUTH
1215 Hospitality Ln (92363)
Rates: $25-$29;
Tel: (619) 326-5131; (800) 440-6000

OLD TRAILS INN BED & BREAKFAST
304 Broadway (92363)
Rates: $40-$65;
Tel: (619) 326-3523

RIVER VALLEY MOTOR LODGE
1707 W Broadway (92363)
Rates: $21-$34;
Tel: (619) 326-3839;
(800) 346-2331 (CA)

Dogs May Be Unleashed Unless Otherwise Indicated

RECREATION

JACK SMITH PARK - Leashes

Info: Roll in and hang out by the Colorado River. Spend an afternoon in the sun-splashed landscape.

Directions: Located at the south end of Bridge Road on the Colorado River.

MOABI REGIONAL PARK/PARK MOABI - Leashes

Info: An afternoon of fun can be yours at this pretty 1,027-acre park. Rent a houseboat and leave the crowds behind as you pursue a wet and wild adventure on the Colorado River. Or just investigate the interesting desert terrain. For more information: (619) 326-3831.

Directions: Located at the intersection of Interstate 40 and Park Moabi Road.

Note: $6 vehicle fee, $1 dog fee.

OLD TRAILS MONUMENT PARK - Leashes

Info: A restored Borax wagon is the highlight of this petite park. Take a leg-stretching break and check it out.

Directions: Located at Broadway and A Streets.

ROADSIDE REST - Leashes

Info: Saunter with your sidekick through the turfed area complete with plenty of shade trees for those toasty afternoons. Railroad devotees can make tracks and have a look-see at several Santa Fe Railroad cars and a caboose.

Directions: Located on Front Street between J and K Streets.

SANTA FE PARK - Leashes

Info: Bench it with Bowser under the shade of towering trees, or sniff out the WWI cannon.

Directions: Located on Front Street between G and F Streets.

NEVADA CITY

LODGING

NEVADA STREET COTTAGES
690 Nevada St (95959)
Rates: $60-$100;
Tel: (916) 265-8071

RECREATION

BULLARDS BAR TRAIL HIKE

Beginner/1.0- 7.0 miles/0.5- 3.5 hours

Info: This popular "do your own thing" trail follows the Bullards Bar Reservoir shoreline. Swim, fish or just dawdle along, there's something for everyone on this relatively flat hike. Ponderosa pine and Douglas fir shade parts of the trail. For more information: (916) 288-3231.

Directions: From Nevada City, take Highway 49 north to Marysville Road (County Road # E 20). Turn west (left) for 2.7 miles to the Dark Day Picnic Area/Boat Ramp turnoff. Make a right for .5 miles, veer left at the fork and continue on to the picnic area and trailhead.

ROCK CREEK NATURE TRAIL HIKE - Leashes

Beginner/0.75 miles/0.5 hours

Info: Before starting out on this interesting trail through various ecosystems, pick up a brochure and make leg stretching time more enjoyable . Pay close attention, you and the sniffer may sniff out some unusual species. By the end of your stroll, you'll be able to identify banana slug, lichens, madrones and much more. For more information: (916) 272-7222.

Directions: From Nevada City, head east 6 miles on Highway 20. Look for the Washington Ridge Conservation Camp sign on the left. Turn and follow the paved road for one mile. Go left onto a gravel road and proceed one mile into the canyon and parking lot.

Dogs May Be Unleashed Unless Otherwise Indicated

ROUND LAKE TRAIL HIKE

Expert/4.5 miles/3.0 hours

Info: Lakes, lakes and more lakes. This trail is heaven for all water-loving pups who are in tip-top shape. Beginning at Feely Lake, the rigorous trail heads east past several picturesque lakes before ending at Milk Lake. The shimmering, blue waters of the trail's lakes make the challenging and sometimes steep hike worth the effort. For more information: (916) 265-4531.

Directions: From Nevada City, take Highway 20 east approximately 22 miles to Bowman Lake Road. Head north on Bowman Lake Road to the sign for Lindsey Lake, Feely Lake, Carr Lake. Go right, following the signs to Carr Lake. Park and walk to the trailhead at Feely Lake.

NEWARK

LODGING

MOTEL 6
5600 Cedar Ct (94560)
Rates: $28-$34;
Tel: (510) 791-5900; (800) 440-6000

WOODFIN SUITES
39150 Cedar Blvd (94560)
Rates: $79-$84;
Tel: (510) 795-1200; (800) 237-8811

NEWBURY PARK

LODGING

MOTEL 6
1516 Newbury Rd (91320)
Rates: $30+;
Tel: (805) 499-0711; (800) 440-6000

NEWHALL

RECREATION
WILLIAM S. HART TRAIL HIKE - Leashes
Beginner/2.0 miles/1.0 hours

Info: Return to the days of yesteryear, to the time of cowboys and Indians on this pleasant hike. The trail loops around the ranch of William S. Hart, one of the early silent screen actors. The hills above the hacienda offer views of the Santa Clara Valley. Westies might recognize the surroundings, many a western was filmed on the ranch. For more information: (805) 259-0855.

Directions: From Newhall, exit Antelope Valley Freeway at San Fernando Road and drive west approximately 1.5 miles to Newhall Avenue. Make a left and follow to Market Street. Turn left to the senior citizens center. The signed trailhead is accessed from the parking lot.

NEWPORT BEACH

LODGING

BALBOA INN
105 Main St (92661)
Rates: $90-$160;
Tel: (714) 675-3412

**FOUR SEASONS HOTEL-
NEWPORT BEACH**
690 Newport Center Dr (92660)
Rates: $205-$305;
Tel: (714) 759-0808; (800) 332-3442
(800) 268-6282 (CAN)

HYATT NEWPORTER
1107 Jamboree Rd (92660)
Rates: $164-$194;
Tel: (714) 729-1234; (800) 233-1234

**NEWPORT BEACH MARRIOTT
HOTEL & TENNIS CLUB**
900 Newport Center Dr (92660)
Rates: $109-$139;
Tel: (714) 640-4000; (800) 228-9290

NEWPORT BEACH MARRIOTT SUITES
500 Bayview Cir (92660)
Rates: $119-$139;
Tel: (714) 854-4500; (800) 228-9290

OAKWOOD CORPORATE HOUSING
880 Irvine Ave (92663)
Rates: $31-$60;
Tel: (714) 574-3725; (800) 456-9351

RECREATION

BALBOA BEACH - Leashes

Info: When the time is right, delight in a morning oceanside jaunt or an early evening sea-misted sojourn with your pooch. Dogs are only permitted on the beach before 9 a.m. and after 5 p.m. and not at all from June 15 to September 15.

Directions: The beach stretches from Main Street to the West Jetty area.

CORONA DEL MAR STATE BEACH - Leashes

Info: Start your day with a brisk pre-breakfast hike along this city beach. Pups are only permitted on the beach before 9 a.m. and after 5 p.m. and not at all from June 15 to September 15. For more information: (714) 644-3047.

Directions: The beach begins at the eastern jetty at the entrance to Newport Harbor.

NEWPORT HARBOR AND NEWPORT DUNES - Leashes

Info: Newport has been called one of the finest and most scenic small boat harbors in the world. This gives water-loving canines something to bark about. The harbor winds its way back to the dunes, a favorite sandy spot complete with hiking trails. For more information: (714) 723-4511.

Directions: The Newport Harbor Office is located in Newport Beach at 1901 Bayside Drive.

UPPER NEWPORT BAY REGIONAL PARK - Leashes

Info: Unpack those binoculars and look to the skies. You'll catch sight of the soaring birds which inhabit this park, especially from Back Bay Road on the east side of the bay. Don't forget about Fido - he'll be anxious for a hilly adventure along the park's dirt trails. For more information: (714) 640-6746.

Directions: From northbound Irvine Avenue, turn right on University Drive. The entrance is on the south side, but you have to park on the north side of the street.

Locate Other Dog-Friendly Activities...Check Nearby Cities

NICE

LODGING

TALLEY'S FAMILY RESORT
3827 E Hwy 20 (95464)
Rates: $50-$85;
Tel: (707) 274-1177

NORTH BLOOMFIELD

RECREATION

MISSOURI BAR TRAIL HIKE

Expert/3.4 miles/2.0 hours

Info: When the hot weather doldrums are wearing you down, make tracks for this cool, serenity-enhanced hike. Be prepared for a high-energy workout along this trail to the South Yuba River. After you and Frisky wind through shady forests of black oak, ponderosa pine, incense cedar and Douglas fir, kick back riverside with some paw dipping in the shallow sections of the South Yuba. Or head upstream and immerse yourself in the deep pools you'll find there. Two paws up for this one. For more information: (916) 265-4538.

Directions: From North Bloomfield, head east on Relief Hill Road toward the town of Washington. Go approximately one of a mile and look for the sign that directs you to the trailhead.

NORTH HIGHLANDS

LODGING

MOTEL 6
4600 Watt Ave (95660)
Rates: $33-$39;
Tel: (916) 973-8637; (800) 440-6000

RODEWAY INN
3425 Orange Grove Ave (95660)
Rates: $40-$65;
Tel: (800) 424-4777

Dogs May Be Unleashed Unless Otherwise Indicated

NORTH HOLLYWOOD

<u>**RECREATION**</u>
NORTH HOLLYWOOD PARK and RECREATION CENTER - Leashes

Info: Head for the section of the park that's south of Magnolia Boulevard where tall shade trees, meadows and a jogging trail will make your visit more pleasurable. For more information: (818) 763-7651.

Directions: From Highway 170, take the Magnolia Boulevard exit east for one block. Turn right on Tujunga Avenue to the park.

NORTH WEDDINGTON PARK - Leashes

Info: This 11-acre urban park offers neighborhood pooches a place to stretch or fetch.

Directions: Located at 10844 Acama Street.

SOUTH WEDDINGTON PARK - Leashes

Info: Romp with Rover along 12 acres of open space. Or pack a basket for your Basset and soak up some California sunshine as furface nibbles on some kibble.

Directions: Located at Valley Heart and Bluffside.

NORTHRIDGE

<u>**RECREATION**</u>
DEARBORN PARK - Leashes

Info: Catch a local game of hoops as you and the mutt munch on lunch in this 9-acre neighborhood park.

Directions: Located at 17141 Nordhoff Street.

LIMEKILN CANYON PARK - Leashes

Info: 133 acres of barely developed land spell a doggone good time for pooches who prefer to pound their paws off the beaten path. Pack a snack and spend some quality time with your loving Lassie in this expansive and scenic park.

Directions: Located at 10300 Limekiln Canyon Road.

PORTER RIDGE PARK - Leashes

Info: Open space and careful landscaping make this 10-acre park a delightful place for Bowser to browser.

Directions: Located at Reseda and Sesnon Boulevard.

VANALDEN PARK - Leashes

Info: Take a break from your busy day and do lunch with the dawgus at this 10-acre neighborhood park.

Directions: Located at 8956 Vanalden.

VIKING PARK - Leashes

Info: This 5.5-acre park is the ideal spot for Spot's constitutional.

Directions: Located at Viking and Nau.

WILBUR-TAMPA PARK - Leashes

Info: Pack a frisbee, a couple of biscuits, a playful attitude and spend some quality time with your favorite furball on the landscaped grounds of this 8.5-acre green scene.

Directions: Located at 12001 Wilbur Avenue.

NORWALK

<u>**LODGING**</u>

ECONO LODGE
12225 E Firestone Blvd (90650)
Rates: $39-$49;
Tel: (800) 424-4777

MOTEL 6
10646 E Rosecrans Ave (90650)
Rates: $30-$34;
Tel: (310) 864-2567; (800) 440-6000

Dogs May Be Unleashed Unless Otherwise Indicated

NOVATO

<u>LODGING</u>

DAYS INN
8141 Redwood Blvd (94945)
Rates: $39-$59;
Tel: (415) 897-7111; (800) 329-7466

RUSH CREEK TRAVELODGE
7600 Redwood Blvd (94945)
Rates: $55-$65;
Tel: (415) 892-7500; (800) 578-7878

<u>RECREATION</u>

DEER ISLAND OPEN SPACE PRESERVE - Leashes

Info: Even a droopy snoopy will love this shaded trail. Enjoy the easy 1.8-mile loop above marshlands and ponds. For more information: (415) 499-6387.

Directions: Head east on San Marin Drive/Atherton Avenue for 1.5 miles, turn right on Olive Avenue, then left on Deer Island Lane. Park in the lot by the trailhead.

INDIAN VALLEY OPEN SPACE PRESERVE - Leashes

Info: There's plenty of wide open, shaded terrain for all those canines who long for hours of unbridled dogplay. For more information: (415) 499-6387.

Directions: Travel west on DeLong Avenue, which becomes Diablo Avenue, turn left on Hill Road, right on Indian Valley Road and follow to the park. Walk left at the spur road with the sign "Not a Through Street", just south of Old Ranch Road. At the entrance, cross Arroyo Avichi Creek.

LUCAS VALLEY OPEN SPACE PRESERVE - Leashes

Info: Delight in a day of frisbee fetching at this hilly oak-shaded preserve. For more information: (415) 499-6387.

Directions: From Lucas Valley Road, go left on Mount Shasta Drive, then right on Vogelsang Drive. Park near the dead end.

MOUNT BURDELL OPEN SPACE PRESERVE - Leashes

Info: Traipse through nearly 10 miles of paths in the largest open space preserve in Marin county. Try the Bay Area Ridge Trail and snake your way through fields of grass and oak. Or pick up the trail starting at San Andreas Drive. There's a seasonal creek about .2 miles into the hike. For more information: (415) 499-6387.

Directions: From San Marin Drive, turn north on San Andreas Drive. Park on the street.

OAK VIEW

LODGING

OAKRIDGE INN
780 N Ventura Ave (93022)
Rates: $50-$100;
Tel: (805) 649-4018

OAKDALE

RECREATION

CHILDREN'S PLAY PARK - Leashes

Info: This park has a little something for everyone. Music mutts, in July and August there are free concerts every Thursday evening.

Directions: Located at the corner of A and Second Streets.

WOODWARD RESERVOIR - Leashes

Info: 23 miles of shoreline spell fun for you and Fido. Hot-diggety dogs will love the cold water on their toasty paws. For more information: (209) 847-3304.

Directions: Located at 26 Mile Road.

OAKHURST

LODGING

**BEST WESTERN-
YOSEMITE GATEWAY INN**
40530 Hwy 41 (93644)
Rates: $44-$82;
Tel: (209) 683-2378; (800) 528-1234

COMFORT INN
40489 Hwy 41 (93644)
Rates: $80;
Tel: (209) 683-8282; (800) 221-2222

PINE ROSE INN BED & BREAKFAST
41703 Road 222 (93644)
Rates: $40-$100;
Tel: (209) 642-2800

RAMADA LIMITED
48800 Royal Oaks Dr (93644)
Rates: $85;
Tel: (209) 658-5500; (800) 272-6232

RECREATION

LEWIS CREEK NATIONAL RECREATION TRAIL HIKE - Leashes

Intermediate/7.3 miles/4.0 hours

Info: When you and the dawgus are seeking beauty and serenity, set your sights on this splendidly peaceful trail. You'll saunter amid forestlands of mixed conifer and black and live oak. You'll also encounter Pacific dogwood and western azalea which add a delightful scent to the air and magnificent colors to the landscape in spring and early summer. The shaded coolness and fragrance of the trail make this outdoor excursion a soothing alternative to just about anything. Pack a picnic lunch, you'll be certain to find many alfresco spots along the way. Plan a visit May through November. Snows often close access roads in winter. For more information: (209) 683-4665.

Directions: From the middle of Oakhurst, turn right on Sky Ranch Road #632 and travel approximately 5 miles to Road #6S47Y. Turn left on #6S47Y, following to where it intersects Road #6S90 and keep right. Continue to the "Y" and keep left. Follow the road to the trailhead at the campground.

NELDER GROVE OF GIANT SEQUOIAS AREA - Leashes

Info: This area encompasses 1,540 acres and contains 101 mature giant sequoias which share the land with a forest of second growth pine, fir and incense cedar. In order to preserve the uniqueness and historical significance of the giant sequoias and the life that thrives beneath their branches, this area has been left in a very natural state. There are no crowds blocking the view of these magnificent giants. An Interpretive Center near Nelder Grove Campground contains interesting displays. There are several trails bound to please you and your tree sniffer. For more information: (209) 683-4665.

Directions: From the middle of Oakhurst turn right on Sky Ranch Road #632 and go approximately 5 miles to Road #6S47Y. Turn left on #6S47Y, following to where it intersects Road #6S90. Go left for one mile to the Shadow of the Giants Nature Trail.

SHADOW OF THE GIANTS NATIONAL RECREATIONAL TRAIL HIKE - Leashes

Beginner/2.0 miles/1.0 hours

Info: Impress your pooch with a stroll on this self-guided trail, located in the southwest corner of Nelder Grove of Giant Sequoias Historical Area. Signs along the path tell the story of the giant sequoias as you amble through woodlands along the banks of Nelder Creek.

Additional trails: If you and your forest Fido are up to more, there's a trail to the Graveyard of the Giants which can be accessed from Nelder Grove Campground. This small grove of immense sequoias was destroyed by a wildfire, an unusual occurrence since the tree's thick bark usually protects them from injury. On a nearby ridge, you'll find a group of sequoias known as "Granddad and the Kids." This enchanting little grouping evokes tender thoughts. Beneath an isolated mature sequoia with one huge branch outstretched like a protective arm, there stand several young sequoias. Another trail, this one from the lower part of the campground leads to the Bull Buck Tree, once a contender for the title of the world's largest tree, with a height of 246 feet and a circumference at ground level of 99 feet. For more information: (209) 683-4665.

Directions: From the middle of Oakhurst, head north on Highway 41 to the Cedar Valley turnoff. Stay on the main road until you see the sign for the trail.

Dogs May Be Unleashed Unless Otherwise Indicated

OAKLAND

LODGING

CLARION SUITES HOTEL-LAKE MERRITT
1800 Madison St (94612)
Rates: $89-$169;
Tel: (510) 832-2300; (800) 933-4683

DAYS INN-OAKLAND AIRPORT
8350 Edes Ave (94621)
Rates: $59-$84;
Tel: (800) 329-7466

HAMPTON INN-OAKLAND AIRPORT
8485 Enterprise Way (94621)
Rates: $64-$75;
Tel: (800) 426-7866

HILTON-OAKLAND AIRPORT
1 Hegenberger Rd (94621)
Rates: $115-$595;
Tel: (510) 635-5000; (800) 445-8667

HOLIDAY INN-OAKLAND AIRPORT
500 Hegenberger Rd (94621)
Rates: $79-$105;
Tel: (510) 562-5311; (800) 465-4329

MOTEL 6
8480 Edes Ave (94621)
Rates: $36-$42;
Tel: (510) 638-1180; (800) 440-6000

MOTEL 6
1801 Embarcadero (94606)
Rates: $45-$51;
Tel: (510) 436-0103; (800) 440-6000

PARC LANE HOTEL
1001 Broadway (94607)
Rates: 105-$150;
Tel: (800) 338-1338

**TRAVELODGE-
OAKLAND AT CHINATOWN**
423 7th St (94607)
Rates: $45-$159;
Tel: (800) 578-7878

RECREATION

BORT MEADOW TRAIL HIKE

Intermediate/5.5 miles/3.0 hours

Info: Once you climb out of Bort Meadow, a kaleidoscope of nature is yours to explore. Start with some stunning ridgetop views of Grass Valley, then traverse dense woodlands before descending a 500-foot canyon to a park of amazing redwoods. For more information: (510) 635-0135.

Directions: From Interstate 580, take 35th Avenue and drive east past where 35th Avenue becomes Redwood Road. 3 miles past Skyline Boulevard is the Bort Meadow Staging Area.

BRIONES REGIONAL PARK

Info: You can't go wrong at this pretty, woodsy park. With north and south entrances, this 5,700-acre paradise is like two parks in one. Interested in burning some calories? Head to the north side, it's all uphill. In the mood for rolling hills and shaded canyons? Try the south entrance at Bear Creek. Or wind your way through groves of bay and oak on the Homestead Valley Trail. Unless you're in the middle of rainy season, bring lots of water. Good news for the pupster – his leash is history once you leave the developed areas. For more information: (510) 635-0135.

Directions: From Highway 24, exit at Orinda and go north on Camino Pablo. Turn right on Bear Creek Road. Follow to Briones Road and the park entrance.

Note: $3 parking fee, $1 dog fee. Avoid in summer.

CHABOT REGIONAL PARK / PROCTOR GATE to BORT MEADOW TRAIL HIKE

Intermediate / 13.0 miles / 7.0 hours

Info: This section of the East Bay National Skyline Trail takes you beside a golf course, up a crest and into Chabot Regional Park. Once you reach Stonebridge, be sure not to veer left, the trail continues on to Grass Valley before reaching Bort Meadow. For more information: (510) 635-0135.

Directions: From Interstate 580, take 35th Avenue exit and drive east past where 35th Avenue becomes Redwood Road. A few miles past Skyline Boulevard is the Proctor Gate Staging Area.

Note: $3 parking fee, $1 dog fee.

DON CASTRO LAKE LOOP TRAIL HIKE

Beginner / 1.7 miles / 1.0 hours

Info: This charming lakeside loop passes a popular swimming lagoon and fishing pier before arriving at San Lorenzo Creek. Cross the creek and continue along the southern shoreline. At the end, climb the staircase, hike over the dam and head back to your car. For more information: (510) 635-0135.

Directions: Take Interstate 580 southeast to Castro Valley, exiting at Center Street and turn right. Make a left on Kelly Street and a left on Woodroe to the park. Head towards the West Lawn to the dam and walk in a clockwise direction.

Dogs May Be Unleashed Unless Otherwise Indicated

EAST RIDGE LOOP TRAIL HIKE

Intermediate/4.0 miles/2.0 hours

Info: Even if you have to huff and puff your way to the top of East Ridge, the loop down leads to refreshing Redwood Creek and a luxuriant forest. Begin the loop with a right on Canyon Trail to East Ridge. Take a left on East Ridge and another left on Prince Road to Stream Trail. For more information: (510) 635-0135.

Directions: From Oakland, go north on Interstate 580 to Highway 13 north. Take a right on Redwood Road and proceed for three miles to the park entrance. There is parking at the Canyon Meadow Staging Area on the left.

GRAHAM LOOP TRAIL HIKE

Beginner/0.75 miles/0.5 hours

Info: This short, undemanding trail sweeps through a magnificent redwood forest, perfect for a morning outing with your pup. For more information: (510) 635-0135.

Directions: Follow Highway 13 south (pay attention to the signs) for 3 miles to Joaquin Miller Road. Head east on Joaquin Miller to Skyline Boulevard and turn left. Continue one mile to park entrance.

GRASS VALLEY LOOP TRAIL HIKE

Beginner/2.8 miles/1.5 hours

Info: Your dog's tail will wag away on this excursion. Surrounded by mountains, Grass Valley is a meadow of peaceful beauty. Visit in the spring and feast your eyes on wild grasses and golden poppies. Take the Grass Valley Trail at the Bort Meadow Trailhead south through Grass Valley and on to Stone Bridge. Return north on the Brandon Trail. For more information: (510) 635-0135.

Directions: From Interstate 580, take 35th Avenue and drive east past where 35th Avenue becomes Redwood Road. 3 miles past Skyline Boulevard is the Bort Meadow Staging Area.

LEONA HEIGHTS REGIONAL OPEN SPACE - Leashes

Info: You and the canine can carouse in a pristine canyon in this 271-acre parkland. Pack some snacks and tote some water, the park is undeveloped. For more information: (510) 562-7275.

Directions: Access from a staging area on Campus Drive off Keller Avenue east of Interstate 580 in Oakland.

MARTIN LUTHER KING JR. REGIONAL SHORELINE - Leashes

Info: Expansive and educational, this 1,220-acre park beside the Oakland International Airport offers plenty of pupportunities for you and Fido. The 50-acre Arrowhead Marsh is a stopping point for migratory birds (hence the leashes) and is part of the Western Hemisphere Shorebird Reserve Network. Picnic areas and pathways are abundant in the region, each having a unique feature or viewing vista. For more information: (510) 562-7275.

Directions: Take Doolittle Drive to Swan Way and turn left. Look for a park road leading north from Swan Way. At the end of the road is the Arrowhead Marsh picnic area. There are several other access points off both Doolittle Drive and Edgewater Drive.

REDWOOD REGIONAL PARK

Info: Spend an exhilarating afternoon hiking and swimming at this gorgeous paw-friendly park. The downhill Stream Trail deposits you at the canyon bottom. When you emerge from the depths of the canyon get set for a wet and wild adventure in the park's lovely watering holes. Take special note of the amazing 150-foot redwood trees scattered throughout the grounds. For more information: (510) 635-0135.

Directions: Head east on Joaquin Miller Road. Turn right on Skyline Boulevard for about four miles to the entrance. There is no parking fee at this entrance.

Note: Dogs must be leashed in developed areas. $3 Parking fee; $1 dog fee.

Dogs May Be Unleashed Unless Otherwise Indicated

REDWOOD REGIONAL PARK /
MACDONALD GATE to SKYLINE GATE TRAIL HIKE

Intermediate/10.0 miles/5.5 hours

Info: Avoid the cyclists by taking the French Trail. You'll start with a 200-foot drop, then a 400-foot climb up the canyon along the redwood-lined Stream Trail. For more information: (510) 635-0135.

Directions: From Interstate 580 in Oakland, take 35th Avenue east past where 35th Avenue becomes Redwood Road. A few miles past Skyline Boulevard is the McDonald Gate Staging Area.

Note: $3 parking fee, $1 dog fee.

ROBERTS REGIONAL RECREATIONAL AREA - Leashes

Info: You and the pupster will have a howl of a good time roaming the grounds in this 82-acre park. Second-growth redwoods shade the area, and hiking trails wind through cool, song-filled forests. For more information: (510) 562-7275.

Directions: The entrance is on Skyline Boulevard one mile north of Joaquin Miller Road.

SIBLEY PRESERVE/SKYLINE GATE through
HUCKLEBERRY PRESERVE TRAIL HIKE

Intermediate/6.0 miles/3.0 hours

Info: Birds serenade you along this wildlife-rich preserve trail. You'll wander amidst a woodland habitat, encounter a 200-foot descent and then a steep 480-foot ascent. For more information: (510) 635-0135.

Directions: Take Highway 24 east to Highway 13 and head south. Or take 580 to Highway 13 and head north. In either case, exit Highway 13 at Joaquin Miller Road and head east to Skyline Boulevard. Turn left and drive to the Skyline Gate Staging Area.

SIBLEY VOLCANIC REGIONAL PRESERVE - Leashes

Info: Lava-sniffers can examine a cross section of a great volcano in this preserve. Folding and erosion caused the Round

Top volcanic complex to tilt on its side, permitting today's visitors to gain a rare perspective of volcanism in an outdoor laboratory setting. For more information: (510) 562-7275.

Directions: The entrance is on Skyline Boulevard just east of the intersection with Grizzly Peak Boulevard in Oakland Hills.

STREAM LOOP TRAIL HIKE

Beginner/Intermediate/3.5 miles/2.0 hours

Info: Within minutes of Oakland, a majestic forest of redwoods and a pretty creek can soothe all city weary souls. Head up Stream Trail .25 miles and go left on French Trail. You'll quickly climb 1,000 feet (the tough part of the hike), then turn right and junction with Stream Trail. The rest of the path is a piece of cake and well worth the initial sweat. For more information: (510) 635-0135.

Directions: Take Highway 24 east to Highway 13 south. Make a left onto Redwood Road and drive for three miles to the park entrance. Park on the left at the Canyon Meadow Staging Area.

TEMESCAL REGIONAL RECREATION AREA - Leashes

Info: Slowly recuperating from the Oakland Tunnel Fire in 1991, the park is a popular swimming, fishing, sunning and picnicking area for people and pooches. Eight acres of lawn provide open, grassy frolicking space. For more information: (510) 562-7275.

Directions: At the junction of Highway 24 and Highway 13.

Note: Parking fee; a $1 dog fee.

1. TILDEN REGIONAL PARK
LOMAS CANTADAS TRAIL HIKE to INSPIRATION POINT

Intermediate/6.0 miles/3.0 hours

Info: As always, those who travel down, must eventually climb up. Get inspired at Inspiration Point, with spectacular views of the East Bay's unsullied foothills. For more information: (510) 635-0135.

Dogs May Be Unleashed Unless Otherwise Indicated

Directions: Take Interstate 580 to Highway 24 and head east. Near the Caldecott Tunnel, take Fish Ranch Road and head west to Grizzly Peak Boulevard. Go north (right) to Lomas Cantadas Road. Turn right, then take an immediate left, following the signs to the Stream Train parking area near the trailhead.

2. TILDEN REGIONAL PARK
SIBLEY PRESERVE to LOMAS CANTADAS TRAIL HIKE

Intermediate/7.0 miles/5.0 hours

Info: Birdwatchers, pack your binoculars, this is hawk country. Cross Caldecott Tunnel and find yourself in the land of an extinct volcano - Mt. Round Top. For more information: (510) 635-0135.

Directions: Take Interstate 580 to the Highway and head east. Near the Caldecott Tunnel, take Fish Ranch Road and head west to Grizzly Peak Boulevard. Turn left (south) and drive to Skyline Boulevard and the park entrance. Near the entrance is the parking area and the staging area.

WILDCAT CANYON REGIONAL PARK / INSPIRATION POINT TRAIL HIKE

Intermediate/Expert/14.0 miles/8.0 hours

Info: The first four miles of this popular trail are paved. The trail continues along picturesque Pablo Ridge where you and fur-face are rewarded with sweeping panoramic views. The trail ends with a steep plunge into Wildcat Canyon Park. For more information: (510) 635-0135.

Directions: Take Interstate 580 to Highway 24 and head east. Near the Caldecott Tunnel, take Fish Ranch Road and head west to Grizzly Peak Boulevard. Turn right (north) and go to south Park Road. Turn right and drive one mile to Wildcat Canyon Drive. Veer right and park at the Inspiration Point parking area.

OCCIDENTAL

LODGING

NEGRI'S OCCIDENTAL LODGE
3610 Bohemian Hwy (95465)
Rates: $38-$56;
Tel: (707) 874-3623

UNION HOTEL
3731 Main St (95465)
Rates: $30-$40;
Tel: (707) 874-3555

OCEANSIDE

LODGING

MOTEL 6-EAST
3708 Plaza Dr (92056)
Rates: $36-$42;
Tel: (619) 941-1011; (800) 440-6000

MOTEL 6-NORTH
1403 Mission Ave (92054)
Rates: $32-$38;
Tel: (619) 721-6662; (800) 440-6000

SANDMAN MOTEL
1501 Carmelo Dr (92054)
Rates: $36-$49;
Tel: (619) 722-7661

OJAI

LODGING

BEST WESTERN CASA OJAI
1302 E Ojai Ave (93023)
Rates: $56-$110;
Tel: (805) 646-8175; (800) 528-1234

LOS PADRES INN
1208 E Ojai Ave (93023)
Rates: $50-$115;
Tel: (805) 646-4365; (800) 228-3744

OJAI MANOR HOTEL
210 E Matilija St (93023)
Rates: $50-$100;
Tel: (805) 646-0961

OJAI VALLEY INN
SR 150 (93023)
Rates: $99-$189;
Tel: (805) 646-5511

RECREATION

COZY DELL TRAIL HIKE

Intermediate/3.6 miles/2.0 hours

Info: Set tails a-wagging on this relatively easy hike through towering oak trees. Fall trekkers will be treated to landscapes splashed with color and Fido will go dog wild rolling in piles of fallen leaves. Retrace your steps once you reach Cozy Dell Creek.

Dogs May Be Unleashed Unless Otherwise Indicated

Directions: From Ojai, take Highway 33 north for 8 miles to the trailhead, located near the Friends Ranch Packing House.

FOSTER PARK - Leashes

Info: This 205-acre park borders Casitas Springs and offers a lovely, expansive landscape for active breeds. It's easy to meet your exercise quotient by doing some hill walking or plain old jogging. When the workout's over, relax with Max in the scenic picnic area. For more information: (805) 654-3951.

Directions: Off Highway 33, south of Ojai. Look for signs.

GENE MARSHALL PIEDRA BLANCA TRAIL to TWIN FORKS CAMP HIKE

Intermediate/6.0 miles/3.0 hours

Info: Enrich your memory banks on this delightful hike through puppy paradise. About a mile into your journey, you'll encounter the Piedra Blanca Rocks. These large sandstone formations are majestic and relatively easy to explore if you stay in sections that are flat and only slightly sloping. Enjoy some waterful fun with your wet wagger as you stroll streamside under a canopy of shade, serenaded by songbirds. Keep a snout out for the everpresent colorful wildflowers. Once you reach Twin Forks, unpack some snacks and dine with your canine in the shade of a large oak. When you can drag the dogster away, retrace your steps. For more information: (805) 646-4348.

Directions: From Ojai, take Highway 33 north 14 miles to Rose Valley Road. Turn right and follow for 6 miles to Lion Campground. The trail begins across the creek and is not always signed.

Note: During most of the year, be prepared for a wet crossing at Lion Camp to the trailhead.

GRIDLEY TRAIL HIKE

Intermediate/8.6 miles/4.5 hours

Info: A very popular hike to the top of Nordhoff Ridge you'll have to tough it out on the tailkicking last leg of your journey.

But if you go the distance, you'll feel like a ridgetop champ as you ponder the Pacific and the incredible vistas. The views of verdant Ojai Valley backdropped by the Topa Topa and Sulphur Mountains are to die for. You might even catch a glimpse of a rare condor in the Sespe Condor Sanctuary. Bow wow! For more information: (805) 646-4348.

Directions: From Ojai, take Highway 150 (Ojai Avenue) for 2.5 miles to Gridley Road. Turn left and drive about 1.8 miles to road's end and the trail on your left.

HOWARD CREEK TRAIL HIKE

Intermediate/6.0 miles/3.0 hours

Info: Shutterbugs will be buzzing about this trail. The hike is one of the shortest to Nordhoff Ridge where Ojai Valley views and spectacular seascapes abound. Pack your Kodak and Bowser's biscuit basket and gear up for a great day hike. For more information: (805) 646-4348.

Directions: From Ojai, take Highway 33 north to Rose Valley Road. Turn right and drive a half-mile to the trail on the right-hand side of the road.

LIBBEY PARK - Leashes

Info: You'll have 15 oak-dotted acres to wander and gad about with your canine companion. This park is home to the world-famous Ojai Music Festival and Tennis Tournament.

Directions: Located across from the Arcade in downtown Ojai.

MATILIJA TRAIL HIKE

Intermediate/1.0 - 14.5 miles/0.5 - 8.0 hours

Info: For an eye-popping experience, visit in early summer and witness the color extravaganza of the five-foot tall Matilija poppy. If and when you've satisfied your visual senses, take care of the physical senses with a splash or swim in one of nature's pools. Pack a picnic lunch and spend the day. The trail leads to a fire road. After crossing the creek two times, go right

Dogs May Be Unleashed Unless Otherwise Indicated

on the trail that leads away from the road and follows the creek. You'll ascend the canyon, pass Middle Matilija Camp and continue to Maple Camp, FSR6N01 and the Cherry Creek Trailhead for Matilija Trail. For more information: (805) 646-4348.

Directions: From Ojai, take Highway 33 north for 5 miles to Matilija Canyon Road (FR5N13), one mile past the Matilija Hot Springs turnoff. Turn left and drive 5 miles to the locked gate.

MURIETTA TRAIL to MURIETTA CAMP HIKE
Beginner/3.0 miles/1.5 hours

Info: Jumpstart a lazy summer day with a jaunt on this easy one-miler which takes you and the dawgus through a canyon bottom. You'll spend the first half-mile walking along a road until the second stream crossing. After some splish-splashing fun, continue another hundred yards to the trail on your left. If you've packed some snacks, Murietta Camp is the ideal place to partake of an afternoon repast. For more information:

Directions: From Ojai, head north on Highway 33 until you reach Matilija Canyon Road on your left. Drive up Matilija Canyon Road to a locked gate. Hike on the road through private property until you reach the trailhead on your left.

Note: Please keep your dog leashed while on private property.

OJAI VALLEY TRAIL HIKE - Leashes
Intermediate/9.0 miles/4.5 hours

Info: This trail rambles through woodlands and hillsides, farms and rural neighborhoods providing excellent views of the valley east of Lake Casitas. For more information: (805) 646-8126.

Directions: Exit Highway 33 at Casitas Vista Road and follow the signs. Or access from Baldwin Avenue, Santa Ana Boulevard, Barbara Street or the San Antonio Creek.

Locate Other Dog-Friendly Activities...Check Nearby Cities

POTRERO JOHN TRAIL HIKE - Leashes

Beginner/3.2 miles/1.5 hours

Info: Give your wagalong something to bark home about on this pine-scented hike that's perfect for all breeds. You'll be serenaded by songbirds and soothed by the sound of rushing water as you amble up the stream channel to Potrero John Camp. The lush landscape and minor creek crossings provide plenty of opportunities for you and your aquatic pup to chill out while you admire the beauty about you. For more information: (805) 646-4348.

Directions: From Ojai, head north on Highway 33 for 21.4 miles to the trailhead on the right-hand side of the road.

PRATT TRAIL HIKE

Intermediate/8.4 miles/4.5 hours

Info: Get ready for a slice of heaven on this somewhat challenging journey to the ridge just west of Nordhoff Lookout Tower. From your vantage point, the Pacific seems to stretch forever as it meshes with the horizon in the distance. You and Old Brown Eyes can ogle the Ojai Valley, nestled quite beautifully between mountains on either side. Breathe deeply of the crisp pine scented mountain air. Whether you click your Canon or not, you're sure to take home memories of a special, peaceful place. Happy tails. For more information: (805) 646-4348.

Directions: From downtown Ojai, head north on Signal Street. Continue until the road curves and park at the turnout. The trailhead is located left of Signal Street.

REYES PEAK TRAIL HIKE - Leashes

Intermediate/11.6 miles/6.0 hours

Info: Strap on the odometer and tick off some miles on your journey through picturesque backcountry along this trail. You and Fido will find yourselves smack dab in the middle of a landscape of sandstone cliffs and spectacular gorges punctuated by 7,000-foot peaks. From bracing pine scents to stunning vistas, your travels atop Pine Mountain will satisfy your inner cravings for peace.

Dogs May Be Unleashed Unless Otherwise Indicated

After about 100 yards on the old road bed you'll reach the trail on your left. Stay on the north slope to Haddock Peak. The views to the northwest encompass the green lowlands of Cuyama Valley and the sandstone Cuyama Badlands. Point your snouts southwest to see the Sespe River Gorge. Cooled by the shade of white fir, Jeffrey, ponderosa and sugar pine, this trail is enjoyable on those dog days of summer. For more information: (805) 646-4348.

Directions: From Ojai, take Highway 33 north about 33 miles to Reyes Peak Road. Go right and continue past Reyes Peak Campground (near the end of Pine Mountain Road) along a rough road for four miles to the parking area.

SANTA PAULA CANYON TRAIL HIKE - Leashes

Beginner/7.0 miles/3.5 hours

Info: You and the sidekick will be astounded by the aesthetic pleasures that await you on this hike. You can amble along a tree-lined canyon, or have a quick paw dip in a sun-drenched stream. The signs at the beginning of the trail will steer you away from the oil field traffic and past an orchard with a few cows grazing on the grassy meadow. Once past the pipe gate, you'll see the Santa Paula Creek and the trailhead. Time for a waterdog experience and a biscuit break when you head into the canyon where the shade of oak and spruce that dot the landscape will cool and refresh, while the sounds of the river will soothe and calm your senses. For more information: (805) 646-4348.

Directions: From Ojai, head east on Highway 150 for 9.5 miles until you cross the Santa Paula River and reach a wide turnout on the south side of the highway. Look for the sign to the Santa Paula Canyon Trail about 500 feet across the highway.

Note: Due to flooding, check with the Ojai Ranger Station on trail conditions in springtime and during heavy rains.

SOULE PARK - Leashes

Info: If you're really seeking scenery, head for this beautiful county park. It's pretty and packed with activity - a perfect place for fun-loving Rovers who happen to have a soft spot for lovely landscapes.

Directions: Just east of downtown Ojai on Boardman Road.

OLEMA

LODGING

RIDGETOP INN & COTTAGES
9865 Sir Francis Drake Blvd (94950)
Rates: $95-$150;
Tel: (415) 663-1500

ONTARIO

LODGING

COUNTRY INN
2359 S Grove Ave (91761)
Rates: $39-$49;
Tel: (800) 770-1887

COUNTRY SUITES BY CARLSON
231 N Vineyard Ave (91764)
Rates: $62-$72;
Tel: (909) 983-8484; (800) 456-4000

DOUBLETREE CLUB HOTEL
429 N Vineyard Ave (91764)
Rates: $65-$69;
Tel: (800) 582-2946

GOOD NITE INN
1801 East G St (91764)
Rates: $67-$80;
Tel: (909) 983-3604; (800) 724-8822

HOLIDAY INN-ONTARIO AIRPORT
3400 Shelby St (91764)
Rates: $62-$76;
Tel: (909) 466-9600; (800) 465-4329

**HOWARD JOHNSON LODGE-
ONTARIO AIRPORT SOUTH**
2425 S Archibald Ave (91761)
Rates: $40-$53;
Tel: (909) 923-2728; (800) 446-4656

MARRIOTT HOTEL-ONTARIO
2200 E Holt Blvd (91764)
Rates: $59-$79;
Tel: (800) 284-8811

MOTEL 6-EAST
1560 E 4th St (91764)
Rates: $30-$36;
Tel: (909) 984-2424; (800) 440-6000

MOTEL 6-WEST
1515 N Mountain Ave (91762)
Rates: $30-$36;
Tel: (909) 986-9932; (800) 440-6000

ONTARIO INN
5361 W Holt Ave (91763)
Rates: $25-$35;
Tel: (909) 625-3806

**RAMADA LIMITED-
ONTARIO AIRPORT NORTHWEST**
1120 E Holt Blvd (91761)
Rates: $34-$55;
Tel: (909) 984-9655; (800) 272-6232

RED LION HOTEL
222 N Vineyard Ave (91764)
Rates: $62-$82;
Tel: (909) 983-0909; (800) 547-8010

RED ROOF INN
1818 E Holt Blvd (91761)
Rates: $51;
Tel: (909) 988-8466; (800) 843-7663

RESIDENCE INN BY MARRIOTT
2025 East D St (91764)
Rates: $99-$129;
Tel: (909) 983-6788; (800) 331-3131

TRAVELODGE-ONTARIO CENTRAL
755 N Euclid Ave (91762)
Rates: $35-$46;
Tel: (909) 984-1775; (800) 578-7878

Dogs May Be Unleashed Unless Otherwise Indicated

ORANGE

LODGING

DOUBLETREE HOTEL-ORANGE COUNTY
100 The City Dr (92668)
Rates: $130-$170;
Tel: (714) 634-4500; (800) 222-8733

GOOD NITE INN
101 N State College Blvd (92668)
Rates: $31-$60;
Tel: (714) 634-9500; (800) 544-6991

HILTON SUITES-ORANGE
400 N State College Blvd (92668)
Rates: $130-$180;
Tel: (714) 938-1111; (800) 445-8667

RESIDENCE INN BY MARRIOTT
201 N State College Blvd (92668)
Rates: $89-$145;
Tel: (714) 978-7700; (800) 331-3131

RECREATION

IRVINE REGIONAL PARK - Leashes

Info: You and your sidekick can enjoy miles of oak and sycamore shaded trails in this 477-acre park. For more information: (714) 633-8074.

Directions: Take Highway 55 south to Chapman Avenue and go east. Continue to Jamboree and turn left to Irvine Park Road and make a right to the park entrance.

1). IRVINE REGIONAL PARK TRAIL HIKE- Leashes

Beginner/2.0 miles/1.0 hours

Info: Avoid the crowds at the zoo, wildlife exhibits and concession stands and "get away from it all" on the William Harding Nature Trail. Learn about the area on this self-guided tour which eventually loops around the park. For more information: (714) 633-8074.

Directions: Take Highway 55 south to Chapman Avenue and go east. Continue to Jamboree and turn left to Irvine Park Road and make a right to the park entrance.

Note: $2 parking fee on weekdays, $4 on weekends, $5 on holidays..

PETERS CANYON REGIONAL PARK - Leashes

Info: Set tails wagging along a variety of hiking trails, or just vege out and enjoy the peaceful hills, lush willow and cottonwood groves, a rolling creek and a sparkling 50-acre lake in this diverse park. For more information: (714) 538-4400.

Directions: Just west of Jamboree Road and Canyon View.

SANTIAGO OAKS REGIONAL PARK TRAIL HIKE - Leashes

Beginner/2.0 miles/1.0 hours

Info: Even tellie bellies will love this cinchy hike. As you saunter along the self-guided Windes Nature Trail, you'll collect exceptional panoramas. For more information: (714) 538-4400.

Directions: Take Highway 55 south. Go east (left) on Chapman Avenue and continue until intersects with Santiago Canyon Road. Take a right onto Santiago Canyon Road and another right onto Windes Drive. Look for the marked park entrance on Windes Drive.

Note: $2 parking fee.

ORICK

LODGING

ROLF'S PARK CAFE & PRAIRIE CREEK MOTEL
Davidson Rd (95555)
Rates: $28-$35;
Tel: (707) 488-3841

ORLAND

LODGING

AMBER LIGHT INN MOTEL
828 Newville Rd (95963)
Rates: $26-$36;
Tel: (916) 865-7655

ORLAND INN
1052 South St (95963)
Rates: $26-$36;
Tel: (916) 865-7632

ORLANDA INN MOTEL
827 Newville Rd (95963)
Rates: $27+;
Tel: (916) 865-4162

Dogs May Be Unleashed Unless Otherwise Indicated

RECREATION

BIG OAK TRAIL HIKE

Beginner/1.0 miles/0.5 hours

Info: This simple walk takes you along the Stony Creek drainage over the Black Butte Reservoir, providing many glimpses of wildlife and birds in a protected state. During the summer, it can be unbearably hot and very crowded. In spring and fall, the weather is better but the trail can be crowded. For more information: (916) 865-4781.

Directions: From Interstate 5 at Orland, exit at Black Butte Lake. Go west 10 miles on Newville Road, then take a left on Road 206. Continue to Road 200A and the trailhead.

BLACK BUTTE LAKE - Leashes

Info: Seclusion is the main attraction at this lake. You and the dogster can traverse three self-guided nature trails. Try the Buckhorn Trail, an easy 1.5 hour stroll. Or take a left at the fork onto County Road 206 to other marked trails. Visit in the spring to experience the most dramatic landscapes. For more information: (916) 824-5550.

Directions: Take Interstate 5 north and exit at Highway 32/Black Butte Lake. Drive northwest (the road will turn into Road 200) about six miles. When you reach a fork in the road, proceed straight for a couple of miles to park headquarters.

Parks in Orland - Leashes
•LELY PARK, Off County Road 200
•LIBRARY PARK, Bounded by 3rd, Mill, 4th and Yolo
•SPENCE PARK, At Monterey and 4th
•VINSONHALER PARK, At Shasta and East Street

OROSI

LODGING

MAMA BEAR'S BED & BREAKFAST
42723 Rd 128 (93647) Rates: $45-$120;
Tel: (209) 528-3614; (800) 530-2327

Locate Other Dog-Friendly Activities...Check Nearby Cities

OROVILLE

LODGING

BEST WESTERN GRAND MANOR INN
1470 Feather River Blvd (95965)
Rates: $53-$91;
Tel: (916) 553-9673; (800) 528-1234

DAYS INN
1745 Feather River Blvd (95965)
Rates: $55-$60;
Tel: (800) 329-7466

ECONO LODGE
1835 Feather River Blvd (95965)
Rates: $32-$79;
Tel: (800) 424-4777

JEAN'S RIVERSIDE BED & BREAKFAST
45 Cabana Dr (95965)
Rates: $55-$125;
Tel: (916) 533-1413

MOTEL 6
505 Montgomery St (95965)
Rates: $29-$35;
Tel: (916) 984-2424; (800) 440-6000

TRAVELODGE
580 Oro Dam Blvd (95965)
Rates: $45+;
Tel: (916) 533-7070

RECREATION

FEATHER FALLS NATIONAL RECREATION TRAIL HIKE

Intermediate/7.6 miles/4.0 hours

Info: Gear up for a hiking excursion that promises to leave you and the pupster breathless - physically and visually. Feather Falls, the 6th highest waterfall in the continental U.S., is a cascading wonder that sends shutterbugs into a clicking frenzy. The trail to the majestic falls climbs through the Sierra Nevada foothills and parts are quite steep. Once you reach the falls overlook, the huffing and puffing will be replaced by oohing and aahing. The sight is spectacular. In springtime, a wildflower extravaganza makes this a popular hike, while soaring temperatures keep the crowds away in the summer. For more information: (916) 534-6500.

Directions: From Oroville, take Oro Dam Boulevard to Olive Highway. Turn right for about 5 miles to Forbestown Road and go right. Continue for approximately 7 miles to Lumpkin Road. Turn left for about 12 miles to the Feather Falls Trailhead turnoff. Go left at the turnoff for 1.5 miles to the trailhead and Feather Falls Parking Area.

HARTMAN BAR NATIONAL RECREATION TRAIL HIKE

Intermediate/Expert/8.0 miles/4.5 hours

Info: You and Fido will experience an aerobic workout on this trail. Don't be fooled by the gradual descent along the first 2 miles. The last 2 miles involve a steep, switchbacking drop to the Middle Fork of the Feather River at Hartman Bar. Take a breather and enjoy some toe dipping at the river before tackling your uphill trek. For more information: (916) 534-6500.

Directions: From Oroville, head north on Olive Highway to Forbestown Road. Turn right, following for 8 miles to Lumpkin Road. Head northeast on Lumpkin Road to the trailhead approximately 31 miles past Feather Falls.

OROVILLE STATE WILDLIFE AREA / THERMALITO AFTERBAY

Info: Over 5,000 acres of diverse terrain, from forests to marshlands, are yours for the viewing. This is birdwatching heaven, so pack those binoculars. For more information: (916) 538-2236.

Directions: From Highway 162, head south on Larkin Road (just east of the Oroville Airport). After a few miles, make a left on Vance Avenue. The wildlife area is another .75 miles.

Note: Voice control obedience is mandatory.

OXNARD

LODGING

AMBASSADOR MOTEL
1631 S Oxnard Blvd (93030)
Rates: $49;Tel: (805) 486-8404

BEST WESTERN OXNARD INN
1156 S Oxnard Blvd (93030)
Rates: $49;
Tel: (805) 483-9581; (800) 528-1234

CITY CENTER MOTEL
550 S Oxnard Blvd (93030)
Rates: $49;Tel: (805) 486-2522

HILTON INN
600 Esplanade Dr (93030)
Rates: $65;
Tel: (805) 485-9666; (800) 445-8667

RADISSON SUITE HOTEL
AT RIVER RIDGE
2101 W Vineyard (93030)
Rates: $85-$129;
Tel: (805) 988-0130; (800) 333-3333

VAGABOND INN
1245 N Oxnard Blvd (93030)
Rates: $40-$60;
Tel: (805) 983-0251; (800) 522-1555

VILLA MOTEL
1715 S Oxnard Blvd (93030)
Rates: $49;
Tel: (805) 487-1370

RECREATION
OXNARD STATE BEACH - Leashes

Info: After hours of exploring the dune trails within this 62-acre beach, unwind with a picnic lunch. For more information: (805) 358-7995.

Directions: Located at 1601 South Harbor Boulevard, just north of Channel Islands Harbor.

Other parks in Oxnard - Leashes
•CHANNEL ISLANDS PARK, 3800 Block South Harbor Blvd.
•PENINSULA PARK, 3800 Block Peninsula Road.
•WEST BANK PARK, 4100 Block of South Victoria

PACIFIC GROVE

LODGING

ANDRIL FIREPLACE COTTAGES
569 Asilomar Blvd (93950)
Rates: $64-$100;
Tel: (408) 375-0994

BEST WESTERN
LIGHTHOUSE LODGE & SUITES
1150 Lighthouse Ave (93950)
Rates: $59-$109;
Tel: (408) 655-2111; (800) 528-1234

BID-A-WEE MOTEL & COTTAGES
221 Asilomar Blvd (93950)
Rates: $49-$95;
Tel: (408) 372-2330

OLD ST. ANGELA'S INN
321 Central Ave (93950)
Rates: $90-$150;
Tel: (408) 372-3246

OLYMPIA MOTOR LODGE
1140 Lighthouse Ave (93950)
Rates: $50-$90;
Tel: (408) 373-2777

RECREATION
ASILOMAR STATE BEACH - Leashes

Info: From whale watching in the fall and winter to tidepooling year round, you're gonna love this beautiful expanse of craggy coastline. Swimming is not a good idea - strong rip tides exist. For more information: (408) 372-4076.

Directions: Parking located on Sunset Drive, across from the Asilomar Conference Grounds.

Dogs May Be Unleashed Unless Otherwise Indicated

GEORGE WASHINGTON PARK - Leashes

Info: A canine hangout, you're sure to meet the locals and their pooches at this town park. A leashed Fido is welcome anytime. Off-leash hours are sunrise to 9 a.m. and 4 p.m. to sunset. For more information: (408) 648-3100.

Directions: The park is bordered by Short Street, Melrose Avenue, Alder Street and Pine Avenue.

LYNN "RIP" VAN WINKLE OPEN SPACE

Info: Come for canine companionship or a pleasant saunter on one of the many trails. The off-leash hours are sunrise to 9 a.m. and 4 p.m. to sunset. For more information: (408) 648-3100.

Directions: Follow the non-toll section of Seventeen Mile Drive south and go left on Sunset Drive. Turn right on Congress Avenue. After you pass Forest Grove Elementary School on your left, the entrance to a dirt parking area is on your right.

PACIFIC PALISADES

<u>RECREATION</u>

RUSTIC CANYON TRAIL HIKE - Leashes

Intermediate/6.0 miles/3.0 hours

Info: This enchanting trail is everything you crave in an outdoor setting. Despite its proximity to civilization, you'll find yourself in a rugged oasis of striking rock walls, wooded glens and a babbling creek. You and Bowser will boogie to Inspiration Point, branch off on Backbone Trail, drop into Rustic Canyon and then circle back to the trailhead. Along the way, you'll get tails wagging with some splish splashing fun in spring-fed Rustic Creek. From the information kiosk near Inspiration Point, the trail heads left on Backbone Trail. After about 1.5 miles, you'll junction with a 3-way trail intersection. Take the rightmost trail for a steep descent to the canyon bottom. This section of trail crisscrosses the creek and loops back to the park. For more information: (310) 454-8212.

Directions: From Sunset Boulevard in Pacific Palisades, turn north on Will Rogers Road and follow to Will Rogers State Historic Park. The trail begins by the tennis courts, west of park headquarters.

Note: $1 dog fee.

WILL ROGERS TRAIL to INSPIRATION POINT HIKE - Leashes

Intermediate/2.0 miles/1.0 hours

Info: Impress your pooch with some pawsitively staggering views from atop Inspiration Point on this charming park trail. For more information: (310) 454-8212.

Directions: From Sunset Boulevard in Pacific Palisades, turn north on Will Rogers Road and follow to Will Rogers State Historic Park. The trail begins by the tennis courts, west of park headquarters.

Note: $1 dog fee.

PACIFICA

<u>LODGING</u>

DAYS INN
200 Rockaway Beach Ave (94044)
Rates: $75;
Tel: (800) 329-7466

LIGHTHOUSE HOTEL
105 Rockaway Beach Ave (94044)
Rates: $55-$295;
Tel: (415) 355-6300; (800) 832-4777

PACOIMA

<u>RECREATION</u>

RITCHIE VALENS PARK - Leashes

Info: This sports-filled park offers 24 acres of open paw-stomping ground for you and the dawgus to enjoy. Hungry pups might tug at that leash and take off for the picnic area.

Directions: Located at 10736 Laurel Canyon Boulevard.

Dogs May Be Unleashed Unless Otherwise Indicated

ROGER JESSUP PARK - Leashes

Info: This 14-acre park fits the bill for a quick leg-stretching jaunt.

Directions: Located at 12467 West Osborne.

PALM DESERT

LODGING

ALADDIN LODGE
73-793 Shadow Mtn Dr (92260)
Rates: $39-$79;
Tel: (619) 346-6816

CASA LARREA RESORT
73-811 Larrea St (92260)
Rates: $47-$98;
Tel: (619) 568-0311

DESERT PATCH INN
73-758 Shadow Mtn Dr (92260)
Rates: $47-$94;
Tel: (619) 346-9161

EMBASSY SUITES
74-700 Hwy 111 (92260)
Rates: $69-$219;
Tel: (619) 340-6600; (800) 633-2843
(800) 223-1679 (CA)

PALM DESERT LODGE
74-527 Hwy 111 (92260)
Rates: $40-$75;
Tel: (619) 346-3875

RECREATION

IRONWOOD PARK - Leashes

Info: You and the Laddie can commune with nature with a sojourn to this pretty park.

Directions: Located off Chia at Haystack.

MAGNESIA FALLS/PALM DESERT COMMUNITY PARK - Leashes

Info: Spend the afternoon relaxing with your best buddy within the boundaries of this lovely parkland.

Directions: Located on Magnesia Falls at Portola.

PALM DESERT CIVIC CENTER PARK

Info: Run, doggie, run! A fenced-in section provides a leash-free area for frolicking and socializing. Your pup will definitely pant with pleasure if you take him to this park.

Directions: Behind City Hall at 73510 Fred Waring Drive.

Locate Other Dog-Friendly Activities...Check Nearby Cities

PALM SPRINGS

LODGING

AMERICAN HOTEL
1200 S Palm Canyon Dr (92264)
Rates: $30-$54;
Tel: (619) 320-4399

A CASA BELLA HOTEL
650 San Lorenzo Rd (92264)
Rates: $40-$70;
Tel: (619) 325-1487

A SUNBEAM INN
291 Camino Monte Vista (92262)
Rates: $35-$75;
Tel: (619) 323-3812

BAHAMA HOTEL
2323 N Palm Canyon Dr (92262)
Rates: $30-$150;
Tel: (619) 325-8190

BEST WESTERN HOST MOTOR HOTEL
1633 S Palm Canyon Dr (92264)
Rates: $39-$98;
Tel: (619) 325-9177; (800) 528-1234

BEST WESTERN ROYAL SUN HOTEL
1700 S Palm Canyon Dr (92264)
Rates: $60-$100;
Tel: (619) 327-1564; (800) 528-1234

BILTMORE HOTEL
1000 E Palm Canyon Dr (92264)
Rates: $60-$250;
Tel: (619) 323-1811

CASA CODY COUNTRY INN
175 S Cahuilla Rd (92262)
Rates: $40-$160;
Tel: (619) 320-9346

CASA DE CAMERO HOTEL
1480 N Indian Canyon Dr (92262)
Rates: $40+;
Tel: (619) 320-1678

DAYS INN TROPICS HOTEL
411 E Palm Canyon Dr (92262)
Rates: $39-$130;
Tel: (800) 329-7466

DESERT RIVIERA HOTEL
610 E Palm Canyon Dr (92264)
Rates: $22-$85;
Tel: (619) 327-5314

DUESENBERG MOTOR LODGE
269 Chuckwalla Rd (92262)
Rates: $45-$65;
Tel: (619) 326-2567

THE DUNES HOTEL
390 S Indian Canyon Dr (92262)
Rates: $29-$79;
Tel: (619) 322-8789

ESTRELLA INN AT PALM SPRINGS
415 S Belardo Rd (92262)
Rates: $69-$200;
Tel: (619) 320-4117; (800) 237-3687

HILTON RESORT-PALM SPRINGS
400 E Tahquitz Canyon Way (92262)
Rates: $90-$205;
Tel: (619) 320-6868; (800) 445-8667
(800) 527-8020 (CAN)

HYATT REGENCY SUITES PALM SPRINGS
285 N Palm Canyon Dr (92262)
Rates: $99-$219;
Tel: (619) 322-9000; (800) 233-1234

INGLESIDE INN
200 W Ramon Rd (92264)
Rates: $76-$375;
Tel: (619) 325-0046; (800) 772-6655

KORAKIA PENSIONE
257 S Patencio Rd (92262)
Rates: $79-$165;
Tel: (619) 864-6411

LA SERENA BUNGALOWS
339 S Belardo Rd (92262)
Rates: $55-$180;
Tel: (619) 325-2805

MOTEL 6-DOWNTOWN
660 S Palm Canyon Dr (92262)
Rates: $30-$37;
Tel: (619) 327-4200; (800) 440-6000

MOTEL 6-EAST
595 E Palm Canyon Dr (92264)
Rates: $28-$35;
Tel: (619) 325-6129; (800) 440-6000

MUSICLAND HOTEL
1342 S Palm Canyon Dr (92264)
Rates: $25-$50;
Tel: (619) 325-1326

Dogs May Be Unleashed Unless Otherwise Indicated

PEPPER TREE INN
645 N Indian Canyon Dr (92262)
Rates: $20-$55;
Tel: (619) 325-9505

PLACE IN THE SUN
754 San Lorenzo Rd (92264)
Rates: $60-$105;
Tel: (619) 325-0254

QUALITY INN RESORT
1269 E Palm Canyon Dr (92264)
Rates: $39-$169;
Tel: (619) 323-2775; (800) 221-2222

RACQUET CLUB
2743 N Indian Canyon Dr (92263)
Rates: $129-$179;
Tel: (619) 325-1281; (800) 367-0946

RIVIERA RESORT & RACQUET CLUB
1600 N Indian Canyon Dr (92262)
Rates: $45-$195;
Tel: (619) 327-8311; (800) 444-8311

SMOKE TREE VILLA
1586 E Palm Canyon Dr (92264)
Rates: $75-$115;
Tel: (619) 323-2231

TRAMWAY INN
2249 N Palm Canyon Dr (92262)
Rates: $39-$55;
Tel: (619) 325-1406

TUSCANY GARDEN RESORT
350 W Chino Canyon Rd (92262)
Rates: $49-$80;
Tel: (619) 325-2349

RECREATION

IDYLLWILD COUNTY PARK - Leashes

Info: Hop on one of the self-guided nature trails at this spacious 202-acre park and learn a little about the area.

Directions: Go north on Highway 243 for about one mile. The park is located at the north end of County Park Road.

Note: $2/ adult, $1/ child under 12 and $2/ dog day-use fee.

PALM SPRINGS INDIAN CANYONS - Leashes

Info: Spend a day with your dog exploring three beautiful canyons. Be sure to pack some snacks and Perrier to satisfy worked-up appetites. For more information: (619) 325-5673.

Directions: South Palm Canyon Drive dead ends into the gate of the park about 5 miles from the center of Palm Springs.

Note: $5 adult fee.

PALMDALE

LODGING

HOLIDAY INN-PALMDALE/LANCASTER
38630 5th St W (93551)
Rates: $50-$70;
Tel: (805) 947-8055; (800) 465-4329

MOTEL 6
407 W Palmdale Blvd (93551)
Rates: $25-$29;
Tel: (805) 272-0660; (800) 440-6000

Locate Other Dog-Friendly Activities...Check Nearby Cities

RECREATION

DEVIL'S PUNCHBOWL NATURAL AREA - Leashes

Info: You and furface will be bowled over by the spectacular scenery in this 1300-acre park. The 2,000-foot change in elevation creates a cornucopia of plant and animal communities, ranging from desert scrub to pine forest. A mile-long loop dips into the punchbowl and winds through the interesting sandstone formations. The more gung-ho can test their stamina with a challenging 7.5-mile roundtrip hike to the fascinating Devil's Chair. Whatever your pleasure, you'll have a howl of a good time exploring this beautiful region. For more information: (805) 944-2743.

Directions: From Palmdale, take Highway 14 south to Highway 138. Travel east to the community of Pearblossom and turn right (south) on County Road N6 and continue to Devils Punchbowl County Park.

Note: $3 parking fee.

PALO ALTO

LODGING

CARDINAL HOTEL
235 Hamilton Ave (94301)
Rates: $60-$125;
Tel: (415) 323-5101

CORONET MOTEL
2455 El Camino Real (94306)
Rates: $38-$40;
Tel: (415) 326-1081

DAYS INN
4238 El Camino Real (94306)
Rates: $49-$100;
Tel: (800) 329-7466

HOLIDAY INN PALO ALTO/STANFORD
625 El Camino Real (94301)
Rates: $124-$152;
Tel: (415) 328-2800; (800) 874-3516

HYATT RICKEYS
4219 El Camino Real (94306)
Rates: $75-$195;
Tel: (415) 493-8000; (800) 233-1234

MOTEL 6
4301 El Camino Real (94306)
Rates: $36-$46;
Tel: (415) 949-0833; (800) 440-6000

RECREATION

ARASTRADERO PRESERVE - Leashes

Info: You'll have it made in the shade on Corte Madera Trail in this open space preserve. During wet season, do some toe dip-

Dogs May Be Unleashed Unless Otherwise Indicated

ping in Arastradero Creek. This trail is accessible from the right end of the parking lot. For more information: (415) 329-2423.

Directions: From Interstate 280, take the Page Mill Road exit south. Go right (west) on Arastradero Road to the parking lot.

Note: Hours: 8 a.m. to sunset.

ESTHER CLARK PARK - Leashes

Info: Open meadows and eucalyptus groves combine to make this undeveloped area an appealing place for both you and your sidekick.

Directions: Located on the right-hand side of Old Adobe Road where it bends to the left and creates a cul-de-sac.

GREER PARK

Info: Your pup's tail will be a-wagging as he cavorts with other canines in the small, enclosed dog run.

Directions: Located at 1086 Amarillo.

HOOVER PARK

Info: Run, Fido, run! Pooches can frolic leash-free in the shade of towering oaks.

Directions: Located at 2901 Cowper Street.

MITCHELL PARK

Info: Visit the largest dog run park in Palo Alto. This fully enclosed area is equipped with water dishes and tennis balls. The shaded area is ideal for a game of fetch.

Directions: Located on East Meadow Drive, south of Middlefield Road.

Locate Other Dog-Friendly Activities...Check Nearby Cities

PARADISE

LODGING
LANTERN MOTEL
5799 Wildwood Ln (95969)
Rates: $37-$46;
Tel: (916) 877-5553

LIME SADDLE MARINA
3428 Pentz Rd (95969)
Rates: $225;
Tel: (916) 877-2414; (800) 834-7571

PALOS VERDES MOTEL
5423 Skyway (95969)
Rates: $35-$39;
Tel: (916) 877-2127

PONDEROSA GARDENS MOTEL
7010 Skyway (95969)
Rates: $50-$95;
Tel: (916) 872-9094

RECREATION
UPPER RIDGE NATURE PRESERVE - Leashes

Info: Nature buffs will love exploring either of the two-mile nature trails at this oak and pine preserve. Even the fair-of-paw will enjoy the pine cushioned trails which wander along streams and springs. For more information: (916) 224-2100.

Directions: From Paradise, head north on Highway 191 to Magalia exit west. Follow Skyway to Ponderosa Way and turn left. After a mile, follow the signs to the preserve. The kiosk near the parking area has trail maps of the preserve.

PARKFIELD

LODGING
PARKFIELD INN
First & Oak Sts (93451)
Rates: $41-$65;
Tel: (805) 463-2323

PASADENA

LODGING
HOLIDAY INN
303 E Cordova St (91101)
Rates: $79-$189;
Tel: (818) 449-4000; (800) 457-7940

HOLIDAY INN EXPRESS
2321 E Colorado Blvd (91107)
Rates: $75;
Tel: (818) 796-9261; (800) 465-4329

Dogs May Be Unleashed Unless Otherwise Indicated

PASADENA HILTON
150 S Los Robles Ave (91101)
Rates: $119-$175;
Tel: (818) 577-1000; (800) 445-8667

PASADENA INN
400 S Arroyo Pkwy (91105)
Rates: $50-$70;
Tel: (818) 795-8401

RAMADA INN
3500 E Colorado Blvd (91107)
Rates: $50-$75;
Tel: (818) 792-1363; (800) 272-6232

VAGABOND INN
2863 E Colorado Blvd (91107)
Rates: $42-$62;
Tel: (818) 449-3020; (800) 522-1555

VAGABOND INN
1203 E Colorado Blvd (91106)
Rates: $36-$48;
Tel: (818) 449-3170; (800) 522-1555

WESTWAY INN
1599 E Colorado Blvd (91106)
Rates: $44-$56;
Tel: (818) 304-9678

RECREATION

ARROYO SECO PARK to ROSE BOWL TRAIL HIKE - Leashes

Intermediate/3.0 miles/1.5 hours

Info: Hop aboard this popular canyon trail and surprise yourself with the diversity of flora you'll encounter in this scenic urban environment. Get your daily dose of Rexercise as you make your way among stands of sycamore, alder, oak, palm, eucalyptus and pepper trees to the stadium. Make note too of some of the exotic plantlife like bougainvillea and bird of paradise that dot and brighten the landscape. When you've had enough of the hiking thing, head to downtown Pasadena for window shopping and people watching along Colorado Avenue. Or stroll this way and that among the pretty, architecturally inspiring neighborhoods of Pasadena. For more information: (213) 255-0370.

Directions: Take the Pasadena Freeway (110) to Marmion Way/Avenue 64. Bear left, following the signs to York Avenue and make a right, then make an immediate left on San Rafael Avenue and continue approximately one mile to Arroyo Seco Park. Park in the softball field parking lot. The trail begins at the San Pasqual Stables.

BROOKSIDE PARK - Leashes

Info: A verdant expanse of open land awaits you and the pupster in this 61-acre park. Tote your tennies and make tracks along one of the pathways.

Directions: Located at 360 North Arroyo Boulevard.

BUCKHORN to COOPER CANYON and LITTLEROCK CREEK TRAIL HIKE

Intermediate/4.5 miles/2.5 hours

Info: This hike takes you through some of the most beautiful country in the San Gabriel mountains. The trail descends through pine, fir and cedar forests to Cooper Canyon where you have two options. The left fork takes you on a moderate climb up Cooper Canyon to Cloudburst Summit. The right fork is a panoramic descent through Cooper Canyon, past cascading Cooper Falls, to Littlerock Creek. The return hike is mostly uphill, so plan accordingly. In spring and summer, expect to be dazzled by exotic blooms and serenaded by birds. For more information: (818) 574-1613.

Directions: From Pasadena, take the 210 Freeway northwest to Angeles Crest Highway northeast (Highway 2). Buckhorn Campground is approximately 8 miles northeast of Chilao. Park to the right in the hiker's parking lot at the end of the side road about halfway through the campgroud.

BUCKHORN to MT. WATERMAN TRAIL HIKE

Intermediate/7.0 miles/3.5 hours

Info: Bring your camera and tons of film. This hike eats Kodak. The reigning queen of trails in the San Gabriels, you'll want the day to last forever. One trip won't be enough to absorb the beauty you'll find in this region. The diversity of trees, the gracefulness of the ferns, the astounding variety of wildflowers and the assortment of birds will leave you craving more. Descend the Burkhart Trail to Cooper Canyon Trail and go right to Little Rock Creek and Burkhart Trail. When your glorious day must end, retrace your steps and partake of the serenery from another vantage point. For more information: (818) 574-1613.

Directions: Take the 210 Freeway northwest to Angeles Crest Highway (Highway 2). Take Angeles Crest Highway north for 34 miles to the Buckhorn Ranger Station. Park on the shoulder and look for the sign for Mount Waterman Trail.

CHARLTON FLAT to DEVIL'S PEAK TRAIL HIKE

Beginner/2.0 miles/1.0 hours

Info: This quick romp provides a fantastic view into the San Gabriel Wilderness from atop Devil Peak. For more information: (818) 574-1613.

Directions: Take the 210 Freeway northwest to Angeles Crest Highway (Highway 2). Continue north for 23 miles to Charlton Flat. Take a left into the Charlton Flat Picnic Area and park. The unmarked trailhead is across the Angeles Highway on a dirt street leading to Mt. Mooney and Devil's Peak.

CHARLTON FLAT to VETTER MOUNTAIN TRAIL HIKE

Beginner/3.0 miles/1.5 hours

Info: You and the pupster are in for a great nature walk up the chasm to a forest service fire station lookout. Along the way, you'll encounter an assortment of birds and flowers. Superb panoramas are also yours at the peak. For more information: (818) 574-1613.

Directions: From Pasadena, take the 210 Freeway northwest to Angeles Crest Highway (Highway 2). Continue north for 23 miles to Charlton Flat. Take a left into the Charlton Flat Picnic Area, then take a right on the first road. Go about a half-mile to a gate. Park, but don't block the gate.

CHILAO to DEVIL'S CANYON TRAIL HIKE

Intermediate/Expert/7.0 miles/4.0 hours

Info: Gear up for a hearty, get-away-from-it-all hike into Devil's Canyon as you and the dawgus earn some hiking points on this challenging trail. You'll hightail it through a forest of pine and big cone Douglas fir, eventually coming upon a small side stream which marks the halfway point and a dramatic change of scenery. The canyon floor is the ideal place for a biscuit break and a bit of a breather. Your uphill return is a guaranteed butt-kicker. This great year-round trek is particularly beautiful in spring and early summer. For more information: (818) 574-1613.

Directions: From Pasadena, take the Foothill Freeway (210) north to the Angeles Crest Highway (Highway 2). Head north to the trailhead about a hundred yards south of the turnoff to Upper Chilao Visitor's Center. Park on the west side of the road directly across from the trailhead.

CRYSTAL LAKE to SOUTH MOUNT HAWKINS TRAIL HIKE

Intermediate/10.0 miles/5.0 hours

Info: Bring your best tracking dog, the trail is a bit difficult to locate. Begin your voyage at the Windy Gap Trail sign at the north edge of the paved road above the parking lot. Keep a snout out for this road, you'll cross it again after a short distance, and a second time after about 3/4 of a mile. When you reach the road the second time, leave the path and follow the road (it will be dirt at this point) to the right as it winds up the mountain and to the summit.

You'll wish you had eyes in the back of your head, the scenery all around you is absolutely stunning. Combine that with the aromatic pine scent of the forest, the views of Crystal Lake and the surrounding mountains and you'll know why the tail-wagger looks like he's grinning. At the summit, do lunch alfresco and simply lounge with the hound or try to capture the beauty with some Kodak snapping. Happy tails to you. For more information: (818) 574-1613.

Directions: From Pasadena, take Highway 210 east to the Highway 39/Azusa Avenue exit. Head north for about 25 miles to Crystal Lake Recreation Area. Continue a short distance past the store and Forest Service Visitor Center to the large dirt parking area. Look for the sign that indicates the Windy Gap Trail.

EATON BLANCHE PARK - Leashes

Info: Take the blahs out of a dogday afternoon and visit this pretty little 5.5-acre park for some Fido fun in the sun.

Directions: Located at 3100 East Del Mar Boulevard.

Dogs May Be Unleashed Unless Otherwise Indicated

EATON CANYON TRAIL to
EATON CANYON FALLS HIKE - Leashes

Beginner/3.0 miles/1.5 hours

Info: Even sofa loafers will take a shine to this pleasant, simple hike. Mature oak trees shade you and the wagger on your way through Eaton Canyon Wash. Be prepared for wet tootsies. The trail crosses the creek a number of times before reaching the falls. For more information: (818) 398-5420.

Directions: From Pasadena, take Altadena Drive north approximately 2 miles to Eaton Canyon County Park. The trail begins from the Nature Center.

GABRIELINO NATIONAL RECREATION TRAIL to
OAKWILDE TRAIL CAMP HIKE - Leashes

Intermediate/10.0 miles/5.0 hours

Info: Jumpstart your day with an outing along this canyon trail. Canopied by oaks, sycamores and bays, you'll traverse the arroyo bottom before beginning a somewhat steep ascent out of the canyon and then a downhill dawdle to trail's end at Oakwilde Camp. Enjoy some trail treats with your pooch or do lunch at one of the picnic areas before tackling the return hike. For more information: (818) 790-1151.

Directions: From Pasadena, head north on Windsor Avenue. The parking area is on the left at the intersection of Windsor Avenue and Ventura Street. Trail begins on the road to the right.

GABRIELINO NATIONAL RECREATION TRAIL to
TEDDY'S OUTPOST HIKE - Leashes

Beginner/3.0 miles/1.5 hours

Info: Leg stretch with Fletch on this pretty, well-shaded canyon hike. Don't forget your biscuit basket- the trail's destination is a delightful picnic spot. For more information: (818) 790-1151.

Directions: From Pasadena, head north on Windsor Avenue. The parking area is on the left at the intersection of Windsor Avenue and Ventura Street. Trail begins on the road to the right.

HAMILTON PARK - Leashes

Info: You'll have a doggone good time with your best buddy in this 6.4-acre city park.

Directions: Located at 3680 Cartwight Street.

ISLIP SADDLE to MT. ISLIP TRAIL HIKE

Intermediate/6.5 miles/3.0 hours

Info: From your perch atop Mt. Islip, you'll reap the rewards of this invigorating hike. Views of the San Gabriel Mountains, the far reaching desert and the San Gabriel Valley are to die for. For more information: (818) 574-1613.

Directions: From Pasadena, take the 210 Freeway northwest to Angeles Crest Highway (Highway 2) and travel north (right) approximately 41 miles to Islip Saddle. The parking area is on the north side of the highway. The trailhead is across the highway.

LOWER ARROYO PARK - Leashes

Info: Take one of the seemingly endless dirt trails or venture into the canyon area and pick a path, any path, and explore away. Keep Rover leashed to protect area wildlife. For more information: (818) 405-4306.

Directions: From the intersection of California Boulevard and Arroyo Boulevard, turn right on Arroyo Boulevard. Follow the road to the left going down the hill to the parking area.

MEMORIAL PARK - Leashes

Info: For an afternoon of fun, you and the dawgus can't go wrong at this 5.3-acre park.

Directions: Located at 85 East Holly.

Dogs May Be Unleashed Unless Otherwise Indicated

MT. WATERMAN TRAIL to SUMMIT HIKE - Leashes

Expert/6.0 miles/3.0 hours

Info: When you crave "serenery" set your sights on this seldom used trail. Trail sniffing canines are a definite bonus to have along. Beginning on a fire road, continue about fifty yards until the unsigned trail on the left-hand side of the road. When you reach the boundary of the San Gabriel Wilderness, the trail turns west and leads to a signed junction with the Twin Peaks Trail. Veer right and follow your Fido-guido through the pines until you reach the trail on your left. Flex those muscles, you're about to begin the final climb to the rugged, secluded summit, where top-of-the-world views await you and your trusty hound. If you've packed a picnic, just pick your pleasure and then enjoy the vistas and the delightful pine-scented air. For more information: (818) 574-1613.

Directions: From Interstate 210 in Pasadena, exit on Highway 2 and drive for 33 miles. A half-mile after the Mt. Waterman ski lift you'll reach a large parking lot on your left. Park and walk along the highway to a dirt fire road on the right secured by a steel yellow gate. You'll know you've found the right road if you spot the Buckhorn Ranger Station (closed) and a phone booth across the highway.

PASADENA CENTRAL PARK - Leashes

Info: Spend an afternoon window shopping in Old Town Pasadena, then treat Fido to a grassy, shaded jaunt around this attractive park.

Directions: At Del Mar Boulevard and Fair Oaks Avenue.

ROBINSON PARK - Leashes

Info: Kick back in the shade of an oak with your pup and enjoy the pleasant outdoors in this 7-acre park.

Directions: Located at 1081 North Fair Oaks Drive.

VICTORY PARK

Info: Happy tails can wag the day away running leash-free in this 24.7-acre park. As a prudent measure, keep a leash handy - the park is fenced and often used for doggie training classes.

Directions: Located at 2575 Paloma Street.

VINCENT GAP to MT. BADEN-POWELL TRAIL HIKE

Intermediate/8.0 miles/4.0 hours

Info: A favorite high country trail, the pathway leads into expansive forests and ancient limber pines. Atop the peak, admire towering Mt. Baldy and the San Gabriel Canyon. For more information: (818) 574-1613.

Directions: From Pasadena, take the 210 Freeway northwest to Angeles Crest Highway (Highway 2) and continue north for 53 miles to the trailhead and parking area.

VINCENT GAP to PRAIRIE FORK TRAIL HIKE - Leashes

Intermediate/Expert/8.8 miles/5.0 hours

Info: Whether you're interested in fishing or simply desire some paw dipping, the icy, snow-fed streams along this trail will satisfy your cravings. Lucky herding dogs may even sniff out bighorn sheep in their wanderings. One things certain - you'll refresh your senses on this journey through calming forests of pine and fir and dense woodlands of towering oak. You've reached the halfway point when Vincent Gulch joins Prairie Fork, an ideal spot for a biscuit break and a bit of splish splashing playtime before the rigorous uphill climb. For more information: (818) 574-1613.

Directions: Take the 210 Freeway northwest to the Angeles Crest Highway (2). Head north to the Vincent Gap Parking Area, 5 miles south of Big Pines. The trailhead is on the south edge of Vincent Gap.

WASHINGTON PARK - Leashes

Info: Even couch-slouch pups will romp with pleasure in this lovely 5.5-acre park.

Directions: Located at Washington Boulevard and El Molino.

Dogs May Be Unleashed Unless Otherwise Indicated

WEST FORK CAMPGROUND to DEVORE TRAIL CAMP HIKE

Beginner/2.0 miles/1.0 hours

Info: An easy jaunt along this pathway will give you a scenic sampling of the 28-mile long Gabrielino Trail. You and Bowser will need some boulder hopping skills as you'll cross the West Fork a dozen times. Or take a more relaxed attitude and plan to get wet. Your journey will be shaded by maples and oaks as you skirt the river's edge. Lucky dogs might even catch a seasonal waterfall halfway to DeVore Camp. For more information: (818) 577-0050.

Directions: From Pasadena, take the Angeles Crest Highway (2) to the Red Box Ranger Station. Turn right on the signed road leading to Mount Wilson. You'll want to bear left immediately onto West Fork Road (a dirt road). Drive six miles to West Fork Campground and look for the sign for the Gabrielino Trail.

Note: High clearance vehicles only. Avoid the trail after severe thunderstorms, the river may be impassable.

Other parks in Pasadena - Leashes
•GRANT PARK, 232 South Michigan Avenue
•JEFFERSON PARK, 1501 East Villa Street
• LA PINTORESCA PARK, 45 East Washington Boulevard
•MCDONALD PARK, 1000 East Mountain

PASO ROBLES

LODGING

BUDGET INN
2745 Spring St (93446)
Rates: $60-$120;Tel: (805) 238-2770

COUNTRY GARDENS INN B & B
2430 Genesco Rd (93446)
Rates: $66-$100; Tel: (805) 238-6639

FARMHOUSE MOTEL
425 Spring St (93446) Rates: $25+;
Tel: (805) 238-1720

MOTEL 6
1134 Black Oak Dr (93446)
Rates: $30-$36;
Tel: (805) 239-9090; (800) 440-6000

SHAMROCK INN BED & BREAKFAST
1640 Circle B Rd (93446)
Rates: $41-$65;
Tel: (805) 239-8585

SUBURBAN LODGE
1955 Theatre Dr (93446)
Rates: $40-$65;
Tel: (805) 238-3814

TRAVELODGE PASO ROBLES
2701 Spring St (93446)
Rates: $34-$75;
Tel: (805) 238-0078; (800) 578-7878

Locate Other Dog-Friendly Activities...Check Nearby Cities

PEBBLE BEACH

LODGING

THE LODGE AT PEBBLE BEACH
1700 17-Mile Dr (93953)
Rates: $295-$450;
Tel: (408) 624-3811; (800) 654-9300

PENN VALLEY

RECREATION

WESTERN GATEWAY PARK - Leashes

Info: Dotted with oak trees and colorful wildflowers, this park is a great place for you and the dawgus to commune with nature. Savor the sounds of songbirds as you skirt Squirrel Creek, or do the calorie-burning thing along the 2-mile exercise trail. Free spirits will love the vast expanse of verdant lawns.

Directions: Located in Penn Valley off Highway 20.

PERRIS

LODGING

BEST WESTERN LAKE PERRIS INN
480 S Redlands Ave (92376) Rates: $45-$53;
Tel: (909) 943-5577; (800) 528-1234

RECREATION

HARFORD SPRINGS RESERVE - Leashes

Info: When you want to be alone, set your sights on this 325-acre oasis and find peacefulness on a hiking excursion amidst the solitude of this beautiful region. For more information: (909) 275-4310.

Directions: Located approximately 7 miles west of Perris; 2 miles south of Cajalco Road on Gavilan Road.

PETALUMA

LODGING

MOTEL 6-NORTH
5135 Montero Way (94954)
Rates: $30-$37;
Tel: (707) 664-9090; (800) 440-6000

MOTEL 6-SOUTH
1368 N McDowell Blvd (94952)
Rates: $30-$37;
Tel: (707) 765-0333; (800) 440-6000

QUALITY INN-PETALUMA
5100 Montero Way (94954)
Rates: $59-$155;
Tel: (707) 664-1155; (800) 221-2222

RECREATION

HELEN PUTNAM REGIONAL PARK - Leashes

Info: Hike your way to panoramic vistas and solitude in this picturesque parkland. Cityslicker canines might prefer the paved pathways or the shaded gazebo. Whatever your pleasure, you and your tailwagger are sure to sniff out a good time in this 200-acre expanse. For more information: (707) 527-2041.

Directions: On Chileno Valley Road near Spring Valley Road.

LUCCHESI PARK - Leashes

Info: Enjoy a promenade with your pooch along the duck-filled pond of this well-maintained community park. Pooches enjoy leashless freedom from 6 a.m. to 9 a.m. Monday - Friday and 6 a.m. to 8 a.m. on Saturday and Sunday. For more information: (707) 778-4380.

Directions: Located at North McDowell Boulevard and Madison Street.

Note: Voice control obedience is mandatory during leash-free hours.

PETROLLA

LODGING

MATTOLE RIVER RESORT
42354 Mattole Rd (95558)
Rates: $35-$90;
Tel: (707) 629-3445; (800) 845-4607

Locate Other Dog-Friendly Activities...Check Nearby Cities

PHELAN

LODGING

ECONOMY INN
8317 Hwy 138 (Cajon Pass 92371)
Rates: $48-$57;
Tel: (619) 249-6777; (800) 826-0778

PIERCY

LODGING

HARTSOOK INN
900 Hwy 101 (95587)
Rates: $39-$100;
Tel: (707) 247-3305

PINE VALLEY

RECREATION

BIG LAGUNA TRAIL HIKE

Intermediate/11.4 miles/6.0 hours

Info: If dense woodlands, verdant meadows and a refreshing lake send Fido's tail a-wagging, this hike's got your name on it. The trail begins in woodlands, enters a meadow, heads back into the woods and passes through another meadow before coming to Big Laguna Lake. You can't beat this hike in spring when wildflowers paint the meadows in a riot of color and the lake is brimming with water. By summer, the lake isn't much more than a big puddle. From the lake, the trail continues north ending at the junction with Noble Canyon National Recreation Trail, near Sunrise Highway and the Penny Pines parking area. For more information: (619) 445-6235.

Directions: From Pine Valley, follow Sunrise Highway (S1) north to the Laguna Campground. The trailhead is located opposite the parking area for the Amphitheater.

Dogs May Be Unleashed Unless Otherwise Indicated

INDIAN CREEK TRAIL to CHAMPAGNE PASS HIKE

Intermediate/8.0 miles/4.0 hours

Info: Enrich your memory banks along this trail through oak, pine and high chaparral. From the Noble Canyon Trail junction, Indian Creek Trail branches to the right heading in a westerly direction to Indian Creek. Depending on the time of year, your toes may get a bit wet crossing the creek but they'll dry quickly as you journey up the trail to Champagne Pass. From the pass, take a quickie jaunt on the spur trail to the ridgetop. Do lunch alfresco while you fill your eyes with some superb vistas. When you've had enough, do an about-face. For more information: (619) 445-6235.

Directions: From Pine Valley, follow Sunrise Highway (S1) north to the Penny Pines parking area, approximately 3.7 miles north of the Forest Service Visitors Center. The Indian Creek Trail is accessed by hiking the Noble Canyon National Recreation Trail for 2 miles.

KWAAYMII INTERPRETIVE TRAIL HIKE

Beginner/0.5 miles/0.5 hours

Info: The Kwaaymii Native Americans were imaginative in their use of plants for food, shelter, clothing and medicine. This interpretive trail and complementary pamphlet explains how. For more information: (619) 445-6235.

Directions: From Pine Valley, take Sunrise Highway (S1) north to the Visitors Information Center at milepost 23.5. The trailhead is located behind the visitors center.

LIGHTNING RIDGE TRAIL HIKE

Beginner/1.5 miles/1.0 hours

Info: Treat the mutt to some fresh air on this easy outdoor excursion. The trail gently switchbacks to a hilltop affording commanding views of Laguna Meadows and the campground. After hiking a short distance, go left where the trail forks. For more information: (619) 445-6235.

Directions: From Pine Valley, follow Sunrise Highway (S1) north to the Laguna Campground. Park in the lot near the Amphitheater. The trailhead is located at the stone monument behind the bleachers.

SUNSET LOOP TRAIL HIKE

Intermediate/8.0 miles/4.0 hours

Info: This hike gives you the chance to explore the western rim plateau of the Laguna Mountains. The surrounding landscape is pretty and the views are excellent. The Big Laguna Trail junction is your sign to head back the way you came. For more information: (619) 445-6235.

Directions: From Pine Valley, take Sunrise Highway (S1) north to the Meadows Information Kiosk at milepost 19.1. The trailhead is located across the highway from the kiosk.

WOODED HILL NATURE TRAIL HIKE

Intermediate/1.5 miles/1.0 hours

Info: Education and Rexercise go hand-in-hand on this self-guided trail. You'll loop through pine and oak woodlands on your climb to 6,223-foot Hill Summit where bird's-eye views of Point Loma, San Diego and the Channel Islands are yours for the looking. For the educational aspect, pick up a trail brochure from the Ranger Station before setting out and learn while you burn. For more information: (619) 445-6235.

Directions: From Pine Valley, follow Sunrise Highway (S1) north approximately 10 miles to signed Wooded Hill Road. Take Wooded Hill Road to the trailhead and parking area.

PINECREST

LODGING

PINECREST CHALET
500 Dodge Ridge Rd (95364)
Rates: $33-$225;
Tel: (209) 965-3276

Dogs May Be Unleashed Unless Otherwise Indicated

PINOLE

LODGING

MOTEL 6
1501 Fitzgerald Dr (94564)
Rates: $36-$42;
Tel: (510) 222-8174; (800) 440-6000

PISMO BEACH

LODGING

KNIGHT'S REST MOTEL
2351 Price St (93449)
Rates: $45-$129;
Tel: (805) 773-4617

MOTEL 6
860 4th St (93449)
Rates: $26-$34;
Tel: (805) 773-2665; (800) 440-6000

OCEAN PALMS MOTEL
390 Ocean View (93449)
Rates: $28-$85;
Tel: (805) 773-4669

QUALITY SUITES
651 Five Cities Dr (93449)
Rates: $83-$136;
Tel: (805) 773-3773; (800) 982-7848

SANDCASTLE INN
100 Stimson Ave (93449)
Rates: $105-$130;
Tel: (805) 773-2422; (800) 822-6606

SEA VIEW MOTEL
230 Five Cats Dr (93499)
Rates: $29-$49;
Tel: (805) 773-1841

RECREATION

PISMO DUNES/PISMO STATE BEACH - Leashes

Info: Make merry on the beach or explore the dunes on miles of trails. Either way, you and your canine will share a delightful afternoon. For more information: (805) 927-4509; (805) 489-2684.

Directions: There's a $6 day-use fee at the Grand Avenue entrance. For no-fee entry, head west on Highway 1 and park on Grand Avenue before the ranger kiosk. Go north on the beach.

PITTSBURG

LODGING

MOTEL 6
2101 Loveridge Rd (94565)
Rates: $28-$34;
Tel: (510) 427-1600; (800) 440-6000

PLACENTIA

LODGING

RESIDENCE INN BY MARRIOTT
700 W Kimberly Ave (92670)
Rates: $69-$145;
Tel: (714) 996-0555; (800) 331-3131

RECREATION

HISTORIC GEORGE KEY RANCH - Leashes

Info: Take Bowser for a browser along the beautifully land-scaped grounds of this historic 1898 home. Sniff out the botanical garden and orange grove for a sense of life in the early days of Orange County. For more information: (714) 528-4260.

Directions: Located at 625 West Bastanchury Road in Placentia. Entry to site is located 1500 feet west of Placentia Avenue on Bastanchury Road across from Sierra Vista School. No on-site parking.

PLACERVILLE

LODGING

BEST WESTERN PLACERVILLE INN
6850 Greenleaf Dr (95667)
Rates: $58-$74;
Tel: (916) 622-9100; (800) 528-1234

MOTHER LODE MOTEL
1940 Broadway (95667)
Rates: $34-$51;
Tel: (916) 622-0895

GOLD TRAIL MOTOR LODGE
1970 Broadway (95667)
Rates: $36-$51;
Tel: (916) 622-2906

Dogs May Be Unleashed Unless Otherwise Indicated

<u>RECREATION</u>

CODY LAKE TRAIL HIKE - Leashes

Beginner/1.0 mile/0.5 hours

Info: A gentle trail takes you to glacier-formed Cody Lake. This secluded paradise is perfect for a boxed lunch with your bow wow and a good read. For more information: (916) 644-6048.

Directions: From Placerville, head east on Highway 50 to the 42 Mile Picnic Area just west of the town of Strawberry. Head south on Packsaddle Pass Road for seven miles towards the Scout Camp. Park by the trailhead on the left side of the road.

HANGTOWN'S GOLD BUG PARK - Leashes

Info: Spend the day milling around the city's largest park, former home to 250 active mines. Explore the dirt paths or relax with Max under the oaks and pines. For more information: (916) 642-5232.

Directions: From Highway 50, take the Bedford Avenue exit north about a mile to the park.

LOVERS LEAP TRAIL HIKE - Leashes

Intermediate/5.0 miles/2.5 hours

Info: You and Fido will break a sweat on this trail to the top of Lovers Leap, a favorite area with rock climbers. The views are staggering as your eyes follow the serpentine path of the American River. For more information: (916) 644-6048.

Directions: From Placerville, head east on Highway 50, turning south at the 42 Mile Picnic Area just west of the town of Strawberry. Continue south on Packsaddle Pass Road for one mile to Strawberry Canyon Road. Follow Strawberry Canyon Road for a half-mile to the trailhead.

RALSTON PEAK TRAIL HIKE - Leashes

Intermediate/6.0 miles/3.0 hours

Info: Don't be fooled by the easy first mile of this trip. Once you enter the Desolation Wilderness, the trail ascends steeply to Mt. Ralston at 9,235 feet, a whopping gain of more than

2,600 feet. Take a deep breath (or pant), and check out the awesome views. That blue gem in the distance is Lake Tahoe. For more information: (916) 644-6048.

Directions: From Placerville, head east on Highway 50 about 48 miles to Camp Sacramento. The trailhead parking is on the north side of the highway, across from Camp Sacramento. The trailhead is 200 yards east of the road to the parking lot.

Note: A wilderness permit is required.

PLAYA DEL REY

<u>RECREATION</u>

DEL REY LAGOON - Leashes

Info: Dine a la blanket while you and the bird-dog do some birdwatching and relaxing along the shore of this tranquil lagoon. If you're feeling more energetic, take advantage of the open space in this 12-acre area.

Directions: Located at 6660 Esplanada.

PLEASANT HILL

<u>LODGING</u>

RESIDENCE INN BY MARRIOTT-PLEASANT HILL
700 Ellinwood Way (94523)
Rates: $89-$119;
Tel: (510) 689-1010; (800) 331-3131

<u>RECREATION</u>

BRIONES CREST LOOP TRAIL HIKE

Intermediate/5.6 miles/3.0 hours

Info: Take Alhambra Creek Trail to the Briones Crest Trail and go left. Cardiovascular training begins here with a 1,483-foot climb in 2.5 miles to the highest point in the park. Admire the outstanding views in peaceful serenity, you've earned it. Finish the loop with a left on Spengler Trail, and a right on a trail that says it all - Diablo View. For more information: (510) 635-0135.

Dogs May Be Unleashed Unless Otherwise Indicated

Directions: From Interstate 680 north of Pleasant Hill, go west on Highway 4 for three miles. Exit and go south on Alhambra Avenue, drive a half-mile and bear right onto Alhambra Valley Road. Proceed another mile to Reliez Valley Road. Take a left and follow Reliez Valley Road a half-mile to the parking area on the right. Find the Alhambra Creek Trailhead.

Note: The trails throughout this 5,700-acre sanctuary are so vast that you'll need a map. Stop at the East Bay Regional Parks District, 2950 Peralta Oaks Court in Oakland.

PLEASANTON

LODGING

DOUBLETREE CLUB HOTEL
5990 Stoneridge Mall Rd (94588)
Rates: $69-$139;
Tel: (510) 463-3330; (800) 222-8733

HILTON-PLEASANTON
7050 Johnson Dr (94588)
Rates: $99-$149;
Tel: (510) 463-8000; (800) 445-8667

HOLIDAY INN
11950 Dublin Canyon Rd (94588)
Rates: $95-$115;
Tel: (510) 847-6000; (800) 465-4329

MOTEL 6
5102 Hopyard Rd (94588)
Rates: $33-$39;
Tel: (510) 463-2626; (800) 440-6000

RECREATION

ANTHONY CHABOT REGIONAL PARK

Info: Seclusion and doggie freedom go hand-in-hand at this 4,900-acre haven. Fun-loving canines will adore the heavily wooded Goldenrod Trail beginning at the southernmost point of Skyline Boulevard and Grass Valley Road. This picture-pretty trail meets up with eucalyptus-lined East Bay Skyline National Trail and slithers through Grass Valley. Fishing hounds may want to try their luck at Lake Chabot. Bass, trout, crappie and catfish await. For more information: (510) 635-0135.

Directions: Travel north on Interstate 680 to Interstate 580 exit. Head northwest to the Castro Valley exit. At the intersection of Redwood Road and Castro Valley Boulevard, turn north on Redwood to Marciel Gate, approximately 4.5 miles.

Note: $4 parking fee; $1 dog fee. Dogs must be leashed in developed areas.

NORTH ARROYO TRAIL HIKE

Beginner/1.3 miles/0.75 hours

Info: For an unusual walk, investigate the Arroyo area, a sequence of small ponds and find yourself in puppy paradise. At the back of the first parking area the trail heads up and then down to the first pond. The North Arroyo Trail continues past several other ponds. The water is beautiful, just the right place for a backstroke or doggie-paddle. For more information: (510) 635-0135.

Directions: From Interstate 580 in Pleasanton, use Santa Rita Road south. Go two miles and take a left on Valley Avenue and continue to Stanley Boulevard. Take a left to the park entrance.

PLEASANTON RIDGE REGIONAL PARK

Info: With nearly 3,200 acres of oak woodlands, verdant grasslands, sparkling canyon streams and spectacular ridgetop panoramas, this is one park outing you shouldn't skip. The park encompasses a 1,600–foot rise in elevation. For more information: (510) 635-0135.

Directions: From Pleasanton travel west on Interstate 580, then south on Interstate 680 exiting at Castlewood Drive. Turn left (west) on Foothill Road to the staging area.

Note: Dogs must be leashed in developed ares.

RIDGELINE TRAIL HIKE

Intermediate/7.0 miles/3.5 hours

Info: The Ridgeline Trail ascends to 1,600 feet, offering expansive views of valleys and rolling hills to the north. The serene, uncultivated setting is a nice change of pace. Begin the hike on the Oak Tree Trail, a challenging 750-foot climb over 1.4 miles, then go right for two miles along the ridge. For more information: (510) 635-0135.

Directions: From Interstate 680 in Pleasanton, exit west at Bernal Road and go to Foothill Road. Go left and travel for three miles to the parking and information area.

Dogs May Be Unleashed Unless Otherwise Indicated

SHADOW CLIFFS REGIONAL RECREATION AREA - Leashes

Info: Fishing fiends can drop a line for the catfish and trout in Shadow Cliffs Lake. Or you and the dawgus can commune with nature beside the tranquil waters in the arroyo of smaller lakes. This region is a haven for pups hoping to chill out in the summertime. For more information: (510) 562-7275.

Directions: From downtown Pleasanton, head east on Stanley Boulevard for about one mile to the park entrance.

Note: Parking fee and $1 dog fee.

PLYMOUTH

LODGING

SHENANDOAH INN
17674 Village Dr (95669)
Rates: $53-$71;
Tel: (209) 245-4491; (800) 542-4549

POINT REYES STATION

LODGING

BERRY PATCH COTTAGE
BED & BREAKFAST
P. O. Box 712 (94956)
Rates: $110;
Tel: (415) 663-1942

GRAY'S RETREAT
P. O. Box 547 (94956)
Rates: $135;
Tel: (415) 663-2000; (800) 887-2880

JASMINE COTTAGE
P. O. Box 547 (94956)
Rates: $125;
Tel: (415) 663-2000; (800) 887-2880

KNOB HILL COTTAGE
P. O. Box 1108 (94956)
Rates: $55-$95;
Tel: (415) 663-1784

THIRTY-NINE CYPRESS
BED & BREAKFAST
39 Cypress Rd, P. O. Box 176 (94956)
Rates: $110-$130;
Tel: (415) 663-1709

POLLOCK PINES

<u>LODGING</u>
STAGECOACH MOTOR INN
5940 Pony Express Tr (95726)
Rates: $50-$68;
Tel: (916) 644-2029

<u>RECREATION</u>
BUCK PASTURE TRAIL HIKE - Leashes
Intermediate/6.0 miles/3.0 hours

Info: This simple hike will lead you to Buck Pasture before rising on the pretty north ridge of Caples Creek Valley. Summer and early fall offer the best hiking conditions, since the area is snow-covered the rest of the year. For more information: (916) 644-6048.

Directions: From Pollock Pines, take Highway 50 east for 18 miles to Kyburz. In Kyburz, take Silver Fork Road for 7 miles to Cody Meadows Road. Turn left and drive for about 5 miles to Negro Flat. At Negro Flat turn right onto the 4-wheel drive road and continue 2 miles to the trailhead.

Note: High clearance vehicles only.

CAPLES CREEK TRAIL HIKE- Leashes
Intermediate/8.0 miles/4.0 hours

Info: For a nature excursion like no other, head for this creekside trail. You and your canine crony will have the unique experience of hiking through a forest in its natural state. That is, a forest virtually untouched by human activity. The trail wanders amidst pretty Jake Schneider's Meadow before packing its final punch - an uphill, one-mile climb to trail's end. Drink in the magnificence of the pristine environment, then retrace your steps. For more information: (916) 644-6048.

Directions: From Pollock Pines, take Highway 50 east for 18 miles to Kyburz. In Kyburz, follow Silver Fork Road for approximately 8 miles, turning left just before Fitch Rantz Bridge. Follow this dirt road a quarter mile to the trailhead.

Note: High clearance vehicles only.

CAPLES CREEK TRAIL to
GOVERNMENT MEADOWS HIKE- Leashes

Intermediate/Beginner/9.0 miles/4.5 hours

Info: You and the pupster must first tackle the four-mile Caples Creek Trail before reaching the Government Meadows Trail (an easy half-mile jaunt). Verdant meadows and refreshing Caples Creek make the effort worthwhile. The creek's a slice of doggie heaven. For more information: (916) 644-6048.

Directions: See Cables Creek Trail Hike.

CAPLES CREEK TRAIL to OLD SILVER LAKE HIKE- Leashes

Intermediate/10.0 miles/5.0 hours

Info: Calling all robust aquatic pups - this paw-wetting hike's for you. Frolic in the chilly waters of Caples Creek before beginning your workout. Follow the Caples Creek Trail about 3.5 miles to Old Silver Lake Trail where you'll switchback through a forest of virgin pine and fir. The Silver Fork Trail junction is your turnaround point. For more information: (916) 644-6048.

Directions: See Cables Creek Trail Hike.

CAPLES CREEK TRAIL to SILVER FORK HIKE- Leashes

Intermediate/12.0 miles/6.0 hours

Info: You and Rover will burn a few calories on this rollercoaster of a hike. Branching off the Caples Creek Trail, Silver Fork begins with a steady ascent, then quickly descends along Silver Creek. Once the trail levels out, your leg muscles get a short respite as you stroll creekside past tranquil pools, aka puppy paradise. This is the perfect place to chill out before the last uphill climb to the junction with the Old Silver Lake Trail. Enjoy the views. For more information: (916) 644-6048.

Directions: See Cables Creek Trail Hike.

EMIGRANT SUMMIT TRAIL HIKE- Leashes

Intermediate/1.0-10.0 miles/0.5-5.0 hours

Info: Journey back in time to the days of settlers and covered wagons on this National Recreation Trail. Spend an hour or a day with your pioneer pup exploring an area once considered a major transportation route. For more information: (916) 644-6048.

Directions: From Highway 50 in Pollock Pines, take the Sly Park/ Jenkinson Lake exit south for 5 miles. The trail is accessible from several locations.

SLY PARK / JENKINSON LAKE - Leashes

Info: At a pleasant elevation of 3,500 feet, this huge recreation site offers year-round fun for you and fur-face. Fishing for trout, bass and bluegill is a popular activity, as is hiking along the several trails located in the area. The Liberty and Miwok Trails are favorites for self-guiding naturalists, while the 8-mile shoreline path is a great way for calorie-burning hounds to spend the day. Abundant wildlife and plantlife thrive in this region, so bring your binoculars. Lucky dogs may even spot a bald eagle. For more information: (916) 644-2545.

Directions: Located off Highway 50. Follow Sly Park Road for five miles until the park entrance.

PONY EXPRESS TRAIL HIKE- Leashes

Expert/1.0-20.0 miles/0.5-10.0 hours

Info: Time and conditioning will determine the length of your Pony Express excursion. Pack plenty of water, an assortment of munchies and get ready to relive the days of the wild, wild west. Every 4th of July, history hounds can witness a reenactment of the mail relay riders. This trail was part of the Pony Express route from Reno to Sacramento. For more information: (916) 644-6048.

Directions: From Pollock Pines, the trail parallels Highway 50.

POMONA

LODGING

MOTEL 6
2470 S Garey Ave (91766)
Rates: $30-$34;
Tel: (909) 591-1871; (800) 440-6000

SHERATON SUITES FAIRPLEX
600 W McKinley Ave (91768)
Rates: $95-$115;
Tel: (909) 622-2220; (800) 722-4055
(800) 325-3535 (CAN)

**SHILO INN HOTEL-
DIAMOND BAR/POMONA**
3200 Temple Ave (91768)
Rates: $90-$100;
Tel: (909) 598-0073; (800) 222-2244

PORT HUENEME

LODGING

SURFSIDE MOTEL
615 E Hueneme Rd (93041)
Rates: $49;
Tel: (805) 488-3686

RECREATION

MORANDA PARK - Leashes

Info: With 8 action-packed acres to explore, this park is a good place to get a bit of Rexercise.

Directions: Located at 200 Moranda Parkway.

Other parks in Port Hueneme - Leashes
•BOLKER PARK, Bolker Drive west of Hueneme Bay

PORTERVILLE

LODGING

MOTEL 6
935 W Morton Ave (93257)
Rates: $23-$29;
Tel: (209) 781-7600; (800) 440-6000

RECREATION
SUCCESS LAKE - Leashes

Info: You'll have 3.5 miles to cruise about if you and aquapup decide to float your boat on your visit to Success Lake. If your paws prefer the terra firma, there are 30 miles of shoreline to explore, including a self-guided nature walk along the Big Sycamore Nature Trail. Pick up a pamphlet at the trailhead and learn about the plants and trees in the area. Lucky dogs may even spot some wildlife. Pack a snack and plan to picnic with the pooch in one of the park's three picnic areas. Tote a fishing rod and drop in on the black bass, white crappie, bluegill and channel catfish. See if you can out fish the world record - a 17-pound, 7-ounce white catfish was caught here in 1982. For more information: (209) 784-0215.

Directions: Located in the Sierra Nevada foothills, 5 miles northeast of Porterville off Highway 190.

PORTOLA

LODGING
SLEEPY PINES MOTEL
74631 Hwy 70 (96122)
Rates: $40+;
Tel: (916) 832-4291

RECREATION
BEAR LAKES TRAIL HIKE
Beginner/2.4 miles/1.25 hours

Info: When you've got a case of the summertime blahs, take your hot diggety dog on a cool lake-hopping adventure. Big Bear Lake, Little Bear Lake and Cub Lake are on the trail's hit list. Pick one or spend time at all three. The trail climbs .7 miles to Big Bear Lake and then within a half-mile passes Little Bear and Cub Lakes, ending at the Silver Lake Trail junction. Happy wet tails to you. For more information: (916) 836-2575.

Directions: From Portola, take Highway 70 west to Highway 89. Head south for 2 miles to the Gold Lake Highway and follow the signs to the Lakes Basin & Recreation Area. The trailhead is in the Lakes Basin Campground.

Dogs May Be Unleashed Unless Otherwise Indicated

DIXIE MOUNTAIN TRAIL HIKE

Beginner/2.2 miles/1.0 hours

Info: You and your canine crony are just a hop, skip and a jump from Dixie Mountain Lookout. Situated at 8,040 feet, the lookout comes complete with outstanding vistas of the surrounding landscape. And we're talking seclusion here. There's a good chance the only things you'll encounter on this trail are peace and quiet. For more information: (916) 253-2223.

Directions: From Portola, take Highway 70 east to State Highway 284 (just west of Chilcoot). Head north following the signs for the Frenchman Recreation Area, for 8 miles to the Frenchman Dam. At the dam, head north on FDR 25N11 (on the west side of Frenchman Reservoir) about eight miles to FDR 25N03 (Lookout Creek Road). Follow FDR 25N03 to the trailhead and limited parking at road's end.

FERN FALLS OVERLOOK TRAIL HIKE

Beginner/0.2 miles/0.25 hours

Info: You and your pooch aren't far from a great photo opportunity- cascading Fern Falls. This easy trail leads to a scenic overlook of the falls. For more information: (916) 836-2575.

Directions: From Portola, take Highway 70 west to Highway 89. Head south for 2 miles to the Gold Lake Highway and follow the signs to the Lakes Basin & Recreation Area. The trailhead is on Gold Lake Highway.

FRAZIER FALLS TRAIL HIKE

Beginner/1.0 miles/0.5 hours

Info: If you're into waterfalls, you'll understand the popularity of this effortless hike. The melting snows June through August make for the best falls. Early summer brings a bonus of copious wildflowers as well. For more information: (916) 836-2575.

Directions: From Portola, go south three miles on Highway 89 (near Blairsden). Go west on Forest Service Road 24 (Gold Lake Highway) and continue until you see the sign for Frazier Falls. Hang a left and proceed to the end of the road.

GOLD LAKE TRAIL HIKE

Beginner/3.0 miles/1.5 hours

Info: This popular walk takes you west to Big Bear Lake. But don't stop there, a slew of magnificent alpine lakes are en route. Hey Rover, last one in the water is a rotten egg. For more information: (916) 283-0555.

Directions: See Frazier Falls Trail for directions.

LAKE DAVIS RECREATION AREA

Info: Once you leave the campgrounds and lake area, your pooch can say hello to freedom. Venture along superb hiking trails and observe bountiful wildlife, including bald eagles and waterfowl. For more information: (916) 283-2050.

Directions: Head north on Highway 70 and take Grizzly Road or Lake Davis Road seven miles north to the lake.

MOUNT ELWELL TRAIL HIKE

Intermediate/6.0 miles/3.0 hours

Info: Awesome sights available; must be willing to travel. Starting at Smith Lake/Gray Eagle Lodge Trail, (6,700 feet), you and Rover will climb 1,100 feet in three miles to Mt. Elwell at 7,812 feet. A tough trek, but well-worth the effort. Check out the spectacular alpine lakes and granite mountains of Gold Lakes Basin. For more information: (916) 836-2575.

Directions: From Portola, travel south three miles on Highway 89 (near Blairsden). Go west on Forest Service Road 24 (Gold Lake Highway) and continue until you see the sign for Gray Eagle Lodge. Take a right and continue to the trailhead.

RED FIR NATURE TRAIL HIKE

Beginner/0.8 miles/0.5 hours

Info: This nature trail is short and sweet, a perfect leg stretcher. As you and Rosie mosey along, take some time to read the interpretive signs on the area's red firs. For more information: (916) 836-2575.

Dogs May Be Unleashed Unless Otherwise Indicated

Directions: From Portola, take Highway 70 west to Highway 89. Head south on Highway 89 for 2 miles to the Gold Lake Highway. Follow the signs on the Gold Lake Highway to the Lakes Basin & Recreation Area. The trailhead is located on the dirt road leading to Mills Peak Lookout.

ROUND LAKE TRAIL HIKE

Beginner/3.4 miles/1.5 hours

Info: All that separates you and Rover from an afternoon of fun in the sun is a simple hike to Round Lake. The invigorating water is most refreshing on a hot summer day. For more information: (916) 836-2575.

Directions: From Portola, take Highway 70 west to Highway 89. Head south on Highway 89 for 2 miles to the Gold Lake Highway. Follow the signs on the Gold Lake Highway to the Lakes Basin & Recreation Area. The trailhead is located in the Gold Lake Lodge parking area.

POWAY

LODGING

POWAY COUNTRY INN
13845 Poway Rd (92064)
Rates: $40-$56;
Tel: (619) 748-6320; (800) 648-6320

QUINCY

LODGING

GOLD PAN MOTEL
200 Crescent St (95971)
Rates: $38-$64;
Tel: (916) 283-3686; (800) 804-6541

RECREATION

BACHS CREEK TRAIL HIKE

Expert/4.8 miles/3.0 hours

Info: Narrow, steep, rugged... get the picture? The trail to Bach Creek is a rigorous hike that should only be tackled by those hikers and canines with a slew of hiking miles under their belts and leashes. For more information: (916) 283-0555.

Directions: From the LaPorte Road turnoff in Quincy, go right for about 7.3 miles to FR 23N92. Turn right for approximately 2.1 miles to the "Y" and take the left fork (FR 23N92A). Follow FR 23N92A for 1 mile to Lost Cabin Springs. The trailhead is located down the road from the springs.

Note: High clearance vehicles only.

BEN LOMOND TRAIL HIKE

Expert/9.6 miles/5.5 hours

Info: Definitely not for the fair-of-paw or out-of-shape, this trail ascends nearly 4,000 feet in under 5 miles. The hike is nothing short of strenuous, but if you and champ can hang in there, the views from atop Ben Lomond Peak are nothing short of spectacular. For more information: (916) 283-0555.

Directions: From Quincy, head west on Highway 70. The trailhead is located at Chips Creek, approximately 25 miles west of the Quincy Ranger Station.

BUCKS LAKE RECREATION AREA

Info: Huck Finn types rejoice. This is rainbow trout fishing at its finest. Or make your own way through the Plumas National Forest which surrounds the lake. For stunning vistas, climb one of the peaks in the scenic Bucks Lake Wilderness Area. For information: (916) 283-0188.

Directions: From Highway 70 in Quincy, take Bucks Lake Road west for 12 miles to the lake.

Dogs May Be Unleashed Unless Otherwise Indicated

CHAMBERS CREEK TRAIL HIKE

Expert/8.2 miles/5.0 hours

Info: Climbing nearly 4,000 feet in just 4 miles, you and Bowser will earn plenty of hiking points on this formidable trail. But what you sacrifice in effort, you get back in far-reaching vistas. The cascading waterfalls by the bridge are also worth a snapshot or two. For more information: (916) 283-0555.

Directions: From Quincy, head west on Highway 70. The trailhead is located across from Indian Jim School, approximately 40 miles west of the Quincy Ranger Station.

GRANITE GAP TRAIL HIKE

Intermediate/1.8 miles/1.0 hours

Info: Exercise and lake hopping go hand-in-hand on this somewhat demanding trail. After traversing about a mile on the Gold Lake Trail, you'll come to the Granite Gap Trail branchoff. Continue trekking, but be certain you don't miss the short sidetrips to sun-sprinkled Mud and Rock Lakes - perfect spots to picnic with Spot. The trail ends after meeting the Pacific Crest Trail. Once back at the Gold Lake/Granite Gap junction, continue on the Gold Lake Trail - it's a short, easy half-mile jaunt to Gold Lake. For more information: (916) 283-0555.

Directions: From Quincy, take Bucks Lake Road west for 9.2 miles through Meadow Valley to FR 24N29X which is marked by the Silver Lake sign. Follow FR 24N29X approximately 6.4 miles to Silver Lake Campground. Hike along the Gold Lake Trail about one mile to the junction with the Granite Gap Trail.

INDIAN SPRINGS TRAIL HIKE

Expert/13.0 miles/7.0 hours

Info: Limber up with your pup before setting out on this lengthy, difficult trail, which covers a 3,700-foot elevation change. Take note of the views on your way. For more information: (916) 283-0555.

Directions: From Quincy, head west on Highway 70. The trailhead is located at the Eby Stamp Mill Rest Area, approximately 25 miles west of the Quincy Ranger Station.

Locate Other Dog-Friendly Activities...Check Nearby Cities

LOST CABIN SPRINGS TRAIL HIKE

Expert/1.6 miles/1.0 hours

Info: This trail may be short, but it's far from sweet. Only diehard hikers and hounds should attempt this steep hike over rough and tumble terrain. Once at the river, chill out while you watch furface do the doggie paddle. Or cast your line and hope for a bite. For more information: (916) 283-0555.

Directions: From the LaPorte Road turnoff in Quincy, go right about 7.3 miles to FR 23N92. Turn right on FR 23N92 for approximately 2.1 miles to the "Y" and take the left fork (FR 23N92A). Continue one mile to Lost Cabin Springs. The trailhead is located down the road from the springs.

Note: High clearance vehicles only.

MCCARTHY BAR TRAIL HIKE

Expert/3.4 miles/2.0 hours

Info: Pretty vistas and biting fish are your rewards for tackling this rigorous hike. Cool your tootsies riverside, break some bread and biscuits with the dogster and drop your line, the fishing's fine. For more information: (916) 283-0555.

Directions: From Quincy, head west on Bucks Lake Road for 4 miles to Slate Creek Road (FR 24N28) and turn left for about 8.8 miles. Once past Dean's Valley Campground, watch for signs and take the left fork onto FR 23N99. Follow FR 23N99 for 2.5 miles to the trailhead. The trailhead is a mile past the sign for the No Ear Bar and Oddie Bar Trails.

Note: High clearance vehicles only.

NO EAR BAR TRAIL HIKE

Expert/3.0 miles/2.0 hours

Info: Get psyched for a steep, calorie burning descent to Feather River - the trail drops 1,500 feet in just 1.5 miles. If you and your hardy hound are up for the challenge and love to fish, you're gonna love this trek. The river offers great bait opportunities. For more information: (916) 283-0555.

Dogs May Be Unleashed Unless Otherwise Indicated

Directions: From Quincy, head west on Bucks Lake Road for 4 miles to Slate Creek Road (FR 24N28) and turn left for about 8.8 miles. Once past Dean's Valley Campground watch for signs and take the left fork onto FR 23N99. Follow FR 23N99 for 1.5 miles to the signed trailhead.

Note: High clearance vehicles only.

ODDIE BAR TRAIL HIKE

Expert/2.6 miles/2.0 hours

Info: You'll definitely work up a sweat on this intense hike. Not only is it exertive but it's unshaded as well. The payoff, refreshing Feather River. Avoid on extremely hot days. For more information: (916) 283-0555.

Directions: See No Ear Bar Trail Hike.

Note: High clearance vehicles only.

YELLOW CREEK TRAIL HIKE

Beginner/2.8 miles/1.5 hours

Info: An easy-does-it, creekside stroll brings you and your puppy pal to a pretty box canyon. Able anglers, don't forget your rods - Yellow Creek is a good fishing hole. For more information: (916) 283-0555.

Directions: See Indian Springs Trail Hike.

RAMONA

LODGING

LAKE SUTHERLAND LODGE
BED & BREAKFAST
24901 Dam Oaks Dr (92065)
Rates: $110-$165;
Tel: (619) 789-6483

RAMONA VALLEY INN
416 Main St (92065)
Rates: $40-$78;
Tel: (619) 789-6433; (800) 648-4618

RANCHO BERNARDO

LODGING

CARMEL HIGHLAND
DOUBLETREE GOLF RESORT
14455 Penasquitos Dr (92129)
Rates: $100-$179;
Tel: (619) 672-9100; (800) 622-9223
(800) 222-8733 (CAN)

HOLIDAY INN
17065 W Bernardo Dr (92127)
Rates: $59-$69;
Tel: (619) 485-6530; (800) 465-4329
(800) 777-0020 (CA)

LA QUINTA MOTOR INN
10185 Paseo Montril (92129)
Rates: $49-$59;
Tel: (619) 484-8800; (800) 531-5900

RADISSON SUITE HOTEL
11520 W Bernardo Ct (92127)
Rates: $79-$119;
Tel: (619) 451-6600; (800) 333-3333

RANCHO BERNARDO INN
17550 Bernardo Oaks (92128)
Rates: $79-$149;
Tel: (619) 487-1611; (800) 542-6096

RESIDENCE INN BY MARRIOTT
11002 Rancho Carmel Dr (92128)
Rates: $79-$149;
Tel: (619) 673-1900; (800) 331-3131

TRAVELODGE
16929 W Bernardo Dr (92127)
Rates: $47-$62;
Tel: (619) 487-0445; (800) 578-7878

RANCHO CALIFORNIA

LODGING

MOTEL 6
41900 Moreno Dr (92390)
Rates: $28-$34;
Tel: (909) 676-7199; (800) 440-6000

RANCHO CORDOVA

LODGING

BEST WESTERN HERITAGE INN
11269 Point East Dr (95742)
Rates: $59-$69;
Tel: (916) 635-4040; (800) 528-1234

COMFORT INN
3240 Mather Field Rd (95670)
Rates: $45-$79;
Tel: (916) 363-3344; (800) 221-2222

DAYS INN
11131 Folsom Blvd (95670)
Rates: $49-$75;
Tel: (800) 329-7466

ECONOMY INNS OF AMERICA
12249 Folsom Blvd (95670)
Rates: $34-$42;
Tel: (916) 351-1213; (800) 826-0778

MOTEL 6-EAST
10694 Olson Dr (95670)
Rates: $28-$32;
Tel: (916) 635-8784; (800) 440-6000

MOTEL 6-WEST
10271 Folsom Blvd (95670)
Rates: $26-$32;
Tel: (916) 362-5800; (800) 440-6000

Dogs May Be Unleashed Unless Otherwise Indicated

RECREATION

FOLSOM LAKE STATE RECREATION AREA - Leashes

Info: A popular park, it's often hot and crowded in summer. Visit in spring for a wildflower extravaganza. Hike on 80 miles of tree-lined trails and ogle an abundance of wildlife, from eagles to red-tailed hawks. For more information: (800) 444-7275.

Directions: From Rancho Cordova, travel northeast on Highway 50 and exit at Folsom. From Folsom, go north a couple of miles on Folsom-Auburn Road.

Note: $6 day-use fee; $1 dog fee.

RANCHO MIRAGE

LODGING

MARRIOTT'S
RANCHO LAS PALMAS RESORT
41000 Bob Hope Dr (92270)
Rates: $75-$175;
Tel: (619) 568-2727; (800) 458-8786

MOTEL 6
69-570 Hwy 111 (92270)
Rates: $29-$36;
Tel: (619) 324-8475; (800) 440-6000

THE WESTIN MISSION HILLS RESORT
71-333 Dinah Shore Dr (92270)
Rates: $109-$390;
Tel: (619) 328-5955; (800) 228-3000;
(800) 999-0287 (CA)

RECREATION

SALTON SEA STATE RECREATION AREA - Leashes

Info: The eerie Salton Sea at 234-feet below sea level is among the largest inland bodies of saltwater in the world. 36 miles long and 15 miles wide, the park area has 16 miles of shoreline and 5 beaches to explore. The high saline content makes staying afloat a cinch and eye irritation a possibility. For more information: (619) 393-3502.

Directions: From Rancho Mirage, take Highway 111 southeast of Mecca about 10 miles. The Visitor's Center is on the west side of the highway.

Note: $5 day-use fee.

Locate Other Dog-Friendly Activities...Check Nearby Cities

RANCHO SANTA FE

LODGING

INN AT RANCHO SANTA FE
5951 Linea del Cielo (92067)
Rates: $95-$510;
Tel: (619) 756-1131; (800) 654-2928

MORGAN RUN RESORT & CLUB
5690 Cancha de Golf (92067)
Rates: $139-$339;
Tel: (619) 756-2471

RAVENDALE

LODGING

RAVENDALE LODGE
Highway 395 (96123)
Rates: $25-$30;
Tel: (916) 728-0028

RED BLUFF

LODGING

CINDERELLA RIVERVIEW MOTEL
600 Rio St (96080)
Rates: $32-$48;
Tel: (916) 527-5490

MOTEL 6
20 Williams Ave (96080)
Rates: $32-$38;
Tel: (916) 527-9200; (800) 440-6000

FLAMINGO HOTEL
250 S Main St (96080)
Rates: $22-$52;
Tel: (916) 527-3454

SUPER 8 MOTEL
203 Antelope Blvd (96080)
Rates: $40-$50;
Tel: (916) 527-8882; (800) 800-8000

KINGS LODGE
38 Antelope Blvd (96080)
Rates: $35-$41;
Tel: (800) 426-5655; (916) 527-6020

VALUE LODGE-IMA
30 Gilmore Rd (96080)
Rates: $35-$60;
Tel: (916) 529-2028; (800) 341-8000

RECREATION

DEER CREEK TRAIL HIKE

Intermediate/2.0-14.0 miles/1.0-7.0 hours

Info: Within the depths of Deer Creek Canyon lies a stream-side hiking opportunity you and the pooch won't want to miss. From basaltic canyon walls and bluffs to the Graham Pinery- a thick mountain oasis of ponderosa pine - this hike

Dogs May Be Unleashed Unless Otherwise Indicated

deserves its popularity. Two trail perks...good trout fishing in Deer Creek and excellent birdwatching. Falcons and hawks favor this area. For more information: (916) 258-2141.

Directions: From Red Bluff and Interstate 5, take Highway 36 east 20 miles to the community of Paynes Creek. At Little Giant Mill Road (Road 202) turn south (right) and drive seven miles to the intersection. Turn south onto Ponderosa Way and drive for another 32 miles to the trailhead.

Note : When fishing please follow the catch and release policy.

DOG ISLAND PARK / SAMUEL AYER PARK - Leashes

Info: This park is the answer to your dog's wildest dreams. Hike one of the many lush trails or cross over the footbridge to alluring Dog Island. For more information: (916) 527-8177.

Directions: Head north on Interstate 5 and exit at Red Bluff/Highway 36 west. Cross the river and turn right on Main Street for a few blocks to the sign for Dog Island Park on your right.

IDES COVE NATIONAL RECREATION TRAIL HIKE

Intermediate/8.8 miles/5.0 hours

Info: A hike along this looping trail through the Yolla Bolly Wilderness is a perfect all-day excursion. After an initial descent to Slide Creek, it's on to the base of 7,361-foot Harvey Peak, a popular picnicking area since it's the loop's halfway point. The trail then takes a sharp turn and continues the return beside the South Yolla Bolly Mountains where you'll come upon Long Lake and Square Lake. Both lakes are small but are trout stocked. For more information: (916) 934-3316.

Directions: From Interstate 5 in Red Bluff, take County Road 356 (Forest Road 22) west for about 41 miles. A signed access road on the right (north) takes you to Ides Cove Trailhead.

McCLURE TRAIL HIKE

Intermediate/12.0 miles/6.5 hours

Info: Nature lovers, take heart. This trail through the Tehama Wildlife Area is a wonderland of flora and abundant fauna, not to mention a refreshing rippling creek. Hike down the steep canyon to Antelope Creek and find yourself surrounded by extravagant greenery, especially in late winter and early spring. Summer can be very hot. For more information: (916) 258-2141.

Directions: From Red Bluff and Interstate 5, take Highway 36 east 20 miles to the community of Paynes Creek. Take Plum Creek Road south (right) 2.5 miles past the Ishi Conservation Camp to the High Trestle and Hogsback Roads intersection and park. The trailhead is .25 miles further on.

REDDING

LODGING

AMERICANA LODGE
1250 Pine St (96001)
Rates: $27-$34;
Tel: (916) 241-7020; (800) 626-1900

BEL AIR MOTEL
540 N Market St (96003)
Rates: $24-$49;
Tel: (916) 243-5291

BEST WESTERN HOSPITALITY HOUSE
532 N Market St (96003)
Rates: $49-$64;
Tel: (916) 241-6464; (800) 528-1234

BEST WESTERN PONDEROSA INN
2220 Pine St (96001)
Rates: $39-$63;
Tel: (916) 241-6300; (800) 528-1234

BRIDGE BAY RESORT
10300 Bridge Bay Rd (96003)
Rates: $55-$150;
Tel: (916) 241-6464; (800) 752-9669

CAPRI MOTEL
4620 Hwy 90 S (96001)
Rates: $30-$40;
Tel: (916) 241-1156; (800) 626-1900

CEDAR LODGE
513 N Market St (96003)
Rates: n/a;
Tel: (916) 244-3251

COMFORT INN
2059 Hilltop Dr (96002)
Rates: $44-$48;
Tel: (916) 221-6530; (800) 221-2222

ECONOMY INN
525 N Market St (96003)
Rates: $35+;
Tel: (916) 246-9803

FAWNDALE LODGE & RV RESORT
15215 Fawndale Rd (96003)
Rates: $30-$75;
Tel: (916) 275-8000

LA QUINTA INN
2180 Hilltop Dr (96002)
Rates: $54-$89;
Tel: (916) 221-8200; (800) 221-4731

MOTEL 6-CENTRAL
1640 Hilltop Dr (96001)
Rates: $38-$44;
Tel: (916) 221-1800; (800) 440-6000

Dogs May Be Unleashed Unless Otherwise Indicated

MOTEL 6-NORTH
1250 Twin View Blvd (96003)
Rates: $33-$41;
Tel: (916) 246-4470; (800) 440-6000

MOTEL 6-SOUTH
2385 Bechelli Ln (96002)
Rates: $34-$42;
Tel: (916) 221-0562; (800) 440-6000

MOTEL 99
533 N Market St (96003)
Rates: $35+;
Tel: (916) 241-4942

NORTH GATE LODGE
1040 Market St (96001)
Rates: $30;
Tel: (916) 243-4900

OXFORD SUITES
1967 Hilltop Dr (96002)
Rates: $65-$105;
Tel: (916) 221-0100; (800) 762-0133

PARK TERRACE INN
1900 Hilltop Dr (96002)
Rates: $68-$75;
Tel: (916) 221-7500

RED LION INN
1830 Hilltop Dr (96002)
Rates: $84-$121;
Tel: (916) 221-8700; (800) 547-8010

REDDING LODGE
1135 Market St (96001)
Rates: $32-$36;
Tel: (916) 243-5141

RIVER INN
1835 Park Marina Dr (96001)
Rates: $40-$60;
Tel: (916) 241-9500; (800) 995-4341

SARATOGA MOTEL
3025 S Market St (96001)
Rates: $25+;
Tel: (916) 243-8586

SHASTA DAM EL RANCHO MOTEL
1529 Cascade Blvd
(Shasta Lake City 96079)
Rates: $28-$38;
Tel: (916) 275-1065

SHASTA LODGE
1245 Pine St (96001)
Rates: $28-$45;
Tel: (916) 243-6133

STAR DUST MOTEL
1200 Pine St (96001)
Rates: $30-$35;
Tel: (916) 241-6121

THRIFTLODGE & CASA BLANCA MOTEL
413 N Market St (96003)
Rates: $25+;
Tel: (916) 241-3010

VAGABOND INN
536 E Cypress Ave (96002)
Rates: $40-$65;
Tel: (916) 223-1600; (800) 522-1555

VAGABOND INN
2010 Pine St (96001)
Rates: $32-$45;
Tel: (916) 243-3336; (800) 522-1555

RECREATION

BAILEY COVE LOOP TRAIL HIKE

Intermediate/2.9 miles/1.5 hours

Info: This picturesque hike offers you and your furry sidekick a glimpse of placid blue waters surrounded by extraordinary limestone rock. The trail loops around the base of what was once a mountain, taking you from groves of oak and pine to dense copse of Douglas fir. Don't forget your rod. The fish are calling your name. For more information: (916) 275-1587.

Directions: Take Interstate 5 north to the O'Brien exit, following the signs to the picnic area at Bailey Cove Public Ramp.

Locate Other Dog-Friendly Activities...Check Nearby Cities

BENTON AIRPARK PARK

Info: Large and entirely fenced, this park is doggie nirvana. Treat your dog to a leash-free day while you kick back and puppy watch.

Directions: Take Interstate 5 and exit at Highway 299. Travel west (turning as needed to stay on 299) to Walnut Street and go left. Continue on Walnut to Placer Street and go right. The park is one block ahead.

HIRZ BAY TRAIL HIKE

Beginner/4.0 miles/2.0 hours

Info: This pleasant amble outlines the lake's shoreline and weaves along small coves and creek inlets. Look out over the lake and take in the unusual limestone outcrops and deep coves at Campbell and Dekkas Creeks. For more information: (916) 275-1587.

Directions: From Redding, take Interstate 5 north to the Gilman Road exit. Head east to the Hirz Bay Campground.

SACRAMENTO RIVER TRAIL HIKE - Leashes

Info: If wet paws equate to happiness, your pooch will be ecstatic romping through this riparian oasis. On weekends and holidays, be prepared to share your space. For more information: (916) 225-4100 or (800) 874-7562.

Directions: Take Market Street/Highway 273 and head west on Riverside Drive to the parking area.

WATERS GULCH OVERLOOK TRAIL HIKE

Intermediate/3.0 miles/1.5 hours

Info: Waters Gulch Loop on Shasta Lake is a nice place to embark on a journey of the largest reservoir in California. The trailhead at Packers Bay bisects with Overlook Trail, climbs a little mountain and provides agreeable views of Waters Gulch. For more information: (916) 246-5222.

Directions: From Interstate 5 head north to Shasta Lake and exit at Packers Bay. Head southwest on Packers Bay Road and you'll reach the trailhead a little before the boat dock.

REDLANDS

LODGING

GOOD NITE INN
1675 Industrial Park Ave (92374)
Rates: $37;
Tel: (909) 793-3723

REDLANDS INN
1235 W Colton Ave (92373)
Rates: $28-$33;
Tel: (909) 793-6648

SUPER 8 MOTEL
1160 Arizona St (92374)
Rates: $26-$32;
Tel: (909) 335-1612; (800) 800-8000

RECREATION

BIG FALLS TRAIL HIKE- Leashes

Beginner/0.6 miles/.50 hours

Info: The highest waterfall in Southern California is less than a hop, skip and a jump away. Simply cross over Mill Creek wash and before you know it, you'll be ogling magnificent Big Falls. Don't stray from the overlook, the terrain is dangerously slippery. For more information: (909) 794-1123.

Directions: From Redlands, take Highway 38 north to Valley-of-the-Falls Boulevard. Follow this road approximately 3 miles to the parking lot adjacent to the Falls Picnic Area. The trailhead is at the north end of the parking lot.

BROOKSIDE PARK - Leashes

Info: 9.3 acres of scenery and serenity can be yours on a visit to this lovely park.

Directions: Located at Brookside and Terracina.

CAROLINE PARK - Leashes

Info: This 16.8-acre park is a nature lover's dream come true. You'll find a nature study area, a water conservation demonstration garden, wildlife areas and rainbow colored wildflower meadows in this delightful parkland.

Directions: Located at Sunset Drive and Mariposa.

COMMUNITY PARK - Leashes

Info: A large, grassy lawn area provides pleasure for padded paws in this 9.1-acre park.

Directions: Located at Church and San Bernardino.

FORD PARK - Leashes

Info: Able anglers, grab your gear and your Golden and get ready for some fun in the sun. This expansive, 19.8-acre park offers a small fishing lake. Lucky dogs can BBQ the day's catch on one of the grills provided.

Directions: Located at Redlands Boulevard and Parkford.

PONDEROSA VISTA NATURE TRAIL HIKE - Leashes

Beginner/0.6 miles/0.25 hours

Info: Learn as you take a turn around this easy, looping trail. Interpretive signs educate you on the area. Stop off at the scenic overlook for some splendid views. For more information: (909) 794-1123.

Directions: Take Highway 38 north to the junction with Jenks Lake Road West. The trail begins on the west side of Highway 38.

PROSPECT PARK - Leashes

Info: Seat yourself on one of the grassy hillside knolls and delight in the stunning vistas and succulent aromas of this idyllic park. The landscape is alive with orange trees, heaven-kissing palms and colorful flowers. For more information: (909) 793-2546.

Dogs May Be Unleashed Unless Otherwise Indicated

Directions: Heading east on Interstate 10, take the Orange Street exit and drive south. After about .25 miles, bear right at Cajon Street and continue about a mile to the park on the right.

SANTA ANA RIVER TRAIL HIKE

Intermediate/9.0 miles/4.5 hours

Info: In early summer, this trail is brimming with paintbrush, lupine, columbine and monkeyflower. Come early in the morning and you and the pupster might just see a bit of wildlife too - the picturesque area is home to fox, deer, raccoon and beaver. Stick to the Santa Ana River Trail signs and you won't go wrong. When you reach the Forest Service Road 1N021 junction, retrace your steps. For more information: (909) 794-1123.

Directions: From Interstate 10 in Redlands, take the Highway 30/38 Interchange north to Highway 38. Head east on Highway 38 for 32 miles to the South Fork Campground. The parking area and trailhead are catty-corner to the campground.

SMILEY PARK - Leashes

Info: You and the dogster will have plenty to smile about as you sniff the stuff in this 9.2-acre park. Complete with the Lincoln Shrine, Redlands Bowl, shuffleboard and horseshoe pits, the area is brimming with recreational opportunities for two-legged and four-legged visitors.

Directions: Located at Eureka and 4th Streets.

SYLVAN PARK - Leashes

Info: Bustling with outdoor activity, this 22.5-acre park can't be beat for sports enthusiasts and social breeds.

Directions: Located at Colton and University.

WHISPERING PINES TRAIL HIKE- Leashes

Beginner/1.0 miles/0.5 hours

Info: Commune with nature and your canine on this simple oak and pine woodland trail. For a more interesting journey, pick up a trail guide before setting out. For more information: (909) 794-1123.

Directions: From Redlands, take Highway 38 north to the trailhead at the junction with Jenks Lake Road West.

YUCAIPA REGIONAL PARK - Leashes

Info: Surrounded by the glorious San Bernadinos and magnificent Mount San Gorgonio, this nearly 900-acre park is a panoramic wonderland. And there's great trout fishing at three stocked lakes. For more information: (909) 790-3120.

Directions: Take Interstate 10 southeast to the Yucaipa exit. Follow the signs for "Regional Park" approximately five miles.

Note: $4 day-use fee on weekdays, $5 on weekends and holidays. $1 dog fee and $4 fishing fee.

Other parks in Redlands - Leashes
•COMMUNITY CENTER PARK, 111 E. Lugonia Avenue
•CRAFTON PARK, on Wabash near Crafton School
•ED HALES PARK, State and 5th Streets
•JENNIE DAVIS PARK, Redlands Boulevard and New York
•TEXONIA PARK, Texas Street and Lugonia

REDONDO BEACH

LODGING

PORTOFINO HOTEL & YACHT CLUB
260 Portofino Way (90277)
Rates: $129-$159;
Tel: (310) 379-8481; (800) 468-4292

TRAVELODGE-REDONDO BEACH PIER
206 S Pacific Coast Hwy (90277)
Rates: $65;
Tel: (310) 318-1811; (800) 578-7878

VAGABOND INN
6226 Pacific Coast Hwy (90277)
Rates: $45-$54;
Tel: (310) 378-8555; (800) 522-1555

Dogs May Be Unleashed Unless Otherwise Indicated

<u>RECREATION</u>

DOMINGUEZ PARK

Info: Although this park is plain and treeless, the 2.25-acre dog area is leashless. Lots of locals congregate A.M. and P.M. so your pooch will have company. Besides, it's the only game in town. For more information: (310) 374-2171 or (800) 282-0333.

Directions: From northbound Highway 1, turn right on Beryl Street. After 10 blocks, go left on Flagler Lane to the second entrance for the park.

Note: Due to renovations, the park will be closed May through August 1996.

REDWAY

<u>LODGING</u>

BUDGET WEST REDWAY INN
3223 Redwood Dr (95560)
Rates: $36;
Tel: (707) 923-2660; (800) 732-5380 (CA)

REDWOOD CITY

<u>LODGING</u>

GOOD NITE INN
485 Veterans Blvd (94063)
Rates: $40-$71;
Tel: (415) 365-5500

<u>RECREATION</u>

HEATHER PARK

Info: Puppy nirvana! This delightful park provides rippling green hills and a labyrinth of paths where your pooch can frolic for hours with other leashless canines. Bring your own water. For more information: (415) 593-8011.

Directions: Head west on Highway 84, then north on Highway 82 to the San Carlos exit. The park is located at Melendy and Portofino Drives, adjacent to Heather Elementary School.

Locate Other Dog-Friendly Activities...Check Nearby Cities

WINDY HILL PRESERVE - Leashes

Info: From grassy ridgetops to the luxuriant forested canyons, this 1,130-acre preserve has it all. In the mood for exercise? Leash Fido and head out for on three miles of diverse trails. At the entrance, go left to the Anniversary Trail. The .75 mile ascent will get your blood pumping. If you're up to more, head down the other side of the hill and go right to Spring Ridge Trail. It's a fairly easy 2.5-mile traipse to a rejuvenating, albeit small creek. Find yourself a shady spot and simply kick back. For more information: (415) 691-1200.

Directions: From Redwood City, take Interstate 280 south to Highway 84 south. The park is located on Skyline Boulevard, 2 miles south of Highway 84.

REEDLEY

LODGING

EDGEWATER INN
1977 W Manning Ave (93654)
Rates: $52;
Tel: (209) 637-7777

RECREATION

HILLCREST TREE FARM - Leashes

Info: Canine companions are welcome to saunter beside you in this peaceful park.

Directions: Located north of Reedley on Reed Road at Adams.

PIONEER PARK - Leashes

Info: Pack a lunch and munch out with the munchkin at this pleasant sun-dappled city park.

Directions: Located on the corner of G and 8th Streets.

Dogs May Be Unleashed Unless Otherwise Indicated

RESEDA

RESEDA RECREATION CENTER - Leashes

Info: From fishing to football, BBQ to baseball, horseshoe pits to open roaming space, this 36-acre green scene provides plenty of entertaining options for you and Fido.

Directions: Located at 18411 Victory Boulevard.

RIALTO

BEST WESTERN EMPIRE INN
475 W Valley Blvd (92376)
Rates: $56-$65;
Tel: (909) 877-0690; (800) 528-1234

RIDGECREST

EL DORADO MOTEL
400 S China Lake Blvd (93555)
Rates: $28-$95;
Tel: (619) 375-1354

EL RANCHO
507 S China Lake Blvd (93555)
Rates: $37-$49;
Tel: (619) 375-9731

HACIENDA COURT
150 W Miguel (93555)
Rates: $50-$70;
Tel: (619) 375-5066

HERITAGE INN
1050 N Norma Dr (93555)
Rates: $75-$95;
Tel: (619) 446-6543; (800) 843-0693

HERITAGE SUITES
919 N Heritage Dr (93555)
Rates: $90-$150;
Tel: (619) 446-7951;

MOTEL 6
535 S China Lake Blvd (93555)
Rates: $25-$29;
Tel: (619) 375-6866; (800) 440-6000

PANAMINT SPRINGS RESORT
Hwy 190 (93555)
Rates: $46-$65;
Tel: (619) 764-2010

RIDGECREST MOTOR INN
329 E Ridgecrest Blvd (93555)
Rates: $30-$50;
Tel: (619) 371-1695

Locate Other Dog-Friendly Activities...Check Nearby Cities

RIO NIDO

<u>LODGING</u>

RIO NIDO LODGE RESORT
1458 River Rd (95471)
Rates: $50-$80;
Tel: (707) 869-0821

RIVERSIDE

<u>LODGING</u>

COURTYARD BY MARRIOTT
1510 University Ave (92507)
Rates: $59;
Tel: (909) 276-1200; (800) 443-6000

DYNASTY SUITES
3735 Iowa Ave (92507)
Rates: $39-$49;
Tel: (909) 369-8200; (800) 842-7899

ECONO LODGE
1971 University Ave (92507)
Rates: $32-$44;
Tel: (909) 684-6363; (800) 424-4777

HAMPTON INN
1590 University Ave (92507)
Rates: $39;
Tel: (909) 683-6000; (800) 426-7866

HOLIDAY INN
1200 University Ave (92507)
Rates: $64-$75;
Tel: (909) 784-8000; (800) 465-4329

MOTEL 6-DOWNTOWN
4045 University Ave (92501)
Rates: $26-$30;
Tel: (909) 686-6666; (800) 440-6000

MOTEL 6-EAST
1260 University Ave (92507)
Rates: $26-$30;
Tel: (909) 784-2131; (800) 440-6000

MOTEL 6-SOUTH
3663 La Sierra Ave (92505)
Rates: $26-$30;
Tel: (909) 351-0764; (800) 440-6000

SUPER 8 MOTEL
1199 University Ave (92507)
Rates: $32-$39;
Tel: (909) 682-9011; (800) 800-8000

TRAVELODGE-LA SIERRA
11043 Magnolia Ave (92505)
Rates: $39-$69;
Tel: (909) 688-5000; (800) 578-7878

<u>RECREATION</u>

BOX SPRINGS MOUNTAIN RESERVE - Leashes

Info: You'll have 1,155 acres of unbridled scenery and trails galore to explore with your wagalong. Tote your own water. For more information: (909) 275-4310.

Directions: Located 5 miles east of Riverside off Highway 60 and Pigeon Pass Road.

Dogs May Be Unleashed Unless Otherwise Indicated

HIDDEN VALLEY WILDLIFE AREA - Leashes

Info: Pack your binocs and a zoom lens for your camera. This gorgeous 1,300-acre region is home to a diverse crosssection of wildlife. Make tracks along the trails for serenity, solitude and a chance to sniff out some photo ops. Tread lightly in this delicate ecosystem and keep your trail-sniffer leashed. For more information: (909) 785-6362.

Directions: Located west of Arlington Avenue, across from Crestlawn Cemetery.

JOSHUA TREE NATIONAL MONUMENT - Leashes

Info: Put this 870-square-mile park at the top of your day's itinerary and you won't soon forget the dazzling display of nature that can be yours. Access the park from the visitors center for amazing vistas of granite rock formations and desert flora and fauna. The west end of the park is home to the elegant Joshua tree. In springtime, this arid terrain comes alive with brilliant wildflowers. Your pup can partake of the nature excursion as long as he remains leashed and on the roads, not the hiking trails.

Directions: Take Highway 60 east to Interstate 10 southeast. Continue to Highway 62 northeast. Follow approximately 39 miles to the town of Twentynine Palms. The visitors center is on the Utah Trail, south of Highway 62, one mile east of town.

Note: $5 entrance fee.

RANCHO JURUPA PARK - Leashes

Info: You'll be surrounded by stately cottonwoods and magnificent meadows as you and your mutt make your way through this 200-acre park. In the cooler months, the 3-acre lake is stocked with trout, so you can try your fly. Visit in summer and drop in on the catfish. Lucky dogs can grill up the day's catch on the BBQ's. Views of the Jurupa Hills and the distant San Bernardino Mountains are incredible. For more information: (909) 684-7032.

Directions: Take Buena Park Avenue across the Santa Ana River. Go left on Crestmore Road. Rancho Jurupa Park is along the Santa Ana River at the end of Crestmore Road.

Note: $2/day dog fee.

Locate Other Dog-Friendly Activities...Check Nearby Cities

SANTA ANA RIVER WILDLIFE AREA - Leashes

Info: This vast 10-mile park runs east to west, enveloping both the Rancho Jurupa Park and the Hidden Valley Wildlife Area. Spend the afternoon hiking the numerous trails near the park's nature center, casting your line or chilling out under a shade tree. For more information: (909) 781-0143.

Directions: To access the fee-free area take Highway 60 to Rubidoux Boulevard Drive southwest a couple of streets and turn right on Mission Boulevard. Travel to Riverview Drive/Limonite Avenue and go left. Half a mile further, Riverview veers to the left and there'll be a sign for the county park. Follow Riverview another 1.5 miles to the park on the left. Park near the nature center. Access fee areas by turning left on Mission Boulevard to Crestmore Boulevard. Follow Crestmore for 1.5 miles to the gate of the park.

Note: $2/adults, $1/child under 12 and $2 dog day-use fee.

ROCKLIN

LODGING

FIRST CHOICE INNS
4420 Rocklin Rd (95677)
Rates: $62-$125;
Tel: (916) 624-4500; (800) 462-2400

ROHNERT PARK

LODGING

BEST WESTERN INN
6500 Redwood Dr (94928)
Rates: $42-$74;
Tel: (707) 584-7435; (800) 528-1234

MOTEL 6
6145 Commerce Blvd (94928)
Rates: $28-$35;
Tel: (707) 585-8888

RED LION HOTEL-SONOMA COUNTY
1 Red Lion Dr (94928)
Rates: $105-$145;
Tel: (707) 584-5466; (800) 547-8010

ROHNERT PARK INN
6288 Redwood Dr (94928)
Rates: $28-$34;
Tel: (707) 584-1005

Dogs May Be Unleashed Unless Otherwise Indicated

RECREATION

CRANE CREEK REGIONAL PARK - Leashes

Info: Meander through meadows, oak and maple woodlands on picturesque creekside trails or just play the day away in this lovely 128-acre park. For more information: (707) 527-2041.

Directions: Just east of Rohnert Park on Pressley Road off the end of Roberts Road, two miles east of Petaluma Hill Road.

ROSAMOND

LODGING

DEVONSHIRE INN MOTEL
P. O. Box 2080 (93560)
Rates: $49-$59;
Tel: (805) 256-3454

ROSEMEAD

LODGING

MOTEL 6
1001 S San Gabriel Blvd (91770)
Rates: $34-$38;
Tel: (818) 572-6076; (800) 440-6000

VAGABOND INN
3633 N Rosemead Blvd (91770)
Rates: $42-$57;
Tel: (818) 288-6661; (800) 522-1555

ROSEVILLE

LODGING

BEST WESTERN ROSEVILLE INN
220 Harding Blvd (95678)
Rates: $49-$80;
Tel: (916) 782-4434; (800) 528-1234

ROWLAND HEIGHTS

LODGING

MOTEL 6
18970 E Labin Ct (91748)
Rates: $30-$34;
Tel: (818) 964-5333; (800) 440-6000

RUNNING SPRINGS

LODGING

GIANT OAKS MOTEL & CABINS
32180 Hilltop Blvd (92382)
Rates: $49-$119;
Tel: (800) 786-1689

SACRAMENTO

LODGING

AAA RESIDENCE INN
3721 Watt Ave (95821)
Rates: $46;
Tel: (916) 485-7125; (800) 786-4926

AMERICANA LODGE
818 15th St (95814)
Rates: $35-$45;
Tel: (916) 444-8085; (800) 645-7318

**BEVERLY GARLAND HOTEL &
CONFERENCE CENTER**
1780 Tribute Rd (95815)
Rates: $74-$145;
Tel: (916) 929-7900; (800) 972-3976

CANTERBURY INN
1900 Canterbury Rd (95815)
Rates: $55-$65;
Tel: (916) 927-3492; (800) 932-3492

CLARION HOTEL-SACRAMENTO
700 16th St (95814) Rates: $79-$109;
Tel: (916) 444-8000; (800) 443-0880

CORAL REEF LODGE
2700 Fulton Ave (95814)
Rates: $45-$80;
Tel: (916) 483-6461; (800) 995-6460

CROSSROADS INN
221 Jibboom St (95814)
Rates: $38-$60;
Tel: (916) 442-7777

DAYS INN-DISCOVERY PARK
350 Bercut Dr (95814)
Rates: $54-$73;
Tel: (916) 442-6971; (800) 329-7746;
(800) 952-5516 (CA)

EXPO INN
1413 Howe Ave (95825)
Rates: $65; Tel: (916) 922-9833

GOLDEN TEE INN
3215 Auburn Blvd (95821)
Rates: $25-$40;
Tel: (916) 482-7440

GUEST SUITES
2806 Grassland Dr (95833)
Rates: $45-$80;
Tel: (916) 641-2617; (800) 227-4903

HILTON INN-SACRAMENTO
2200 Harvard St (95815)
Rates: $99-$109;
Tel: (916) 922-4700; (800) 344-4321

Dogs May Be Unleashed Unless Otherwise Indicated

HOLIDAY INN CAL EXPO
1780 Tribute Rd (95815)
Rates: $69-$89; Tel: (800) 465-4329

HOLIDAY INN-CAPITOL PLAZA
300 J St (95814); Rates: $86-$120;
Tel: (916) 446-0100; (800) 465-4329

HOLIDAY INN NORTH EAST
5321 Date Ave (95841)
Rates: $56-$74;
Tel: (916) 338-5800; (800) 465-4329

HOWARD JOHNSON HOTEL
3343 Bradshaw Rd (95827)
Rates: $50-$60;
Tel: (916) 366-1266; (800) 446-4656

INNS OF AMERICA
25 Howe Ave (95826)
Rates: $35-$50;
Tel: (916) 386-8408; (800) 826-0778

LA QUINTA INN
4604 Madison Ave (95841)
Rates: $52-$65;
Tel: (916) 348-0900; (800) 531-5900

LA QUINTA INN
200 Jibboom St (95814)
Rates: $52-$68;
Tel: (916) 448-8100; (800) 531-5900

MANSION VIEW LODGE
771 16th St (95814); Rates: $36-$42;
Tel: (916) 443-6631; (800) 409-9595

MOTEL ORLEANS
228 Jibboom St (95814)
Rates: $40-$62;
Tel: (916) 443-4811; (800) 626-1900

MOTEL 6
7407 Elsie Ave (95828)
Rates: $32-$38;
Tel: (916) 689-6555; (800) 440-6000

MOTEL 6-CENTRAL
7850 College Town Dr (95826)
Rates: $31-$37;
Tel: (916) 383-8110; (800) 440-6000

MOTEL 6-DOWNTOWN
1415 30th St (95816);
Rates: $35-$41;
Tel: (916) 457-0777; (800) 440-6000

MOTEL 6-NORTH
5110 Interstate Ave (95842)
Rates: $33-$39;
Tel: (916) 331-8100; (800) 440-6000

MOTEL 6-OLD SACRAMENTO
227 Jibboom St (95814)
Rates: $34-$40;
Tel: (916) 441-0733; (800) 440-6000

MOTEL 6-SOUTHWEST
7780 Stockton Blvd (95823)
Rates: $31-$37;
Tel: (916) 689-9141; (800) 440-6000

POINT WEST APARTMENTS
1761 Heritage Ln (95815)
Rates: $80+;
Tel: (916) 922-5882

RADISSON HOTEL
500 Leisure Ln (95815)
Rates: $72-$82;
Tel: (916) 922-2020; (800) 333-3333

RED LION HOTEL-SACRAMENTO
2001 Point West Way (95815)
Rates: $85-$145;
Tel: (916) 929-8855; (800) 547-8010

RED LION'S SACRAMENTO INN
1401 Arden Way (95815)
Rates: $68-$120;
Tel: (916) 922-9391; (800) 547-8010

RESIDENCE INN BY MARRIOTT
2410 W El Camino (95833)
Rates: $59-$129;
Tel: (916) 649-1300; (800) 331-3131

SIERRA INN
2600 Auburn Blvd (95821)
Rates: $36-$125;
Tel: (916) 482-4770; (800) 757-4377

SKY RIDERS MOTEL
6100 Freeport Blvd (95822)
Rates: $45-$80;
Tel: (916) 421-5700

SUPER 8 MOTEL
7216 55th St (95823);
Rates: $40-$56;
Tel: (916) 427-7925; (800) 800-8000

TRAVELODGE-CAPITOL CENTER
1111 H St (95814)
Rates: $39-$54;
Tel: (916) 444-8880; (800) 578-7878

VAGABOND INN-MIDTOWN
1319 30th St (95816)
Rates: $39-$49;
Tel: (916) 454-4400; (800) 522-1555

Locate Other Dog-Friendly Activities...Check Nearby Cities

RECREATION

AMERICAN RIVER PARKWAY TRAIL HIKE

Beginner/1.0 to 23.0 miles/0.5 to 11.0 hours

Info: This trail along the American River stretches from Discovery Park in Sacramento to Folsom. The popular multi-use trail attracts walkers, cyclists, joggers and equestrians. The bike and horse trails are separate. It's prettiest in spring and fall and very hot in summer. For more information: (916) 366-2061.

Directions: From Sacramento, take Interstate 5 south to the Richards Boulevard exit. Head west to Jibboom Street, turn north following the road into the park.

GIBSON RANCH COUNTY PARK - Leashes

Info: A 40-acre picnic area is part of this 325-acre park. Relax in the sunshine or work off some kibble on one of the hiking trails. Pups are prohibited on the horse trails. For more information: (916) 366-2066.

Directions: Located at 8554 Gibson Ranch Road.

LOCH LEVEN LAKES TRAIL HIKE

Intermediate/7.0 miles/3.5 hours

Info: Get a jump start on your day and make the most of this spectacular hike. Spend hours "oohing and aahing" over granite cliffs, alpine meadows, verdant valleys, Jeffrey and lodgepole pine woodlands, sun-drenched lakes, glacial mountain terrain and of course, the three beautiful Loch Leven Lakes. Just follow the path across a creek, over railroad tracks, through a forest and down to Lower Loch Leven Lake. But don't stop there. Go for the last mile around Middle Loch then continue eastward to High Loch. Not having enough time to spend will be your only regret of the day. For more information: (916) 265-4531.

Directions: From Sacramento, take Interstate 80 east to the Big Bend exit. Follow the signs to the visitors center. Both the trailhead and parking are .25 miles east of the visitors center.

Dogs May Be Unleashed Unless Otherwise Indicated

SALINAS

LODGING

DAYS INN
1226 De La Torre Blvd (93905)
Rates: $35-$90;
Tel: (800) 329-7466

EL DORADO MOTEL
1351 N Main St (93906)
Rates: $28-$60;
Tel: (408) 449-2442; (800) 523-6506

MOTEL 6-CENTRAL
1010 Fairview Ave (93905)
Rates: $26-$34;
Tel: (408) 758-2122; (800) 440-6000

MOTEL 6-NORTH
140 Kern St (93901)
Rates: $28-$35;
Tel: (408) 753-1711; (800) 440-6000

MOTEL 6-SOUTH
1275 De La Torre Blvd (93905)
Rates: $27-$35;
Tel: (408) 757-3077; (800) 440-6000

RAMADA INN
808 N Main St (93906)
Rates: $49-$89;
Tel: (800) 272-6232

TRAVELODGE OF SALINAS
555 Airport Blvd (93905)
Rates: $36-$99;
Tel: (408) 424-1741; (800) 578-7878

VAGABOND INN
131 Kern St (93905)
Rates: $45-$95;
Tel: (408) 758-4693; (800) 522-1555

RECREATION

ROYAL OAKS PARK - Leashes

Info: Velvet hills roll through an expansive oak forest and create a shade-filled verdant oasis for you and Fido. Stroll among trees or kick back on the soft grass. For more information: (408) 755-4899.

Directions: From Salinas, take Highway 101 to San Miguel Canyon Road. Turn left onto Echo Valley Road and then right onto Maher Road. The park is on the left-hand side.

TORO REGIONAL PARK - Leashes

Info: As you ascend along 12 miles of trails, you'll be rewarded with outstanding vistas of Salinas Valley and Monterey Bay. This 4,800-acre wilderness area also offers a self-guided interpretive trail beside a tranquil stream. Summer can be hot. Tote your own water. For more information: (408) 755-4899.

Directions: Head west on Highway 68 for five miles. Follow the signs to the park.

Note: $3 car fee Monday-Thursday and $5 Friday-Sunday.

Locate Other Dog-Friendly Activities...Check Nearby Cities

SAN ANDREAS

LODGING

BLACK BART INN & MOTEL
35 Main St (95249)
Rates: $47-$55;
Tel: (209) 754-3808; (800) 225-3764

RECREATION

SPICER RESERVOIR to SAND FLAT TRAIL HIKE

Intermediate/Expert/10.0 miles/5.0 hours

Info: This calorie burning hike leads you among dense woodlands, through Corral Meadow, and over rough and tough but beautiful terrain to Sand Flat. Once you reach Sand Flat, or you've simply had enough, turn the hound around and retrace your steps. For more information: (209) 795-1381.

Directions: From San Andreas, take Highway 49 south 13 miles to Angels Camp and Highway 4. Continue 43 miles northeast. After the Big Meadows Campground turn right (south) onto Forest Road 7N01. Follow the paved road for approximately 9.5 miles to the trailhead. For an area map and more information, stop by the Ranger Station.

SAN ANSELMO

RECREATION

MEMORIAL PARK - Leashes

Info: Lounge with the hound in this lovely community park. Step lively through the open spaces or break some biscuits with Bowser on the shaded ground.

Directions: Located at 1000 Sir Francis Drake Boulevard.

ROBSON HERRINGTON PARK - Leashes

Info: Complete with a pretty garden, this park provides pleasant sniffing space for you and your canine companion.

Directions: Located at 237 Crescent Road.

Dogs May Be Unleashed Unless Otherwise Indicated

SAN BERNARDINO

LODGING

BEST WESTERN SANDS MOTEL
606 North H St (92410)
Rates: $52-$60;
Tel: (909) 889-8391; (800) 528-1234;
(800) 331-4409 (CA)

HILTON-SAN BERNARDINO
285 E Hospitality Ln (92408)
Rates: $85-$95;
Tel: (909) 889-0133; (800) 445-8667;
(800) 446-1065 (CA)

LA QUINTA INN
205 E Hospitality Ln (92408)
Rates: $52-$67;
Tel: (909) 888-7571; (800) 531-5900

MOTEL 6-NORTH
1960 Ostrems Way (92407)
Rates: $28-$32;
Tel: (909) 887-8191; (800) 440-6000

MOTEL 6-SOUTH
111 Redlands Blvd (92408)
Rates: $26-$32;
Tel: (909) 825-6666; (800) 440-6000

RECREATION

BLUFF MESA TRAIL HIKE

Beginner/0.8 miles/1.0 hours

Info: Sofa loafers rejoice. Here's a trail through towering Jeffrey pines that's short on effort, long on beauty. Start at the Champion Lodgepole Pine and head north to Bluff Mesa Group Camp. For more information: (909) 866-3437.

Directions: From Interstate 15 at Cajon Junction go east on the Rim of the World Highway (Highway 18) to Big Bear Lake, and turn right onto Tulip Lane. About a half-mile from the highway, go right onto Forest Service Road 2N11. Follow the Champion Lodgepole signs for the next five miles until you reach the marked trailhead. Park by the road.

CASTLE ROCK TRAIL HIKE

Intermediate/1.6 miles/1.5 hours

Info: Towering above Big Bear Lake, Castle Rock stands guard over a magnificent landscape. Summer and fall are the seasons of vibrant colors. For more information: (909) 866-3437.

Directions: From Interstate 15 at Cajon Junction, go east on the Rim of the World Highway (Highway 18) to Big Bear Lake. Go about one mile past the dam on Highway 18 to a parking area next to the highway.

Locate Other Dog-Friendly Activities...Check Nearby Cities

GLORY RIDGE TRAIL HIKE

Expert/2.0 miles/1.0 hours

Info: The hike to Bear Creek is a short but steep descent. Once you arrive, relax to the soothing sounds of the stream before tackling the 1,100-foot return climb. This challenging trail separates the dogs from the pups. For more information: (909) 866-3437.

Directions: From Interstate 15 at Cajon Junction, go east on the Rim of the World Highway (Highway 18). Take a right onto Forest Service Road 2N15, and travel about 1.5 miles until arriving at Big Bear Lake. Parking is at the end of the road.

WOODLAND TRAIL HIKE

Beginner/1.5 miles/1.0 hours

Info: Become one with nature along this interpretive trail. Learn about the natural history of Big Bear Lake. Before you start, pick up a brochure at the Ranger Station. For more information: (909) 866-3437.

Directions: From Interstate 15 at Cajon Junction, go east on the Rim of the World Highway (Highway 18) to Big Bear Lake. Travel north onto Highway 38 and proceed to the marked trailhead and parking area located on the north side of the highway. It's a little past the Big Bear Ranger Station and across from the MWD East Launch Boat Ramp.

SAN BRUNO

LODGING

SUMMERFIELD SUITES HOTEL
1350 Huntington Ave (94066)
Rates: $129-$189;
Tel: (800) 833-4353

Dogs May Be Unleashed Unless Otherwise Indicated

<u>RECREATION</u>
CARL SANDBURG PARK

Info: How convenient, a dedicated dog park equipped with the basics - pooper scoopers, water and benches - all in one enclosed area.

Directions: On Evergreen behind Carl Sandburg School.

SAN CARLOS

<u>RECREATION</u>
PULGAS RIDGE PRESERVE - Leashes

Info: Three miles of trails zig and zag their way through oak and chapparal-strewn terrain in this 293-acre preserve. Come in springtime when the landscape is dotted with colorful wildflowers. For more information: (415) 691-1200.

Directions: From Highway 280, take the Edgewood Road exit east approximately one mile. Turn left on Crestview Drive and a quick left on Edmonds Road. Follow the signs to the preserve.

SAN CLEMENTE

<u>LODGING</u>
HOLIDAY INN-SAN CLEMENTE RESORT
111 S Avenida de Estrella (92672)
Rates: $70-$95;
Tel: (714) 361-3000; (800) 465-4329

SAN DIEGO

<u>LODGING</u>
ARENA INN
3330 Rosecrans St (92110)
Rates: $44-$78;
Tel: (619) 224-8266; (800) 742-4627

BEACH HAVEN INN
4740 Mission Blvd (92109)
Rates: $60-$140;
Tel: (619) 272-3812; (800) 831-6323

Locate Other Dog-Friendly Activities...Check Nearby Cities

BEST WESTERN HANALEI HOTEL
2270 Hotel Circle N (92108)
Rates: $69-$109;
Tel: (619) 297-1101; (800) 882-0858

CATAMARAN RESORT HOTEL
3999 Mission Blvd (92109)
Rates: $140-$900;
Tel: (619) 488-1081; (800) 288-0770

CROWN POINT VIEW SUITE-HOTEL
4088 Crown Point Dr (92109)
Rates: $70-$150;
Tel: (619) 272-0676; (800) 338-3331

DAYS INN-JACK MURPHY STADIUM
9350 Kearny Mesa Dr (92126)
Rates: $40-$70;
Tel: (619) 578-4350; (800) 329-7466

DAYS INN-MISSION BAY/SEA WORLD
2575 Clairemont Dr (92117)
Rates: $56-$71;
Tel: (619) 275-5700; (800) 329-7466

EMBASSY SUITES-SAN DIEGO BAY
601 Pacific Hwy (92101)
Rates: $119-$169;
Tel: (619) 239-2400; (800) 362-2779

E-Z 8 MOTEL
2484 Hotel Circle Pl (92018)
Rates: $35-$50;
Tel: (619) 291-8252; (800) 326-6835

E-Z 8 MOTEL-OLD TOWN
4747 Pacific Hwy (92110)
Rates: $35-$50;
Tel: (619) 294-2512; (800) 326-6835

E-Z 8 MOTEL-SPORTS ARENA
3325 Midway Dr (92110)
Rates: $35-$50;
Tel: (619) 223-9500; (800) 326-6835

GOOD NITE INN
4545 Waring Rd (92120)
Rates: $35-$53;
Tel: (619) 286-7000; (800) 648-3466

GOOD NITE INN-SEA WORLD
3880 Greenwood St (92110)
Rates: $46-$70;
Tel: (619) 543-9944; (800) 648-3466

GROSVENOR INN-DOWNTOWN
810 Ash St (92101)
Rates: $40-$50;
Tel: (619) 233-8826; (800) 232-1212

HOLIDAY INN ON THE BAY
1355 N Harbor Dr (92101)
Rates: $68-$98;
Tel: (619) 232-3861; (800) 465-4329;
(800) 877-8920

THE HORTON GRAND HOTEL
311 Island Ave (92101)
Rates: $99-$129;
Tel: (619) 544-1886; (800) 542-1886

HOTEL CIRCLE INN & SUITES
2201 Hotel Circle S (92108)
Rates: $49-$99;
Tel: (619) 291-2711; (800) 772-7711
(800) 621-4222 (CAN)

LAMPLIGHTER INN & SUITES
6474 El Cajon Blvd (92115)
Rates: $39-$64;
Tel: (619) 582-3088; (800) 545-0778

**MARRIOTT HOTEL & MARINA-
SAN DIEGO**
333 W Harbor Dr (92101)
Rates: $149-$179;
Tel: (619) 234-1500; (800) 228-9290

MARRIOTT SUITES-DOWNTOWN
701 A St (92101)
Rates: $170-$180;
Tel: (619) 696-9800; (800) 962-1367

MOTEL 6-HOTEL CIRCLE
2424 Hotel Circle N (92108)
Rates: $36-$42;
Tel: (619) 296-1612; (800) 440-6000

MOTEL 6-NORTH
5592 Clairemont Mesa Blvd (92117)
Rates: $34-$38;
Tel: (619) 268-9758; (800) 440-6000

OLD TOWN INN
4444 Pacific Hwy (92110)
Rates: $35-$50;
Tel: (619) 260-8024

OUTRIGGER MOTEL
1370 Scott St (92106)
Rates: $35-$50;
Tel: (619) 223-7105

**PACIFIC SANDS MOTEL &
CONDOMINIUMS**
4449 Ocean Blvd (92109)
Rates: $40-$60;
Tel: (619) 483-7555

Dogs May Be Unleashed Unless Otherwise Indicated

PACIFIC SHORES INN
4802 Mission Blvd (92109)
Rates: $58-$95;
Tel: (619) 483-6300; (800) 826-0715

PARK MANOR SUITES
525 Spruce St (92103)
Rates: $69-$149;
Tel: (619) 291-0999; (800) 874-2649

PICKWICK HOTEL
132 W Broadway (92101)
Rates: $35-$50;
Tel: (619) 234-0141

QUALITY INN-AIRPORT
2901 Nimitz Blvd (92106)
Rates: $75;
Tel: (619) 224-3655; (800) 221-2222

QUALITY SUITES
9880 Mira Mesa Blvd (92131)
Rates: $69-$99;
Tel: (619) 530-2000; (800) 221-2222

RADISSON HOTEL HARBOR VIEW
1646 Front St (92101)
Rates: $99-$129;
Tel: (619) 239-6800; (800) 333-3333

RADISSON HOTEL-SAN DIEGO
1433 Camino Del Rio S (92108)
Rates: $79-$135;
Tel: (619) 260-0111; (800) 333-3333

RAMADA INN-SAN DIEGO NORTH
5550 Kearny Mesa Rd (92111)
Rates: $52-$84;
Tel: (619) 278-0800; (800) 447-2637

RED LION INN
7450 Hazard Center Dr (92108)
Rates: $130-$165;
Tel: (619) 297-5466; (800) 547-8010

RESIDENCE INN BY MARRIOTT-KEARNY MESA
5400 Kearny Mesa Rd (92111)
Rates: $69-$175;
Tel: (619) 278-2100; (800) 331-3131

**SAN DIEGO HILTON
BEACH & TENNIS RESORT**
1775 E Mission Bay Dr (92109)
Rates: $145-$225;
Tel: (619) 276-4010; (800) 445-8667;
(800) 962-6307 (CA)

**SAN DIEGO MARRIOTT
MISSION VALLEY**
8757 Rio San Diego Dr (92108)
Rates: $99-$149;
Tel: (619) 692-3800; (800) 228-9290

SAN DIEGO MISSION VALLEY HILTON
901 Camino Del Rio S (92108)
Rates: $109-$179;
Tel: (619) 543-9000; (800) 445-8667;
(800) 733-2332 (CA)

SAN DIEGO PRINCESS RESORT
1404 W Vacation Rd (92109)
Rates: $130-$345;
Tel: (619) 274-4630; (800) 344-2626

SHERATON INN-SAN DIEGO CENTRAL
8110 Aero Dr (92123)
Rates: $89-$122;
Tel: (619) 277-8888; (800) 325-3535

SOUTH BAY LODGE
1101 Hollister St (92154)
Rates: $27-$47; Tel: (619) 428-7600

SUPER 8 MISSION BAY
4540 Mission Bay Dr (92109)
Rates: $45-$58;
Tel: (619) 274-7888; (800) 800-8000

U.S. GRANT HOTEL
326 Broadway (92101)
Rates: $135-$195;
Tel: (619) 232-3121; (800) 237-5029

VAGABOND INN-BY THE BAY
1655 Pacific Hwy (92101)
Rates: $38-$67;
Tel: (619) 232-6391; (800) 522-1555

VAGABOND INN-MISSION VALLEY
625 Hotel Circle South (92108)
Rates: $50-$73;
Tel: (619) 297-1691; (800) 522-1555

VAGABOND INN-POINT LOMA
1325 Scott St (92106) Rates: $47-$70;
Tel: (619) 224-3371; (800) 522-1555

VAGABOND INN-UNIVERSITY
6440 El Cajon Blvd (92115)
Rates: $38-$53;
Tel: (619) 286-2040; (800) 522-1555

WAYFARER'S INN
3275 Rosecrans St (92110)
Rates: $32-$60;
Tel: (619) 224-2411; (800) 266-2411

RECREATION

BLACK MOUNTAIN OPEN SPACE - Leashes

Info: This 200-acre primitive area offers both tranquility and rustic charm. Venture to the 1,552-foot summit of Black Mountain to get a sense of the surrounding landscape. For more information: (619) 525-8281.

Directions: From Interstate 15, take the Rancho Penasquitos Boulevard/Mountain Road exit and head west for two miles to Black Mountain Road. Go right and travel north approximately 2.5 miles to just before a dead end. Turn right on the dirt road and continue up the mountain. The road will curve sharply to the right and become a paved road. Follow to the parking lot and look for the start of the trail.

BLUE SKY ECOLOGICAL PRESERVE HIKE

Beginner/3.0 miles/1.5 hours

Info: Visit between April and June and behold a wildflower frenzy. Shaded by oak and sycamores, the dirt path wanders creekside through the preserve. For more information: (619) 486-7238.

Directions: From Interstate 15 north of San Diego, exit on Poway Road (S4) and go through the city of Poway to Espola Road (S5). Go left (north) onto Espola Road and continue past the entrance to Lake Poway and Lake Poway Road to the marked entrance for Blue Sky Ecological Preserve, about a half mile past Lake Poway.

FIESTA ISLAND

Info: This island is every dog's version of Fantasy Island. Swim, socialize, fetch and frolic... on land, sand or in the surf. The south side of the island provides outstanding views of downtown San Diego and Mission Bay. Remember a ball or frisbee. For more information: (619) 221-8901.

Directions: From Interstate 5, exit at Sea World Drive/Tecolote Road heading southeast to Fiesta Island Road, your first right. Follow Fiesta Island Road onto the island.

Note: Voice control obedience is mandatory.

Dogs May Be Unleashed Unless Otherwise Indicated

KATE O. SESSIONS PARK - Leashes

Info: Admire the spectacular city views of San Diego as you loll about this charmingly serene park. For more information: (619) 581-9924.

Directions: Located on Soledad Road at Park Drive.

LOS PENASQUITOS CANYON PRESERVE HIKE

Beginner/Intermediate/7.0 miles/3.5 hours

Info: If Rover's tail is wagging, he's picked up the scent of shady oak groves and water, water everywhere. This creek-side trail to the canyon's belly puts you and the pooch smack dab in the middle of a water wonderland, where alluring pools beg to be doggie paddled. Further along through a slender canyon, waterfalls await your ogling. Come in early spring and double the beauty with a flamboyant wildflower show. When day is done, head back over the same route. For more information: (619) 685-1350.

Directions: Take Interstate 15 north from San Diego to Mira Mesa/Scripps Ranch. Take the Mira Mesa Boulevard exit west for .5 miles to Black Mountain Road. Turn north (right) and drive to the equestrian staging area parking area (opposite Marcy Road).

MISSION BAY PARK - Leashes

Info: Visit this vast aquatic park during summer months when days last longer. You and your pup are in for a sand and surf good time. Pooches are only permitted before 9 a.m. and after 6 p.m. For more information: (619) 221-8901.

Directions: There are dozens of entry points located north of the San Diego River and south of Pacific Beach Drive. The east-west perimeters are East Mission Bay Drive and Mission Boulevard. From Interstate 5 at the Clairemont Drive/Visitor Center turnoff, follow signs to the center.

MISSION BEACH/PACIFIC BEACH - Leashes

Info: Meander along two adjoining beaches that offer miles of sandy coastline. Or stroll the promenade paralleling the beaches. Pooch hours are restricted - before 9 a.m. or after 6 p.m. For more information: (619) 221-8901.

Directions: Mission Beach is located behind the amusement park at West Mission Bay Drive and Mission Boulevard. Pacific Beach starts at Tournament Street, north of Mission Beach.

MISSION TRAILS REGIONAL PARK - Leashes

Info: Green terrain and scenic trails beckon at this 5,700-acre urban park - one of the largest in the U.S. History buffs, make your way to the Old Mission Dam Historical Site which was built by Native Americans. Hiking hounds, try your paws at the trail up Cowles Mountain. The summit views are terrific. For more information: (619) 533-4051.

Directions: From Interstate 8, take the College Avenue exit north to Navajo Road and turn right. Continue to the parking area and trailhead at Golfcrest Drive. This trail leads to Cowles Mountain.

MOUNT WOODSON HIKE

Beginner/3.6 miles/2.0 hours

Info: A haven for rock climbers, if you want peaceful serenity, you won't find it here. What you will find though are some gorgeous views of Poway and the Pacific. For more information: (619) 695-1400

Directions: From Interstate 15 north of San Diego, use the Poway Road (S4) exit and go through the city of Poway to Highway 67. Go left (north) onto Highway 67 and travel about three miles to a California Division of Forestry Fire Station. Park across the station in the dirt turnouts. Hike past the fire station to a paved service road all the way to the summit.

OCEAN BEACH PARK/DOG PARK

Info: Chill out at the most popular, well-loved beach in the area. Dogs smile when they know their destination is Dog Beach. The off-leash section is at the north end of the beach. For more information: (619) 221-8901.

Directions: From Interstate 5, take the Interstate 8 exit west. Follow the signs to Sunset Cliffs Boulevard. Bear right onto Voltaire Street to the end and the entrance to Dog Beach.

Note: Voice control obedience mandatory.

PRESIDIO PARK - Leashes

Info: Experience a bit of history when you visit this park which encompasses the hill known as the "Plymouth Rock of the West"- the birthplace of California. The trails of this hilly park are well shaded and offer spectacular city views. For more information: (619) 297-3258.

Directions: From Highway 8, take the Taylor Street exit west. Turn left at Presidio Drive, which leads into the park. Maps of the area are available at the museum.

SWEETWATER RIVER HIKE

Intermediate/5.0 miles/3.0 hours

Info: Walk alongside the golf course and then head northeast over rippling hillsides. You'll snake up a succession of switchbacks to a lookout point. For more information: (619) 765-0755.

Directions: From Interstate 805, going south from San Diego, exit at Bonita Road and travel about four miles to where Bonita Road bears left and crosses a narrow bridge over Sweetwater River. Park near the bridge or on any of the nearby side streets. The trailhead is directly beneath the bridge, by the golf course.

TECOLOTE CANYON NATURAL PARK - Leashes

Info: Learn about the area's natural history and its geologic makeup at the 9-acre nature center. Or challenge yourself to a vigorous hike into the canyon. This passage is not for the fair of paw but if you get as far as the northern Clairemont section, you'll find yourself in an Eden-like spot complete with rejuvenating Tecolote Creek. For more information: (619) 581-9930.

Directions: From Interstate 5, exit at Seaworld Drive/Tecolote Drive east. Follow to park.

WOODED HILL NATURE TRAIL HIKE

Intermediate/3.0 miles/1.5 hours

Info: This interpretive trail takes you to the highest wooded summit in the Laguna Mountains. On a clear day, you're rewarded with seemingly endless vistas of San Diego and Catalina Island. For more information: (619) 445-6235.

Directions: From Interstate 8 east of San Diego, go north on County Road S1 (Sunrise Highway) about 21.5 miles. Turn left on the road leading to Wooded Hill Campground and the Wooded Hill Trailhead.

SAN DIMAS

LODGING

MOTEL 6
502 W Arrow Hwy (91773)
Rates: $30-$34;
Tel: (909) 592-5631; (800) 440-6000

RED ROOF INN-SAN DIMAS
204 N Village Ct (91773)
Rates: $65-$85;
Tel: (909) 599-2362; (800) 843-7663

RECREATION

BONELLI REGIONAL PARK - Leashes

Info: Hike, boat or fish with your hot diggety dog in this beautiful park. Pack the pup's brown bagger and do lunch lakeside or drop a line and try your luck at catching dinner. For more information: (909) 599-8411.

Directions: Located at 120 Via Verde.

Dogs May Be Unleashed Unless Otherwise Indicated

MARSHALL CANYON TRAIL HIKE - Leashes

Intermediate/7.0 miles/3.5 hours

Info: This secluded, rustic canyon getaway is the ideal place for you and aqua pup to share a wet and wild adventure. The trail drops into Marshall Canyon, branching left at the fork. You'll crisscross the creek and climb out of the canyon toward the water tower, to a scenic ridgetop. From the ridgetop, the trail follows a yoyo-like course to signed Miller Road. Go left to begin your descent into lush Live Oak Canyon. At the 3-way intersection, you'll need the pupster's help in sniffing out the unsigned trail that descends through a grabbag forest of walnut, oak, cottonwood and sycamore to the canyon's bottom. When the trail splits, bear right and head back through Marshall Canyon to the trailhead. For more information: (909) 599-8411.

Directions: From San Dimas, take the Foothill Freeway (210) east to Highway 30 east to Foothill Boulevard. Continue to Wheeler Avenue and turn left (north). Go right on Golden Hill Road to Stevens Ranch Road and turn left. The trail begins at the staging area at the top of the hill.

SAN FRANCISCO

LODGING

ALEXANDER INN
415 O'Farrell St (94102)
Rates: $48-$84;
Tel: (415) 928-6800; (800) 843-8709

BERESFORD ARMS
701 Post St (94109)
Rates: $79-$135;
Tel: (415) 673-2600; (800) 533-6533

BERESFORD HOTEL
635 Sutter St (94102)
Rates: $79-$99;
Tel: (415) 673-9900; (800) 533-6533

**BEST WESTERN
CIVIC CENTER MOTOR INN**
364 9th St (94103)
Rates: $65-$95;
Tel: (415) 621-2826; (800) 528-1234

CAMPTON PLACE HOTEL
340 Stockton St (94108)
Rates: $185-$320;
Tel: (415) 781-5555; (800) 235-4300

CHANCELLOR HOTEL
433 Powell St (94102)
Rates: $69-$250;
Tel: (415) 362-2004; (800) 428-4748

DAYS INN
2600 Sloat Blvd (94116)
Rates: $60-$95;
Tel: (800) 329-7466

DAYS INN-AIRPORT/OYSTER POINT
1113 Airport Blvd S (94080)
Rates: $55-$79;
Tel: (415) 873-9300; (800) 329-7466

DAYS INN-FISHERMAN'S WHARF
2358 Lombard St (94123)
Rates: $50-$65;
Tel: (415) 922-2010; (800) 329-7466

EXECUTIVE SUITES
One St Francis Pl (94107)
Rates: $125-$189;
Tel: (415) 495-5151

GRAND HERITAGE HOTEL
495 Geary St (94102)
Rates: $215-$360;
Tel: (415) 775-4700; (800) 437-4824

GROSVENOR HOUSE
899 Pine St (94108)
Rates: $99-$169;
Tel: (415) 421-1899; (800) 999-9189

HAUS KLEEBAUER BED & BREAKFAST
225 Clipper (Noe Valley 94114)
Rates: $65-$85;
Tel: (415) 821-3866

HOLIDAY INN-FINANCIAL DISTRICT
750 Kearny St (94108)
Rates: $125-$170;
Tel: (415) 433-6600; (800) 465-4329

HOLIDAY LODGE & GARDEN HOTEL
1901 Van Ness Ave (94109)
Rates: $89-$139;
Tel: (800) 738-7477

HOTEL BERESFORD MANOR
860 Sutter St (94102)
Rates: $60-$70;
Tel: (415) 673-3330; (800) 533-6533

HOTEL NIKKO
222 Mason St (94102)
Rates: $225-$1300;
Tel: (415) 394-1111; (800) 645-5687

THE INN SAN FRANCISCO
BED & BREAKFAST
943 S Van Ness Ave (94110)
Rates: $75-$195;
Tel: (415) 641-0188; (800) 359-0913

THE JULIANA HOTEL
590 Bush St (94108) Rates: $125-$185;
Tel: (415) 392-2540; (800) 328-3880

LAUREL MOTOR INN
444 Presidio Ave (94115)
Rates: $75-$99;
Tel: (415) 567-8467; (800) 928-1866

THE MANSIONS HOTEL
2220 Sacramento St (94115)
Rates: $114-$350;
Tel: (415) 929-9444; (800) 826-9398

MARRIOTT-FISHERMAN'S WHARF
1250 Columbus Ave (94133)
Rates: $148-$450;
Tel: (415) 775-7555; (800) 228-9290

MARRIOTT-SAN FRANCISCO
55 Fourth St (94103)
Rates: $140-$185;
Tel: (415) 896-1600; (800) 228-9290

OCEAN PARK MOTEL
2690 46th Ave (94116)
Rates: $53-$65;
Tel: (415) 566-7020

PACIFIC HEIGHTS INN
1555 Union St (94123)
Rates: $65-$105;
Tel: (415) 776-3310; (800) 523-1801

THE PAN PACIFIC HOTEL
500 Post St (94102)
Rates: $185-$350;
Tel: (415) 771-8600; (800) 327-8585

THE PHILLIPS HOTEL
205 Ninth St (94109)
Rates: $23-$35;
Tel: (415) 863-7652

THE PHOENIX INN
601 Eddy St (94109)
Rates: $79-$99;
Tel: (415) 776-1380; (800) 248-9466

RAMADA HOTEL-
FISHERMAN'S WHARF
590 Bay St (94133)
Rates: $89-$175;
Tel: (415) 885-4700; (800) 228-8408

RODEWAY INN-BY THE BAY
1450 Lombard St (94123)
Rates: $49-$125;
Tel: (415) 673-0691; (800) 424-4777

SAN FRANCISCO AIRPORT HILTON
P. O. Box 8355, San Francisco
International Airport (94128)
Rates: $139-$175;
Tel: (415) 589-0770; (800) 445-8667

Dogs May Be Unleashed Unless Otherwise Indicated

SAN FRANCISCO HILTON & TOWERS
333 O'Farrell St (94102)
Rates: $170-$250;
Tel: (415) 771-1400; (800) 445-8667

SHEEHAN HOTEL
620 Sutter St (94102)
Rates: $40-$99;
Tel: (415) 775-6500; (800) 848-1529

SIR FRANCIS DRAKE HOTEL
450 Powell St (94102)
Rates: $95-$155;
Tel: (415) 392-7755; (800) 227-5480

THE STEINHART
952 Sutter St (94109)
Rates: $70-$135;
Tel: (415) 928-3855

STOUFFER STANFORD COURT-NOB HILL
905 California St (94108)
Rates: $205-$2000;
Tel: (800) 227-4736

TUSCAN INN AT FISHERMAN'S WHARF
425 N Point St (94133)
Rates: $158-$198;
Tel: (415) 561-1100; (800) 648-4626

THE WESTIN ST. FRANCIS
335 Powell St (94102)
Rates: $150-$1500;
Tel: (415) 397-7000; (800) 228-3000

RECREATION

ALTA PLAZA PARK

Info: Your pooch will have a paw-stomping good time fraternizing with canine locals at this leash-free neighborhood park. Don't forget a tennis ball or frisbee.

Directions: Bordered by Jackson, Clay, Steiner and Scott Streets. The off-leash area is located on the second level above Clay.

BERNAL HEIGHTS PARK

Info: Get your day off to an energizing start. The craggy hillsides of this treeless park provide a robust workout. Climb to the top and feast your eyes on magnificent views of the Golden Gate and Bay Bridges. Dress warmly - the wind-chill factor can send shivers through your fur. Brrr!

Directions: At Folsom Street and Bernal Heights Boulevard.

BUENA VISTA PARK

Info: Finish a morning of browsing and people watching in Haight Ashbury with a visit to this park. Dozens of eucalyptus and redwood encircled trails run up and down the hillsides. Or cling to the park's summit for seemingly endless vistas.

Directions: Access the park from Buena Vista Avenue west and Waller Street, or from Haight Street. The shaded west side of the park is the leash-free section.

CORONA HEIGHTS PARK/RED ROCK PARK

Info: Begin your day's excursion at the foot of the park where Fido and his canine cronies can scamper in green grass glee. Or get the juices flowing with a steep, shadeless climb to the top where great city views abound. Bring plenty of water.

Directions: Located at Museum Way and Roosevelt Avenue.

GOLDEN GATE PARK - Leashes

Info: Hot diggety dog. 1,000 acres await your exploration in this amazing urban oasis. Sniff out the leash-free areas, there are several within the park's boundaries. Pack snacks and plan to picnic with the pup - you're sure to work up an appetite strolling this verdant expanse.

Directions: The park is bounded by Fulton, Lincoln and Stanyan Streets, and the Great Highway.

GOLDEN GATE BRIDGE HIKE - Leashes

Beginner/3.0 miles/1.5 hours

Info: Nothing compares to the views from the center of the Golden Gate Bridge. On a clear day you'll see Alcatraz, Angel Island, the San Francisco waterfront and the East Bay Hills. After parking, you and your Golden Gate Retriever will walk through a tunnel under Highway 101, before looping up to the pathway entrance. Dress warmly, it gets cool out there. For more information: (415) 556-0560

Directions: From Highway 101 at the south end of Golden Gate Bridge, use the toll plaza parking exit. Parking directly east and west of the toll plaza. Walk through the tunnel to the bridge.

Note: Leash-free from Marina Green to the west gate of Crissy Field.

GOLDEN GATE NATIONAL RECREATION AREA

Info: An interesting array of natural beauty, historic features and urban development, this region offers tons of tailwagging adventures for you and your pal. Keep a snout out for hawks, deer, seabirds and whales when you visit. Wander amid

Dogs May Be Unleashed Unless Otherwise Indicated

windswept ridges, verdant valleys and beautiful beaches. A dozen opportunities are outlined below just waiting for you and the pup. For more information: (415) 663-1092.

Note: Voice control obedience or leashes are mandatory. Policies are strictly enforced.

1). BAKER BEACH

Info: Even in summer, there's a breeze and a nip in the air. Dogs and people go au natural at the north end of this sandy beach. Make sure Fido's leashed if you plan to hit the hiking trails. For more information: (415) 556-8371.

Directions: Take Lincoln Boulevard, from either direction, to Bowley Street, make the first turn into the parking lots. The leash-free beach north of HoBo's Creek Beach is easily accessible from the first lot.

Note: Voice control obedience or leashes are mandatory. Policies are strictly enforced.

2). CRISSY FIELD

Info: Crissy Field is everything you've wanted in the outdoors and more. Stunning views. Gentle bay swimming. Sailboat watching. Endless beach walking. Water, picnic tables, shade trees, leashless freedom and sunsets are to die for. For more information: (415) 556-0560.

Directions: There are many access points off Mason Street in the Marina District.

Note: Voice control obedience or leashes are mandatory. Policies are strictly enforced.

3). FORT FUNSTON

Info: Feel the wind in your hair and smell the tangy sea air at this duney location. Begin on ice-plant lined Sunset Trail and wander through dunes to the Battery. From there, pick up a trail on either side, or access the beach by the slender trails in the dunes. For more information: (415) 556-8371.

Locate Other Dog-Friendly Activities...Check Nearby Cities

Directions: From Geary Boulevard, follow the brown signs on the Great Highway, located about one-half mile south of the John Muir Drive turnoff. Bear right on the main drive, follow to main parking area. Sunset Trail is just north of the parking lot.

Note: Voice control obedience or leashes are mandatory. Policies are strictly enforced.

4). FORT MASON - Leashes

Info: Quieter breeds will enjoy the serene setting and the stunning views of the city and bay. You'll have lawns to laze on, gardens to sniff through and fishing piers to drop in on. For more information: (415) 556-0560.

Directions: From the Golden Gate Bridge, take Doyle Drive to Lombard Street and follow to Van Ness. The Fort Mason Information and Park Headquarters are located at the intersection of Lombard and Van Ness.

5). GOLDEN GATE PROMENADE TRAIL HIKE - Leashes

Beginner/3.0 miles/1.5 hours

Info: This gentle, paved trail provides stunning panoramas of the Golden Gate Bridge, Alcatraz, Tiburon, Sausalito, and the Bay. Mornings are popular with joggers and walkers, while afternoons are great for kite enthusiasts. But any time of the day is perfect for city-weary pooches. For more information: (415) 663-1092.

Directions: From Highway 101 at the south end of Golden Gate Bridge in San Francisco, exit on Marina Boulevard. Go southwest toward Fisherman's Wharf. Parking lots are available off Marina Boulevard at Fort Mason, Marina Green, Crissy Field and close to St. Francis Yacht Club. The area from Marina Green to the west gate of Crissy Field is leash-free.

6). LAND'S END - Leashes

Info: A walk along this craggy, pristine coastline park is like a walk back in time, when people were few and nature was abundant. Birds soar high above the crashing surf, and your pup might make the only paw prints on the beach. From the

Dogs May Be Unleashed Unless Otherwise Indicated

end of the parking lot, descend the staircase and go right. Admire the powerful Pacific from one of the beaches en route. Resist the temptation to explore the paths down the cliff face. When you've had your fill, turn around and head back. For more information: (415) 556-8371.

Directions: Located at the end of Camino del Mar.

Note: Heed the warning signs.

7). MI-WOK LOOP HIKE - Leashes

Intermediate/3.5 miles/2.0 hours

Info: Traipse through lush grasslands on this elliptical course. From the Mi-Wok stables, head north on the trail. Finish the loop by turning left on Ridge Road. The never-ending views continue another mile. Return by taking a left at the Fox Trail. Go 1.1 miles and take another left on Tennessee Valley Trail for the last half-mile to the stables. For more information: (415) 663-1092.

Directions: From San Francisco, go north on Highway 101 to Marin City. Exit and travel west on Stinson Beach/Highway 1. After the overpass, take a left on Tennessee Valley Road and drive until it dead ends at the trailhead.

8). MUIR BEACH - Leashes

Info: Muir Beach - small on size, big on beauty. There's a little bit of everything here - sand dunes, a fresh water creek, a lagoon and an almost constant breeze. Take a book or dine à la blanket with your best buddy. For more information: (415) 388-2596.

Directions: From Mill Valley, take Highway 1 north to the signed Muir Beach turnoff.

9). OCEAN BEACH - Leashes

Info: Your beach-loving pooch will have a sand-stomping good time at this four-mile, wind-whipped stretch of coastline. And he won't be alone. This is a popular canine hangout. Dress warmly, tote your own water and a toy. If your pooch doesn't like the leash thing, head for the leash-free area from Lincoln Way to Sloat Boulevard. For more information: (415) 556-8642.

Directions: Several access points: between Cliff House and Balboa Street, between Fulton Street and Lincoln Way or from Sloat Boulevard.

10). OCEAN BEACH ESPLANADE TRAIL HIKE - Leashes

Beginner/6.0 miles/3.0 hours

Info: Choose the paved trail or the beach walk. This threemile beach runs from Seal Rock to Fort Funston and continues to the north end of Pacifica. There's also a jogging trail just east of the Great Highway. Your paw pal will get all the Rexercise he needs on this stimulating hike. If your pooch doesn't like the leash thing, head for the leash-free area from Lincoln Way to Sloat Boulevard. For more information: (415) 663-1092.

Directions: From San Francisco, take Geary Boulevard west until it dead ends at the ocean and the Cliff House Restaurant. Turn left onto the Great Highway and go one mile to the parking area on the right.

11). RODEO BEACH AND LAGOON

Info: Water-loving mutts will love swimming in the protected saltwater/freshwater lagoon. When playtime ends, take the wooden walkway to the small, but appealing beach. Don't let your dog swim or wander away, the surf here can be unpredictable and deadly. For more information: (415) 331-1540.

Directions: From Sausalito, go south on Alexander Avenue towards the Golden Gate Bridge (do not get on the freeway). About .25 miles before the bridge, make a right on Bunker Road. This road leads to a one-way tunnel equipped with a traffic light directing opposing traffic. Continue on Bunker Road to the beach. Follow the signs west of the visitor center.

Note: Check tide tables. High tide can be dangerous. Voice control obedience or leashes are mandatory. Policies are strictly enforced.

12). SWEENEY RIDGE TRAIL HIKE

Intermediate/4.4 miles/2.25 hours

Info: The reward for finishing this steady 2.2-mile climb is a sensational summit view of Mt. Tamalpais, Mt. Diablo and Montara Mountain. You'll be stomping your paws among coastal scrub and grasslands until you top out at at 1,200 feet. Come in springtime and double your pleasure with a psychedelic profusion of wildflowers. For more information: (415) 663-1092.

Directions: From Interstate 280 in San Bruno, exit on Westborough and head west up the hill to Highway 35 (Skyline Boulevard) and go left a short distance to College Drive. Turn right and enter the Skyline College campus on the left. Proceed to lot #2, the trailhead is at the southeast corner of the parking lot.

Note: Voice control obedience or leashes are mandatory. Policies are strictly enforced.

INSPIRATION POINT TRAIL HIKE - Leashes

Beginner/2.6 miles/1.5 hours

Info: Inspiration Point says it all. From the trailhead, don't head up East Peak. Head the opposite way and go right on Eldridge Grade. You'll encounter two hairpin turns. At the second one, take the cutoff trail on your left to the top. Be prepared to see forever. For more information: (415) 388-2070 or (415) 456-1286.

Directions: Head north on Highway 101 to Larkspur. Exit and head west on Tamalpais Drive. Turn right on Corte Madera Avenue and travel about a half-mile. Take a left on Madrone Avenue and go to Valley Way. The trailhead is at the end of the road.

MOUNTAIN LAKE PARK

Info: This paw-friendly park has a leash-free area on the east side where you're sure to meet other socially-minded canines. For more information: (415) 666-7200.

Directions: Access the dog-run area from 8th Avenue at Lake Street.

Locate Other Dog-Friendly Activities...Check Nearby Cities

SAN GABRIEL

LODGING

QUALITY INN
1114 E Las Tunas Dr (91776)
Rates: $50-$110;
Tel: (818) 285-0921; (800) 221-2222

SAN JACINTO

LODGING

CROWN MOTEL
138 S Ramona Blvd (92583)
Rates: $36-$54;
Tel: (909) 654-7133

SAN JOSE

LODGING

AIRPORT INN INTERNATIONAL
1355 N 4th St (95112)
Rates: $49-$64; Tel: (408) 453-5340

BEST WESTERN GATEWAY INN
2585 Seaboard Ave (95131)
Rates: $59-$79;
Tel: (408) 435-8800; (800) 528-1234;
(800) 437-8855 (CA)

BEST WESTERN SAN JOSE LODGE
1440 N First St (95112)
Rates: $56-$68;
Tel: (408) 453-7750; (800) 528-1234

COMFORT INN-AIRPORT
1310 N 1st St (95112)
Rates: $65;
Tel: (408) 453-1100; (800) 221-2222

DAYS INN
4170 Monterey Rd (95111)
Rates: $50-$75;
Tel: (408) 224-4122; (800) 329-7466

EXECUTIVE INN SUITES
3930 Monterey Rd (94111)
Rates: $65; Tel: (408) 281-8700

FRIENDSHIP INN
2188 The Alameda (95126)
Rates: $35-$45;
Tel: (408) 248-8300; (800) 424-4777

HOLIDAY INN PARK CENTER PLAZA
282 Almaden Blvd (95113)
Rates: $72-$89;
Tel: (408) 998-0400; (800) 465-4329

HOMEWOOD SUITES
10 W Trimble Rd (95131)
Rates: $89-$159;
Tel: (408) 428-9900; (800) 225-5466

HOWARD JOHNSON LODGE
1755 N First St (95112)
Rates: $49-$89; Tel: (800) 446-4656

HYATT SAN JOSE
1740 N First St (95112)
Rates: $69-$154;
Tel: (408) 993-1234; (800) 223-1234

LE BARON HOTEL
1350 N First St (95112)
Rates: $54-$105;
Tel: (408) 453-6200; (800) 538-6818;
(800) 662-9896 (CA)

Dogs May Be Unleashed Unless Otherwise Indicated

MOTEL 6-SOUTH
2560 Fontaine Rd (95121)
Rates: $35-$39;
Tel: (408) 270-3131; (800) 440-6000

MOTEL 6-AIRPORT
2081 N First St (95131)
Rates: $35-$41;
Tel: (408) 436-8180; (800) 440-6000

RED LION HOTEL
2050 Gateway Pl (95110)
Rates: $135-$600;
Tel: (408) 453-4000; (800) 547-8010

SAN JOSE HILTON & TOWERS
300 Almaden Blvd (95110)
Rates: $80-$600;
Tel: (408) 287-2100; (800) 445-8667

SUMMERFIELD SUITES
1602 Crane Ct (95122)
Rates: $119-$149;
Tel: (408) 436-1600; (800) 833-4353

VAGABOND INN
1488 N First St (95112)
Rates: $54-$64;
Tel: (408) 453-8822; (800) 522-1555

RECREATION

ALMADEN QUICKSILVER COUNTY PARK - Leashes

Info: This 3,600-acre park is laced with 15 miles of dog-friendly trails. Sniff out the Guadalupe, Hacienda, Mine Hill, No Name, Senator Mine and the Mockingbird Picnic Area. On cool spring days, your pooch can chase after butterflies as you ooh and aah on wildflower-flecked hillsides. For more information: (408) 268-3883.

Directions: From Highway 85, take the Almaden Expressway exit south for 4.5 miles to Almaden Road, continuing south for .5 miles to Mockingbird Hill Lane. Turn right for .4 miles to the parking area.

ANDERSON LAKE PARK - Leashes

Info: Leashed pooches are allowed anywhere within the boundaries of this vast, 2,365-acre park. You can stroll along the 15-mile paved pathway that follows Coyote Creek north through stands of oak, cottonwood, and sycamore. Or hop on the one-mile, self-guided nature trail for an education on the riparian habitat and the abundant wildlife found in this area. Sofa-loafers and sun-worshippers may prefer a chill-out afternoon riverside. Come prepared, Anderson Reservoir is open to line-droppers year round, and you can try your fly in Coyote Creek from April-November. For more information: (408) 779-3634.

Directions: Anderson Lake and the picnic areas along Coyote Creek are located on Cochrane Road in Morgan Hill, east of Highway 101. Woodchopper's Picnic Area and Jackson Ranch can be found by following Dunne Avenue east from Highway 101. The Coyote Creek multiple use trails can be accessed by following Cochrane Road west from Highway 101 to Monterey Road. Turn right onto Monterey Road and drive about a mile until you reach Burnett Avenue. Turn right (east) onto Burnett to the trailhead.

Note: Fees required for entry. Posted at gate.

CALERO PARK - Leashes

Info: Scenery sniffers will love this park with its spectacular views of the surrounding Santa Cruz Mountain Range. Pack some picnic goodies and do lunch. Visit in spring and be dazzled by dizzying displays of wildflowers. Frolic in the fall in piles of colorful leaves. If you're itching to go fishing, bass, bluegill, sunfish and crappie are abundant. No pups are allowed on the trails or beaches. For more information: (408) 268-3883.

Directions: Take the Almaden Expressway south to Harry Road and turn right. Then go left onto McKean Road to the park entrance.

Note: Catch and release fish. Mercury in the reservoir makes the fish unsafe for consumption. Vehicle entrance fees are posted at the kiosk.

COYOTE HELLYER PARK - Leashes

Info: 223 acres of roaming room can be yours in this pretty parkland. Lead your Laddie along lovely pathways amidst thick, streamside growths of tall trees. Forget the hurley-burley of city life and enjoy the sweet sounds of songbirds and the diversity of nature. Summer strollers will love the abundance of soothing shade and cool, toe-dipping water. A 15-mile hike south along Coyote Creek escorts you to expansive, dog-friendly Anderson Park. Barbecue pits are available for kibble cook-outs. Whatever your pleasure, you and furface will find it here. For more information: (408) 225-0225.

Directions: Located west of the Hellyer Avenue exit along Highway 101.

Note: Fees for vehicle entrance are posted at the Ranger Station.

JOSEPH D. GRANT COUNTY PARK - Leashes

Info: Nestled between two ridges in the Diablo Range of the Coastal Mountains, scenery sniffers and their camera toting cohorts will have a howl of a good time snapping stunning photos for the family album at this pretty park. Picnicking, hiking and wildlife watching are the main attractions in this oak-clad area. In springtime, the air is filled with the sweet trill of songbirds and the landscape is splashed with colorful wildflowers. For more information: (408) 274-6121.

Directions: Located on Mount Hamilton Road, 8 miles east of Alum Rock Avenue.

Note: Fees posted at park entrance. Dogs are allowed in designated areas only and leash laws are strictly enforced.

KELLEY PARK - Leashes

Info: This popular park has a pleasant social atmosphere. Stroll the walking paths and check out the old orchard behind the museum.

Directions: Located on Senter Road, between Tully Road and Keyes Street.

Note: $3 parking fee on weekends and holidays.

LEXINGTON COUNTY PARK - Leashes

Info: You and Fido can float your boats on the 450-acre lake or drop in a line at this lazy day kind of park. For more information: (408) 867-0190.

Directions: Take Interstate 880 (17) to Old Santa Cruz Highway. Continue until you reach Aldercroft Heights Road. Take Aldercroft Heights Road to Alma Bridge Road and follow to the parking area.

Note: Fees posted at park entrance. Dogs are allowed in designated areas only and leash laws are strictly enforced.

PENITENCIA CREEK COUNTY PARK - Leashes

Info: This 83-acre park is comprised of a chain of smaller park units located along lovely Penitencia Creek. You and the pooch can chill out with some snacks as you repose on the banks of the stream and listen to the water's soothing serenade. For more information: (408) 358-3741.

Directions: Noble Avenue is the northernmost tip of the park, while Jackson and Mabury Streets mark the southern boundary.

Note: Fees posted at park entrance. Dogs are allowed in designated areas only and leash laws are strictly enforced.

Other parks in San Jose - Leashes
•SANTA TERESA COUNTY PARK, midway between San Jose and Morgan Hill on Bernal Road.

SAN JUAN BAUTISTA

<u>LODGING</u>
SAN JUAN INN
410 The Alameda St (95045)
Rates: $42-$60;
Tel: (408) 623-4380

SAN JUAN CAPISTRANO

<u>LODGING</u>
BEST WESTERN CAPISTRANO INN
27174 Ortega Hwy (92675)
Rates: $59-$75;
Tel: (714) 493-5661; (800) 441-9438

<u>RECREATION</u>
BEAR CANYON TO PIGEON SPRINGS TRAIL HIKE
Intermediate/5.5 miles/2.5 hours

Info: Experience the Santa Ana Mountains first-hand with Old Brown Eyes on this scenic hike. The trail ascends a hillside and crosses a creek before entering the San Mateo Canyon

Dogs May Be Unleashed Unless Otherwise Indicated

Wilderness. After about 2 miles, head right on Verdugo Trail for .75 miles to Pigeon Springs. Do lunch alfresco under a large oak before heading back. If your timing is right and the water is flowing, cool your heels in the refreshing seasonal creek on the return trip. For more information: (909) 736-1811.

Directions: From the intersection of Interstate 5 and Highway 74, head east on Highway 74 approximately 20 miles to a large parking area across from the Ortega Oaks store. The signed trailhead is just west of the store on Highway 74.

CHIQUITO TRAIL HIKE

Expert/11.5 miles/6.0 hours

Info: Although the beginning section of this trail is relatively easy, once you and Fido hook up with the Chiquito Trail, the going gets tough. In just over a mile on the San Juan Loop Trail, you'll reach the signed Chiquito Trail. Follow this pathway as it crosses the San Juan Creek and continues creekside before the cardiovascular workout begins-an unshaded, switchbacking haul up the west slope of Lion Canyon. Five miles into the hike, you'll round a ridge, bearing north to where the trail ends in an oak-filled meadow. Come springtime, the canyon slopes are colorfully painted with beautiful wildflowers. For more information: (909) 736-1811.

Directions: From the intersection of Interstate 5 and Highway 74, head east on Highway 74 approximately 20 miles to a large parking area across from the Ortega Oaks store. The trailhead is at the east end of the parking area. The sign reads the San Juan Loop Trail.

EL CARISO NATURE TRAIL HIKE

Beginner/1.5 miles/0.75 hours

Info: Talk about easy. This self-guided looping trail is sure to get two paws up even from the most devoted couch slouch. For more information: (909) 736-1811.

Directions: From the intersection of Interstate 5 and Highway 74, head east on Highway 74 approximately 24 miles to the trailhead at the El Cariso Fire Station.

SAN JUAN LOOP TRAIL HIKE

Beginner/2.1 miles/1.0 hours

Info: Three words describe this hike - piece of cake. Along the trail, you and your barking buddy will encounter a variety of vegetation ranging from riparian to chaparral. The flora changes as you loop from the creek, into the canyon and back again. For more information: (909) 736-1811.

Directions: From the intersection of Interstate 5 and Highway 74, head east on Highway 74 approximately 20 miles to a large parking area across from the Ortega Oaks store. The signed trailhead is at the east end of the parking area.

SAN LEANDRO

LODGING

ISLANDER LODGE MOTEL
2398 E 14th St (94577)
Rates: $33-$45;
Tel: (510) 352-5010

SAN LUIS OBISPO

LODGING

AVILA HOT SPRINGS SPA
250 Avila Beach Dr (93405)
Rates: $35+;
Tel: (805) 595-2359; (800) 332-2359

BEST WESTERN OLIVE TREE INN
100 Olive St (93405)
Rates: $48-$85;
Tel: (805) 544-2800; (800) 528-1234

**BEST WESTERN ROYAL OAK
MOTOR HOTEL**
214 Madonna Rd (93405)
Rates: $61-$89;
Tel: (805) 544-4410; (800) 528-1234

BEST WESTERN SOMERSET MANOR
1895 Monterey St (93401)
Rates: $38-$72;
Tel: (805) 544-0973; (800) 528-1234

CAMPUS MOTEL
404 Santa Rosa St (93405)
Rates: $44-$89;
Tel: (805) 544-0881; (800) 447-8080

HERITAGE INN BED & BREAKFAST
978 Olive St (93405)
Rates: $65-$150;
Tel: (805) 544-7440

HOWARD JOHNSON HOTEL
1585 Calle Joaquin (93405)
Rates: $49-$79;
Tel: (805) 544-5300; (800) 446-4656

MOTEL 6-NORTH
1433 Calle Joaquin (93401)
Rates: $29-$38;
Tel: (805) 549-9595; (800) 440-6000

Dogs May Be Unleashed Unless Otherwise Indicated

MOTEL 6-SOUTH
1625 Calle Joaquin (93401)
Rates: $29-$38;
Tel: (805) 541-6992; (800) 440-6000

SANDS MOTEL & SUITES
1930 Monterey St (93401)
Rates: $54-$109;
Tel: (805) 544-0500; (800) 441-4657

TRAVELODGE
1825 Monterey St (93401)
Rates: $39-$99;
Tel: (805) 543-5110; (800) 367-2250;
(800) 578-7878 (US)

TRAVELODGE SOUTH
950 Olive St (93405)
Rates: $40-$115;
Tel: (805) 544-8886; (800) 578-7878

VAGABOND INN
210 Madonna Rd (93401)
Rates: $48-$74;
Tel: (805) 544-4710; (800) 522-1555

RECREATION

EL CHORRO REGIONAL PARK - Leashes

Info: Come to this blissful 1,730-acre park when you're craving seclusion. Refresh yourself with a pleasant walk along an uncrowded four-mile pathway. For more information: (805) 541-8000.

Directions: Take Highway 101 to the Santa Rosa Street/ Highway 1 exit. Head northeast for seven miles. The park is on the right.

Note: $1 car fee and $1.50 dog fee.

LAGUNA LAKE PARK - Leashes

Info: This pretty city oasis is the ideal place for an early morning jog. Take the Fitness Trail and combine a little Rexercise with cool piney air. For more information: (805) 781-3000.

Directions: From Highway 101, exit at Los Osos Valley Road and head northwest. After several blocks, turn right on Madonna Road, left on Dalido Drive.

OLDE PORT BEACH - Leashes

Info: Small but lovely, take advantage of this picturesque, paw-pleasing beach. For more information: (805) 595-2381.

Directions: From San Luis Obispo, travel south on Highway 1/Highway 101. Exit at Avila Beach west. Once you reach town, continue west on Harford Drive, the beach is on the left.

SANTA MARGARITA RECREATION AREA - Leashes

Info: Get all the exercise you desire on ten miles of trails around Santa Margarita Lake. For more information: (805) 438-5485.

Directions: From San Luis Obispo, take Highway 101 north, exit at Highway 58 and head east four miles. Follow the signs.

Note: $4 car fee and $1.50 dog fee.

SAN MARCOS

<u>LODGING</u>

QUAILS INN-LAKE SAN MARCOS RESORT
1025 La Bonita Dr (92069)
Rates: $85-$225;
Tel: (619) 744-0120; (800) 447-6556

<u>RECREATION</u>

LOVE VALLEY TRAIL HIKE

Beginner/2.0 miles/1.0 hours

Info: They don't call it Love Valley for nothing. Pack a lunch and take your Honey and your hound on an unhurried excursion. Picnic in the meadow or beneath a sprawling oak. In springtime, wildflowers add a glamorous touch of color to the day. For more information: (619) 788-0250.

Directions: From San Marcos, travel north on Interstate 15. Head east on Highway 76, then left on East Grade Road (just before Lake Henshaw). Go 3.3 miles to a turnout on the south side of the road. The trailhead is at the locked gate.

SAN MATEO

<u>LODGING</u>

BEST WESTERN LOS PRADOS
2940 S Norfolk St (94403)
Rates: $62-$84;
Tel: (415) 341-3300; (800) 528-1234

DUNFEY SAN MATEO HOTEL
1770 S Amphlett Blvd (94402)
Rates: $59-$89;
Tel: (415) 573-7661

Dogs May Be Unleashed Unless Otherwise Indicated

HOLIDAY INN-SAN MATEO
330 N Bayshore Blvd (94401)
Rates: $79-$200;
Tel: (800) 465-4329

RESIDENCE INN BY MARRIOTT
2000 Winward Way (94404)
Rates: $129-$155;
Tel: (800) 331-3131

VILLA HOTEL AIRPORT SOUTH
4000 S El Camino Real (94403)
Rates: $56-$149;
Tel: (415) 341-0966; (800) 341-2345

RECREATION

LAURELWOOD PARK - Leashes

Info: Hike streamside and enjoy the simple pleasures of a tree-laden countryside.

Directions: Located at Glendora and Cedarwood Drives.

SAN MIGUEL

LODGING

SAN MIGUEL MISSION INN
P. O. Box 58 (93451)
Rates: $30-$45;
Tel: (805) 467-3674

SAN PEDRO

LODGING

SHERATON LOS ANGELES HARBOR
601 S Palos Verdes St (90731)
Rates: $95-$695;
Tel: (310) 519-8200; (800) 325-3535

VAGABOND INN
215 S Gaffey St (90731)
Rates: $50-$60;
Tel: (310) 831-8911; (800) 522-1555

RECREATION

AVERILL PARK - Leashes

Info: Munch on a brown bag lunch as you and Lassie listen to the gentle sounds of a tumbling waterfall. Or toe-dip in the creek that rolls through this beautiful 10-acre park.

Directions: Located at 1300 Dodson Avenue.

Locate Other Dog-Friendly Activities...Check Nearby Cities

FERMIN PARK - Leashes

Info: Tangy salt air, swaying palms and thick grassy areas combine to make this oceanfront park an agreeable interlude.

Directions: Located on Paseo del Mar, west of Gaffey Street.

LOOKOUT POINT PARK - Leashes

Info: Beautiful and petite, this park is a nice resting spot for weary drivers and their pooches.

Directions: Located at Gaffey and San Pedro Streets.

PECK PARK COMMUNITY CENTER - Leashes

Info: This park is definitely something to bark about. 75 expansive acres of green comprise this beautiful area. Whether you saunter along the simple, scenic pathway or tough it out on the more challenging and secluded trail, you're sure to rack up some fun points.

Directions: Located at 560 North Western Avenue.

SAN RAFAEL

LODGING

CASA SOLDAVINI GUESTHOUSE
531 C St (94901)
Rates: n/a;
Tel: (415) 454-3140

VILLA INN
1600 Lincoln Ave (94901)
Rates: $62-$85;
Tel: (415) 456-4975; (800) 228-2000

WYNDHAM GARDEN HOTEL-MARIN/SAN RAFAEL
1010 Northgate Dr (94903)
Rates: $79-$109;
Tel: (415) 479-8800; (800) 996-3426

RECREATION

BOYD PARK - Leashes

Info: Take time to smell the flowers or just roam amid the lush landscape in this 42-acre park.

Directions: Located at 8th Street and Mission Avenue.

Dogs May Be Unleashed Unless Otherwise Indicated

CIVIC CENTER PARK LAGOON - Leashes

Info: Soak up some scenery and repast with Rover in this lush 20-acre park.

Directions: Take the San Pedro turnoff from Highway 101. The park is located on Civic Center Drive.

GERSTLE PARK - Leashes

Info: Relax with Max in the redwood grove or fill your snouts with the scent of fresh flowers as you take a gander at the gardens.

Directions: Located at San Rafael Avenue and Clark Street.

PEACOCK GAP PARK - Leashes

Info: Jog with your dog along the pathway in this pretty 7-acre park.

Directions: Located on Biscayne Drive off San Pedro Road.

SAN PEDRO MOUNTAIN OPEN SPACE PRESERVE - Leashes

Info: You and Fido can have a doggone good time exploring this vast area. Test your perseverance on a steady uphill climb through a madrone forest and you'll be greeted with spectacular bay and mountain views. For more information: (415) 499-6387.

Directions: At the end of Woodoaks Drive, just off North Point San Pedro Road and just north of the Marin Jewish Community Center.

SANTA MARGARITA ISLAND OPEN SPACE PRESERVE - Leashes

Info: Solitude and adventure team up at this preserve. Traverse the embankments and piers of Gallinas Creek. Or venture across the footbridge to an idyllic island setting. Pack plenty of water for you and the pooch. For more information: (415) 499-6387.

Directions: From North Point San Pedro Road, turn west on Meadow Drive. Follow to the end. The footbridge is at the western end of Vendola Drive. Park on the street.

Locate Other Dog-Friendly Activities...Check Nearby Cities

SANTA VENETIA MARSH OPEN SPACE PRESERVE - Leashes

Info: Visit Santa Venetia and surround you hound with salt-water marshes, pleasant breezes and swooping swallows. For more information: (415) 499-6387.

Directions: From North Point San Pedro Road, turn west on Meadow Drive. Follow to the end. The footbridge is at the western end of Vendola Drive. Park on the street.

SOBRANTE RIDGE REGIONAL PRESERVE

Info: Discover a little known 277-acre preserve in which the rare Alameda Manzanita flourishes. Snout out a short fire trail to a number of non-looping ridgetop trails and hike to your heart's content. For more information: (510) 635-0135.

Directions: Travel southeast on Interstate 580 to Interstate 80 towards Richmond. Exit at San Pablo Dam Road and travel south to Castro Ranch Road and make a left. Make another left at Conestoga Way and enter the Carriage Hills housing development. Turn left on Carriage Drive and right on Coach Drive. Park at the end of Coach and walk into the preserve.

Note: Dogs must be leashed in developed areas.

VICTOR JONES PARK - Leashes

Info: Plenty of open fields await Fido and his frisbee at this parkland.

Directions: Located at Robinhood and Maplewood Drives.

Other parks in San Rafael - Leashes
- BRET HARTE PARK, Irwin Street near Hazel Court
- FREITAS MEMORIAL PARK, Montecillo Road at Trellis Drive
- HARTZELL PARK, Golden Hinde and Los Ranchitos
- MUNSON PARK, Freitas Parkway
- OLEANDER PARK, Oleander Drive off Las Gallinas Road
- SANTA MARGARITA VALLEY PARK, end of De La Guerre Road
- SCOEN PARK, Canal Street and Bahia Way
- SUN VALLEY PARK, Solano and K Streets

SAN RAMON

LODGING

RESIDENCE INN BY MARRIOTT
1071 Market Pl (94583)
Rates: $69-$179;
Tel: (510) 277-9292; (800) 331-3131

**SAN RAMON MARRIOTT
AT BISHOP RANCH**
2600 Bishop Dr (94583)
Rates: $72-$125;
Tel: (800) 228-9290

RECREATION

BISHOP RANCH REGIONAL OPEN SPACE - Leashes

Info: Solitude seekers will love this serene park. This ridge-top refuge is a haven for deer, red-tailed hawks and turkey vultures, so wildlife watchers will want to keep a keen snout out. For more information: (510) 562-7275.

Directions: The park is located on Morgan Drive, accessible from Bollinger Canyon Road and San Ramon Valley Boulevard.

ROCKY RIDGE LOOP TRAIL HIKE

Intermediate/4.4 miles/3.0 hours

Info: This grassy ridge in the Las Trampas Regional Wilderness is filled with multi-hued outcrops that have been shaped by the wind. Your remarkable journey begins at the end of Bollinger Road and steeply climbs 800 feet in just 1.5 miles. After that, the toughest part of the trail is behind you. You and furball can let your hair down and let the good times roll. For more information: (510) 635-0135.

Directions: From Interstate 680 in San Ramon, exit on Crow Canyon Road and travel west to Bollinger Canyon Road. Head north five miles to the parking area.

SAN SIMEON

LODGING

BEST WESTERN CAVALIER INN
9415 Hearst Dr (93452)
Rates: $59-$118;
Tel: (805) 927-4688; (800) 826-8168

BEST WESTERN COURTESY INN
9450 Castillo Dr (93452)
Rates: $50-$175;
Tel: (805) 927-4691; (800) 528-1234

Locate Other Dog-Friendly Activities...Check Nearby Cities

MOTEL 6-PREMIERE
9070 Castillo Dr (93452)
Rates: $41-$48;
Tel: (805) 927-8691; (800) 440-6000

RAGGED POINT INN
Hwy 1 (93452)
Rates: $40-$120;
Tel: (805) 927-4502

SILVER SURF MOTEL
9390 Castillo Dr (93452)
Rates: $39-$99;
Tel: (805) 927-4661; (800) 621-3999

RECREATION

SAN SIMEON STATE BEACH - Leashes

Info: Expect company on this popular two-mile beach. But if the tide is right, you'll love beachcombing and tidepooling along the rocky coastline. For more information: (805) 927-2035.

Directions: Located on Highway 1, between Cambria and San Simeon, about six miles south of Hearst Castle.

SAN YSIDRO

LODGING

ECONOMY INNS OF AMERICA
230 Via de San Ysidro (92173)
Rates: $25-$40;
Tel: (800) 826-0778

INTERNATIONAL MOTOR INN
190 E Calle Primera (92173)
Rates: $39-$42;
Tel: (619) 428-4486

MOTEL 6
160 E Calle Primera (92173)
Rates: $26-$30;
Tel: (619) 690-6663; (800) 440-6000

SANGER

RECREATION

CITY PARK - Leashes

Info: Even sofa-loafing canines will love a trip to this park.

Directions: Located on the corner of 5th and Academy just north of Jensen.

Dogs May Be Unleashed Unless Otherwise Indicated

SANTA ANA

LODGING

**COMFORT SUITES-
JOHN WAYNE AIRPORT**
2620 Hotel Terrace Dr (92705)
Rates: $49-$69;
Tel: (714) 966-5200; (800) 221-2222

CROWN STERLING SUITES
1325 E Dyer Rd (92705)
Rates: $79-$99;
Tel: (800) 433-4600

HOLIDAY INN EXPRESS
1600 E First St (92701)
Rates: $55-$75;
Tel: (714) 835-3051; (800) 959-4654

HOWARD JOHNSON MOTOR LODGE
939 E 17th St (92701)
Rates: $55-$75;
Tel: (714) 558-3700; (800) 654-8778

MOTEL 6
1623 E First St (92701)
Rates: $30-$34;
Tel: (714) 558-0500; (800) 440-6000

RADISSON HOTEL
2720 Hotel Terrace Dr (92705)
Rates: $85-$105;
Tel: (714) 556-3838; (800) 333-3333

**TRAVELODGE-
ORANGE COUNTY AIRPORT**
1400 SE Bristol St (92707)
Rates: $43-$47;
Tel: (714) 557-8700; (800) 578-7878

SANTA BARBARA

LODGING

ALPINE MOTEL
2824 State St (93105)
Rates: $75;
Tel: (805) 687-2821

BAYBERRY INN BED & BREAKFAST
111 W Valerio St (93101)
Rates: $85-$135;
Tel: (805) 682-3199; (800) 528-9691

BEACH HOUSE MOTEL
320 W Yanonali St (93101)
Rates: $75-$125;
Tel: (805) 966-1126

BLUE SANDS MOTEL
421 S Milpas (93103)
Rates: $75;
Tel: (805) 965-1624

CASA DEL MAR INN
18 Bath St (93101)
Rates: $59-$194;
Tel: (805) 963-4418; (800) 433-3097

EAST BEACH LODGE
1029 Orilla Del Mar St (93103)
Rates: $75-$125;
Tel: (805) 965-0546

FESS PARKER'S RED LION RESORT
633 E Cabrillo Blvd (93103)
Rates: $195-$295;
Tel: (805) 564-4333; (800) 879-2929

FOUR SEASONS BILTMORE HOTEL
1260 Channel Dr (93108)
Rates: $290-$595;
Tel: (805) 969-2261; (800) 332-3442

HOTEL STATE STREET
121 State St (93101)
Rates: $75;
Tel: (805) 966-6586

IVANHOE INN BED & BREAKFAST
1406 Castillo St (93101)
Rates: $95-$195;
Tel: (805) 963-8832

Locate Other Dog-Friendly Activities...Check Nearby Cities

LA PLAYA INN
212 W Cabrillo Blvd (93102)
Rates: $45-$150;
Tel: (805) 962-6436

MOTEL 6
443 Corona Del Mar (93103)
Rates: $48;
Tel: (805) 564-1392; (800) 440-6000

MOTEL 6
3505 State St (93105)
Rates: $46;
Tel: (805) 687-5400; (800) 440-6000

OCEAN PALMS RESORT HOTEL
232 W Cabrillo Blvd (93101)
Rates: $75-$125;
Tel: (805) 966-9133

PACIFICA SUITES
5490 Hollister Ave (93111)
Rates: $120-$180;
Tel: (805) 683-6722; (800) 338-6722

PLAZA INN
3885 State St (93105)
Rates: $75;
Tel: (805) 687-3217

SAHARA MOTEL
2800 State St (93105)
Rates: $75-$125;
Tel: (805) 687-2500

SANDY BEACH INN
122 W Cabrillo Blvd (93102)
Rates: $55-$150;
Tel: (805) 963-0405; (800) 662-1451

TRAVELER'S MOTEL
3222 State St (93105)
Rates: $75-$125;
Tel: (805) 687-6009

RECREATION

ALAMEDA PARK - Leashes

Info: Come to this city park before the workday begins or after it ends and you're sure to find other canines carousing about. Take a moment to admire the diversity of trees and palms - some of them are truly magnificent. Rover will love the cool, thick grass underpaw.

Directions: Located at 1400 Santa Barbara Street.

ALICE KECK PARK MEMORIAL GARDENS - Leashes

Info: Beautiful shade trees, a small lily pond, glorious flowers and heavenly scents go hand in paw at this garden park.

Directions: Bounded by Arrellaga, Santa Barbara, Garden and Micheltorena Streets, just east of State.

ALISO CANYON INTERPRETIVE TRAIL HIKE

Intermediate/3.5 miles/2.0 hours

Info: Before you begin on this excursion, pick up a free guide to help you and the pupster appreciate this pretty Santa Barbara backcountry trail. Your self-guided stroll will escort you

Dogs May Be Unleashed Unless Otherwise Indicated

through chaparral, grasslands, oak and sycamore woodlands. Wet waggers will love a little paw dipping en route. Once you leave the creek area, you'll have a steep switchbacking ascent. If you're visiting in spring, the meadow beside the upper trail will color your world in rainbow hues. California poppies, purple lupine, popcorn flowers and Indian paintbrush vie for your attention. At the signed junction, turn right and continue uphill to the ridgetop where you'll be greeted with some impressive views of the San Rafael and Santa Ynez Mountains. The trail then descends to Aliso Creek and rejoins the canyon trail for the return leg of your trip. For more information: (805) 683-6711.

Directions: From Santa Barbara, take Highway 101 north and exit at Highway 154, proceeding east. A short distance over San Marcos Pass (about 10 miles from Santa Barbara), take a right on Paradise Road, and drive 4 miles to the Los Prietos Ranger Station on your left. Pick up the interpretive guide at the Ranger Station. Follow the winding road across the Santa Ynez River through Sage Hill Campground to the trailhead.

AQUA CALIENTE TRAIL HIKE

Beginner/6.0 miles/3.0 hours

Info: Your hot diggety dog will be in paradise along this trail which skirts Aqua Caliente Creek. After about a mile, you'll reach the Big Caliente Debris Dam built in the 1930s to keep sediment from flowing into Gibralter Reservoir. There's a large pool at the base of the dam that's perfect for puppy paddling. When you can coax your water-logged dog from his swimming hole, continue through the canyon admiring the verdant meadows on your way to Big Caliente picnic area, your lunch spot and turnaround point. For more information: (805) 683-6711.

Directions: From Santa Barbara, take Highway 101 north to Highway 154, proceeding east 8 miles to East Camino Cielo. Turn right and continue past the Forbush Flat and Blue Canyon Trailheads. When you reach the upper Santa Ynez River, continue to Juncal Camp. Turn left and continue past the Pendola Ranger Station for 3 miles to Big Caliente Hot Springs and park.

Note: Due to primitive road conditions, it takes two hours to reach this trail in the Upper Santa Ynez Recreation Area.

ARROYO BURRO COUNTY BEACH - Leashes

Info: Meander along one of the few county beaches that allows dogs or dine alfresco at the small beachside cafe. For more information: (805) 963-7109.

Directions: Located at 2981 Cliff Drive, west of Las Positas Road.

ARROYO BURRO TRAIL HIKE

Intermediate/7.0 miles/3.5 hours

Info: Amble up the north slope to the ridgetop, paying particular attention to the madrone trees. This species, distinguished by smooth, red bark is rarely seen so far south. The trail merges with Arroyo Burro Road near the top of the ridge and leads to East Camino Cielo Road. For more information: (805) 683-6711.

Directions: From Santa Barbara, take Highway 101 north and exit at Highway 154, proceeding east. Continue 4 miles to a saddle where Arroyo Burro Road begins. The trail is a quarter-mile down this dirt road.

BLUE CANYON TRAIL HIKE

Intermediate/10.0 miles/5.0 hours

Info: Tiptoe through the small, year-round creek along this pretty hike delightfully shaded by alder, oak and sycamore. Frolic with Fido through the blue-green serpentine formations of this narrow canyon. There are several campgrounds creekside where you can stop and break biscuits together. Then turn the hound around, you're homeward bound. For more information: (805) 683-6711.

Directions: From Santa Barbara, take Highway 101 north to Highway 154, proceeding east for 8 miles to East Camino Cielo. Turn right and continue 3.2 miles from the point where the pavement ends to the trailhead.

Note: Due to primitive road conditions, it takes two hours to reach this trail in the Upper Santa Ynez Recreation Area.

Dogs May Be Unleashed Unless Otherwise Indicated

CHASE PALM PARK TRAIL HIKE - Leashes

Beginner/2.0 miles/1.0 hours

Info: Explore this section of East Beach with a stroll through Chase Palm Park. From Stearns Wharf at the foot of State Street, your hike parallels the Pacific. Take the paved path or go shoeless on the thick, moist manicured grass, which is shaded by towering, elegant Washington palms. After about a mile, you'll reach Cabrillo Pavillion ideal for a refreshment break. On Sundays throughout the year, there's a delightful arts and crafts show along Cabrillo Boulevard. Join the other walkers and their pooches and check out the artwork on display.

Directions: The park runs south from State Street/Stearn's Wharf for approximately one mile.

COLD SPRINGS TRAIL TO SANTA YNEZ RIVER HIKE

Intermediate/6.0 miles/3.0 hours

Info: The first 1.5 miles comprise a steady descent of 1,000 feet and bring you to Forbush Flat Camp. The well-shaded camp is beside Gidney Creek and a once prosperous apple orchard planted by homesteader Fred Forbush in the early 1900s. Take a cool break before continuing on to the Santa Ynez River where picnicking and riverside frolicking spell fun for you and furface. When you can drag yourself and your pooch away from this cool oasis, retrace your steps. For more information: (805) 683-6711.

Directions: Take Highway 101 north to Highway 154, proceeding east 8 miles to East Camino Cielo. Turn right and continue to the trailhead on the north side of the road.

Note: Due to primitive road conditions, it takes two hours to reach this trail in the Upper Santa Ynez Recreation Area.

GIBRALTER RECREATION AREA TRAIL HIKE

Beginner/6.0 miles/3.0 hours

Info: You and the dawgus can dawdle riverside to a slew of swimming holes, complete with Tarzan swings. When you've had your fill of this delightful water wonderland, continue your journey to Gibralter Reservoir where fishing is allowed if you have a permit. For more information: (805) 683-6711.

Locate Other Dog-Friendly Activities...Check Nearby Cities

Directions: From Santa Barbara, take Highway 101 north and exit at Highway 154, proceeding east. A short distance over San Marcos Pass (about 10 miles from Santa Barbara), take a right on Paradise Road and continue approximately 10 miles to the dirt parking lot at road's end.

INDIAN CREEK TRAIL HIKE

Beginner/8.0 miles/4.0 hours

Info: The tailwagger will love you forever after a visit to this puppy paradise. This journey along Indian Creek is the perfect way to beat the heat during the dog days of summer. When you reach Lower Buckhorn Camp, break out the bread and biscuits before retracing those wet pawprints to your starting point. For more information: (805) 683-6711.

Directions: From Santa Barbara, take Highway 101 north to Highway 154, proceeding east 8 miles to East Camino Cielo. Turn right and continue past the Forbush Flat and Blue Canyon trailheads. When you reach the Upper Santa Ynez River, continue to Juncal Camp. Turn left and continue 2 miles beyond Mono Camp to a trailhead sign and a wide parking turnout on the north side of the road.

Note: Due to primitive road conditions, it takes two hours to reach this trail in the Upper Santa Ynez Recreation Area.

JAMESON RESERVOIR AND ALDER CREEK TRAIL HIKE

Intermediate/8.0 miles/4.0 hours

Info: Your excursion begins behind the locked gate at the east end of Juncal Campground. You'll traverse an oak-shaded dirt road for the first 2.5 miles before encountering a short climb up the south side of the reservoir. At the turnoff to Alder Creek, the landscape becomes much more interesting. Aquatic pups will love this part of the trail which travels past pools and waterfalls for about a mile until Alder Camp. Do the lunch thing before heading back the way you came. For more information: (805) 683-6711.

Directions: From Santa Barbara, take Highway 101 north to Highway 154, proceeding east 8 miles to East Camino Cielo. Turn right and continue past the Forbush Flat and Blue Canyon trailheads. When you reach the Upper Santa Ynez River, continue to Juncal Camp. The trailhead is located at the east end of Juncal Campground.

Note: Due to primitive road conditions, it takes two hours to reach this trail in the Upper Santa Ynez Recreation Area.

KNAPP'S CASTLE TRAIL HIKE

Beginner/1.0 miles/0.5 hours

Info: History hounds will love this simple hike to the ruins of George Knapp's one-time hideaway. Knapp's Castle provides a keyhole peek into a time gone by as well as some enchanting views of the Pacific, the Channel Islands and the Santa Barbara backcountry. For more information: (805) 683-6711.

Directions: Take Highway 101 north to Highway 154 and proceed east eight miles to East Camino Cielo. Turn right and continue 2.5 miles to a parking area and a locked gate.

Note: Due to primitive road conditions, it takes two hours to reach this trail in the Upper Santa Ynez Recreation Area.

MISSION PARK - Leashes

Info: Sniff out more than 1,000 roses in the garden at this lovely, aromatic park. And then check out the Santa Barbara Mission, queen of the California missions.

Directions: The park is located directly across from the Old Mission at the intersection of Laguna and Mission Drives.

RATTLESNAKE CANYON TRAIL HIKE

Intermediate/3.5 miles/2.0 hours

Info: Nestled in a deep canyon, you'll find waterfalls, deep pools and quiet, out-of-the-way places. Pack a biscuit basket, there are plenty of secluded spots where you can do lunch. For more information: (805) 683-6711.

Locate Other Dog-Friendly Activities...Check Nearby Cities

Directions: From Santa Barbara, take Mission Canyon Road past its intersection with Foothill Road and go right on Los Canoas Road. Continue to Skofield Park. There's a large parking area near the picnic grounds.

RED ROCK TRAIL HIKE

Intermediate/7.0 miles/3.5 hours

Info: Two dirt roads leading up river to the Gibralter Reservoir combine to form this popular hike. Start on the low road which is called the Red Rock Trail. You and the pupster will delight in the multitude of swimming holes along this looping trail. For more information: (805) 683-6711.

Directions: From Santa Barbara, take Highway 101 north and exit at Highway 154, proceeding east. A short distance over San Marcos Pass (about 10 miles from Santa Barbara), take a right on Paradise Road for approximately 10 miles to the parking lot. The trail begins beyond the locked gates.

SAN ANTONIO CANYON PARK - Leashes

Info: Hike with your wagalong and sniff out the awesome scenery. Or just laze away the day and soak up some sun in this beautiful 16-acre park.

Directions: Located on San Antonio Creek Road.

SANTA BARBARA BOTANIC GARDEN - Leashes

Info: This 65-acre, ever-blooming garden oasis is home to over 1,000 species of native California plants, some quite rare. More than five miles of trails escort you on a kaleidoscopic color journey. Visit on a cool day, this canyon area is often warmer than the beach in Santa Barbara. For more information: (805) 563-2521.

Directions: Take Mission Street northeast. After 10 blocks, the road curves to the left and becomes Mission Canyon Drive. Follow to Foothill Road, bear right, then make a quick left to continue on Mission Canyon Drive. It's about half a mile to the park.

Note: $3 adult admission fee.

Dogs May Be Unleashed Unless Otherwise Indicated

SANTA CRUZ to LITTLE PINE MOUNTAIN TRAIL HIKE

Intermediate/Expert/12.0 miles/6.5 hours

Info: The beginning of this trail along the Camuesa Fire Road is a simple hike to Oso Canyon and some excellent swimming holes, ideal stops for water hijinks. Once you reach the junction with the Santa Cruz Trail, the leisurely pace gives way to a steep zigzag ascent across pretty trailside meadows. Atop the saddle, you'll know why you made the effort. The views of the Santa Ynez Valley, Channel Islands and Lake Cachuma are exquisite. All around is a grabbag of trees - from Coulter, yellow and sugar pine, to live oak, spruce and Douglas fir. Break out the snack pack, you can't beat the top of Little Pine Mountain as a picnic spot. When you've had your fill, retrace your steps. For more information: (805) 683-6711.

Directions: From Santa Barbara, take Highway 101 north and exit at Highway 154, proceeding east. A short distance over San Marcos Pass (about 10 miles from Santa Barbara), take a right on Paradise Road and continue east for 6 miles along the Santa Ynez River. Cross the river, go through a parking area and turn left on Oso Road. Follow for one mile to Upper Oso Campground and trailhead parking at the eastern end of the camp.

SANTA CRUZ TRAIL to NINETEEN OAKS CAMP HIKE

Beginner/3.5 miles/2.0 hours

Info: Fix a brown bagger, pack the pooch and head out for some splish-splashing fun in the delightfully cool waters of Oso Creek. Do lunch at Nineteen Oaks Camp before returning the way you came. For more information: (805) 683-6711.

Directions: From Santa Barbara, take Highway 101 north and exit at Highway 154, proceeding east. A short distance over San Marcos Pass (about 10 miles from Santa Barbara), take a right on Paradise Road and continue east for 6 miles along the Santa Ynez River. Cross the river, go through a parking area and turn left on Oso Road. Follow for one mile to Upper Oso Campground and trailhead parking at the eastern end of the camp.

SHORELINE PARK - Leashes

Info: An ideal park for your pooch's daily constitutional, the path parallels the off-limits beach. Between the tangy ocean breezes and the cushy green grass, you're sure to find this walk invigorating. For more information: (805) 966-9222.

Directions: Located at Marina and Shoreline Drives.

TUNNEL TRAIL to SEVEN FALLS HIKE

Intermediate/3.0 miles/1.5 hours

Info: The trail to Seven Falls of Mission Creek is one of the most popular and picturesque hikes in Santa Barbara. And with good reason. All along the creek, you'll encounter deep pools just perfect for swim breaks or dirty dog antics. A verdant canyon, it's alive with chaparral and oak. Sweet birdsongs fill the air and mingle with the rushing water, soothing your senses. To reach the falls, you and the dawgus will need some boulder hopping and rock scrambling experience. If you decide to forgo the falls and just chill out creekside, you won't regret a moment spent on this idyllic hideaway trail. Two paws up. For more information: (805) 683-6711.

Directions: From Santa Barbara, take Mission Canyon Road turning right for one block on Foothill Road, then immediately turning left back onto Mission Canyon Road. At a distinct V-intersection, veer left onto Tunnel Road and drive to the end. Park along the road.

SANTA CLARA

LODGING

BUDGET INN
2499 El Camino Real (95051)
Rates: $44-$52;
Tel: (408) 244-9610

DAYS INN
4200 Great America Pkwy (95054)
Rates: $59-$89;
Tel: (408) 980-1525; (800) 329-7466

DAYS INN-SANTA CLARA
859 El Camino Real (95050)
Rates: $59-$89;
Tel: (408) 255-2840; (800) 329-7466

ECONO LODGE-SILICON VALLEY
2930 El Camino Real (95051)
Rates: $50-$105;
Tel: (408) 241-3010; (800) 424-4777

Dogs May Be Unleashed Unless Otherwise Indicated

HOWARD JOHNSON LODGE
5405 Stevens Creek Blvd (95051)
Rates: $75-$90;
Tel: (800) 446-4656

MARRIOTT HOTEL
2700 Mission College Blvd (95054)
Rates: $69-$400;
Tel: (408) 988-1500; (800) 228-9290

MOTEL 6
3208 El Camino Real (95051)
Rates: $33-$39;
Tel: (408) 241-0200; (800) 440-6000

TRAVELODGE
3477 El Camino Real (95051)
Rates: $45-$55;
Tel: (408) 984-3364; (800) 578-7878

VAGABOND INN
3580 El Camino Real (95051)
Rates: $44-$55;
Tel: (408) 241-0771; (800) 522-1555

THE WESTIN HOTEL-SANTA CLARA
5101 Great America Pkwy (95054)
Rates: $135-$169;
Tel: (408) 986-0700; (800) 228-3000

RECREATION

CENTRAL PARK - Leashes

Info: Jumpstart your day with a jog along the pathways that lace this expansive 52-acre park. Or plan a brown bagger and an afternoon interlude.

Directions: Off Kiely Boulevard at the entrance to the CRC.

EARL R. CARMICHAEL PARK - Leashes

Info: Soak up some sunshine with your canine in this lovely 10.5-acre park.

Directions: Located at 3445 Benton Street.

HENRY SCHMIDT PARK - Leashes

Info: You and Fido will have a howl of a good time stomping your paws through this 8-acre park.

Directions: Located at 555 Los Padres.

LEXINGTON RESERVOIR - Leashes

Info: Pups are welcome anywhere except on the Sierra Azul Trail. You can row, row, row your pooch, or fish for dinner as you enjoy your day in this lovely park. For more information: (408) 358-3741.

Directions: Located off Highway 17 at Alma Bridge Road.

Locate Other Dog-Friendly Activities...Check Nearby Cities

LICK MILL PARK - Leashes

Info: Start your day with a kick by heading down to the "Lick." If you have time to kill, take a pup stroll at the Mill.

Directions: Located at 4750 Lick Mill Boulevard.

MAYWOOD PARK - Leashes

Info: Make your pup's day with a stroll through this pretty, 7-acre park.

Directions: Located at 3330 Pruneridge Avenue.

SANTA CLARA DOG PARK

Info: Dog owners will be happy to see pooper scoopers, water and benches at this small enclosed dog run, the only leash-free area in Santa Clara. Canine mingling peaks in early evening.

Directions: Located at 3445 Lochinvar Avenue near Lawrence Expressway and Homestead Road.

Other parks in Santa Clara - Leashes
- AGNEW PARK, 2250 Agnew Road
- BOWERS PARK, 2582 Cabrillo Avenue
- BRACHER PARK, 2560 Alhambra Drive
- CITY PLAZA PARK, Lexington and Main
- EVERETT ALVAREZ PARK, 2280 Rosita Drive
- FAIRWAY GLEN PARK, 2051 Calle de Primavera
- HOMERIDGE PARK, 2985 Stevenson Street
- JENNY STRAND PARK, 250 Howard Drive
- MACHADO PARK, 3360 Cabrillo Avenue
- MEMORIAL CROSS PARK, Martin Avenue and De La Cruz
- PARKWAY PARK, 3675 Forest Avenue
- ROTARY PARK, 1490 Don Avenue
- WESTWOOD OAKS PARK, 460 La Herran Drive

Dogs May Be Unleashed Unless Otherwise Indicated

SANTA CLARITA

LODGING

BEST WESTERN RANCH HOUSE INN
27143 N Tourney Rd (91355)
Rates: $70-$100;
Tel: (800) 528-1234

HAMPTON INN-MAGIC MOUNTAIN
25259 The Old Rd (91381)
Rates: $74-$89;
Tel: (805) 253-2400; (800) 426-7866

SANTA CRUZ

LODGING

BEST WESTERN TORCH-LITE INN
500 Riverside Ave (95060)
Rates: $49-$83;
Tel: (408) 475-5600; (800) 528-1234

CANDLELITE INN
1101 Ocean St (95060)
Rates: $35-$140;
Tel: (408) 427-1616

CHAMINADE AT SANTA CRUZ
1 Chaminade Ln (95065)
Rates: $125-$145;
Tel: (408) 475-5600; (800) 283-6569

COMFORT INN
110 Plymouth St (95060)
Rates: $39-$149; Tel: (800) 221-2222

EDGEWATER BEACH MOTEL
525 Second St (95060)
Rates: $48-$100;
Tel: (408) 423-0440

HOLIDAY INN EXPRESS
600 Riverside Ave (95060)
Rates: $45-$175;
Tel: (408) 458-9660; (800) 465-4329

THE INN AT PASATIEMPO
555 Hwy 17 (95060)
Rates: $74-$175;
Tel: (408) 423-5000; (800) 834-2546

MISSION INN
2250 Mission St (95060)
Rates: $110;
Tel: (408) 425-5455

MOTEL CONTINENTAL
414 Ocean St (95060)
Rates: $38-$98;
Tel: (408) 429-1221

OCEAN FRONT HOUSE
1600 W Cliff Dr (95060)
Rates: $850-$1320 Weekly;
Tel: (408) 266-4453; (800) 801-4453

OCEAN PACIFIC LODGE
120 Washington (95060)
Rates: $55-$185;
Tel: (408) 457-1234; (800) 995-0289

PACIFIC INN
330 Ocean St (95060)
Rates: $38-$98
Tel: (408) 425-3722

SANTA CRUZ INN
2950 Soquel Ave (95062)
Rates: $32-$85;
Tel: (408) 475-6322

SUNNY COVE MOTEL
2-1610 E Cliff Dr (95062)
Rates: $40-$95;
Tel: (408) 475-1741

SUNSET INN
2424 Mission St (95060)
Rates: $40-$95;
Tel: (408) 423-3471

TERRACE COURT MOTEL
125 Beach St (95060)
Rates: $62-$105;
Tel: (408) 423-3031

TRAVELODGE RIVIERA MOTEL
619 Riverside Ave (95060)
Rates: $34-$254;
Tel: (408) 423-9515; (800) 578-7878

Locate Other Dog-Friendly Activities...Check Nearby Cities

RECREATION

ANTONELLI POND - Leashes

Info: Make tracks along the trails that lace this beautiful area.

Directions: Located on Delaware Avenue, next to Natural Bridges State Park.

BONNY DOON BEACH - Leashes

Info: Spend a peaceful afternoon at this isolated beach shrouded by craggy bluffs. For more information: (408) 462-8333.

Directions: Head northwest on Highway 1 to Davenport. The beach is located at Highway 1 and Bonny Doon Road. Look for a small parking area on the side of the road.

EAST CLIFF DRIVE COASTAL ACCESS POINTS - Leashes

Info: This coastal road offers many small, paw-friendly beaches. Look for them by the following streets: 12th, 13th, 20th, 21st, 22nd, 23rd, 26th, 36th, 38th, and 41st.

Directions: All access points are off East Cliff Drive.

MITCHELL'S COVE BEACH - Leashes

Info: For an early morning romp with your leashless pup, this beach is the place to be. You might even meet a local pooch or two. Off-leash hours are sunrise to 10:00 a.m. and 4:00 p.m. to sunset. For more information: (408) 429-3777.

Directions: Located on the south side of West Cliff Drive, between Almar and Woodrow Avenues.

PLEASURE POINT BEACH - Leashes

Info: Laze with Lassie on the sand and watch the surfers strut their stuff. Or hop on the trail around the cliff's edge for outstanding views.

Directions: Located off East Cliff Drive at Pleasure Point Drive.

Dogs May Be Unleashed Unless Otherwise Indicated

SCOTT CREEK BEACH - Leashes

Info: Soak up some rays as you and the pupster prance along this lovely beach.

Directions: Located north of Greyhound Rock off Highway 1.

SEABRIGHT/CASTLE BEACH - Leashes

Info: This long beach is a great place for Sandy to leg stretch.

Directions: Located off East Cliff Drive at Seabright, between the Boardwalk and the Yacht Harbor.

WEST LIGHTHOUSE BEACH - Leashes

Info: Despite the limited off-leash hours, Fido will still love the blissful freedom he'll experience at this less frequented beach. Off-leash hours are sunrise to 10:00 a.m. and 4:00 p.m. to sunset. For more information: (408) 429-3777.

Directions: Located on the south side of West Cliff Drive, west of Point Santa Cruz.

SANTA FE SPRINGS

LODGING

DYNASTY SUITES
13530 E Firestone Blvd (90670)
Rates: $35-$40;
Tel: (310) 921-8571; (800) 842-7899

MOTEL 6
13412 Excelsior Dr (90670)
Rates: $30-$34;
Tel: (310) 921-0596; (800) 440-6000

SANTA MARIA

LODGING

BEST WESTERN BIG AMERICA
1725 N Broadway (93454)
Rates: $55-$90;
Tel: (805) 922-5200; (800) 426-3213

HUNTER'S INN
1514 S Broadway (93454)
Rates: $49-$95;
Tel: (805) 922-2123; (800) 950-2123

HOWARD JOHNSON LODGE
210 S Nicholson Ave (93454)
Rates: $39-$64;
Tel: (805) 922-5891; (800) 446-4656

MOTEL 6-NORTH
2040 N Preisker Ln (93454)
Rates: $28-$34;
Tel: (805) 928-8111; (800) 440-6000

Locate Other Dog-Friendly Activities...Check Nearby Cities

MOTEL 6-SOUTH
839 E Main St (93454)
Rates: $26-$32;
Tel: (805) 925-2551; (800) 440-6000

RAMADA SUITES
2050 N Preisker Ln (93454)
Rates: $55-$150;
Tel: (805) 928-6000; (800) 272-6232

ROSE GARDEN INN
1007 E Main St (93454)
Rates: $49-$79;
Tel: (805) 922-4505

RECREATION

ADAM PARK - Leashes

Info: Every dog should have his day in a park this pretty. 30 acres offer plenty of paw-pleasing recreation. Chill out in the shade at the gazebo or sunbathe on the grass.

Directions: Located at 600 West Enos Drive.

ATKINSON PARK - Leashes

Info: Break some bread with Bowser and bask in the sunshine at this lovely 6.5-acre park.

Directions: Located at 1000 North Railroad Avenue.

GROGAN PARK - Leashes

Info: Promenade with your pup through 6 acres of parkland.

Directions: Located at 1155 West Rancho Verde.

MARAMONTE PARK - Leashes

Info: Pack some Scooby snacks and plan an outdoor biscuit break with your bowwow in this 9-acre park.

Directions: Located at 620 East Sunrise Drive.

PREISKER PARK - Leashes

Info: This beautiful, 40-acre park can make for a doggone great afternoon. Ducks and geese glide across the peaceful pond, while dozens of monarch butterflies flutter through Grandchildrens Grove in the southwest corner of the region. Listen to the serenades of songbirds while you stroll or loll with your pup on the grass.

Directions: Located at 2301 North Broadway.

Dogs May Be Unleashed Unless Otherwise Indicated

WALLER COUNTY PARK - Leashes

Info: Grassy and woodsy, this park is perfect for playtime or walktime. For more information: (805) 934-6211.

Directions: From Highway 135, take Waller Lane about half a block west.

WALLER PARK - Leashes

Info: Shaded by towering pines surrounding a tranquil lake, this park is a pooch paradise with plenty of room for pup-prancing. For more information: (805) 934-6211.

Directions: Located at South Broadway and Goodwin Road.

Other parks in Santa Maria - Leashes
• ALICE TREFTS PARK, 510 East Park Avenue
• ARMSTRONG PARK, 1000 East Chapel Street
• BUENA VISTA PARK, 800 South Pine Street
• CENTRAL PLAZA PARK, 100 North Broadway
• JOE WHITE PARK, 500 South Palisade Drive
• MEMORIAL PARK, 200 North Pine Street
• OAKLEY PARK, 1300 North Western Avenue
• RICE PARK, 700 East Sunset Avenue
• RUSSELL PARK, 1000 West Church Street
• SIMAS PARK, 500 South McClelland
• TUNNELL PARK, 1100 North Palisade Drive

SANTA MONICA

LODGING

DAYS INN
3007 Santa Monica Blvd (90404)
Rates: $64-$94;
Tel: (310) 829-6333; (800) 329-7466

THE GEORGIAN
1415 Ocean Ave (90401)
Rates: $125;
Tel: (310) 395-9945

HOLIDAY INN SANTA MONICA
120 Colorado Blvd (90401)
Rates: $69-$99;
Tel: (310) 451-0676; (800) 465-4329

LOEWS-
SANTA MONICA BEACH HOTEL
1700 Ocean Ave (90401)
Rates: $195-$450;
Tel: (310) 458-6700; (800) 223-0888

RECREATION

ARROYO SEQUIT PARK TRAIL HIKE - Leashes

Beginner/2.4 miles/1.25 hours

Info: To witness the best of what this easy trail has to offer, you and the pupster should plan an après rain hike. Not only will the creek be gurgling with paw dipping opportunities, but the waterfall will be cascading and gorgeous. The trail parallels a creek (wet those paws), crosses a meadow (check out the flowers) and encounters a waterfall (kick back and enjoy) before coming to an end. For more information: (818) 880-0350.

Directions: From Santa Monica, head northwest on Pacific Coast Highway to Mulholland Highway. Turn north approximately 6 miles to the park entrance and parking area. Even though the gate to the park is only open on weekends, hiking is permitted daily. Just squeeze through and head towards the barn, following the signs to the trail.

MALIBU SPRINGS TRAIL HIKE - Leashes

Beginner/1.0 miles/0.5 hours

Info: Leg stretch with Fletch on this short, easy trail. If wet paws equate to happiness, then plan an outing after a rainstorm has filled the Malibu Springs Stream. For more information: (818) 880-0350.

Directions: Head northwest on Pacific Coast Highway to Mulholland Highway. Turn north approximately 4 miles to the signed trailhead on the left-side of the highway.

NICHOLAS FLAT TRAIL HIKE - Leashes

Beginner/2.0 miles/1.0 hours

Info: You'll want to pack a biscuit basket and a camera for your day's outing. From the trailhead, you'll encounter two junctions. Head right at the first one. When you reach the second junction, go left for a short, half-mile jaunt to Nicholas Flat Pond or stay on the main trail for a mile walk to the scenic overlook. The pond is surrounded by sandstone outcroppings which make for great picnic spots, while the overlook affords terrific views of the dramatic landscape. For more information: (818) 880-0350.

Dogs May Be Unleashed Unless Otherwise Indicated

Directions: From Santa Monica, head northwest on Pacific Coast Highway to Mulholland Highway. Turn north approximately 8 miles to the State 23 intersection. Make a right, following approximately 2.5 miles to Decker School Road (not to be confused with Decker School Lane). Continue on Decker School Road for 1.5 miles to the trailhead at road's end.

SANTA NELLA

LODGING

BEST WESTERN ANDERSEN'S INN
12367 S Hwy 33 (95322)
Rates: $47-$65;
Tel: (209) 826-5534; (800) 527-5534

MOTEL 6
12733 S Hwy 33 (95322)
Rates: $32-$38;
Tel: (209) 826-6644; (800) 440-6000

HOLIDAY INN MISSION DE ORO
13070 S Hwy 33 (95322)
Rates: $45-$72;
Tel: (209) 826-5555; (800) 465-4329

SUPER 8 MOTEL
28821 W Gonzaga Rd (95322)
Rates: $40-$56;
Tel: (209) 827-8700; (800) 800-8000

RECREATION

O'NEILL FOREBAY WILDLIFE AREA

Info: This 700-acre wildlife area, rife with trees and grassy areas is a welcome sight to weary highway travelers. Access is by foot only. Hunting dog tests and trials are frequently held here. For more information: (209) 826-0463.

Directions: Take Highway 33 south for two miles to the wildlife area on the west side of the road.

Note: Open year-round except for two weekends in November. Dogs must be leashed from April 1 - June 30.

SANTA PAULA

LODGING

SANTA PAULA TRAVELODGE
350 S Peck Rd (93060)
Rates: $46-$62;
Tel: (805) 525-1561; (800) 578-7878

SANTA ROSA

LODGING

BEST WESTERN GARDEN INN
1500 Santa Rosa Ave (95404)
Rates: $48-$75;
Tel: (707) 546-4031; (800) 528-1234

BEST WESTERN HILLSIDE INN
2901 4th St (95409)
Rates: $44-$54;
Tel: (707) 546-9353; (800) 528-1234

ECONO LODGE
1800 Santa Rosa Ave (95407)
Rates: $36-$66;
Tel: (800) 424-4777

HERITAGE INN
870 Hopper Ave (95403)
Rates: $47-$68;
Tel: (707) 545-9000

LOS ROBLES LODGE
1985 Cleveland Ave (95401)
Rates: $65-$95;
Tel: (707) 545-6330; (800) 255-6330

MOTEL 6-NORTH
3145 Cleveland Ave (95403)
Rates: $30-$36;
Tel: (707) 525-9010; (800) 440-6000

MOTEL 6-SOUTH
2760 Cleveland Ave (95403)
Rates: $30-$36;
Tel: (707) 546-1500; (800) 440-6000

RAMADA LIMITED
866 Hopper Ave (95403)
Rates: $45-$85;
Tel: (707) 575-0945; (800) 272-6232

TRAVELODGE
1815 Santa Rosa Ave (95407)
Rates: $48-$65;
Tel: (707) 542-3472; (800) 578-7878

TRAVELODGE-DOWNTOWN
635 Healdsburg Ave (95401)
Rates: $45-$70;
Tel: (707) 544-4141; (800) 578-7878

RECREATION

DOYLE PARK - Leashes

Info: In summer, find a shady spot under the spreading oaks or toe dip in Spring Creek.

Directions: From Sonoma Avenue, turn south on Doyle Park. Drive to the parking lot.

HOOD MOUNTAIN REGIONAL PARK - Leashes

Info: With lots of trails to pick from, it's no wonder this park is a local favorite. The four-mile drive to the entrance is pretty and offers a good view of Hood Mountain. But the narrow, steep and twisting road to the park is not for the faint-hearted. Open only on weekends and holidays. Closed during the summer when the threat of fire is extreme. For more information: (707) 527-2041.

Directions: From Highway 12, turn east on Los Alamos Road (not Adobe Canyon Road). The entrance is four miles below.

Note: Parking fee of $2.

Dogs May Be Unleashed Unless Otherwise Indicated

SPRING LAKE COUNTY PARK - Leashes

Info: Strut with your mutt along the 2-mile trail that encircles the lake or take a path less traveled. Pack a biscuit basket and plan a picnic lunch in this lovely 320-acre park. For more information: (707) 539-8092.

Directions: The west entrance is on Newanga Avenue off Summerfield Road. The east entrance is on Violetti Drive, off Montgomery Road.

SANTA YNEZ

<u>LODGING</u>

SANTA COTA MOTEL
3099 Mission Dr (93460)
Rates: $75-$125;
Tel: (805) 688-5525

<u>RECREATION</u>

ZACA LAKE - Leashes

Info: Pick up a trail guide at Zaca Lake Lodge and shake a leg through miles of dense oak and pine woodlands. Or stroll the lake's perimeter, find that perfect picnic spot and do lunch. In the mood to do nothing? Then simply laze the day away under a shade tree with your best Buster beside you. For more information: (805) 688-4891.

Directions: From Santa Ynez, take Foxen Canyon Road north through the wine country of Santa Ynez Valley to a rough road leading to the lake. This road will be on your right about a mile south of the Zaca Mesa Winery.

Note: High clearance vehicles only. $5.00 day-use entrance fee, and $3.00 dog entrance fee.

SANTA YSABEL

LODGING

APPLE TREE INN
4360 Hwy 78 (92070)
Rates: $45-$79;
Tel: (619) 765-0222

SANTEE

LODGING

CARLTON OAKS COUNTRY CLUB
9200 Inwood Dr (92071)
Rates: $40-$75;
Tel: (619) 448-4242

SARATOGA

RECREATION

BROOKGLEN PARK - Leashes

Info: Make tracks with Max along the bike path that twists through this lovely 7-acre park.

Directions: Located at 2734 Brookglen Court.

CONGRESS SPRINGS PARK - Leashes

Info: Open fields and pathways provide the space for furface to get his daily dose of exercise in this 19-acre park.

Directions: Located at 12970 Glen Brae Drive.

EL QUITO PARK - Leashes

Info: Burn some kibble on the fitness course in this pleasant 6-acre community park.

Directions: Located at 12855 Paseo Presada.

Dogs May Be Unleashed Unless Otherwise Indicated

HAKONE GARDENS - Leashes

Info: Huff up the hill, or browse through the bamboo gardens in this scenic 15.5-acre park.

Directions: Located at 21000 Big Basin Way.

KEVIN MORAN PARK - Leashes

Info: Pack the pupster's basket and do lunch alfresco. Then burn off the calories with a jaunt on the bike path.

Directions: Located at 12415 Scully Avenue.

SANBORN COUNTY PARK - Leashes

Info: The 40-acre grassed picnic area is a lovely place for a brown bagger with your best buddy beside you. The park harbors a variety of flora and fauna that make this area a sensory delight for serenity-seeking picnickers. For more information: (408) 867-9959.

Directions: From Saratoga, take Highway 9 two miles west to Sanborn Road. Turn left onto Sanborn and travel one mile to the park entrance.

Note: Fees posted at park entrance. Dogs are allowed in designated areas only and leash laws are strictly enforced.

Other parks in Saratoga - Leashes
•FOOTHILL PARK, 20654 Seaton Avenue
•GARDINER PARK, 19085 Portas Drive
•SARATOGA HISTORICAL HALF-ACRE, 20460 Saratoga-Los Gatos Road
•WILDWOOD PARK, 20764 4th Street

SCOTTS VALLEY

<u>**LODGING**</u>

BEST WESTERN INN-SCOTTS VALLEY
6020 Scotts Valley Dr (95066)
Rates: $50-$75;
Tel: (408) 438-6666; (800) 528-1234

SEAL BEACH

LODGING

RADISSON INN SEAL BEACH
600 Marina Dr (90740)
Rates: $89-$109;
Tel: (310) 493-7501; (800) 333-3333

SEASIDE

LODGING

BAY BREEZE INN
2049 Fremont Blvd (93955)
Rates: $33-$102;
Tel: (408) 899-7111

SEASIDE MOTEL
81131 Fremont Blvd (93955)
Rates: $50-$95;
Tel: (408) 394-8881

DAYS INN
1400 Del Monte Blvd (93955)
Rates: $53-$115;
Tel: (408) 394-5335; (800) 325-2525

THUNDERBIRD MOTEL
1933 Fremont Blvd (93955)
Rates: $29-$95;
Tel: (408) 394-6797; (800) 848-7841

SEBASTOPOL

RECREATION

RAGLE RANCH PARK - Leashes

Info: For some R&R, plan to spend an afternoon at this beautiful parkland. Picnic in the shade of a massive oak tree, toss a frisbee in the verdant expanse, or wander along the nature trails while you and the dogster are serenaded by songbirds. For more information: (707) 527-2041.

Directions: Located at 500 Ragle Ranch Road.

Other parks in Sebastopol - Leashes
• CLAHAN PARK, 390 Morris Street
• IVES POOL/LIBRARY PARK, 7985 Valentine Avenue

SELMA

LODGING

BEST WESTERN JOHN JAY INN
2799 Floral Ave (93662)
Rates: $45-$55;
Tel: (209) 891-0300; (800) 528-1234

SUPER 8 MOTEL
3142 S Highland Ave (93662)
Rates: $44-$48;
Tel: (800) 800-8000

SEPULVEDA

LODGING

COMFORT INN
8657 Sepulveda Blvd (91343)
Rates: $35-$65;
Tel: (800) 221-2222

MOTEL 6
15711 Roscoe Blvd (91343)
Rates: $33-$39;
Tel: (818) 894-9341; (800) 440-6000

SEQUOIA / KINGS CANYON NATIONAL PARKS

LODGING

GRANT GROVE LODGE
SR 180 (93633)
Rates: $33-$90;
Tel: (209) 561-3314

SHASTA LAKE

LODGING

BRIDGE BAY RESORT
10300 Bridge Bay Rd (Redding 96003)
Rates: $55-$89;
Tel: (916) 275-3021; (800) 752-9669

Locate Other Dog-Friendly Activities...Check Nearby Cities

SHAVER LAKE

<u>RECREATION</u>

BLACK POINT TRAIL HIKE - Leashes

Intermediate/1.2 miles/1.0 hours

Info: When you only have time for a leg-stretching saunter but you still want to be surrounded by beauty and coolness, this hike's for you. Most of the trail follows a path through a true fir plant community that includes whitethorn, gooseberry and chinquipin. Elevation at the trailhead is 7,640 feet and then rises to 8,111 feet at the top of Black Point where you'll also encounter sierra juniper, Jeffrey pine and green manzanita. From atop Black Point, you and Fido will feast your eyes on scenic vistas of Huntington Lake, Shaver Lake, the crest of Kaiser Ridge and the San Joaquin River Canyon. Best times to visit are June through October. In winter, access roads and the trail are snow covered. For more information: (209) 855-5360.

Directions: Take Highway 168 north to Huntington Lake Road (Big Creek turnoff) and continue into Big Creek to Forest Road 8S32. Follow 8S32 approximately 4 miles to the trailhead.

RANCHERIA FALLS TRAIL HIKE - Leashes

Beginner/2.0 miles/1.0 hours

Info: Sunday strollers will love this rather simple trail leading to beautiful Rancheria Falls. You and the pupster will step lively in a forest of fragrant fir trees. In early summer, wildflowers add dazzling colors to the forest floor. This shaded, delightfully cool trail leads to beautiful Rancheria Falls, the perfect chill out spot. Rancheria Falls is approximately 150 feet high and 50 feet wide and is best viewed in June and July. Even during low water years, the falls keep flowing and present a beautiful slice of Mother Nature. For more information: (209) 855-8321.

Directions: Take Highway 168 north to Rancheria Falls Road (FR 8S31), approximately one mile past the Sierra Summit Ski Resort. Follow FR 8S31 one mile to the signed trailhead.

SHELL BEACH

LODGING

THE CLIFFS AT SHELL BEACH
2757 Shell Beach Rd (93449)
Rates: $70+;
Tel: (805) 773-5000; (800) 826-7827

SPYGLASS INN
2705 Spyglass Dr (93449)
Rates: $64-$124;
Tel: (805) 773-4855;
(800) 824-2612 (CA)

SHELTER COVE

LODGING

MARINA MOTEL
533 Machi Rd (95589)
Rates: $52-$62;
Tel: (707) 986-7595

SHELTER COVE MOTOR INN
205 Wave Dr (95589)
Rates: $63-$78;
Tel: (707) 986-7521

SHERMAN OAKS

RECREATION

VAN NUYS - SHERMAN OAKS PARK - Leashes

Info: Take the pupster for a jaunt along the jogging trail in this vast 67-acre park. Get your daily dose along the exercise course.

Directions: Located at 14201 Huston Street.

SIERRA CITY

LODGING

HERRINGTON'S SIERRA PINES
SR 49 (96125)
Rates: $55-$75;
Tel: (916) 862-1151

Locate Other Dog-Friendly Activities...Check Nearby Cities

RECREATION

BUTCHER RANCH to PAULEY CREEK TRAIL HIKE

Beginner/3.0 miles/1.5 hours

Info: All you want in a trail and more is found on this cinchy hike. This mountainous canyon is crammed with wildflowers and excellent fishing opportunities. You'll hike along Butcher Creek to the confluence of Butcher Ranch and Pauley Creeks where you and your pooch can spend the afternoon in one of the refreshingly cool, deep pools. You'll never want to leave. For more information: (916) 288-3231.

Directions: From Sierra City, take Highway 49 east for 5 miles to Gold Lake Highway at Bassetts Station. Head north for 1.4 miles and turn left over the Salmon Creek Bridge. Drive for .3 miles to Packer Lake Road. Turn right for 2.5 miles to where the road forks at Packer Lake. Take the left fork which is Forest Road 93 (Packer Saddle Road) for 2.1 miles to Packer Saddle and turn left, following the sign reading "Sierra Buttes Lookout 3 and Pauley Creek 5". After .5 miles, the road makes a 90° turn to the right. Follow this another .5 miles to the sign "Butcher Ranch 1, Pauley Creek 4". Take the right fork for .7 miles to the sign for the trailhead.

Note: High clearance vehicles only.

CHAPMAN CREEK TRAIL HIKE

Beginner/3.0 miles/1.5 hours

Info: Saunter around the babbling creek, skim rocks over the water and simply enjoy the surroundings with Fido on this easy hike. For more information: (916) 288-3231.

Directions: From Sierra City, go eight miles east on Highway 49 to Chapman Creek Campground. At the north end of the campground, you'll see the trailhead and parking area.

Dogs May Be Unleashed Unless Otherwise Indicated

DEER LAKE TRAIL HIKE
Intermediate/5.0 miles/ 2.5 hours

Info: Avid hikers take heart. This well-loved trail includes near-ly everything you and your city-weary dog have on your wish list. From cobalt blue waters to the gorgeous Sierra Buttes, col-orful wildflowers to elusive eastern brook trout, you're gonna love this hike. For more information: (916) 288-3231.

Directions: From Sierra City, take Highway 49 east for five miles to Gold Lake Highway at Bassetts Station. Head north 1.4 miles, turn left and cross over the Salmon Creek Bridge. Drive for .3 miles and take a right on Packer Lake Road. Travel for 2 miles to the marked trailhead on the right-side of the road. Parking is available at the Packsaddle Camping Ground.

HASKELL PEAK TRAIL HIKE
Expert/3.0 miles/2.0 hours

Info: This trail clamors up 1,100 feet and tops out at 8,107-foot Haskell Peak. The first mile climbs through a thick forest, then levels out and offers a great view of the trail's namesake. But it's the last quarter-mile that will give your leg muscles a real workout. This part of the hike is steep, four-paw terrain with spectacular mountain vistas and unusual volcanic rock formations. For more information: (916) 288-3231.

Directions: Head five miles east on Highway 49, then go north on Gold Lake Highway at Bassetts. Continue 3.7 miles, then hang a right on Forest Service Road 9 (Haskell Peak Road) and travel 8.4 miles to the trailhead. Park on either side of the road.

HAYPRESS CREEK TRAIL HIKE
Expert/6.0 miles/4.0 hours

Info: Discover a canyon with a secluded stream and waterfall in the midst of an ancient red fir forest. But as with all great things, there's a price to be paid. You and Rover will definite-ly pay your dues as you climb nearly 1,400 feet in just 3 miles. Even though the first half-mile is quite simple, don't be fooled. The next 2.5 miles are sure to separate the dogs from the pups.

Catch your breath and throw Rover a power snack before heading back. For more information: (916) 288-3231.

Directions: Take Highway 49 northeast to Wild Plum Road opposite the Yuba River Inn. Follow for one mile to the trail-head parking area. Walk across the bridge and through the campground. The trail branches from the road to the left about a half-mile past the campground. Once you cross the bridge over Haypress Creek, the Haypress Creek Trail is to the right.

SAND POND INTERPRETIVE TRAIL HIKE

Beginner/0.8 miles/0.5 hours

Info: Even telly bellies will dig this effortless hike through marshland and forests. Take some time to read the interpretive signs along the trail - they're very educational. Come spring, the melodic songs of birds fill the air. For more information: (916) 288-3231.

Directions: Take Highway 49 east for 5 miles to Gold Lake Highway at Bassetts Station. Head north for 1.4 miles, turn left and cross over the Salmon Creek Bridge. Continue west for approximately one mile to the Sand Pond Swim Area parking lot. The trailhead is at the gate on the west (right) side of the parking lot near the sign explaining the history of Sand Pond.

UPPER SALMON LAKE TRAIL HIKE

Intermediate/4.0 miles/2.0 hours

Info: For the first half-mile you and furface will enjoy an easy amble along the east side of Upper Salmon Lake. Let your hot diggety dog do a refreshing doggie paddle in Horse Lake Creek before heading south past Horse Lake. And then get psyched for a series of steep switchbacks that zigzag to a saddle and merge with the Deer Lake Trail. Your reward, panoramic views of Horse Lake and Upper Salmon Lake, backdropped by an enormous glacial moraine. Take the short trek to beautiful Deer Lake, unpack your snacks and picnic with your precious pup before heading home. For more information: (916) 288-3231.

Directions: From Sierra City, head east on Highway 49 for five miles to Gold Lake Highway at Bassetts Station. Continue for four miles to the clearly marked Salmon Lake junction. Turn left and proceed to Upper Salmon Lake. The trailhead will be on your right.

SIMI VALLEY

LODGING
CLARION HOTEL-SIMI VALLEY
1775 Madera Rd (93065)
Rates: $70-$100;
Tel: (805) 584-6300; (800) 221-2222

RADISSON HOTEL-SIMI VALLEY
999 Enchanted Way (93065)
Rates: $69-$109;
Tel: (805) 583-2000; (800) 333-3333

MOTEL 6
2566 N Erringer Rd (93065)
Rates: $36-$42;
Tel: (805) 526-3533; (800) 440-6000

RECREATION
CHUMASH PARK - Leashes

Info: Shuffle along the Chumash Trail or just relax with Max in this beautiful park.

Directions: Located at Flanagan Drive and Broken Arrow.

RANCHO MADERA COMMUNITY PARK - Leashes

Info: The park encompasses 35 acres. Ten are developed for town hounds to enjoy.

Directions: Located at 556 Lake Park Drive.

RANCHO SANTA SUSANA - Leashes

Info: Expansive and open best describe this 55-acre park. Take the dog for a jog or play the day away.

Directions: Located at 50057 Los Angeles Avenue.

Locate Other Dog-Friendly Activities...Check Nearby Cities

RANCHO SIMI - Leashes

Info: 45 acres of fun and adventure await you and Fido in this pleasant community park.

Directions: Located at 1765 Royal Avenue.

RANCHO TAPO COMMUNITY PARK - Leashes

Info: Commune with canine comrades and nature in this lovely 35-acre park.

Directions: Located at 3700 Avenida Simi.

Other parks in Simi Valley - Leashes
• ARROYO PARK, 2105 Socrates Avenue
• ARROYOSTOW PARK, 1700 North Stow Street
• ATHERWOOD PARK, 2271 Alamo Street
• BERYLWOOD PARK, 1955 Bridget Avenue
• CITRUS GROVE PARK, 2100 North Marvel Court
• DARRAH VOLUNTEER PARK, Royal Avenue and Darrah Avenue
• FOOTHILL PARK, 1850 Ardenwood Avenue
• FRONTIER PARK, 2163 Elizondo Avenue
• HOUGHTON-SCHRELBER PARK, 4333 Township Avenue
• KNOLLS PARK, 1300 West Katherine Road
• LINCOLN PARK, 1215 First Street
• MAYFAIR PARK, 2550 Caldwell Street
• SIMI HILLS NEIGHBORHOOD PARK, 5031 Alamo Street
• STARGAZE PARK, Tierra Rejada Road and Stargaze Place
• STRATHEARN HISTORICAL PARK, 137 Strathearn Place
• VERDE PARK, 6045 East Nelda Street
• WILLOWBROOK PARK, Willowbrook Lane and Arroyo Simi

SMITH RIVER

LODGING

BEST WESTERN SHIP ASHORE RESORT
12370 Hwy 101 N (95567)
Rates: $44-$83;
Tel: (707) 487-3141; (800) 528-1234

SEA ESCAPE MOTEL
15370 Hwy 101 N (95567)
Rates: $40-$60;
Tel: (707) 487-7333

CASA RUBIO BEACH HOUSE
17285 Crissey Rd (95567)
Rates: $78-$88;
Tel: (800) 357-6199

RECREATION

SMITH RIVER COUNTY PARK - Leashes

Info: This splendid park is directly at the mouth of the Smith River. Birdwatch at Pyramid Point, roam the pebbly beach or toss a frisbee to Rover. For more information: (707) 464-7230.

Directions: The park is at the end of Mouth of Smith River Road.

SODA SPRINGS

RECREATION

PALISADE CREEK TRAIL to
PALISADE CREEK BRIDGE HIKE - Leashes

Expert/10.0 miles/6.0 hours

Info: The not so gung-ho will love the first two miles of this hike. A relatively flat section leads through areas of glacier-polished granite and along a small tranquil lake that reflects the surrounding stands of timber. The padded of paw may want to retrace their steps from the lake, while sturdier breeds can wiggle their tails on the switchbacks to the Palisade Creek Bridge. Take a munchie break at the creek before your about-face and homeward trek. For more information: (916) 587-3558.

Directions: From Interstate 80 in Soda Springs, follow Old Highway 40 east for 0.8 miles to Soda Springs Road. Turn south and continue another 0.8 miles to Pahatsi Road on the right. Follow Pahatsi until it turns to dirt Kidd Lakes Road.

Follow this dirt road for 1.5 miles to the fork. Do not take the road to Palisade Lake, go straight instead. Continue for 2.5 miles (Kidd Lake will be on your left) until you reach the trailhead on the north side of Cascade Lakes.

SOLEDAD

LODGING

MOTEL 8-SOLEDAD
1013 S Front St (93960)
Rates: $39-$64;
Tel: (408) 678-3814; (800) 800-8000

PARAISO HOT SPRINGS LODGE
Paraiso Springs Rd (93960)
Rates: $110-$160;
Tel: (408) 678-2882

SOLVANG

LODGING

BEST WESTERN KRONBORG INN
1440 Mission Dr (93463)
Rates: $65-$85;
Tel: (805) 688-2383; (800) 528-1234

MEADOWLARK MOTEL
2644 Mission Dr (93463)
Rates: $40-$70;
Tel: (805) 688-4631; (800) 549-4658

HAMLET MOTEL
1532 Mission Dr (93463)
Rates: $35-$95;
Tel: (805) 688-4413; (800) 253-5033

VIKING MOTEL
1506 Mission Dr (93463)
Rates: $32-$85;
Tel: (805) 688-1337; (800) 368-5611

RECREATION

HANS CHRISTIAN ANDERSEN PARK - Leashes

Info: About half of this 52-acre park has been left in its natural, rugged state. Loaded with shaded trails, you'll be able to hike to your heart's content. For more information: (800) 468-6765.

Directions: From Highway 246, exit at Atterdag Road north. The park is three blocks further on the left.

NOJOQUI FALLS COUNTY PARK - Leashes

Info: This micro-Yosemite encompasses 82 acres of dense woodlands and lush hillsides. Visit in the spring, you might be lucky enough to behold breathtaking Nojoqui Waterfall. For more information: (805) 568-2461.

Dogs May Be Unleashed Unless Otherwise Indicated

Directions: Head south on Alisal Road for about 10 miles to the park on your left. After about six miles, the road veers sharply to the right, follow it.

SOMES BAR

LODGING

MARBLE MOUNTAIN RANCH CABINS
92520 Hwy 96 (95568)
Rates: $27-$200;
Tel: (800) 552-6284

SONOMA

LODGING

BEST WESTERN SONOMA VALLEY INN
550 2nd St W (95476)
Rates: $79-$149;
Tel: (707) 938-9200; (800) 334-5784

MARTHA'S COTTAGE
BED & BREAKFAST
19377 Orange Ave (95476)
Rates: $110-$125;
Tel: (707) 996-6918

SPARROW'S NEST INN
BED & BREAKFAST
425 Denmark St (95476)
Rates: $85-$105;
Tel: (707) 996-3750

STONE GROVE BED & BREAKFAST
240 2nd St E (95476)
Rates: $65-$115;
Tel: (707) 939-8249

TREE HOUSE BED & BREAKFAST
431 2nd St E (95476)
Rates: $125-$150;
Tel: (707) 938-1628

VILLA CASTILLO BED & BREAKFAST
1100 Castle Rd (95476)
Rates: $150;
Tel: (707) 996-4616

RECREATION

LAKE SONOMA

Info: The stunning coastal foothills provide the backdrop for this fun-filled lake. Float, paddle or power your way over the tranquil waters. If your paws are grounded, head to the trails. Over 40 miles of pathways zigzag through this pretty area. Leashes are recommended. For more information: (707) 433-9483.

Directions: The lake is accessible via Canyon Road or Dry Creek Road off Highway 101.

Locate Other Dog-Friendly Activities...Check Nearby Cities

MAXWELL FARMS REGIONAL PARK - Leashes

Info: Traverse the paths that follow Sonoma Creek and admire the laurel trees wrapped in untamed grapevines. The creek is dry in summer months. For more information: (707) 527-2041.

Directions: The park is off Verano Avenue, west of Highway 12.

Note: $2 day-use fee.

SONOMA VALLEY REGIONAL PARK - Leashes

Info: Relish in the bucolic setting of this enchanting park. Spend an afternoon hiking beside Sonoma Creek or wandering amidst the oak forest and wildflower-filled meadows. For more information: (707) 527-2041.

Directions: From Sonoma, take Highway 12 north to the park entrance (south of Glen Ellen between Arnold Drive and Highway 12). Once you park, walk one mile west across the park to Glen Ellen to reach the creek.

Note: $2 parking fee.

SONORA

LODGING

ALADDIN MOTOR INN
14260 Mono Way (95370)
Rates: $49-$67;
Tel: (209) 533-4971

**BEST WESTERN
SONORA OAKS MOTOR HOTEL**
19551 Hess Ave (95370)
Rates: $56-$80;
Tel: (209) 553-4400; (800) 528-1234

KENNEDY MEADOWS RESORT CABINS
P. O. Box 4010 (95370)
Rates: $52-$105;
Tel: (209) 965-3900

MINERS MOTEL
18740 Hwy 108 (95370)
Rates: $40-$75;
Tel: (209) 532-7850;
(800) 4451-4176 (CA)

RAIL FENCE MOTEL
19950 Hwy 108 (95370)
Rates: $35-$47;
Tel: (209) 532-9191

SONORA INN HOTEL
160 S Washington St (95370)
Rates: $49-$59;
Tel: (209) 532-7468

RECREATION

BEARDSLEY NATURE TRAIL HIKE - Leashes

Beginner/2.5 miles/1.25 hours

Info: This instructive walk explores a beautiful geologic phenomenon. Pick up a free pamphlet at the trailhead for a quickie education. For more information: (209) 965-3434.

Directions: From Sonora, head northeast on Highway 108 towards Sonora Pass, past the turnoff for Pinecrest. Pass through Strawberry, turning left on Beardsley Road (FR 5N01). Continue for 7 miles to Beardsley Day-Use Road. Follow for 1.5 miles to the trailhead at the Beardsley Day-Use Area.

CLARK FORK MEADOW TRAIL HIKE - Leashes

Intermediate/5.0 miles/2.5 hours

Info: Treat your pooch pal to a touch of the Carson Iceberg Wilderness with an afternoon hike on this trail. This section of the 8-mile (one way) trail gives you a feel for the beautiful area without any of the hassles. Only experienced hikers should attempt to complete the entire hike. For more information: (209) 965-3434.

Directions: Head east on Highway 108 to Tuolumne Country Road (FR 7N83), approximately 5 miles east of Niagara Creek Campground. Turn left to the trailhead at Iceberg Meadow.

COLUMNS OF THE GIANTS TRAIL HIKE - Leashes

Beginner/0.5 miles/0.5 hours

Info: Learn as you journey. This interpretive trail leads past two volcanic formations which cooled at different speeds and caused unusual specimens of columnar basalt. There's a free pamphlet at the trailhead which explains all. For more information: (209) 965-3434.

Directions: From Sonora, head east on Highway 108 approximately 24 miles past Pinecrest to Pigeon Flat Campground. The trailhead and parking area are next to the campground.

Locate Other Dog-Friendly Activities...Check Nearby Cities

CRABTREE TRAIL to CAMP LAKE and BEAR LAKE HIKE - Leashes

Beginner/Intermediate/8.0 miles/4.0 hours

Info: Play lake hop-scotch with your Scottie and treat your pooch to some water-filled fun. The first 3 miles of this pupular wilderness hike to Camp Lake are somewhat demanding and merit a lakeside luncheon and a bit of paw dipping. The next mile will ensconce you in solitude as you make your way along a flat and easy course to Bear Lake - a picturesque and isolated spot. Happy wet wags to you. For more information: (209) 965-3434.

Directions: Head east on Highway 108 for 28 miles to signed Crabtree Road. Follow Crabtree Road approximately 6 miles to the paved parking area for the trailhead. Take the 3-mile trail to Camp Lake and then follow the signed spur trail to Bear Lake.

DONNELL VISTA TRAIL HIKE - Leashes

Beginner/0.5 miles/0.5 hours

Info: This interpretive trail provides an education along with some first-rate views of Dardanelle Cones and Dardanelle Reservoir. For more information: (209) 965-3434.

Directions: From Sonora, head east on Highway 108 to the trailhead and parking area approximately 18 miles past Pinecrest on the north side of the highway.

EAGLE CREEK to DARDANELLE TRAIL HIKE - Leashes

Intermediate/8.0 miles/4.0 hours

Info: This fairly easy hike is splendid in springtime when wildflowers cover the meadows. Retrace your steps after reaching Dardanelle. Leave a car at either end of the trail if you're traveling in a group, and hike to or from Dardanelle. For more information: (209) 965-3434.

Directions: From Sonora, head east on Highway 108 approximately 15 miles past Pinecrest to Eagle Meadow Road. Turn right for 8 miles to the trailhead at Eagle Meadow.

Dogs May Be Unleashed Unless Otherwise Indicated

PINECREST LAKE LOOP TRAIL HIKE - Leashes

Beginner/4.0 miles/2.0 hours

Info: Couch potatoes will love this easy trail. Do a picnic style lunch at any of the blanket - spreading spots that encircle pretty Pinecrest Lake. Birdwatchers, bring your binoculars. For more information: (209) 965-3434.

Directions: Head east on Highway 108 for 30 miles to the Pinecrest exit. The Pinecrest Lake parking area is one mile from the exit.

PINECREST LAKE LOOP TRAIL to CLEO'S BATHS HIKE - Leashes

Beginner/Intermediate/7.0 miles/3.5 hours

Info: The hike around Pinecrest Lake may be a cinch, but the going gets a bit rough once you branch off on the trail to Cleo's Baths. This section involves a moderately difficult climb, but the refreshing pools of the Stanislaus River are definitely worth the sweat. Kick back or kick up some water fun with your aquapup before heading back. For more information: (209) 965-3434.

Directions: From Sonora, head east on Highway 108 for 30 miles to the Pinecrest exit. The Pinecrest Lake parking area is one mile from the exit. Follow the Pinecrest Lake Loop Trail to where the trail forks at the lake's inlet near the bridge. The spur trail to Cleo's Baths is signed.

SHADOW OF THE MI-WOK TRAIL HIKE - Leashes

Beginner/0.5 miles/0.5 hours

Info: This enlightening walk through history provides insight into the lifestyle of the Mi-Wok Indians, Native Americans who lived in the area around 1,000 A.D. For more information: (209) 965-3434.

Directions: From Sonora, head east on Highway 108 for 30 miles to the Pinecrest exit. Follow Pinecrest Lake Road to the Summit Ranger Station parking area. The trailhead is located across the road from ranger headquarters.

Note: No smoking on the trail.

Locate Other Dog-Friendly Activities...Check Nearby Cities

TRAIL OF THE SURVIVORS HIKE - Leashes

Beginner/0.5 miles/0.5 hours

Info: For an informative look at how trees survive in a rugged mountain environment, take this field trip. It's a wonderful introduction to the region's ecology. For more information: (209) 965-3434.

Directions: Go northeast on Highway 108 to the Pinecrest exit. Make a right on Pinecrest Lake Road for .5 miles to Dodge Ridge Road. Turn right for .2 miles to the sign for Pinecrest Community Center. Turn right and the trailhead is on the left.

WOODS CREEK ROTARY PARK - Leashes

Info: Pack the picnic baskets and head for shade. Indulge in a hearty lunch or a good read while your water-loving pup splashes to his heart's content. For more information: (209) 532-4541.

Directions: On Stockton Street and Woods Creek Drive, just southwest of town.

SOUTH EL MONTE

LODGING

RAMADA SUITES
1089 Santa Anita Ave (91733)
Rates: $79-$107;
Tel: (818) 350-9588; (800) 272-6232

SOUTH LAKE TAHOE

LODGING

ALDER INN
1072 Ski Run Blvd (96150)
Rates: $42-$95;
Tel: (916) 544-4485; (800) 544-0056

BEACHSIDE INN & SUITES
930 Park Ave (96150)
Rates: $30-$125;
Tel: (916) 544-2400; 800 884-4920

BEST WESTERN LAKE TAHOE INN
4110 Lake Tahoe Blvd (96150)
Rates: $65-$165;
Tel: (916) 541-2010; (800) 528-1234

BLUE JAY LODGE
4133 Cedar Ave (96150)
Rates: $39-$99;
Tel: (916) 544-5232; (800) 258-3529

Dogs May Be Unleashed Unless Otherwise Indicated

BLUE LAKE MOTEL
1055 Ski Run Blvd (96150)
Rates: $50-$80;
Tel: (916) 541-2399

CARNEY'S CABINS
P. O. Box 601748 (96153)
Rates: $70-$100;
Tel: (916) 542-3361

**DAYS INN-STATELINE/
SOUTH LAKE TAHOE**
968 Park Ave (96150)
Rates: $49-$120;
Tel: (916) 541-4800; (800) 325-2525

ECHO CREEK RANCH
P. O. Box 20088 (96151)
Rates: $101+;
Tel: (916) 544-5397; (800) 462-5397

EMBASSY SUITES RESORT
4130 Lake Tahoe Blvd (96150)
Rates: $139-$500;
Tel: (916) 544-5400; (800) 362-2779

HEAVENLY VALLEY MOTEL & SPA
1261 Ski Run Blvd (96150)
Rates: $101+;
Tel: (916) 544-4244; (800) 692-2246

HIGH COUNTRY LODGE
1227 Emerald Bay Rd (96150)
Rates: $30-$70;
Tel: (916) 541-0508

LA BAER INN
4133 Lake Tahoe Blvd (96150)
Rates: $40-$53;
Tel: (916) 544-2139; (800) 544-5575

LAKEPARK LODGE
4081 Cedar Ave (96150)
Rates: $40-$65;
Tel: (916) 541-5004

LAMPLITER MOTEL
4143 Cedar Ave (96150)
Rates: $45-$70;
Tel: (916) 544-2936

MATTERHORN MOTEL
2187 Lake Tahoe Blvd (96150)
Rates: $39-$150;
Tel: (916) 541-0367

MOTEL 6
2375 Lake Tahoe Blvd (96150)
Rates: $30-$44;
Tel: (916) 542-1400; (800) 440-6000

THE MONTGOMERY INN
966 Modesto Ave (96150)
Rates: $49-$69;
Tel: (916) 544-3871; (800) 624-8224

PARK AVENUE/MEADOWOOD LODGE
904 Park Ave (96150)
Rates: $70-$100;
Tel: (916) 544-3503

RAVEN WOOD HOTEL
4075 Manzanita Ave (96150)
Rates: $52-$169;
Tel: (800) 659-4185

RED CARPET INN
4100 Lake Tahoe Blvd (96150)
Rates: $40-$70;
Tel: (916) 544-2261; (800) 851-7952

RIVIERA INN
890 Stateline Ave (96150)
Rates: $40-$70;
Tel: (916) 544-3448; (800) 358-2463

RODEWAY INN
4082 Lake Tahoe Blvd (96150)
Rates: $39-$79;
Tel: (916) 541-7900; (800) 424-4777

SAFARI MOTEL
966 LaSalle St (96150)
Rates: $70-$100;
Tel: (916) 544-2912

SIERRA-CAL LODGE
3838 Lake Tahoe Blvd (96150)
Rates: $70-$100;
Tel: (916) 541-5400; (800) 245-6343

SLEEPY RACCOON MOTEL
1180 Ski Run Blvd (96150)
Rates: $40-$70;
Tel: (916) 544-5890

SUPER 8 MOTEL
3600 Lake Tahoe Blvd (96150)
Rates: $53-$78;
Tel: (916) 544-3476; (800) 237-8882

TAHOE COLONY INN
3794 Montreal (96157)
Rates: $40-$70;
Tel: (916) 655-6481

TAHOE KEYS RESORT
599 Tahoe Keys Blvd (96150)
Rates: $200-$300;
Tel: (916) 544-5397; (800) 438-8246

Locate Other Dog-Friendly Activities...Check Nearby Cities

TAHOE MARINA INN
930 Bal Bijou Rd (96150)
Rates: $56-$140;
Tel: (916) 541-2180

TAHOE QUEEN MOTEL
932 Poplar St (96150)
Rates: $40-$70;
Tel: (916) 544-2291

TAHOE TROPICANA LODGE
4132 Cedar Ave (96150)
Rates: $40-$70;
Tel: (916) 541-3911

TAHOE VALLEY MOTEL
2241 Lake Tahoe Blvd (96150)
Rates: $85-$150;
Tel: (916) 541-0353; (800) 669-7544

TORCHLITE INN
965 Park Ave (96150)
Rates: $38-$78;
Tel: (916) 541-2363; (800) 455-6060

TRADE WINDS MOTEL
944 Friday Ave (96150)
Rates: $35-$125;
Tel: (916) 544-6459; (800) 628-1829

RECREATION

See "Lake Tahoe Area" for additional recreation listings

FOREST TREE TRAIL HIKE - Leashes

Beginner/0.25 miles/0.25 hours

Info: Here's your chance to learn about the towering and majestic Jeffrey pine. The life cycle of this tree species, from germination to termination, is interpreted along this enjoyable jaunt. For more information: (916) 573-2600.

Directions: The trailhead is located in the northwest corner of the parking lot, across from the visitor center, 3 miles from South Lake Tahoe on Highway 89.

MEEKS BAY to LAKE GENEVIEVE TRAIL HIKE - Leashes

Intermediate/9.0 miles/5.0 hours

Info: This somewhat challenging hike takes you into the Desolation Wilderness, where serenery awaits. Make your way through the shaded woodlands of pine to the lake and do lunch with Lassie. If you want to accumulate more hiking miles, continue along the trail to a series of scenic alpine lakes. Keep track of the time and allow enough daylight hours for the return trip. For more information: (916) 573-2600.

Directions: Take Highway 89 to Meeks Bay Resort. Parking is located across the highway from the resort in a small dirt parking lot.

Note: Wilderness permit required.

Dogs May Be Unleashed Unless Otherwise Indicated

MOUNT TALLAC to CATHEDRAL LAKE TRAIL HIKE - Leashes

Intermediate/5.0 miles/2.5 hours

Info: Solitude can be yours as you and pooch-face saunter along this trail to Cathedral Lake. You'll hear the wind whistling through stands of Jeffrey pine and songbirds serenading you as they flutter through the azure blue sky. Take a biscuit basket and kick back at the picturesque lake.

If you're up to some Rexercise, don't stop at the lake. Continue a couple of miles further up the front face of Mt. Tallac. Reach the summit and enjoy panoramic vistas in every direction. You'll be awestruck by the views of Fallen Leaf Lake, Desolation Wilderness and Lake Tahoe. Altogether, the round-trip journey to the peak adds 5 butt-kicking miles to your trek. For more information: (916) 573-2600.

Directions: The trailhead is located approximately 3.5 miles from South Lake Tahoe on Highway 89. Look for the Mt. Tallac Trailhead sign directly across the entrance to Baldwin Beach and turn left down the dirt road. Continue to the trailhead parking area.

Note: Wilderness permit required.

RAINBOW TRAIL HIKE - Leashes

Beginner/0.5 miles/0.5 hours

Info: Fill your snouts with the crisp scent of Jeffrey pine as the pathway leads you and furface to a soothing mountain meadow. Admire the wildflowers that splash the landscape in rainbow-like colors all the way to the Stream Profile Chamber. Snap up some great scenery shots before continuing your journey along this short loop trail. For more information: (916) 573-2600.

Directions: The trailhead is located at the visitor center, 3 miles north of South Lake Tahoe on Highway 89.

SMOKEY'S TRAIL HIKE - Leashes

Beginner/0.15 miles/0.10 hours

Info: This is an important educational walk for all outdoor types. Let Fido sniff his way around as you check out the instructions for building a safe campfire. If you brought the kids, let them learn too. They'll receive a reward from the visitor center if they can remember the procedures for a safe campfire. For more information: (916) 573-2600.

Directions: The trailhead is located at the visitor center, 3 miles north of South Lake Tahoe on Highway 89.

TRAIL OF THE WASHOE HIKE - Leashes

Beginner/0.75 miles/0.5 hours

Info: History buffs take heart - this easy, woodsy trail provides insight into the area's first inhabitants. Environmentally attuned, you'll be surprised to learn how the Washoe survived without detrimentally impacting their surroundings. For more information: (916) 573-2600.

Directions: The trailhead is located in the southwest corner of the visitor center's parking lot, 3 miles north of South Lake Tahoe on Highway 89.

SOUTH SAN FRANCISCO

LODGING

COMFORT SUITES
121 E Grand Ave (94080)
Rates: $59-$89;
Tel: (800) 221-2222

LA QUINTA MOTOR INN
20 Airport Blvd (94080)
Rates: $64-$70;
Tel: (415) 583-2223; (800) 531-5900

RADISSON HOTEL
275 S Airport Blvd (94080)
Rates: $85-$160;
Tel: (800) 333-3333

RAMADA INN NORTH
245 S Airport Blvd (94080)
Rates: $82-$150;
Tel: (415) 589-7200; (800) 452-3456

TRAVELODGE-AIRPORT NORTH
326 S Airport Blvd (94080)
Rates: $55-$80;
Tel: (415) 583-9600; (800) 578-7878

VAGABOND INN-AIRPORT
222 S Airport Blvd (94080)
Rates: $48-$95;
Tel: (415) 692-4040; (800) 522-1555

Dogs May Be Unleashed Unless Otherwise Indicated

SPRING VALLEY

LODGING

SUPER 8 MOTEL-SPRING VALLEY
9603 Campo Rd (91977)
Rates: $37-$49;
Tel: (619) 589-1111; (800) 800-8000

SPRINGVILLE

RECREATION

FORKS OF THE KERN to KERN RIVER TRAIL HIKE

Intermediate/5.0 miles/2.5 hours

Info: For a waterful adventure your aquatic pup won't soon forget, hot dog it to the Little Kern River for some paw dipping fun. Don't attempt to cross the river during times of spring meltoff. Bring along a fishing rod - there might be a fish with your name on it. For more information: (209) 539-2607.

Directions: From Springville, head east on Highway 190 for 28 miles, continuing on Western Divide Highway for 17 miles. Turn left on Tulare County Road M-50 for 7 miles to FR 22S82. Turn left for 21 miles to FR 20S67. Make a right on FR 20S67 for 2 miles to the trailhead at road's end.

FREEMAN CREEK TRAIL HIKE

Intermediate/8.6 miles/4.5 hours

Info: Cram your RAM with memories along this trail. From giant sequoias and verdant meadows to paw-wetting creek crossings and abundant fishing opportunities, this hike has something for everyone. Beginning with a 1,500-foot descent to Freeman Creek, the trail then hugs the creek and leads you to the Freeman Creek Giant Sequoia Grove. For more information: (209) 539-2607.

Locate Other Dog-Friendly Activities...Check Nearby Cities

Directions: From Springville, head east on Highway 190 for 28 miles to FR 21S50. Turn left for a half-mile to an intersection marked with an island in the middle of the road. Turn left, then make a quick right on to FR 20S99. Follow FR 20S99 for a quarter-mile to the trailhead at road's end.

LEWIS CAMP to TROUT MEADOW RANGER STATION TRAIL HIKE

Intermediate/14.0 miles/7.5 miles

Info: You'll have to step lively on this trail if you expect to go the distance. And don't forget to pack some snacks and lots of Perrier. The trail travels in an eastwardly direction and sets tails wagging with great views of the Sierras. You and the panter can do some paw dipping when you cross the Little Kern River where you'll traverse a bridge and arrive at the Ranger Station. For more information: (209) 539-2607.

Directions: Take Highway 190 east for 28 miles to FR 21S50. Turn left on FR 21S50 for 4 miles to FR 21S79 and go right. Follow FR 21S79 for 4 miles to the trailhead at road's end.

NEEDLES TRAIL HIKE

Beginner/4.4 miles/2.25 hours

Info: Get an eyeful of fabulous views of Lloyd Meadow and the Golden Trout Wilderness from atop the Needles Fire Lookout. You and the dawgus can access the lookout by following the trail as it gently climbs the north slopes of Needles Ridge. For more information: (209) 539-2607.

Directions: Head east on Highway 190 for 28 miles, continuing on Western Divide Highway for one mile to FR 21S05 (Needles Road). Turn left for 4.5 miles to the trailhead at road's end.

NELSON TRAIL HIKE

Expert/7.4 miles/4.0 hours

Info: This difficult trail is for experienced hikers and hounds only. Starting from the upper trailhead, you'll descend rather steeply to the Tule River. On your way down take some time to admire the Belknap Giant Sequoia Grove, or click your Kodak and take home a memory of the sequoias. Once you reach the river, it's splish-splashing time in this mini puppy paradise. Save some energy, it's an uphill return. For more information: (209) 539-2607.

Directions to the upper trailhead; Head east on Highway 190 for 27.5 miles to the trailhead at the large turnout on the right-hand side of the highway.

Directions to the lower trailhead; Head east on Highway 190 for 16 miles to Camp Nelson. Turn right on Nelson Drive for 3 miles to the trailhead at road's end.

WISHON TRAIL HIKE

Intermediate/12.0 miles/6.0 hours

Info: Spend some quality time with your pooch on this outdoor excursion. Breathe deeply and delight in the aromatic air as you make tracks to trail's end at Mt. Home State Forest. Your course will follow along a road, climb up and over Doyle Springs, cross the Tule River, cross Silver Creek and finally end at the state forest boundary. If wet paws equate to your pup's happiness, he'll rate this as a bonafido great hike. For more information: (209) 539-2607.

Directions: From Springville, head east on Highway 190 for 8 miles to Tulare Co. Road M-208 (Wishon Road). Turn left for 4 miles to the trailhead at road's end.

ST. HELENA

LODGING

EL BONITA MOTEL
195 Main St (94574)
Rates: $46-$115;
Tel: (707) 963-3216; (800) 541-3284

HARVEST INN
1 Main St (94574)
Rates: $100-$350;
Tel: (707) 963-9463; (800) 950-8466

HYPHEN INN
P. O. Box 190 (94574)
Rates: $135;
Tel: (707) 942-0434

STANTON

LODGING

MOTEL 6
7450 Katella Ave (90680)
Rates: $27-$41;
Tel: (714) 891-0717; (800) 440-6000

STOCKTON

LODGING

BEST WESTERN CHARTER WAY INN
550 W Charter Way (95206)
Rates: $45-$62;
Tel: (209) 948-0321; (800) 528-1234

DAYS INN
33 N Center St (95202)
Rates: $45-$65;
Tel: (209) 931-3131; (800) 329-7466

HOLIDAY INN STOCKTON
111 E March Ln (95207)
Rates: $85-$93;
Tel: (209) 474-3301; (800) 465-4329;
(800) 633-3737

LA QUINTA INN
2710 W March Ln (95219)
Rates: $46-$72;
Tel: (209) 952-7800; (800) 531-5900

MOTEL 6
4100 Waterloo Rd (95205)
Rates: $28-$42;
Tel: (209) 931-9511; (800) 440-6000

MOTEL 6
1625 French Camp Tpk (95206)
Rates: $27-$33;
Tel: (209) 467-3600; (800) 440-6000

MOTEL 6
817 Navy Dr (95206)
Rates: $27-$33;
Tel: (209) 946-0923; (800) 440-6000

MOTEL 6
6717 Plymouth Rd (95207)
Rates: $28-$42;
Tel: (209) 951-8120; (800) 440-6000

SUNSHINE INN
8009 N Hwy 99 (95212)
Rates: $25-$50;
Tel: (209) 956-5200

RECREATION

OAK GROVE REGIONAL COUNTY PARK - Leashes

Info: Although dogs are banned from the trails, there are plenty of open spaces where you and the pupster can admire over 1,500 oaks that shade and color the area. For more information: (209) 953-8800.

Directions: Take Interstate 5 north to the Eight Mile Road exit. The park is on the corner of Eight Mile Road and Interstate 5.

Note: $2 car fee on weekdays, $4 on weekends and holidays.

Dogs May Be Unleashed Unless Otherwise Indicated

STRAWBERRY

LODGING
THREE RIVERS RESORT
P. O. Box 81 (95375)
Rates: $85-$185;
Tel: (209) 965-3278; (800) 514-6777

STUDIO CITY

RECREATION
COLDWATER CANYON PARK - Leashes

Info: Hooray! Hooray! Fido can frolic and play in the scenic surroundings of this 81-acre partially developed park. Take a tennis ball - this could be Fido's lucky day.

Directions: Located at 12601 Mulholland Drive.

DEARING MOUNTAIN TRAIL to
COLDWATER CANYON PARK HIKE - Leashes
Beginner/2.5 miles/1.25 hours

Info: Leash up the Laddie and let the good times roll as you follow the simple trail from one verdant park to another. When you arrive at Coldwater Canyon Park, climb one of the stairways for a quick stroll along the Magic Forest Nature Trail. This trail laces through the Tree People's Preserve. For more information: (818) 756-8188.

Directions: From Studio City, take Laurel Canyon Boulevard south to Wilacre Park. The trailhead is in the park.

DEARING MOUNTAIN TRAIL to
FRYMAN OVERLOOK HIKE - Leashes
Intermediate/6.0 miles/3.0 hours

Info: Spend a pleasant afternoon with the pupster on this scenic, up and down trail. Keep your cool under the shade of pine, toyon and walnut trees as you climb to Coldwater Canyon Park and clear day views of the San Fernando Valley. The trail then takes a downhill turn to Irdell Street before returning to the trail at the yellow gate. After about 100 yards, the trail branches left and climbs a steep slope before descending again to a eucalyptus-clad ravine and down again to another ravine. The final stretch traverses the chaparral slopes of Fryman Canyon to Fryman Overlook. If you've packed a biscuit basket, the views from atop the overlook provide the scenery for a great outdoor repast. For more information: (818) 756-8188.

Directions: From Studio City take Laurel Canyon Boulevard south to Wilacre Park. The trailhead is in the park.

SUISUN CITY

LODGING
ECONOMY INNS OF AMERICA
4376 Central Pl (94585)
Rates: $30-$42;
Tel: (707) 864-1728; (800) 826-0778

RECREATION
CARL E. HALL PARK - Leashes

Info: Packed with plenty of pupportunities, this park has 10 acres of grass, picnic tables and a jogging path.

Directions: Located in Denver Terrace South, on Pintail Drive at East Wigeon Way.

GRIZZLY ISLAND WILDLIFE AREA - Leashes

Info: Calling all nature enthusiasts, anglers and adventurous pooches. You'll love this 14,300-acre wildlife area. The island complex offers wetlands, artificially-diked marshes and more than 8,000 acres of seasonal ponds. Keep a snout out for tule elk, egrets, blue herons and otters; keep a line in for striped bass, sturgeon and catfish. Drive to that perfect photo spot or study nature as you and your leashed Laddie hike along the trails. Please obey all leash laws, many birds nest in the area. For more information: (707) 425-3828.

Dogs May Be Unleashed Unless Otherwise Indicated

Directions: The recreation area is located in the heart of Suisan Marsh, off Highway 12 on Grizzly Island Road.

SAMUEL W. GOEPP PARK-Leashes

Info: Do a lap or two on the pathway through this 5-acre neighborhood park and then kick back in the cool, grassy area.

Directions: Located on Pintail Drive at Harrier Drive.

SUN CITY

LODGING

SUNSET INN
27955 En Canto (92586)
Rates: $20-$35;
Tel: (909) 679-1133

SUN VALLEY

LODGING

SCOTTISH INNS
8365 Lehigh Ave (91352)
Rates: $40+;
Tel: (818) 504-2671; (800) 251-1962

RECREATION

STRATHERN PARK WEST - Leashes

Info: Greenery sniffing canines will adore this 12-acre landscaped park smack dab in the center of a greenbelt. Playful pooches can enjoy a game of fetch. Hot dogs can chill out in the moist grass of this urban oasis.

Directions: Located at 12541 Saticoy.

SUNNYVALE

LODGING

BEST WESTERN SUNNYVALE INN
940 Weddell Dr (94089)
Rates: $56-$60;
Tel: (408) 734-3742; (800) 528-1234

CAPTAIN'S COVE MOTEL
600 N Mathilda Ave (94086)
Rates: $59-$61;
Tel: (800) 322-2683

COMFORT INN
820 E El Camino Real (94087)
Rates: $49-$65;
Tel: (800) 221-2222

MAPLE TREE INN
711 E El Camino Real (94087)
Rates: $72-$83;
Tel: (408) 720-9700; (800) 423-0243;
(800) 262-2624 (CA)

MOTEL 6
775 N Mathilda Ave (94086)
Rates: $39-$52;
Tel: (408) 736-4595; (800) 440-6000

MOTEL 6
806 Ahwanee Ave (94086)
Rates: $33-$39;
Tel: (408) 720-1222; (800) 440-6000

RESIDENCE INN BY MARRIOTT
750 Lakeway Dr (94086)
Rates: $78-$157;
Tel: (408) 720-1000; (800) 331-3131

RESIDENCE INN BY MARRIOTT
1080 Stewart Dr (94086)
Rates: $78-$157;
Tel: (408) 720-8893; (800) 331-3131

SUMMERFIELD SUITES
900 Hamlin Ct (94089)
Rates: $79-$159;
Tel: (800) 833-4353

VAGABOND INN
816 Ahwanee Ave (94086)
Rates: $40-$55;
Tel: (408) 734-4607; (800) 522-1555

WOODFIN SUITES MOTOR HOTEL
635 E El Camino Real (94087)
Rates: $79-$152;
Tel: (408) 738-1700; (800) 237-8811

RECREATION

BAYLANDS PARK - Leashes

Info: Saunter along great walking trails and enjoy the scenery in this beautiful, 177-acre park.

Directions: Located at 999 E. Caribbean Drive.

BRALY PARK - Leashes

Info: A Japanese-style wooden bridge sets this park apart from others. So, leash up the pup and snout out this interesting little green scene.

Directions: Located at 704 Daffodil Court.

Dogs May Be Unleashed Unless Otherwise Indicated

COLUMBIA PARK - Leashes

Info: 15 acres of fun await you and your ground-sniffer. Explore the woodsy region in this pleasant park.

Directions: Located at 739 Morse Avenue.

DEANZA PARK - Leashes

Info: Take Fido for a sun-filled fiesta or an afternoon siesta in this lovely 9-acre park.

Directions: Located at 1150 Lime Drive.

LAS PALMAS PARK - Leashes

Info: A pretty pond is the centerpiece of this charming park. Plenty of water and paw-friendly space pack this park with fun. A dog run for leash-free furballs creates a social, tailwagging scene.

Directions: Located at 850 Russet Drive.

ORTEGA PARK - Leashes

Info: Enjoy an afternoon interlude while you and Rover check out the green scene in this 21-acre park.

Directions: Located at 238 Gardner Drive.

RAYNOR PARK - Leashes

Info: You and your canine cohort can cavort in 15 acres of sun-filled scenery.

Directions: Located at 1565 Quail Avenue.

SERRA PARK - Leashes

Info: Take the pupster for a walk through the pretty grounds in this 18-acre park.

Directions: Located at 730 the Dalles.

Other parks in Sunnyvale - Leashes
•CANNERY PARK, 900 West California Avenue
•ENCINAL PARK, 445 North Macara Avenue

Locate Other Dog-Friendly Activities...Check Nearby Cities

- MARTIN MURPHY JUNIOR PARK, 260 North Sunnyvale
- ORCHARD GARDENS PARK, 238 Garner Drive
- PANAMA PARK, 755 Dartshire Way
- PONDEROSA PARK, 811 Henderson Avenue
- WASHINGTON PARK, 840 West Washington Avenue

SUSANVILLE

LODGING

BEST WESTERN TRAILSIDE INN
2785 Main St (96130)
Rates: $44-$83;
Tel: (916) 257-4123; (800) 528-1234

COZY MOTEL
2829 Main St (96130)
Rates: $25-$30;
Tel: (916) 257-2319

DIAMOND VIEW MOTEL
1529 Main St (96130)
Rates: $27-$34;
Tel: (916) 257-4585

FRONTIER INN MOTEL
2685 Main St (96130)
Rates: $30-$55;
Tel: (916) 257-4141

KNIGHTS INN MOTEL
1705 Main St (96130)
Rates: $37-$49;
Tel: (916) 257-2168

MT. LASSEN HOTEL
27 S Lassen St (96130)
Rates: $37+;
Tel: (916) 257-6609

RIVER INN MOTEL
1710 Main St (96130)
Rates: $32-$45;
Tel: (916) 257-6051

SIERRA VISTA MOTEL
1067 Main St (96130)
Rates: $29-$34;
Tel: (916) 257-6721

SUPER BUDGET MOTEL
2975 Johnstonville Rd (96130)
Rates: $36-$44;
Tel: (916) 257-2782

RECREATION

BIZZ JOHNSON NATIONAL RECREATION TRAIL HIKE - Leashes

Info: This 25-mile trail from Susanville to Mason Station wanders along a 1914 railroad line, passing through an old logging camp and loading stations. This do-your-own-thing trail is ideal for an unhurried saunter or an energetic workout. For more information: (916) 257-2151.

Directions: Take Highway 36 from Susanville and make a left on South Lassen Street. The trail is four blocks ahead.

Dogs May Be Unleashed Unless Otherwise Indicated

CRATER LAKE

Info: An unforgettable, wet and wild adventure awaits you at this 27-acre lake. The sun dappled, azure blue water makes for an afternoon of fun in the sun. You and your wagabout can make your own trail on the logging roads which surround the lake or kick back lakeside, cooling your paws in the refreshing water. Fishing hounds, remember your trusty rod, brook trout make for a tasty din din. Come fall, aspens shimmer and shake in a frenzy of gold. Bring your camera, we're talking postcard perfect shots. For more information: (916) 257-4188.

Directions: Take Highway 36 west for 5 miles to the junction of Highway 44. Head northwest approximately 27 miles. Just north of the state rest stop on Highway 44, turn right on the dirt road. Follow this signed road for 7 miles to Crater Lake Campground.

Note: High clearance vehicles only.

EAGLE LAKE - Leashes

Info: From luxuriant pine forests on the south shore to high chaparral on the north, you and Fido will find plenty of wide open spaces to investigate. Pristine and uncrowded, Eagle Lake is the state's second largest natural lake. For more information: (916) 257-4323.

Directions: Head west on Highway 36 for 2 miles to Highway A-1. Turn right approximately 15 miles to Eagle Lake.

EAGLE LAKE SOUTH SHORE TRAIL HIKE

Beginner/10.0 miles/5.0 hours

Info: Strap on the odometer and click off some miles on this piece of cake hike. Starting at Gallatin Beach, the paved trail wanders this way and that through pine forests on the south side of sun-sprinkled, fun-filled Eagle Lake. Plenty of pretty picnic spots abound - ideal places to chow down with your chow. Christie Campground marks the end of your nature excursion. For more information: (916) 257-4188.

Directions: Head west on Highway 36 for 2 miles to Highway A-1. Turn right for 14 miles to the south shore of Eagle Lake. Follow the signs to Gallatin Beach and the trailhead.

HIDDEN CHANGE INTERPRETIVE TRAIL HIKE
Beginner/0.25 miles/0.5 hours

Info: Pick up a brochure and learn as you loop around with your hound on this nature trail. The handy guide explains the biological process of succession, the natural change from one plant community to another. For more information: (916) 257-6952.

Directions: From Susanville, head west on Highway 36 for 2 miles to Highway A-1. Turn right after approximately 15 miles, following the signs to the Eagle Lake Visitor Information Center.

SYLMAR

LODGING
MOTEL 6
12775 Encinitas Ave (91342)
Rates: $32-$38;
Tel: (818) 362-9491; (800) 440-6000

RECREATION
SYLMAR PARK-Leashes

Info: Make your merry way with Marmaduke through the open fields in this 19-acre park.

Directions: Located at 13109 Borden Avenue.

TAHOE VISTA

LODGING
BEESLEY'S COTTAGES
6674 N Lake Blvd (96148)
Rates: $70-$140;
Tel: (916) 546-2448

HOLIDAY HOUSE-LAKESIDE CHALETS
7276 N Lake Blvd (96148)
Rates: $85-$125;
Tel: (916) 546-2369; (800) 294-6378

TATAMI COTTAGE RESORT
7449 N Lake Blvd (96148)
Rates: $69-$129;
Tel: (916) 546-3523

RECREATION
See "Lake Tahoe Area" listings for recreation

Dogs May Be Unleashed Unless Otherwise Indicated

TAHOMA

LODGING

NORFOLK WOODS COUNTRY INN
6941 W Lake Blvd (96142)
Rates: $100-$150;
Tel: (916) 525-5000

TAHOE LAKE COTTAGES
7030 W Lake Blvd (96142)
Rates: $237 (Three nights lodging);
Tel: (800) 824-6348

TAHOMA LODGE
7018 W Lake Blvd (96142)
Rates: $213 (Three nights lodging);
Tel: (800) 824-6348

RECREATION

See "Lake Tahoe Area" listings for recreation

TEHACHAPI

LODGING

BEST WESTERN MOUNTAIN INN
416 W Tehachapi Blvd (93561)
Rates $45-$59;
Tel: (805) 822-5591; (800) 528-1234

GOLDEN HILLS MOTEL
22561 Woodford-
Tehachapi Rd (93561)
Rates: $25+;
Tel: (805) 822-4488; (800) 434-1118

TRAVELODGE-TEHACHAPI SUMMIT
500 Steuber Rd (93581)
Rates: $46-$60;
Tel: (805) 823-8000; (800) 578-7878

RECREATION

TEHACHAPI MOUNTAIN PARK - Leashes

Info: Fill your snouts with pine-scented air as you hike along a scenic trail. Or, just relax and enjoy a brown bag lunch. In winter, Snowball can frolic and play in pure white powder. For more information: (805) 822-4180.

Directions: From Highway 58, take the Highway 202 exit south. When Highway 202 veers west, stay straight on Tucker Road. After a mile, turn right on Highline Road. After 1.5 miles, turn left on Water Canyon Road. Follow the road about 2 miles to the park.

Locate Other Dog-Friendly Activities...Check Nearby Cities

TEMECULA

LODGING

COMFORT INN
27338 Jefferson Ave (92590)
Rates: $39-$75;
Tel: (909) 699-5888; (800) 221-2222

RAMADA INN
28980 Front St (92592)
Rates: $39-$54;
Tel: (909) 676-8770; (800) 272-6232

TEMECULA CREEK INN
44501 Rainbow Canyon Rd (92592)
Rates: $115-$150;
Tel: (909) 694-1000

RECREATION

AGUA CALIENTE TRAIL HIKE - Leashes

Intermediate/8.0 miles/4.0 hours

Info: This is one helluva great scenic day hike. From the Agua Caliente Bridge, follow the Pacific Crest Trail upstream into the Cleveland National Forest. You'll lose the creek for a few miles, but when you join up with the creek again, you'll find yourself in a deep, willow-shaded gorge. Turn around at any time and head back. For more information: (619) 788-0250.

Directions: Take Interstate 15 south to Highway 79 and head southeast towards Warner Springs. Drive until one mile before Warner Springs to milepost marker 36.7 and parking. Hike east over the bridge to milepost 36.6 and the trailhead.

BARKER VALLEY TRAIL HIKE - Leashes

Intermediate/7.0 miles/3.5 hours

Info: Beat the heat in Barker Valley, an ever-cool oasis. Descend the old roadbed about 2 miles to a trail on the right that meanders slopeside to Barker Valley. If you've got the time, let Rover romp around the falls and grottos you'll encounter downstream. Two paws up for this heavenly oasis. For more information: (619) 788-0250.

Directions: Take Interstate 15 south to Highway 79 and head southeast towards Warner Springs. Drive about 35 miles to Palomar Divide Road (milepost 41.9). Turn right onto this high clearance vehicle road and go for eight miles to the Barker Valley Spur Trailhead on your left.

Note: High clearance vehicles only.

Dogs May Be Unleashed Unless Otherwise Indicated

DRIPPING SPRINGS to GIANT CHAPARRAL TRAIL HIKE

Expert/7.0 miles/4.0 hours

Info: This hike is not for the fair of paw or the out of shape. But, if you and your fit Fido are craving an aerobic workout in beautiful surroundings, you can't beat this hike. You'll zigzag up the mountainside on a series of switchbacks, with views in every direction. Vail Lake and the San Jacintos form a pretty backdrop, while a look-see northwest treats you to a sighting of Mt. Baldy in the distance. Point your snout due north for a peek at the San Gorgonio Peak. You'll want to pack plenty of Perrier since the trail is practically shadeless.

At the Giant Chaparral, kick back and enjoy a well-deserved rest. If you're hiking in winter, the massive manzanitas will be covered in glorious white blossoms. When you can pull yourself away from this pristine spot, make a 180° and head for home. Gung-ho hikers can continue another three miles to the Palomar Divide Truck Trail. Your huffing and puffing will end in oohing and aahing - the panoramic vistas are extraordinary. For more information: (619) 788-0250.

Directions: From Interstate 15 in Temecula, take Highway 79 east for approximately 10 miles to the Dripping Springs Campground on your right. The trailhead is located at the south end of the campground.

FRY CREEK TRAIL HIKE

Beginner/1.5 miles/0.75 hours

Info: When you're short on time but yearn for a taste of the outdoors, make tracks for this simple, looping trail through a mixed conifer forest. Even couch potatoes will love this one. For more information: (619) 788-0250.

Directions: Head south on Interstate 15 to Highway 76. Go east to County Road S6. Turn left, following to the trailhead and parking area at Fry Creek Campground.

Locate Other Dog-Friendly Activities...Check Nearby Cities

LAKE SKINNER COUNTY PARK - Leashes

Info: Dogs aren't permitted in the lake area, but you'll still have over 4,000 acres of rolling chaparral-covered hillsides, trails and grassy terrain to canvas. For more information: (909) 926-1541.

Directions: From Interstate 15, take the Rancho California Avenue exit northeast about nine miles to the park.

Note: $2/adult, $1/child under 12 and $2/dog day-use fee. Can be closed during rainy season.

OAK GROVE TRAIL HIKE

Intermediate/4.0 miles/2.0 hours

Info: If you and the pupster are looking to stay fit and trim, then this is your hike. Your journey to High Point Lookout is steep at times, traversing rough, chaparral-clad terrain. But the 4,200-foot perch treats you to fabulous vistas of the San Bernardino Mountains and surrounding valleys. For more information: (619) 788-0250.

Directions: From Interstate 15 in Temecula, take Highway 79 east to the trailhead at the Oak Grove Station.

OBSERVATORY NATIONAL RECREATION TRAIL HIKE - Leashes

Beginner/4.4 miles/2.5 hours

Info: You and the dawgus could do a drive by and zoom up to the observatory on wheels, but then you'd miss this soothing, pine-scented forest hike. Either watch Fido's ears flap in the breeze as he hangs out the car window or wander amidst the flower-filled meadows of the Palomars as you're serenaded by songbirds. Even sofa loafers will enjoy a sojourn to the renowned Great Glass Telescope. The paw-friendly path wiggles through whispering woodlands of conifers and chaparral. Fido will think he's found pup's paradise before he even reaches the top.

The telescope isn't the only way to observe those heavenly views. Never-ending mountain and ocean vistas are yours for the taking. You'll barely have time to catch your breath before another stunning panorama takes it away again. Pack lots of film, this place eats Fuji. For more information: (619) 788-0250.

Dogs May Be Unleashed Unless Otherwise Indicated

Directions: Head south on Interstate 15 to Highway 76 and go east to County Road S6. Turn left, following to the trailhead and parking area on the east side of Observatory Campground.

Other parks in Temecula - Leashes
- BAHIA VISTA PARK, 41566 Avenida de la Reina
- CALLE ARAGON PARK, 41621 Calle Aragon
- LOMA LINDA PARK, 30877 Loma Linda Road
- SAM HICKS MONUMENT PARK, 41970 Moreno Drive
- VETERANS PARK, 30965 La Serena Way

THOUSAND OAKS

LODGING

BEST WESTERN OAKS LODGE
12 Conejo Blvd (91360)
Rates: $47-$62;
Tel: (805) 495-7011; (800) 528-1234

E-Z 8 MOTEL
2434 W Hillcrest Dr (91360)
Rates: $31+;
Tel: (805) 499-0755; (800) 326-6835

HOLIDAY INN
495 N Ventu Park Rd (91360)
Rates: $69+;
Tel: (805) 498-6733; (800) 465-4329

MOTEL 6
1516 Newbury Rd (91360)
Rates: $30-$36;
Tel: (805) 499-0711; (800) 440-6000

THOUSAND OAKS INN
75 W Thousand Oaks Blvd (91360)
Rates: $47-$70;
Tel: (805) 497-3701; (800) 600-6878

RECREATION

BORCHARD COMMUNITY PARK - Leashes

Info: The paved footpath through this grassy, tree-laden park is a lovely place for a morning outing.

Directions: From Highway 101, take the Borchard Road/Rancho Conejo Road exit and travel southwest on Borchard Road. It's another mile to the park on your right at Reino Road.

CONEJO COMMUNITY PARK - Leashes

Info: Expansive and picturesque, this 27-acre park is a haven for scenery sniffing canines. Two ponds and a connecting creek are nestled among acres of open lawn.

Directions: Located at James Road and Highway 23.

Locate Other Dog-Friendly Activities...Check Nearby Cities

WILDWOOD PARK - Leashes

Info: Gaze at a spectacular 60-foot plunging waterfall or traverse miles of serpentine trails through brush-covered hillsides in this enchanting 1,700-acre park. A visit in springtime will delight the senses. Tote your camera and lots of film. For more information: (805) 495-6471.

Directions: From Highway 101, take the Thousand Oaks Freeway/Highway 23 exit north. After approximately 2.5 miles, turn left on Avenida de los Arboles and follow 3 miles to the end. Park in the lot on your left. Pick up an area map and brochure at the kiosk.

THREE RIVERS

LODGING

BEST WESTERN HOLIDAY LODGE
40105 Sierra Dr (93271)
Rates: $46-$76;
Tel: (209) 561-4119; (800) 528-1234

BUCKEYE TREE LODGE
46000 Sierra Dr (93271)
Rates: $39-$61;
Tel: (209) 561-5900

LAZY J RANCH MOTEL
39625 Sierra Dr (93271)
Rates: $40-$80;
Tel: (209) 561-4449; (800) 341-8000

THE RIVER INN
45176 Sierra Dr (93271)
Rates: $35-$59;
Tel: (209) 561-4367

SEQUOIA VILLAGE INN
45971 Sierra Dr (93271)
Rates: $35-$90;
Tel: (209) 561-3652

SIERRA LODGE
43175 Sierra Dr (93271)
Rates: $35-$65;
Tel: (209) 561-3681

TIBURON

RECREATION

RICHARDSON BAY PARK - Leashes

Info: A very popular bike path extends nearly the length of Tiburon's peninsula, with parking at either end. Enter at the northern end and take Brunini Way to a peaceful, natural bay shoreline. Or continue to McKegney Green, a large paw pleasing grassy picnic area. Views of Mt. Tamalpais, the Bay Bridge

Dogs May Be Unleashed Unless Otherwise Indicated

and San Francisco surround you. Pack a sweatshirt for yourself and drinking water for the pooch. For more information: (415) 435-7373.

Directions: The park parallels Tiburon Boulevard with parking lots at either end.

TORRANCE

LODGING
DAYS INN
4111 Pacific Coast Hwy (90505)
Rates: $55-$70;
Tel: (800) 329-7466

HOLIDAY INN TORRANCE-DEL AMO
21333 Hawthorne Blvd (90503)
Rates: $89-$119;
Tel: (800) 465-4329

HOWARD JOHNSON LODGE
2880 Pacific Coast Hwy (90505)
Rates: $79-$94;
Tel: (310) 325-0660; (800) 446-4656

RESIDENCE INN BY MARRIOTT
3701 Torrance Blvd (90503)
Rates: $124-$162;
Tel: (310) 543-4566; (800) 331-3131

SUMMERFIELD SUITES HOTEL
19901 Prairie Ave (90503)
Rates: $89-$159;
Tel: (310) 371-8525

TRACY

LODGING
BEST WESTERN JOHN JAY INN
811 Clover Rd (95376)
Rates: $53-$65;
Tel: (209) 832-0271; (800) 528-1234

MOTEL 6
3810 Tracy Blvd (95376)
Rates: $28-$34;
Tel: (209) 836-4900; (800) 440-6000

PHOENIX LODGE
3511 N Tracy Blvd (95376)
Rates: $45;
Tel: (209) 835-1335

TRINIDAD

LODGING

BISHOP PINE LODGE
1481 Patricks Point Dr (95570)
Rates: $50-$75;
Tel: (707) 677-3314

SHADOW LODGE
687 Patricks Point Dr (95570)
Rates: $59-$95;
Tel: (707) 677-0532

TRINIDAD INN
1170 Patricks Point Dr (95570)
Rates: $50-$100;
Tel: (707) 677-3349

VIEW CREST LODGE
3415 Patricks Point Dr (95570)
Rates: $50-$120;
Tel: (707) 677-3393

RECREATION

REDWOOD NATIONAL PARK - Leashes

Info: You and Fido are in for a humbling experience at this 106,000-acre park. Simply stand next to one of the largest trees in the world - a 350-foot redwood - for an ant's view of the world. Some of these giants are 1,500 years old. There's a one-mile nature trail, named after Lady Bird Johnson, that escorts you through the magnificent redwood forest. For more information: (707) 464-6101.

Directions: Take Highway 101 north. Once past the Orick exit, follow the signs to the park's information center. Maps and literature are available.

Note: Dogs are prohibited from trails unless otherwise specified.

TRINITY CENTER

LODGING

BECKER'S BOUNTY LODGE
HCR 3, Box 4659 (96091)
Rates: $400-$650 Weekly;
Tel: (916) 266-3277

CEDAR STOCK RESORT
45810 Hwy 3 (96091)
Rates: $350-$2,300 Weekly;
Tel: (916) 286-2225; (800) 982-2279

ENRIGHT GULCH CABINS & MOTEL
3500 Hwy 3, P. O Box 244 (96091)
Rates: $30-$35;
Tel: (916) 266-3600

RIPPLE CREEK CABINS
Rt 2, Box 4020 (96091)
Rates: $60-$115;
Tel: (916) 266-3505

WYNTOON RESORT
Hwy 3, P. O. Box 70 (96091)
Rates: $16-$110;
Tel: (916) 266-3337; (800) 715-3337

Dogs May Be Unleashed Unless Otherwise Indicated

<u>RECREATION</u>
BIG BEAR LAKE TRAIL HIKE
Intermediate/8.0 miles/4.0 hours

Info: The hike to pretty Big Bear Lake is a strenuous uphill climb combined with a bit of stream hopping. Once you reach the lake, kick back and relax, you've earned it. For more information: (916) 623-2121.

Directions: Take Highway 3 north about 13 miles to the Bear Creek Parking Area. Turn left (west) and go to the trailhead.

SCOTT MOUNTAIN to BOULDER LAKES TRAIL HIKE
Intermediate/11.0 miles/6.0 hours

Info: Upper Boulder Lake, East Boulder Lake, Mid Boulder Lake and Telephone Lake are just samplings of the beautiful lakes in the Trinity Alps Wilderness found along this stretch of the Pacific Crest Trail. You and your wagalong will head due west for about five miles. The lakes are then within .5 miles of the trail. Bring a tennis ball for a bit of water retrieving. For more information: (916) 623-2121.

Directions: Drive about 22 miles north on Highway 3 to Scott Mountain Campgrounds and the trailhead.

TRINITY LAKE

Info: Rent a boat and set your rudder for a secluded section of the lake. Early summer is prettiest. The snow-capped Trinity Alps provide a dramatic backdrop to the shimmering blue waters. For more information: (916) 623-6101 or (800) 421-7259.

Directions: The lake is just east of Highway 3.

TRONA

<u>LODGING</u>
DESERT ROSE MOTEL
84368 Trona Rd (93562)
Rates: $30-$42;
Tel: (619) 372-4572

TRUCKEE

LODGING

ALPINE VILLAGE MOTEL
12660 Deerfield Dr (96161)
Rates: $50-$79;
Tel: (916) 587-3801; (800) 933-1787

RICHARDS MOTEL
15758 Donner Pass Rd (96160)
Rates: $60-$110;
Tel: (916) 587-3662

SUPER 8 LODGE-TRUCKEE
11506 Deerfield Dr (96161)
Rates: $57-$94;
Tel: (916) 587-8888; (800) 800-8000

RECREATION

GLACIER MEADOW LOOP TRAIL HIKE

Beginner/0.5 miles/0.5 hours

Info: 30 minutes are all you and the pupster need for a quick lesson in glaciology. The self-guided trail makes for a pleasant jaunt. For more information: (916) 587-3558.

Directions: Take Interstate 80 west from Truckee to the Castle Peak Area/Boreal Ridge exit. The sign for the Pacific Crest Trailhead is on the south side of the highway. Follow the signs for .5 miles to the trailhead. Glacier Meadow Loop intersects with the larger trail.

HEATH FALLS OVERLOOK TRAIL HIKE

Intermediate/10.0 miles/5.0 hours

Info: Dramatic, plunging Heath Falls is the rainbow at the end of this invigorating hike - particularly in the spring and summer. Once you and your hiking hound hook up with this trail, the falls are a short, half-mile away. Resist the urge to climb on or around the cascades, it's dangerous and illegal. The falls are on private land. For more information: (916) 587-3558.

Directions: Take Interstate 80 west from Truckee for about 12 miles to the Soda Springs-Norden exit. Take Old Highway 40 east for about .8 miles to Soda Springs Road. Take Soda Springs south to Pahatsi Road. Turn right (west) and drive past where it becomes dirt to the fork. At the fork, continue straight for 2.5 miles to the Palisade Creek Trail on the north side of Cascade Lakes. Follow this trail for 4.5 miles to the Heath Falls Overlook Trail.

Dogs May Be Unleashed Unless Otherwise Indicated

LOWER LOLA MONTEZ LAKE TRAIL HIKE

Intermediate/6.0 miles/3.0 hours

Info: After a brief quarter-mile hike, follow the road crossing over Lower Castle Creek. During times of high water, use extreme caution. Continue another .25 miles up a small incline to another road. Travel one mile under the cooling tree cover to the end of the road and a meadow. Then it's only a short distance to pretty Lower Lola Montez Lakes - a sight well worth the effort. The fishing's not bad either. For more information: (916) 587-3558.

Directions: Take Interstate 80 west from Truckee for about 12 miles to the Soda Springs-Norden exit. Don't cross over the Interstate, but rather remain on the unsigned road north of the freeway. Go east on this road for .25 miles to the trailhead parking area just east of the fire station.

MARTIS CREEK LAKE - Leashes

Info: Soaring hawks and whimsical looking mule deer are just two of the wildlife species you might see in this charming lake area. Luxuriant meadows and conifer forests beckon you and your pooch to spend an hour or a day. Visit in springtime and behold acres upon acres of gorgeous wildflowers. For more information: (916) 639-2342.

Directions: From Truckee, take Highway 267 southeast approximately six miles. The lake entrance is just past the airport. The lake area is only open between May and September.

TUJUNGA

RECREATION

MCGROARTY PARK - Leashes

Info: Beat the summer heat and catch some shade in the lovely oak grove of this 16-acre park. The soothing setting is a great place to spend some R&R.

Directions: Located at 7570 McGroarty Terrace.

Locate Other Dog-Friendly Activities...Check Nearby Cities

TULARE

LODGING

**BEST WESTERN-
TOWN & COUNTRY LODGE**
1051 N Blackstone (93274)
Rates: $47-$52;
Tel: (209) 688-7537; (800) 528-1234

FRIENDSHIP INN
26442 SR 99 (93274)
Rates: $30-$60;
Tel: (800) 424-4777

GREEN GABLE INN
1010 E Prosperity Ave (93274)
Rates: $42;
Tel: (209) 686-3432

INNS OF AMERICA
1183 N Blackstone (93274)
Rates: $30-$42;
Tel: (209) 686-0985; (800) 826-0778

MOTEL 6
1111 N Blackstone (93274)
Rates: $28-$34;
Tel: (209) 686-1611; (800) 440-6000

TULARE INN MOTEL
1301 E Paige (93274)
Rates: $29-$38;
Tel: (800) 333-8571

RECREATION

MOUNTAIN HOME DEMONSTRATION STATE FOREST

Info: On a hot summer day, cool off with a journey to this 4,800-acre forest. Trails usher you and the pupster past giant sequoia, ponderosa, and sugar pine, fir and cedar. For more information: (209) 539-2855.

Directions: Take Highway 137 east for 13 miles to Highway 65 south approximately 7 miles to Country Road J28 east. Continue 12 miles to 190 east in Springville. Travel north on Balch Park Drive 3 miles and go east on Bear Creek Road about 15 miles. Access points to the forest continue for another 6 miles.

TURLOCK

LODGING

**BEST WESTERN-
THE GARDENS MOTOR INN**
1119 Pedras Rd (95380)
Rates: $46-$64;
Tel: (209) 634-9351; (800) 528-1234

BEST WESTERN ORCHARD INN
5025 N Golden State Blvd (95380)
Rates: $47-$63;
Tel: (209) 667-2827; (800) 528-1234

COMFORT INN-TURLOCK
200 W Glenwood Ave (95380)
Rates: $40-$50;
Tel: (209) 668-3400; (800) 221-2222

MOTEL 6
250 S Walnut Ave (95380)
Rates: $25-$31;
Tel: (209) 667-4100; (800) 440-6000

Dogs May Be Unleashed Unless Otherwise Indicated

RECREATION

FRANK RAINES REGIONAL PARK - Leashes

Info: 2,000 wonderful acres of hilly seclusion are the main attraction of this park. Hike backcountry dirt trails through wildlife-inhabited woodlands. Visit in the spring and take pleasure in the paint box display of wildflowers. For more information: (209) 525-4107.

Directions: From the Del Puerto Canyon Road exit off I-5, head west for 18 twisting miles. Follow the signs to the park.

TWAIN HARTE

LODGING

ELDORADO MOTEL
P. O. Box 368 (95383)
Rates: $40-$60;
Tel: (209) 586-4479

TWENTYNINE PALMS

LODGING

CIRCLE "C" MOTEL
6340 El Rey Ave (92277)
Rates: $85;
Tel: (619) 367-7615

MOTEL 6
72562 Twentynine Palms
Hwy (92277)
Rates: $32-$40;
Tel: (619) 367-2833; (800) 440-6000

RECREATION

JOSHUA TREE NATIONAL MONUMENT - Leashes

Info: Encompassing both the Mojave and Colorado Deserts, the western half of this 874-square-mile park is home to the elegant and graceful Joshua tree, also called the praying plant because of its upstretched arms. The diverse landscape includes stunning granite formations surrounded by vast arid terrain. In springtime, wildflowers sweep over the desert floor leaving patches of color everywhere. Use the paved and dirt roads to explore this intriguing region. Carry plenty of water year-round.

Locate Other Dog-Friendly Activities...Check Nearby Cities

Directions: The visitors center is on Utah Trail, just south of Highway 62 about a mile east of Twentynine Palms.

Note: $5 entrance fee (includes maps).

TWIN PEAKS

LODGING

ARROWHEAD PINE ROSE CABINS
Hwy 189 at Grand View (92391)
Rates: $49-$69;
Tel: (909) 337-2341; (800) 429-7463

UKIAH

LODGING

DAYS INN-
REDWOODS/WINE COUNTRY
950 N State St (95482)
Rates: $48-$70;
Tel: (707) 462-7584; (800) 329-7466

HOLIDAY LODGE
1050 S State St (95482)
Rates: $27-$40;
Tel: (707) 462-2906; (800) 300-2906

MOTEL 6
1208 S State St (95482)
Rates: $29-$38;
Tel: (707) 468-5404; (800) 440-6000

TRAVELODGE-UKIAH
406 S State St (95482)
Rates: $39-$58;
Tel: (707) 462-8611; (800) 578-7878

WESTERN TRAVELER MOTEL
693 S Orchard Ave (95482)
Rates: $32-$56;
Tel: (707) 468-9167

RECREATION

COW MOUNTAIN RECREATION AREA

Info: Throw Fido's leash to the wind and watch him sprint across 27,000 acres of doggie freedom. The varied terrain rises from 800 to 4,000 feet, offering a range of hikes, from gentle to rugged. For more information: (707) 465-4000.

Directions: From Highway 101 south, take the Talmage Road exit east to the dead end at the City of 10,000 Buddhas. Turn right on East Side Road, then left on Mill Creek Road. The entrance is on the left.

Dogs May Be Unleashed Unless Otherwise Indicated

FAULKNER COUNTY PARK - Leashes

Info: Immerse yourself in a 12-stop nature trail filled with flowering shrubs and towering redwoods or venture to the ridgetop on a short hiking trail in this 40-acre park. For more information: (707) 463-4267.

Directions: Head south on Highway 101 to Highway 253. Head west for 20 miles to Boonville. The park is located on Mountain View Road, two miles west of Boonville.

LOW GAP REGIONAL COUNTY PARK - Leashes

Info: Enjoy a day of cavorting with your canine along 6.5 miles of hiking trails. In summer, the path is tucked away under a shady canopy of trees. For more information: (707) 463-4267.

Directions: Take Highway 101 south from Ukiah and exit at Perkins Street. Head west to State Street and go north. Go west on Brush Street/Low Gap Road. The park entrance is one mile on the left.

MILL CREEK COUNTY PARK - Leashes

Info: This 400-acre park has something for every breed. Hike nature trails, wade streams, relax in shaded knolls, picnic in meadows, photograph distant vistas...you and your shadow can do it all. For more information: (707) 463-4267.

Directions: From Highway 101 south, take the Talmage Road exit east to the dead end at the City of 10,000 Buddhas. Turn right on East Side Road, then left on Mill Creek Road. Continue on Mill Creek Road until you pass the pond. Look for signs to the park. Additional entrances are around the creek near the small parking areas.

UPPER LAKE

LODGING

NARROWS LODGE RESORT
5690 Blue Lakes Rd (95485)
Rates: $50-$85;
Tel: (707) 275-2718

PINE ACRES BLUE LAKE RESORT
5328 Blue Lakes Rd (95485)
Rates: $85+;
Tel: (707) 275-2811

Locate Other Dog-Friendly Activities...Check Nearby Cities

VACAVILLE

LODGING

BEST WESTERN HERITAGE INN
1420 E Monte Vista Ave (95688)
Rates: $42-$48;
Tel: (707) 448-8453; (800) 528-1234

DAYS INN
1571 E Monte Vista Ave (95688)
Rates: $45-$75;
Tel: (800) 329-7466

MOTEL 6
107 Lawrence Dr (95688)
Rates: $29-$35;
Tel: (707) 447-5550; (800) 440-6000

RECREATION

ALAMO-BUCK PARK - Leashes

Info: Active Rovers will be certain to sniff out the jogging trails in this park. Lace up your tennies and hightail it.

Directions: At the corner of Buck Avenue and Alamo Drive.

ANDREWS PARK - Leashes

Info: Head east of the creek and make your own path through a landscape of rolling hills, trees and thick lawns.

Directions: At East Monte Vista Avenue and School Street.

DOS CALLES PADAN PARK - Leashes

Info: Laze with your Lassie in the grassie or amble along the asphalt walkways in this pleasant city park.

Directions: Between Padan and Alonzo Streets near Padan School.

LAGOON VALLEY COUNTY PARK - Leashes

Info: Take to the lake's loop trail or hop on the path to town. If you'd rather just relax with Max, pack a biscuit basket and enjoy the sunshine in the expansive picnic area. Or try your luck and line on black bass, catfish and sunfish in 105-acre Lagoon Valley Lake. For more information: (707) 449-5654.

Directions: On Lagoon Valley Road off Rivera Road.

Dogs May Be Unleashed Unless Otherwise Indicated

NORTH ORCHARD PARK - Leashes

Info: Enjoy the greenery and the scenery along the walkway in this pretty park.

Directions: Located at North Orchard and Crestview Streets.

PATWIN PARK - Leashes

Info: Get some Rexercise along the trails in this 10-acre park.

Directions: Located at Elmira and Leisure Town Roads.

TROWER PARK - Leashes

Info: Frolic with Frisky in the grass or hop on the walkway in this lovely park for your daily dose.

Directions: Located at Harkham Avenue and Holly Lane.

Other parks in Vacaville - Leashes

- ALAMO SCHOOL PARK, 500 South Orchard Avenue at Alamo School
- ELM SCHOOL NEIGHBORHOOD PARK, William and Elm Streets
- FAIRMONT-BEELARD PARK, end of Beelard Street
- FAIRMONT SCHOOL PARK, 1355 Marshall Road
- WILLIAM KEATING PARK, Alamo Road at California Drive

VALENCIA

LODGING

HILTON GARDEN INN-VALENCIA
27710 The Old Rd (91355)
Rates: $99-$129;
Tel: (805) 254-8800; (800) 445-8667

Locate Other Dog-Friendly Activities...Check Nearby Cities

VALLEJO

LODGING

E-Z 8 MOTEL
4 Mariposa St (94590)
Rates: $25-$32;
Tel: (800) 326-6835

**HOLIDAY INN-
MARINE WORLD/AFRICA USA**
1000 Fairgrounds Dr (94590)
Rates: $55-$80;
Tel: (707) 644-1200; (800) 465-4329

MOTEL 6
458 Fairgrounds Dr (94589)
Rates: $30-$36;
Tel: (707) 642-7781; (800) 440-6000

MOTEL 6
1455 Marine World Pkwy (94589)
Rates: $26-$30;
Tel: (707) 643-7611; (800) 440-6000

MOTEL 6
597 Sandy Beach Rd (94590)
Rates: $28-$34;
Tel: (707) 552-2912; (800) 440-6000

RAMADA INN
1000 Admiral Callaghan Ln (94591)
Rates: $61-$98;
Tel: (707) 643-2700; (800) 228-2828

ROYAL BAY INN
44 Admiral Callaghan Ln (94590)
Rates: $35-$68;
Tel: (707) 643-1061; (800) 643-8887

THRIFTLODGE
160 E Lincoln (94591)
Rates: $43+;
Tel: (800) 255-3050

VALU INN BY NENDELS
300 Fairgrounds Dr (94590)
Rates: $32-$59;
Tel: (707) 554-8000

**WINDMILL INN-
MARINE WORLD/AFRICA USA**
1596 Fairgrounds Dr (94589)
Rates: $45-$69;
Tel: (707) 554-9655; (800) 547-4747

RECREATION

BEVERLY HILLS PARK - Leashes

Info: 11 acres of open space spell fun for you and your sidekick.

Directions: Located at Del Sir Street, Davidson School.

CREST RANCH PARK - Leashes

Info: Trod the turf and steal the sunshine in this pleasant 11-acre park.

Directions: Located at Gateway and Nicole.

DAN FOLEY PARK - Leashes

Info: Tumbling hills dotted with willow and pine and a refreshing lake breeze make this park a pleasant stop.

Directions: On Camino Alto North, east of Tuolumne Street.

Note: $1 parking fee.

Dogs May Be Unleashed Unless Otherwise Indicated

HANNS MEMORIAL PARK - Leashes

Info: Rove over the rustic area with Rover in this expansive park.

Directions: Located on Redwood Parkway at Skyline.

MARINA VISTA PARK - Leashes

Info: Float your boat or just enjoy the scenery in this beautiful park.

Directions: Located on Mare Island Drive.

RICHARDSON PARK - Leashes

Info: Get out and surf the turf with Spot in this pretty park.

Directions: Located at the end of Richardson Drive.

SETTERQUIST PARK - Leashes

Info: Paw-friendly fun combined with a pleasant atmosphere make for a delightful outdoor excursion in this 10-acre park.

Directions: Located at Mini and Standord Drive.

TERRACE PARK - Leashes

Info: 12 acres of paw-stomping space can be yours in this parkland.

Directions: Located at Selfridge and Rodgers Streets.

WILSON PARK/LAKE DALWIGK - Leashes

Info: Partake of some California sunshine on the grounds of this vast, open park.

Directions: Located on Solano Avenue at Stewart Street.

Other parks in Vallejo - Leashes
• BORGAS PARK, Borgas Lane and Kenyon Way
• CARQUINEZ HEIGHTS PARK, Sandy Beach and Sonoma Boulevard

- CASTLEWOOD PARK, 700 block of Heartwood Avenue
- CITY PARK, Marin and Louisiana Streets
- DELTA MEADOWS, Jack London and Candy Drives
- FAIRMONT PARK, between Viewmont and Edgemont
- GRANT MAHONEY PARK, Mariposa and Arkansas Streets
- HENRY RANCH PARK, Newport Drive
- HIGHLANDS PARK, Columbus Parkway and Regents Park
- INDEPENDENCE PARK, Sonoma Boulevard
- NORTH VALLEJO COMMUNITY PARK, 1121 Whitney
- SHEVELAND PARK, top of Coughlan Street
- WASHINGTON PARK, Napa and Ohio Streets

VALLEY SPRINGS

LODGING

10th GREEN INN BED & BREAKFAST
14 St. Andrews Rd (95252)
Rates: $59-$89;
Tel: (209) 772-1084

VENICE

LODGING

LINCOLN INN
2447 Lincoln Blvd (90291)
Rates: $86;
Tel: (310) 822-0686

MARINA MOTEL
3130 Washington Blvd (90291)
Rates: $45-$50;
Tel: (310) 821-5086

RECREATION

VENICE RECREATION CENTER/BEACH - Leashes

Info: Take a stroll on the walkway alongside the beach any weekend day and get an eyeful of an eclectic beach scene. Body builders and bikinied blondes, rollerbladers and street entertainers, are sure to provide a fun excursion.

Directions: Located at 1800 Ocean Front Walk.

VENTURA

LODGING

LA QUINTA INN
5818 Valentine Rd (93003)
Rates: $48-$60;
Tel: (805) 658-6200; (800) 221-4731

MOTEL 6
2145 E Harbor Blvd (93001)
Rates: $32-$36;
Tel: (805) 643-5100; (800) 440-6000

MOTEL 6
3075 Johnson Dr (93003)
Rates: $35-$39;
Tel: (805) 650-0080; (800) 440-6000

PACIFIC INN
350 E Thompson Blvd (93001)
Rates: $35-$63;
Tel: (805) 653-0879

PIERPONT INN
550 Sanjon Rd (93001)
Rates: $99;
Tel: (805) 658-6200; (800) 285-4667

RAMADA CLOCKTOWER INN
181 E Santa Clara (93001)
Rates: $75-$80;
Tel: (805) 652-0141; (800) 272-6232

VAGABOND INN
756 E Thompson Blvd (93001)
Rates: $43-$65;
Tel: (805) 648-5371; (800) 522-1555

VICTORIA MOTEL
2350 S Victoria Ave (93003)
Rates: $33-$60;
Tel: (805) 642-2173

RECREATION

GRANT MEMORIAL PARK - Leashes

Info: This well-liked park offers a get-away-from-it-all dirt trail on the opposite side of the parking lot. It's unshaded, so tote your own water. For some terrific city and Channel Island views, head to the grassy knoll at the park's crest.

Directions: From Cedar Street, located 2 blocks east of Ventura Avenue, turn east on Ferro Drive. Follow to the top.

VICTORVILLE

LODGING

BEST WESTERN GREEN TREE INN
14173 Green Tree Rd (92392)
Rates: $50-$80;
Tel: (619) 245-3461; (800) 528-1234

BUDGET INN
14153 Kentwood Blvd (92392)
Rates: $30-$42;
Tel: (619) 241-8010

HI DESERT/RED ROOF INN MOTEL
13409 Mariposa Rd (92392)
Rates: $45-$51;
Tel: (619) 241-1577; (800) 843-7663

HOLIDAY INN MOTOR HOTEL
15494 Palmdale Rd (92392)
Rates: $51-$61;
Tel: (619) 245-6565; (800) 465-4329

Locate Other Dog-Friendly Activities...Check Nearby Cities

MOTEL 6
16901 Stoddard Wells Rd (92392)
Rates: $24-$28;
Tel: (619) 243-0666; (800) 440-6000

SCOTTISH INNS
15499 Village Dr (92392)
Rates: $22-$36;
Tel: (800) 251-1962

SUNSET INN
15765 Mojave Dr (92392)
Rates: $25-$36;
Tel: (619) 243-2342

TRAVELODGE NORTH MOTEL
16868 Stoddard Wells Rd (92392)
Rates: $31-$39;
Tel: (619) 243-7700; (800) 578-7878

RECREATION

CENTER STREET PARK - Leashes

Info: This 7-acre park is a pleasant place to wag away the afternoon with your best buddy.

Directions: Located at 15413 Center Street.

EVA DELL PARK - Leashes

Info: Strut with your mutt through this attractive 10-acre park.

Directions: Located at 15714 First Street.

LAKE GREGORY - Leashes

Info: Take a spin around the 2.75-mile exercise path bordering sun-splashed Lake Gregory. You'll be surrounded by cedar, ponderosa and sugar pines. For more information: (909) 338-2233.

Directions: Take Interstate 15 south to Highway 138 east towards Crestline. Highway 138 joins with Highway 18. From Highway 18, take the Crestline exit which turns into Lake Drive. Follow to the park. The hiking section begins at the south shore.

MOJAVE NARROWS REGIONAL PARK - Leashes

Info: Explore the forested area of this 840-acre triangular shaped park. Or throw in a line in the Mojave River, maybe you'll catch dinner. For more information: (619) 245-2226.

Directions: Located at 18000 Yates Road.

Note: $4 day-use fee, $1 dog fee. Extra $4 fishing fee.

Dogs May Be Unleashed Unless Otherwise Indicated

PEBBLE BEACH PARK - Leashes

Info: Grass, sunshine, pretty open spaces and walking paths make this 30-acre park a great place to visit with the dawgus.

Directions: Located at 16300 Pebble Beach Road.

Other parks in Victorville - Leashes
- AVALON PARK, 16338 Avalon Drive
- BRENTWOOD PARK, 14026 Hook Boulevard
- FORREST PARK, 16858 D Street
- GRADY TRAMMEL PARK, 17184 Stoddard Wells Road
- HOOK PARK, 14793 Joshua Street

VISALIA

LODGING

BEST WESTERN VISALIA INN MOTEL
623 W Main St (93277)
Rates: $55-$64;
Tel: (209) 732-4561; (800) 528-1234

HOLIDAY INN PLAZA PARK
9000 W Airport Dr (93277)
Rates: $74-$94;
Tel: (209) 651-5000; (800) 465-4329

OAK TREE INN
401 Woodland Dr (93277)
Rates: $30-$36;
Tel: (209) 732-8861; (800) 554-7664

THRIFTLODGE
4645 W Mineral King Ave (93277)
Rates: $35-$75;
Tel: (209) 732-5611; (800) 525-9055

RECREATION

ALEJANDRO R. RUIZ SR. PARK - Leashes

Info: 10 leg-stretching acres await your visit in this pretty neighborhood park.

Directions: Located on North Burke at Vista and Margalo.

BLAIN PARK - Leashes

Info: Discover this charming park nestled in a quiet suburban neighborhood. What a perfect place for a peaceful promenade.

Directions: Located on the west side of South Court Street, just north of Caldwell Avenue.

FAIRVIEW VILLAGE PARK - Leashes

Info: You'll find splendor in the grass as you mosey with Rosie through this park's 10 acres of open play space.

Directions: Located at North Highland and Wren, adjacent to Fairview School.

MILL CREEK GARDEN - Leashes

Info: If flowers make your Fido sneeze, no problem. This 8-acre park has an allergy-free demo garden made for sniffing. No excuses now - take some time to smell the flowers.

Directions: At North Lovers Lane and Mill Creek Parkway.

PLAZA PARK - Leashes

Info: There's a hiking path and a delightful pond in this popular city park. Or you and Rover can kick back under a shade tree for a dog nap.

Directions: At Highway 198 and Road 80, east of Highway 99.

RECREATION PARK - Leashes

Info: Race through the open space with your pooch-face as you enjoy an afternoon in this 14-acre community park.

Directions: Located at North Jacob and West Center Streets.

WHITENDALE PARK - Leashes

Info: Get your daily Rexercise in this neat 10-acre park.

Directions: The park is adjacent to Community Center and Mountain View School on South West and West Beech Streets.

Other parks in Visalia - Leashes
- CONSTITUTION PARK, West Tulare and Crenshaw Court
- CRESTWOOD PARK, SW County Circle and Whitendale
- HOUK PARK, South Woodland and Dartmouth
- ICEHOUSE PARK, North Bridge and Race
- JEFFERSON PARK, South Watson and Myrtle

Dogs May Be Unleashed Unless Otherwise Indicated

- •KAWEAH PARK, North West and West Mineral King
- •LINCOLN OVAL PARK, North Court and NW 2nd
- •MAYORS PARK, SW Hall and Main
- •MEMORIAL PARK, NW Hall and Main
- •PINKHAM PARK, South Pinkham and Tulare
- •ROTARY PARK, South Divisadero and Harvard
- •SOROPTIMIST PARK, On Douglas at Sante Fe and Burke
- •ST. JOHNS RIVER PARK, North Ben Maddox to McAuliff
- •SUMMERS PARK, Summers Lane and West Ferguson
- •VILLAGE PARK, North Court and Pearl
- •WILLOW GLEN PARK, North Akers and Hurley

VISTA

LODGING

HILLTOP MOTOR LODGE
330 Mar Vista Dr (92083)
Rates: $36-$44;
Tel: (619) 726-7010

LA QUINTA INN
630 Sycamore Ave (92083)
Rates: $46-$61;
Tel: (619) 727-8180; (800) 221-4731

WALNUT CREEK

LODGING

EMBASSY SUITES HOTEL
1345 Treat Blvd (94596)
Rates: $119-$134;
Tel: (415) 934-2500; (800) 362-2779

WALNUT CREEK MOTOR LODGE
1960 N Main St (94596)
Rates: $65-$90;
Tel: (415) 932-2811; (800) 824-0334

MOTEL 6
2389 N Main St (94596)
Rates: $38-$46;
Tel: (415) 935-4010; (800) 440-6000

RECREATION

CHINA WALL LOOP TRAIL HIKE

Intermediate/3.0 miles/1.5 hours

Info: Formed by natural, neolithic-looking sandstone configurations, the China Wall is a spectacle worth seeing. The hike begins at Borges Ranch Trailhead and heads off into the Briones-to-Mt.

Diablo Trail. Turn right at the trail junction. Finish the loop by going right on Hanging Valley Trail. Watch for golden eagles, hawks and falcons. For more information: (510) 635-0135.

Directions: From Interstate 680 northbound in Walnut Creek, exit and go right on Ignacio Valley Road. Take a right on Walnut Avenue, another right on Oak Grove Road, and then another right on Castle Rock Road. Follow to Borges Ranch Road. The parking area is at the end of Borges Ranch Road.

LAFAYETTE / MORAGA TRAIL HIKE

Beginner/7.75 miles/4.0 hours

Info: Ranging from paved to dirt, this trail extends from the Olympic Staging Area in Lafayette to the Valle Vista Staging Area in Moraga. A gentle hike, the trail meanders along Las Trampas Creek to Bollinger Canyon and proceeds through the heart of downtown Moraga before ending at the staging area on Canyon Road. Be prepared to share your space with cyclists. For more information: (510) 635-0135.

Directions: Take Highway 80 to Highway 24 toward the bay to the Pleasant Hill exit south. Turn right onto Olympic Boulevard and park at the Olympic Staging Area. Look for the trailhead.

LAS TRAMPAS REGIONAL WILDERNESS

Info: From the wooded canyons of Corduroy Hills to the unique stone outcroppings of Rocky Ridge, this 3,600+ acre wilderness park gets two paws up on the scenery scale. Civilization will seem worlds away as the park's whisper-quiet atmosphere and spectacular ridgetop vistas pervade your senses along the numerous trails. Be sure to bring plenty of water for you and the pupster. For more information: (510) 635-0135.

Directions: Take Interstate 680 southeast to the Bollinger Canyon Road exit, located about 6 miles north of where Interstates 680 and 580 intersect. Head north on Bollinger Canyon Road to the park entrance. Park in the lot at the end of the road and take the Rocky Ridge Trail.

Note: Dogs must be leashed in developed areas.

Dogs May Be Unleashed Unless Otherwise Indicated

NIMITZ WAY TRAIL HIKE

Beginner/4.0 miles/2.0 hours
Intermediate/6.0 miles/3.0 hours

Info: The first four miles of this hike are a breeze, they're paved and the views are splendid. But if you still want more, continue past the gate onto a dirt road and start your ascent to San Pablo Ridge. Talk about incredible vistas. Finish this invigorating hike with a final climb to Wildcat Peak at 1,250 feet before doing the descent thing. For more information: (510) 635-0135.

Directions: Take Highway 80 north to Highway 24 towards the bay. Near the Caldecott Tunnel is the Fish Ranch Road exit. Take it west to Grizzly Peak Boulevard. Turn right (north) and go to South Park Drive. Turn right and drive one mile to Wildcat Canyon Road. Veer right and proceed to the parking area for Inspiration Point on your left.

WATSONVILLE

LODGING

BEST WESTERN INN
740 Freedom Blvd (95076)
Rates: $42-$98;
Tel: (408) 724-3367; (800) 528-1234

COUNTRY SUNRISE BED & BREAKFAST
3085 Freedom Blvd (95076)
Rates: $70-$95;
Tel: (408) 722-4793

EL RANCHO MOTEL
976 Salinas Rd (95076)
Rates: $30-$69;
Tel: (408) 722-2766

MONTEREY BAY/SANTA CRUZ RESORT
1186 San Andreas Rd (95076)
Rates: $26-$39;
Tel: (408) 722-0551

MOTEL 6
125 Silver Leaf Dr (95076)
Rates: $33-$42;
Tel: (408) 728-4144; (800) 440-6000

NATIONAL 9 MOTEL
1 Western Dr (95076)
Rates: $55-$80;
Tel: (408) 724-1116

RECREATION

PINTO LAKE COUNTY PARK - Leashes

Info: Pack your rods and set your course for Pinto Lake. Trout, bluegill, catfish, crappie and bass thrive in this small lake. Rover can munch on a rawhide under a shade tree while you catch dinner. For more information: (408) 454-2777.

Locate Other Dog-Friendly Activities...Check Nearby Cities

Directions: From Highway 1 southeast, exit at Airport Boulevard. Turn left on Green Valley Road and follow to the marked entrance.

Note: $2 day-use fee.

WEAVERVILLE

LODGING

49er MOTEL
718 Main St (96093)
Rates: $34-$50; Tel: (916) 623-4937

MOTEL TRINITY
1112 Main St (96093)
Rates: $30-$65; Tel: (916) 623-2129

WEAVERVILLE VICTORIAN INN
1709 Main St (96093)
Rates: $49-$80; Tel: (916) 623-4432

RECREATION

ADAMS LAKE TRAIL HIKE

Intermediate/Expert/5.0 miles/3.0 hours

Info: When you and the dawgus crave peace and solitude, you can't go wrong on this hike. But you'll pay for the quietude with a strenuous climb through a steep forest to this small, pretty lake. For more information: (916) 623-2121.

Directions: Take Highway 3 north 38 miles, turning left on Coffee Creek Road (County Road 104) for 14 miles to the trailhead.

BEAR LAKES TRAIL HIKE

Expert/10.0 miles/5.0 hours

Info: You'll need some bonafido hiking experience to deal with the steepness of this hike but the exceptional views and pretty lakes are certainly worth the workout. The cross-country climb to these isolated lakes takes the easterly ridge leading away from the mouth of Big Bear and then contours around to Little and Wee Bear Lakes. Pack some snacks for a biscuit break lakeside, where your wet wagger can feel like a lucky dog. For more information: (916) 623-2121.

Directions: Take Highway 3 north 46 miles to County Road 137. Turn left and follow for 2.5 miles to the trailhead.

BIG and LITTLE BOULDER LAKES TRAIL HIKE

Beginner/4.0 miles/2.0 hours to Little Boulder
Beginner/6.0 miles/3.0 hours to Big Boulder

Info: Plan a doggie paddle once you reach the deep waters of granite-ensconced Little Boulder Lake. Woof. Lots of ideal chill out spots abound lakeside. Continue another mile to Big Boulder for a lake encounter of a different kind. Woof. Big Boulder Lake is large and shallow, adorned with pretty lily-pads and surrounded by forestlands and a granite dome. Woof, woof. Photo ops and picnic spots are everywhere. For more information: (916) 623-2121.

Directions: Take Highway 3 north for approximately 38 miles (1/4 mile before Coffee Creek Road), turning left on Forest Road 37N52. Follow FR 37N52 for 3.1 miles to FR 37N53. Make a right on FR 37N53 and continue to the trailhead.

EAST FORK LAKE TRAIL HIKE

Expert/7.0 miles/4.0 hours

Info: You and your hiking hound will ascend this steep streamside trail to a small but scenic lake with several smaller lakes just above it. Pack some high energy treats and take a restful break before retracing your steps. For more information: (916) 623-2121.

Directions: From Weaverville, take Highway 299 west 8 miles to Junction City and County Road 401. Turn right on County Road 401, following for 10.4 miles to Forest Road 35N47Y. Make a right on FR 35N47Y for 1.8 miles to the trailhead.

EAST WEAVER LAKE TRAIL HIKE

Beginner/2.0 miles/1.0 hours

Info: Lake loving Laddies will jump at the chance to hike up and over a ridge to this small picturesque lake surrounded by granite and forests. Chill out with a brown bag lunch and a wet and wild attitude. For more information: (916) 623-2121.

Directions: On the west edge of Weaverville, take County Road 40 (Memorial Lane) to Forest Road 33N38 (the Weaver Dally Lookout Road). Turn left on FR 33N38, following for 10 miles to the trailhead. The trail takes off to the right.

GRANITE PEAK TRAIL HIKE

Expert/9.2 miles/5.0 hours

Info: Don't even consider this hike unless you've got lots of hiking points under your collar. For the physically fit only, this very steep trail does have a payoff. Once you reach the top, you'll be rewarded with outstanding, unforgettable views. For more information: (916) 623-2121.

Directions: Take Highway 3 north for 16.5 miles to Forest Road 35N28Y. Turn left for approximately 3 miles to the trailhead.

HOBO GULCH TRAIL to BACKBONE CREEK HIKE

Beginner/1.5 miles/1.0 hours

Info: For a small taste of nature's best, you and Bowser will definitely want to browser this trail. Settle in for some paw-stomping fun in the cold waters of Backbone Creek before traipsing through a grabbag forest of giant madrone and Douglas fir. A visit in autumn will reward your color senses with a pretty showing from the oak and dogwood that compete for attention in this pretty forest region. For more information: (916) 623-2121.

Directions: Take Highway 299 west to Helena (17 miles) and County Road 421. Turn right and follow for 4 miles to the intersection with Forest Road 34N07Y. Make a left and continue for 12 miles to the trailhead.

HOBO GULCH TRAIL to RATTLESNAKE CREEK HIKE

Beginner/Intermediate/10.0 miles/6.0 hours

Info: Get ready to step lively on this pretty, sometimes challenging trail. You'll skirt the North Fork of the Trinity River where your soon to be dirty dog will think he's found puppy paradise. Shaded by giant Douglas fir and towering ponderosa pine, a journey through the picturesque landscape is a fun way to spend the day. For more information: (916) 623-2121.

Directions: See Hobo Gulch Trail to Backbone Creek Hike.

LAKE ELEANOR and SHIMMY LAKE TRAIL HIKE

Beginner/1.0 miles/0.5 hours to Lake Eleanor
Beginner/8.2 miles/4.5 hours to Shimmy Lake

Info: Splish-splashers will adore you forever after a trip to one or both of these pretty lakes. Stop at Lake Eleanor, and just idle your day away while Sammy does the dog paddle or continue on to Shimmy Lake. Enjoy the meadows and forests all around you. You won't regret a moment spent on this waterful trail. For more information: (916) 623-2121.

Directions: Take Highway 3 north for 30 miles to County Road 123. Turn left for 1.5 miles to Forest Road 36N24. Make a right following about 6 miles to the trailhead.

STODDARD and McDONALD LAKES TRAIL HIKE

Intermediate/7.0 miles/4.0 hours

Info: A wet and wild adventure beckons you and your wagabout at the end of this scenic trail. Shake a tail through meadows and dense forests to your reward, large deep blue lakes sitting amidst conifer forests. Ah, let the fun begin. When you can drag your dirty dog away, retrace your steps. For more information: (916) 623-2121.

Directions: Take Highway 3 north for 41 miles to County Road 135. Turn left following for 1 mile to Forest Road 38N22. Make a right for 4.3 miles to FR 38N27. Turn left and follow to the trailhead.

WEED

LODGING

GRAND MANOR INN
1844 Shastina Dr (96094)
Rates: $64-$92;
Tel: (916) 938-1982

MOTEL 6
6466 N Weed Blvd (96094)
Rates: $32-$38;
Tel: (916) 938-4101; (800) 440-6000

SIS-Q-INN MOTEL
1825 Shastina Dr (96094)
Rates: $29-$46;
Tel: (916) 938-4194

STEWART MINERAL SPRINGS CABINS
4617 Stewart Springs Rd (96094)
Rates: $25-$65;
Tel: (916) 938-2222; (800) 322-9223

TOWN HOUSE MOTEL
157 S Weed Blvd (96094)
Rates: $36-$33;
Tel: (916) 938-4431

Y MOTEL
90 N Weed Blvd (96094)
Rates: $27-$40;
Tel: (916) 938-4481

RECREATION

DEER MOUNTAIN TRAIL HIKE

Beginner/Intermediate/4.0 miles/2.5 hours

Info: The Deer Mountain Trail encompasses an 800-foot climb to the summit at 7,000 feet. Your pooch will love the soft pine needles that carpet the forest floor and you'll love the scent. For more information: (916) 398-4391.

Directions: From Interstate 5 at Weed, use the "Weed/ College of the Siskiyous" exit and head north through town to the Highway 97 turnoff. Travel north about 15 miles, then go right on Deer Mountain Road and continue four miles to Deer Mountain Snowmobile Park. Take a right on Forest Service Road 44N23 and go about two miles. You won't see a designated trailhead, so park off the road and hike to the mountain from anywhere along Forest Service Road 43N69.

JUANITA LAKE TRAIL HIKE - Leashes

Beginner/1.5 miles/1.0 hours

Info: Unknown to many, this trail follows an easy loop around Juanita Lake. The lake sits in a mixed conifer forest where dwellers such as osprey and bald eagles make their home. Bring the binoculars. For more information: (916) 398-4391.

Dogs May Be Unleashed Unless Otherwise Indicated

Directions: From Interstate 5 use the "Weed/College of the Siskiyous" exit and head north through town to the Highway 97 turnoff. Proceed about 35 miles northeast, then make a left on Ball Mountain Road and go two miles. Take a right at the sign for Juanita Lake and follow the signs for three miles to the lake. The trailhead is at the campground by the boat dock.

THE WHALEBACK TRAIL HIKE

Intermediate/3.0 miles/1.5 hours

Info: Possibly the offspring of once active Mt. Shasta, Whaleback at 8,528 feet is a volcanic cinderdome that sports a large crater at the top. Take the challenging climb to the summit for first-class views of Mt. Shasta complete with seclusion and quiet that you and your canine won't soon forget. For more information: (916) 398-4391.

Directions: From Interstate 5 at Weed, use the "Weed/College of the Siskiyous" exit and head north through town to the Highway 97 turnoff. Travel north about 15 miles, then go right on Deer Mountain Road and continue four miles to Deer Mountain Snowmobile Park. Go three miles east on Forest Service Road 19. Take a right on Forest Service Road 42N24 and continue three miles to a gate. Just park and hike in. Since there is no designated trail, you should hike cross-country from the road. The peak is about 1.5 miles from the gate.

WEST HILLS

<u>RECREATION</u>

CHASE PARK- Leashes

Info: This 5.9-acre park is ideal for a quickie stroll.

Directions: Located at 22525 Chase Street.

WEST HOLLYWOOD

LODGING

LE MONTROSE
SUITE HOTEL DE GRAN LUXE
900 Hammond St (90069)
Rates: $185-$300;
Tel: (310) 855-1115; (800) 776-0666

LE PARC DE GRAN LUXE HOTEL
733 N West Knoll Dr (90069)
Rates: $165-$205;
Tel: (310) 855-8888; (800) 578-4837

MONDRIAN HOTEL
8440 Sunset Blvd (90069)
Rates: $185-$325;
Tel: (213) 650-8999; (800) 525-8029

RAMADA PLAZA HOTEL
8585 Santa Monica Blvd (90069)
Rates: $80;
Tel: (310) 652-6400; (800) 272-6232

SUMMERFIELD SUITES HOTEL
1000 Westmount Dr (90069)
Rates: $149-$179;
Tel: (310) 657-7400; (800) 833-4353

WYNDHAM BELAGE MOTEL
1020 N San Vicente Blvd (90069)
Rates: $149-$175;
Tel: (310) 854-1111; (800) 996-3426

WEST SACRAMENTO

LODGING

BEST WESTERN-
HARBOR INN & SUITES
1250 Halyard Dr (95691)
Rates: $59-$159;
Tel: (916) 922-9833; (800) 528-1234

MOTEL 6
1254 Halyard Dr (95691)
Rates: $31-$37;
Tel: (916) 372-3624; (800) 440-6000

WESTLEY

LODGING

DAYS INN
7144 McKraken Rd (95387)
Rates: $37+;
Tel: (209) 894-5500; (800) 325-2525

Dogs May Be Unleashed Unless Otherwise Indicated

WESTMINSTER

LODGING

BEST WESTERN WESTMINSTER INN
5755 Westminster Ave (92683)
Rates: $42-$57;
Tel: (714) 898-4043; (800) 528-1234

MOTEL 6
6266 Westminster Ave (92683)
Rates: $30-$34;
Tel: (714) 891-5366; (800) 440-6000

MOTEL 6
13100 Goldenwest (92683)
Rates: $30-$34;
Tel: (714) 895-0042; (800) 440-6000

WESTPORT

LODGING

BLUE VICTORIAN INN
38921 N Hwy 1 (95488)
Rates: $75-$130;
Tel: (707) 964-6310

**HOWARD CREEK RANCH
BED & BREAKFAST**
40501 N Hwy 1 (95488)
Rates: $50-$90;
Tel: (707) 964-6725

RECREATION

WESTPORT-UNION LANDING STATE BEACH - Leashes

Info: Astound your hound with playtime on this isolated beach. Bring a blanket, a good book and a biscuit or two, and set up a picnic on the blufftop. Whale-watchers, even if Orca doesn't shoot a spray your way, you're gonna love the tranquility of this coastal region. For more information: (707) 937-5804.

Directions: Take Highway 1 north about 2.5 miles. Follow the signs.

WESTWOOD

LODGING

HOTEL DEL CAPRI
10587 Wilshire Blvd (90024)
Rates: $85-$140;
Tel: (800) 444-6835

**WESTWOOD MARQUIS
HOTEL AND GARDENS**
930 Hilgard Ave (90024)
Rates: $220-$325;
Tel: (310) 208-8765; (800) 421-2317

Locate Other Dog-Friendly Activities...Check Nearby Cities

RECREATION

WESTWOOD PARK - Leashes

Info: Break out the red and white checkered cloth, stake out a shaded picnic table and enjoy a relaxing respite. If Rover gets restless, take a stroll around the sculpture-embellished paths.

Directions: From Wilshire Boulevard, head south on Veteran Avenue. A short distance past the federal building, look for the park on your right.

WHITTIER

LODGING

BEST WHITTIER INN
14226 Whittier Blvd (90606)
Rates; $34-$80;
Tel: (310) 698-0323

MOTEL 6
8221 S Pioneer Blvd (90606)
Rates: $30-$34;
Tel: (310) 692-9101; (800) 440-6000

VAGABOND INN
14125 E Whittier Blvd (90605)
Rates: $35-$55;
Tel: (310) 698-9701; (800) 522-1555

WILLIAMS

LODGING

MOTEL 6
455 4th St (95987)
Rates: $32-$38;
Tel: (916) 473-5337; (800) 440-6000

STAGE STOP MOTEL
330 7th St (95987)
Rates: $33-$50;
Tel: (916) 473-2281

WOODCREST INN
400 C St (95987)
Rates: $54;
Tel: (916) 473-2381

RECREATION

WILLIAMS CITY PARK - Leashes

Info: When it's time for some fresh air and a bit of turf this park has both.

Directions: Head west to 9th Street. The park will be on your left.

Dogs May Be Unleashed Unless Otherwise Indicated

WILLITS

LODGING

BAECHTEL CREEK INN
101 Gregory Ln (95490)
Rates: $65-$105;
Tel: (707) 459-9063; (800) 459-9911

HOLIDAY LODGE
1540 S Main St (95490)
Rates: $45-$65;
Tel: (707) 459-5361

LARK MOTEL
1411 S Main St (95490)
Rates: $30-$40;
Tel: (707) 459-2421

PEPPERWOOD MOTEL
452 S Main St (95490)
Rates: $30-$40;
Tel: (707) 459-2231

PINE CONE MOTEL
1350 S Main St (95490)
Rates: $29-$32;
Tel: (707) 459-5044

SKUNK TRAIL MOTEL
500 S Main St (95490)
Rates: $38+;
Tel: (707) 459-2302

WESTERN VILLAGE INN
1440 S Main St (95490)
Rates: $34+;
Tel: (707) 459-4011

RECREATION

BATHHOUSE TRAIL HIKE

Intermediate/4.0 miles/2.0 hours

Info: Late fall, winter or early spring are the best times to experience this diverse trail. Admire the woodland, as you and the dawgus amble this way and that among stands of chaparral, oak and pine, interspersed by glades, meadows and rock outcrops. You'll also collect some excellent views of Stony Creek Canyon. Happy tails to you. For more information: (707) 275-2361.

Directions: From Willits, take Highway 101 south to Highway 20 east for 28 miles to the town of Upper Lake. Turn left at Treasure Cove Pizza Parlor and drive .75 miles to a stop sign. The Upper Lake Ranger District will be on your left. Stop at the station, check with the forest rangers on trail conditions, as well as specific directions to the trailhead. Or call first.

BEARWALLOW TRAIL HIKE

Beginner/6.0 miles/3.0 hours

Info: If you're looking for pretty views, shaded, forests and refreshing creeks, this hike's got your name on it. Beginning on Forest Road 18N06.2 the trail contours the west flank of St. John Mountain. This relatively level pathway wanders among a cornucopia of trees, offering superb views of Snow Mountain, the Middle Fork of Stony Creek Gorge and rugged Bear Wallow Creek Canyon. For the water fun part of your excursion, take the short side trail to Bear Wallow Creek, throw in your fishing line and simply chill out. Fido is sure to amuse you with his creekside capers. For more information: (707) 275-2361.

Directions: See Bathhouse Trail Hike for directions to the Upper Lake Ranger Station.

BENMORE TRAIL HIKE

Intermediate/6.0 miles/3.0 hours

Info: Get ready for a wet and wetter adventure along this pretty trail with several creek crossings. The pup will think he's found paradise. And perhaps he has. The trailhead begins in the Pine Mountain area at the junction of Benmore Creek and Eel River. You'll get tails wagging with a run through forests of Douglas fir and oak in Montgomery Glade where fine views of Hull Mountain are yours for the looking. After you cross Benmore Creek twice and a beautiful meadow once, the vegetation changes to madrone and manzanita on your approach to the Eel River. Picnic spots abound creekside or in the meadowlands. For more information: (707) 275-2361.

Directions: See Bathhouse Trail Hike for directions to the Upper Lake Ranger Station.

Dogs May Be Unleashed Unless Otherwise Indicated

BLOODY ROCK TRAIL HIKE

Beginner/6.0 miles/3.0 hours

Info: Located in the Eel River area within the State Game Refuge, this trail ambles through glades and passes near historic Bloody Rock before entering a woodland. When you reach the Eel River, do a biscuit break, share some riverside fun with furface and then retrace your steps. For more information: (707) 275-2361.

Directions: See Bathhouse Trail Hike for directions to the Upper Lake Ranger Station.

DEAFY GLADE TRAIL HIKE

Intermediate/3.2 miles/2.0 hours

Info: After passing among forests of oak and pine, the trail descends into the South Fork of Stony Creek Canyon and brings you and your hot diggety dog to a bonafido water wonderland. At the crossing, you'll be treated to views of the sheer face of Deafy Rock which rises several hundred feet above the cascading stream waters. The trail climbs through Deafy Glade and zigzags up through second growth forests to the wilderness boundary where it connects to the Summit Springs Trail. You'll traverse some private land where the route becomes somewhat indistinct. Follow the old blazes in the trees or let the hound sniff the way. For more information: (707) 275-2361.

Directions: See Bathhouse Trail Hike for directions to the Upper Lake Ranger Station.

EAST PEAK LOOP TRAIL HIKE

Beginner/7.5 miles/4.0 hours

Info: Hop on this trail and join other outdoor enthusiasts who love this popular loop in the Snow Mountain Area. You and the dogster will get an eyeful of some of the best high country scenery along the way. Take your camera and try to capture the glorious beauty of this rugged canyon and mountain country. You'll traverse several vegetative regions and high meadows before reaching the top of East Peak, Snow Mountain's highest point. Carpe diem Duke. For more information: (707) 275-2361.

Directions: See Bathhouse Trail Hike for directions to the Upper Lake Ranger Station.

LAKE SHORE LOOP TRAIL HIKE

Beginner/4.0 miles/2.0 hours

Info: Sunday strollers will love this scenic trail beside the shore of Lake Pillsbury. Your initial journey traverses scrub oak vegetation and several species of chaparral before reaching Horsepasture Gulch Creek. The Horsepasture Gulch area is level, verdant and very picturesque in the spring. About 150 yards from the lakeshore, you'll want to take the east/left route through a grabbag forest of fir, pine, oak, madrone and manzanita. When you reach the ridgetop, you and the dogster will get an eyeful of Lake Pillsbury. Your descent will be along the lakeshore where it junctions back to the fork. For more information: (707) 275-2361.

Directions: See Bathhouse Trail Hike for directions to the Upper Lake Ranger Station.

MILE RANCH LOOP TRAIL HIKE

Beginner/9.5 miles/5.0 hours

Info: This trail is one of the most popular loops on Snow Mountain, and with good reason. Starting at the Summit Springs Trailhead, you'll experience the best of Snow Mountain - dense red fir forests, lush meadows and a barren peak. Take notice of the eerie, severely fire-scarred areas resulting from the Fouts Fire. You and furface will also sojourn through Milk Ranch Meadow which is privately owned. Hikers are welcome to walk through this pretty meadowland. For more information: (707) 275-2361.

Directions: See Bathhouse Trail Hike for directions to the Upper Lake Ranger Station.

Dogs May Be Unleashed Unless Otherwise Indicated

OVERLOOK LOOP TRAIL HIKE

Expert/6.5 miles/4.0 hours

Info: This looping trail is not for the fair of paw. Only fit Fidos should attempt this strenuous hike, which covers an elevation change of nearly 1,400 feet. Beginning at the Summit Springs Trailhead, this interesting loop allows you a peek at the recovery stage of a fire-ecology area. It continues on to impressive vistas of Mt. Shasta, Mt. Lassen and the Yolla-Bollys. When you've taken in the beauty all around, do the descent thing to Appletree Camp and the headwaters of Dark Hollow Creek, aka paradise for aquatic pups. From compressed ecological zones, unusual plant communities and the refreshing creek, this adventure is well-worth the sweat. For more information: (707) 275-2361.

Directions: See Bathhouse Trail Hike for directions to the Upper Lake Ranger Station.

PACKSADDLE TRAIL HIKE

Beginner/3.2 miles/1.5 hours

Info: For an easy-does-it hike that combines wet tootsies and cool forests, set your sights on this trail. Beginning in woodlands of Douglas fir, madrone and black oak, you'll eventually make your way to mixed chaparral. Paw dunking delights await in Packsaddle Creek, approximately 300 yards from Lake Pillsbury. Continue to Swallow Rock on the shores of Lake Pillsbury, do the doggie paddle, break some biscuits and bread and end your afternoon on a high note. Two paws up for this day. For more information: (707) 275-2361.

Directions: See Bathhouse Trail Hike for directions to the Upper Lake Ranger Station.

WATERFALL LOOP TRAIL HIKE

Beginner/6.8 miles/3.0 hours

Info: This pretty trail is a perfect antidote to the summertime blahs. Pack some snacks, your pooch, and let the good times roll. Beginning at the West Crockett Trailhead, you'll pass a beautiful cascading waterfall. Take the spur trail and revel in some excellent views. When you reach the Middle Fork of Stony Creek, take a break and let the wet wagger enjoy a bit of water playtime. As the trail heads south, Lake Pillsbury Basin and the surrounding mountains can be seen to the west while the Middle Fork of Stony Creek Canyon can be spotted to the east. Do the distance on this one and you'll cross through Milk Ranch, one of the largest meadow areas on Snow Mountain. Milk Ranch Meadow is private property but hikers are welcome to pass through. If you're hiking in the springtime, you won't believe the crayola wildflower show. The dramatic vistas of forested mountains and rugged river canyons from the ridgetop are memorable. Get your fill and then hop back on the trail. As you approach West Crockett Trailhead, you'll switchback down to Stony Creek before ascending to the trailhead. For more information: (707) 275-2361.

Directions: See Bathhouse Trail Hike for directions to the Upper Lake Ranger Station.

WILLOWS

LODGING

**BEST WESTERN-
GOLDEN PHEASANT INN**
249 N Humboldt Ave (95988)
Rates: $31-$77;
Tel: (916) 934-4603; (800) 528-1234

BLUE GUM INN
Rt 2, Hwy 99 W (95988)
Rates: $26-$42;
Tel: (916) 934-5401

CROSS ROADS WEST INN
452 N Humboldt Ave (95988)
Rates: $26-$36;
Tel: (916) 934-7026

DAYS INN
475 N Humboldt Ave (95988)
Rates: $38-$52;
Tel: (916) 934-4444; (800) 329-7466

ECONOMY INN
435 N Tehama (95988)
Rates: $30+;
Tel: (916) 934-4224

GROVE MOTEL
Rt 2, Hwy 99 W (95988)
Rates: $30+;
Tel: (916) 934-5067

SUPER 8 MOTEL
457 N Humboldt Ave (95988)
Rates: $36-$38;
Tel: (916) 934-2871; (800) 800-8000

WESTERN MOTEL
601 N Tehama (95988)
Rates: $27+;
Tel: (916) 934-3856

RECREATION

BEARWALLOW TRAIL HIKE

Beginner/5.0 miles/2.5 hours

Info: After hiking for 2 miles on the Bearwallow Trailhead, you and the pupster will come to a trail junction on the left. Follow it for .25 miles to Bearwallow Creek where you'll find yourself in a picturesque little spot beside a small feeder stream. If you miss the turn, you'll end up on waterless Windy Point Trailhead. Avoid in summer - too hot. For more information: (916) 963-3128.

Directions: From Willows on Interstate 5, travel west on Highway 162 and continue to the town of Elk Creek. Leave Highway 162 and go south to Stonyford. Then go west on Fouts Springs Road and travel about eight miles. Go north on Forest Service Road 18N06 to the parking area.

SACRAMENTO NATIONAL WILDLIFE REFUGE - Leashes

Info: Pack your binoculars and get ready to explore 10,700 acres of marshland, home to over 300 species of mammals and birds. For more information: (916) 934-2801.

Directions: From Willows, take the Road 57 exit and travel south along frontage road about six miles to the entrance.

Note: Refuge is sometimes closed, call first.

WILMINGTON

RECREATION

BANNING PARK AND RECREATION CENTER - Leashes

Info: Bring a frisbee and a fun attitude to this 20-acre park.

Directions: Located at 1331 Eubank Street.

EAST WILMINGTON GREENBELT PARK - Leashes

Info: This 5-acre greenbelt park harbors a variety of flora and fauna, making this area a sensory delight for serenity-seeking parkgoers. And there's a grassy picnic section that's ideal for a brown bag lunch hour.

Directions: On Drumm Avenue between M and Sanford Streets.

WINDSOR

<u>RECREATION</u>

ESPOSTI PARK - Leashes

Info: Take a trip with Skip to the expansive, grassy area in this friendly neighborhood park.

Directions: Located at 6000 Old Redwood Highway.

KEISER PARK - Leashes

Info: Stroll through the open space or lead Fido along the walking trail in this pleasant city park.

Directions: Located at 700 Windsor River Road.

Other parks in Windsor - Leashes
•LAKEWOOD MEADOWS PARK, 9150 Brooks Road
•LOS ROBLES PARK, 10860 Rio Russo Drive
•MICHAEL A. HALL PARK, 431 Jane Drive
•ROBBINS PARK, 100 Billington Lane
•SUTTON PARK, 1030 Robbie Way

WISHON

<u>LODGING</u>

MILLER'S LANDING
37976 Rd 222 (93669)
Rates: $40-$125;
Tel: (209) 642-3633

Dogs May Be Unleashed Unless Otherwise Indicated

WOODLAND

LODGING

CINDERELLA MOTEL
99 W Main St (95695)
Rates: $35-$42;
Tel: (916) 662-1091; (800) 782-9403

COMFORT INN
1562 E Main St (95695)
Rates: $45-$65;
Tel: (916) 666-3050; (800) 221-2222

MOTEL 6
1564 E Main St (95695)
Rates: $29-$36;
Tel: (916) 666-6777; (800) 440-6000

RECREATION

BLUE RIDGE TRAIL HIKE

Intermediate/Expert/6.0 miles/4.0 hours

Info: You and the pupster will certainly get your Rexercise on this outing. But every huff and puff will be rewarded with an ooh and aah. Do the distance on this one and you'll feel like you're on top of the world when you reach ridgetop and memorable views of the central valley and coastal mountain ranges. Don't be surprised to see hummingbirds, hawks, eagles and even an occasional falcon as you enjoy delightful mountaintop breezes. Ranked as one of the top 100 hikes in Northern California, this trail rises a strenuous 2,000 feet in three miles from the trailhead to the crest of Blue Ridge. An extraordinary journey, your RAM will go into overload. Be sure to carry plenty of water whenever you hike. And be prepared for extreme temperatures in the summer months. For more information: (707) 263-9544.

Directions: From Woodland, travel northwest on Highway 16 through Esparto for about 40 miles. At the Lower Cache Creek Canyon Regional Park Recreation Site, make a left onto County Road 40 (Bayhouse Road) and look for a concrete bridge. Across the bridge and just downstream look for a small unpaved access road that opens up into a primitive group campground. The trailhead is located near the group site on the north side. Park on the south side of the low water bridge in the dry season. In the wet season, Country Road 40 is closed but non-vehicular access is usually possible.

Locate Other Dog-Friendly Activities...Check Nearby Cities

WOODLAND HILLS

LODGING

VAGABOND INN
20157 Ventura Blvd (91364)
Rates: $47-$67;
Tel: (818) 347-8080; (800) 522-1555

RECREATION

ORCUTT RANCH HORTICULTURE CENTER - Leashes

Info: Mosey with Rosie through the lush, verdant grounds of this 24-acre park. Take some time to smell the flowers at the rose garden or sniff the fragrant air in the sun-ripened orange groves along one of the park's nature trails. There's a massive 700-year-old, valley oak that's definitely worth a look-see. For more information: (818) 883-6641.

Directions: Located at 23600 Roscoe Boulevard.

Note: Hours- 8 a.m. to 5 p.m. daily. Closed major holidays.

SERRANIA PARK-Leashes

Info: This spacious, beautifully landscaped park is ideal for an afternoon of R&R.

Directions: Located at 20865 Wells Drive.

SERRANIA RIDGE TRAIL HIKE - Leashes

Intermediate/2.5 miles/1.25 hours

Info: When you want to combine a hearty workout with some outstanding views, you can't beat this short, albeit steep trail. Mulholland Highway marks the end of your ascent and the beginning of your descent. For more information: (818) 756-8190.

Directions: Take De Soto Avenue south past Ventura Boulevard, where it becomes Serrania Avenue. Continue for one mile to Serrania Park. The trailhead is located at the east end of the park.

STAGECOACH TRAIL to DEVIL'S SLIDE HIKE - Leashes

Intermediate/2.5 miles/1.25 hours

Info: This rough, dirt trail was once the main route of early pioneers traveling between Los Angeles and San Francisco. The covered wagons are gone, but Devil's Slide still offers hikers and hounds terrific views of the San Fernando Valley. As you and the pupster ascend the semi-eroded dirt trail, take note of the spectacular, age-old rock configurations of the Simi Hills. For more information: (818) 756-8188.

Directions: From Woodland Hills, exit the San Fernando Valley Freeway (118) at Topanga Canyon Boulevard. Head south approximately 1.5 miles to Devonshire Street, turning right to Chatsworth Park South. The trailhead begins just below the water tower.

WOODLAND HILLS PARK- Leashes

Info: This 19-acre parkland has all the amenities needed for active breeds to enjoy their day. Pack a fuzzy Penn and some power snacks and go for it.

Directions: Located at 5858 Shoup Avenue.

YORKVILLE

LODGING

SHEEP DUNG ESTATES COTTAGES
P. O. Box 49 (95494)
Rates: $75;
Tel: (707) 894-5322

YOSEMITE AREA

LODGING

DEER VALLEY INN BED & BREAKFAST
45013 Hwy 49 (Nipinnawasee 93601)
Rates: $49-$175;
Tel: (800) 676-5647

Locate Other Dog-Friendly Activities...Check Nearby Cities

YOSEMITE NATIONAL PARK

LODGING

THE REDWOODS GUEST COTTAGES
P. O. Box 2085
(Wawona Station 95389)
Rates: $82-$365;
Tel: (209) 375-6666

YOSEMITE VIEW LODGE
11159 Hwy 140, P. O. Box D
(El Portal 95318)
Rates: $62-$135;
Tel: 209 379-2681; (800) 321-5261

YOUNTVILLE

LODGING

VINTAGE INN
6541 Washington St (94599)
Rates: $134-$204;
Tel: (707) 944-1112; (800) 351-1133

YREKA

LODGING

BEST WESTERN MINER'S INN
122 E Miner St (96097)
Rates: $44-$55;
Tel: (916) 842-4355; (800) 528-1234

MOTEL ORLEANS
1804-B Fort Jones Rd (96097)
Rates: $32-$39;
Tel: (916) 842-1612; (800) 626-1900

MOTEL 6
1785 S Main St (96097)
Rates: $32-$38;
Tel: (916) 842-4111; (800) 440-6000

THUNDERBIRD LODGE
526 S Main St (96097)
Rates: $32-$76;
Tel: (916) 842-4404; (800) 554-4339

WAYSIDE INN
1235 S Main St (96097)
Rates: $30-$150;
Tel: (916) 842-4412; (800) 795-7974

RECREATION

BIG MILL CREEK TRAIL HIKE

Beginner/6.0 miles/3.0 hours

Info: Leave the crowds behind as you and your canine crony roam amidst the whisper-quiet Salmon-Trinity Alps Primitive Area. After traversing a once booming chromium mining

Dogs May Be Unleashed Unless Otherwise Indicated

sight, the trail ends on a scenic ridgetop. If Rover thinks that cattle chasing is the cat's meow, keep him leashed in this heavily used grazing area. For more information: (916) 468-5351.

Directions: From Yreka, take Highway 3 southwest approximately 20 miles to the Scott River Ranger Station. Once at the station, check with the forest rangers on trail conditions, as well as specific directions to the trailhead. Or call first.

BLUE GOOSE STEAM TRAIN - Leashes

Info: All aboard for a unique 3-hour steam train adventure through beautiful Shasta Valley. If yours is a lap size pup, bring him along but don't forget his leash. Big Bowsers, fret not. You'll be given the V.I.P. (very important pooch) treatment while you wait. The train depot offers a complimentary dog sitting service, complete with air conditioned facilities, water, and at least one leg stretching jaunt. For more information: (916) 842-4146.

Directions: The train depot is located on the east side of Interstate 5 at the Central Yreka exit.

Note: Season runs from Memorial Day weekend to the end of October. $9.00 per adult, $4.50 per child, dogs ride free.

BOX CAMP to BOX CAMP RIDGE TRAIL HIKE

Intermediate/2.0 miles/1.0 hours

Info: Take a few minutes to limber up with the pup before tackling this short but steep hike. You'll ascend 1,200 feet in just one mile and be rewarded with some outstanding views. Look south to magnificent Sky High Lakes Basin or east to Canyon Creek and Boulder Peak. At 8,299 feet it's the highest peak in the Marble Mountain Wilderness. When you've had your fill, do an about-face. Or continue further by hooking up with one of the interconnecting trails. For more information: (916) 468-5351.

Directions: See Big Mill Creek Trail Hike for directions to the Scott River Ranger Station.

CHILCOOT TRAIL HIKE

Beginner/3.0 miles/1.5 hours

Info: This simple trail makes for a great day hike with your pooch. Wander through a verdant botanical area and collect some terrific views along the way. Remember, cattle and canines don't mix. Bring Rex's leash if he's easily tempted. For more information: (916) 468-5351.

Directions: See Big Mill Creek Trail Hike for directions to the Scott River Ranger Station.

EAST BOULDER TRAIL HIKE

Beginner/6.0 miles/3.0 hours

Info: Simple and scenic, sun-splashed East Boulder Lake is your destination. Aka puppy paradise, you and your pup can vege out lakeside, crack into your biscuit basket and relish in the magnificence of this beautiful basin surrounded by towering peaks. For more information: (916) 468-5351.

Directions: See Big Mill Creek Trail Hike for directions to the Scott River Ranger Station.

FOX CREEK RIDGE TRAIL HIKE

Intermediate/9.0 miles/4.5 hours

Info: Take along a wet and wild attitude and a cache of trail mix on this somewhat difficult trail. Your soon-to-be dirty dog can have his pick of three lakes, each encased in a picturesque setting. For more information: (916) 468-5351.

Directions: See Big Mill Creek Trail Hike for directions to the Scott River Ranger Station.

HIDDEN LAKE TRAIL HIKE

Beginner/2.0 miles/1.0 hours

Info: This one-mile jaunt to Hidden Lake is an easy one. Fishing hounds, tote your poles and try your luck. From Carter Meadows, take the Pacific Crest Trail about 100 yards to the signed junction for Hidden Lake - the trail branches right. The path gets quite rocky in one section, so use caution. For more information: (916) 468-5351.

Directions: See Big Mill Creek Trail Hike for directions to the Scott River Ranger Station.

HIGH CAMP TRAIL HIKE

Intermediate/2.0 miles/1.0 hours

Info: Boogie with Bowser to the ridgetop for your daily dose of exercise. Then partake of the pretty scenery from your lofty perch. For more information: (916) 468-5351.

Directions: See Big Mill Creek Trail Hike for directions to the Scott River Ranger Station.

HOUSTON CREEK TRAIL HIKE

Intermediate/5.0 miles/2.5 hours

Info: Exercise and panoramic views go hand-in-hand on this trail. Even though certain sections along the hike are steep, you and the pupster will be happy with your choice. Depending upon the time of year, you might be able to do some paw dipping in the creek. This area is known for cattle grazing. If your canine is a cattle chaser, bring his leash. For more information: (916) 468-5351.

Directions: See Big Mill Creek Trail Hike for directions to the Scott River Ranger Station.

JONES BEACH

Info: If sandy paws equate to a happy Sandy, then yours will be in for a tailwagging good time. Pack the beach balls and boogie boards, it's time for some fun in the sun. For more information: (916) 468-5351.

Directions: From Yreka, take Highway 3 southwest approximately 20 miles to the Scott River Ranger Station. Turn right on Scott River Road. Follow to the beach about 6 miles past the old red schoolhouse.

LITTLE MILL CREEK TRAIL HIKE

Beginner/7.0 miles/3.5 hours

Info: An A-one recommended hike of local forest rangers, this simple trail has it all - refreshing lakes, terrific views, fish à-plenty and best of all, quiet solitude. Heads up while hiking through the meadows, the trail is not well-blazed. Keep Fido leashed if he's a bovine bounder, this is cattle grazing country. For more information: (916) 468-5351.

Directions: See Big Mill Creek Trail Hike for directions to the Scott River Ranger Station.

LONG GULCH TRAIL HIKE

Expert/4.5 miles/3.0 hours

Info: After climbing the trail about two miles, you'll arrive at Long Gulch Lake. Stocked with small trout, this pretty lake is northeast of Deadman Peak at 7,741 feet. For more information: (916) 468-5351.

Directions: See Big Mill Creek Trail Hike for directions to the Scott River Ranger Station.

NOLAND GULCH TRAIL HIKE

Beginner/3.0 miles/1.5 hours

Info: Solitude and gentle terrain combine for a great day hike. Enjoy the peacefulness as you and the pooch stroll along the old road trail, which ends after junctioning with the Pacific Crest Trail, your about-face point. Up for more? Hop on the PCT and do your own thing. Leash your cattle chaser if bovines are a temptation. For more information: (916) 468-5351.

Directions: See Big Mill Creek Trail Hike for directions to the Scott River Ranger Station.

Dogs May Be Unleashed Unless Otherwise Indicated

PARADISE LAKE TRAIL HIKE

Intermediate/4.0 miles/2.0 hours

Info: Starting at an elevation of 4,880 feet, the trail takes you and your hiking hound on a steep, two-mile climb. Your efforts will be rewarded with the trail's namesake. Paradise Lake is prettily nestled in a mountain pocket beckoning you and aquapup to have a hot diggety dog day. Expect to encounter campers. For more information: (916) 468-5351

Directions: See Big Mill Creek Trail Hike for directions to the Scott River Ranger Station.

SHACKLEFORD CREEK to CAMPBELL LAKE TRAIL HIKE

Intermediate/11.0 miles/6.0 hours

Info: There's no better way to spend a hot summer day than hiking a creekside trail through the scenic Marble Mountain Wilderness with your wagalong. Your destination - Campbell Lake - a refreshing mountain oasis. For more information: (916) 468-5351.

Directions: See Big Mill Creek Trail Hike for directions to the Scott River Ranger Station.

SISSON TRAIL HIKE

Beginner/3.0 miles/1.5 hours

Info: Even couch potatoes will love this easy trail. This historic hike to Mt. Shasta is short and sweet and the vistas are excellent. For more information: (916) 468-5351.

Directions: See Big Mill Creek Trail Hike for directions to the Scott River Ranger Station.

TAYLOR LAKE TRAIL HIKE

Beginner/1.0 miles/0.5 hours

Info: This leg stretcher brings you to Taylor Lake - a long, narrow body of water in the Russian Wilderness, where a fishing pole or a small raft will add to a fun day. You might even catch a trout or two. For more information: (916) 467-5757.

Directions: From Yreka, take Highway 3/Fort Jones south 25 miles to Etna. Head west on Etna-Somes Bar Road (Main Street in town) and continue for 10.25 miles. Take a left on Taylor Lake Road just past Etna Summit to reach the trailhead.

TRAIL GULCH LAKE HIKE

Intermediate/9.0 miles/5.0 hours

Info: Long but lovely, the hike to Trail Gulch Lake is pawsitively one of the area's best. Kick back and enjoy the surrounding beauty. Aquatic Retrievers probably wouldn't mind a bit of doggie paddling for a tennis ball either. When you can drag yourself away and coax the wet wonder from the water, retrace your steps. For more information: (916) 468-5351.

Directions: See Big Mill Creek Trail Hike for directions to the Scott River Ranger Station.

YUBA CITY

LODGING

GARDEN COURT INN
4228 S Hwy 99 (95991)
Rates: $26-$38;
Tel: (916) 674-0210

MOTEL ORLEANS-YUBA CITY
730 Palora Ave (95991)
Rates: $32-$40;
Tel: (916) 674-1592; (800) 626-1900

MOTEL 6
700 N Palora Ave (95991)
Rates: $30-$36;
Tel: (916) 674-1710; (800) 440-6000

YUCCA VALLEY

LODGING

OASIS OF EDEN INN & SUITES
56377 Twentynine Palms Hwy (92284)
Rates: $44-$80;
Tel: (619) 365-6321

SUPER 8 MOTEL
57096 Twentynine Palms Hwy (92284)
Rates: $42-$46;
Tel: (619) 228-1773; (800) 800-8000

YUCCA INN
7500 Camino Del Cielo (92284)
Rates: $39-$55;
Tel: (619) 365-3311

LET'S GET READY TO TRAVEL

LET'S GET READY TO TRAVEL BY CAR

"Kennel Up"...the magical, all-purpose command

When Rosie and Maxwell's training began, I used a metal kennel which they were taught to regard as their spot, their sleeping place. Whenever they were left at home and then again when they were put to bed at night, I used the simple command, "Kennel Up," as I pointed to and touched their kennel. They quickly learned the command. As they outgrew the kennel, the laundry room became their "kennel up" place. As full-grown dogs, the entire kitchen became their "kennel up" spot. Likewise, when they began accompanying me on trips, I reinforced the command each time I told them to jump into the car. They soon understood that being in their "kennel up" place meant that I expected them to stay quietly and behave, whether they were at home, in the car or in a hotel room. Teaching your dog to "kennel up" will make travels easier.

Old dogs can learn new tricks

When we first began vacationing with Rosie and Max, some friends decided to join us on a few of our local jaunts. Their dog Brandy, a ten year-old Cocker Spaniel, had never traveled with them. Other than trips to the vet and the groomer, she'd never been in the car. The question remained... would Brandy adjust? We needn't have worried. She took to the car immediately. Despite her small size, she quickly learned to jump in and out of the rear of their station wagon. She ran through the forests with Rosie and Max, playing and exploring as if she'd always had free run. To her owners and to Brandy, the world took on new meaning. Nature as seen through the eyes of their dog became a more exciting place of discovery.

Can my pooch be trained to travel?

Dogs are quite adaptable and responsive and patience will definitely have its rewards. Your pooch loves nothing more than to be with you. If it means behaving to have that privilege, he'll respond.

Now that you've decided to travel and vacation with your dog, it's probably a good idea to get him started with short trips. Before you go anywhere, remember two of the most important items for happy dog travel, a leash for safety and the proper paraphernalia for clean up. There's nothing more frustrating or scary than a loose, uncontrolled dog. And nothing more embarrassing than being without clean-up essentials when your dog unexpectedly decides to relieve himself.

Make traveling an enjoyable experience. Stop every so often and do fun things. As you lengthen travel times, don't think that you have to stop every hour or so. Handle your dog as you would at home. He won't have to walk any more frequently. But when you do stop to let him out, leash him before you open the car doors.

When the walk or playtime is over, remember to use the "Kennel Up" command when you tell your pooch to get into the car or into his kennel. And use lots of praise when he obeys the command.

You'll find that your dog will most likely be lulled to sleep by the motion of the car. When I travel with Rosie and Maxwell, after less than fifteen minutes, they're both asleep. When we vacation together, I stop every few hours to give them water and let them "stretch their legs." They've become accustomed to these short stops and anticipate them. The moment the car is turned off and the hatch-back popped open, they anxiously await their leashes. When our romping time is over and we're back at the car, a simple "kennel up" gets them into their travel area.

To kennel or not to kennel?

Whether or not you use a kennel for car travel is a personal choice. Safety should be your primary concern. Yours and your dog's. Whatever method of travel you choose, be certain that your dog will not interfere with your driving. If you plan to use a kennel, line the bottom with an old blanket, towel or shredded newspaper. Include a treat or chew toy to keep him amused. When you're vacationing by car and not using a kennel, consider a car harness.

If it's your habit not to use a kennel or harness, confine your dog to the back seat and command him to "kennel up." Protect your upholstery by covering the rear seat with an old blanket. The blanket will make clean up that much easier at the end of your trip. To keep my car fresh smelling and free from doggie odors, I keep a deodorizer tucked under the front seat.

How often should I stop?

Many people think that when their dogs are in the car, they have to "go" more often. Not true. Whenever you stop for yourself, let your pooch have a drink and take a walk. It's not necessary to make extra stops along the way unless your dog has a physical problem and must be walked more often. Always pull your car out of the flow of traffic so you can safely care for your pooch. Never let your dog run free. Use a leash at all times. Since your pooch is in unfamiliar territory, he can bolt into traffic, be injured, become lost or run away.

Can my dog be left alone in the car?

Even if you think you'll only be gone a few minutes, that's all it takes for a dog to become dehydrated. Even if all the windows are open, even if your car is parked in the shade, even when the outside temperature is only 85° the temperature in a parked car can reach 100° to 120° in thirty minutes. Exposure to high temperatures, even for short periods, can cause brain damage and possibly death.

NEVER LEAVE YOUR DOG UNATTENDED IN WARM WEATHER.

During the winter months, you should also be aware of hypothermia, a life threatening condition when an animal's body temperature falls below normal. In particular, short-haired dogs and toys are very susceptible to illness in extremely cold weather.

FIDO FACT:

- *Hot pavement can damage your dog's sensitive footpads. In the summer months, walk your pooch in the morning or evening or on grassy areas and other cool surfaces.*

What about carsickness?

Just like people, some dogs are queasier than others. And for some reason, puppies suffer more frequently from motion sickness. It's best to wait a couple of hours after your dog has eaten before beginning your trip. Or better yet, feed your dog after you arrive at your destination. Keep the windows open enough to allow in fresh air. If your pooch has a tendency to be carsick, sugar can help. Give your dog a tablespoon of honey or a small piece of candy before beginning your trip (**NO CHOCOLATE**).   That should help settle his stomach. If you notice that he still looks sickly, stop and allow him some additional fresh air or take him for a short walk.

What about identification if my dog runs off?

As far as identification, traveling time is no different than staying at home. Never allow your pooch to be anywhere without proper identification. ID tags should provide your dog's name, your name, address and phone number. Most states require dog owners to purchase a license every year. The tag usually includes a license number that is registered with your state. If you attach the license tag to your dog's collar and you become separated, your dog can be traced. There are also local organizations that help reunite lost pets and owners. The phone numbers of these organizations can be obtained from local police authorities.

Use the form on the facing page to record your pooch's description so that the information will be handy should the need arise.

MY POOCH'S IDENTIFICATION

In the event that your dog is lost or stolen, the following information will help describe your pooch. Before leaving on your first trip, take a few minutes to fill out this form, make a duplicate, and then keep them separate but handy.

Answers to the name of: _____

Breed or mix: _____

Sex: _____ Age: _____ Tag ID#: _____

Description of hair (color, length and texture): _____

_____

Indicate unusual markings or scars: _____

_____

TAIL: ( ) Short   ( ) Screw-type   ( ) Bushy   ( ) Cut

EARS: ( ) Clipped   ( ) Erect   ( ) Floppy

Weight: _____ Height: _____

If you have a recent photo of your pet, attach it to this form.

27
Things To Know
When Driving To Your Destination

1. Keep your dog confined with either a crate, barrier or car seat.

2. To avoid sliding in the event of sharp turns or sudden stops, be certain that your luggage, as well as your dog's crate are securely stored or fastened.

3. Be certain your vehicle is in good working order. Check brakelights, turn signals, hazard and headlights. Clean your windshield and top off washer fluid whenever you fill up. You'll be driving in unfamiliar territory so keep an eye on the gas gauge. Fill up when half full during daylight hours or at well-lit service stations.

4. A first aid kit, blanket, and sweets like hard candy will come in handy. When packing, include a flashlight, tool kit, paper towels, an extra leash, waterproof matches and a supply of plastic bags. During the winter months, keep an ice scraper, snow brush and small shovel in your car.

5. Never drive tired. Keep the music on, windows open. Fresh air can help you remain alert.

6. Keep your windshield clean, inside and out.

7. Avoid using sedatives or tranquilizers when driving.

8. Don't drink and drive.

9. Never try to drive and read a map at the same time. If you're driving alone, pull off at a well-lit gas station or roadside restaurant and check the map. If you're unsure of directions, ask for assistance from a safe source.

10. Wear your seatbelt. They save lives.

11. Keep car doors locked.

12. Good posture is especially important when driving. Do your back a favor and sit up straight. For lower back pain, wedge a small pillow between your back and the seat.

13. If you're the driver, eat frequent small snacks rather than large meals. You'll be less tired that way.

14. Don't use high beams in fog. The light will bounce back into your eyes as it reflects off the moisture.

15. When pulling off to the side of the road, use your flashers to warn other cars away.

16. Before beginning your drive each day, do a car check. Tire pressure okay? Leakage under car? Windows clean? Signals working? Mirrors properly adjusted? Gas tank full?

17. Roads can become particularly slippery at the onset of rain, the result of water mixing with dust and oil on the pavement. Slow down and exercise caution in wet weather.

18. Every so often, turn off your cruise control. Overuse can often lull you into inattention.

19. If you'll be doing a lot of driving into the sun, put a towel over the dashboard. It will provide some relief from the heat and brightness.

20. Even during the cooler months, your car can become stuffy. Keep your windows or sun roof open and let fresh air circulate.

21. Kids coming along? A small tape or CD player can amuse youngsters. Hand-held video games are also entertaining. And action figures are a good source for imaginary games. Put together a travel container and include markers or colored pencils, stamps, stickers, blunt safety scissors, and some pads of paper, both colored and lined.

22. If your car trip requires an overnight stay on route to your destination, pack a change of clothing and other necessities in a separate bag. Keep it in an accessible location.

23. When visiting wet and/or humid climates, take along insect repellent.

24. Guard against temperature extremes. In hot weather, protect your skin from the effects of the sun. Hazy days are just as dangerous to your skin as sunny ones. Pack plenty of sunscreen. Apply in the morning and then again in the early afternoon. The sun is strongest midday so avoid overexposure at that time. To remain comfortable, wear lightweight, loose fitting cotton clothing. Choose light colors. Dark ones attract the sun. In dry climates, remember to drink lots of liquids. Because the evaporation process speeds up in arid areas, you won't be aware of how much you're perspiring.

25. In cold climes, protect yourself from frostbite. If the temperature falls below 32° fahrenheit and the wind chill factor is also low, frostbite can occur in a matter of minutes. Layer your clothing. Cotton next to your skin and wool over that is the best insulator. Wear a hat to keep yourself warm - body heat escapes very quickly through your head.

26. Changes in altitude can cause altitude sickness. Whenever possible, slowly accustom yourself to the altitude change. Don't overexert yourself either. Symptoms of high altitude sickness occur more frequently over 8,000 feet and include dizziness, shortness of breath and headaches.

27. Store your maps, itinerary and related travel information in a clear plastic container (shoe box storage type with a lid works best). Keep it in the front of your vehicle in an easy-to-reach location.

WHAT YOU SHOULD KNOW ABOUT DRIVING IN THE DESERT

Water: Check your radiator before journeying into the desert. Outside of metropolitan areas, service stations are few and far between, even on major roads. Always carry extra water.

Gasoline: Since you'll be traveling through sparsely populated areas, fill up before beginning your desert adventure. When you have half a tank or less, refuel whenever you come upon a service station - you never know when you'll come across another.

Flashfloods: Summer thunderstorms in the desert can wreak havoc on the California road system, especially where roads dip into washes. The runoff quickly fills the washes, creating hazardous driving conditions and impassable roads. Heed the warning signs which pinpoint flash flood areas.

Dust storms: When a dust storm approaches, pull your vehicle off the road as far as possible, switch off your headlights and wait until the storm passes.

Breakdowns: Put on your hazard lights or raise the hood of your vehicle and remain with your vehicle until help arrives. Keep doors locked and do not open doors except for police officers. If you break down on a secluded back road and must seek help, retrace your route. Don't take any short cuts.

FIDO FACT:

- *Never leave your dog unattended in the car during the warm weather months or extremely cold ones.*

Desert survival

Acquiring the skills necessary to survive in the desert isn't the responsibility of just hikers and campers - any one of us could end up lost or stranded in the desert. All it takes is a flat tire, a wrong turn or a sprained ankle/paw and suddenly you're faced with a dire situation which requires survival skills you may or may not have. Remain calm. Think through your options. Use common sense and remain focused. Survivalists recommend that you stay with your vehicle. Do not attempt to walk through the desert. Dehydration, exposure and exhaustion are killers.

The best way to handle survival situations is to avoid them. But when you find yourself in a survival situation, the following tips may help.

- Pre-plan your hike and become familiar with the area.
- Know where the water sources are in the area you're hiking.
- Familiarize yourself with the local weather conditions.
- Avoid intense desert heat by taking early morning or evening hikes.
- Always carry a topographical map of the area you're hiking.
- Avoid sidetrips, they may only confuse you and cause you to lose your bearings.
- Carry as much drinking water as possible - it can save your life.
- If you're planning an overnight, establish camp near water.
- Inform a third party where you're going and when you'll be home. And then contact the person upon your return.
- Never overestimate your hiking abilities - know your limits.

Heat Stroke / Exhaustion

Both newcomers and longtime desert dwellers are susceptible to these potentially serious medical conditions. Early heat exhaustion indicators include: weakness, pale skin, dizziness, nausea, dehydration, muscle cramping and profuse sweating. Heat stroke symptoms include the above along with hot, dry, red skin. In either case, seek shade, cool off by fanning and apply damp cloths to face, neck and ears. Cases of heat stroke demand immediate medical attention.

Hypothermia

Although hypothermia is a serious medical condition most commonly associated with mountain hiking, desert hikers and campers are also susceptible. Temperatures do not have to dip below freezing for exposure to occur. In fact, hypothermia strikes most often in the 30-50° temperature range - a common temperature for winter nights in the desert. Damp clothing and a cool breeze can sometimes be enough to cause the body to lose heat faster than it can be replaced - causing cold shivers. If you experience unstoppable shivering, it's imperative that you put on dry clothes, wrap yourself in a blanket and drink hot liquids. Without these precautions, you can lapse into the second, and often fatal stage of hypothermia. When that occurs, there is little chance of the body rewarming itself without the aid of internal heating, conventional heating methods and immediate medical attention.

Keep your cool

- When traveling with Fido, it's a good idea to keep a cooler of cold towels in the car. Cold towels help to bring down a dog's body temperature after a long afternoon of hiking

- A wet handkerchief wrapped around your neck can keep you and Fido cool while hiking.

TRAVEL TRAINING

A well-trained, well-behaved dog is easy to live with and especially easy to travel with. There are basics other than "sit," "down," "stay" which you might want to incorporate into your training routine. Whenever you begin a training session, remember that your patience and your dog's attention span are the key elements. Training sessions should be 5-10 minutes each. Don't let yourself become discouraged or frustrated. Stick with it. After just a few lessons, your dog will respond. Dogs love to learn, to feel productive and accomplished. Training isn't punishment. It's a gift. A gift of love. You'll quickly see the difference training can make. Being with your dog will become a pleasant experience, something you'll anticipate, not dread. Most of all, keep a sense of humor. It's not punishment for you either.

Throughout this section, many references are made to puppies. But it's never too late for training to begin. The adage that you can't teach an old dog new tricks just isn't true. Patience and consistency combined with a reward system will provide excellent results.

Let's get social

When it comes to travel training, not enough can be said about the benefits of socialization. I regard the lessons of socialization as the foundation of a well-trained, well-behaved dog.

Whenever possible socialize your dog at an early age. Allow your puppy to be handled by many different people. Include men and children since puppies are inherently more fearful of both. At three months, you can join a puppy class. These classes are important because they provide puppies with the experience of being with other dogs. Your puppy will have the opportunity of putting down other dogs without inflicting harm and he'll also learn how to bounce back after being put down himself. Socialization can also be accomplished through walks around your neighborhood, visits to parks frequented by other dogs and children, or by working with friends who have dogs they also want to socialize.

❖₀

FIDO FACT:

- *Dog ownership is a common bond and the basis of impromptu conversations as well as lasting friendships.*

Walking on a leash

The same "paying attention" rules apply here. It's only natural for a puppy to pull at his leash. Instead of just pulling back, stop walking. Hold the leash to your chest. If your dog lets the leash slacken, say GOOD DOG. If he sits, say GOOD SIT. Then begin your walk again. Stop every ten feet or so and tell your dog to sit. Knowing he'll only be told to sit if he pulls, he'll eventually learn to pay attention to the next command. It makes sense to continue your training while on walks because your dog will learn to heed your commands under varying circumstances and environments. This will be especially important when traveling together. The lack of "tug of war" can mean the difference between enjoying or disliking the company of your pooch at home or away.

Chewing

Most dogs chew out of boredom. Teach your dog constructive chewing and eliminate destructive chewing. Teach your dog to chew on chew toys. An easy way to interest him in chewing is to stuff a hollow, nonconsumable chew toy with treats such as peanut butter, kibble or a piece of hard cheese. Once the toy is stuffed, attach a string to it and tempt your dog's interest by pulling the toy along. He'll take it from there.

Until you're satisfied that he won't be destructive, consider confining your pooch to one room or to his crate with a selection of chew toys. This is a particularly important training tool for dogs who must be left alone for long periods of time, and for dogs who travel with their owners. If your pooch knows not to chew destructively at home, those same good habits will remain with him on the road.

Bite inhibition

The trick here is to keep a puppy from biting in the first place, not break the bad habit after it's formed, although that too can be accomplished. Your puppy should be taught to develop a soft mouth by inhibiting the force of his bites. As your dog grows into adolescence, he should continue to be taught to soften his bite and as an adult dog should learn never to mouth at all.

Allow your puppy to bite but whenever force is exhibited, say OUCH! If he continues to bite, say OUCH louder and then leave the room. When you return to the room, let the puppy come next to you and calm down. Your pup will begin to associate the bite and OUCH with the cessation of playtime and will learn to mouth more softly. Even when your puppy's bites no longer hurt, pretend they do. Once this training is finished, you'll have a dog that will not mouth. A dog who will not accidentally injure people you meet during your travels.

Jumping dogs

Dogs usually jump on people to get their attention. A fairly simple way to correct this habit is to teach your dog to sit and stay until released.
When your dog is about to meet new people, put him in the sit/stay position. Be sure to praise him for obeying the command and then pet him to give him the attention he craves. Ask friends and visitors to help reinforce the command.

Come

The secret to this command is to begin training at an early age. But as I've said before, older dogs can also learn. It might just take a little longer. From the time your pup's brought home, call him by name and say COME every time you're going to feed him. The association will be simple. He'll soon realize that goodies await him if he responds to your call. Try another approach as well. Sit in your favorite armchair and call to your dog every few minutes. Reward him with praise and sometimes with a treat. Take advantage of normally occurring circumstances, such as your dog approaching you. Whenever you can anticipate that your dog is coming toward you, command COME as he nears you. Then reward him with praise for doing what came naturally.

NEVER order your dog to COME for a punishment. If he's caught in the act of negative behavior, walk to him and then reprimand.

Pay attention

Train your dog to listen to you during his normal routines. For example, when your dog is at play in the yard, call him to you. When he comes, have him sit and praise him. Then release him to play again. It will quickly become apparent that obeying will not mean the end of playtime. Instead it will mean that he'll be petted and praised and then allowed to play again.

Communication - talking to your dog

Training isn't just about teaching your dog to sit or give his paw. Training is about teaching your pooch to become an integral part of your life. To fit into your daily routine. And into your leisure time. Take notice of how your dog studies you, anticipates your next move. Incorporate his natural desire to please into your training. Let him know what you're thinking, how you're feeling. Talk to him as you go about your daily routines. He'll soon come to understand the differences in your voice, your facial expressions, hand movements and body language. He'll know when you're happy or angry with him or with anyone else. If you want him to do something, speak to him. For example, if you want him to fetch his ball, ask him in an emphatic way, stressing the word ball. He won't understand at first, so fetch it yourself and tell him ball. Put the ball down and then later repeat the command. He'll soon know what you want when you use the term ball with specific emphasis.

Training Do's & Don'ts

1. Never hit your dog.

2. Praise and reward your dog for good behavior. Don't be embarrassed to lavish praise upon a dog who's earned it.

3. Unless you catch your dog in a mischievous act, don't punish him. He will not understand what he did wrong. And when you do punish, go to your dog. Never use the command COME for punishment.

4. Don't repeat a command. Say the command in a firm voice only once. If your dog doesn't obey, return to the training method for the disobeyed command.

5. Don't be too eager or too reticent to punish. Most of all, be consistent.

6. Don't encourage fearfulness. If your dog has a fear of people or places, work with him to overcome this fear rather than ignoring it, or believing it can't be changed.

7. Don't ignore or encourage aggression.

8. Don't use food excessively as a reward. Although food is useful in the beginning of training, it must be phased out as the dog matures.

8 Ways To Prevent Aggression in Your Dog

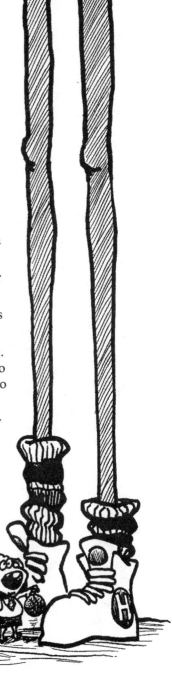

1. Socialize him at an early age.

2. Under your supervision, let him play with children.

3. Never be abusive towards your dog by hitting or yelling at him.

4. Offer plenty of praise when he's behaving himself.

5. Be consistent with training. Make sure your dog responds to your commands before you do anything for him.

6. Don't handle your dog roughly or play aggressively with him.

7. Neuter your dog.

8. Your dog is a member of the family. Treat him that way. Tied to a pole is not a life.

Lodging Guidelines For You and Your Pooch

Conduct yourself in a courteous manner and you'll continue to be welcome anywhere you travel. Never do anything on vacation with your pooch that you wouldn't do at home. Some quick tips that can make traveling with your pooch more enjoyable.

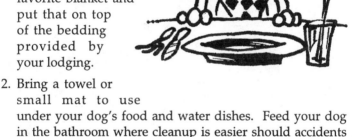

1. Don't allow your dog to sleep on the bed with you. If that's what your dog is accustomed to doing, take along a sheet or favorite blanket and put that on top of the bedding provided by your lodging.

2. Bring a towel or small mat to use under your dog's food and water dishes. Feed your dog in the bathroom where cleanup is easier should accidents occur.

3. Try to keep your dog off the furniture. Take along a washable lint and hair remover to remove unwanted hairs.

4. When you walk your dog, carry plastic bags and/or paper towels for clean up.

5. Always keep your dog on a leash on the hotel and motel grounds.

Can my pooch be left alone in the room?

Only you know the answer to that. If your dog is not destructive, if he doesn't bark incessantly, and the hotel allows unattended dogs, you might consider leaving him in the room for short periods of time —
say when you dine out. In any case, hang the "Do Not Disturb" sign on your door to alert the chambermaid or anyone else that your room shouldn't be entered.

Consider doing the following when you plan to leave your dog unattended:

1. Walk or otherwise exercise your pooch. An exercised dog will fall asleep more easily.

2. Provide a chew or toy.

3. Turn on the TV or radio for audio/visual companionship.

4. Make sure there is an ample amount of fresh water available.

5. Calm your dog with a reassuring goodbye and a stroke of your hand.

Take your dog's temperament into account:

- Is he a pleaser?
- Is he the playful sort?
- Does he love having tasks to perform?
- Does he like to retrieve? To carry?

Dogs, like people, have distinct person-alities...mellow, hyper, shy or outgo-ing. Take advan-tage of your dog's unique charac-teristics. A hyper dog can amuse you with hours of playful frolicking. A laid-back pooch will

cuddle beside you offering warm companionship. An outgo-ing dog will help you make friends.

If you can combine what you know of your dog's personality with what you want to teach, your dog will train more easily. Together you'll achieve a unique compatibility.

WHAT AND HOW DO I PACK FOR MY POOCH?

Be prepared

Dogs enjoy the adventure of travel. If your dog is basically well behaved and physically healthy, he will make an excellent traveling companion. But traveling times will be more successful with just a little common sense and preparation.

Just as many children (and adults I might add) travel with their own pillow, your pooch will also enjoy having his favorites with him. Perhaps you'll want to include the blanket he sleeps with or his favorite toy or chew. Not only will a familiar item make him feel more at ease but he'll have a toy along to keep him occupied and give him something to do.

To keep things simple from vacation to vacation, I use two travel bags which I restock at the end of each vacation. That way, I'm always prepared for the next one. You'll want to include some or all of the following:

- A blanket to cover the back seat of your car.
- Two or three old towels for emergencies.
- Two bowls, one for water, the other for food.
- Plastic clean up bags (supermarket produce bags work well).
- Paper towels — for spills, clean up and everything in between.
- A long line of rope. You'll be surprised how often you'll use this very handy item.
- An extra collar and lead.
- Can opener and spoon.
- Flashlight.
- An extra flea and tick collar.
- Dog brush.

- Small scissors.
- Blunt end tweezers — great for removing thorns and cactus needles.
- Chew toys, balls, frisbees, treats — whatever your pooch prefers.
- Nightlight.
- A room deodorizer.
- A handful of zip-lock bags in several sizes.
- Pre-moistened towelettes. Take along two packs. Put one in your suitcase, the other in the glove compartment of your car. More than just great for cleaning your hands, they'll serve a dozen uses.
- Dog food — enough for a couple of days. Most brands are available throughout the country — either at pet stores, supermarkets or veterinary offices. But, you'll want to take enough to eliminate having to find a store that's open the first night or two of your vacation.
- Water — a full container from home — top off as needed to gradually accustom your dog to his new water supply.

Special tip: When hiking with your dog, large zip-lock bags make great portable water bowls. Just roll down the sides to form a bowl and add water.

Packing made easy...12 tips!

I've said it before but I'll say it again. No matter where your travels take you, whether it's to the local park or on a cross-country trip, never leave home without your dog's leash and a handful of plastic bags or pooper scooper. I still remember those awful moments when I ended up without one or both.

1. Consolidate. Even if you're traveling as a family, one tube of toothpaste and one hair dryer should suffice.

2. Avoid potential spills by wrapping perfume, shampoo and other liquids together and placing them in large zip-lock plastic bags.

3. When packing, layer your clothing using inter-locking patterns. You'll fit more into your suitcase and have less shifting and wrinkling.

4. Keep a duplicate copy of your itinerary in a safe place. Record flight info, car rental confirmation numbers, travel agent telephone numbers, lodging info, etc.

5. Take along a night light, especially if you're traveling with a child.

6. Stash a supply of zip-lock plastic bags, moist towelettes, several trash bags, an extra leash (or rope) and a plastic container in an accessible place.

7. If you plan to hike with your children, give each a whistle; they're great for signaling help.

8. Include a can opener and a flashlight.

9. Comfortable walking shoes are a must. If you plan on hiking, invest in a sturdy pair of hiking boots, but be sure to break them in before your trip. Take along an extra pair of socks whenever you hike.

10. Don't forget to include first aid kits. One for dogs and one for people.

11. Include an extra pair of glasses or contact lenses. And don't forget to take a copy of your eyeglass prescription.

12. Keep medications in separate, clearly marked containers.

CRATE TRAINING IS GREAT TRAINING

Many people erroneously equate the crate to jail. But that's only a human perspective. To a dog who's been properly crate trained, the crate represents a private place within your home where your dog will feel safe and secure. It is much better to prevent behavioral problems by crate training than to merely give up on an unruly dog.

4 REASONS WHY CRATE TRAINING IS GOOD FOR YOU

1. You can relax when you leave your dog home alone. You'll know that he is safe, comfortable and incapable of destructive behavior.

2. You can housebreak your pooch faster. The confinement encourages control and helps establish a regular walk-time routine.

3. You can safely confine your dog to prevent unforseen situations. For example, if he's sick, if you have workers or guests that are either afraid or allergic to dogs, or if your canine becomes easily excited or confused when new people enter the scene.

4. You can travel with your pooch. Use of a crate eliminates the potential for distraction and assures that your dog will not get loose during your travels.

FIDO FACT:

- *If your dog is lonely for you when he's left alone, try leaving your voice on a tape and let it play during your absence.*

5 REASONS WHY CRATE TRAINING IS GOOD FOR THE POOCH

1. He'll have an area for rest when he's tired, stressed or sick.

2. He'll be exposed to fewer bad behavior temptations which can result in punishment.

3. He'll have an easier time learning to control calls of nature.

4. He'll feel more secure when left alone.

5. He'll be thrilled to join you in your travels.

SOME DO'S AND DONT'S

- DO exercise your dog before crating and as soon as you let him out.

- DO provide your pooch with his favorite toy and blanket.

- DO place the crate in a well-used, well-ventilated area of your home.

- DO make sure that you can always approach your dog while he is in his crate. This will insure that he does not become overly protective of his space.

- DON'T punish your dog in his crate or banish him to the crate.

- DON'T leave your pooch in the crate for more than four hours at a time.

- DON'T let curious kids invade his private place. This is his special area.

- DON'T confine your dog to the crate if he becomes frantic or completely miserable.

- DON'T use a crate without proper training.

Hiking...
a walk through nature

Hiking conjures up images of rugged outdoor types, standing tall on mountaintops, wind in their hair, outfitted with sturdy, specially designed vests, pockets filled with intriguing paraphernalia.

While there might have been a time when hiking was an activity with limited appeal, America's obsession with physical fitness has changed all that. Hiking has become a popular pastime. In addition to the physical benefits associated with hiking, consider the pleasures to be found in nature. And other than the simple gear and supplies you might want to include, hiking is free.

There's something special about hiking, particularly with a canine companion. It's truly time of the highest quality. Time when the phone isn't ringing, when hours seem endless and when a little dirt is part of the experience, not a disaster. Share an invigorating hike with your pooch. It will be an experience you'll want to repeat again and again.

Hiking on a marked trail provides a sense of fulfillment and security. Both goal-oriented types who like to feel they've accomplished something and novices who want to know what to expect will appreciate marked hiking trails. Knowing the length of the trail, the time required, a bit about the terrain and the sights to be expected also adds to the pleasures of hiking.

Hiking can be a total exploration of a defined area or merely a slice of nature. You set the distances and the time. Hike in for half an hour and then retrace your steps. Do a loop trail with predetermined mileage. Or do it all, see it all.

Some words of advice for novice hikers

Begin with easy trails. Learn what to take along, what to leave at home. Find a pace that suits your walking style. For that's what hiking is — walking with a purpose. Easy trails are usually found in low lying areas. Although the terrain might change from level, even ground to more hilly contours, for the most part, you'll experience a trail without obstacles.

Intermediate level trails are more rugged. Typically, they might be found in mountainous areas. Along the trail you might have to wade through shallow streams, make your way through brush, among rocks and fallen trees. You can expect changes in elevation that will require some exertion and provide more of an aerobic workout. If you're new to hiking but in good physical condition, you shouldn't have difficulty with intermediate hiking trails. Set a comfortable pace and rest whenever you feel tired.

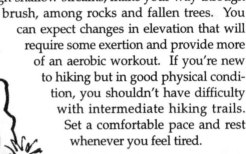

Expert trails are usually steeper and more challenging. Stamina, agility and fitness all come into play. You might have to scale boulders, ascend and descend precipitous escarpments or maintain your balance on slippery rocks. Expert trails should not be attempted by beginner hikers. Even intermediates should only hike the more difficult trails after they've accumulated some "hiking points" in the intermediate arena. Take into account your dog's ability as well as your own when deciding where to hike. In any case, don't hike expert trails alone, and let someone know where you're hiking and when to expect your return.

Hiking is an experience that's enjoyable to share. With your pooch, with your friends. That's not to say that solitary hikers don't enjoy themselves — many solitary hikers prefer the peacefulness of nature without the distractions of other people.

Eileen's "BE PREPARED" approach to hiking

The day hikes I've detailed in *Doin' California With Your Pooch!* will be more pleasurable if you travel with a light load. Invest in a well-made, lightweight fanny pack with built-in water bottles and several zippered compartments, large enough to hold the following items.

1. Penlight size flashlight with fresh batteries and bulb.

2. A small box of waterproof matches - the type that light when scratched on just about anything.

3. A large trash bag, folded into a small square. This serves three purposes. It's an instant raincoat (just punch out arm and head holes), a receptacle for trash and a seat covering for cold/wet ground.

4. A bandana. This simple cotton garment serves as a washcloth, headband, cool compress, etc. It folds up into nothing or can be worn around your neck to save fanny pack room.

5. Lip balm with UV protection.

6. Small travel size tube of sunscreen. Use in sunny or hazy weather, especially at high altitudes.

7. Nylon windbreaker. Many sporting goods stores sell the type that fold up and fit into their own case.

8. Soft felt hat. Great protection from the sun, it's easily stored or safety pinned to your pack.

9. A whistle. Wear it around your neck on a tripled piece of string which is also handy to have along. Three whistle blasts are the signal for help.

10. Small map magnifier (doubles as a fire starter).

11. Water bottle(s) with squirt top. If water supplies run low, a squirt in your mouth or your dog's will temporarily relieve thirst.

12. Sunglasses with UV protective lenses can be worn or left dangling on an eyeglass holder.

13. Travel-size first aid kit.

14. An extra pair of socks.

15. Grocery produce bags. They're great for doggie clean up and as an emergency barrier between wet socks and dry feet.

16. A small, non-aerosol spray can of insect repellent. Spray yourself and your pooch before the hike and leave the can in the car.

17. A couple of safety pins.

18. A multi-use, swiss army-type knife.

19. A compass if you know how to use one.

20. A map of the area or a copy of the trail description/information.

Depending on conditions, weather and personal preferences, you might also want to include:

- A walking stick for the extra balance it provides (ski poles are great).

- An extra sweater or jacket. Two or three lighter layered articles of clothing are better than one heavy garment. Layering locks in air between garments, warms the air and then warms you.

FIDO FACT:

- *Fido's fitness counts towards insuring a longer, healthier life. In this arena, you're the one in control. The most common cause of ill health in canines is obesity. Approximately 60% of all adult dogs are overweight or will become overweight due to lack of physical activity and overfeeding. Much like humans, the medical consequences of obesity include liver, heart and orthopedic problems. As little as a few extra pounds on a small dog can lead to health-related complications.*

What about the pooch

Your pooch can be outfitted with side saddle bags —
small but roomy enough to carry all his needs. When you
pack his saddle bags, keep the weight even on both sides for
balance. Include the following:

1. Water bottles with spritzer tops
2. Bones, biscuits or treats
3. Small grooming brush
4. A chamois for drying
5. An extra leash
6. A line of rope
7. A ball, soft frisbee or other favorite toy

100
Ways To Be A Better Hiker

The following tips and info will add to your enjoyment of the outdoors and help prepare you for the unexpected.

1. Never hike in a new pair of hiking boots. Always break in boots before hiking.

2. Buy smart. To get a good fit, try boots on with the type of socks you'll be wearing. COMFORT is the key word in boot selection. After comfort, look for support and traction. For day hikers, a lightweight, well-made, sturdy boot is the number one choice.

3. Water, water everywhere, but not a drop to drink. Drink plenty of water before you begin and pack enough to last through your hike. Although there may be water available trailside in the form of lakes and streams, unless you're experienced and properly prepared to purify the water, don't drink it.

4. Carry a generous supply of grocery-type plastic bags for clean up. Keep extras in your car and suitcase.

5. Dress in layers. Peel off or add clothing as weather dictates. Cotton next to the skin with wool over it is the most comfortable. The exception is during wet weather when cotton is a negative because it takes too long to dry and offers little insulation.

6. Pack extra clothing, most importantly a second pair of socks and a nylon windbreaker.

7. If your feet are cold, put on a hat. Body heat escapes through the head.

8. Before you begin your trip, make sure all hiking apparel is in good repair. Check for loose buttons, open seams, stuck zippers. Lubricate zipper slides and teeth with wax or a spray lubricant.

9. Don't litter, carry out your trash.

10. Leave only footprints, take only memories.

11. Carry a small first-aid kit and learn some basic skills.

12. Avoid wet, soggy socks and boots. If you know the trail includes crossing streams or creeks, pack a pair of all-terrain sandals to use instead of your boots. Or use plastic grocery bags under your wool socks.

13. Carry your own water and top off at every opportunity.

14. In warm weather hiking, freeze your filled water bottles the night before your trip, leaving room for expansion. Your water supply will remain cooler.

15. Take along an extra leash or line of rope for unforeseen emergencies.

16. Set a comfortable pace. Don't overexert yourself, there's always tomorrow.

17. Ski poles make great walking sticks.

18. Before you begin any hiking trip, tell a reliable person your plans. Include an estimated time for your return and make sure you let them know when you've returned.

19. Pack picnic goodies in reusable containers or plastic zip-lock bags.

20. For an instant water bowl, include a large size zip-lock bag. With the sides rolled down, it makes a terrific water bowl for your pooch.

21. Spray exposed arms, legs and face area with insect repellent. Spray your pooch too but remember to avoid spraying near the eyes.

22. Sites containing Native American relics should be treated with respect. Do not disturb or remove anything.

23. Nature is soft and serene - behave accordingly.

24. Blend in with your surroundings.

25. Wear light colored clothing. When it's warm and sunny, dark colors attract the sun and mosquitoes.

26. Every hour or so, take a ten-minute break. In warm weather, select a shady spot. In cooler weather, find a sunny, wind-protected area. In cold weather, sit on something other than the ground.

27. Should a lightning or thunderstorm occur, find shelter away from mountain peaks or exposed slopes.

28. Stow some high energy snacks in your pack. Include some biscuits and a chew for your pooch.

29. A small roll of duct tape can repair just about anything.

30. Consider your dog's age and physical capabilities when you plan trips.

31. Stop and look around and in back of you as you hike. The views are always different.

32. A large garbage bag can double as an emergency rain coat. Just punch holes for your head and arms.

33. Some basic geology knowledge will go a long way towards enhancing your outdoor experience.

34. View your surroundings as if you're in an outdoor museum, you'll see and enjoy more.

35. Wear sunglasses to protect your eyes and a hat to protect your scalp from UV rays and direct sunlight.

36. Apply a minimum 15 SPF sunscreen to all exposed parts of your body, particularly your face. Reapply after swimming or after several hours.

37. Carry a UV-protected lip balm and apply frequently.

38. Always clean up after your pooch. The fact that dog owners don't clean up after their dogs is the number one complaint to federal, state and local agencies governing public lands. In some areas, dogs have been banned because of these complaints. Do your share so dogs will continue to be welcome.

39. A box of waterproof matches can be a lifesaver.

40. Keep a multi-purpose knife in your hiking gear.

41. Remember you have to walk out as far as you've walked in.

42. Don't begin a hike towards evening. Hiking in darkness is dangerous.

43. Practice trail etiquette. Allow fast-walking hikers to pass you.

44. Carry your dog's leash even in areas where he is permitted to run free.

45. Keep your dog on a leash in wildlife areas, for his protection and the protection of wildlife.

46. Dogs must be leashed in all developed campgrounds.

47. Dogs are not permitted to swim in public pools.

48. Control your dog at all times. One unruly dog can cause problems for every dog.

49. Unless your dog responds to voice commands, keep him leashed in crowded areas or on well-used trails.

50. Certain breeds of dogs are inclined to chase wildlife. Know your own dog. If you feel he might do harm to the wildlife, the terrain or himself, keep him leashed.

51. Get into shape before your trip. Start with short walks and lengthen them, increasing your pace as you do. Take your dog along and get him in shape too.

52. Make exercise an integral part of your daily routine. Whenever there's a choice, take the stairs. Park a few streets from your destination and then walk.

53. Ten minutes of easy stretching before any physical activity will minimize the chance of injury. Avoid jerky movements. Stretch the hamstrings, shoulders, back, legs, arms and Achilles tendon.

54. Go for comfort. Avoid tight constrictive clothing.

55. Socks should fit well and be clean. Loose, ill-fitting or dirty socks can cause blisters.

56. Educate yourself on the area's flora and fauna and you'll have a more interesting hike.

57. During warmer months or in desert terrain, drink plenty of water before and during your hike. You won't always know when your body is becoming dehydrated because perspiration dries very quickly. You might not feel thirsty but your body will be.

(DON'T FORGET TO WATER THE POOCH!)

58. If you use a backpack, buy one with wide straps so it won't dig into your skin.

59. Pack a whistle - a series of three blasts is the recognized distress signal.

60. Even if you intend to begin and end your hike during daylight hours, pack a small flashlight with fresh batteries and bulb for emergencies.

61. Wear a watch or keep one handy. Time flies by without reference points. Remember, it's going to take as long to hike out as it did to hike in.

62. As the name implies, trail mix makes a great hiking snack.

63. Be prepared for unexpected weather changes. Tune in to a local radio station before beginning your hiking.

64. Hypothermia is the number one outdoor killer. As soon as you feel chilled, put on an extra layer of clothing. Don't wait until you're cold.

65. Feeling warm, remove a layer.

66. If you're hiking and rain or wet conditions are expected, don't wear cotton. Synthetic fabrics and wool offer the best insulation when wet.

67. A long time favorite of hikers are wool rag socks. Thick and absorbent, they'll keep your feet warm even when wet. They'll also provide cushioning. Take along an extra pair.

68. Liner socks are also popular. Similar to the thin socks worn under ski boots, they're usually made of wool, silk or a synthetic. Liner socks are softer to the touch and can be worn under heavier socks.

69. When hiking in cooler temperatures, two light sweaters are better than one heavy sweater.

70. Slow your pace when descending a trail to avoid potential injury.

71. If the weather turns unpredictably cold but you still want to hike, plastic produce bags can be used to keep your feet warm. Put them on your bare feet, wrap the top around your ankles and put on your socks. The plastic becomes a barrier and prevents body heat from escaping.

72. Wide brimmed soft felt hats are great for hiking. They fold up into nothing and even in hot summer months, they can be comfortable. Simply air condition them by cutting out hearts or triangles with a pair of scissors.

73. Disposable polyethylene gloves, the kind sold in paint stores, make great glove liners. They'll keep your hands toasty warm in the coldest climes.

74. An old-fashioned bandana can become a washcloth, head-band, cool compress, napkin and a dozen other useful items. Wrap one around your dog's neck too.

75. Consider side saddle bags for your pooch to wear. He'll feel productive and help carry the load.

76. A small map magnifier can double as a fire starter.

77. Disposable cameras are lightweight and easy to include on a day hike. The panoramic-type captures California the best.

78. In the summer, fannypacks are cooler to use than backpacks.

79. Fruit, fresh or sun dried, is a quick energy source. Peel a couple of oranges or tangerines before your hike and store in zip-lock baggies. You'll always have a light snack at your fingertips.

80. Cut your toenails a few days before your hike or trip. Long toenails can cripple a hiker, especially descending a steep trail.

81. Before your trip, wear your pack at home with a typical load until you're certain it's comfortable.

82. If your feet or hands begin to feel swollen during your hike, find a shady tree and elevate your feet higher than your head. Hold your arms up in the air at the same time. Three minutes ought to do the trick and redistribute the blood throughout your body.

83. Begin a hike wearing only enough clothing to keep you just shy of comfortable. After the first ten minutes of exertion, you'll feel warmer and be happier with less on.

84. After walking through mud, loose dirt, sand or other clogging substances, clear your boot's cleats and restore their traction with a sharp kick at a sturdy tree or boulder.

85. Use your arms to make hiking more controlled and aerobic. Don't let them hang limply beside you. Swing them as you walk; use them for balance.

86. Take along a package of pre-moistened towelettes and travel-size tissues.

87. Take a trash bag along and clean the trail on your way out.

88. Puffy cumulus clouds usually mean fair weather.

89. A ring around the moon forecasts rain or snow.

90. Bad weather warnings — a red sky at dawn, the absence of dew on the grass or an early morning rainbow.

91. When bad weather threatens, avoid high, open places, lakes, meadows, exposed slopes and lone or towering trees. Seek shelter in caves, canyon bottoms or areas of the forest with shorter, relatively equal sized trees.

92. To gauge lightning- every five seconds between flash and boom equals a mile in distance.

93. When cumulus clouds blend together and the bottoms darken, a storm is on the way.

94. Yellow sunsets and still moist air can signal bad weather.

95. Make your own folding cup. Flatten a waxed paper cup or a paper cone cup and tuck into your pocket. Unfold when needed.

96. Carry safety pins.

97. To prevent spillage, store your canteen or water bottle in a plastic bag.

98. Do not undertake more than you can handle. Recognize your limitations and the limitations of your canine.

99. While you're hiking, if you become too hot, too cold, too tired, too anything, other than ecstatic, take a rest or begin your return.

100. High altitude sickness can occur in elevations over 7,000 feet. Whenever possible, slowly accustom yourself to changes in altitude. Symptoms include lightheadedness, faintness, headaches and dryness. If you experience any of these symptoms, stop, rest, seek shade, and drink plenty of water.

TIPS FOR TIDEPOOLING

View tidepools during a minus tide.

At minus tide you'll be able to observe the full intertidal zone. Local newspapers publish high and low tides, but to anticipate the season's best days, you'll need a yearly table, available at stores specializing in marine items.

Don't turn your back to the ocean.

Avoid being swept away by rogue waves.

Observe posted rules at each location.

Most places forbid collecting of live creatures.

Watch your step.

Green algae areas aren't the only slippery ones. Rocks with a dark, almost black covering can also be slick as ice.

Watch the rising tide.

The route you took at low tide may be underwater when the high tide comes back in.

Wear shorts.

Or wear a pair of long pants that you can easily roll up.

Put rocks back into place.

Exposed animals can die. Be careful when you replace the rock that you don't crush the animal.

CANINE CAMPER

Traditionally canine campers have been welcome in our national forests. Owners however should be aware that problems with dogs in many recreation areas have increased in recent years. The few rules that apply to dogs are meant to assure that you and other visitors have enjoyable outdoor experiences. Although it's fun to treat Rover to a day or night in the forest, not everyone appreciates his behavior.

In a study done several years ago in developed recreation areas, one of every eight dogs was involved in either a complaint as a result of their behavior or a warning to the owner for not observing rules. If the situation worsens, more rules and stronger enforcement action will be necessary, possibly resulting in a ban on pets in some areas. Dog owners must be responsible for their pets.

Your fellow visitor's reaction will be a major factor in determining whether or not dogs continue to be welcome in national forest recreation and wilderness areas. To avoid complaints from other visitors, please follow these rules:

- When you bring your dog, assume responsibility for him. Be courteous and remember not all visitors like dogs in their campsites and that dogs are not permitted on beaches that are designated for swimming.

- Leave vicious or unusually noisy dogs at home. If they disturb or threaten anyone, they will not be allowed in public recreation areas.

- The law requires that you have your dog on a leash at all times in developed areas.

- Developed campgrounds are for people, not animals. Please do not bring more than two dogs or other pets into any one campsite.

- Make preparations for your dog before bringing him into wilderness areas. Remember that you have hiking boots to protect your feet. Consider your dog's pads and feet. Keep your pet leashed in the wild. Dogs are predators by nature and will chase wildlife and stock animals. Any dog found running at large in national forest areas may be captured and impounded.

After you return home from a backcountry trip, keep an eye on your pet for any signs of illness. If your pet develops diarrhea, have a vet check him for giardia. This small parasite is often found in streams and lakes. Check your pooch for ticks, foxtails and burrs as well.

ROCKHOUNDING WITH THE HOUND

California is a rockhound's dream. From agate to multi-colored onyx, quartz crystals to jasper, garnet clusters to chalcedony roses, gold nuggets to azurite, obsidian to geode, chrysocolla to selenite clusters, California is world renowned as a rockhounder's heaven. For more detailed information on houndable gems and minerals, along with the top hounding hotspots, contact your local gem and mineral club or Chamber of Commerce.

Since most rockhounding adventures take you into remote areas, it's a good idea to hound with a group. But if you and Digger are treasure seeking loners, inform a third party where you're going and when you'll be back. Also, pack plenty of drinking water along with an updated map of the area.

Regardless of the temptation, stay out of mines. They are deathtraps capable of caving in with the smallest disturbance. They are also home to rattlesnakes and other poisonous creatures. For the most part, mines are privately owned and marked with "No Trespassing" signs or surrounded by a fence. For your safety and your pooch's - keep out and keep safe. Leave things as they are unless you've been told that it is okay to remove rocks, or you're in an area designated specifically for rockhounding.

❧ ❧ ❧ ❧ ❧ ❧ ❧ ❧ ❧ ❧ ❧ ❧ ❧ ❧ ❧ ❧ ❧ ❧ ❧ ❧

FIDO FACT:

- *Former First Lady Barbara Bush: "An old dog that has served you long and well is like an old painting. The patina of age softens and beautifies, and like a master's work, can never be replaced by exactly the same thing, ever again."*

37
WAYS TO HAVE A BETTER VACATION WITH YOUR POOCH

Some tips and suggestions to increase your enjoyment when you and the pooch hit the road.

1. Don't feed or water your pooch just before starting on your trip. Feed and water your dog approximately two hours before you plan to depart. Or better still, if it's a short trip, wait until you arrive at your destination.

2. Exercise your pooch before you leave. A tired dog will fall off to sleep more easily and adapt more readily to new surroundings.

3. Take along a large container of water to avoid potential stomach upset. Your dog will do better drinking from his own water supply for the first few days. And having water along will mean you can stop wherever you like and not worry about finding water. Gradually accustom your pooch to his new source of water by topping off your water container with local water.

4. Plan stops along your trip. Just like you, your pooch will enjoy stretching his legs. Along your route, there will be many areas conducive to dog freedom. And you'll be surprised how satisfying these little stops will be for you as well. If you make the car ride an agreeable part of your trip, your vacation will begin the moment you leave home - not just when you reach your ultimate destination.

5. While driving, keep windows open enough to allow the circulation of fresh air but not enough to allow your dog to jump out. If you have air conditioning, that will keep your dog cool enough.

6. Don't let your dog hang his head out of the window. Eyes, ears and throats can become inflamed.

7. Use a short leash when walking your pooch through public areas — he'll be easier to control.

8. Take along your dog's favorite objects from home. If they entertain him at home, they'll entertain him on vacation.

9. Before any trip, allow your pooch to relieve himself.

10. Cover your back seat with an old blanket or towel to protect the upholstery.

11. A room freshener under the seat of your car will keep it smelling fresh. Take along an extra deodorizer for your room.

12. If your dog has a tendency for carsickness, keep a small packet of honey (many restaurants offer them with toast) in the glove compartment or carry a roll of hard candy — like Lifesavers — with you. Either of these might help with carsickness.

13. Use a flea and tick collar on your pooch.

14. When traveling in warm weather months, drape a damp towel over your dog's crate. This allows ventilation and the moist, cooler air will reduce the heat.

15. Before you begin a trip, expose your pooch to experiences he will encounter while traveling; such as crowds, noise, people, elevators, walks along busy streets, and stairs (especially those with open risers).

16. Shade moves. If you must leave your dog in the car for a short period of time, make sure the shade that protects him when you park will be there by the time you return. As a general rule though, it's best not to leave your dog in a parked car. <u>NEVER LEAVE YOUR DOG IN THE CAR DURING THE WARM SUMMER MONTHS</u>. In the colder months, beware of hypothermia, a life threatening condition that occurs when an animal's body temperature falls below normal. Short-haired dogs and toys are very susceptible to illness in extremely cold weather.

17. Take along a clip-on minifan for airless hotel rooms.

18. When packing, include a heating pad, ice pack and a few safety pins.

19. A handful of clothespins will serve a dozen purposes, from clamping motel curtains shut to sealing a bag of potato chips... they're great.

20. A night light will help you find the bathroom in the dark.

21. Don't forget that book you've been meaning to read.

22. Include a journal and record your travel memories.

23. Pack a roll of duct tape. Use it to repair shoes, patch suitcases or strap lunch onto the back of a rented bicycle, to name just a few.

24. Never begin a vacation with a new pair of shoes.

25. Pooper scoopers make clean up simple and sanitary. Plastic vegetable bags from the supermarket are great too.

26. FYI, in drier climates, many accommodations have room humidifiers available for guest use. Arrange for one when you make your reservation.

27. Use unbreakable bowls and storage containers for your dog's food and water needs.

28. Don't do anything on the road with your pooch that you wouldn't do at home.

29. Brown and grey tinted sun lenses are the most effective for screening bright light. Polarized lenses reduce the blinding glare of the sun.

30. Before you leave on vacation, safeguard your home. Either ask neighbors to take in your mail and newspapers, or arrange with your mail carrier to hold your mail. Stop newspaper delivery. Use timers and set them so that a couple of lights go on and off. Unplug small appliances and electronics. Lock all doors and windows. Place steel bars or wooden dowels in the tracks of all sliding glass doors or windows. Ladders or other objects that could be used to gain entrance into your home should be stored in your garage or inside your home. Arrange to have your lawn mowed. And don't forget to take out the garbage.

31. Pack some snacks and drinks in a small cooler.

32. As a precaution when traveling, once you arrive at your final destination, check the yellow pages for the nearest vet and determine emergency hours and location.

33. NEVER permit your dog to travel in the bed of a pickup truck. If you must, there are safety straps available at auto supply stores that can be used to insure the safety of your dog. Never use a choke chain, rope or leash around your dog's neck to secure him in the bed of a pickup.

34. Take along a spray bottle of water. A squirt in your dog's mouth will temporarily relieve his thirst.

35. Heavy duty zip-lock type bags make great traveling water bowls. Just roll down edges, form a bowl and fill with water. They fold up into practically nothing. Keep one in your purse, jacket pocket or fanny pack. Keep an extra in your glove compartment.

36. Arrange with housekeeping to have your room cleaned while you're present or while you're out with your pooch.

37. Traveling with children too? Keep them occupied with colored pencils and markers. Avoid crayons — they can melt in the sun. Take along question cards from trivia games as well as a pack of playing cards. Travel size magnetic games like checkers and chess are also good diversions. Don't forget those battery operated electronic games either. Include a book of crossword puzzles, a pair of dice and a favorite stuffed animal for cuddling time. In the car, games can include finding license plates from different states, spotting various makes or colors of cars, saying the alphabet backwards, or completing the alphabet from roadsigns.

TRAVELING BY PLANE

Quick Takes:

- Always travel on the same flight as your dog. And personally ascertain that your dog has been put on board before you board the plane.

- Book direct, nonstop flights.

- Upon boarding, inform a flight attendant that your pooch is traveling in the cargo hold.

- Early morning or late evening flights are best in the summer, while afternoon flights are best in the winter.

- Fill the water tray of your dog's travel carrier with ice cubes rather than water. This will prevent spillage during loading.

- Clip your dog's nails to prevent them from hooking in the crate's door, holes or other openings.

Dog carriers/kennels

Most airlines require pets to be in specific carriers. Airline regulations vary and arrangements should be made well in advance of travel. Some airlines allow small dogs to accompany their owners in the passenger cabins. The carrier must fit under the passenger's seat. These regulations also vary and prior arrangements should be made. In addition, airlines require that your dog remain in the carrier for the duration of the flight.

Airlines run hot and cold on pet travel

Many airlines won't allow pets to travel in the cargo hold if the departure or destination temperatures are over 80°. The same holds true if the weather is too cold. Check with the airlines to ascertain policies.

What about the size of the carrier?

Your dog should have enough room to stand, lie down, sit and turn around comfortably. Larger doesn't equate to more comfort. If anything, larger quarters only increase the chances of your dog being hurt because of too much movement. Just like your dog's favorite place is under the kitchen desk, a cozy, compact kennel will suit him much better than a spacious one.

Should anything else be in the carrier?

Cover the bottom with newspaper sheets and cover that with additional shredded newspaper. This will absorb accidents and provide a soft, warm cushion for your dog. Include a soft blanket, or an old flannel shirt of yours, some article that will remind your pooch of home and provide a feeling of security. You might want to include a hard rubber chew. But forget toys. They can increase the risk of accidents.

How will my pooch feel about a kennel?

Training and familiarization are the key elements in this area. If possible, buy the kennel (airlines and pet stores sell them) several weeks before your trip. Leave it in your home in the area where your dog spends most of his time. Let him become accustomed to its smell, feel and look. After a few days, your pooch will become comfortable around the kennel. You might even try feeding him in his kennel to make it more like home. Keep all the associations friendly. Never use the kennel for punishment. Taking the time to accustom your dog with his traveling quarters will alleviate potential problems and make vacationing more enjoyable.

What about identification?

The kennel should contain a tag identifying your dog and provide all pertinent information including the dog's name, age, feeding and water requirements, your name, address and phone number and your final destination. In addition, it should include the name and phone number of your dog's vet. A "luggage-type" ID card will function well. Use a waterproof marker. Securely fasten the ID tag to the kennel. Your dog should also wear his state ID tag. Should he somehow become separated from his kennel, the information will travel with him. Using a waterproof pen, mark the kennel "LIVE ANIMAL" in large letters at least an inch or more. Indicate which is the top and bottom with arrows or more large lettering of "THIS END UP."

How can I make plane travel comfortable for my pooch?

If possible, make your travel plans for weekday rather than weekend travel. Travel during off hours. Direct and nonstop flights reduce the potential for problems and delays. Check with your airline to determine how much time they require for check in. Limiting the amount of time your dog will be in the hold section will make travel time that much more comfortable. Personally ascertain that your dog has been put on board your flight before you board the aircraft.

Will there automatically be room on board for my pooch?

Not always. Airline space for pets is normally provided on a first-come, first-served basis. As soon as your travel plans are decided, contact the airline and confirm your arrangements.

What will pet travel cost?

Prices vary depending on whether your dog travels in the cabin or whether a kennel must be provided in the hold. Check with the airlines to determine individual pricing policies.

What about food?

It's best not to feed your dog at least six hours before departure.

What about tranquilizers?

Opinions vary on this subject. Discuss this with your vet. But don't give your dog any medication not prescribed by a vet. Dosages for animals and humans vary greatly.

What about after we land?

If your pooch has not been in the passenger cabin with you, you will be able to pick him up in the baggage claim area along with your luggage. Since traveling in a kennel aboard a plane is an unusual experience, he may react strangely. Leash him before you let him out of the kennel. Having his leash on will avoid mishaps. Once he's leashed, give him a cool drink of water and then take him for a walk.

Dogs who shouldn't fly

In general, very young puppies, females in heat, sickly, frail or pregnant dogs should not be flown. In addition to the stress of flying, changes in altitude and cabin pressure might adversely effect your pooch. Also, pug-nosed dogs are definite "no flys". These dogs have short nasal passages which limit their intake of oxygen. The noxious fumes of the cargo hold can severely limit their supply of oxygen, leaving them highly susceptible to heatstroke.

Health certificates - will I need one?

Although you may never be asked to present a health certificate, it's a good idea to have one with you. Your vet can supply a certificate listing the inoculations your dog has received, including rabies. Keep this information with your travel papers.

Airlines have specific regulations regarding animal flying rights. Make certain you know your dog's rights.

29
TIPS FOR TRAVEL SAFETY

Whether you're at home doing errands or on a far-flung travel adventure, you should practice travel safety. A few minutes of preparation and an extra moment of prevention can help you from becoming a statistic, no matter where you travel.

Safety Tips:

1. When returning to your room late at night use the main entrance of your hotel.

2. Don't leave your room key within sight in public areas, particularly if it's numbered instead of coded.

3. Store valuables in your room safe or in a safety-deposit box at the front desk.

4. Don't carry large amounts of cash; use traveler's checks and credit cards.

5. Avoid flaunting expensive watches and jewelry.

6. When visiting a public attraction like a museum or amusement park, decide where to meet should you become separated from your traveling companions.

7. Use a fanny pack and not a purse when touring.

8. Make use of the locks provided in your room. In addition to your room door, be certain all sliding glass doors, windows and connecting doors are locked.

9. If someone knocks on your room door, the American Hotel and Motel Association advises guests to ascertain the identity of the caller before opening the door. If you haven't arranged for room service or requested anything, call the front desk and determine if someone has been sent to your room before you open the door.

10. Carry your money (or preferably traveler's checks) separately from credit cards.

11. Use your business address on luggage tags, not your home address.

12. Be alert in parking lots and underground garages.

13. Check back seat of your car before getting inside.

14. In your car, always buckle up. Seatbelts save lives.

15. Keep car doors locked.

16. When you stop at traffic lights, leave enough room (one car length) between your vehicle and the one in front so you can quickly pull away.

17. AAA recommends that if you're hit from behind by another vehicle, motion the other driver to a public place before getting out of your car.

18. When driving at night, stay on main roads.

19. Fill your tank during daylight hours. If you must fill up at night, do so at a busy, well-lit service station.

20. If your vehicle breaks down, tie a white cloth to the antenna or the raised hood of your car to signal other motorists. Turn on your hazard lights. Remain in your locked car until police or road service arrives.

21. Don't pull over for flashing headlights. Police cars have red or blue lights.

22. Lock video cameras, car phones and other expensive equipment in your trunk. Don't leave them in your vehicle.

23. Have car keys ready as you approach your car.

24. At an airport, allow only uniformed airport personnel to carry your bags or carry them yourself. Refuse offers of transportation from strangers. Use the services of the airport's ground transportation center or a uniformed taxi dispatcher.

25. Walk purposefully.

26. When using an ATM, choose one in a well-lit area with heavy foot traffic. Look for machines inside establishments - they're the safest.

27. Avoid poorly lit areas, shrubbery or dark doorways.

28. When ordering from an outside source, have it delivered to the front desk or office rather than to your room.

29. Trust your instincts. If a situation doesn't feel right - it probably isn't.

11
TIPS THAT TAKE THE STRESS OUT OF VACATIONS

Vacations are intended to be restful occasions but sometimes the preparations involved in "getting away from it all" can prove stressful. The following are proven stress reducers to help you cope before, during and after your trip.

1. Awaken fifteen minutes earlier each day for a couple of weeks before your trip and use that extra time to plan your day and do "vacation" chores.

2. Write down errands to be done. Don't rely on your memory. The anticipation of forgetting something important can be stressful.

3. Don't procrastinate. Whatever has to be done tomorrow, do today. Whatever needs doing today, do NOW.

4. Take stock of your car. Get car repairs done. Have your car washed. Your journey will be more pleasant in a clean car. Fill up with gas the day before your departure. And check your tires and oil gauge. Summertime travel, check your air conditioning. In the winter, make sure your heater and defroster work. Make sure wiper blades are in good working condition.

5. Learn to be more flexible. Not everything has to be perfect. Compromise, you'll have a happier life.

6. If you have an unpleasant task to do, take care of it early in the day.

7. Ask for help. Delegating responsibility relieves pressure and stress. It also makes others feel productive and needed.

8. Accept that we are all part of this imperfect world. An ounce of forgiveness will take you far.

9. Don't take on more tasks than you can readily accomplish.

10. Think positive thoughts and eliminate negativism, like, "I'm too fat, I'm too old, I'm not smart enough."

11. Take 5-10 minutes to stretch before you begin your day or before bedtime. Breathe deeply and slowly, clearing your mind as you do.

TIPS ON MOVING WITH YOUR DOG

During this coming year, one out of five Americans will be moving. Of those, nearly half will be moving with their pets. If you're part of the "pet half", you should understand that your dog can experience the same anxiety as you. The following tips can make moving less stressful for you and your dog.

1. Although moving companies provide information on how to move your pet, they are not permitted to transport animals. Plan to do so on your own.

2. Begin with a visit to your vet. Your vet can provide a copy of your dog's medical records. Your vet might even be able to recommend a vet in the city where you'll be moving.

3. If you'll be traveling by plane, contact the airlines ASAP. Many airlines offer in-cabin boarding for small dogs, but only on a first-come, first-served basis. The earlier you make your reservations, the better chance you'll have of securing space.

4. If you'll be driving to your new home, use ***Doin' California With Your Pooch!*** (or our national lodging directory, ***Vacationing With Your Pet!)*** for your lodging reservations. By planning ahead, your move will proceed more smoothly .

5. Buy a special toy or a favorite chew that's only given to your dog when you're busy packing.

6. Don't feed or water your pooch for several hours before your departure. The motion of the ride might cause stomach upset.

7. Keep your dog kenneled up on moving day to avoid disasters. Never allow your pet to run free when you're in unfamiliar territory.

8. Pack your dog's dishes, food, water, treats, toys, leash and bedding in an easy-to-reach location. Take water and food from home. Drinking unfamiliar water or eating a different brand of food can cause digestion problems. And don't forget those plastic bags for clean-up.

9. Once you've moved in and unpacked, be patient. Your pooch may misbehave. Like a child, he may resent change and begin acting up. Deal with problems in a gentle and reassuring manner. Spend some extra time with your canine during this upheaval period and understand that it will pass.

FIRST-AID EMERGENCY TREATMENT

Having a bit of the Girl Scout in me, I like being prepared. Over the years, I've accumulated information regarding animal emergency treatment. Although I've had only one occasion to use this information, once was enough. I'd like to share my knowledge with you.

Whether you're the stay-at-home type who rarely travels with your dog, or a gadabout who can't sit still, every dog owner should know these simple, but potentially lifesaving procedures.

The Basics

Assemble your own first-aid kit by including some or all of the following:

- Two-inch bandages
- Antibiotic ointment
- Scissors
- Rectal thermometer
- Boric acid
- Baking soda
- Lighter fluid
- 3% hydrogen peroxide
- Blunt tweezers
- Tomato juice
- Cotton gauze
- Flea powder
- Flashlight (with new batteries)
- Extra flea and tick collar

The following are only guidelines to assist you during emergencies. Whenever possible, seek treatment from a vet if your animal becomes injured and you don't feel qualified to administer first aid. I have not personally experienced any of the emergencies outlined, but these tips may help you with initial treatment.

Allergies: One in five dogs suffers from some form of allergy. Sneezing and watery eyes can be an allergic reaction caused by pollen and smoke. Inflamed skin can indicate a sensitivity to grass or to chemicals used in carpet cleaning. See your vet.

Bites and stings: Use ice to reduce swelling. If your animal has been stung in the mouth, take him to the vet immediately. Swelling can close the throat. If your dog experiences an allergic reaction, an antihistamine may be needed. For fast relief from a wasp or bee sting, dab the spot with plain vinegar and then apply baking soda. If you're in the middle of nowhere, a small mud pie plastered over the sting will provide relief. Snake bites: seek veterinary attention ASAP.

Bleeding: If the cut is small, use tweezers to remove hair from the wound. Gently wash with soap and water and then bandage (not too tightly). Severe bleeding, apply direct pressure and seek medical attention ASAP.

Burns: <u>First degree burns:</u> Use an ice cube or apply ice water until the pain is alleviated. Then apply vitamin E, swab with honey or cover with a freshly brewed teabag.

<u>Minor burns:</u> Use antibiotic ointment.

<u>Acid:</u> Apply dampened baking soda.

<u>Scalds:</u> Douse with cold water. After treatment, bandage all burns for protection.

Earache: A drop of warm eucalyptus oil in your dog's ear can help relieve the pain.

Eye scratches or inflammation: Make a solution of boric acid and bathe eyes with soft cotton.

Falls or impact injuries: Limping, pain, grey gums or prostration need immediate veterinary attention. The cause could be a fracture or internal bleeding.

Fire: Friends of Animals, Inc. will send you a decal for your window alerting fire fighters to the presence of a pet and the area in your home where the pet may be found. Charge for one decal is $1. Write to them at 1841 Broadway, #212, New York, NY 10023 or call 212-247-8120.

Fleas: Patches of hair loss, itching and redness are common signs of fleas, particularly during warm months. Use a flea bath and a flea collar to eliminate and prevent infestation. Ask your vet about new oral medication now available for flea control.

Heatstroke: Signs include lying prone, rapid breathing and heartbeat, difficulty in breathing, rolling eyes, panting, high fever, a staggering gait. Quick response is essential. Move your pooch into the shade. Generously douse with cold water or if possible, partially fill a tub with cold water and immerse your dog. Remain with him and check his temperature. Normal for dogs: 100°-102°. Don't let your dog's temperature drop below that.

Prevent common heatstroke by limiting outdoor exercise in hot or humid weather, provide plenty of fresh, cool water and access to shade. Never leave your dog in a car on a warm day, even for "just a few minutes."

Poisons: Gasoline products, antifreeze, disinfectants, and insecticides are all poisonous. Keep these products tightly closed and out of reach. Vomiting, trembling, and convulsions can be symptoms of poisoning. If your dog suffers from any of these symptoms, get veterinary attention. (See listings on Poison Control Centers in section "Everything You Want to Know About Pet Care...".)

Poison ivy: Poison ivy or oak on your dog's coat will not bother him. But the poison can be passed on to you. If you believe your dog has come in contact with poison ivy or oak use rubber gloves to handle your dog. Rinse him in salt water, then follow with a clear water rinse. Shampoo and rinse again.

Shock: Shock can occur after an accident or severe fright. Your animal might experience shallow breathing, pale gums, nervousness or prostration. Keep him still, quiet and warm and have someone drive you to a vet.

Skunks: Hopefully, you and your pooch will never encounter one of Rover's favorite furry friends during your travels. But, unfortunately, dogs and skunks have a way of sniffing each other out and establishing a very smelly relationship. Here are some tips if you encounter a skunk on the trail. You'll be surprised at how persistent the little black and white fellows can be, even when Fido is perfectly behaved.

1. Try to keep your pooch quiet. Skunks have an unforgettable way of displaying their dislike of barking.

2. Try to ignore the little critter. Distract Rover, and hasten your pace down the pathway.

3. Don't try to scare the skunk away, they'll spray!

If you end up in a very stinky situation, here are three home remedies recommended by groomers. (Of course, it is always a good idea to consult with a veterinarian before dousing your dog with foreign substances.) Time is of the essence for your nose's sake and for Fido's sake. So, if possible, act quickly.

1. The old tomato juice method might work for you. Saturate Fido's fur with the juice and wait for it to dry. Brush and shampoo later. This method may prove effective, but is quite messy.

2. A 5-part water, 1-part vinegar ratio is an alternative. Pour the solution over Rover and let it soak for 10-15 minutes. Shampoo.

3. Use 1 quart 3% hydrogen peroxide, 1/4 cup baking soda and a small amount of liquid soap. Apply on your pal and let him sit for 15 minutes. Shampoo.

Note: Immediately wash eyes with boric acid solution. Always apply any solution with care around the eyes and face.

Snake bites:

1. Immobilization and prompt medical attention are key elements to handling a poisonous snake bite. Immediate veterinary care is essential to recovery this means within 2 hours of the bite. DO NOT try to treat this yourself.

2. If the bite occurs while in a remote location, immediately immobilize the bitten area and carry the dog to the vehicle. If the dog walks on his own, the venom will spread quicker.

3. Most snake bites on dogs occur in the head or neck area, especially on the nose. The front leg is the second most common place.

4. Severe swelling within 30 to 60 minutes of the bite is the first indication that your dog is suffering from a venomous snake bite.

5. Excessive pain and slow, steady bleeding are other indicators - hemotoxins in the venom of certain snakes prevent the clotting of blood.

6. If your dog goes into shock or stops breathing, CPR (cardiopulmonary resuscitation) is your only option. CPR for dogs is the same as for humans - push on the dog's chest to compress his heart and force blood to the brain, then hold his mouth closed and breathe into his nose.

7. DO NOT apply ice to the bite - venom constricts the blood vessels and ice only compounds the constriction.

8. DO NOT use a tourniquet - the body's natural immune system fights off the venom and by cutting off the blood flow you'll either minimize or completely eliminate this fight.

Ticks: Use lighter fluid (or other alcohol) and loosen by soaking. Then tweeze out gently. Make sure you get the tick's head.

Winter woes: Rock salt and other commercial chemicals used to melt ice can be very harmful to your dog. Not only can they burn your dog's pads, but ingestion by licking can result in poisoning or dehydration. Upon returning from a walk through snow or ice, wash your dog's feet with a mild soap and then rinse. Before an outdoor excursion, you can also try spraying your dog's paws with cooking oil to deter adherence.

❧❧❧❧❧❧❧❧❧❧❧❧❧❧❧❧❧❧❧❧❧❧❧❧❧❧❧

FIDO FACT:

- *It's easier than you might think to help your dog lose those extra pounds. Begin by eliminating unnecessary table scraps. Cut back a small amount on the kibble or canned dog food you normally feed your pooch, if he's accustomed to two full cups each day, reduce that amount to 1 3/4 cups instead. If you normally give your pooch biscuits every day, cut the amount in half. And don't feel guilty. Stick with the program and you'll eventually see a reduction in weight. Slow and steady is the best approach. And don't let yourself imagine that your dog is being deprived of anything. Even when he looks at you with a woebegone expression, remember you're doing him a favor by helping him reduce and you're adding years of good health to his life.*

STEPS TO BETTER GROOMING

Grooming is another way of saying "I love you" to your pooch. As pack animals, dogs love grooming rituals. Make grooming time an extension of your caring relationship. Other than some breeds which require professional grooming, most canines can be groomed in about 10 minutes a day.

1. Designate a grooming place, preferably one that is not on the floor. If possible, use a grooming table. Your dog will learn to remain still and you won't trade a well-groomed pooch for an aching back.

2. End every grooming session with a small treat. When your dog understands that grooming ends with a goodie, he'll behave better.

3. Brush out your dog's coat before washing. Wetting a matted coat only tightens the tangles and makes removal more difficult.

4. Using a soft tissue, wipe around your dog's eyes daily, especially if his eyes tend to be teary.

5. When bathing a long-haired dog, squeeze the coat, don't rub. Rubbing can result in snarls.

6. To gently clean your dog's teeth, slip your hand into a soft sock and go over each tooth.

<u>FIDO FACT:</u>
- *Stroke a dog instead of patting it. Stroking is soothing. Patting can make a dog nervous.*

Grooming tips...sticky problems

Chewing gum: There are two methods you can try. Ice the gum for a minimum of ten minutes to make it more manageable and easier to remove. Or use peanut butter. Apply and let the oil in the peanut butter loosen the gum from the hair shaft. Leave on about 20 minutes before working out the gum.

Tar: This is a tough one. Try soaking the tarred area in vegetable or baby oil. Leave on overnight and then bathe your dog the following day. The oil should cause the tar to slide off the hair shaft. Since this method can be messy, shampoo your dog with Dawn dishwashing soap to remove the oil. Follow with pet shampoo to restore the pH balance.

Oil: Apply baby powder or cornstarch to the oily area. Leave on 20 minutes. Shampoo with warm water and Dawn. Follow with pet shampoo to restore the pH balance.

Burrs:

1. Burrs in your dog's coat may be easier to remove if you first crush the burrs with pliers.

2. Slip a kitchen fork under the burr to remove.

3. Soak the burrs in petroleum jelly before working them out.

Keep cleaning sessions as short as possible. Your dog will not want to sit for hours. If your dog's skin is sensitive, you might want to simply remove the offending matter with a scissors. If you don't feel competent to do the removal yourself, contact a grooming service in your area and have them do the job for you.

FIDO FACT:

- *Inflamed skin can indicate a sensitivity to grass or chemicals used in carpet cleaning. Patches of hair loss, itching and redness are common signs of fleas, particularly during warm months.*

FITNESS FOR FIDO

A daily dose of exercise is as important for the pooch's health as it is for yours. A 15-30 minute walk twice daily is a perfect way to build muscles and stamina and get you and the dogster in shape for more aerobic workouts. If you're a summer hound, beat the heat by walking in the early hours of the morning or after sundown. Keep in mind that dogs don't sweat, so if you notice your pooch panting excessively or lagging behind, stop in a cool area for a water break.

Be especially careful when beginning an exercise program with a young dog or an overweight pooch. Consult with your veterinarian about a fitness program that would be best for your furry friend before leashing him up and pooping him out. Obese dogs may have other health problems which should be considered before taking to the trail. Young dogs are still developing their bones and may not be ready for rigorous programs. Use common sense when beginning any exercise program.

❄·❄

FIDO FACT:

- *Fido's fitness counts towards insuring a longer, healthier life. The most common cause of ill health in canines is obesity. About 60% of all adult dogs are or will become overweight due to lack of physical activity and overfeeding.*

MASSAGE, IT'S PETTING WITH A PURPOSE

After a tough day of hiking, nothing is more appealing than a soak in a hot tub. Since that won't work for your pooch, consider a massage. All it takes is twenty minutes and the following simple procedures:

1. Gently stroke the head.

2. Caress around the ears in a circular fashion.

3. Rub down both the neck and the shoulders, first on one side of the spine, and then the other continuing down to the rump.

4. Turn Rover over and gently knead the abdominal area.

5. Rub your dogs legs.

6. Caress between the paw pads.

After his massage, offer your pooch plenty of fresh, cool water to flush out the toxins released from the muscles.

Massages are also therapeutic for pooches recovering from surgery and/or suffering from hip dysplasia, circulatory disorders, sprains, chronic illnesses and old age. Timid and hyperactive pooches can benefit as well.

FIDO FACT:

- *Is your pooch pudgy? Place both thumbs on your dog's backbone and then run your fingers along his rib cage. If the bony part of each rib cannot be easily felt, your dog may be overweight. Another quickie test - stand directly over your dog while he's standing. If you can't see a clearly defined waist behind his rib cage, he's probably too portly.*

10

REASONS WHY DOGS ARE GOOD FOR YOUR HEALTH

Adding a dog to your household can improve your health and that of your family. In particular, dogs seem to help the very young and seniors. The following is based on various studies.

1. People over 40 who own dogs have lower blood pressure. 20% have lower triglyceride levels. Talking to dogs has been shown to lower blood pressure as well.

2. People who own dogs see their doctor less than those who don't.

3. Dogs have been shown to reduce depression, particularly in seniors.

4. It's easier to make friends when you have a dog. Life is more social with them.

5. It's healthier too. Seniors with dogs are generally more active because they walk more.

6. Dogs are friends. Here again, seniors seem to benefit most.

7. Dogs can help older people deal with the loss of a spouse. Seniors are less likely to experience the deterioration in health that often follows the stressful loss of a mate.

8. Dogs ease loneliness.

9. Perhaps because of the responsibility of dog ownership, seniors take better care of themselves.

10. Dogs provide a sense of security to people of all ages.

CALIFORNIA'S NATIONAL FORESTS AND WILDERNESS AREAS

Sunrise in the Sierras. As morning's glow lights up the mountain snowpack, a jumping trout sends ripples across the still surface of a mountain lake. Sunset in the desert mountains, the rocks, heated by the midday sun, are warm to the touch as the sun drops below the western horizon and the dry air cools. Uncountable stars, unseen by those who remain in the city, fill the sky. A coyote howls in the distance as darkness brings the desert to life. Wilderness areas in California's national forests range from woodlands in the north to desert mountains in the south. Visitors are welcome to enjoy California's wilderness areas and national forests, but are asked to leave only footprints and take only memories.

With care our children's grandchildren will be able to cherish the same sight of a crystal clear mountain lake or an elk crossing a meadow. To preserve wilderness areas for future generations, the Forest Service asks people to be sensitive to their surroundings and observe the rules and guidelines designed to protect the wilderness areas. Unfortunately, rules alone can't preserve a wilderness. Users need to make protection of these areas a personal ethic.

Green forests and tumbling rivers, small mountain lakes tucked behind towering peaks, desert vistas stretching as far as the eye can see, these scenes and a multitude of others greet visitors to forest service wilderness areas in California. The Wilderness Act of 1964 set aside wilderness areas "where the earth and its community of life are untrammeled by man, where man himself is a visitor who does not remain."

You enter the wilderness at your own risk and must be prepared to take care of yourself. There are no bathrooms, rest stops, food or drink. In turn, however, you will find unspoiled vistas, solitude and escape from the fast pace of civilization. Although many non-wilderness areas in the national forests provide similar opportunities for camping and hiking in an isolated, undeveloped setting, wilderness areas in particular are managed to preserve their natural conditions.

Recreation use of national forest wilderness areas in California averages about 2 million visitors a year, but varies according to weather and travel conditions that affect access to the areas. Preserving the wilderness quality of these unique lands while accommodating increased recreation use is one of the major challenges faced by national forest managers.

What Is Wilderness?

Land designated by Congress as wilderness:

- Is affected primarily by the forces of nature; people visit, but don't remain. It may contain ecological, geological or other features with scientific, educational, scenic or historical values.

- Has outstanding opportunities for solitude or primitive recreation.

- Is large enough so continued use won't change its unspoiled, natural condition.

Preserving Wilderness

The forest service manages wilderness areas to:

- Perpetuate a high-quality wilderness system that represents natural ecosystems.

- Maintain native plants and animals by protecting complete biological communities.

- Preserve healthy watersheds.

- Protect threatened or endangered species.

- Maintain the primitive character of wilderness as a benchmark for developed lands.

Permits

A visitor permit may be required to enter some national forest wilderness areas. Some have a quota system for peak season use that admits visitors gradually in order to reduce adverse impacts on the wilderness quality of the areas. The forest service offices listed for the areas you intend to visit will provide you with information about permit requirements and permit application forms. A campfire permit is required if you plan to build a wood fire or use a portable stove during your trip. During periods of severe fire danger, campfires may be prohibited and some areas or parts of areas closed to public entry. Be sure to inquire at the forest service office at your point of entry for complete information about any fire restrictions in effect. Group size is limited. No matter how careful, very large groups tend to compact campsites and have a greater impact on wilderness than small groups.

Fishing and hunting are permitted in season in many wilderness areas. State fish and game laws apply to all national forest land. If you don't want to camp in an area during hunting season, be sure to inquire about the effective dates when you plan your trip.

To ensure preservation of this unique area and a quality experience for all who visit it, please abide by the Forest Service guidelines.

Pooch Rules & Regulations:

THEY CAN'T BE AVOIDED. AND THEY'RE REALLY QUITE EASY TO LIVE WITH. BE A RESPONSIBLE DOG OWNER AND OBEY THE RULES.

- Clean up after your dog even if no one has seen him do his business.
- Leash your dog in areas that require leashing.
- Train your dog to be well behaved.
- Control your dog in public places so that he's not a nuisance to others.

Camp With Courtesy

- Burn all paper.
- Pack out all cans, bottles and metal foil.

Refuse & Garbage

- Don't bury your trash, animals dig it up.
- Don't leave leftover food for the next party, it teaches bears to rob camps.

Smoking

Don't smoke on trails. You may smoke at your campsite - sit down and dig a small area to be used as an ashtray. Always take your cigarette butt with you - filters don't easily decompose.

Bicycles

Motor vehicles and bicycles are prohibited. Travel is restricted to foot or horseback.

Small Groups

Travel in groups of 15 or fewer. Give others as much privacy as possible. Leave radios and tape players at home.

Stay On Trails

To preserve plants and prevent erosion, don't take shortcuts. Don't cut your own trails. This contributes to trail erosion and destroys plant life. Stick to marked trails. Whenever possible, walk on rocks or dry ground. Tread lightly in meadows which are home to many sensitive plants.

Horses

Some restrictions exist, check with the ranger district.

Hunting

Hunting is allowed with the proper permits. Check with the California Department of Fish and Game for regulations.

FIDO FACT:

- *When dogs first meet, it's uncommon for them to approach each other head on. Most will approach in curving lines. They'll walk beyond each other's noses sniffing at rear ends while standing side by side.*

Fishing License

The state of California requires that any person 16 years or older possess a valid fishing license in order to partake in any fishing activity throughout the state. A license is not required of those persons under the age of 16. A license may be purchased at any State Department of Fish and Game Office or at most sporting goods and outdoor stores. Or call the California Department of Fish & Game, License & Revenue Branch at (916) 227-2246. They accept both Visa and Mastercard. The average cost of an annual resident license is $25 and the average cost of an annual non-resident license is $67. A one-day fishing permit may be purchased for $9 (both residents and non-residents). Prices of fishing licenses are subject to change. Call (916) 227-2244 for exact fees or additional information.

TRAIL MANNERS & METHODS

Trails are both a convenience for wilderness users and a way to minimize human impact on an area. Cutting switchbacks or cutting through trail sections can cause serious erosion. Walking on the shoulder of a wet or muddy trail creates ruts along the trail. If you aren't following the trail, stay well away from it. Use caution when crossing dangerous sections, such as swampy areas, potential slide areas, deep snowdrifts, slippery trails on slopes or rapid streams.

For everyone's safety, hikers should stand quietly on the downhill side to allow horses to pass. Don't try to touch the pack animals or hide from them. Startled horses can be dangerous.

Be prepared

Be sure you and your fellow campers are in shape. Take weekend hikes and exercise with a full backpack for several weeks before your trip. Clothing is the most important precaution against hypothermia, exhaustion and exposure. Pack a waterproof poncho for stormy weather. Dressing in layers lets you adapt to temperatures that can change as much as 80° between day and night in mountainous areas. Be sure your sleeping bag keeps you warm when outdoor temperatures are well below freezing. Your boots should be sturdy, well insulated and waterproof, fit comfortably over two pairs of socks (cotton inner, wool outer), protect the ankle and support the foot.

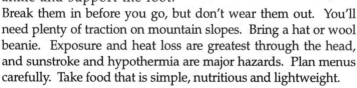

Break them in before you go, but don't wear them out. You'll need plenty of traction on mountain slopes. Bring a hat or wool beanie. Exposure and heat loss are greatest through the head, and sunstroke and hypothermia are major hazards. Plan menus carefully. Take food that is simple, nutritious and lightweight.

California hiking etiquette

- Respect the land - don't shortcut the trail.
- Avoid wet trails if possible, and avoid cutting new trails.
- Keep to the right of the trail - left is for passing.
- Downhill traffic yields to uphill traffic.
- Adjust your pace when approaching other users.
- When overtaking a hiker, announce your intentions.
- Don't block the trail. Allow room for others.
- Joggers yield to trail stock and hikers.
- Bicyclists yield to all other users.
- Some trails have steep grades, natural hazards, variable terrain conditions, and limited visibility. Observe and heed all signs.

Trip checklist

You will find greater enjoyment in the wilderness if you are properly prepared. The following checklist is important for your safety and enjoyment.

- Clothing and shelter for rain, wind and cold
- Map and compass
- First-aid kit
- Sunglasses or hat
- Flashlight
- Knife
- Waterproof matches
- Nylon twine or cord
- Sun lotion and lip ointment
- Mosquito repellent
- Notification of your trip route and time

First aid

Blisters, headaches or other ailments can ruin a trip. Wilderness users should carry a first-aid kit to treat common medical problems. The following supplies should handle most cases. Additional supplies should be carried based on the size of the party and specific needs.

- Pain medication such as aspirin (25 tablets)

- Antacid (25 tablets)

- Antihistamine (12 tablets)

- Bandages (12, 1-inch size)

- Sterile gauze pads (6, 4-inch squares)

- Adhesive tape (2-inch roll)

- Elastic bandages (3-inch)

- Tweezers (1 pair)

- Moleskin (1/2 package)

- Antibacterial soap (small bottle)

- Roll gauze (2, 2-inch rolls)

- Oral thermometer

- Personal prescription drugs

- Space blanket

- Pencil and paper

- Change for a telephone

- Arm and leg inflatable splints (1 each)

- Safety pins (3 large)

Get ready to go

Plan your trip from start to finish at home. Use topographic maps and trail guides, and get the advice of experienced back-country travelers. Check elevations and total distance to be traveled up and down. Allow plenty of time for moving over hilly, rugged terrain. Before entering the wilderness, leave your itinerary with a relative or friend. Write a full account of who is going, where you are going, when you will be back, where you will exit, and the approximate location of each overnight campsite. Carry a map and compass and stick to the planned route. It is wise never to travel alone, but if you must, stick to frequently used trails in case you become sick or injured.

Buying Equipment

Acquiring equipment requires a little research and the advice of experienced backpackers. You can refer to the many camping guides commercially available, but don't rely on printed information alone. Talk to an experienced backpacker or your local camping supplier. They can help you select basic equipment.

Wildlife

Many of the hikes will bring you in close proximity to wildlife. Please do not disturb the natural habitat or get too close to the animals. If you know that you will encounter wildlife and you do not feel you have total voice control over your dog, leash him to prevent mishaps. Elk, for example, have been known to charge when they sense danger or feel threatened.

When hiking in a marshland or other bird sanctuary, keep your dog leashed, particularly if he's a hunting or bird dog. It's up to you to protect our wildlife.

Regardless of where you hike, whether it's through a red-walled canyon, in a heavily wooded forest or on granite mountaintops, clean up after your dog. Let's work together to preserve dog-friendly attitudes and policies.

Bears are not cuddly

Most large mammals stay away from anything that smells of humans, but some bears are exceptions. Bears are intelligent, adaptable animals, and some have changed their natural foraging habits to take advantage of hikers bringing food into wilderness areas. Some basic rules - stay away from bears and don't harass them. Here are some additional suggestions when traveling in bear country:

Keep your camp clean and counterbalance anything that has an odor, including soap, toothpaste and trash. To counterbalance your load, place the items in two bags so they weigh about the same. Find a tree with a good branch about 20 feet off the ground. Toss a rope over the branch far enough from the trunk so cubs can't crawl along the branch and reach the bags. Tie the first sack on one end of the rope and hoist the sack up to the branch. Tie the second sack to the other end of the rope. The rope should be about 10 feet long, tuck any excess in the bag. Tie a loop in the rope near the second bag. Toss the second bag into position so both bags are hanging about 12 feet off the ground. To retrieve them, hook the loop with a long stick and pull the bags down.

Don't hang packs in trees. Leave them on the ground with zippers and flaps open so bears can nose through them without doing any damage.

If a bear approaches your camp, yell, bang pans and wave coats in the air. In many cases, the bear will retreat. If the bear doesn't retreat, get yourself out of camp.

Bears may only enter camp looking for food, but they still are potentially dangerous. Never try to take food away from a bear. Never approach a bear, especially a cub. You may lose a meal to animals, but they pay a higher price for human carelessness. Bears that become accustomed to getting food from campers sometimes become too aggressive and have to be destroyed. Animals that spend the summer getting food from campers also can be in trouble when the first snow falls and their food supply quits for the year.

Rattlesnakes

Rattlesnakes inhabit much of California but they prefer dry, rocky areas below the 6,000 foot elevation. Active in warmer months, they will not normally attack unless they are cornered or touched. Be aware of your surroundings. If a bite occurs, do not panic. Remain calm, immobilize the bitten area below the level of the heart and get to a hospital ASAP for an anti-venom shot.

Don't get ticked off

Ticks are prevalent in many areas of California. They prefer brushy areas and tall grass so avoid both whenever possible and keep your dog away as well. When hiking in tick country, wear long pants and a long sleeve shirt to minimize contact. It's also easier to spot a tick on light colored clothing. At the end of your outing or hike, carefully inspect yourself and your canine for ticks. Deep Woods OFF!, an insect repellent, can help repel ticks. To remove a tick, use lighter fluid (or other alcohol) and loosen by soaking. Then tweeze out gently, being sure to remove the tick's head.

Poison oak

Found throughout California, poison oak can be either a vine or a shrub. The leaves are red in fall, green in spring and summer. They usually form clusters of three. If you come into contact with poison oak, wash with soap and cool water ASAP. Remove and wash all clothing as well. Over-the-counter medicines are available to help relieve symptoms. If your dog comes in contact with poison oak, he won't experience any ill effects, but the poison will remain on his coat. Do not pet him. Use rubber gloves to handle your dog. Rinse him in salt water, followed with a clear water rinse. Then shampoo and rinse again.

Foxtails

Foxtails are those annoying, prickly shafts of dried grass which always seem to fasten themselves to your clothing. Unfortunately, pooches are more susceptible to foxtails and they don't have the added protection of clothing. If you happen to be hiking through dry grass, be certain to thoroughly check your pooch for this nasty grass, especially his paws, eyes, nose, mouth and ears. Left untreated, foxtails can cause serious medical problems.

The Pacific Ocean

Unpredictable, particularly in winter. Never turn your back on the Pacific. Headlands, cliffs, and rocky outcroppings can be very dangerous as well. Even if your dog is an excellent swimmer, don't let him swim when the waters are too turbulent or too cold. And be sure to watch for rogue waves.

The California deserts

Desert education and familiarity are recommended before any desert excursion. The following are some basics: Dress in light colored/lightweight clothing. Wear a hat, and sunscreen and reapply as needed. Carry plenty of water. And don't overdo it. These guidelines and a heavy dose of common sense will go a long way toward helping you enjoy and appreciate the grandeur and beauty of the desert.

Take it easy

Once in the wilderness, take it easy for a day or two. Getting out of your living room and into the wild takes some adjustment. Walk slowly and steadily, and eat dried fruit or other quick energy food from time to time.

Remember, if you overexert yourself at high elevations you may experience altitude sickness or hyperventilation. Most of the time these attacks are the result of traveling too fast. Never joke about a person's ability to keep up when traveling in the wild. A good principle of wilderness travel is to take it slow, rest often and snack frequently to restore body energy.

Stoves & fire

Take a lightweight camping stove specifically designed for backpackers, and plenty of fuel. Don't rely on finding firewood for cooking. Cutting wood from standing trees is prohibited, and heavy use of dead and down wood means that many areas don't have a reliable supply of wood fuel. Standing dead trees are used by cavity nesting birds, small mammals and other wilderness inhabi-

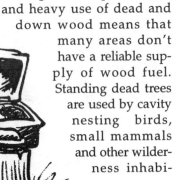

tants. Pulling limbs off trees also scars campsites for future users. In addition, wood fires may be prohibited in some wilderness areas. A portable stove cooks efficiently and reliably, and never gets so wet it won't burn.

If you plan to use a portable stove or build a wood fire you must obtain an California campfire permit from the forest service office listed for the area you plan to visit. Some areas restrict the use of campfires or portable stoves.

Use only dead and down wood. Never break branches from standing trees, even if they look dead. The trees may be alive and breaking branches can cause injury. To build the fire, select a level spot away from overhanging trees, bushes or dry grass. Keep away from the base of steep hills; fire travels uphill fast. With your shovel, clear a circle 10 feet across down to bare dirt. Hollow out a firehole 2 feet across and 5 to 6 inches deep. Pile the soil around the edge of the firehole. Keep the fire small and never start a fire in windy weather. Put out your fires at least a half hour before you start to break camp. First let it die down. Then pour water over the wood and ashes, and spread soil over that. Mix soil, water and ashes until the fire is OUT.

No trace camping

Camp on mineral soil, never in meadows or soft grassy areas that compact easily. Locate your campsite at least 100 feet from water or trail. Pick a place where you won't have to clear vegetation or level a tent site. Do not bury trash. Burn it or pack it out. You must pack out cans, bottles or metal foil. If you bury trash, animals will dig it up. Keeping trails and campsites clean helps preserve the wilderness experience for all.

Before leaving camp, naturalize the area. Scatter any rocks and wood you used, and scout the area to be sure you're leaving nothing behind. Try to make the site look as if no one had been there. Even if you have to pack out trash left by careless campers.

The natural balance of an area around a campsite can be destroyed by such things as building rock walls or cutting branches. Plants and animals depend on the micro-habitats for their survival, and the actions alter the area for the next camper.

Water

Lakes and streams are gathering points for wilderness users, so protecting water quality becomes more critical with growing wilderness use. Hikers and hounds can contract diseases such as giardiasis from drinking impure water. Improper disposal of human waste can contaminate water supplies. Soaps and other wastes add nutrients that can upset the biological balance of water bodies. Water problems can be reduced by following these guidelines.

- Camp at least 100 feet from any water source.

- Carry water to camp for cooking and washing.

- Protect water sources by keeping wash water, food scraps, fish entrails and other wastes at least 100 feet from water.

- Don't use soaps, including "biodegradable" soap near lakes and streams.

- Waste sites should be at least 100 feet from the nearest water supply. Dig a hole 8 to 10 inches wide and 6 to 8 inches deep. After use, fill the hole with loose soil and tamp in the sod.

- Purify even clear, running water before drinking. A recommended treatment is to bring water to a rolling boil for five minutes.

THUMBNAIL DESCRIPTIONS OF CALIFORNIA'S NATIONAL FORESTS

The Mission of the National Forests of the United States:

"Caring for the land and serving people."

ANGELES NATIONAL FOREST

Over 650,000 acres of mountainous, labyrinth-like terrain await you at this national forest spread throughout Los Angeles County in southern California. The forest is a phenomenon of nature laced with 525 miles of hiking trails winding through verdant meadows, wildflower-clad hills, cascading waterfalls, canyons and groves of 2,000 year old Limber pines.

The trails range in difficulty from cinchy to rigorous. Even the fair-of-paw can appreciate the astounding beauty of this forestland. Experienced hikers should set their sights on the 10,064-foot peak of Mount San Antonio, the highest point in the forest. Old Baldy offers sweeping panoramic vistas of the surrounding landscape.

Angeles National Forest encompasses the San Gabriel Mountains, as well as the Sheep Mountain, San Gabriel and Cucamonga Wilderness Areas, home to bighorn sheep, coyotes and black bears.

See the NATIONAL FOREST HIKING TRAIL LOCATOR for a complete list of dog-friendly hikes in the Angeles National Forest.

CLEVELAND NATIONAL FOREST

Between the roaring ocean and the arid desert of southern California, you'll find 420,000 acres of diverse terrain. Filled with dense pine and oak woodlands, the Cleveland National Forest is situated a mere five miles from the Mexican border. Over 200 miles of nature trails escort you up mountains, past bottomless chasms and into four separate wilderness areas - Agua Tibia, Hauser, Pine Creek and San Mateo Canyon.

Remember that coyotes, mountain lions, bobcats and mule deer inhabit many areas of this woodland. Be certain that your pooch's leash is easily accessible!

See the NATIONAL FOREST HIKING TRAIL LOCATOR for a complete list of dog-friendly hikes in the Cleveland National Forest.

ELDORADO NATIONAL FOREST

Spend hours or days hiking and camping in the Sierra Nevada at this 669,000-acre national forest, southwest of Lake Tahoe. The strenuous climb up to the 10,000-foot Pyramid Peak will reward you with magnificent vistas.

Over 350 miles of trails usher you through wildflower-strewn meadows, glacial lakes, canyons and whitebark fir, hemlock and lodgepole pine forests. The Desolation Wilderness and Mokelumne Wilderness are within this forest area. Gray fox, bobcats, mountain lions, mule deer, coyotes and black bear all populate these regions.

Spring and summer attract the most visitors to Eldorado National Forest, but there are also several ski resort areas that are popular in winter months.

See the NATIONAL FOREST HIKING TRAIL LOCATOR for a complete list of dog-friendly hikes in the Eldorado National Forest.

INYO NATIONAL FOREST

When you visit this 1.8 million acre national forest situated between Inyokern and Lee Vining in eastern California, you're sure to be awestruck by its vast grandeur and beauty. Nearly 1,200 miles of trails traverse the varying terrain of lakes, waterfalls, rocky bluffs and outcrops, bottomless granite gorges, verdant meadows and lush hillsides.

The Ancient Bristlecone Pine Forest, home to the oldest living things on earth and 14,495-foot Mount Whitney, the highest mountain peak in the contiguous United States are within the forest's boundaries.

The John Muir, Golden Trout, Ansel Adams and South Sierra Wilderness Areas can be found in Inyo National Forest, along with black bears, coyotes, deer, bobcats, foxes and bighorn sheep.

See the NATIONAL FOREST HIKING TRAIL LOCATOR for a complete list of dog-friendly hikes in the Inyo National Forest.

KLAMATH NATIONAL FOREST

An escape from civilization is one of the lures at this 1.7 million acre national forest, the least populated national forest in California. Explore over 1,100 miles of trails with elevations ranging from 1,000 to over 8,000 feet. Rugged mountain granite and marble ridges, boulder-scattered chasms, mixed conifer forests and the powerful Klamath River embody the landscape of this region.

Accomplished hikers, head for Boulder Peak in the Marble Mountain Wilderness. Situated 8,299-feet above sea level, the vistas are breathtaking! Fishermen, bring your rods and cast your lines in one of the major rivers. Maybe you'll catch dinner. The forest is home to elk, black bears, wolverine, gray foxes, black-tailed deer and antelope.

See the NATIONAL FOREST HIKING TRAIL LOCATOR for a complete list of dog-friendly hikes in the Kalamath National Forest.

LAKE TAHOE BASIN MANAGEMENT UNIT

This 148,000 acre national forest embraces the southern half of Lake Tahoe. The forest serves as the lake's guardian, protecting the land from further development.

Over 100 miles of trails lace both the Desolation Wilderness Area and the Mount Rose Wilderness Area, rising from 6,300 feet to over 10,000. A jaunt to Fallen Leaf Lake and Echo Lake provides an escape from the crowds. Pooches must be leashed in all areas of this jurisdiction.

LASSEN NATIONAL FOREST

A day of volcanic adventures can be yours at this 1.2 million acre national forest which encircles Lassen Volcanic National Park (dogs are not permitted in the park). Hike the 1.5 mile Spattercone Trail and observe fascinating volcanic craters and unusual lava formations.

The vast terrain of this forest is filled with 135 miles of trails which rise in elevation from 1,500 feet to 8,677-foot Crater Peak, the highest point. Ishi, Caribou and Thousand Lakes Wilderness Areas are contained within the forest. Black bears, mountain lions and coyotes are a few of the wildlife species which reside there.

Fishermen will be happy to learn that Eagle Lake, Hat Creek and Lake Almanor offer trout-filled waters, a perfect way to end an exhausting day of exploring caves, canyons and volcanic-made lakes.

See the NATIONAL FOREST HIKING TRAIL LOCATOR for a complete list of dog-friendly hikes in the Lassen National Forest.

LOS PADRES NATIONAL FOREST

From the Big Sur coastline and natural hot springs, to a refuge for endangered California condors and the redwood-shaded Ventana Wilderness Area, this spectacular 1.7 million acre national forest has it all.

Spend hours hiking over 1,200 miles of trails through rugged mountainous terrain. Five wilderness areas filled with streams, waterfalls, steep craggy bluffs, deep chasms and rock formations are located within this region. Feeling extremely energetic? Set your sights on Mount Pinos, situated at 8,831 feet above sea level, the highest point in the forest. The five wilderness areas include: Ventana, Machesna Mountain, San Rafael, Santa Lucia and Dick Smith.

Best hiking conditions are in winter and spring. Trails may be closed July through November due to high fire danger.

See the NATIONAL FOREST HIKING TRAIL LOCATOR for a complete list of dog-friendly hikes in the Los Padres National Forest.

MENDOCINO NATIONAL FOREST

Nearly 900,000 acres of peaceful abandonment can be yours at this national forest in the North Coast Mountain Range just north of San Francisco. Take a panoramic journey along 600 miles of trails through dense woodlands, lush grasslands and deep gorges.

Both the northern Yolla Bolly-Middle Eel Wilderness and the southern Snow Mountain Wilderness provide beautiful and tranquil nature experiences. Visit in the spring or early summer when orange poppies, red bud, blue lupine and bush lilac carpet the meadow floors. Some areas require leashes. Check with local rangers.

See the NATIONAL FOREST HIKING TRAIL LOCATOR for a complete list of dog-friendly hikes in the Mendocino National Forest.

MODOC NATIONAL FOREST

What do bald eagles, ancient Indian petroglyphs and pictographs, lava formations and glacial lakes have in common? The answer is Modoc National Forest, nearly 1.7 million acres of pure natural beauty.

The interesting terrain is comprised of pine and fir woodlands, grassy meadows, wetlands, cliffs and canyons. Two of the most remarkable sights can be seen in the Medicine Lake highlands; Glass Mountain, formed by a massive flow of obsidian and the Burnt Lava Flow, formed by a mound of black lava. Medicine Lake was once an old volcanic crater.

South Warner Wilderness is the only wilderness area within this forest's boundry. Trek to Eagle Peak, the highest point in the forest, and treat yourself to incredible panoramic views.

See the NATIONAL FOREST HIKING TRAIL LOCATOR for a complete list of dog-friendly hikes in the Modoc National Forest.

PLUMAS NATIONAL FOREST

Sandwiched between the Sierra Nevada and the Cascades lies a beautiful, mountainous, water-rich national forest containing over 1,000 miles of rivers and streams and nearly 100 lakes. Anglers, you may have found your heaven on earth!

In addition to 640-foot Feather Falls (the 6th highest waterfall in the U.S.) more than 300 miles of hiking trails lead you over rocky cliffs, bluffs and chasms of surging white water carved by Feather River. Experienced hikers should head for the 7,017-foot Spanish Peak in Bucks Lake Wilderness Area for outstanding views.

See the NATIONAL FOREST HIKING TRAIL LOCATOR for a complete list of dog-friendly hikes in the Plumas National Forest.

SAN BERNARDINO NATIONAL FOREST

Lake Arrowhead and Big Bear Lake resorts are encircled by this scenic 660,000-acre forest in Southern California. From cactus-filled desert regions to dense pine, fir and juniper woodlands, granite chasms to remote canyons, there are over 500 miles of trails - each offering unique and spectacular panoramic vistas.

San Bernardino National Forest is home to the highest point in Southern California, the 11,502-foot San Gorgonio Mountain. The forest also encompasses four wilderness areas: Cucamonga, San Gorgonio, Santa Rosa and San Jacinto. Dogs are not permitted in most of the San Jacinto Wilderness.

See the NATIONAL FOREST HIKING TRAIL LOCATOR for a complete list of dog-friendly hikes in the San Bernadino National Forest.

SEQUOIA NATIONAL FOREST

This vast 1.1 million acre national forest situated in the southern Sierras, affords you the opportunity of experiencing nature at its best. Witness firsthand the awe-inspiring giant sequoias on the lower slopes of the forest. You can't miss Boole Tree, the largest tree in any national forest. This mammoth sequoia stands 270 feet tall with a 90-foot circumference.

The forest's more than 900 miles of trails usher you through oak woodlands, flower-scented meadows, desert areas, steep canyons, granite peaks, lakes and waterfalls. White-water rafting on the fast moving Kern and Kings Rivers is an added bonus.

The Golden Trout, Monarch, Jennie Lakes, South Sierra and Dome Land comprise the wilderness areas of the forest. Mount Florence at 12,432 feet is the highest peak.

See the NATIONAL FOREST HIKING TRAIL LOCATOR for a complete list of dog-friendly hikes in the Sequoia National Forest.

SHASTA-TRINITY NATIONAL FOREST

The king of California's national forests is the colossal 2.1 million acre Shasta-Trinity National Forest. Canvas the remarkable terrain via 1,400 miles of trails. Wander through meadows alive with vibrant wildflowers, splash in beautiful mountain creeks twinkling with waterfalls, swim in sparkling lakes, hike over steep granite ridges, bluffs, glaciers and dried mounds of lava.

Glaciers and lava together? Yes, both of these extraordinary sights are compliments of Mount Shasta, a towering 14,162 feet high and 17 miles wide. This dormant, snow and glacier-covered volcano is the second highest in the Cascades.

The lakes of this forest beckon all anglers. Cast your line into Trinity Lake or find a secluded spot along 370-mile Shasta Lake. Five separate wilderness areas are within the forest's boundaries: Castle Crags, Chanchelulla, Mount Shasta, Trinity Alps and Yolla Bolly-Middle Eel.

See the NATIONAL FOREST HIKING TRAIL LOCATOR for a complete list of dog-friendly hikes in the Shasta-Trinity National Forest.

SIERRA NATIONAL FOREST

Situated between Yosemite and Kings Canyon National Parks, the beauty of this 1.3 million acre forest includes snow-covered peaks and glaciers of the High Sierra, fathomless chasms and ravines carved by the San Joaquin and Kings Rivers and magnificent groves of giant sequoias.

A true appreciation of this majestic forest can be gained by hiking your choice of 1,100 miles of trails. Five wilderness areas, Ansel Adams, Dinkey Lakes, John Muir, Kaiser and Monarch offer distinctly beautiful landscapes. Mount Humphreys at nearly 14,000 feet is the highest point in the forest. High elevation areas are usually snow covered until July.

See the NATIONAL FOREST HIKING TRAIL LOCATOR for a complete list of dog-friendly hikes in the Sierra National Forest.

SIX RIVERS NATIONAL FOREST

1,500 miles of waterways flow through this 990,000-acre national forest, heaven for all water-loving humans and canines. A wet-and-wild adventure awaits in the waters of six major rivers - Smith, Klamath, Trinity, Mad, Van Duzen and Eel. Or stay on terra firma and explore over 200 miles of trails. Pack binoculars as sightings of the endangered bald eagle and Peregrine falcon are fairly common.

Four wilderness areas are part of Six Rivers National Forest: North Fork, Siskiyou, Trinity Alps and Yolla Bolly-Middle Eel.

See the NATIONAL FOREST HIKING TRAIL LOCATOR for a complete list of dog-friendly hikes in the Six-Rivers National Forest.

STANISLAUS NATIONAL FOREST

More than 700 miles of trails can be explored in this beautiful 900,000-acre national forest. Hike alpine grasslands or dense pine and fir woodlands. The panoramic trails pass river-carved canyons, granite cliffs, volcanic peaks and glacial lakes and offer outstanding views.

Lake Alpine and 11,520-foot Leavitt Peak, the forest's highest point, are two main attractions. High elevation areas are usually snow covered from October to June. The Emigrant, Mokelumne and Carson-Iceberg Wilderness areas are within the forest.

See the NATIONAL FOREST HIKING TRAIL LOCATOR for a complete list of dog-friendly hikes in the Stanislaus National Forest.

TAHOE NATIONAL FOREST

Nestled in the majestic snow-capped Sierra Nevada, this 830,000-acre national forest offers 500 miles of trails through dense woodlands, mountain meadows, alpine lakes, rock outcrops, steep-walled chasms and plunging waterfalls.

Take the trail past the vintage quartz mines of the Sierra Buttes. Or on a hot sultry day, cool off beside the North Fork American National Wild and Scenic River. The Granite Chief Wilderness Area is located within the forest's boundaries. Most high trails are snow-covered until July.

See the NATIONAL FOREST HIKING TRAIL LOCATOR for a complete list of dog-friendly hikes in the Tahoe National Forest.

TOIYABE NATIONAL FOREST

The majority of this 3.8 million acre spectacle of nature lies in Nevada, but California is still home to a portion of the largest national forest in the continental United States.

Hundreds of miles of trails wander among glacial lakes, alpine meadows and cascading waterfalls in the Hoover and Carson-Iceberg Wilderness Areas. Vistas are plentiful in this enchanting forest, especially near Lake Tahoe.

See the NATIONAL FOREST HIKING TRAIL LOCATOR for a complete list of dog-friendly hikes in the Toiyabe National Forest.

DEATH VALLEY NATIONAL PARK

Ancient does not even begin to describe this enormous 2 million acre national park which has been forming for over 3 million years. Within this geological phenomenon, you'll discover archaic salt deposits, giant sand dunes and volcanic craters. The unearthly landscape changes dramatically from desert to snow-dappled mountains. A spectacular sight is the changing color of canyon and mountain walls which occurs with the shifting sunlight.

Elevations within the valley range from 282 feet below sea level (Badwater Basin) to 11,049 feet above sea level (Telescope Peak). Not only is Badwater Basin the lowest point in the valley, it's the lowest point in the Western Hemisphere.

Death Valley Tips:

- Dogs are not allowed on the trails, but are allowed on the roadways.
- Coyote, mountain lions, bighorn sheep and mule deer inhabit the area.
- Hiking Death Valley is not recommended between April and September.
- Pack plenty of water for both you and your pooch.
- Pick up a brochure of the area at the visitor's center.
- $5 parking fee.

JOSHUA TREE NATIONAL MONUMENT

Nestled in southern California, just east of the San Bernardino National Forest are 548,000 acres of vast desert terrain, stunning granite rock formations and deep gorges.

The monument's elegant namesake, the unusual and intriguingly shaped Joshua Trees, can be found in the western half of the park. You will not soon forget the sight of the "praying plants" with their upstretched arms backdropped by mountain ranges rising to nearly 6,000 feet. Everywhere you turn, springtime fills the desert with gorgeous multi-hued wildflowers.

Joshua Tree Tips:

- $5 entrance fee.
- Bighorn sheep, cougars and bobcats roam the desert.
- Avoid in warm months.
- Pooches are not permitted on the trails, but are allowed on the roadways.

POINT REYES NATIONAL SEASHORE

Pretty beaches, limestone cliffs, freshwater lakes and woodsy Inverness Ridge are all part of Point Reyes National Seashore. This ruggedly picturesque area stretches along the northern coast of California and encircles 65,303 acres.

Many of the secluded beaches of Point Reyes National Seashore offer whale and seal sightings, as well as over 350 species of birds and 72 species of mammals. Dogs are not permitted on the 75 miles of hiking trails or in the campgrounds. Where permitted on beaches, they must be leashed to protect the harbor seals and snowy plovers, an endangered shorebird.

National Forest Tips & Info

- April through July are the driest months, increasing the threat of forest fires.

- Be certain that your campfire is completely out. Use your hands to spread dirt and water over the coals.

- If you smoke, adhere to these precautions. Don't smoke on trails. Clear a small area to be used as an ashtray. Pack out your cigarette butts, filters don't easily decompose.

- Water hemlock, mushrooms and berries can be deadly. If you are unsure of a plant's identity, leave it alone.

- Afternoon thunderstorms are a common occurrence from July to summer's end.

- Flash floods are common after heavy rains, especially in canyons and washes.

- Carry tire chains. They are extremely helpful on mud slicked, snow covered and ice coated roads.

- When hiking into a forest, identify landmarks for your hike out. Build cairns along the way, except in wilderness areas.

- Inform a third party of your itinerary and when you expect to return. Upon your return, contact that person.

- From mid-May to July, deerflies and horseflies are troublesome above 7,000 feet.

- Summer rains bring a profusion of mosquitos.

- Learn to identify poison oak. Leaves are usually shiny, bright green in the spring, bright red, or maroon in the fall. In the winter, there are no leaves. Poison oak can look like a shrub or vine always with three-lobed leaves. Remember: "Leaves of three, let it be."

- Dogs must be leashed in all developed areas.

- It's illegal to remove or disturb historic and/or prehistoric artifacts.

- Pack enough water to last the extent of your trip and then some - untreated stream or lake water can cause illness.

- Begin car travel with a full tank of gas.

- A shovel is an invaluable tool to store in your car.

- Don't litter. Litter lasts this long:

Cigarette butts...................1 - 5 Years
Aluminum cans..................80 - 100 Years
Orange peels......................Up to 2 Years
Plastic bags......................10 - 20 Years
Glass bottles......................1 Million Years
Tin cans..............................50 Years
Wool socks..........................1 - 5 Years
Plastic bottles....................Indefinitely

IF YOU PACK IT IN... PACK IT OUT

EVERYTHING YOU WANT TO KNOW ABOUT PET CARE AND WHO TO ASK

Whether you've always had dogs or you're starting out with your first, the following organizations and hotlines can provide information on the care, feeding and protection of your loyal companions.

Pet behavior information

Tree House Animal Foundation: If you are concerned with canine aggression, nipping, biting, housebreaking or other behavioral problems, the Tree House Animal Foundation will try to help. But don't wait until the last minute. Call for advice early on and your animal's problems will be easier to correct. Consultation is free, except for applicable long distance charges. Call (312) 784-5488, 9AM to 5PM CST, seven days a week.

Dial-Pet: Health and care topics for pets including dogs, cats, horses, small animals, exotics and fish. Call (312) 342-5738 any time. (You must have a touch-tone phone to use the service.) Basically, it's a hotline sponsored by the Chicago Veterinary Medical Association. Vets who belong to the organization write and then record 5-7 minute messages on subjects ranging from ear problems to training tips. There's no charge except applicable long distance charges. Or, if you prefer, write for a list of topics to: DIAL-PET, Chicago Veterinary Medical Association, 161 S. Lincolnway, North Aurora, IL 60542.

Animal Behavior Helpline: This organization is sponsored by the San Francisco Society for the Prevention of Cruelty to Animals. It will assist you in solving canine behavioral problems. Staffed by volunteers, you may reach a recorded message. However, calls are returned within 48 hours by volunteers trained in animal behavior. Problems such as chewing, digging and barking are cited as the most common reason dog owners call. House-breaking tips, how to deal with aggression and other topics are covered. Callers are first asked to speak about the problem and describe what steps have been taken to correct inappropriate behavior. After evaluating the information, specific advice is given to callers. The consultation is free, except for applicable long distance charges or collect call charges when a counselor returns your call. Messages can be left any time. Call (415) 554-3075.

Poison Control Center: There are two telephone numbers for this organization. The 800 number is an emergency line for both veterinarians and pet owners for emergency poisoning information. Calls are taken by the veterinarian-staffed National Animal Poison Control Center at the University of Illinois. When calling the 800 number, there is a charge of $30 per case. Every call made to the 800 number is followed up by the NAPCC. Callers to the 900 line pay $20 for the first 5 minutes and $2.95 for every minute thereafter with a minimum charge of $20 and a maximum of $30. The 900 number is for non-emergency questions and there is no follow up.

When calling the NAPCC, be prepared to provide your name and address and the name of the suspected poison (be specific). If the product is manufactured by a company that is a member of the Animal Product Safety Service - the company may pay the charge.

In all other cases, you pay for the consultation. You must also provide the animal species, breed, sex, and weight. You will be asked to describe symptoms as well as unusual behavior. This detailed information is critical - it can mean the difference between life or death for your dog.

For emergencies only, call (800) 548-2423. Major credit cards are accepted. For non-emergency questions, call (900) 680-0000. The Poison Control Center offers poison control information by veterinarians 24 hours a day, 7 days a week.

Poinsettias and other toxic plants... pretty but deadly

During the Christmas holidays, the risk of poisoning and injury is greater for your dog. If eaten, poinsettias and holly berries for example, can be fatal. Although there are conflicting reports on the effects of mistletoe, play it safe and keep your dogs away from this plant. Be alert - swallowed tree ornaments, like ribbon and tinsel can cause choking and/or intestinal problems.

Christmas wiring is another potential problem. Your dog can be electrocuted by chewing on it. And don't forget about the dangers of poultry bones. The same goes for aluminum foil including those disposable pans so popular at holiday time.

Keep your trash inaccessible. And remember that the holidays are a source of excitement and stress to both people and animals. Maintain your dog's feeding and walking schedules and provide plenty of TLC and playtime. Then everyone, including your pooch, will find the holidays more enjoyable.

FYI...
common plants that are toxic to dogs*

Amaryllis (bulbs)

Appleseeds (cyanide)

Azalea

Boxwood

Caladium

Cherry Pits (cyanide)

Climbing Lilly

Daffodil (bulb)

Delphinium

Dumb Cane

English Ivy

Foxglove

Holly

Hydrangea

Japanese Yew

Jerusalem Cherry

Laburnum

Laurel

Marigold

Mistletoe (berries)

Mushrooms

Nightshade

Peach

Poinsettia

Privet

Rhubarb

Stinging Nettie

Tobacco

Walnuts

Yew

Andromeda

Arrowglass

Bittersweet

Buttercup

Castor Bean

Chokecherry

Crown of Thorns

Daphne

Dieffenbachia

Elephant Ear

Elderberry

Hemlock

Hyacinth (bulbs)

Iris (bulb)

Jasmine (berries)

Jimsonweed

Larkspur

Locoweed

Marijuana

Monkshood

Narcissus (bulb)

Oleander

Philodendron

Poison Ivy

Rhododendron

Snow on the Mountain

Toadstool

Tulip (bulb)

Wisteria

NOTE: This is only a partial list.

PET LOSS SUPPORT HELPLINES

Chicago Veterinary Medical Association:

If you are experiencing the loss of a beloved pet, there is help provided by the Chicago Veterinary Medical Association. Call and leave a voice mail message. A counselor will return your call. Veterinarians staff the hotline and are trained to help owners accept the loss of a pet. Written materials are sent on request. When needed, referrals to professional grief counselors are also provided. Consultation and call are free except for applicable long distance charges. Call (708) 603-3884, any time. Calls are returned from 7PM to 9PM, Monday through Friday.

University of California at Davis:

Another valuable hotline, calls are staffed and answered by veterinary students. Whether you're grieving for a pet who has already died or in anticipation of a sick or elderly pet dying, the Pet Loss Hotline will help you deal with your grief. Parents may also call to learn how to explain the loss of a pet to a child. Consultation is free except for applicable long distance charges. Return calls are COLLECT. Messages can be left any time. The Hotline is staffed 6:30PM to 9:30PM EST, Monday through Friday during the school year. Call (916) 752-4200.

University of Florida at Gainesville College:

Their hotline is staffed by veterinary students as well as other volunteers who provide grief counseling for pet owners. Owners leave a message on a voice mail system and calls are returned by a counselor (at no charge) between 7PM and 9PM EST. Counselors are trained to help grieving owners and will provide written materials upon request. Call (904) 392-4700, Ext. 4080, any time. Consultation is free, except for applicable long distance charges.

College of Veterinary Medicine at Michigan:

Provides a Pet Loss Support Hotline staffed by veterinary students trained in crisis intervention. Volunteers help owners cope with their loss. Calls are followed up with pet loss related materials as well as information about the pet loss support group. Consultation and call are free except for applicable long distance charges. Return calls are *COLLECT*. Call (517) 483-2692, any time. Hotline is staffed on Tuesday, Wednesday and Thursday, from 6:30PM to 9:30PM EST.

Pet nutrition information — ALPO, HILLS, IAMS

These three organizations are manufacturers of products to the animal market. Each has a Pet Nutrition Hotline offering information on their own products as well as pet health and other pet-related questions. Free written materials are also available on such topics as canine obesity, pet loss, training, feeding guidelines and puppy-proofing a house. All consultations and printed materials are free.

ALPO: (800) 366-6033 9AM to 5PM EST, Monday through Friday.

HILLS: (800) 445-5777 8AM to 6PM CST, Monday through Friday.

IAMS: (800) 525-4267 8AM to 8PM EST, Monday through Saturday. This hotline is also available to international calls, with translation in 140 languages.

FIDO FACT:

- *Want to register your puppy, or locate a breeder? The American Kennel Club's customer service line is (919) 233-9767. Their interactive voice processing telephone system is open twenty-four hours a day, seven days a week. Information is available on dog and litter registrations.*

ANIMAL ETHICS ORGANIZATIONS

American Humane Association:

63 Inverness Drive East, Englewood, CO 80112; (303) 792-9900 or toll-free at (800) 227-4645.

This national, non-profit animal welfare organization has been dedicated to the prevention of cruelty, neglect, and exploitation of animals since it's founding in 1877. Key programs include: improving the care and welfare of pet animals, developing training and resources for animal shelters and humane societies across the country, strengthening animal cruelty laws and enforcement, being a national coordinator of emergency animal relief for natural disasters and legislative advocacy for pets, wildlife and lab animals. $15/year includes updates and quarterly magazine.

American Society For Prevention of Cruelty to Animals:

424 E. 92nd St., New York, NY 10128; (212) 876-7711; 9AM to 5PM EST, Monday through Friday.

An organization that places emphasis on prevention of cruelty to animals.

Humane Society of the United States:

2100 L St., NW, Washington, DC 20037; (202) 452-1100.

Non-profit animal welfare organization involved in numerous animal welfare issues.

National Animal Interest Alliance:

P. O. Box 66579, Portland, OR 97290; (503) 761-1139.

A national animal welfare umbrella organization that provides factual information on issues that may be unknown or confusing to the public. $25/year includes "The Alliance Alert" newsletter.

National Anti-Vivisection Society:

53 West Jackson Boulevard, Chicago, IL 60604;
(800) 888-NAVS.

Non-profit, charitable animal welfare organization devoted to stopping the use of animals in biomedical research. $25/year (discounts for students and seniors) includes updates and a quarterly publications, plus special publications, such as "Personal Care for People Who Care," a guide to over 750 companies that are cruelty-free.

People for the Ethical Treatment of Animals (PETA):

P. O. Box 42516, Washington, DC 20015;
(301) 770-7444.

Non-profit, animal rights organization that works through undercover investigations and research, and grass-roots activist and public education campaigns, to teach people about the cruelties involved in beef production, the fur trade, laboratory experiments, and various animal entertainment acts. $15/year includes "Guide to Compassionate Living," the quarterly magazine "PETA News," action alerts and updates.

FIDO FACTS

The following assortment of facts, tidbits and data will increase your knowledge of our canine companions.

- Gain the confidence of a worried dog by avoiding direct eye contact or by turning away, exposing your back or side to the dog.

- When dogs first meet, it's uncommon for them to approach each other head on. Most will approach in curving lines. They'll walk beyond each other's noses sniffing at rear ends while standing side by side.

- Dog ownership is a common bond and the basis of impromptu conversations as well as lasting friendships.

- Chemical salt makes sidewalks less slippery but can be harmful to your dog's footpads. Wash you dog's paws after walks to remove salt. Don't let him lick the salt either. It's poisonous.

- Vets warn that removing tar with over-the-counter petroleum products can be highly toxic.

- Although a dog's vision is better than humans in the dark, bright red and green are the easiest colors for them to see.

- Puppies are born blind. Their eyes open and they begin to see at 10 to 14 days.

- The best time to separate a pup from his mother is seven to ten weeks after birth.

- It's a sign of submission when a dog's ears are held back close to his head.

- Hot pavement can damage your dog's sensitive footpads. In the summer months, walk your pooch in the morning or evening or on grassy areas and other cool surfaces.

- Never leave your dog unattended in the car during the warm weather months or extremely cold ones.

- Always walk your dog on a leash on hotel/motel grounds.

- Want to register your puppy, or locate a breeder in your area? The American Kennel Club has a new customer service line at (919) 233-9767. Their interactive voice processing telephone system is open twenty-four hours a day, seven days a week. Information is available on dog and litter registrations. You can also use the number to order registration materials, certified pedigrees, books and videos. If you want to speak with a customer service rep, call during business hours.

- Stroke a dog instead of patting it. Stroking is soothing. Patting can make some dogs nervous.

- If your dog is lonely for you when he's left alone, try leaving your voice on a tape and let it play during your absence.

- When a dog licks you with a straight tongue, he's saying "I Love You."

- Don't do anything on the road with your dog that you wouldn't do at home.

- Never put your dog in the bed of a pickup truck as a means of transportation.

- Black dogs and dark colored ones are more susceptible to the heat.

- When traveling, take a spray bottle of water with you. A squirt in your dog's mouth will temporarily relieve his thirst.

- Changing your dog's water supply too quickly can cause stomach upset. Take along a container of water from home and replenish with local water, providing a gradual change.

- One in five dogs suffers from some form of allergy. Sneezing and watery eyes could be an allergic reaction caused by pollen or smoke.

- Inflamed skin can indicate a sensitivity to grass or chemicals used in carpet cleaning.

- Patches of hair loss, itching and redness are common signs of fleas, particularly during warm months.

- Normal temperature for dogs: 100° to 102°.

- No matter how much your dog begs, do not overfeed him.

- Housebreaking problems can sometimes be attributed to diet. Consult with your vet about one good dog food and be consistent in feeding. A change in your dog's diet can lead to digestive problems.

- Spay or neuter your dog to prevent health problems and illnesses that plague the intact animal. Contrary to popular belief, spaying or neutering your canine will not result in weight gain. Only food and lack of exercise can do that.

- Spend ample quality time with your canine every day. Satisfy his need for social contact.

- Obedience train your dog, it's good for his mental well being and yours too.

- If you make training fun for you and Fido, he'll learn faster.

- Always provide cool fresh drinking water for your dog.

- If you have an outdoor pooch, make sure he has easy access to shade and plenty of water.

- If your pooch lives indoors, make certain he has access to cool moving air and ample fresh water.

- In the summertime, avoid exercising your dog during the hottest parts of the day.

- Never tie your dog or let him run free while he's wearing a choke collar. Choke collars can easily hook on something and strangle him.

- The Chinese Shar-Pei and the Chow have blue-black tongues instead of pink ones.

- The smallest breed of dog is the Chihuahua.

- Poodles, Bedlington Terriers, Bichon Frises, Schnauzers and Soft-Coated Wheaten Terriers don't shed.

- Terriers and toy breeds usually bark the most.

- The Basenji is often called the barkless dog.

- Golden Labs and Retrievers are fast learners, making them easy to train.

- Climate counts when deciding on a breed. Collies and Pugs will be unhappy in hot, humid climates. But the Italian Greyhound and Chihuahua originated in hot climes, the heat won't bother them, but winter will. They'll need insulation in the form of dog apparel to protect them from the cold. And as you might think, heavy-coated dogs like the Saint Bernard, Siberian Husky and the Newfy thrive in cooler weather.

- Apartment dwellers, consider the Dachshund and Cairn Terrier. Both can be content in small quarters.

- Fido's fitness counts towards insuring a longer, healthier life. In this arena, you're the one in control. The most common cause of ill health in canines is obesity. Approximately 60% of all adult dogs are overweight or will become overweight due to lack of physical activity and overfeeding. Much like humans, the medical consequences of obesity include liver, heart and orthopedic problems. As little as a few extra pounds on a small dog can lead to health-related complications.

- Is your pooch pudgy? Place both thumbs on your dog's backbone and then run your fingers along his rib cage. If the bony part of each rib cannot be easily felt, your dog may be overweight. Another quickie test - stand directly over your dog while he's standing. If you can't see a clearly defined waist behind his rib cage, he's probably too portly.

- It's easier than you might think to help your dog lose those extra pounds. Begin by eliminating unnecessary table scraps. Cut back a small amount on the kibble or canned dog food you normally feed your pooch, if he's accustomed to two full cups each day, reduce that amount to 1 3/4 cups instead. If you normally give your pooch biscuits every day, cut the amount in half. And don't feel guilty. Stick with the program and you'll even-tually see a reduction in weight. Slow and steady is the best approach. And don't let yourself imagine that your dog is being deprived of anything. Even when he looks at you with a woebegone expression, remember you're doing him a favor by helping him reduce and you're adding years of good health to his life.

- Exercise. Not enough can be said about the benefits. Establish a daily exercise routine. Awaken twenty minutes earlier every morning and take a brisk mile walk. Instead of immediately watching TV after dinner, walk off some calories. Your pooch's overall good health, as well as your own, will be vastly enhanced.

- According to a survey, 90% of dog owners speak to their dogs like humans, walk or run with their dogs and take pictures of them; 72% take their pups for car rides and discuss Digger with their friends; 51% hang Christmas stockings for their dogs; 41% watch movies and TV with their pooches; 29% sign Rover's name to greeting cards and more than 20% buy homes with their dogs in mind, carry photos of Fido with them and arrange the furniture so FiFi can see outside.

- Lewis and Clark traveled with a 150-pound Newfoundland named "Seamen". This pooch was a respected member of the expedition, and his antics were included in the extensive diaries of these famous explorers.

- The infamous Red Baron owned a Great Dane named Moritz who lived on the military base with the pilot. The Red Baron fondly referred to Moritz as his "little lapdog."

- Frederick the Great owned an estimated 30 Greyhounds. His love of these animals led him to coin the saying: "The more I see of men, the more I love my dogs."

- The English have a saying: The virtues of a dog are its own, its vices those of its master.

- Lord Byron, in his eulogy to his dog Boatswain, wrote, "One who possessed beauty without vanity, strength without insolence, courage without ferocity, and all the virtues of man without his vices."

- "Be Kind To Animals Week" (May 7-13) was established in 1915. Recognized by Congress, this is the oldest week of its kind in the nation.

- The "Always Faithful" Memorial, which honors Dogs of War, was unveiled on June 20, 1994. It now stands on the US Naval Base in Orote Point, Guam.

- During WWII, the Doberman was an official member of the US Marine Corps combat force.

- The domestic dog dates back more than 50,000 years.

- Ghandi once said, "The greatness of a nation and its moral progress can be judged by the way its animals are treated."

- England's Dickin Medal is specifically awarded to dogs for bravery and outstanding behavior in wartime.

- Napoleon's wife, Josephine, had a Pug named Fortune. She relied on the animal to carry secret messages under his collar to Napoleon while she was imprisoned at Les Carnes.

- Former First Lady Barbara Bush: "An old dog that has served you long and well is like an old painting. The patina of age softens and beautifies, and like a master's work, can never be replaced by exactly the same thing, ever again."

- Dogs and Halloween don't mix. Even the mellowest of pooches can become frightened and overexcited by all the commotion. Save the candy collecting and chocolate for the kids, and leave the dog at home.

- Most outdoor dogs suffer from unnoticed parasites like fleas.

- In winter, the water in an outdoor dog dish can freeze within an hour.

- In summer, dogs consume large quantities of water. Bowls need frequent refilling.

PET POEMS, PROCLAMATIONS, PRAYERS...& HOMEMADE DOG BISCUITS!

Ode to Travel with Pets

We're all set to roam

Going far from home

With doggies in tow

Off shall we go

To wander and gadabout

Since travel we're mad about

With Rosie and Max by my side

We'll all go for a ride

As we travel for miles

And bring about smiles

Rosie will grin

Max will chime in

Driving into the sunset

Odometers all set

But enough of these word rhymes

Let's roll with the good times!

— Eileen Barish, November 1994

Alone Again

I wish someone would tell me what it is
    That I've done wrong.
Why I have to stay chained up and
    Left alone so long.
They seemed so glad to have me
    When I came here as a pup.
There were so many things we'd do
    While I was growing up.
They couldn't wait to train me as a
    Companion and a friend.
And told me how they'd never fear
    Being left alone again.
The children said they'd feed me and
    Brush me every day.
They'd play with me and walk me
    If only I could stay.
But now the family "Hasn't time,"
    They often say I shed.
They do not even want me in the house
    Not even to be fed.
The children never walk me.
    They always say "Not now!"
I wish that I could please them.
    Won't someone tell me how?
All I had, you see, was love.
    I wish they would explain
Why they said they wanted me
    Then left me on a chain?

— Anonymous

A Dogs Bill of Rights

I have the right to give and receive
   unconditional love.
I have the right to a life that is beyond
   mere survival.
I have the right to be trained so I do not become
   the prisoner of my own misbehavior.
I have the right to adequate food and
   medical care.
I have the right to fresh air and green grass.
I have the right to socialize with people
   and dogs outside my family.
I have the right to have my needs
   and wants respected.
I have the right to a special time with
   my people .
I have the right to only be bred
   responsibly if at all.
I have the right to be foolish and silly, and
   to make my person laugh.
I have the right to earn my person's trust
   and be trusted in return.
I have the right to be forgiven.
I have the right to die with dignity.
I have the right to be remembered well.

A Dog's Prayer

Treat me kindly, my beloved master, for no heart in all the world is more grateful for kindness, than the loving heart of mine.

Do not break my spirit with a stick, for though I should lick your hand between the blows, your patience and understanding will more quickly teach me the things you would have me do.

Speak to me often, for your voice is the world's sweetest music as you must know by the fierce wagging of my tail when your footstep falls up on my waiting ear.

When it is cold and wet, please take me inside...for I am now a domesticated animal, no longer used to bitter elements...and I ask no greater glory than the privilege of sitting at your feet beside the hearth...though had you no home, I would rather follow you through ice and snow, than rest upon the softest pillow in the warmest home in all the land...for you are my God...and I am your devoted worshipper.

Keep my pan filled with fresh water, for although I should not reproach you were it dry, I cannot tell you when I suffer thirst. Feed me clean food, that I may stay well, to romp and play and do your bidding, to walk by your side, and stand ready willing and able to protect you with my life, should your life be in danger.

And beloved master, should the Great Master see fit to deprive me of my health or sight, do not turn away from me. Rather hold me gently in your arms, as skilled hands grant me the merciful boon of eternal rest...and I will leave you knowing with the last breath I draw, my fate was ever safest in your hands.

Rainbow Bridge

There is a bridge connecting Heaven and Earth. It is called the Rainbow Bridge because of its many colors. Just this side of the Rainbow Bridge there is a land of meadows, hills and valleys with lush green grass.

When a beloved pet dies, the pet goes to this place. There is always food and water and warm spring weather. The old and frail animals are young again. Those who are maimed are made whole again. They play all day with each other.

There is only one thing missing. They are not with their special person who loved them on Earth. So each day they run and play until the day comes when one suddenly stops playing and looks up! The nose twitches! The ears are up! The eyes are staring! And this one suddenly runs from the group!

You have been seen, and when you and your special friend meet, you take him or her in your arms and embrace. Your face is kissed again and again, and you look once more into the eyes of your trusting pet.

Then you cross Rainbow Bridge together, never again to be separated.

Anonymous

HOMEMADE DOG BISCUITS
(Makes about 8 dozen biscuits)

3 1/2 cups all-purpose flour

2 cups whole wheat flour

1 cup rye flour

1 cup cornmeal

2 cups cracked wheat bulgur

1/2 cup nonfat dry milk

4 tsp. salt

1 package dry yeast

2 cups chicken stock or other liquid

1 egg and 1 tbsp. milk (to brush on top)

Combine all the dry ingredients except the yeast. In a separate bowl, dissolve the yeast in 1/4 cup warm water. To this, add the chicken stock. (You can use bouillon, pan drippings or water from cooking vegetables.) Add the liquid to the dry ingredients. Knead mixture for about 3 minutes. Dough will be quite stiff. If too stiff, add extra liquid or an egg. Preheat oven to 300 degrees. Roll the dough out on a floured board to 1/4" thickness, then immediately cut into shapes with cookie cutters. Place on an ungreased cookie sheet and brush with a wash of egg and milk. Place in oven. After 45 minutes, turn off the heat and leave biscuits overnight in the oven to get bone hard.

General Information
&
Visitor Information Bureaus

GENERAL INFORMATION

OBSERVED STATE HOLIDAYS

Below is a list of holidays observed by the state of California. New Year's Day, July 4 and Christmas are observed on the actual date of the holiday; however, if a holiday falls on a Saturday, it is celebrated on the preceding Friday and if a holiday falls on a Sunday, it is celebrated on the following Monday.

New Year's Day*	Memorial Day*
Martin Luther King's Birthday	Independence Day*
	Lincoln's Birthday*
Labor Day*	President's Day*
Columbus Day*	Veterans Day*
Thanksgiving*	Easter*
Christmas Day*	Cinco de Mayo

*National holidays- all banks and government agencies are closed.

CALIFORNIA'S STATE AND NATIONAL PARKS

California is home to 270 state parks, that include over 250 miles of lakes, rivers, coastal beaches, hiking trails, campsites, recreational areas and historic sites. For information, contact: Publications, California Department of Parks & Recreation, P.O. Box 942896, Sacramento, CA 94296-0001.

The state of California encompasses 17 national parks, historic sites and monuments, recreational facilities and campsites. For more information, contact: Western Region Information Center, National Park Service, Fort Mason, Bldg. 201, San Francisco, CA 94123, (415) 556-0560, TTY (415) 556-2766.

Note: State parks require that dogs be leashed and attended at all times. They are prohibited from trails and undeveloped areas unless otherwise specified.

Road Safety Tips:

- Don't drink and drive - a blood alcohol level of .08% or higher is considered legally intoxicated.

- Open alcohol containers in a moving vehicle are illegal.

- A blood alcohol test is mandatory for anyone arrested for driving while under the influence.

- Seatbelts are the law.

- Child safety seats are mandatory for children ages 4 years and under or who weigh under 40 lbs.

- Adhere to the maximum speed limit of 55 mph (90 km). Several freeways are marked as 65 mph (105 km).

- Helmets are the law for all motorcyclists and passengers.

For information on road conditions, contact Caltrans 24-hour service:

Northern California...(916) 445-7623

Southern California...(213) 628-7623

Statewide..(800) 427-7623

CALIFORNIA VISITOR INFORMATION BUREAUS

ALPINE COUNTY CHAMBER OF
COMMERCE
P.O. Box 265, Markleeville, CA 96120,
(916) 694-2475.

ALTURAS CHAMBER OF COMMERCE
522 S. Main St., P.O. Box 1170,
Alturas, CA 96103,
(916) 233-4434.

AMADOR COUNTY CHAMBER OF
COMMERCE
125 Peek St., P.O. Box 596,
Jackson, CA 95642,
(209) 223-0350 or (800) 649-4988.

ANAHEIM/ORANGE COUNTY VISITOR
AND CONVENTION BUREAU
800 W. Katella Ave., Anaheim, CA 92802,
(714) 999-8999; Fax: (714) 991-8963.

ANDERSON CHAMBER OF COMMERCE
1856 Hwy. 273, P.O. Box 1144,
Anderson, CA 96007,
(916) 365-8095, Fax: (916) 365-4561.

ANDERSON VALLEY CHAMBER OF
COMMERCE
P.O. Box 275, Boonville, CA 95415,
(707) 895-2379.

ARCATA CHAMBER OF COMMERCE
1062 G St., Arcata, CA 95521,
(707) 822-3619 or (800) 553-6569 (CA).

ARROYO GRANDE CHAMBER OF
COMMERCE
800 W. Branch St.,
Arroyo Grande, CA 93420,
(805) 489-1488.

ATASCADERO CHAMBER OF
COMMERCE
6550 El Camino Real,
Atascadero, CA 93422,
(805) 466-2044.

AUBURN AREA CHAMBER OF
COMMERCE
601 Lincoln Way, Auburn, CA 95603,
(916) 885-5616, Fax: (916) 885-5854.

AVENUE OF THE GIANTS
ASSOCIATION
P.O. Box 1000, Miranda, CA 95553,
(707) 923-2555, Fax: (707) 923-2547.

BAKERSFIELD (GREATER)
CONVENTION AND VISITORS BUREAU
1033 Truxtun Ave., Bakersfield, CA 93301,
(805) 325-5051 or (800) 325-6001.

BANNING CHAMBER OF COMMERCE
123 W. Ramsey, P.O. Box 665,
Banning, CA 92220,
(909) 849-4695.

BARSTOW AREA CHAMBER OF
COMMERCE
222 E. Main St., Ste. 216,
Barstow, CA 92311,
(619) 256-8617 or (800) CALICO-9.

BASS LAKE CHAMBER OF COMMERCE
54432 N. Shore Rd., P.O. Box 126,
Bass Lake, CA 93604, (209) 642-3676.

BEAUMONT CHAMBER OF
COMMERCE
450 E. Fourth St., P.O. Box 291, Beaumont,
CA 92223, (909) 845-9541.

BELVEDERE-TIBURON CHAMBER OF
COMMERCE
96-B Main St., P.O. Box 563,
Tiburon, CA 94920, (415) 435-5633.

BERKELEY CONVENTION AND
VISITORS BUREAU
1834 University Ave., 1st Fl.,
Berkeley, CA 94703,
(510) 549-7040 or (800) 847-4823,
Fax: (510) 644-2052.

BEVERLY HILLS VISITORS BUREAU
239 S. Beverly Dr., Beverly Hills, CA 90212,
(310) 271-8174 or (800) 345-2210,
Fax: (310) 858-8032.

BIG BEAR LAKE RESORT ASSOCIATION
P.O. Box 1936, Big Bear Lake, CA 92315,
(909) 866-6190, Fax: (909) 866-5671.

BIG SUR CHAMBER OF COMMERCE
P.O. Box 87, Big Sur, CA 93920,
(408) 667-2100.

BISHOP CHAMBER OF COMMERCE
690 N. Main St., Bishop, CA 93514,
(619) 873-8405, Fax: (619) 873-6999.

BLUE LAKE CHAMBER OF COMMERCE
P.O. Box 476, Blue Lake, CA 95525
(no telephone).

BLYTHE CHAMBER OF COMMERCE
201 S. Broadway, Blythe, CA 92225,
(619) 922-8166 or (800) 445-0541.

BODEGA BAY CHAMBER OF
COMMERCE
850 Coast Hwy. 1, P.O. Box 146,
Bodega Bay, CA 94923, (707) 875-3422.

BORREGO SPRINGS CHAMBER OF
COMMERCE
622 Palm Canyon Dr., P.O. Box 66,
Borrego Springs, CA 92004,
(619) 767-5555.

BRAWLEY CHAMBER OF COMMERCE
204 S. Imperial Ave., P.O. Box 218,
Brawley, CA 92227, (619) 344-3160.

BRIDGEPORT CHAMBER OF
COMMERCE
Hwy. 395, Main St., P.O. Box 247,
Bridgeport, CA 93517, (619) 932-7500.

BUELLTON VISITORS BUREAU
376 Ave. of Flags, P.O. Box 231,
Buellton, CA 93427,
(805) 688-7829 or (800) 324-3800,
Fax: (805) 688-5399.

BUENA PARK CONVENTION AND
VISITORS OFFICE
6280 Manchester Blvd., Ste. 103,
Buena Park, CA 90621,
(714) 562-3560 or (800) 541-3953,
Fax: (714) 562-3569.

BURLINGAME CHAMBER OF
COMMERCE
290 California Dr., Burlingame, CA 94010,
(415) 344-1735.

CALAVERAS LODGING AND VISITORS
ASSOCIATION
1211 S. Main St., P.O. Box 637,
Angels Camp, CA 95222,
(209) 736-0049 or (800) 225-3764.

CALEXICO CHAMBER OF COMMERCE
1100 Imperial Ave., P.O. Box 948,
Calexico, CA 92231, (619) 357-1166.

CALIFORNIA DESERTS TOURISM
ASSOCIATION
37-115 Palm View Rd., P.O. Box 364,
Rancho Mirage, CA 92270,
(619) 328-9256, Fax: (619) 340-4281.

CALIFORNIA HISTORIC ROUTE 66
ASSOCIATION
2127 Foothill Blvd., #66, LaVerne, CA
91750, (909) 593-4853 or (909) 593-4046,
Fax: (909) 593-1468.

CALISTOGA CHAMBER OF
COMMERCE
1458 Lincoln Ave., Calistoga, CA 94515,
(707) 942-6333.

CAMBRIA CHAMBER OF COMMERCE
767 Main St., Cambria, CA 93428,
(805) 927-3624.

CARLSBAD CONVENTION AND
 VISITORS BUREAU
400 Carlsbad Village Dr., P.O. Box 1246,
Carlsbad, CA 92018,
(619) 434-6093 or (800) 227-5722.

CARMEL BUSINESS ASSOCIATION
San Carlos and 6th,
Carmel-by-the-Sea, CA 93921,
(408) 624-2522.

CARMEL VALLEY CHAMBER OF
COMMERCE
71 W. Carmel Valley Rd., P.O. Box 288,
Carmel Valley, CA 93924,
(408) 659-4000 or (800) 543-8343.

CARPINTERIA VALLEY CHAMBER OF
COMMERCE
5320 Carpinteria Ave.,
Carpinteria, CA 93014,
(805) 684-5479, Fax: (805) 684-3477.

CATALINA ISLAND CHAMBER OF
COMMERCE
One Green Pleasure Pier, P.O. Box 217,
Avalon, CA 90704,
(310) 510-1520, Fax: (310) 510-7606.

CAYUCOS CHAMBER OF COMMERCE
80 N. Ocean Ave., P.O. Box 141,
Cayucos, CA 93430, (805) 995-1200.

CENTURY CITY CHAMBER OF
COMMERCE
1801 Century Park East, Ste. 300,
Los Angeles, CA 90067, (310) 553-2222.

CHANNEL ISLANDS HARBOR VISITOR
CENTER
3600 S. Harbor Blvd., #234,
Oxnard, CA 93035.

CHESTER/LAKE ALMANOR CHAMBER
OF COMMERCE
529 Main St., P.O. Box 1198,
Chester, CA 96020, (916) 258-2426.

CHICO CHAMBER OF COMMERCE
500 Main St., P.O. Box 3038,
Chico, CA 95927, (916) 891-5556 or
(800) 852-8570, Fax: (916) 891-3613.

CHULA VISTA VISITOR INFORMATION
CENTER
750 E St., Chula Vista, CA 91910,
(619) 425-4444.

CLAREMONT CHAMBER OF
COMMERCE AND VISITORS CENTER
205 Yale Ave., Claremont, CA 91711,
(909) 624-1681.

CLEARLAKE CHAMBER OF
COMMERCE
14335 Lakeshore Dr., P.O. Box 629,
Clearlake, CA 95422, (707) 994-3600.

CLOVERDALE CHAMBER OF
COMMERCE
132 S. Cloverdale Blvd., P.O. Box 356,
Cloverdale, CA 95425,
(707) 894-4470, Fax: (707) 894-4470.

COACHELLA CHAMBER OF
COMMERCE
1258 Sixth St., P.O. Box 126,
Coachella, CA 92236, (619) 398-5111.

COALINGA AREA CHAMBER OF
COMMERCE
380 Coalinga Plaza, Coalinga, CA 93210,
(209) 935-2948 or (800) 854-3885,
Fax: (209) 935-9044.

CONEJO VALLEY CHAMBER OF
COMMERCE
625 W. Hillcrest Dr.,
Thousand Oaks, CA 91360, (805) 499-1993.

CONTRA COSTA CONVENTION AND
VISITORS BUREAU
2151 Salvio St., Ste. N, Concord, CA 94520,
(510) 685-1184, Fax: (510) 685-8190.

CORNING CHAMBER OF COMMERCE
1401 Solano St., P.O. Box 871,
Corning, CA 96021, (916) 824-5550.

CORONA CHAMBER OF COMMERCE
904 E. Sixth St., Corona, CA 91719,
(909) 737-3350, Fax: (909) 737-3531.

CORONADO VISITOR INFORMATION
1111 Orange Ave., Ste. A,
Coronado, CA 92118, (619) 437-8788 or
(800) 622-8300, Fax: (619) 437-0384.

COSTA MESA CHAMBER OF
COMMERCE
1835 Newport Blvd., Ste. E-270,
Costa Mesa, CA 92627, (714) 574-8780.

COULTERVILLE CHAMBER OF
COMMERCE
5007 Main St., P.O. Box 333,
Coulterville, CA 95311, (209) 878-3074.

CRESCENT CITY-DEL NORTE COUNTY
CHAMBER OF COMMERCE
1001 Front St.,
Crescent City, CA 95531-0433,
(707) 464-3174 or (800) 343-8300,
Fax: (707) 464-9676.

CROWLEY LAKE CHAMBER OF
COMMERCE
Rte. 1, Box 1111,
Crowley Lake, CA 93546, (619) 935-4556.

DANA POINT CHAMBER OF
COMMERCE
24681 La Plaza, Dana Point, CA 92629,
(800) 248-DANA, Fax: (714) 496-5321.

DAVIS AREA CHAMBER OF
COMMERCE
228 B St., Davis, CA 95616, (916) 756-5160.

DEATH VALLEY CHAMBER OF
COMMERCE
118 Hwy. 127, P.O. Box 157,
Shoshone, CA 92384, (619) 852-4524.

DEL MAR (GREATER) CHAMBER OF
COMMERCE
1104 Camino del Mar,
Del Mar, CA 92014, (619) 793-5292.

DESERT HOT SPRINGS CHAMBER OF
COMMERCE
11711 West Dr., P.O. Box 848,
Desert Hot Springs, CA 92240,
(619) 329-6403 or (800) 346-3347.

DINUBA CHAMBER OF COMMERCE
210 N. L St., Dinuba, CA 93618,
(209) 591-2707.

DUNSMUIR CHAMBER OF COMMERCE
4841 Dunsmuir Ave., P.O. Box 17,
Dunsmuir, CA 96025, (916) 235-2177.

EASTERN PLUMAS CHAMBER OF
COMMERCE
P.O. Box 1370, Portola, CA 96122,
(916) 832-5444 or (800) 995-6057.

EL CAJON CHAMBER OF COMMERCE
109 Rea Ave., El Cajon, CA 92020,
(619) 440-6161.

EL CENTRO CHAMBER OF COMMERCE
1100 Main St., P.O. Box 3006,
El Centro, CA 92244, (619) 352-3681.

EL DORADO COUNTY CHAMBER OF
COMMERCE
542 Main St., Placerville, CA 95667,
(916) 621-5885 or (800) 457-6279,
Fax: (916) 642-1624.

ENCINITAS CHAMBER OF COMMERCE
345 N. First St., Encinitas, CA 92024,
(619) 753-6041, Fax: (619) 753-6270.

ESCONDIDO CHAMBER OF
COMMERCE
720 N. Broadway, Escondido, CA 92025,
(619) 745-2125.

EUREKA CHAMBER OF COMMERCE
2112 Broadway, Eureka, CA 95501,
(707) 442-3738 or (800) 356-6381,
Fax: (707) 442-0079.

EUREKA/HUMBOLDT COUNTY
CONVENTION AND VISITORS BUREAU
1034 Second St., Eureka, CA 95501,
(707) 443-5097, (800) 338-7352 (CA),
(800) 346-3482 (USA), Fax: (707) 443-5115.

FAIRFIELD-SUISUN CHAMBER OF
COMMERCE
1111 Webster St.,
Fairfield, CA 94533, (707) 425-4625 or
(800) 400-0446, Fax: (707) 425-0826.

FALLBROOK CHAMBER OF
COMMERCE
233-A E. Mission Rd.,
Fallbrook, CA 92028, (619) 728-5845.

FALL RIVER VALLEY CHAMBER OF
COMMERCE
P.O. Box 475, Fall River Mills, CA 96028,
(916) 336-5840 or (916) 335-2111.

FERNDALE CHAMBER OF COMMERCE
P.O. Box 325, Ferndale, CA 95536,
(707) 786-4477.

FOLSOM CHAMBER OF COMMERCE
200 Wool St., Folsom, CA 95630,
(916) 985-2698, Fax: (916) 985-4117.

FORESTHILL DIVIDE CHAMBER OF
COMMERCE
P.O. Box 346, Foresthill, CA 95631,
(916) 367-2474.

FORT BRAGG-MENDOCINO COAST
CHAMBER OF COMMERCE
332 N. Main St., P.O. Box 1141, Fort Bragg,
CA 95437, (707) 961-6300 or (800) 726-2780,
Fax: (707) 964-2056.

FORTUNA CHAMBER OF COMMERCE
735 14th St., P.O. Box 797,
Fortuna, CA 95540, (707) 725-3959.

FREMONT CHAMBER OF COMMERCE
2201 Walnut Ave., Ste. 110,
Fremont, CA 94538, (510) 795-2244.

FRESNO CITY AND COUNTY
CONVENTION AND VISITORS BUREAU
808 M St., Fresno, CA 93721,
(209) 233-0836 or (800) 788-0836,
Fax: (209) 445-0122.

GARBERVILLE-REDWAY CHAMBER OF
COMMERCE
773 Redwood Dr., P.O. Box 445,
Garberville, CA 95542,
(707) 923-2613, Fax: (707) 923-4789.

GILROY VISITORS BUREAU
7780 Monterey St., Gilroy, CA 95020,
(408) 842-6436, Fax: (408) 842-6438.

GLENDALE CHAMBER OF COMMERCE
200 S. Louise St., P.O. Box 112,
Glendale, CA 91209,
(818) 240-7870, Fax: (818) 240-2872.

GLENN COUNTY CHAMBER OF
COMMERCE
410 W. Sycamore St., P.O. Box 1277,
Willows, CA 95988,
(916) 934-2841 or (916) 934-8150.

GOLETA VALLEY CHAMBER OF
COMMERCE
5730 Hollister Ave., Ste. 1, P.O. Box 781,
Goleta, CA 93116, (805) 967-4618.

GRASS VALLEY/NEVADA COUNTY
CHAMBER OF COMMERCE
248 Mill St., Grass Valley, CA 95945,
(916) 273-4667.

GROVER BEACH CHAMBER OF
COMMERCE
177 S. Eighth St., Grover Beach, CA 93433,
(805) 489-9091, Fax: (805) 489-9091.

GUSTINE CHAMBER OF COMMERCE
462 Fourth Ave., P.O. Box 306, Gustine,
CA 95322, (209) 854-6975.

HALF MOON BAY/COASTSIDE
CHAMBER OF COMMERCE
225 S. Cabrillo Hwy., P.O. Box 188,
Half Moon Bay, CA 94019, (415) 726-5202.

HANFORD VISITOR AGENCY
200 Santa Fe, Ste. D, Hanford, CA 93230,
(209) 582-0483 or (800) 722-1114,
Fax: (209) 582-0960.

HAYWARD CHAMBER OF COMMERCE
22320 Foothill Blvd., Ste. 600,
Hayward, CA 94541, (510) 537-2424.

HEALDSBURG AREA CHAMBER OF
COMMERCE
217 Healdsburg Ave.,
Healdsburg, CA 95448,
(707) 433-6935 or (800) 648-9922.

HEMET CHAMBER OF COMMERCE
395 E. Latham Ave., Hemet, CA 92543,
(909) 658-3211, Fax: (909) 766-5013.

HERMOSA BEACH CHAMBER OF
COMMERCE
323 Pier Ave., P.O. Box 404,
Hermosa Beach, CA 90254, (310) 376-0951.

HOPLAND CHAMBER OF COMMERCE
P.O. Box 677, Hopland, CA 95449,
(707) 744-1047.

HUNTINGTON BEACH CONFERENCE
AND VISITORS BUREAU
2100 Main St., Ste. 190, Huntington Beach,
CA 92648, (714) 969-3492 or (800) 729-6232,
Fax: (714) 969-5592.

IDYLLWILD CHAMBER OF COMMERCE
P.O. Box 304, Idyllwild, CA 92549,
(909) 659-3259.

IMPERIAL BEACH CHAMBER OF
COMMERCE
600 Palm Ave., Ste. 221, Imperial Beach,
CA 91932, (619) 424-3151.

INDIAN VALLEY CHAMBER OF
COMMERCE
P.O. Box 516, Greenville, CA 95947,
(916) 284-6633.

INLAND EMPIRE TOURISM COUNCIL,
P.O. Box 1593, Upland, CA 91785,
(909) 624-5651, Fax: (909) 624-5651.

IRVINE CHAMBER OF COMMERCE
17200 Jamboree, Ste. A, Irvine, CA 92714,
(714) 660-9112.

JULIAN CHAMBER OF COMMERCE
P.O. Box 413, Julian, CA 92036,
(619) 765-1857.

JUNE LAKE LOOP CHAMBER OF
COMMERCE
P.O. Box 2, June Lake, CA 93529,
(619) 648-7584.

KERN COUNTY BOARD OF TRADE
2101 Oak St., P.O. Bin 1312,
Bakersfield, CA 93302,
(805) 861-2367 or(800) 500-KERN,
Fax: (805) 861-2017.

KERN RIVER VALLEY VISITOR
COUNCIL
P.O. Box O, Lake Isabella, CA 93240,
(619) 379-3867.

KERNVILLE CHAMBER OF COMMERCE
11447 Sierra Way, P.O. Box 397,
Kernville, CA 93238, (619) 376-2629.

KING CITY AND SOUTHERN
MONTEREY COUNTY CHAMBER OF
COMMERCE
203 Broadway St., King City, CA 93930,
(408) 385-3814.

KLAMATH CHAMBER OF COMMERCE
P.O. Box 476, Klamath, CA 95548,
(707) 482-7165.

LAGUNA BEACH HOSPITALITY
ASSOCIATION
252 Broadway, Laguna Beach, CA 92651,
(714) 497-9229 or (800) 877-1115.

LA JOLLA TOWN COUNCIL
1055 Wall St., Ste. 110, P.O. Box 1101,
La Jolla, CA 92037, (619) 454-1444.

LAKE ARROWHEAD COMMUNITIES
CHAMBER OF COMMERCE
28200 Hwy. 189, P.O. Box 219,
Lake Arrowhead, CA 92352,
(909) 337-3715, Fax: (909) 336-1548.

LAKE BERRYESSA CHAMBER OF
COMMERCE
4310 Knoxville Rd., P.O. Box 9164,
Napa, CA 94558, (800) 726-1256.

LAKE COUNTY VISITOR
INFORMATION CENTER
875 Lakeport Blvd., Lakeport, CA 95453,
(707) 263-9544 or (800) 525-3743,
Fax: (707) 263-9564.

LAKE ELSINORE (CITY OF)
130 S. Main St., Lake Elsinore, CA 92530,
(909) 674-3124, Fax: (909) 674-2392.

LAKE ISABELLA CHAMBER OF
COMMERCE
P.O. Box 567, Lake Isabella, CA 93240,
(619) 379-5236.

LAKEPORT (GREATER) CHAMBER OF
COMMERCE
P.O. Box 295, Lakeport CA 95453,
(707) 263-5092, Fax: (707) 263-5104.

LAKE TAHOE VISITORS AUTHORITY
P.O. Box 16299,
South Lake Tahoe, CA 96151,
(916) 544-5050 or (800) AT-TAHOE,
Fax: (916) 544-2386.

LANCASTER CHAMBER OF
COMMERCE
44335 Lowtree Ave.,
Lancaster, CA 93534, (805) 948-4518.

LARKSPUR CHAMBER OF COMMERCE
P.O. Box 315, Larkspur, CA 94993,
(415) 257-8338.

LASSEN COUNTY CHAMBER OF
COMMERCE
84 N. Lassen St., P.O. Box 338,
Susanville, CA 96130, (916) 257-4323.

LEGGETT VALLEY CHAMBER OF
COMMERCE
P.O. Box 105, Leggett, CA 95585,
(707) 925-6385.

LEMOORE DISTRICT CHAMBER OF
COMMERCE
218 W. D St., Lemoore, CA 93245,
(209) 924-6401, Fax: (209) 924-4520.

LEE VINING CHAMBER OF
COMMERCE
Hwy. 395 and Main St., P.O. Box 130,
Lee Vining, CA 93541, (619) 647-6629.

LINDSAY CHAMBER OF COMMERCE
147 Gale Hill, P.O. Box 989,
Lindsay, CA 93247,
(209) 562-4929, Fax: (209) 562-5219.

LIVERMORE CHAMBER OF
COMMERCE
2157 First St., Livermore, CA 94550-4543,
(510) 447-1606, Fax: (510) 447-1641.

LODI DISTRICT CHAMBER OF
COMMERCE
1330 S. Ham Lane, P.O. Box 386,
Lodi, CA 95241, (209) 367-7840 or
(800) 304-LODI.

LOMPOC VALLEY CHAMBER OF
COMMERCE
111S I St., P.O. Box 626,
Lompoc, CA 93436, (805) 736-4567.

LONE PINE CHAMBER OF COMMERCE
126 S. Main St., P.O. Box 749,
Lone Pine, CA 93545, (619) 876-4444.

LONG BEACH AREA CONVENTION
AND VISITORS BUREAU
One World Trade Center, Ste. 300,
Long Beach, CA 90831, (310) 436-3645 or
(800) 4LB-STAY, Fax: (310) 435-5653.

LOS ALTOS CHAMBER OF COMMERCE
321 University Ave., P.O. Box 1820,
Los Altos, CA 94022, (415) 948-1455.

LOS ANGELES CONVENTION AND
VISITORS BUREAU
633 W. Fifth St., Ste. 6000,
Los Angeles, CA 90071,
(213) 624-7300, Fax: (213) 624-9746.

DOWNTOWN LOS ANGELES VISITOR
INFORMATION CENTER,
685 S. Figueroa St., Los Angeles, CA 90017,
(213) 689-8822.

HOLLYWOOD VISITOR INFORMATION
CENTER, 6541 HOLLYWOOD BLVD.,
Hollywood, CA 90028, (213) 689-8822.

LOS BANOS CHAMBER OF COMMERCE
503 J St., P.O. Box 2117,
Los Banos, CA 93635, (209) 826-2495 or
(800) 336-6354, Fax: (209) 826-9689.

LOS GATOS CHAMBER OF COMMERCE
180 S. Market St.,
San Jose, CA 95113,
(408) 354-9300, Fax: (408) 395-6593.

MADERA CHAMBER OF COMMERCE
131 W. Yosemite, P.O. Box 307,
Madera, CA 93639, (209) 673-3563.

MADERA (EASTERN) COUNTY
CHAMBER OF COMMERCE
49074 Civic Circle, P.O. Box 1404,
Oakhurst, CA 93644, (209) 683-4636.

MALIBU CHAMBER OF COMMERCE
23805 Stuart Ranch Rd., Ste. 100,
Malibu, CA 90265-4897,
(310) 456-9025, Fax: (310) 456-0195.

MAMMOTH LAKES VISITORS BUREAU
3399 Main St., P.O. Box 48,
Mammoth Lakes, CA 93546,
(619) 934-2712 or (800) 367-6572,
Fax: (619) 934-7066.

MARIN (WEST) CHAMBER OF
COMMERCE
11431 State Rte. 1, #17,
Point Reyes Station, CA 94956,
(415) 663-9232.

MARINA DEL REY CHAMBER OF
COMMERCE
4629-A Admiralty Way,
Marina del Rey, CA 90292, (310) 821-0555.

MARTINEZ AREA CHAMBER OF
COMMERCE
620 Las Juntas St., Martinez, CA 94553,
(510) 228-2345.

MARYSVILLE
(See Yuba-Sutter Chamber of Commerce.)

MCKINLEYVILLE CHAMBER OF
COMMERCE
2196 Central Ave., P.O. Box 2144,
McKinleyville, CA 95521, (707) 839-2449.

MENDOCINO COUNTY TOURISM
BOARD
239 S. Main St., Willits, CA 95490,
(707) 459-7910 or (800) 94-MENDO.

MENLO PARK CHAMBER OF
COMMERCE
1100 Merrill St., Menlo Park, CA 94025,
(415) 325-2818, Fax: (415) 325-0920.

MERCED CONFERENCE AND VISITORS
BUREAU
690 W. 16th St., Merced, CA 95340,
(209) 384-3333 or (800) 446-5353,
Fax: (209) 384-8472.

MODESTO CONVENTION AND
VISITORS BUREAU
1114 J St., P.O. Box 844,
Modesto, CA 95353, (209) 577-5757 or
(800) 266-4CVB, Fax: (209) 577-2673.

MOJAVE CHAMBER OF COMMERCE
15836 Sierra Hwy., Mojave, CA 93501,
(805) 824-2481.

MONO LAKE CHAMBER OF
COMMERCE
Hwy. 395 at Third St., P.O. Box 29,
Lee Vining, CA 93541, (619) 647-6595.

MONTEREY COUNTY TOURISM
CENTER
San Lorenzo Park, 1160 Broadway St.,
King City, CA 93930, (408) 385-1484.

MONTEREY COUNTY VISITORS AND
CONVENTION BUREAU
380 Alvarado St., P.O. Box 1770,
Monterey, CA 93942, (408) 649-1770,
Fax: (408) 649-3502.

MORENO VALLEY CHAMBER OF
COMMERCE
22620 Goldencrest Dr., Ste. 110,
P.O. Box 524, Moreno Valley, CA 92553,
(909) 697-4404, Fax: (909) 697-4767.

MORGAN HILL CHAMBER OF
COMMERCE
25 W. First St., P.O. Box 786,
Morgan Hill, CA 95037,
(408) 779-9444, Fax: (408) 779-6798.

MORRO BAY CHAMBER OF
COMMERCE
895 Napa St., Ste. A-1, P.O. Box 876,
Morro Bay, CA 93442, (805) 772-4467.

MOUNTAIN VIEW CHAMBER OF
COMMERCE
580 Castro St., Mountain View, CA 94041,
(415) 968-8378.

MT. BALDY CHAMBER OF COMMERCE
70 Mt. Baldy Rd., P.O. Box 399,
Mt. Baldy, CA 91759,
(909) 931-4458, Fax: (909) 931-7681.

MT. SHASTA VISITORS BUREAU
300 Pine St., Mount Shasta, CA 96067,
(916) 926-4865 or (800) 926-4865.

NAPA VALLEY CONFERENCE AND
VISITORS BUREAU
1310 Napa Town Center, Napa, CA 94559,
(707) 226-7459, Fax: (707) 255-2066.

NEEDLES AREA CHAMBER OF
COMMERCE
100 G St., P.O. Box 705,
Needles, CA 92363, (619) 326-2050.

NEVADA CITY CHAMBER OF
COMMERCE
132 Main St., Nevada City, CA 95959,
(916) 265-2692 or (800) 655-6569
(CA & NV).

NEWMAN CHAMBER OF COMMERCE
P.O. Box 753, Newman, CA 95360,
(209) 862-3776.

NEWPORT BEACH CONFERENCE AND
VISITORS BUREAU
366 San Miguel Dr., Ste. 200,
Newport Beach, CA 92660, (714) 722-1611
or (800) 94-COAST, Fax: (714) 644-1180.

NORTH LAKE TAHOE CHAMBER OF
COMMERCE
245 N. Lake Blvd., P.O. Box 884,
Tahoe City, CA 96145,
(916) 581-6900, Fax: (916) 581-6904.

NOVATO CHAMBER OF COMMERCE
807 DeLong Ave., Novato, CA 94947,
(415) 897-1164, Fax: (415) 898-9097.

OAKDALE CHAMBER OF COMMERCE
590 N. Yosemite Ave., Oakdale, CA 95361,
(209) 847-2244.

OAKLAND CONVENTION AND
VISITORS BUREAU
1000 Broadway, Ste. 200,
Oakland, CA 94607, (510) 839-9000 or
(800) 262-5526, Fax: (510) 839-9960.

OCEANSIDE VISITORS INFORMATION
928 N. Hill St., Oceanside, CA 92054,
(619) 721-1101 or (800) 350-7873.

OJAI VALLEY CHAMBER OF
COMMERCE
338 E. Ojai Ave., P.O. Box 1134,
Ojai, CA 93024,
(805) 646-8126, Fax: (805) 646-9762.

ONTARIO (GREATER) VISITORS AND
CONVENTION BUREAU
421 N. Euclid Ave., Ontario, CA 91762,
(909) 984-2450, Fax: (909) 984-7895.

ORICK CHAMBER OF COMMERCE
P.O. Box 234, Orick, CA 95555,
(707) 488-6755.

ORLAND AREA CHAMBER OF
COMMERCE
401 Walker St., Orland, CA 95963,
(916) 865-2311.

OROVILLE AREA CHAMBER OF
COMMERCE
1789 Montgomery St., Oroville, CA 95965,
(916) 533-2542 or (800) 655-4653,
Fax: (916) 533-5990.

OXNARD (GREATER) AND HARBORS
TOURISM BUREAU
711 S. A St., Oxnard, CA 93030,
(805) 385-7545, Fax: (805) 385-7452.

PACIFIC GROVE CHAMBER OF
COMMERCE
P. O. Box 167, Pacific Grove, CA 93950,
(408) 373-3304.

PACIFICA CHAMBER OF COMMERCE
450 Dondee Way, Ste. 2,
Pacifica, CA 94044,
(415) 355-4122, Fax: (415) 355-6949.

PAJARO VALLEY CHAMBER OF
COMMERCE
444 Main St., P.O. Box 1748,
Watsonville, CA 95077,
(408) 724-3900, Fax: (408) 728-5300.

PALMDALE CHAMBER OF COMMERCE
38260-A 10th St. East, Palmdale, CA 93550,
(805) 273-3232, Fax: (805) 273-8508.

PALM SPRINGS DESERT RESORTS
CONVENTION AND VISITORS BUREAU
69-930 Hwy. 111, Ste. 201,
Rancho Mirage, CA 92270, (619) 770-9000
or (800) 41-RELAX, Fax: (619) 770-9001.

PALM SPRINGS TOURISM
401 S. Pavilion, Palm Springs, CA 92262,
(619) 778-8418 or (800) 347-7746,
Fax: (619) 323-8279.

PASADENA CONVENTION AND
VISITORS BUREAU
171 S. Los Robles Ave.,
Pasadena, CA 91101,
(818) 795-9311, Fax: (818) 795-9656.

PASO ROBLES CHAMBER OF
COMMERCE
1225 Park St., Paso Robles, CA 93446,
(805) 238-0506, Fax: (805) 238-0527.

PATTERSON-WESTLEY CHAMBER OF
COMMERCE
2 Plaza, P.O. Box 365,
Patterson, CA 95363, (209) 892-2821.

PENN VALLEY CHAMBER OF
COMMERCE
P.O. Box 202, Penn Valley, CA 95946,
(916) 272-4320.

PETALUMA VISITORS PROGRAM
799 Baywood Dr., Ste. #1,
Petaluma, CA 94954,
(707) 769-0429, Fax: (707) 762-4721.

PISMO BEACH CONVENTION AND
VISITORS BUREAU
581 Dolliver St., Pismo Beach, CA 93449,
(805) 773-4382 or (800) 443-7778 (CA).

PLACER COUNTY VISITOR
INFORMATION CENTER
13460-A Lincoln Way, Auburn, CA 95603,
(916) 887-2111 or (800) 427-6463,
Fax: (916) 887-2134.

PLEASANT HILL CHAMBER OF
COMMERCE
91 Gregory Lane, Ste. 11,
Pleasant Hill, CA 94523, (510) 687-0700.

PLEASANTON CONVENTION AND
VISITORS BUREAU
10 W. Neal St., Pleasanton, CA 94566-6632,
(510) 846-8910.

PLUMAS COUNTY VISITORS BUREAU
91 Church St., P.O. Box 4120,
Quincy, CA 95971, (916) 283-6345 or
(800) 326-2247, Fax: (916) 283-5465.

POLLOCK PINES-CAMINO CHAMBER
OF COMMERCE
6532 Pony Express Trail, P.O. Box 95,
Pollock Pines, CA 95726, (916) 644-3970.

POMONA CHAMBER OF COMMERCE
485 N. Garvey Ave., P.O. Box 1457,
Pomona, CA 91769,
(909) 622-1256, Fax: (909) 620-5986.

PORTERVILLE CHAMBER OF
COMMERCE
36 W. Cleveland Ave.,
Porterville, CA 93257, (209) 784-7502.

PORT HUENEME CHAMBER OF
COMMERCE
220 N. Market St., P.O. Box 465,
Port Hueneme, CA 93041, (805) 488-2023.

POWAY CHAMBER OF COMMERCE
12709 Poway Rd., Ste. 101,
Poway, CA 92074,(619) 748-0016.

QUINCY MAIN STREET CHAMBER OF
COMMERCE
P.O. Box 4120, Quincy, CA 95971,
(916) 283-0188, Fax: (916) 283-0188.

RAMONA CHAMBER OF COMMERCE
1306 Main St., Ste. 106, Ramona, CA 92065,
(619) 789-1484.

RANCHO CORDOVA CHAMBER OF
COMMERCE
11070 White Rock Rd., Ste. 170,
Rancho Cordova, CA 95670,
(916) 638-8700.

RED BLUFF-TEHAMA COUNTY
CHAMBER OF COMMERCE
100 Main St., P.O. Box 850,
Red Bluff, CA 96080,
(916) 527-6220 or (800) 655-6225.

REDDING CONVENTION AND
VISITORS BUREAU
777 Auditorium Dr., Redding, CA 96001,
(916) 225-4100 or (800) 874-7562,
Fax: (916) 225-4354.

REDLANDS CHAMBER OF COMMERCE
1 E. Redlands Blvd., Redlands, CA 92373,
(909) 793-2546, Fax: (909) 335-6388.

REDONDO BEACH VISITORS BUREAU
200 N. Pacific Coast Hwy.,
Redondo Beach, CA 90277,
(310) 374-2171 or (800) 282-0333,
Fax: (310) 374-7373.

REDWOOD EMPIRE ASSOCIATION
The Cannery-2801 Leavenworth St.,
San Francisco, CA 94133, (415) 543-8334,
Fax: (415) 543-8337.

REEDLEY DISTRICT CHAMBER OF
COMMERCE AND VISITORS BUREAU
1613 12th St., Reedley, CA 93654,
(209) 638-3548, Fax: (209) 638-8479.

RIDGECREST AREA CONVENTION
AND VISITORS BUREAU
100 W. California Ave.,
Ridgecrest, CA 93555, (619) 375-8202 or
(800) 847-4830, Fax: (619) 371-1654.

RIO DELL-SCOTIA CHAMBER OF
COMMERCE
715 Wildwood Ave., Rio Dell, CA 95562,
(707) 764-3436.

RIVERSIDE VISITORS AND
CONVENTION BUREAU
3443 Orange St., Riverside, CA 92501,
(909) 787-7950, Fax: (909) 787-4940.

ROHNERT PARK CHAMBER OF
COMMERCE
Rohnert Park, CA 95928, (707) 584-1415.

ROSAMOND CHAMBER OF
COMMERCE
2861 Diamond St., P.O. Box 365,
Rosamond, CA 93560,
(805) 256-3248, Fax: (805) 256-3249.

ROSEMEAD CHAMBER OF COMMERCE
9054 E. Garvey Ave., Rosemead, CA 91770,
(818) 288-0811.

ROSEVILLE AREA CHAMBER OF
COMMERCE
650 Douglas Blvd., Roseville, CA 95678,
(916) 783-8136.

ROUGH AND READY CHAMBER OF
COMMERCE
P.O. Box 801, Rough and Ready, CA 95975,
(916) 272-4320.

ROUTE 66 TERRITORY VISITORS
BUREAU
7965 Vineyard Ave., Ste. F-5, Rancho
Cucamonga, CA 91730, (909) 948-9166 or
(800) JOG-RT66, Fax: (909) 599-5308.

RUSSIAN RIVER CHAMBER OF
COMMERCE
16200 First St., P.O. Box 331,
Guerneville, CA 95446,
(707) 869-9000, Fax: (707) 869-9009.

RUSSIAN RIVER REGION
14034 Armstrong Woods Rd.,
P.O. Box 255, Guerneville, CA 95446,
(707) 869-9212 or (800) 253-8800,
Fax: (707) 869-9215.

SACRAMENTO CONVENTION AND
VISITORS BUREAU
1421 K St., Sacramento, CA 95814,
(916) 264-7777, Fax: (916) 264-7788.

SACRAMENTO VISITOR CENTER
1104 Front St., Old Sacramento, CA 95814,
(916) 442-7644.

SALINAS AREA CHAMBER OF
COMMERCE
119 E. Alisal St., Salinas, CA 93901,
(408) 424-7611, Fax: (408) 424-8693.

SAN ANSELMO CHAMBER OF
COMMERCE
P.O. Box 2844, San Anselmo, CA 94979,
(415) 454-2510, Fax: (415) 258-9458.

SAN BENITO COUNTY CHAMBER OF
COMMERCE
649C San Benito St., Hollister, CA 95023,
(408) 637-5315, Fax: (408) 637-1008.

SAN BERNARDINO CONVENTION
AND VISITORS BUREAU
201 N. E St., Ste. 103, San Bernardino, CA
92401, (909) 889-3980 or (800) TO-RTE-66,
Fax: (909) 888-5998.

SAN BRUNO CHAMBER OF
COMMERCE
618 San Mateo Ave., P.O. Box 713,
San Bruno, CA 94066,
(415) 588-0180, Fax: (415) 588-7545.

SAN CLEMENTE CHAMBER OF
COMMERCE
1100 N. El Camino Real,
San Clemente, CA 92672,
(714) 492-1131, Fax: (714) 492-3764.

SAN DIEGO CONVENTION AND
VISITORS BUREAU
401 B St., Ste. 1400, San Diego, CA 92101,
(619) 232-3101, Fax: (619) 696-9371.

SAN DIEGO INTERNATIONAL VISITOR
INFORMATION CENTER,
11 Horton Plaza, San Diego, CA 92101,
(619) 236-1212
(For public information and walk-in
visitor services.)

SAN DIEGO NORTH COUNTY
CONVENTION AND VISITORS BUREAU
720 N. Broadway, Escondido, CA 92025,
(619) 745-4741 or (800) 848-3336,
Fax: (619) 745-4796.

SAN DIEGO VISITOR CENTER
2688 E. Mission Bay Dr.,
San Diego, CA 92109,
(619) 276-8200, Fax: (619) 276-6041.

SAN DIMAS CHAMBER OF COMMERCE
246 E. Bonita Ave., P.O. Box 175,
San Dimas, CA 91773,
(909) 592-3818, Fax: (909) 592-8178.

SAN FERNANDO (MID) VALLEY
CHAMBER OF COMMERCE
14540 Victory Blvd., #100,
Van Nuys, CA 91411, (818) 989-0300.

SAN FRANCISCO CONVENTION AND
VISITORS BUREAU
201 Third St., Ste. 900,
San Francisco, CA 94103,
(415) 974-6900, Fax: (415) 227-2602.

SAN FRANCISCO VISITOR
INFORMATION CENTER
Hallidie Plaza, Lower Level, 900
Market St., P.O. Box 429097,
San Francisco, CA 94142,
(415) 391-2000; TTY: (415) 392-0328.

SAN JACINTO CHAMBER OF
COMMERCE
188 E. Main St., San Jacinto, CA 92583,
(909) 654-9246, Fax: (909) 654-5007.

SAN JOSE CONVENTION AND
VISITORS BUREAU
333 W. San Carlos St., Ste. 1000,
San Jose, CA 95110,
(408) 295-9600, Fax: (408) 295-3937.

SAN JOSE VISITOR INFORMATION
CENTER
150 W. San Carlos St., San Jose, CA 95110,
(408) 283-8833, Fax: (408) 283-8862.

SAN JUAN BAUTISTA CHAMBER OF
COMMERCE
402A Third St., P.O. Box 1037,
San Juan Bautista, CA 95045,
(408) 623-2454, Fax: (408) 623-0674.

SAN JUAN CAPISTRANO CHAMBER OF
COMMERCE
26832 Ortega Hwy., San Juan Capistrano,
CA 92675, (714) 493-4700.

SAN LUIS OBISPO CHAMBER OF
COMMERCE
1039 Chorro St., San Luis Obispo, CA
93401, (805) 781-2777, Fax: (805) 543-1255.

SAN LUIS OBISPO COUNTY VISITORS
AND CONFERENCE BUREAU
1041 Chorro St., Ste. E,
San Luis Obispo, CA 93401,
(805) 541-8000 or (800) 634-1414,
Fax: (805) 543-9498.

SAN MARCOS CHAMBER OF
COMMERCE
144 W. Mission Rd.,
San Marcos, CA 92069, (619) 744-1270.

SAN MATEO COUNTY CONVENTION
AND VISITORS BUREAU
111 Anza Blvd., Ste. 410,
Burlingame, CA 94010,
(415) 348-7600 or (800) 288-4748,
Fax: (415) 348-7687.

SAN PEDRO PENINSULA CHAMBER OF
COMMERCE
390 W. Seventh St., P.O. Box 167,
San Pedro, CA 90731, (310) 832-7272.

SAN RAFAEL CHAMBER OF
COMMERCE
817 Mission Ave., San Rafael, CA 94901,
(415) 454-4163.

SAN SIMEON CHAMBER OF
COMMERCE
9255 Hearst Dr., P.O. Box 1,
San Simeon, CA 93452,
(805) 927-3500 or (800) 342-5613,
Fax: (805) 927-1929.

SANTA ANA CHAMBER OF
COMMERCE
801 Civic Center Dr., Ste. 110,
P.O. Box 205, Santa Ana, CA 92702,
(714) 541-5353.

SANTA BARBARA CONFERENCE AND
VISITORS BUREAU
510 State St., Ste. A, Santa
Barbara, CA 93101, (805) 966-9222 or
(800) 927-4688, Fax: (805) 966-1728.

SANTA CLARA CONVENTION AND
VISITORS BUREAU
2200 Laurelwood Rd., 2nd Fl.,
P.O. Box 387, Santa Clara, CA 95054,
(408) 296-7111 or (800) 2-SANTA CLARA,
Fax: (408) 970-8864.

SANTA CLARA VISITOR
INFORMATION CENTER
1515 El Camino Real,
Santa Clara, CA 95050,
(408) 296-7111, Fax: (408) 246-7705.

SANTA CLARITA VALLEY TOURISM
BUREAU
23920 Valencia Blvd., Ste. 125,
Santa Clarita, CA 91355
(805) 259-4787 or (800) 718-TOUR, ext. 123,
Fax: (805) 259-8628.

SANTA CRUZ COUNTY CONFERENCE
AND VISITORS COUNCIL
701 Front St., Santa Cruz, CA 95060,
(408) 425-1234 or (800) 833-3494,
Fax: (408) 425-1260.

SANTA MARIA VALLEY CHAMBER OF
COMMERCE
614 S. Broadway, Santa Maria, CA 93454,
(805) 925-2403 or (800) 331-3779,
Fax: (805) 928-7559.

SANTA MONICA CONVENTION AND
VISITORS BUREAU
2219 Main St., Santa Monica, CA 90405,
(310) 392-9631, Fax: (310) 392-6907 (trade).

SANTA MONICA VISITOR CENTER
1400 Ocean Ave., Santa Monica, CA 90401,
(310) 393-7593 (public information).

SANTA NELLA CHAMBER OF
COMMERCE
12310 S. Hwy. 33, Santa Nella, CA 95322,
(209) 826-0741.

SANTA ROSA (GREATER)
CONFERENCE AND VISITORS BUREAU
637 First St., Santa Rosa, CA 95404,
(707) 577-8674 or (800) 404-ROSE (CA),
Fax: (707) 545-6914.

SARATOGA CHAMBER OF COMMERCE
20460 Saratoga-Los Gatos Rd.,
Saratoga, CA 95070, (408) 867-0753.

SAUSALITO CHAMBER OF COMMERCE
333 Caledonia St., P.O. Box 566,
Sausalito, CA 94966,
(415) 332-0505, Fax: (415) 332-0323.

SEASIDE-SAND CITY CHAMBER OF
COMMERCE
505 Broadway, Seaside, CA 93955,
(408) 394-6501.

SEBASTOPOL AREA CHAMBER OF
COMMERCE
265 S. Main St., P.O. Box 178,
Sebastopol, CA 95473, (707) 823-3032.

SELMA DISTRICT CHAMBER OF
COMMERCE
1802 Tucker St., Selma, CA 93662,
(209) 896-3315, Fax: (209) 896-1068.

SEQUOIA AND KINGS CANYON
NATIONAL PARKS GUEST SERVICES
P.O. Box 789, Sequoia National Parks,
Three Rivers, CA 93271, (209) 561-3314.

SEQUOIA REGIONAL VISITORS
COUNCIL
4125 W. Mineral King, Ste. 104,
Visalia, CA 93277,
(209) 733-6284, Fax: (209) 730-2604.

SHAFTER CHAMBER OF COMMERCE
AND AGRICULTURE
150 Central Valley Hwy., P.O. Box 1088,
Shafter, CA 93263, (805) 746-2600.

SHASTA CASCADE WONDERLAND
ASSOCIATION
14250 Holiday Rd., Redding, CA 96003,
(916) 275-5555 or (800) 326-6944,
Fax: (916) 275-9755.
(Visitor information for entire Shasta
Cascade region.)

SHINGLE SPRINGS/CAMERON PARK
CHAMBER OF COMMERCE
4065 Mother Lode Dr., P.O. Box 341,
Shingle Springs, CA 95682, (916) 677-8000,
Fax: (916) 676-8313.

SIERRA COUNTY CHAMBER OF
COMMERCE
P.O. Box 222, Downieville, CA 95936,
(916) 993-6900 or (800) 200-4949.

SIMI VALLEY CHAMBER OF
COMMERCE
40 W. Cochran St., #100, Simi Valley, CA
93065, (805) 526-3900, Fax: (805) 526-6234.

SISKIYOU COUNTY VISITORS BUREAU
808 W. Lennox St., Yreka, CA 96097,
(916) 842-7857 or (800) 446-7475,
Fax: (916) 842-7666.

SOLANA BEACH CHAMBER OF
COMMERCE
210 W. Plaza, P.O. Box 623,
Solana Beach, CA 92075, (619) 755-4775.

SOLEDAD CHAMBER OF COMMERCE
248 Main St., P.O. Box 156, Soledad, CA
93960, (408) 678-3963, Fax: (408) 678-3965.

SOLVANG VISITORS BUREAU
1511-A Mission Dr., P.O. Box 70, Solvang,
CA 93463, (805) 688-6144 or (800) 468-6765,
Fax: (805) 688-8620.

SONOMA COUNTY CONVENTION
AND VISITORS BUREAU
5000 Roberts Lake Rd.,
Rohnert Park, CA 94928,
(707) 586-8100, Fax: (707) 326-7666.

SONOMA VALLEY VISITORS BUREAU
453 First St. East, Sonoma, CA 95476,
(707) 996-1090, Fax: (707) 996-9212.

SOUTH COAST METRO ALLIANCE
611 Anton Blvd., Ste. 760,
Costa Mesa, CA 92626,
(714) 435-2109, Fax: (714) 668-0972.

SOUTH ORANGE COUNTY CHAMBER
OF COMMERCE
25431 Cabot Rd., Ste. 205,
Laguna Hills, CA 92653, (714) 837-3000.

SPRINGVILLE CHAMBER OF
COMMERCE
35625 Hwy. 190, Springville, CA 93265,
(209) 539-2312.

ST. HELENA CHAMBER OF
COMMERCE
1080 Main St., P.O. Box 124,
St. Helena, CA 94574, (707) 963-4456.

STOCKTON-SAN JOAQUIN
CONVENTION AND VISITORS BUREAU
46 W. Fremont St., Stockton, CA 95202,
(209) 943-1987 or (800) 350-1987,
Fax: (209) 943-6235.

SUNNYVALE CHAMBER OF
COMMERCE
499 S. Murphy Ave., Sunnyvale, CA 94086,
(408) 736-4971.

TAHOE NORTH VISITORS BUREAU
950 N. Lake Blvd., Ste. 3, P.O. Box 5578,
Tahoe City, CA 96145, (916) 581-3494 or
(800) 824-6348, Fax: (916) 581-4081.

TEHACHAPI (GREATER) CHAMBER OF
COMMERCE
209 E. Tehachapi Blvd., P.O. Box 401,
Tehachapi, CA 93581,
(805) 822-4180, Fax: (805) 822-9036.

TEMECULA VALLEY CHAMBER OF
COMMERCE
27450 Ynez Rd., #104, Temecula, CA
92591,
(909) 676-5090, Fax: (909) 694-0201.

TORRANCE VISITORS BUREAU
3400 Torrance Blvd., Suite 100,
Torrance, CA 90503, (310) 792-2341 or
(800) 228-8890, Fax: (310) 540-7662.

TRINIDAD (GREATER) CHAMBER OF
COMMERCE
P.O. Box 356, Trinidad, CA 95570,
(707) 677-0591.

TRINITY COUNTY CHAMBER OF
COMMERCE
317 Main St., P.O. Box 517, Weaverville,
CA 96093, (916) 623-6101 or (800) 421-7259.

TRUCKEE-DONNER CHAMBER OF
COMMERCE AND VISITORS CENTER
12036 Donner Pass Rd., P.O. Box 2757,
Truckee, CA 96160,
(916) 587-2757 or (800) 548-8388.

TULARE CHAMBER OF COMMERCE
260 N. L St., Tulare, CA 93274,
(209) 686-1547.

TUOLUMNE COUNTY VISITORS
BUREAU
55 W. Stockton Rd., P.O. Box 4020,
Sonora, CA 95370, (209) 533-4420 or
(800) 446-1333, Fax: (209) 533-0956.

TURLOCK CONVENTION AND
VISITORS BUREAU
115 S. Golden State Blvd.,
Turlock, CA 95380, (209) 632-2221 or
(800) 508-2221, Fax: (209) 632-5289.

TWENTYNINE PALMS CHAMBER OF
COMMERCE
6136 Adobe Rd., 29 Palms, CA 92277,
(619) 367-3445 or (800) 533-7104,
Fax: (619) 367-4890.

UKIAH CHAMBER OF COMMERCE
200 S. School St., Ukiah, CA 95482,
(707) 462-4705.

VACAVILLE CHAMBER OF
COMMERCE
300 Main St., Vacaville, CA 95688,
(707) 448-6424.

VALLEJO CONVENTION AND
VISITORS BUREAU
495 Mare Island Way, Vallejo, CA 94590,
(707) 642-3653 or (800) 4-VALLEJO,
Fax: (707) 644-2206.

VENICE CHAMBER OF COMMERCE
2904 W. Washington Blvd. #100,
P.O. Box 202, Venice, CA 90291, (
310) 827-2366.

VENTURA VISITORS BUREAU
89-C S. California St., Ventura, CA 93001,
(805) 648-2075 Fax: (805) 648-2150.

VICTORVILLE CHAMBER OF
COMMERCE
14174 Green Tree Blvd., P.O. Box 997,
Victorville, CA 92393,
(619) 245-6506, Fax: (619) 951-1375.

VISALIA CONVENTION AND VISITORS
BUREAU
815 W. Center St., Visalia, CA 93291,
(209) 738-3435 or (800) 524-0303,
Fax: (209) 738-3577.

VISTA CHAMBER OF COMMERCE
201 E. Washington St., Vista, CA 92084,
(619) 726-1122.

WALNUT CREEK CHAMBER OF
COMMERCE
1501 N. Broadway, #110,
Walnut Creek, CA 94596,
(510) 934-2007, Fax: (510) 934-2404.

WEED CHAMBER OF COMMERCE
34 Main St., P.O. Box 366,
Weed, CA 96096,(916) 938-4624.

WEST COVINA CHAMBER OF
COMMERCE
811 S. Sunset Ave., West Covina, CA
91790, (818) 338-8496, Fax: (310) 301-2022.

WEST HOLLYWOOD MARKETING
CORPORATION
9000 Sunset Blvd., West Hollywood, CA
90069, (310) 274-7294 or (800) 368-6020.

WEST SACRAMENTO CHAMBER OF
COMMERCE
1414 Merkley Ave., Ste. 1,
P.O. Box 404, West Sacramento, CA 95691,
(916) 371-7042 or (800) 350-7210.

WEST SHORES CHAMBER OF
COMMERCE
2114 Haven, P.O. Box 5185, Salton City,
CA 92275, (619) 394-4112.

WESTWOOD CHAMBER OF
COMMERCE
315 Ash St., P.O. Box 1235,
Westwood, CA 96137, (916) 256-2456.

WILLITS CHAMBER OF COMMERCE
239 S. Main St., Willits, CA 95490,
(707) 459-7910.

WILLOW CREEK CHAMBER OF
COMMERCE
Hwy. 299 and 96, P.O. Box 704,
Willow Creek, CA 95573, (916) 629-2693.

WILLOWS AREA CHAMBER OF
COMMERCE
410 W. Sycamore St., Willows, CA 95988,
(916) 934-8150, Fax: (916) 934-2844.

WINDSOR CHAMBER OF COMMERCE
8499 Old Redwood Hwy., Ste. 202,
Windsor, CA 95492, (707) 838-7285.

WOODLAND CHAMBER OF
COMMERCE
520 Main St., Woodland, CA 95695,
(916) 662-7327.

WRIGHTWOOD CHAMBER OF
COMMERCE
P.O. Box 416, Wrightwood, CA 92397,
(619) 249-4320, Fax: (619) 249-4021.

YOSEMITE CONCESSION SERVICES
CORPORATION
5410 E. Home, Fresno, CA 93727,
(209) 252-4848, Fax: (209) 456-0542.

YOSEMITE-MARIPOSA COUNTY
CHAMBER OF COMMERCE
5158 Hwy. 140, P.O. Box 425,
Mariposa, CA 95338, (209) 966-2456 or
(800) 208-2434, Fax: (209) 742-5409.

YOSEMITE (SOUTHERN) VISITORS
BUREAU
49074 Civic Circle, Oakhurst, CA 93644,
(209) 683-4636, Fax: (209) 683-0784.

YREKA CHAMBER OF COMMERCE
117 W. Miner St., Yreka, CA 96097,
(916) 842-1649 or (800) ON-YREKA.

YUBA-SUTTER CHAMBER OF
COMMERCE
429 10th St., P.O. Box 1429,
Marysville, CA 95901, (916) 743-6501.

YUCAIPA VALLEY CHAMBER OF
COMMERCE
35144 Yucaipa Blvd., P.O. Box 45,
Yucaipa, CA 92399, (909) 790-1841.

YUCCA VALLEY CHAMBER OF
COMMERCE
56300 29 Palms Highway, Ste. D,
Yucca Valley, CA 92284,
(619) 365-6323, Fax: (619) 365-0763.

National Forest Hiking Trail Index

GENERAL INDEX

City Names Are In ALL CAPITAL LETTERS

City Names Are In ALL CAPITAL LETTERS

City Names Are In ALL CAPITAL LETTERS

City Names Are In ALL CAPITAL LETTERS

City Names Are In ALL CAPITAL LETTERS

City Names Are In ALL CAPITAL LETTERS

City Names Are In ALL CAPITAL LETTERS

City Names Are In ALL CAPITAL LETTERS

City Names Are In ALL CAPITAL LETTERS

City Names Are In ALL CAPITAL LETTERS

City Names Are In ALL CAPITAL LETTERS

City Names Are In ALL CAPITAL LETTERS

City Names Are In ALL CAPITAL LETTERS

City Names Are In ALL CAPITAL LETTERS

City Names Are In ALL CAPITAL LETTERS